RICHARD REEVES

PRESIDENT REAGAN

The Triumph of Imagination

SIMON & SCHUSTER

NEW YORK LONDON TORONTO SYDNEY

SIMON & SCHUSTER
Rockefeller Center
1230 Avenue of the Americas
New York, NY 10020

The author and publisher gratefully acknowledge permission to reprint material from
the following work: "Trying to Repeal Keynes: Economic Analysis" by Leonard Silk.
Copyright © 1981 by The New York Times Co. Reprinted with permission.

Photography credits on page 572.

For information about special discounts for bulk purchases,
please contact Simon & Schuster Special Sales at
1-800-456-6798 or business@simonandschuster.com.

Designed by Karolina Harris

Manufactured in the United States of America
10   9   8   7   6   5   4   3   2   1

Library of Congress Cataloging-in-Publication Data

Reeves, Richard.
    President Reagan : the triumph of imagination / Richard Reeves.
       p.   cm.
    Includes bibliographical references and index.
    1. Reagan, Ronald.   2. Presidents—United States—Biography.   3. United States—
Politics and government—1981–1989.   4. United States—Politics and government—
1981–1989—Decision making.   5. United States—Foreign relations—
1981–1989.   I. Title.

    E877.R44 2005
    973.927092—dc22
    [B]   2005054198

ISBN-13: 978-0-7432-3022-3
ISBN-10:   0-7432-3022-1

This book is for my daughter,
FIONA O'NEILL REEVES

CONTENTS

INTRODUCTION

I FIRST MET RONALD REAGAN in November of 1967. I was a reporter for *The New York Times* traveling with the mayor of New York, John V. Lindsay, who was then a Republican. There was a lot of talk that year about a Republican "dream ticket" of Governor Nelson Rockefeller of New York for President and Governor Reagan of California, in office for less than a year, for Vice President. The idea seemed to make some sense, or it was good copy. The energetic leader of liberal Republicans in the East and the new conservative darling from the West might have made an exciting ticket, uniting the party's left and right wings. Part of Lindsay's mission that day was to size up the ex-actor and self-proclaimed "citizen politician." We walked down a long hallway to the Presidential Suite of the Biltmore Hotel in Los Angeles. As the mayor raised his hand to knock on the double doors, they popped open and there stood Reagan. "Welcome to California," he said. "I've always wanted to ask a real New Yorker a question: Have you ever been to the top of the Empire State Building or visited the Statue of Liberty?"

I was not impressed.

I saw Reagan next half a year later at the 1968 Republican National Convention in Miami Beach. By then he was more politician than citizen. He had declared himself a candidate for President rather late in the game on the chance that the party's front-runner, former Vice President Richard Nixon, might not get enough delegate votes to win on the first ballot, and conservatives would reject both Nixon and Rockefeller and turn to Reagan. It almost happened. Nixon did not have enough votes at the end of the roll call of states and won only when a few dozen delegates switched their votes. Reagan ran again in 1976, losing a very close race to President Gerald Ford 1,187 to 1,070 when delegates voted at that Republican convention.

By then, I was impressed. In the fall of 1975, I had traveled the country promoting a book, *A Ford, Not a Lincoln,* answering what seemed like thousands of questions on radio call-in shows. In early December that year I wrote a magazine story predicting that Reagan, or perhaps Jimmy Carter, the former governor of Georgia, would be the next President. All the night talk on radio had persuaded me that the real issue in 1976 would be Washington. The people who were driven to call those talk shows used their few minutes to complain about Washington and government. Carter was anti-Washington. Reagan was anti-government.

Pretty soon I received a letter from Reagan: "This is just a line to thank you for your article in *New York.* I'm aware our viewpoints may differ, indeed you so indicated, but I appreciate your fairness. Perhaps one day our paths may cross and who knows, we may discover our differences are not so terribly great. I look forward to a meeting and in the meantime thanks again."

Our paths did cross over the next fifteen years. He did not change my liberal mind and I did not dent his conservatism, but we did agree on some important things, particularly that the Soviet Union and communism itself were collapsing of their own weight and contradictions, hardly an accepted idea in the late 1970s, and on what historians called "American exceptionalism." I think Americans are different and I had written about that in a book, *American Journey,* which retraced the American travels of Alexis de Tocqueville in the 1830s. Reagan thought Americans were simply better than other people and that God meant it to be that way. He was a man of ideas—good ones, bad ones, and odd ones. He understood that words are often more important than deeds. One of his forgotten hired hands, James Lake, a campaign press secretary in 1980, said he saw Reagan lose his temper only once. Lake had walked into the candidate's section of a plane to say he needed to talk to him about some issue. Reagan snapped at him: "No, I'm busy. Can't you see I'm working on my speech? Just go away. We will be there in 20 minutes and I have to give this speech."

The speech was the real work. No one ever called Reagan an intellectual, but he did see the world in terms of ideas. He was an ideologue with a few ideas that he held with stubborn certainty. His rhetorical gift was to render those ideas into values and emotions. He was capable of simplifying ideas to the point of dumbing-down the nation's dialogue by brilliantly confusing fact and fiction. He made politics, and governing, too, into a branch of his old business, entertainment.

President Reagan is the third of my books about Presidents important in my professional lifetime. With each of them, John F. Kennedy, Richard M. Nixon, and Reagan, I have tried to reconstruct a President's world from his own perspective. I am interested in what he knew and when he knew it, what he actually saw and did—sometimes day by day, sometimes hour by hour, sometimes minute by minute. I have tried to show what it was like for each of these men to be President.

President Reagan did not "do" as much as Kennedy and Nixon. They were younger men who wanted to know as much as they could and control as much as possible. Kennedy and Nixon cared greatly about what people were saying about them. Reagan had the virtues and failings of an old man: He already knew what he wanted to know, he was set in his ways, stubborn, and he did not generally care what journalists or the hired help thought of him. He was not obsessed by history, as were Kennedy and Nixon. His wife, Nancy, would become the shaper and keeper of the legacy. In 1985 he told one of his assistants, political director Ed Rollins: "First of all, the history will probably get distorted when it's written. And I won't be around to read it."

President Reagan did not so much do things as persuade others to do them. His official role model was a President generally judged unimportant, Calvin Coolidge. Young Ronald Reagan, growing up in Illinois river towns, read Coolidge's autobiography, and he read it again while in the White House. One Coolidge paragraph struck me: "In the discharge of the duties of the office there is one rule of action more important than all others. It consists in never doing anything that some one else can do for you."

In *An American Life,* the autobiography he wrote in 1990, Reagan compares his boyhood on the river to the adventures of Tom Sawyer. Exactly right. President Reagan could have been a barefoot hustler in overalls, chewing on a stick of hay, sitting on a barrel in the shade, munching on someone else's apple, a shrewd kid watching other kids whitewash his fence because he had persuaded them it was fun.

THIS book is a narrative of what President Reagan did at crucial points of his eight years in office. What I searched for was what he knew or heard, said and read. In my account, all of what he says and is said to him is taken from recordings, documents, journals, notes, and interviews, including my own reporting over the years. Where someone's thoughts are mentioned, it is because he or she told me those thoughts, or told someone at the time, or recorded their thinking in journals or memoranda. In some cases, usually in tape-recorded and telephone conversations, I have edited out "uhs," repetitions, and confusing errors of grammar.

I do not subscribe to the many theories of Reagan's passivity. It is true that much of any presidency is essentially reactive, dealing with crises unpredictable and unanticipated—strikes, bombings, market crashes, revolutions, plagues—but the President Reagan I found in the course of my research was a gambler, a bold, determined guy. On Halloween night in 1975, he told his wife he was running for President again, no matter what: "I'm entering the race. Otherwise I'd feel like the guy who always sat on the bench and never goes into the game." Reagan came to the White House more than five years later with an agenda: a few simple ideas about taxes and prosperity, the moral and economic bankruptcy of communism, and a remaking of America back into remembrances of his own boyhood and a *Reader's Digest* version of the 1950s. He remembered happy times.

Or perhaps it was just what he imagined, a gentle God-fearing and whitewashed American past that never was, happy times he convinced himself and many others were real and wonderful. He also saw or imagined an American future of lower taxes, less government, reduced taxation, military superiority, and a world where Americans would walk proudly and safely on the meanest streets and trails of the world. He believed everyone admired or envied Americans—if they did not, they were evil. He imagined a future, and he made some of it happen.

Reagan was dismissed as a lightweight with no strategy and he resented that. Asked before he was President about how he would deal with communism and the Soviet Union, he replied: "We win. They lose." And that's what happened, though he did not reach his imagined end all by himself, as his champions now claim in television commentary and volumes of hero worship. "Reagan's admirers should not claim that without him the collapse of communism would never happen," editorialized *The Economist* in the week of his death in June 2004. "It would have collapsed anyway, in the end. . . . A system which believes that a small group of self-selected possessors of the truth knows how to run everything is sooner or later going to run into the wall. But Reagan brought the wall closer. . . . The result: maybe 20 years less of Marxist-Leninist ideological arrogance, and of the cold war's dangers."

Former President Gerald Ford added to that, saying bringing down communism was not a one-man job: "I feel very strongly that our country's policies, starting with Harry Truman and those who followed him—Democratic and Republican presidents and Democratic and Republican Congresses—brought about the collapse of the Soviet Union."

That is true, of course. President Reagan did not win the Cold War and end communism, but he knew that it was going to happen. No small thing. He had imagined it for a long time and his vision traveled further than he knew. On the morning of April 1, 1985, James Buckley, a former senator from New York, serving as president of Radio Free Europe, came into the Oval Office. He was holding a couple of tiny pieces of rice paper. "This is a message to you from a hundred women who are locked in the pokey"—meaning a Soviet prison camp.

Buckley had a magnifying glass. "This is what they say: 'We women political prisoners congratulate you on your reelection to the post of President of the U.S.A. We look with hope to your country which is on the road to freedom and respect for human rights. We wish you success.' "

"Oh, golly," said the President. "Golly, how could anyone write that small? Good Lord. Oh, Lord. Damnit it is an evil empire. . . . The system is barbarism!"

I DO NOT think Reagan was an unwitting tool of a manipulative staff. Quite the opposite. This was a man, a failing president in 1986, who turned around history by understanding and then trusting his greatest adversary—as his own chorus of advisers and conservative commentators were treating him as a fool being tricked into surrendering to evil communism. The first and most effective chief of staff in Reagan's White House, James A. Baker III, once said of the boss: "He treats us all the same, as hired help." Could the talented Mr. Baker have changed the tax code or doubled to 14 percent the portion of the federal budget devoted to interest payments? Could the shrewd Secretary of Defense, Caspar Weinberger, have more than doubled the Pentagon budget? Could the experienced Secretary of State, George Shultz, have believed Russia would be applying for membership in NATO by 1993? Could Donald Regan, another Reagan chief of staff, have raised the morale of a nation?

"What was the biggest problem in the White House when you were there?" I asked Don Regan.

"Everyone there thought he was smarter than the President," he said.

"Including you?"

"Especially me."

Smart they might be, but in the end they were just part of "Reaganism," a word that defined his dominance. No other President became a noun in that way. Amazing things, good and bad, happened in the 1980s because President Reagan wanted them to happen. He knew how to be President. The job does not pay by the hour. Presidential naps don't endanger the country or the world. And Reagan's ignorance of detail and his many blunders did not change the way people felt about him as a leader. His personal popularity remained remarkably high in the years after the recession of 1982, even though a majority of Americans disapproved of what he was doing in driving the country deep into debt, fighting little wars in Central America, secretly selling arms to Iran, or refusing to acknowledge the lethal spread of AIDS across the nation.

Governor Reagan won the Republican nomination for President on his third try. He won the presidency because President Jimmy Carter had failed. Inflation, interest rates, and rising energy costs seemed out of control in Carter's last year. In July of 1979, President Carter went on national television, seeming to blame the American people for those troubles in one of the most pessimistic speeches in American history. "I want to talk to you tonight about a fundamental threat to American democracy. . . . It is a crisis of confidence. It strikes at the very heart and soul and spirit of our national will. . . . We've always had a faith that the days of our children would be better than our own. Our people are losing that faith." That November, Iranians, driven by a zealous theocracy, seized the United States embassy in Tehran, taking more than fifty Americans hostage. In December, the Soviet Union invaded Afghanistan to preserve a communist government in Kabul.

In contrast to Carter, Reagan was the voice of optimism and national destiny, saying, as he always had, that Americans were God's chosen, the world's last best hope. He defeated Carter with just over

50 percent of the popular vote. Through good times and bad for eight years, according to Gallup polls, he was the most admired man in America. He had a 63 percent approval rating when he left the White House, higher than the other popular Presidents in the last half of the century—Dwight Eisenhower (59 percent) and John F. Kennedy (58 percent). Among Americans between eighteen and twenty-nine, Reagan's approval rate was 87 percent. There are debates about whether he realigned the country's political structure in the manner of Franklin D. Roosevelt, but there is no doubt that he established the Republicans as the country's governing party. There is also no doubt that many Americans paid a high price for President Reagan's certainty. None of us can be certain of the "opportunity costs" of Reaganism; the money going to tax breaks and defense may have cost decades of lost opportunities for better education and health care. The rich got richer and Reagan told them they deserved it. The poor got poorer and he told them it was their own fault. It was his policy. In its 1982 annual report to the President, the Council of Economic Advisers stated that cash transfers to the poor interfere with the workings of the private marketplace and weaken the national economy, concluding: "Transfers reduce the incentive of recipients to work and taxes imposed on the rest of society to finance those transfers also cause losses in efficiency."

For American conservatives he became what Franklin Roosevelt was to liberals. Larger than life. Indispensable. Almost all those I interviewed, during the five years I worked on this book, said that they considered Ronald Reagan a great man. Many had worked for him, of course, but his adversaries no longer laughed at the question. One of those, Robert Rubin, Secretary of the Treasury under President Bill Clinton, did not smile as he told me: "Reagan is above the debate for them; it is like reciting Mao Zedong's *Little Red Book*. He is like a religious figure. Conservatives have to hold him up as an icon to preserve the agenda, to protect the ideology." And so they do, writing books, renaming airports, raising statues. They keep the faith. Returning to the White House on March 30, 1981, the day President Reagan was shot, Vice President Bush said it all:

"We will act as if he were here."

CHAPTER 1

JANUARY 20, 1981

THE THIRTY-NINTH PRESIDENT OF THE UNITED STATES, Jimmy Carter, had not slept for almost forty-eight hours when he telephoned the President-elect, Ronald Reagan, just before seven o'clock on the morning of January 20, 1981. "We have good news on the hostages," he said to the Reagan assistant who answered the phone, Michael Deaver.

Carter had spent those sleepless hours in the Oval Office and in the subbasement Situation Room of the White House, personally supervising intricate negotiations between diplomats in Washington, Tehran, and Algiers, and bankers in New York and London, attempting to free fifty-two American hostages held in captivity in Iran for 444 days. The last step was a complex series of bank cash transfers releasing $12 billion in Iranian assets seized by the United States government after the diplomats, their staff, spies, and Marine guards were taken at the embassy in Tehran in November of 1979. At 6:47 A.M., the last transfer was done and planes were waiting on the runway of the Tehran airport to take the Americans out of Iran.

Reagan was sleeping just across Pennsylvania Avenue, in Blair House. Deaver told President Carter that Reagan had left orders that he was not to be disturbed unless the hostages were actually free, in the air and out of Iranian airspace. The former governor of California had left a wake-up call for eight o'clock, four hours before he would be sworn in as the fortieth President. At the appointed hour, Deaver knocked on the door. Reagan grunted and Deaver heard him roll over, so he knocked again, saying: "It's eight o'clock. You're going to be inaugurated as President in a few hours."

"Do I have to?" Reagan called back. Then he laughed.

The President called again at 8:30. Reagan was up. Carter said that planes were still on the runway in Tehran. The takeoff was being delayed by the Iranians and it looked as if the planes would not be out of Iran before noon in Washington, the hour at which Reagan would become the fortieth President. Reagan said he was sorry about that and he meant it. The hostage crisis, along with soaring inflation and interest rates at home, had doomed the Carter presidency and the next President did not want it to take over his as well. He told the President what he had told his own men, that he did not want to say anything about the hostages in public until they were all safely out of Iranian airspace. "It's very close," Carter said. Reagan was not unsympathetic to the man he had defeated in November. He thought Carter deserved both the blame and the credit for the Iranian crisis and resolution. The President-elect's major contribution to the negotiations were campaign statements designed to persuade the Iranians that he would be a tougher adversary than Carter, and they would be well advised to release the Americans before he took office. As the conversation wound down, Reagan asked the exhausted President if he would be willing to go to West Germany, to the United States Air Force base and hospital at Wiesbaden, to greet the hostages once they were finally released. Carter immediately said yes.

A couple of hours later the two men rode together side by side in a limousine, up Pennsylvania Avenue to the Capitol for Reagan's inaugural. They did not much like each other and conversation was hard. Reagan took the initiative as he often did; entertainment after all had been his business for more than thirty years. Trying to make his beaten and bitter predecessor feel more comfortable, he rolled out old Hollywood stories, a couple of them about his days at Warner Brothers studios under Jack Warner.

"He kept talking about Jack Warner," Carter said later to his communications director, Gerald Rafshoon. "Who's Jack Warner?"

The Presidents, old and new, shared only one moment of true personal communication. Reagan hoped to announce the release and credit Carter during his inaugural remarks. Just before noon, as he stood to take his oath of office, he turned to look at Carter, who shook his head slightly and whispered the words, "Not yet." Back in the Situation Room, eighteen feet under the West Wing of the White House, Carter's chief of staff, Hamilton Jordan, and Rafshoon were working, still on open phone lines back and forth to Algiers. As Reagan stood to deliver his inaugural address a mile away, a White House secretary came down and told them, a bit frantically, "You've got to get out of here. The Reagans will be on their way." As the Carter men hustled up the stairs from the Situation Room, they realized that the photographs on the wall of the corridor leading to the press room had all been changed. Carter images were gone, the framed Reagans smiled at them now.

Reagan, who took pride in the fact that he wrote or at least carefully edited most of his own speeches before and after he became a politician, had begun working on his inaugural speech the day after he defeated Carter. Actually he had been working on it for twenty-five years, beginning on the day in 1954 when he was hired by General Electric to translate his fading fame as a movie star into being the company's traveling spokesman and morale booster, speaking to more than 250,000 GE employees at 139 plants. That experience catapulted him into politics at the highest levels when he adapted his standard GE speech into a half-hour 1964 fund-raising speech for the Republican presidential candidate, Senator Barry Goldwater of Arizona. Goldwater was crushed in that election, but Reagan soared, replacing Goldwater as the public voice of American conservatism and becoming governor of California within two years. It was a wonderful voice, husky and honeyed, but not greatly respected. In one of his first presidential campaign memos, Reagan's pollster, Richard Wirthlin, told him:

> We can expect Ronald Reagan to be pictured as a simplistic and untried lightweight (Dumb), a person who consciously misuses facts to overblow his own record (Deceptive) and, if president, one who would be too anxious to engage our country in a nuclear holocaust (Dangerous).

When Reagan won the Republican nomination in 1980 on his third try—he lost to Richard Nixon in 1968 and to President Gerald Ford in 1976—it marked a peak for movement conservatives but still frightened many Republicans who more or less agreed with the premises of the Wirthlin memo. Led by former Secretary of State Henry Kissinger, the party's elders came within minutes of persuading Reagan to take Ford as his running mate, not so much as Vice President but as a kind of co-president in charge of foreign affairs and budgetary matters. A joke, which took notice of Reagan's supposed laziness, made the rounds on the floor of the Republican convention: "Ford will be president before nine, after five, and on weekends."

In the weeks before his inaugural, with staff and press concentrating on who would man the new government, the President-elect spent his own time outlining the inaugural address. To him, the words were more important than the men who served him, aides he usually just called "the fellas," often because he could not remember all their names. He was helped this time by a fellow named Ken Khachigian, a Los Angeles lawyer who had written for President Nixon and done a good deal of the heavy word-lifting on the 1980 campaign speeches. As he always did, Reagan began by chatting for twenty minutes or so about his ideas and gave Khachigian a six-inch pile of the four-by-six index cards he had used and edited for speeches over the years. In his transition meetings with Carter, Reagan had not taken a note nor made a serious comment during the President's long and complicated issue briefings, but at the end of the first and most important session— use of nuclear weapons was one topic—he noticed that Carter used three-by-five cards listing the subjects of the hour-long talk. "Can I get copies of those?" Reagan asked as he stood up to leave.

With his writer taking notes, Reagan began dictating themes:

The system: everything we need is here. It is the people. This ceremony itself is evidence that government belongs to the people. . . . Under that system: our nation went from peace to war on a single morning, we had the depression etc. . . . We showed that they, the people, have all the power to solve things. . . . Want optimism and hope, but not "goody-goody." . . . There's no reason *not* to believe that we have the answer to things that are wrong.

He also told Khachigian to find the script of a World War II movie. "It was about Bataan," he said. An actor named Frank McHugh, Reagan remembered, said something like: "We're Americans. What's happening to us?" The writer found the line, which was somewhat different from what Reagan recalled, and used it as a finale in the first draft of the speech he brought to the President-elect on January 4: "We have great deeds to do. . . . But do them we will. We are after all Americans."

The new President, unlike most of his predecessors, wanted to give his inaugural address from the back of the Capitol, facing west toward the monuments to Washington, Jefferson, and Lincoln—and toward Arlington National Cemetery, the final resting place of many American heroes. He told Khachigian that a friend from California had written him a letter about a soldier buried there, a World War I battlefield courier named Martin Treptow, a boy from Wisconsin killed in action in France in 1917. Treptow had kept a diary, Reagan said, with this on the flyleaf: "My Pledge: America must win this war. Therefore I will work. I will save, I will sacrifice, I will endure, I will fight cheerfully and do my utmost, as if the issue of the whole struggle depended on me alone."

"Can I see the letter?" asked Khachigian. "We have to check this out."

Reagan looked hurt, at least that's what Khachigian thought.

The writer met again with Governor Reagan on January 18, two days before the inauguration. It was a Sunday. The President-elect had already been to church and was sitting in bed, under the covers. He had hung up his pants—so they wouldn't wrinkle, Khachigian thought—and was having coffee and toast with honey. Reagan immediately noticed that the Treptow story was not in the final draft of his speech. Why? Khachigian nervously said that researchers could not find a diary and the soldier was not buried at Arlington but in his hometown, Boomer, Wisconsin.

"Put it back in," Reagan said.

The writer came back an hour later with the changes Reagan wanted. Richard Allen, a conservative veteran of President Nixon's National Security Council scheduled to be Reagan's NSC director, was there with a couple of other staffers to talk about the latest word on the hostages in Iran. They were watching television. Steve Bell of ABC News was talking about the crisis, about Carter and his men working on the details of transferring money to the Iranians. The image of an Iranian mob appeared; the President-elect pursed his lips and muttered: "Shitheels!"

On Tuesday, Reagan's men circulated among reporters, making sure the ladies and gentlemen of the press understood the symbolism of facing westward: a new direction opened by a man of the West. But it was the Californian's words that marked the most radical departure from presidential tradition. And the words were Reagan's own. He wrote the final version of the speech out in longhand on a yellow legal pad—waking once at 4 A.M. to write for twenty minutes—changing the speechwriter's phrasing, changing "they" to "you," adding old favorites of his own, among them: "Those who say we are in a time when there are no heroes just don't know where to look." He followed that with his own ode to the common people: "You can see heroes every day going in and out of factory gates . . . producing food enough to feed all of us and the world beyond. . . . You meet heroes across a counter."

He said nothing he had not said before in his years as spokesman and speechman for General Electric and then as governor of California and as the post-Goldwater icon of the conservative wing of the Republican Party. As he had during the campaign, he touched four simple themes: (1) reducing taxes and deficits, thus reducing the power and size of the federal government; (2) rebuilding the American military; (3) confronting communism around the world; (4) restoring American patriotism and pride.

Ronald Reagan wanted to destroy communism. He had long ago rejected words like "containment" and "détente," instead preaching a victory of right over wrong. In 1977, he had listened to a long briefing by Richard Allen about the need for an overall strategy for dealing with Soviet communism and interrupted to say, "I do have a strategy: 'We win, they lose!' " Talk like that and the repeated anti-communist sermons were what had worried Kissinger and others. But this inaugural day, Reagan's first speech as President focused on America and Americans, just as his campaign had.

Rather than repeat economic statistics, which he often mangled anyway, Reagan tried to change the way people thought. Importantly, he redefined populism, the old American idea that someone up there was screwing the little guy. In the past, in the agricultural South and in the Midwest, the homegrown oppressor of the hardworking little guy was traditionally big business, the banks, the railroads, Wall Street. In Reagan's new populism the bad guys were not businessmen and financiers—they were heroes to Reagan—his bad guy was big government. Speaking to and for all his fellow Americans, their brand-new President said:

> These United States are confronted with an economic affliction of great proportions. . . . In this present crisis, government is not the solution, government is the problem. . . .
>
> It is time to reawaken this industrial giant, to get government back within its means, and to lighten our punitive tax burden. And these will be our first priorities. . . .

Those who do work are denied a fair return for their labor by a tax system which penalizes successful achievement and keeps us from maintaining full productivity. . . . For decades we have piled deficit upon deficit, mortgaging our future and our children's future for the temporary convenience of the present. . . .

"We the people," this breed called Americans . . . special among the nations of the Earth. . . . And as we renew ourselves here in our own land, we will be seen as having greater strength throughout the world. We will again be the exemplar of freedom and a beacon of hope for those who do not now have freedom.

Conservative intellectuals called that a revolution. But to Reagan it was a restoration. He wanted to take America back to a past imagined, a time of hard work, generosity, and patriotism, all under a God on our side.

He ended his speech with the Treptow story, talking of the crosses at Arlington and saying the dead soldier lay under "one such marker" and quoted the young soldier's pledge. "The crisis we are facing today does not require the kind of sacrifice that Martin Treptow and so many thousands of others were called on to make. It does require, however, our best effort and our willingness to believe in our capacity to perform great deeds, to believe that together with God's help, we can and will resolve the problems which now confront us. . . .

"And after all, why shouldn't we believe that? We are Americans."

Reagan, too old to change his mind about much, knew one very big thing about leadership and leaders: Words are usually more important than deeds. And words of hope and destiny had elected him over a failing President. When Jimmy Carter said the nation faced "a crisis of confidence," Reagan said no, it was Jimmy Carter who had lost confidence, adding: "I find nothing wrong with the American people." Carter, the former governor of Georgia, was the last of a line of Democratic and liberal leaders and liberal commentators who consistently reminded Americans of what was wrong with them, citing milestones of failure, from the racism of the old South to the folly of the war in Vietnam and the lying of Watergate. But it was not an easy election. With an independent candidate, John Anderson, a moderate anti-Reagan Republican congressman from Illinois, winning 7 percent of the vote, the new President won just 50.75 percent of the voters who went to the polls that day. So, now Reagan was proceeding down Pennsylvania Avenue to move into the White House and Carter was on a helicopter headed for Andrews Air Force Base and a flight back to Georgia. He met Jordan at Andrews and asked him to check on the hostages. Jordan called the White House to ask his old military liaison whether the hostages were safe yet. "I'm sorry, sir," said the officer. "You are no longer authorized to receive that information."

In a special Inaugural Section of *The Washington Post,* James David Barber, a political scientist from Duke, writer of a best-selling book, *The Presidential Character,* said: "Reagan floated into the presidency on a recurrent tide that swells through politics with remarkable regularity—the tide of reaction against too long and hard a time of troubles, too much worry, too much tension and anxiety. Sometimes people want a fighter in the White House and sometimes a saint. But the time comes when all we want is a friend, a pal, a guy to reassure us that the story is going to come out all right. . . . In short, Reagan was elected because he is not Carter." Then Barber added an important perception of the old entertainer: "Reagan has a propensity to be more interested in theatrical truth than in empirical truth." Reagan was not a man of vision, he was a man of imagination—and he believed in the past he imagined.

Reagan's triumph on November 4, 1980, also swept in Republican congressional candidates across the country, giving the party control of the Senate for the first time since 1954—the new Senate was made up of fifty-three Republicans and forty-seven Democrats—and among the losers that day was a roster of the Senate's liberal all-stars, including George McGovern, Birch Bayh, Frank Church, and John Culver. In the House of Representatives the Democrats retained control with 243 members, while Republicans won 192 races. But several prominent Democratic liberals lost, beginning with Minority Whip John Brademas. "An across-the-board rejection of the Democratic Party," wrote William Schneider, a poll analyst writing in the *Los Angeles Times.*

Still, there seemed to be no consensus that Reaganism or Republicanism were being accepted across the country. The inaugural address got mixed reviews. The conservative editorial page of *The Wall Street Journal* cheered: "President Reagan said what needed to be said. . . . His address was delivered by a man to whom the world has come around and who knows it. It was a radical speech, and it felt good to hear it." The *Baltimore Sun* disagreed: "What an insult to language and logic! It showed a willingness to distort a perfectly valid idea mainly for effect." The *Philadelphia Inquirer* stood somewhere in the middle: "The deep underlying question raised by Mr. Reagan's address, as by his candidacy for President, was unspoken. . . . It is: Can the federal government be significantly dismantled, can the authority of the central government be broadly reduced, programs and spending cut, without savaging the lives and hopes of those Americans who are least equipped to defend themselves?"

The Algerian airliner lifting the hostages out of Iran took off at 12:33 P.M. Washington time. At his formal inaugural lunch, in the Statuary Hall of the Capitol, President Reagan rose to offer a toast, saying: "With thanks to Almighty God, I have been given a tagline . . . some thirty minutes ago, the planes bearing our prisoners left Iranian airspace and are now free." Then, in a viewing stand outside the White House, the new President watched 8,000 marchers and 450 equestrian teams parade by in his honor. With each passing flag, he leaped to his feet and put his right hand over his heart. He leaped again later that night in a holding room with his wife at the Washington Hilton before the first of eight inaugural balls. Straightening his tie in a full-length mirror, he jumped, clicked his heels, and said: "I'm the president of the United States of America!"

On January 29, the new President held his first press conference, nationally televised from the auditorium of the Old Executive Office Building next to the White House. After he recited a short list of symbolic anti-government acts—a civilian hiring freeze, a 5 percent reduction in travel expenses for all federal employees, a reduction in the number of consultants attached to government—Reagan spoke for the first time, as President, about the Soviet Union and communism. For him, after decades of crusading anti-communism, the words were routine. For a President they were harsh. The question was about détente, and he answered: "Well, so far détente's been a one-way street that the Soviet Union has used to pursue its own aims. I don't have to think of an answer as to what I think their intentions are . . . they have openly and publicly declared that the only morality they recognize is what will further their cause, meaning they reserve unto themselves the right to commit any crime, to lie, to cheat, in order to attain that. . . . I think that when you do business with them, even at a détente, you keep that in mind."

Earlier that day, it was reported that his Secretary of State, Alexander Haig, had sent a "sharp message," in State Department jargon, to his Soviet counterpart, Foreign Minister Andrei Gromyko, warning that there would be "dire consequences" if the Soviet Union sent troops into Poland to put down anti-communist strikes and demonstrations. A sharp rise in food prices in the summer of 1980 had triggered protests led by shipyard workers who organized themselves under the banner "Solidarity," which quickly grew into a makeshift national movement of more than five million workers, led by a shipyard electrician named Lech Walesa. The first National Intelligence Estimate sent to President Reagan, fifteen pages prepared by the Central Intelligence Agency and the intelligence divisions of the Pentagon, was titled "Poland's Prospects Over the Next Six Months."

"The present crisis in Poland constitutes the most serious and broadly based challenge to communist rule in the Warsaw Pact in more than a decade," the secret NIE began, then warned that Soviet intervention of thirty Red Army divisions was a possibility if the country's own communist leadership could not control events that seemed to be spinning out of control. The conclusion read: "The Soviets' reluctance to intervene militarily derives above all from the enormous costs they probably anticipate in eliminating Polish armed and passive resistance. . . . We believe that Soviet pressure on the Polish regime will increase and that, if the pattern of domestic confrontation continues, the trend is toward ultimate intervention."

It was a document that played to one of Reagan's core convictions: The point was dramatized in a rather petty way when Soviet ambassador Anatoly Dobrynin arrived at the State Department to deliver a message from Foreign Minister Gromyko. The Soviet limousine was turned away from the department's private garage entrance. The driver was blocked by security guards and told to drop his passenger at the main entrance—let the Russian sign in at the same door used by lesser nations.

The White House announced that the President would make his first speech from the Oval Office on his sixteenth day in office, February 5. The subject would be economics. That timing was purposeful. Reagan wanted to create a sense of urgency, to declare, as he had during the campaign, that the United States was in its worst economic crisis since the Great Depression of the 1930s. When the old Reagan hands from California saw the next-to-final draft of the speech, they were surprised to see that the usual attacks on Washington liberals had been stricken from the text. When one of the Californians, press assistant Lyn Nofziger, asked Reagan about that, he laughed and said, "Listen, if I were making this speech from the outside, I'd kick their balls off."

He was inside now, a new role for the old drumbeater, but as he had during the campaign, he did solemnly recite the alarming statistics that marked the end of Carter's presidency: high inflation, high interest rates, unemployment, and increased deficit spending. He showed graphs with the good lines going down and the bad lines going up. He took a quarter, a dime, and a penny out of his pocket—he had gotten the change from his young personal assistant, Dave Fischer—to illustrate the fact that a 1980 dollar was worth only 36 cents compared with the purchasing power of a 1960 dollar. Then he said: "It's time to try something different, and that's what we're going to do."

He was more specific than politicians usually are on what was to be done, declaring that he wanted to reduce government spending and graduated federal income taxes. On spending, Reagan used a tried-and-true line he had repeated a thousand times in after-dinner speeches: "Over the past decades we've talked of curtailing government spending so that we can lower the tax burden. Sometimes we've even taken a run at doing that. But there were always those who told us that taxes couldn't be cut until spending was reduced. Well, you know, we can lecture our children about extravagance until we run out of voice and breath. Or we can cure their extravagance by simply reducing their allowance."

That was old-time religion to American conservatives. This is what Reagan had told them for years: "It is a myth that our graduated income tax has any resemblance to proportionate taxation. The entire structure was created by Karl Marx. It simply is a penalty on the individual who can improve his own lot; it takes his earnings from him and redistributes them to people who are incapable of earning as much as he can." Ronald Reagan, the movie star making $3,500 a week before World War II, had paid 91 percent in income tax on much of that money. He had hated that, and he promised this night to cut taxes 10 percent a year for three years. The fundamental question for more literal conservatives then was: How do you raise military spending, cut taxes, and reduce deficit spending and the federal deficit itself?

"Voodoo Economics," one Republican, his own Vice President, George H. W. Bush, had called Reagan's numbers games when he was running against him in the 1980 primaries. "Supply-side Economics" was the name put forth by younger conservatives who argued that putting more money back in the pockets of taxpayers would jump-start the economy and lift it to new heights—in earnings, spending, and investment—and actually increase federal revenues to wipe out deficits. That trick was new to the old conservative from California. Whether or not he actually believed in it was a subject of endless argument in conservative journals, but it worked rhetorically as a rationale for Reagan's four goals—and it was at least as true as some of his stock of old anecdotes.

Nice work if you can get it, *The New York Times* reported when the Reagan plan was proposed before the Senate Budget Committee: "Surprise swept over the Democrats when the new Treasury Secretary, Donald Regan, the former chairman of Merrill Lynch, acknowledged that the highly optimistic forecast was based on Administration economists' views of how Americans are likely to respond to the program and not on any existing model."

Reagan did not think in models. He often said he had always believed that economics, his major at Eureka College fifty years before, was at least 50 percent psychology. Times were good if you thought they were good. Or, in this case, the disastrous Carter inflation would go away if people thought it would, because lower inflation would affect, positively, people's attitudes about spending and investing.

The new President laid out his old thinking in simple language in his first budget message to Congress, saying: "First, we must cut the growth of federal spending. Second, we must cut tax rates so that once again work will be rewarded and savings encouraged. Third, we must carefully remove the tentacles of excessive government regulation. . . . Fourth, we must work with the Federal Reserve Board to develop a monetary policy that will rationally control the money supply. Fifth, we must move, surely and predictably, toward a balanced budget."

The old and the new taken together became "Reaganomics." The details of squeezing it all together into a budget and tax legislation was the job of the President's new director of the Office of Management and Budget, a thirty-four-year-old congressman from rural Michigan named David Stockman. During the campaign, Stockman had impressed Reagan and his men when he played his former boss, John Anderson of Illinois, in rehearsals for a September 1980 debate against Carter. Stockman/Anderson clobbered Reagan in secret. The young winner was shocked by the old man's mumbling confusion—at least in those rehearsals. "Sorry, fellas," Reagan would say. "I just lost that one."

Brilliant, confident and overconfident, lean and hungry, Stockman's personal politics had swung in one decade from "a soft-core Marxist," his words, and full-time anti–Vietnam War organizer to a zealous libertarian conservative. A month after election, Reagan had called him and said: "Dave, I've been thinking about how to get even with you for that thrashing you gave me in the debate rehearsals. So I'm going to send you to OMB." Now the new budget director, the youngest Cabinet officer in more than 150 years, was delegated to transform the muddle of Reaganomics into hard numbers by February 18, the day the President intended to present "America's New Beginning: A Program for Economic Recovery" as his first State of the Union message. The kid from Michigan was quite suddenly the fourth or fifth most important man in the White House, behind the President and his "Troika," or as some called it, his triumvirate: chief of staff James A. Baker III, a smooth Houston lawyer who had been Vice President Bush's campaign manager during the Republican primaries; Edwin Meese, a former California prosecutor who served as Governor Reagan's ideological memory; and Deaver, a California public relations man who protected and burnished the governor's persona. In the closing days of the 1980 presidential campaign, Deaver had turned to another old Reagan hand, Martin Anderson, and said, "You know, I am Ronald Reagan. Where do you think he got most of those ideas over the years? Every morning after I get up I make believe I am him and ask what should he do and where should he go." But, in fact, whatever Deaver thought, the staff was not the real Reagan. The old actor was staff-dependent but not staff-driven. He went where he was told to go—taking direction they called it in his old business—but possibly more than any politician of his time he said what he actually thought, often to a fault. Most of the staff also talked as if their man was wife-driven, but he was actually wife-dependent. He might never have become President without his Nancy, but there were many times he was heard saying, "That's enough, Nancy!"

Stockman was the new boy in every way. He signed on to "Supply Side," as he was supposed to, but he certainly never believed it. Young as he was, he was old-school, a cost-cutter and a low-tax man. Supply side was a useful if questionable political doctrine for him. "Starve the beast" were his more brutal codewords for the way to reduce government's role in American life. Sitting in the Old Executive Office Building at the center of piles of black notebooks, chain-smoking Salems, Stockman told a *New York Times* reporter: "I don't feel vulnerable. I'm used to being attacked. That's what all these books are, people losing their benefits from government. There's a lot of enemies in those pages. . . . Most of them have unjust claims."

The Reagan White House was up and running in only a few days, smoothly, or so it seemed to outsiders shielded from the usual arm-wrestling over organization charts and offices with a view. The new President was an old man set in his ways, seventy on February 6, post-ambition in his way, with the certainty of the self-educated. He was quite different from his recent predecessors—John F. Kennedy, Lyndon Johnson, Nixon, and Carter—not obsessed with what other people thought of him. He had been famous for most of his life outside politics and he felt no great need to know what the newspapers were saying about him or anything else each morning. He skimmed *The New York Times* and *Washington Post* each morning at breakfast—fruit or juice, bran cereal, and decaffeinated coffee. He looked at the *Post* first because the *Times* had no comics page, and that was where Reagan had begun his reading since he was a kid. Part of Meese's job was shielding the President from most disagreement. When internal debate could not be avoided, Meese did what he had done when Reagan was governor: call a meeting and let the boss listen to the arguments of Cabinet members and senior officials. When disagreement rose, so did Meese, taking the disputants outside as Reagan waved and said, "Right, fellas, you work that out and get back to me."

"Fellas" put them in their place, at some distance from the boss, and reminded them that throughout his career the people around him were more or less interchangeable, whether they were cameramen on a three-week movie shoot or the drivers he had in eight years as governor of California. Reagan's first chief of staff in Washington, Jim Baker, put it this way: "He treats us all the same, as hired help."

"It isn't that he doesn't like people, because he's very friendly," Martin Anderson told newcomers. "It's that he doesn't need people. Except for Nancy. He's the most warmly ruthless man I've ever seen." Later he added: "When he decided to get something done, you did not want to be in his way. He didn't take any pleasure in hurting people, but you were gone if you were in his way."

Reagan intended to be a President of big things. Baker, Meese, and Deaver handled smaller things, the day-to-day, week-to-week stuff. "I have never seen this man enjoy himself as much as he has in the last few weeks," said Deaver, who had worked for the Reagans for almost twenty years, in an interview with *The New York Times*. "More than anything else, he enjoys presiding over Cabinet meetings and listening to the give-and-take. And he realizes that he is finally doing the things he's been talking about for years." That talking had mostly been public. When the boss did speak in private to the fellows, it was usually cryptic, often confusing. It was the job of everyone else, staff and Cabinet included, to figure out what to do about it. His typical Cabinet meeting exit lines were: "Maybe we should sleep on this," or "You fellas work it out."

That was Reagan's way. After a Cabinet meeting, he stopped by at a meeting of Latin American editors and commentators invited to the White House for a briefing after a conference at the Woodrow Wilson Center. As the participants were sitting down, the President suddenly popped his head in the door and said only a few pointed words: "Sorry I can't stay with you. But there is something I want you to know. We are going to turn Latin America into a beacon of freedom."

Then, with a wave, he was gone.

An early memo from his Secretary of State, Alexander Haig, a veteran of two White Houses, briefly mentioned Latin America and "steps being taken to implement your decisions." The "decisions" were actually presidential musings on the possibilities of covert aid to the government of El Salvador, where a right-wing government was fighting left-wing insurgents, and covert opposition to the government of Nicaragua, where a left-wing government, the Sandinistas, had driven out a right-wing military dictatorship supported for decades by Washington. The "decisions" were Reagan's talking points on a single card dated in February: "Covert dimension to what must be a comprehensive strategy for dealing with Cuba throughout Central America. . . . Where will we get the money? . . . Cannot some of the items be funded by Defense? . . . Can we not get some help from [other countries]? . . . Come back with a refined proposal in a week."

The idea might be the President's, but in his memo, the Secretary of State kept the initiative for himself, adding a final sentence that began: "Unless you prefer otherwise . . ." The administration and the men in it went their own way unless the boss said he preferred otherwise.

Talking among themselves, the conferees at the Wilson Center meeting decoded Reagan's "beacon of freedom" remark as: There will be a lot more military aid, a lot more covert action, and a lot more killing in Central America. That was rather dramatically confirmed a bit later during the same conference. One of the scheduled briefers, the United States ambassador to El Salvador, Robert White, walked in and said, "I've just been fired by Haig." The reason, leaked to newspapers by Haig's people, was that White had gone to the press with his complaints that the Reagan administration was considering covertly aiding right-wing death squads responsible for the murders of hundreds of Salvadorans and several Americans, including three nuns raped and killed on the road from the capital, San Salvador, to the airport on December 2, 1980.

The President was a clean-desk man. James Baker's deputy, Richard Darman, served as Reagan's "In Box" and "Out Box." When the President came down from the living quarters, his schedule for the day was there in a leather folder. He liked to draw a line through each appointment as it ended. Next to that were papers collected and compiled by Darman, most of them approved in advance by Baker. The documents, briefings, clippings, and memos were usually short and direct, light on numbers and other complexities. The papers and notes that Darman brought in late in the afternoon, usually at 5 P.M., for Reagan's evening work at a small study upstairs—often he read them while watching television with his wife—were the same, most of them summaries or talking points on a single page, or two at most.

Many of the pages waiting on Reagan's desk each morning were "Recommended Telephone Call" memos. Usually the calls were to members of Congress: "Thank Lloyd for his support," things like that, a dozen or so most days. The memos came back each evening marked, in the President's handwriting, "Mission Accomplished, RR." He arrived in the Oval Office each morning at nine o'clock or a few minutes after, had lunch with his wife upstairs in the living quarters, came back at two o'clock, and left before six each afternoon. Most days there was also morning and afternoon "staff time"—usually reading and writing letters, sometimes taking a nap. After supper, Darman would deliver a package of readings, placing them on a table upstairs. They were sorted in colored folders—red for "Classified," green for "Action," gray for speech material, blue for general information. Darman nodded to the Reagans sitting at opposite ends of a long couch, watching television, or tapes of the evening newscasts, or an old film, often munching popcorn. He tried to keep the reading material to an hour and a half, and the President methodically went though the folders, putting a small check or his initials on each document as he finished it.

Those beginnings seemed so even-tempered and orderly that Reagan was comfortable, and then some, walking through an hourlong NBC News show titled *Day in the Life of the President* after only twenty days in office. Already, his days were pretty much the same. Early on, Jim Baker realized that his boss, the old actor, was used to working from a script and used to taking direction. "Mr. President," he said at the beginning, "if you agree, we think we ought to concentrate on your economic agenda, to the exclusion of everything else, for the first three months of your administration." So, each day, Baker or Darman would appear, saying, "Here's what the day looks like." If the President preferred otherwise, which he rarely did, he would say so—if not, he would methodically begin crossing off the meetings and briefings, making the phone calls until it was time to leave his bare desk.

For the NBC cameras, the President arrived an hour earlier than on most other days, coming downstairs just after 8:15 A.M. for a breakfast meeting with labor leaders who had supported him against Carter. Then there was his usual 9:15 meeting with Baker, Meese, and Deaver, and at 9:30 with the three of them and Richard Allen, the National Security Adviser, who delivered the "Morning Summary," a dozen or so short intelligence reports and analyses of the state of the world. The civil war in El Salvador and the strikes and demonstrations in Poland usually dominated the first pages the President saw, but there were other topics, too, including: "Giscard Proposes International Conference on Afghanistan" . . . "Israel: Likud Government Begins Final Settlement Push" . . . "West Germany: Unrest in Schmidt Coalition" . . . "Soviet Assessment of Impact of Hostage Release" . . . "Italian Communist Party Wants Role in Government."

On February 10, before the cameras were allowed in, Allen did have real business, arriving with a short and classified Central Intelligence Agency biography of Poland's new leader, General Wojciech Jaruzelski, who was trying to bring military order to the country after weeks of Solidarity strikes. At 9:45, with the cameras rolling, Max Friedersdorf, his congressional liaison, arrived with Press Secretary James Brady. As broadcast three days later on *NBC Magazine*, the network host, David Brinkley, put those scripted little sessions in a favorable and dramatic frame, saying:

> There are those who say he can't do it, that the political pressure against cutting federal payrolls, contracts, subsidies, grants, benefits are so great that Washington and particularly Congress cannot stand up to them. Well, that may be true. Modern history suggests it is true. Since 1933 and Franklin D. Roosevelt and the Depression

nobody has changed the thrust of the United States government. More taxes and more spending. And no one has really tried. Reagan will try.

Those words segued on screen to a full Cabinet meeting, which the President opened with a small joke, telling them the subject was the economy, "So try not to smile too much."

The agenda in front of him said: "Announce that the focus of the Cabinet meeting is on the Economic Program. . . . Indicate that Don Regan and Dave Stockman have been working day and night to meet our schedule. . . . Before getting into the details of the program, ask Dave Stockman for an overview . . . (Stockman will deliver a list of programs that will not be cut in any substantial way.) . . ."

"Don Regan and Dave Stockman have been working night and day," the President said. "Before we get into details, I'd like to ask Dave for an interview . . . I mean an overview."

As Stockman began, Brinkley's voice overrode him, saying, "Stockman is the big number now. He's so fast with big figures that he scares old Washington hands."

Stockman was pretty fast with words, too, beginning with the job of meeting Reagan's campaign promises—cutting taxes, building up the military, and then somehow cutting the federal budget enough to balance it. He began with budget cuts for the fiscal year 1982, which would begin in eight months, on October 1, 1981. "The goals you gave us are extraordinarily difficult," he said. "But I'm pleased to report today that we're almost there. . . . We have $49.8 billion of savings in the fiscal 1982 budget. We only have about $4.3 million to go. . . . We're 93 percent of the way to the goal you set."

Whatever those numbers meant—and no one at the table knew—Stockman did know they were wrong and impossible, too. The numbers he was using were based on January projections that the 1982 budget would have a deficit—the gap between revenues and spending—of $75 billion. But factoring in Reagan's proposed tax cuts and defense spending increases, Stockman's computer was calculating $600 billion of deficits over the next five years. Moving right along as the President nodded, Stockman changed one promise with a muttering reference to balancing the budget by 1984, a year later than Reagan had promised. No one noticed. Stockman sounded sure and confident, but when he finished his recitation, his hands were shaking when he pushed at the mop of long hair that helmeted his face. But the President, who had not really spoken to him since he was appointed, seemed pleased, saying, "Good work, Dave."

Then, as directed, for the cameras, Stockman began reciting a list of programs protected against Reagan's promised budget cuts—he meant "so far," but he never said that—beginning with the great middle-class entitlements, Social Security and Medicare. Suddenly the room came alive. "That's great!" someone said. "This is just wonderful," Reagan added.

Leaving the room, away from the cameras, Meese and Brady began talking about how to get the great news to the press. "No, no," Stockman tried to explain, telling Meese, "We can't imply that they're exempted from cuts entirely." They ignored him. They had heard what they wanted to hear and they were preparing press releases. The misunderstood misinformation was the lead three-deck headline of the next morning's *New York Times:*

> REAGAN WON'T CUT
> 7 SOCIAL PROGRAMS
> THAT AID 80 MILLION
>
> ANNUAL COST IS $210 BILLION
>
> White House Says That Retaining
> Medicare and Other Services
> Will Benefit 'Truly Needy'

On another morning, the President's script was titled "Cabinet Talking Points" and began with an introduction of Secretary of Defense Caspar Weinberger:

"Turn to Cap Weinberger who will outline where he and Dave Stockman have found savings within the Department of Defense." But there were no real savings in military spending. Quite the opposite. Another series of misunderstandings and miscalculations—Weinberger budget tricks and Stockman mistakes—was producing fuzzy budget numbers and footnotes that could produce a 10 percent a year increase in defense spending for at least six years. That represented double what candidate Reagan had proposed during the campaign. "What happened?" Stockman asked one of his assistants when he saw the talking points.

Three things happened. Reagan had escalated his promises during the campaign. And the budget director and the Defense Secretary had agreed on a 7 percent a year increase on Carter's defense budget. Stockman used the 1980 Carter budget of $142 million. But Weinberger used the 1981 number, which included a congressionally mandated, built-in 9 percent a year increase that had been added after the national humiliation of the failed Iranian hostage rescue mission called Desert One. Finally, Reagan himself had ordered a onetime "Get well" package of expenditures that amounted to growth increments of 12 percent in 1981 and 15 percent in 1982. So, the 7 percent increase was on a $222 billion base rather than the $142 billion base Stockman had in mind.

Even with the date for balancing the budget quietly extended to 1984, Stockman's projections indicated that the tax cut and the defense buildup would create the greatest budget deficits in history, growing to $130 billion in that year alone. He was dealing with the fuzziness of the numbers by placing asterisks all over the budget; each asterisk represented "Future savings to be identified." On camera, the President nodded occasionally and said more than once, "Good job, Dave. We're here to do whatever it takes." Stockman was telling himself that he could still make the numbers balance with what he called "Chapter Two" cuts in Social Security, Medicare, and other entitlement programs, which accounted for more than 40 percent of the total budget. That fantasy strategy collapsed with the press release that led the *Times* and most other newspapers on the morning of February 11. Whatever the numbers showed, the President's breezy optimism held, and leaving a dinner that night Reagan said he still believed the budget could be balanced by 1983, then added: "If we try for '83, we're sure to get it by '84."

The first Harris poll of the Reagan presidency was published that same morning, February 11, and *The Washington Post* reported it this way: "By 77 to 17 percent, the majority of Americans give the new president positive marks on 'inspiring confidence in the White House.' This contrasts sharply with the 64 to 34 percent negative rating on the confidence issue Jimmy Carter was given as he left office. . . . An 87 to 10 percent majority rates Reagan favorably for deciding to give priority to improving the economy."

On February 14, at Camp David, the presidential retreat in Maryland's Catoctin Mountains, Reagan sat down with a speech draft by Khachigian, and memos from Stockman, and began writing out his

"Economic Address" in longhand. Twenty pages. That was the way he had worked for almost forty years, from the time he became a member of the board of directors of the Screen Actors Guild in 1941.

"I'm here tonight," he wrote in the second paragraph, "to ask that we share in restoring the promise that is offered to every citizen by this, the last best hope of man on earth."

That was how he began before Congress on the night of February 18, and then, following a Stockman suggestion—"An opening in which old, failed policy principles are set up in straw-man fashion: this sets the strategy for a totally new framework for national economic policy" read a memo from the budget director—he continued:

All of us are aware of the punishing inflation which has for the first time in sixty years held to double-digit figures for two years in a row. Interest rates have reached absurd levels of more than twenty percent and over fifteen percent for those who would borrow to buy a home. . . . Almost eight million Americans are out of work. . . . Hourly earnings of the American worker, after adjusting for inflation, declined five percent over the past five years, Federal personal taxes for the average family have increased 67 percent. . . .

Our national debt is approaching $1 trillion. A few weeks ago I called such a figure, a trillion dollars, incomprehensible, and I've been trying ever since to think of a way to illustrate how big a trillion really is. And the best I could come up with is that if you had a stack of thousand-dollar bills in your hand only four inches high, you'd be a millionaire. A trillion dollars would be a stack of thousand-dollar bills 67 miles high. The interest on the public debt this year we know will be over $90 billion.

Reagan proposed cutting the funding of eighty-three major programs, proposed his tax cuts and increased military spending, and then said, as he had written himself on the nineteenth page of his speech draft:

We're in control here. There's nothing wrong with America that together we can't fix. . . . The substance and prosperity of our nation is built by wages brought home from the factories and the mills, the farms, and the shops. . . . For too long now, we've removed from our people the decisions on how to dispose of what they created. We've strayed from first principles. We must alter our course.

The taxing power of government must be used to provide revenues for legitimate government purposes. It must not be used to regulate the economy or bring about social change. We've tried that and we must be able to see it doesn't work.

"This was the big night," he wrote carefully in the diary he had decided to keep as President. "It was a thrill and something I will long remember."

"REAGAN: NOTHING WRONG THAT WE CAN'T FIX" headlined the *New Orleans Times-Picayune*. "REAGAN ROLLS ECONOMIC DICE TO GET U.S. BACK ON COURSE," said the *Omaha World Herald*. "A Bold and Risky Venture" said *The New York Times* over an analysis by the paper's chief Washington correspondent, Hedrick Smith, that said: "Much attention has focused on the specific numbers and programs involved. . . . Only now have some politicians begun to comment that the new President is staking the Republicans' future on achieving a philosophical sea change in American politics. . . . Democrats and Republicans remarked that in his straight-talking, figure-studded speech, Mr. Reagan had confronted Congress with a set of decisions on domestic policy that were of greater magnitude of any since the early New Deal period." The paper's economic correspondent, Steven Rattner, added: "President Reagan's economic program represents a daring gamble that a sweeping application of an untested economic theory can improve the American economy radically and quickly."

"Figure-studded" the speech might be, but there were no numbers in the President's handwritten draft—just blanks. Someone else filled in those blanks. The speech defined itself in its final sentences: "The people are watching and waiting. They don't expect miracles. They do expect us to act. Let us act together."

It was a stunning speech. Two days later a *Washington Post*/ABC News poll showed that two-thirds of respondents across the nation said they agreed with the President, although there were indications in other answers that they recognized his will and confidence better than they understood his economic arguments. *The Times,* which often set the agenda for the rest of the press and of the Washington political establishment, too, began to catch up with what had happened. "Trying to Repeal Keynes—President's Plans Considered as Revolutionary as Those Espoused by the New Deal in the 30's" was the headline over a front-page analysis by the paper's chief economic correspondent, Leonard Silk:

> He is urging tighter eligibility rules and reduced spending in food stamps, student loans, welfare, free school lunches, aid to the arts, humanities, sciences, public-service jobs, and much else. . . . But in economic terms, something even larger is afoot. The most remarkable aspect of Mr. Reagan's program is his effort to repeal the so-called Keynesian revolution: the transformation of economic theory that flowed from the mind of John Maynard Keynes in the 1930's and came to dominate the thinking of Presidents and Prime Ministers for almost half a century.
>
> The Keynesian doctrine sought economic growth and stable prices through the manipulation of Government budgets. Governments were counseled that in a lagging underemployed economy, revival lay in generating demand by cutting taxes and raising public spending. Conversely the remedy for an over-heated economy was to raise taxes and curb spending to avoid inflation.
>
> In crisp contrast, President Reagan . . . has declared new guidelines for public policy that stress stimulating not demand but production and supply, mainly by lowering business taxes, while relying on other measures—budget cuts and tight money—to rein in inflation. And, more fundamental, the President's overriding purpose is to bring about a permanent shrinkage of Government's place in the American economy.

Rudolph Penner, the assistant director of President Ford's Office of Management and Budget, was even blunter, writing in the *Times*: "President Reagan has proposed a huge restructuring of government, and people are actually taking him seriously. The man, whom we call a conservative, turns out to be downright radical. . . . It is Mr. Reagan's goal to lower budget outlays to 19 percent of the gross national product by fiscal year 1986, compared with an estimated level of 23 percent in 1981."

Penner used a telling anecdote about the power of a determined President who instinctively understood the Oval Office's agenda-setting power: "Mr. Reagan proposes reducing food stamps by $1.8 billion in 1982. One newspaper story quoted an unnamed Congressional staff member who said that the Budget Committee would not accept more than $1 billion in cuts. It is probably safe to say that two years ago, a similar Congressional staff member would have ruled out any cuts at all. Four years ago, he might have been demanding increases."

On the other hand, the right hand, *Human Events,* a sixty-thousand-circulation weekly newspaper favored by conservative activists and Reagan's favorite reading for years—which featured headlines such as "State Department Spreading Marxism in Central America"—began its coverage of the speech with: "President Reagan's economic package, less bold than many of his supporters would have wished . . . is nevertheless a strong attempt to rescue the economy, tether the runaway government, restore a good measure of economic liberty to the people and repair our crumbling defense posture. And considering the efforts of past chief executives, the proposal is almost revolutionary."

Human Events, however, was no favorite of the new men around Reagan. Baker and Darman, and Deaver, too, did their best each week to keep it out of the reading material they gave the President as he headed up to the living quarters and an evening of television. *Human Events* was also promoting the idea of "defensive weapons," specifically "Space Lasers," a kind of electronic umbrella to destroy ballistic missiles fired from the Soviet Union. "The first space-based lasers could be in orbit by the mid or late 1980s," wrote Senator Malcolm Wallop of Wyoming in a January issue. "Two dozen of these lasers would have to be orbiting in order to cover every spot on the globe at any given time. Each station would have enough fuel for hundreds of 'shots'—meaning that each could cope with the possibility of a thousand missiles being launched in an almost simultaneous barrage."

The conservative journal was already deeply suspicious of the men around their old hero, the new President. "Is Reagan Ignoring Activists?" by William A. Rusher captured that uneasiness. Rusher, publisher of a newer and slicker conservative journal, *National Review,* pointed out that many of the best jobs in the administration were going to moderate Republicans with Ivy League degrees and names like J. Parmalee Butterthorpe III—or James Addison Baker III—rather than to people with names like Fred Bezirk, who led young conservative groups on middle-class campuses.

In the same issue *Human Events* promoted a book titled *Wealth and Poverty* by George Gilder, which attacked heavy taxation of wealthy investors and emphasized the moral and spiritual superiority of capitalism over other economic systems: "A must-read for those conservatives concerned about the future of capitalism . . . a refreshing departure from the spate of no-growth, the world-is-ending books on economics which have been in vogue in recent years." *

Rusher's complaints aside—and he knew that Reagan's Sacramento was a place of talking right and governing from somewhere near the center—ideas and optimism were in the air and so was the President. By ten o'clock the next morning, the Reagans were on Air Force One, flying west for a few days at Rancho del Cielo, his California ranch in the Santa Ynez Mountains, more than 2,200 feet above the Pacific beaches of Santa Barbara. During the flight, Reagan talked a bit to the pool reporters, a half-dozen men and women seated in the rear of the plane, who would later brief other reporters. They asked him whether he felt good about the big speech and the old star charmed them, saying: "Yes, well, I'm in good spirits, but then you're always in good spirits when you figure you got by without losing your place—or forgetting your lines."

---

* In this case the President outwitted the men who would be his handlers. According to Lou Cannon of *The Washington Post*, Reagan arranged to have *Human Events* delivered directly to the White House living quarters on weekends.

CHAPTER 2
MARCH 30, 1981

"THE MOST TRUSTED MAN IN AMERICA," as national polls crowned him, Walter Cronkite did his last regular *CBS Evening News* broadcast during the first week of March 1981. It featured a long exclusive interview with President Reagan, taped in the Oval Office on the afternoon of March 3. It was quite different from the understated and scripted *Day in the Life of the President* done two weeks earlier by his old rival, NBC's David Brinkley. Cronkite went after Reagan.

One of the anchorman's early questions focused on the business of making Anatoly Dobrynin use the same State Department entrance as everybody else. "What advantage is there in embarrassing the Soviet Ambassador like that? Was that just a macho thing for domestic consumption?"

Reagan, as avuncular as "Uncle Walter," chuckled for a moment, then answered: "I have to tell you, I didn't know anything about it until I read it in the paper, saw it on television myself. I don't know actually how that came about."

And, he went on, he never asked anyone about it. Cronkite persisted, asking: "Don't you think the Russians kind of think we're childish when we pull something like that?"

Reagan chuckled again: "I don't know. I don't know, or maybe they got a message."

"Your hard line toward the Soviet Union . . . There are some who, while applauding that stance, feel that you might have overdone the rhetoric a little bit in laying into the Soviet leadership as being liars and thieves, et cetera?"

"I was asked a question. . . . I said we're naive if we don't remember their ideology is without God, without our idea of morality in the religious sense—their statement about morality is that nothing is immoral if it furthers their cause, which means that they can resort to lying or stealing or cheating or even murder if it furthers their cause. . . . If we're going to deal with them, then we have to keep that in mind."

Later, when Cronkite asked again whether Reagan's rhetoric was eliminating any chance to talk about arms control with the Soviets, the President said:

"I remember when Hitler was arming and had built himself up—no one's created quite the military power that the Soviet Union has, but comparatively he was in that way—Franklin Delano Roosevelt made a speech in Chicago at the dedication of a bridge over the Chicago River. And in that speech he called on the free world to quarantine Nazi Germany, to stop all communication, all trade, all relations with them until they gave up that militaristic course—"

Cronkite interjected: "That did a whale of a lot of good."

"The funny thing was," Reagan continued, "he was attacked here in our own country for having said such a thing. Can we honestly look back now and say that World War II would have taken place if we had done what he wanted us to do back in 1938? I think there's a very good chance it wouldn't have taken place."

Hostile questions did not seem to bother Reagan, or if they did, he did not show it. He was not in awe of the job. As Deaver first noticed, Reagan loved the job. The work, so far, seemed not so different from being governor. He wrote or edited speeches pointing the way he wanted to go, knowing that more often than not what he said was far more important than what his men did. Speeches were marching orders. Meese, the keeper of the Reagan flame, told newcomers and anyone else who would listen: "We all know what the President wants and our job is simply to go out and do it."

Reagan was uncomfortable with confrontation but he was not infected by the tension of others. At the Cabinet meeting called to discuss the State Department budget—Stockman's OMB wanted to cut 591 of the department's 22,000 positions—Secretary of State Haig stood up, tapping charts with a metal pointer, and said: "Mr. President, if you accept the OMB proposal, your entire foreign policy will go right down the drain. . . . I cannot tolerate being micro-managed by OMB accountants. Now, Mr. President, they're simply asking you to rear back and"—Haig's voice rose—"shove your head into a pencil sharpener."

The President continued doodling and doing numbers on a yellow pad. He looked up and said: "Now I've done some figuring here on this 591. Couldn't you fellas live with 295 each way?"

Splitting the difference, jokes, quick exits, and silence in private served him well; but when he cleared his throat the others stopped and waited for his benediction. So this was what it was like being President. Carter had told him of the burdens of the job; he concluded there was something wrong with Carter. On March 13, the Reagans went to New York, stayed in the Presidential Suite of the Waldorf-Astoria, ate at Le Cirque, and went to Lincoln Center to see their son, Ron Jr., perform with the Joffrey Ballet—"He was great!" said his father—then they caught up with old Hollywood friends Mickey Rooney and Ann Miller, doing star turns at the Mark Hellinger Theatre in the musical *Sugar Babies*. When the curtain fell, Rooney stepped out and asked the rest of the audience to wait while the Reagans left. As Ron and Nancy walked up the aisle, people began singing "America the Beautiful."

On March 17, St. Patrick's Day, back in the Oval Office, Reagan met with the leaders of the new Republican Senate in the office of the Majority Leader, Senator Howard Baker of Tennessee. The jokes were Irish, the talk was about cutting the budget by eliminating or reducing cost-of-living adjustments (COLAS) that ratcheted up Social Security payments to compensate for inflation. For twenty minutes the senators and Reagan's team, led by Stockman, talked about how to do that. Then Reagan spoke up: "Fellas, I promised I wouldn't touch Social Security. We just can't get suckered into it. The other side's waiting to pounce. So let's put this one behind us and get on with the budget cutting."

"Mr. President, we hear you loud and clear," said Senator Baker. That was it. The meeting was over. The Republicans were back in power, a more disciplined bunch than the Democrats, and their President had spoken. Sitting across from his boss, Stockman knew budget-balancing was a dead letter. Reagan was a politician, a good one, not a revolutionary. When he was governor he had told an aide, Peter Hannaford: "Anytime I can get 70 percent of what I am asking for out of a hostile legislative body, I'll take it. I figure that it will work well enough for me to go back later and get a little more of it here and a little more of it there."

His voice had been just as clear at an earlier meeting, a bipartisan session with governors. There was the opening joke, then just listening for more than a half-hour as governors related their budget concerns. The governor of New York, Hugh Carey, a Democrat, finally rose and said: "Mr. President, I hear your theory, but I don't see the evidence that we can afford this big giveaway to the rich. Do you realize how many needy people are going to be hurt?"

Reagan's face was red, his fists clenched. "I'm not going to sit still for the notion that we're hurting anyone. We've tried your way for decades and millions have been hurt by runaway inflation and unemployment. We didn't invent deficit spending. We didn't advocate tax and spend until the economy was a mess. The American people want a change and to say our tax benefits only help the wealthy, well that's a deliberate distortion and I'm not going to put up with hearing it!"

And that meeting was over.

The President's men knew or were learning how to read Reagan's music. Attorney General William French Smith reversed OMB's proposal to eliminate 2,000 of the Justice Department's 54,000 employees by telling the President at one Cabinet session: "The Justice Department is not a domestic agency. It is"—his cadence slowed—"the internal arm of the nation's defense. Our budget is less than one percent of Defense's, and dollar for dollar we provide far more actual security for the American people."

"Bill is right," Reagan said. "Law enforcement is something that we have always believed was a legitimate function of government."

The trick was to arrange the lyrics, the facts and figures, to fit into the Reagan ideology. At a Cabinet meeting on March 19, Secretary of Transporation Drew Lewis used the President's dislike of government as a wedge to persuade him that import quotas on Japanese automobiles were necessary because American manufacturers were handicapped by government safety standards. "Yes," said Reagan. "We believe in free trade, but there's something different here. Government regulation is responsible for this."

"We're *all* for free enterprise," echoed Vice President Bush, who rarely spoke at such meetings, "but would any of us find fault if Japan announced without any request from us that they were going to *voluntarily* reduce their export of autos to America?"

The President said nothing after that, but when the meeting broke up he asked the Secretary of State to come into the Oval Office. He told him he liked Bush's idea and wanted Haig to call Ambassador Mike Mansfield in Tokyo and have him informally suggest to Foreign Minister Masayoshi Ito that a voluntary quota on auto exports to the United States might relieve congressional pressure for mandated quotas. It was the first time Reagan and Haig met one-on-one for more than a few minutes, and the President was surprised by the rage that seemed to fuel the Secretary's intensity. Haig pounded the President's desk, complaining that White House people—Baker, Deaver, and Bush—were trying to take over his turf.

There was some truth in Haig's complaints, but he also had a very expansive view of his place in the world and his role in the administration—and obvious contempt for Baker, Meese, and Deaver, for Bush, and especially for National Security Adviser Richard Allen. "Second-rate hambones" he called the White House people. On inaugural day, before he was formally sworn in as Secretary of State, Haig had given Reagan a twenty-page draft titled "National Security Decision Directive 1," which essentially gave the State Department control over both diplomacy and national security. It was never signed. Baker, Meese, and Deaver blocked it. They interrogated Haig at length about what he wanted and finally said NSDD 1 would have to be read and approved by the Secretary of Defense, the National Security Adviser, and William Casey, Reagan's campaign manager who had been named director of the Central Intelligence Agency.

Haig blamed the Troika, never seeming to understand that they were doing what they were told to do by the President. For weeks after that, Haig was both puzzled and angry by what he saw as the President's seeming lack of interest in foreign affairs, including the potential threat of leftist movements in El Salvador and the other small countries of Central America.

He did not get it. Reagan was greatly interested in going after Central American Marxists, but he was a more focused and disciplined man than Haig in his arrogance could imagine. Reagan was following his own script: the story line was the domestic economy. The star was motivating bipartisan supporters for his tax and budget cuts—and arguments over foreign policy could split both parties. The Secretary of State took the President too seriously and not seriously enough. In a larger meeeting that same day, March 19, Haig, talking about Cuban influence in Central American conflicts during a White House meeting, said: "Give me the word and I'll turn that island into a fucking parking lot."

Walking out of that meeting, Deaver turned to Bill Clark, another old Reagan hand who was Haig's principal deputy, and said: "Good God, I can't believe that I'm in the room with the President of the United States and the Secretary of State's talking about bombing

Cuba. . . . It scared the shit out of me." Clark said that Haig just talked that way for effect, but Deaver was sure Reagan was just as shaken as he was. Later, he talked with Baker about never letting the Secretary of State be alone again with the President.

Reagan, meanwhile, was preparing for a speech the next day to the 1981 Conservative Political Action Conference at the Mayflower Hotel, close to the White House. "Fellow conservatives," he said. "Our moment has arrived." Speaking to people who were bringing the language and agenda of post-Goldwater conservativism to the capital city—people who read *Human Events* and the *National Review* and knew the difference—the President was direct in stating purpose and theory that had been ignored or dismissed for years by most of the people of power in Washington. "We're not cutting the budget simply for the sake of sounder financial management," Reagan said. "This is only a first step toward reordering the relationship between citizen and government. We can make government again responsive to people . . . by cutting its size and scope and thereby insuring that its legitimate functions are performed efficiently and justly."

"Starve the beast"—the President was what he said he was, an anti-government conservative ready to cut down government by cutting its revenues. This was an audience which understood that "legitimate functions" of government was a euphemism for only two functions: national defense and public order.

On March 24, Foreign Minister Ito of Japan arrived in Washington on an official visit and the President invited him to the White House, telling him privately of strong congressional pressure for auto import quotas. "I don't know whether I'll be able to stop them," said Reagan in a classic political maneuver. "But I think if you voluntarily set a limit on your automobile exports to this country, it would probably head off the bills." Just a suggestion.

As the President and two senators met with Ito, Press Secretary James Brady was preparing a six-paragraph "Statement by the Press Secretary on Foreign and Domestic Crisis Management." The paper announced that Vice President Bush would be in overall charge of crisis planning and operations, with staff work on foreign situations to be handled by the National Security Council. The Secretary of State was not mentioned.

Haig was crazed when he heard that, or rather read it in the *Washington Star*. He was almost uncontrollable in his anger, telling Clark that the President had lied to him. He dictated a resignation letter—

"Members of your personal staff have consistently undermined your stated intention that the Secretary of State be your principal foreign policy adviser. . . . I hereby tender my resignation"—and then demanded to see Reagan. He got the President on the phone, saying that he believed the Vice President should have no foreign policy authority whatever and he was thinking of resigning. Reagan told him to come in the next morning at 8:45. He expected Haig to resign right there and he intended to try to talk him out of it; a resignation by his Secretary of State after eight weeks in office was unthinkable. Haig might sound crazy—as his mentor, Henry Kissinger, sometimes did to get his way—but Reagan would look the fool. The pretender from Hollywood. But Haig came and did not mention resignation when he saw Reagan. He seemed calm, asking the President to issue a statement saying that he alone was in charge of foreign affairs of all kinds.

Reagan avoided agreeing to that. Instead, he issued a public statement saying, "The Secretary of State is my primary adviser on foreign affairs." At the same time, he sent a memo to Baker and Meese saying: "This is to confirm my prior verbal directive to you to attend all meetings of the National Security Council and to participate in such meetings and the activities of the Council as representatives of the President."

What followed was a classic Washington routine. Deaver and Baker, who acted as though they believed the Secretary of State was indeed a crazy man, were whispering anti-Haig stories to White House correspondents day after day, telling reporters on background that the Secretary was threatening to resign every other week. He was being set up for death by a thousand cuts or leaks. "Mr. Haig's rush for the throne has been slowed by a significant public stumble," said a *Philadelphia Inquirer* editorial. The *Gainesville Sun* in Florida was more blunt: "The man is dangerous. Somebody better pay attention because Haig is going to get a lot of people killed—a lot of people— for no good purpose at all. He is the perfect example of the old men who dream up wars for the young to fight." *The New York Times* said in an editorial: "So the single voice the Reagan administration intended to speak to the world has been saying nothing more urgent than 'I quit.' For a Secretary of State to threaten resignation eight or nine times in sixty-five days must be a record."

Deaver, who was pushing out numbers like that, told the President exactly what he thought about Haig: "He's a cancer that has to be cut out." This time, Deaver misjudged his boss. The President's take on the anti-Haig stories was that the press was maliciously trying to tear up his team and his turf. He decided to tidy the place up, stopping at the White House press room on his way to Virginia for his usual Wednesday afternoon of riding at Quantico Marine Base.

"Mr. President," a surprised reporter asked, "can't you give us your own reaction to what you read about the Secretary—?"

"My reaction was that maybe some of you were trying to make the news instead of reporting it."

That night, though, Reagan traded jokes with some of those same reporters at the annual dinner of the Gridiron Club, an organization of one hundred of the capital's most important or self-important journalists who got together once a year in the main ballroom of the Washington Hilton Hotel. He got laughs by saying that in his administration one of the problems was: "Sometimes our right hand doesn't know what our far right hand is doing." In turn he was ritually lampooned in songs that did have a good deal of truth in their bite: One, to a familiar tune from the show *The King and I*, went:

He will not say what you would have him say,
But now and then he'll say . . . something won-derful

Just put it on a card he cannot disregard
Then every time he will say . . . something won-derful!

He knows a thousand things that aren't quite true;
And you know he believes in them
And that's enough for you

You'll always go along
And help him be less wrong
And even when he's wrong
He is— Wonderful.

Two days later the President was headed back to the Hilton, a dozen blocks from the White House, for a speech to a national conference of the AFL-CIO's Building Construction Trades Department. His warm-up joke was about the wife of a baseball player telling him how to put on their baby's diaper: "Look, buster, you lay the diaper out like a diamond, you put second base on home plate, put the baby's bottom on the pitcher's mound, hook up first and third, slide home underneath, and if it starts to rain, the game ain't called, you start all over again."

It was not a particularly friendly audience—most of the labor officials opposed the economic program he was trying to sell them—but they laughed with the President, like many of them a man who enjoyed his own old stories. As always with union audiences, he reminded them that he had been president of the Screen Actors Guild and was a lifetime member of the AFL-CIO. The speech itself was a variation on his basic pitch: "We've been left with a legacy of almost eight million people out of work, 666,000 of them construction workers. . . . The annual inflation rate has soared to nearly 12 percent making a mockery of hard work and savings. And our national debt has grown to more than $950 billion despite taxes that eat up an ever-increasing share of the family dollar. If we don't get control of the budget and stop wild and irresponsible spending . . ."

He left the hotel by a side entrance on T Street at 2:25 P.M., waving to the small crowd waiting to see him, turning toward Michael Putzel, an Associated Press reporter who had called, "Mr. President . . ." He heard a *pop-pop-pop* sound.

"What the hell's that?" Reagan said to Jerry Parr, the Secret Service agent in charge of his guard unit. Parr was already moving, tackling the President, pushing him toward the ground as another agent, Ray Shaddick, pushed both Reagan and Parr into the back of the President's bulletproof limousine, onto the floor of the big car.

"Take off," Parr yelled to the driver, Agent Drew Unrue.

Reagan was in great pain, the worst he had ever felt. "Jerry," he said. "Get off. I think you've broken one of my ribs."

"Rawhide returning to Crown," Parr shouted to Unrue. "Get the President to the White House." *

The agent slid onto a jump seat. Reagan climbed up onto the back seat as Parr ran his hands along his side and back feeling for blood or injury. The pain was paralyzing; Reagan sat stiff on the edge of the seat. He coughed up bright red, frothy blood. "I think I've cut my mouth," he said.

"Go to GW!" Parr yelled. The emergency room of George Washington University Hospital. Sirens were screaming all around the limousine. The route to the White House along Connecticut Avenue to

---

* "Rawhide" was the President's Secret Service code name. Mrs. Reagan was "Rainbow."

17th Street had been cleared by District of Columbia police. But at Pennsylvania Avenue, Unrue turned right into traffic, away from the White House for the five-block run to the hospital.

David Prosperi, an assistant to Press Secretary James Brady, watched the limousine roar away and ran back into the Hilton, looking for a phone to call the White House. He reached the deputy press secretary, Larry Speakes, gasping as he said: "Shots have been fired. Brady's down. I don't know about the President." Brady was on the ground in a pool of his own blood from a head wound. A Secret Service agent and a Washington policeman had also been hit.

As the limousine reached the GW Emergency Room at 2:35 P.M., Reagan, in pain, was having trouble breathing, afraid he was suffocating. But he was able to stand and tell Parr, "I'll walk in."

He made it, a brave man, a great performance, going twenty feet until he was inside the emergency entrance. Then he sagged to the floor. Parr and Shaddick carried him along to Trauma Bay 5. Nurses and doctors were cutting off his clothes. The President was naked on a gurney, his mouth and teeth red from bubbling blood. "I can't breathe," he gasped. The doctors made a quick incision and inserted a breathing tube into his throat. It did not help much; the trouble was deeper. His blood pressure was down to 78, compared to his normal reading of 140, and he passed out. Doctors made three intravenous incisions, to pump in new blood and liquids. The frothy blood meant lung damage, a collapsed left lung. Catheters were inserted to try to drain the blood in the lung. It was coming out dark, steadily pouring out as doctors tried to reinflate the lung. "I don't hear anything," a nurse said, feeling for his pulse.

"Oh my God, we've lost him." Parr said silently. He was praying, "Lord, be with him. Let him live."

The nurse, Kathy Paul, and a surgical resident, Dr. Wesley Price, noticed the small slit under Reagan's left armpit, a half-inch long. The President had been shot. Another nurse, Marisa Mize, held his hand. He came out of it. "Who's holding my hand? Who's holding my hand? Does Nancy know about us?"

Deaver called Jim Baker at 2:38, just as Speakes came running into the chief of staff's office. Baker called several Cabinet members, telling them to come to the White House Situation Room, under the West Wing. Staff members were already crowding around the long conference table in the windowless fifteen-by-twenty-five-foot room.

Next door a larger L-shaped room was crammed with Teletypes, phones, and other communications equipment.

In the emergency room hallway at GW Hospital, FBI agents and military officers were fighting over the President's dark blue suit and monogrammed shirt, the thousand-dollar suit Reagan called it, custom-tailored and hand-sewn by Mariani of Beverly Hills. The officers, including Lieutenant Colonel Jose Muratti, the man holding the football—the black leather attaché case holding the codes and targeting options necessary to launch American nuclear missiles—wanted the nuclear code card in Reagan's wallet. Card #1 was a piece of plastic, like a credit card, with printed numerical and letter codes that identified the President of the United States to military officers at the consoles used to command the launch of American nuclear warheads. The FBI wanted everything as evidence—and they got it. Agents walked out of the hospital with the code card in a sealed evidence bag.*

Nancy Reagan, who had been having lunch at the White House, was at the hospital less than ten minutes later. The President opened his eyes and saw her. "Honey," he said, "I forgot to duck." It was what heavyweight champion Jack Dempsey said after he lost the championship to Gene Tunney—when Reagan was a teenager back in Illinois. Lyn Nofziger, a press assistant who had worked on and off for Reagan for fifteen years, arrived in a car with Jim Baker, Ed Meese, and Speakes. The three had left just as Secretary of State Haig arrived at the Situation Room and took the big chair at the end of the conference table. Nofziger looked around, asked a few questions of anyone he could grab, then telephoned an assistant back at the White House, Ed Rollins, saying: "The guy's in really bad shape. They don't know if he's gonna make it or not." Speakes stood against a wall, taking notes: "Doctors believe bleeding to death. . . . 'Think we're going to lose him.' Rapid loss of blood pressure."

"Has the Vice President been called?" Haig asked. George Bush was in the air aboard Air Force Two, flying from the Dallas–Fort Worth Airport to Austin. He was doing what Vice Presidents do, making little speeches and dedicating things, this time a plaque outside the Texas Hotel in Fort Worth, the place where President Kennedy had stayed the night before he was assassinated on November 22, 1963. Bush had been called by his press secretary, Pete Teeley, who

---

* The President's card was not returned by the FBI until two days later. Vice President Bush had Card #2, Secretary of Defense Weinberger had #3.

had told him there were shots but President Reagan had not been hit. Haig was patched through to the plane.

"This is Secretary Haig, Mr. Vice President . . ." He could not really hear Bush on the scrambled ground-to-air call, finally shouting, "George! This is Al Haig," telling him he should return to Washington. Air Force Two landed at Austin and began refueling. Bush, who had been scheduled to address the state legislature, stayed on board.

At 3:10 P.M., the White House press office released a short statement saying that contrary to earlier reports the President had been shot, but was in stable condition. Haig ordered the State Department to prepare a cable for United States ambassadors around the world.

"Flash. Please deliver following message to the government to which you are accredited. You will have heard that there was an attempt on the life of President Reagan. His condition is stable . . . the government in Washington continues to carry out its obligations to its people and its allies."

Haig crossed out the last sentence and wrote: "His condition is stable and he is conscious." The Secretary ordered the cable sent as Allen said: "Well, just let me point out to you that the President is not now conscious."

"No, of course not," said Haig.

A Secret Service man called Treasury Secretary Donald Regan out of the room—the Secret Service is supervised by Treasury—and Regan came back to say that the gunman was a twenty-three-year-old white man from Colorado named John W. Hinckley Jr. He was identified by a Texas Tech student identification card in his wallet. "This is apt to be a loner," he added.

At GW someone was asking the President permission to operate, to stop the internal bleeding, to find the bullet. There was no exit wound. An X-ray to find the position of the bullet showed nothing. Parr heard himself saying, "We must have the bullet for evidence." The President was wheeled into the operating room at 3:24 P.M. The senior surgeon in the room, Dr. Benjamin Aaron, GW's chief of thoracic surgery, widened the incision under Reagan's armpit, then inserted another catheter worming into the little wound. The bullet, a hollow .22-caliber slug meant to explode in the body, was flattened like a dime, apparently because it had ricocheted off the bulletproof presidential limousine before hitting one of the President's ribs and being redirected toward his heart. It was an inch behind Reagan's heart. Aaron inched it out, dropped it into a cup, and handed it to

Parr. The chest cavity was filled with blood. Reagan had lost half the blood in his body, eight or nine or ten pints. He was dying, kept alive by transfusions of blood and other fluids.

Outside the operating room, Baker and Meese went to the chief of GW's trauma unit, Dr. Joseph Giordano, and asked him whether the President would be able to function after surgery. "Not immediately," Giordano said. "The anesthesia affects the mind, the brain."

"How long will it take?" one of them asked.

"A couple of days," Dr. Giordano answered.

Inside, Dr. Aaron decided immediate surgery was necessary to stop the bleeding. Reagan opened his eyes as the surgeons made ready and said: "I hope you're a Republican." Dr. Giordano, who was not, said: "Mr. President, we're all Republicans today."

Back at the White House, more and more people crowded into the Situation Room. "The football is near the Vice President," Haig said.

"We should get one over here," said Allen. They found one in a closet in the White House Military Office.

The Secretary of State had taken charge in the Situation Room, but the highest officials of the land were getting their basic information in the same way as ordinary Americans, from a single television set in the room, located just behind Haig. They did not know much and they were arguing in polite, but tense, terms about what should happen before the Vice President returned to Washington. Haig and Caspar Weinberger were in quiet confrontation over the ready status of United States military forces around the world, when David Gergen, whose title was communications director, interrupted: "Al, a quick question. We need some sense, better sense of where the President is. Is he under sedation now?"

"He's not on the operating table," Haig answered.

"He *is* on the operating table!" Gergen said.

"So the . . ." Haig began, "the helm is right here. And that means right in this chair for now, constitutionally, until the Vice President gets here."

That was not constitutionally correct, and several of the men in the room knew that. The Twenty-fifth Amendment to the Constitution, ratified in 1967, had established the succession as, first, the Vice President, then the Speaker of the House and the President pro tempore of the Senate—all elected officials—followed by the members of the Cabinet in the order their departments had been established, beginning with State. Military command authority, however, went from the

President, to the Vice President, then to the Secretary of Defense. But Haig seemed testy, ready for a fight, so Weinberger decided not to push the matter. After quietly conferring with Weinberger away from the crowded table—and telling him he was right and Haig wrong—Fred Fielding, the White House counsel, hurried to his office to bring back the documents the Cabinet could use to begin the Twenty-fifth Amendment process of temporarily replacing the President if a majority of the members agreed he was incapable of functioning. When Richard Darman, Baker's principal assistant, saw the papers on the table in front of Haig—prewritten letters to the Speaker of the House, Thomas P. "Tip" O'Neill of Massachusetts, and the President pro tempore of the Senate, Strom Thurmond of South Carolina—he walked around the table and picked them up and left, locking them in his safe. He had no authority whatsoever to do that, but he knew that if the Twenty-fifth Amendment discussion began in that room this day, it would be in the newspapers by the next—and the world would never again see Reagan as a whole man in charge of the government of the most powerful country in the world.

Two miles away, in the Capitol, there were only two senators on the floor of the Senate, Republican Majority Leader Howard Baker of Tennessee and Daniel Patrick Moynihan of New York, a Democrat. Baker received word of the shooting and announced it, really for the benefit of the correspondents in the press gallery above the chamber, saying that the President was apparently in good shape. Moynihan, one of the most articulate of the hundred and a member of John F. Kennedy's sub-Cabinet when he was assassinated on November 22, 1963, rose to say: "I was glad to hear how well the President is recovering, but there is something larger at stake. Ernest Hemingway once described courage as grace under pressure. I do not know that in our time we have seen so great a display. It makes us proud of our President. It is perhaps no time to talk about the Nation, but it is the Nation that nurtured that quality in him, and we are all enhanced by it. . . . We are surely proud of him."

The President was still on the operating table, fighting for his life. Just before 4 P.M., Larry Speakes returned from a trip to the hospital and was quickly surrounded by reporters as he went to his first-floor office, just above the Situation Room. He decided to hold a formal briefing right there.

"Is the President in surgery?" a reporter asked.

"I can't say . . ."

"Has the U.S. military been put on any higher alert readiness?"

"Not that I'm aware of . . ."

"Who's running the government right now . . . ?"

"I cannot answer that question at this time . . ."

"Larry, who'll be determining the status of the President and whether the Vice President should, in fact, become the acting President?"

"I don't know the details on that."

Speakes's impromptu briefing was live on national television—and Haig noticed it on the set behind his chair. "How do you get up to the press room?" he demanded of Allen.

"Up here," said Allen, pointing to the small staircase near the Situation Room.

"Yeah," said Haig, moving toward the staircase. "He's turning this into a goddamned disaster!"

He ran up, followed by Allen, who said, "Christ almighty, why's he doing that?"

"They want to know who's running the government," said an assistant in the press office, Frank Ursomarso. Speakes was leaving the rostrum and Ursomarso called out: "The Secretary of State! The Secretary of State!"

Haig grabbed the lectern. He was out of breath and sweating. Standing behind him, Allen saw his arms shaking and legs wobbling. He thought he might faint and stepped forward to catch him. But Haig began speaking: "I just want to touch on a few matters . . ." He said the Cabinet was assembled downstairs, allies had been informed, and the Cabinet had concluded that there was no need for and no consideration of increased military alerts around the world. Then he asked for questions.

"Who is making decisions for the government right now? Who's making the decisions?"

"Constitutionally, gentlemen, you have the President, the Vice President, and the Secretary of State in that order. . . . As of now, I am in control here, in the White House, pending the return of the Vice President and in close touch with him."

Downstairs in the Situation Room, Weinberger stood up and said: "I can't believe this. He's wrong. He doesn't have any such authority." The others could not believe what Haig looked like; he seemed out of control. "Is he mad?" said Donald Regan. When Haig came back downstairs, he immediately got into a more heated argument with

Weinberger over what constituted combat alert escalation, and the fact that Soviet submarines did seem to have moved a bit closer to the East Coast than their usual deployment. At that point, the Secretary of Defense asserted himself: "Until the Vice President actually arrives here, the command authority is what I have . . . and I have to make sure that it is essential that we do everything that seems proper."

"You better read the Constitution," said Haig.

"What?"

Haig laughed and said it again: "You better read the Constitution." No one else laughed.

At GW, with the President still in the operating room, Lyn Nofziger met with reporters shortly after 5 P.M. in a hospital auditorium. He, too, on live television, had to answer most questions by saying, "I don't know." As he was turning away to go back toward the emergency room, someone called, "Did he say anything?"

Nofziger stepped back to the microphone and fished into his pockets, pulling out a wad of crumpled notes on GW notepads. "I have some stuff here," he said. "I'm glad you reminded me of that because I took some notes. As he was going down the hall into surgery he winked at Baker, James Baker. . . . He had earlier told Senator [Paul] Laxalt, who was there, 'Don't worry about me. I'll make it.' "

He also passed on the "Honey, I forgot to duck" and "Are you all Republicans?" lines. Then he said that as they were rolling him into surgery, the President saw Baker, Meese, and Deaver standing together and quipped, "Who's minding the store?"

The cameras were rolling and print reporters were scribbling like mad—and laughing. How bad could it be if the man was still telling jokes?

The surgery was finished at 6:20 P.M., though the President, still under anesthesia and on a respirator, remained in the room under close observation. Ten minutes later, Air Force Two landed at Andrews Air Force Base and taxied into a hangar, so that no outsider (or sniper) could see the Vice President disembark. Bush told the waiting helicopter crew to take him to his own official residence rather than to the White House. Only then, from there, would he be driven to the White House. "The more normal things are, the better," he said when he arrived in the Situation Room at one minute before 7 P.M. "We want to make the government function as normally as possible."

The President began to regain consciousness at 7:30 P.M., but then, a half-hour later, was given morphine because of his chest pain. At one point he asked whether the shooter had been caught. "Why did he do it?" Reagan wanted to know. "What's his beef?"

As Reagan began to talk upstairs, the first official medical briefing began at GW Hospital. After meeting with Lyn Nofziger, Dr. Dennis O'Leary, the dean of clinical affairs at the medical school, said with calm authority: "The President's vital signs were absolutely rock stable through this whole thing. . . . He was at no time in any serious danger." All that was a good deal more reassuring than true. Other physicians watching Dr. O'Leary knew that the performance was more politics than medicine. He was assuring the American people, and foreign leaders, that the President was functioning. In fact, he was a seventy-year-old man who had just been shot, lost half his blood, had a collapsed lung, surgery, and anesthesia, and was being pumped with drugs that were killing pain but were also scrambling his brain. In addition to morphine, he was administered codeine, Demerol, and Valium, as well as the anesthesia Pentothal, which would be slowly metabolized over a week or so.

The Vice President came into the press briefing room at 8:20 P.M. to say, "I can reassure this nation and the watching world that the American government is functioning fully and effectively." When he left, Speakes and Gergen took questions from reporters crowded into the room. One of them asked: "What precautions are being taken that Haig is not going to try a coup d'état?"

A few hours after that, Dr. O'Leary, who knew better, had another statement for the world: "The President is obviously able to function . . . in terms of the capacity to make decisions and so forth, he can probably put in a full-time day today as long as he gets a nap this afternoon."

In the recovery room at GW hospital, the President was awake and in pain most of the night. At 2:15 A.M., after being given more morphine, he was taken off the respirator, but was still unable to speak because of the endotracheal tube in his throat. He had a felt-tip pen in his hand and wrote notes on pink paper, brave and fearful, too.

"All in all, I'd rather be in Philadelphia"—an old line from the comedian W. C. Fields, when he was asked what he wanted on his gravestone. When he heard a technician say, "This is it," he became agitated and scrawled, "What does he mean?" A nurse said it meant they were ready to remove the tube. That was at 2:50 A.M.

One of the notes said: "Where am I?"

CHAPTER 3
APRIL 28, 1981

THE WOUNDED PRESIDENT had been in George Washington Hospital for less than thirty-six hours when *The Washington Post* hit the streets just before midnight on March 31. The lead headline of that paper, dated April 1, read: "REAGAN IN GOOD SPIRIT, MAKING A FAST RECOVERY." A second page-one headline added: "Reagan Staff Plan for Interim Rule: Business as Usual."

The *Washington Star* was more explicit: "REAGAN WORKS FROM HOSPITAL: Sees Visitors, Signs Bill on Dairy Prices, 'Business as Usual' White House Insists." The network news the night before was reported on the first page of the daily White House News Summary this way: "REAGAN—Doing extremely well, signs milk bill and receives visitors. White House staff continues work on a 'business as usual' basis. (ABC, CBS, NBC—lead.)"

That was the way the story was told across the country. An overnight national *Washington Post*/ABC News poll indicated that the President's approval rating had jumped from 62 to 73 percent. A front-page box in *The New York Times* added: "Business leaders were relieved by developments and some thought the outlook for the President's economic program was enhanced. Stocks rallied with the Dow Jones Industrial average up 11.71 points to 1003.87."

Baker, Meese, and Deaver had brought the eighteen-page News Summary, put together each weekday by staffers and interns in the press secretary's office, to the recovery room for what was announced as a regular 7 A.M. planning meeting—except that it was being held in the Intensive Care Unit. The President was there, though he never had been at the early meeting before. The windows were covered with blankets so that no one, gawker or assassin, could look inside.

Reagan had dozed on and off through the dark morning hours of Tuesday, March 31. Oxygen tubes were clipped into his nose. By 6:45 he had been propped up in bed and was able to brush his teeth. Deaver began the meeting by telling the President not to worry, that the White House was still functioning like a well-oiled machine. Reagan's response was breathless and garbled, but it was a good line: "What makes you think I'd be happy to hear *that*?"

The event of the day was the President's signing of a piece of legislation, S-509, the first bill-signing of the administration, canceling some price supports for dairy farmers. He received morphine just before that and his signature was so shaky that reporters questioned whether it was a forgery. But it did the trick, as one newspaper, the *Los Angeles Herald Examiner,* ran the signature across a full page under the headline "President Reagan's pen is mightier than the bullet." It's bigger rival, the *Los Angeles Times,* accepting Washington's official version, said in an editorial: "The President's excellent prognosis rendered academic the sections of the 25th Amendment that provide for the continuing firm government when a President is disabled and unable to execute his duties."

For the rest of the day, sleeping on and off, Reagan wrote more notes—"Will I be able to ride my horses again? Will I be able to cut brush?"—and exchanged a few words with his wife and his children, who had flown in from California and from Omaha, where his son, Ron, had been appearing with the Joffrey Ballet. At midday, his White House physician, Dr. Daniel Ruge, told him that Jim Brady, Secret Service agent Tim McCarthy, and a Washington policeman named Thomas Delahanty had been shot—and that Brady had severe brain damage. "Oh damn, oh damn," Reagan said, his eyes filling with tears. "We must pray. That means four bullets hit. Good Lord." All that was reported in an afternoon press conference by Jim Baker, who emphasized: "I would like to reiterate that we at all times had full communication between the hospital, the Situation Room here at the White House and Air Force Two."

At 9 P.M., Tuesday night, Reagan was moved to a suite on the third floor of the hospital. He was in great pain and still needed oxygen to breathe.

The Wednesday morning papers—and the White House summary—carried the news that the gunman, John Hinckley, was an obviously disturbed young man who had arrived in Washington just after noon on Sunday, March 29, on a Greyhound bus. He had a ticket through to New Haven, Connecticut, because he wanted to see Jodie Foster, a teenage movie star who was a student at Yale. He wanted to tell her he loved her. He checked in at the Park Central Hotel, at 18th and G Streets. On Monday, he bought a copy of the *Washington Star* and saw the President's daily schedule, including the speech at the Washington Hilton. At 12:45, he wrote a letter to Foster, whom he had seen in a movie called *Taxi Driver,* saying he intended to kill President Reagan to prove his love for her. "I would abandon the idea of getting Reagan in a second, if only I could win your heart," he said in an unmailed letter.

So, it seemed, there was no reason for the assassination attempt beyond the fantasies of a sick young man. But there was great impact beyond the personal tragedies of the victims, beginning with the President. Columnists in Wednesday's *Washington Post* realized that everything would be different after the attempt and that Reagan always would be a leader seen as somehow above or distanced from more ordinary politicians.

David Broder, the newspaper's political editor, whose identification usually began with "the most respected . . ." wrote:

> A new legend has been born. The gunfire that shattered the stillness of a rainy Washington Monday afternoon . . . created a new hero in Reagan, the chipper "Gipper" who took a .22-caliber slug in his chest but walked into the emergency room on his own power and joked with the anxious doctors on his way into surgery. . . . As long as people remember the hospitalized President joshing his doctors and nurses—and they will remember—no critic will be able to portray Reagan as a cruel or callow or heartless man.

On the same page, the team of Rowland Evans and Robert Novak put Reagan in a context that explained both the way he governed and his unique importance as the leader of a movement:

> The assassination attempt Monday afternoon left those who share Reagan's dream cold with fear at the futility of going on without Reagan. . . . Far from being the irrelevancy of his caricatures, Reagan is the vital spark that moves his Administration. Even if Bush, with vastly more governmental experience, fully agreed with Reagan's ideological revolutionary goals, he could not match Reagan's ideological commitment. That is what makes the Presi-

dent personally irreplaceable if his Administration is to change the nation. . . . If he had been killed or incapacitated, its radical quality would have been ended.

There was, it seemed, no Reaganism without Reagan. The man was a noun, whereas even the greatest of his predecessors were remembered with adjectives, Jeffersonian or Lincolnesque.

The Wall Street Journal, the newspaper most supportive of Reagan's tax-cutting, added: "During the brief time Monday when President Reagan's life was in danger, something came into focus that we had not thought much about before: There really is a great deal riding on this particular President."

By Wednesday, April 1, the Vice President was publicly calling the President's recovery "amazing." Capitalized, the word dominated headlines around the country. Inside the White House Bush told staffers: "We will act as if he were here." At the hospital, where Reagan actually was, Dr. O'Leary, in one of his twice-daily briefings, declared that Reagan had not really collapsed inside the hospital and was certainly never in danger of dying. The White House began issuing three daily "Notice to the Press" accounts of what the President ate, beginning with a Wednesday breakfast of "Fresh orange juice, honeydew melon, two soft-boiled eggs, whole wheat toast and decaffeinated coffee"—and said he walked fifty yards down a guarded hallway with his wife. When he was helped back into bed, Nancy Reagan and her stepdaughter, Maureen Reagan, daughter of the President's first wife, Jane Wyman, sat quietly on a couch in the next room, hearing the thumping noise made by a nurse pounding the President's chest to bring up phlegm. Then they talked, softly, and held hands, ending years of suspicion and estrangement.

"He's so sick, oh, he may die," the daughter told a friend. No postoperation photos had been allowed or released, and that began to raise some suspicion, accounting for about half the reporters' questions at the daily scrums in the White House press room.

By late the next day, Thursday, April 2, the President was running a fever of almost 103 degrees. His white blood count was up and the color had drained from his face. He was spitting up small amounts of blood. GW doctors put him back on antibiotics, and a chest X-ray showed cloudy areas along the bullet's track through his lung. "We've been living in a dream world," said Dr. Aaron, who told the Reagans that he was considering another operation to remove the damaged lobe of his lung. But at the same time, he issued a statement saying that it was no more than "a little bit of setback" in a "remarkable recovery."

The fever was still at 102 on Friday morning, but dropped some at midday. Michael Evans, the White House photographer, was called in to take the first postoperation pictures of the President. One was released to the press that evening for use Saturday morning. It showed the President in a bathrobe, a little bit bent over, smiling and holding hands, tightly, with his wife. By that time his temperature was climbing again to 101. It was a busy medical day, with new X-rays and a flexible fiber bronchoscopy snake inserted through Reagan's throat to clear the left lung of blood particles. Dr. Aaron issued a statement saying the President would probably be discharged early the next week, but other physicians were more worried, believing that Reagan had developed pneumonia. He slept through most of Saturday and Sunday, being treated intravenously with a range of stronger antibiotics.

The world was also busier that weekend. "POLAND: Back to the Brink" was the cover headline of *Time* magazine on the day Reagan was shot. Soviet troops and tanks, along with units from other Warsaw Pact countries, were on the borders of Poland—two Red Army divisions were permanently stationed inside the country—on "maneuvers" and "war games" called Soyuz-81 that had already lasted three weeks. The Soviet leader, Leonid Brezhnev, flew to Prague on Sunday to make an unusual appearance at a Czech Communist Party Congress. He then sat behind the Czech party leader, Gustav Husak, applauding as Husak compared the threat of Solidarity union unrest and strikes in Poland to the situations that led to Soviet invasions of East Germany in 1953, Hungary in 1956, and Czechoslovakia itself in 1968. Warnings of the "gravest consequences for East-West relations" were issued from the White House—along with statements that the President was conferring with aides as the crisis deepened. The American television networks were breaking into regular programming for live coverage of speeches by Lech Walesa, the Solidarity leader, and the new Polish leader, General Jaruzelski. During one of their televised speechs, an intern checking Reagan's room noticed that the President was sitting up, happily watching television cartoons.*

---

* On that day, Sunday, April 5, Dr. Dennis O'Leary, the GW dean and spokesman, said his press briefings were meant to be "as upbeat as possible without damaging my credibility." *The New York Times* story that day, written by their medical correspondent, Dr. Lawrence Altman, was headlined: "Physician Says Reports on Reagan Were Optimistic but Hid Nothing."

On Monday, one week after the shooting, the White House began issuing new proposals under the President's name, the first one relaxing or delaying thirty-five air-quality and safety regulations on new American automobiles. Reagan's fever was just below 100 and X-rays showed his left lung beginning to clear up. He was in good spirits, feeling well enough for his first meeting with someone outside his family and his White House people. The Democratic Speaker of the House, Tip O'Neill, who got on well personally with Reagan, came over at midday. He was shocked. Reagan's men had gradually become used to how their boss looked.

Some of Reagan's men, including Darman, were speaking the unspeakable among themselves: "Woodrow Wilson"—wondering whether their leader would end his White House days pathetically disabled but hidden and protected from the public by a loyal wife and trusted aides. That certainly seemed possible to O'Neill. Instead of a President cracking jokes and reading briefing papers—that was what he had been told on television—the Speaker saw a sick old man in terrible pain. Reagan was feverish and obviously medicated. "Doped up," O'Neill thought. He suddenly realized that the President had been near death. They shook hands, O'Neill gave Reagan a small book of Irish jokes, then got out of there as fast as he could.

The chest X-rays looked a little better the next day, Tuesday, April 7. So did the world. In Prague, Brezhnev announced the end of Soyuz-81 and said the Polish government should be able to solve its own problems. The next day, Wednesday, Reagan was exhausted but he managed to work for more than an hour, writing a little piece about his America. One of the memos that got through to him, delivered by Deaver, was from speechwriter Anthony Dolan, saying that the White House had promised a July 4 message to *Parade* magazine, the Sunday supplement to hundreds of newspapers. Deaver thought the President might want to do it himself and that it might cheer him up as well. He was right on both counts. In the strongest handwriting any of them had seen since the shooting, the President wrote on both sides of Dolan's memo, telling of the boyish thrill of blowing tin cans thirty feet into the air with giant firecrackers, and then:

> Enough of nostalgia. Somewhere in our growing up we began to be
> aware of the meaning of the day . . . the birthday of our nation. I
> believed then and even more so today that it is the greatest nation
> on earth. In recent years I've come to think of that day as more than

just the birthday of a nation. It commemorates the only true philosophical revolution in all history. Oh there have been revolutions
before and since ours. But those revolutions simply exchanged one
set of rulers for another. Ours was a revolution that changed the
very concept of government. . . . In this land for the first time it was
decided that man is born with certain God-given rights; that government is only a convenience. . . . Happy 4th of July.

By Thursday, the President's fever was gone. He celebrated with a
little more of his own patriotic rhetoric, sending this message to the
crew of the spaceship *Columbia,* the first reusable shuttle, ready for
its maiden voyage into space and back to a landing strip in the California desert, the culmination of a ten-year, $10 billion project: "You
go in the hand of God. Through you, today, we all feel as giants once
again. Once again we feel the surge of pride that comes from knowing
we are the first and we are the best and we are so because we are free."
God and country—and Reagan!
In the thirteen days in the hospital, Reagan had lost a dozen pounds
or more. Despite the doctors and spokesmen saying he was "wolfing
down" food, even his wife was having trouble getting him to eat. Mrs.
Reagan had friends from California transport soups—the President's
favorites, split pea, turkey, and hamburger soup—made by Anne All-
man, who had been their cook for years in Pacific Palisades. That
didn't work either. He wanted to go home to the White House and the
departure was set for Saturday morning, April 11.
The arrangements were made by Deaver after meetings with a press
pool, led by Steven Weisman of *The New York Times,* who reported
back to other reporters on that Friday and Saturday:

Deaver asked that the questions be limited to how he was feeling,
and not to weightier matters, and the pool informally agreed. Reagan will say good-bye to the hospital staff gathered at both sides of
the exit of the hospital. . . . The President, before leaving the hospital entrance, received warm applause from what looked like about
forty or fifty people inside. It seemed he was making some comments to all of them, because they applauded him again as he
headed toward the door. As you saw on television, Reagan emerged
with Nancy clutching his right arm and daughter Patti holding his
left. He seemed pale and a little stiff but he was grinning broadly.
He said a total of five words upon leaving. Asked how he was feel-

ing he said: "Great . . . great." Asked what he was going to do first when he got to the White House he said: "What?" and when the question was repeated he said, "Sit down." He then got slowly into the pearl gray Lincoln that served as his limo today. . . . On the way back, in the rain, a few hundred people lined the street along State Place as Reagan pulled up to the southwest entrance of the White House. They cheered and clapped under their umbrellas.

There was more cheering and applause as the President walked into the White House under the canopy of the diplomatic entrance on the South Lawn in the back. He was wearing a red sweater and a grin, too, waving and quickly covering the fifty feet to the elevator up to the family quarters on the second floor. No one was close enough to see how drawn he looked or the way he collapsed into a chair upstairs. That night, in his diary, he wrote: "Whatever happens now I owe my life to God and will try to serve him in every way I can."

He asked to be awakened early the next morning, a Sunday. He sat up in the hospital bed that had been installed in the Lincoln Bedroom to watch the launch of *Columbia,* which had been delayed for two days because of computer problems. At 7 A.M., the spaceship blasted into the sky for a planned trip of thirty-six orbits of the earth in about fifty-four hours. It took the first Americans, two pilots, into space in six years, riding a new kind of vehicle, one of four 122-foot-long shuttles designed to lift off attached to a rocket, cruise in space, and then glide to earth for a soft landing at two hundred miles per hour in the California desert. Reagan was thrilled, and he loved seeing NASA scientists and technicians at Houston Control waving small American flags when the launch was declared a success despite the fact that a dozen or so insulation tiles seemed to fly off the tail section as *Columbia* left the earth's atmosphere.

It was not an easy day for Reagan. The few people who saw him were surprised at how pale and disoriented he was, moving stiffly and cautiously, like a very old man. He tried to work, but that lasted less than an hour, and he could concentrate for only a few minutes. That night he wrote in his diary: "The first full day at home. I'm not jumping any fences and the routine is still one of blood tests, X-rays, bottles dripping into my arms but I'm home. With the let-up on antibiotics, I'm beginning to have an appetite and food tastes good for the first time."

Each day, the press office would release a schedule reporting that the President was upstairs working four or five hours a day. But, most days, the only meetings he had were short ones with Baker, Meese, and Deaver. The situation in Poland had calmed down some, and the Vice President was handling public appearances and presiding at Cabinet meetings. Reagan still felt terrible and looked worse. Upstairs, sitting in the solarium, he was a guy around the house—and his wife ran the house. Nancy Reagan was a fiercely protective wife, determined that her "Ronnie" was going to get the rest he so obviously needed. She did not like his staff—the feeling was mutual—and they were on her turf now. When Dick Darman arrived for the first time with papers for the President, he was accompanied by Helene von Damme, his longtime secretary who was no favorite of Mrs. Reagan. The First Lady walked into the room and told everyone there that they had to move because someone was measuring for new drapes. The President painfully pulled himself out of his chair, and said softly to Darman, "I've never understood why she cares so much about those things."

But by April 17, only nineteen days after being wounded, Reagan began to spend a couple of hours a day doing some of the things he would have been doing if there had been no shooting: writing letters and calling members of Congress—ten or so each day for two or three minutes each—cranking up pressure and support for his economic program. Under "Topics for Discussion," the call sheets read: "1. I need your help on my Economic Recovery Progam. . . . 2. Reduction of Federal spending is essential if we are to reduce the deficit and get inflation under control. . . . 3. Can I count on you next week in the House? Will you be with me?"

Some momentum had been lost while the President was hospitalized, particularly in congressional committees, and Reagan's original budget proposals had been morphed into a bipartisan substitute called "Gramm-Latta," put forward with White House backing by Representative Phil Gramm, a conservative Texas Democrat, and Republican Delbert Latta of Ohio. Some promising economic numbers had also been released—gross national product growth for the first quarter of 1981 was 6.5 percent on an annual basis and the Consumer Price Index for March was only 0.6 percent—so Reagan's rhetoric of crisis was fading a bit. But his aura of heroism was not fading at all, and his poll numbers were still on the rise. An NBC News/Associated Press survey in mid-April reported that 77 percent of Americans had a favorable opinion of the man, compared with 58 percent on the day he was inaugurated. Among Democrats, the loyal opposition, his approval rate was at 64 percent. When Reagan called, most members of Congress reacted as if they were hearing the voice of God Himself. *The New York Times* put his activities in some context by quoting President Harry S Truman: "All the President is, is a glorified public relations man who spends his time flattering, kissing and kicking people to get them to do what they're supposed to be doing anyway."

By that definition, and others, too, Reagan was great at being President. The call lists prepared by his congressional liaison, Max Friedersdorf, handed to him each morning by Baker or Meese, began with a short biographical and political summary, like this one for Representative Margaret Heckler, a Massachusetts Republican: "North suburbs of Boston and Fall River. Member of the Science and Technology and Veterans' Affairs Committees . . . Peggy wants to support the President but feels vulnerable because her district is likely to be reapportioned and she will be pitted against Barney Frank, a liberal Democrat." Reagan carefully wrote out notes after the Heckler call: "Has a very real problem. . . . Many of our cuts are extremely sensitive in her area. There is no doubt of her personal support & desire to be of help. We need to give her good rational explanations re: the cuts such as college loans etc." For a conservative Democrat, D. Douglas Barnard, the summary read: "Barnard represents Athens and Augusta, Georgia. He was elected with former President Carter in 1976. He never received a call from Carter during his Presidency. A Presidential phone call would do much to solidify the Congressman's support of the Administration on future votes." After the call, Reagan wrote at the bottom of his sheet: "He's gung ho and working all out for Gramm-Latta. Claims his district is solidly behind us."

Half the ten calls that day, April 22, were to Northeastern Republicans, men and women with instincts and constituencies generally more liberal than their party colleagues from the West and the South—Heckler of Massachusetts was one of them—and half to conservative Democrats, most from the South. Only one did not go well, to Representative James Jeffords, a liberal Republican from Vermont. "Not locked in" was the last summary line. Reagan's note after making the call said: "I don't know why I call one like him. Did say he would keep an open mind—but I wouldn't count on him."

Reagan was also spending time writing and rewriting a personal letter to the leader of the Soviet Union, Leonid Brezhnev. Sitting alone in pajamas and robe, at a table in the solarium, he composed thirteen paragraphs on a yellow legal pad, referring to a March 6 letter in which Brezhnev had formally repeated pages of routine Soviet rhetoric blaming United States "imperialistic designs" for the Cold War and most everything else going bad in the world. Draft answers to that letter were still bouncing between the White House and the State Department when Reagan was shot. His draft, in the language of Everyman rather than diplomacy, began:

> My Dear Mr. President:
>   I regret yet can understand the somewhat intemperate tone of your recent letter. After all, we approach the problems confronting us from opposite philosophical points of view. . . . Is it possible that we have let ideology, political and economical philosophy and governmental policies keep us from considering the very real, everyday problems of the people we represent?

Two of those paragraphs laid out Reagan's personal view of America's postwar policies, a view undoubtedly shared by the great majority of his countrymen:

> When WWII ended the United States had the only undamaged industrial power in the world. Its military might was at its peak— and we alone had the ultimate weapon, the nuclear bomb with the unquestioned ability to deliver it anywhere in the world. If we had sought world domination who could have opposed us?
>   But the United States followed a different course—one unique in all the history of mankind. We used our power and wealth to rebuild the war-ravaged economies of all the world including those nations who had been our enemies.

Reagan also wrote that he intended to lift the embargo on American grain sales to the Soviet Union, an embargo ordered by President Carter when the Soviets invaded Afghanistan on Christmas Day in 1979. Reagan had always opposed the embargo, claiming that it hurt American farmers more than the Soviets, who began buying wheat and other commodities from other countries, particularly Argentina and Australia. When Secretary of State Haig had argued against lifting the embargo, saying it would send the wrong conciliatory message to Brezhnev, Reagan cut him off with: "I promised to do it in the campaign, Al." The rest of Reagan's draft was greeted with the same low level of enthusiasm at State and the National Security Council. Haig sent back a State Department rewrite, a completely different letter.

"This isn't what I had written, but I suppose they are the experts," Reagan told Deaver one morning.

"You know, Mr. President," Deaver said, "those assholes have been running the Soviet business for the last forty years, and they haven't done a very good job of it. None of them ever got elected to anything; you got elected. Why don't you just tell them to stick it and send the goddamn letter?"

"That's a good idea. Thank you," Reagan said. Deaver, the most senior of the hired hands, calculated that that was about the third time in twenty years he had heard Reagan use those words in private. Then the boss said: "I need to follow my own instincts. And I'm going to."

In the end, on April 25, the State Department version was delivered to the Soviet embassy in Washington: "The USSR's unremitting and comprehensive military build up over the past fifteen years, a build up which in our view exceeds purely defensive requirements and carries disturbing implications of a search for military superiority."

The President signed the diplomatic language. But on top of it he clipped a cover letter in his own hand, which said, in part:

Mr. President, in writing the attached letter I am reminded of our meeting in San Clemente a decade or so ago. I was Governor of California at the time, and you were concluding a series of meetings with President Nixon. Those meetings had captured the imagination of all the world. Never had peace and good will among men seemed closer at hand.

When we met I asked if you were aware that the hopes and aspirations of millions and millions of people throughout the world were dependent on the decisions that would be reached in your meetings. You took my hand in both of yours and assured me that you were aware of that and that you were dedicated with all your heart and mind to fulfilling those hopes and dreams.

The people of the world still share that hope. Indeed, the peoples of the world, despite differences in racial and ethnic origin, have very much in common. They want the dignity of having some control over their individual destiny. They want to work at the craft or trade of their own choosing and to be fairly rewarded. They want to raise their families in peace without harming anyone or suffering harm themselves. Government exists for their convenience, not the other way around. . . .

It is in this spirit, in the spirit of helping the people of both our nations, that I have lifted the grain embargo. Perhaps this decision will contribute to creating the circumstances which will lead to the meaningful and constructive dialogue which will assist us in fulfilling our joint obligation to finding lasting peace.*

His work on the letter had been interrupted that last week in April by a call from Ed Meese, saying he wanted to come upstairs with Attorney General William French Smith. "We've got some news," he said. It was important: Supreme Court Justice Potter Stewart had told Vice President Bush that he intended to resign from the court after twenty-three years. Reagan told Smith and Meese to prepare a list of possible replacements, reminding them of his campaign pledge to appoint the first woman to the high court.

On April 28, the President made his first public appearance since the shooting twenty-nine days before, a 9 P.M. speech to a joint session of Congress gathered in the House of Representatives—on live television. "The place went nuts," in the words of a television commentator. Representatives and senators stood and applauded, then cheered and whistled for three long minutes. They knew what he was going to say—vote for Gramm-Latta—but that was not what they were cheering. They were cheering him! The gallant American hero.

"Thanks to some very fine people, my health is much improved," he said. "I'd like to be able to say that with regard to the health of the economy. . . .

"Where have we come in this 6 months? Inflation, as measured by the Consumer Price Index, has continued at a double-digit rate. Mortgage interest rates have averaged almost 15 percent for these 6 months, preventing families across America from buying homes. There are still almost 8 million unemployed. The average worker's hourly earnings after adjusting for inflation are lower today than they were 6 months ago, and there have been over 6,000 business failures."

Then he got to the specifics: "The House will soon be choosing between two different versions of measures to deal with the econ-

* Brezhnev replied in a letter that, in Reagan's words, "Blamed the United States for starting and perpetuating the Cold War, and then said we had no business telling the Soviets what they could or could not do anywhere in the world."

omy. One is the measure offered by the House Budget Committee. The other is a bipartisan measure, a substitute introduced by Congressmen Phil Gramm of Texas and Del Latta of Ohio." The administration, he said, was going to embrace Gramm-Latta.

"Let us cut through the fog for a moment. The answer to a government that's too big is to stop feeding its growth. Government spending has been growing faster than the economy itself. The massive national debt which we accumulated is the result of the government's high spending diet. Well, it's time to change the diet and to change it in the right way. . . .

"Now, I know that over the recess in some informal polling some of your constituents have been asked which they'd rather have, a balanced budget or a tax cut, and with the common sense that characterized the people of this country, the answer, of course, has been a balanced budget. But may I suggest . . .

"Our choice is not between a balanced budget and a tax cut. Properly asked, the question is, 'Do you want a great big raise in your taxes this coming year or, at the worst, a very little increase with the prospect of tax reduction and a balanced budget down the road a ways?' "

He had already been interrupted by cheering and applause thirteen times when he began to close, saying:

"The space shuttle did more than prove our technical abilities. It raised our expectations once more. It started us dreaming again.

"The poet Carl Sandburg wrote, 'The republic is a dream. Nothing happens unless first a dream.' And that's what makes us, as Americans, different. We've always reached for a new spirit and aimed at a higher goal. We've been courageous and determined, unafraid and bold. Who among us wants to be the first to say we no longer have those qualities?"

Back at the White House, the President was excited. He said he was amazed when he saw forty or so Democrats standing and applauding. "Boy, that took guts," he said. Then he joked: "That reception was almost worth getting shot."

Late that night, the Democratic Majority Leader of the House, Jim Wright of Texas, wrote in his diary: "We've just been outflanked and outgunned. The aura of heroism which has attended him since his wounding, deserved in large part by his demeanor under the extreme duress of his physical ordeal, assured a tumultuous welcome. It was a very deceptive, extremely partisan and probably very effective presentation. Tip and I are embattled, trying to stem the flow of conservative sands through the sieve."

As for O'Neill himself, the Speaker said: "The President has become a hero. We can't argue with a man as popular as he is. . . . I've been in politics a long time and I know when to fight and when not to fight."

CHAPTER 4

AUGUST 8, 1981

IN THE MIDDLE OF THE DAY ON MAY 17, President Reagan, with his
wife, boarded a helicopter on the south grounds of the White
House for the short hop to Andrews Air Force Base and a one-
hour-and-twenty-minute flight to South Bend, Indiana. He was scheduled to give the commencement address to the 1,977 members of the
Class of 1981 at the University of Notre Dame, the storied Roman
Catholic university. It was not the first time Reagan had been there.

The event was a triumph of the life imagined. Forty years before, in
the first act of a legend, actor Ronald Reagan had come to the campus
to play in a film the part of a Notre Dame halfback named George
Gipp, a gifted athlete who died in 1920, during his senior year. The
Notre Dame legend had it that Gipp, who was nicknamed "The Gipper" by the sportswriters of his day, had, on his deathbed, told his
coach, the great Knute Rockne, that there would come a day when a
discouraged Notre Dame team would need inspiration to win a big
game—and that Rockne should pull the players together and tell them
to "Win one for the Gipper!" Eight years later, the story goes, Rockne
did just that, and it worked. Notre Dame won, with Gipp smiling
down on them.

The film, a great success, was titled *Knute Rockne—All American*.
Now, forty years later, the Gipper was back, but there were no quota-
tion marks around his name anymore. Ronald Reagan had practically
become George Gipp. The movie was part of his life, imagined and
real. Rockne was there, too, this day, or at least the actor who played
him, Pat O'Brien, who was receiving an honorary Doctor of Laws degree along with the President.

It was not promoted as an important speech. Reagan, wearing a bulletproof vest under his suit, compared Notre Dame football with another winning team, the Founding Fathers of the Republic, saying America was better for the exploits of both. Then he casually attacked both the government he presided over now and its enemies abroad, saying:

"Central government has usurped powers . . . government has been fixing things that aren't broken and inventing miracle cures for unknown diseases. . . . All of this has led to the misuses of power and preemption of the prerogatives of the people and their social institutions."

Then: "The years ahead are great ones for this country, for the cause of freedom and the spread of civilization. The West won't contain communism, it will transcend communism. . . . It will dismiss it as some bizarre chapter in human history, whose last pages are even now being written."

The Reagans were back at the White House for dinner. An ordinary Reagan day, inspiring, with a comfortable blend of fiction, fact, and crusading ideology. He looked good; he had begun exercising for an hour a day in a new gym installed in the living quarters. How he looked, this man of courage and humor, was the first thing people talked about. Aides, guards, reporters, even his wife and children suspected or knew the Reagan presidency had been turned by the insane act of a demented man-child with a little gun. Darman changed the autopenning system so that more official papers were signed by the autograph machines—and so were letters to friends. The machines were more personal now, signing "Ron" or "Dutch," Reagan's nickname as a kid. At the same time, the Secret Service was keeping ordinary people farther and farther away from the President. Reagan was not going to be allowed to see or shake hands with uninvestigated, uncredentialed people again. It would be all speeches now, all television and waving to ordinary people from an armored limousine with loudspeakers all around.

Lou Cannon, Reagan's journalistic shadow since 1965 in California, when he first covered the actor who would be governor, noticed the change as well. He understood Reagan was a mythic figure now, but he sensed the presidency would become more ceremonial and, worse, that the education of Ronald Reagan was ended.

Nancy Reagan, the wife proud to say her husband was her life, had been both frantic and depressed in the weeks following March 30. She could not sleep and her weight dropped from 112 pounds to 100. She was haunted by the thought that assassination was her husband's destiny. A friend, Merv Griffin, the entertainer and hotel owner, trying to comfort her, said that there was an astrologer in San Francisco, a friend of his named Joan Quigley, who had told him she could have prevented the shooting by warning the President that the day, March 30, was dangerous for him. So her charts of the stars told her. Mrs. Reagan called Quigley, saying, "I am so scared. I am scared every time he leaves the house. . . . I cringe every time we step out of a car or leave the building."

She began to call the astrologer every week or so, with word of the President's advance schedule. And the astrologer would do her charts, telling the wife of dangerous days, hours, minutes, places. Then, working through Deaver, Mrs. Reagan would get the schedules adjusted. Deaver had been around the Reagans long enough to know that a happy Nancy meant a happy Ronnie—and the opposite. Mrs. Reagan was frantic, afraid every time her husband left the White House, insisting that he wear a new lead-lined raincoat over the bulky bulletproof vest—and that he be kept away from crowds. Her son, Ronald Reagan Jr., was worried for different reasons. He could see that his father was just slower, speaking less, pausing longer, making less effort to remember. Lesley Stahl of CBS News saw him walk up to his Secretary of Housing and Urban Development, Samuel Pierce, the only prominent black man in the administration, at a reception for big city mayors and say: "How are you, Mr. Mayor? How are things in your city?"

IN THE three weeks before the Notre Dame speech, the President had spent almost all of his working time—three or four hours most days—continuing to try to win votes for the fiscal year 1982 budget. His job, done on the telephone and in small receptions in the White House, was to hold the 193 Republicans in the 435-member House, and to win over the votes of a few dozen conservative Democrats. Reagan met or talked with 479 members of Congress—about 400 more, they said, than Jimmy Carter had spoken to in four years. He also received a daily "Log of Selected Senate Mail" and "Log of Selected House Mail," one-paragraph summaries of letters from members that he dutifully read, and, more often than not, he scratched a note or two in a "Comments" column. Usually it was "?" or "I know" or "We're already doing that." Those little notes, returned to Darman each evening, like his quips and nods at meetings, were the marching orders of the administration, often the only words from on high. Martin Anderson, an old Sacramento hand who was in charge of domestic policy for the first two years, had to explain the Reagan style to new faces in the White House: "He makes no demands and gives no instructions." Adding later: "He made decisions like an ancient king. . . . He just sat back in a supremely calm manner and waited until important things were brought to him. And then he would act, quickly, decisively, and usually, very wisely."

The budget debate began in the House on April 30, with the House equally divided between supporters of the $689 billion Gramm-Latta plan and supporters of a $714 billion Democratic plan based on higher social spending and a lower tax-cut plan than the President's proposed 36 percent cut over three years. Reagan heard some good news that day. After weeks of pressure from American officials, led by trade representative William Brock, the Japanese Ministry of International Trade and Industry announced that the country's automakers, now winning more than a quarter of the American market, had decided to "voluntarily" restrict imports to the United States to 1.68 million vehicles in the coming year. A victory for free trade, proclaimed the President.

Reagan also made a characteristic mistake that day. He got carried away with emotion at a White House meeting of the President's Commission on the Holocaust. After talking with several Jewish survivors of Nazi death camps, he added a sentence to his State Department–approved text: "Never shall it be forgotten for a moment that the persecution of people for their religious belief that is [not] a matter to be on the negotiating table, for the United States does not belong at that table."

Within minutes, the White House press office produced an even more confusing statement saying the President did not mean what he had just said. His words were a direct contradiction of administration policy—not that unusual for him—in this case the more pragmatic types on his staff wanted to reassure other countries, beginning with the Soviet Union, South Africa, Chile, China, Guatemala, and El Salvador, that negotiations involving war and peace and trade would not be complicated by such idealism.

On May 2, a Saturday, the President went down to the Oval Office for the first time since the shooting, but stayed less than an hour. Back upstairs, he took a couple of phone calls, talking with Meese for a total of eight minutes.

A newspaper story was among the papers Darman delivered that evening to the living quarters upstairs. A *New York Times* headline of the day before had read: "Air Controllers Halt Talks with F.A.A.; Budget Office Opposes Demands." That story and dozens of others were summarized in the White House News Summary, which he was reading again. Its audience was tiny but elite and the journal was both balanced and irreverent, putting out a special seventeen-page issue on Reagan's hundredth day in office with a cartoon of him in his hospital bed over a couple of real headlines. One of them was: "Thus Far, He Seems Little More than a Likeable Ideologue." Perhaps he did seem that way, but a more perceptive analysis of his first hundred days was a quote in *U.S. News & World Report* by Edwin C. Hargrove, director of the Institute of Public Policy Studies at Vanderbilt University and author of a 1974 book titled *The Power of the Modern Presidency:* "Reagan has demonstrated in a way that Jimmy Carter never did, that he understands how to be President. He knows that a President can deal with only a relatively small number of issues at a time. He also understands that his principal task is public leadership . . . and developing a working relationship with Congress."

The air controllers' story was familiar to Reagan. The Professional Air Traffic Controllers Organization had played a significant role in his campaign—PATCO was one of the very few unions to endorse him in 1980—and the autopen machine downstairs was being cranked up to sign the President's name to a letter congratulating Robert Poli, the union's president, on the occasion of PATCO's twenty-fourth anniversary convention: "Let me take this opportunity to thank PATCO for its support last November. . . . I am confident that, together, we can achieve the vital common goals which will benefit all Americans."

Poli wanted—and Stockman wanted to block—wage increases of up to 40 percent, which would mean senior controllers would get $73,420 a year, $4,000 more than Cabinet members. The 17,500 men and women in airport towers also wanted a cutback in duty time from forty hours to thirty-two hours a week. And Poli obviously thought candidate Reagan had agreed to those demands in an October 20, 1980, letter that began: "I have been thoroughly briefed by members of my staff as to the deplorable state of our nation's air traffic control system. They have told me that too few people working unreasonable hours with obsolete equipment has placed the nation's air travellers in unwarranted danger. . . . I pledge to you that my administration will work very closely with you to bring about a spirit of cooperation between the President and the air traffic controllers."

The "cooperation" was laid out more specifically in a letter drafted that same day by Richard Leighton, PATCO's counsel, and filed in Reagan-Bush campaign headquarters in Arlington, Virginia. The letter, addressed to a campaign assistant named Michael Balzano, was an extraordinary document that Reagan may not have actually seen but that did seem to summarize commitments he or his personal staff had made to the controllers' union, including giving the controllers the right to strike under "certain circumstances":

This is the letter of understanding that I read to you relating to the endorsement of Governor Reagan. . . . Reagan, through you, Bob Garrick, and other agents, has agreed that the following will take place after the Governor is elected to the Presidency: 1. The present Administrator of the Federal Aviation Administration will be replaced by a competent administrator; 2. PATCO will play a role in the process for replacing the FAA administrator; 3. The Reagan Administration will commit itself to improving air traffic control by taking actions to assure that outdated air traffic control is replaced as soon as feasible; 4. The Reagan Administration will support legislation designed to reduce the hours of air traffic controllers (but not their annual salaries) if PATCO can demonstrate that such a reduction is needed to assure safety.

On Monday, May 4, Reagan returned to work in the Oval Office and began doing budget business there, meeting for three hours with four groups of congressmen, all Democrats, all but seven from the Deep South. The issue of *Business Week* that came out that day speculated on the possibility of an illegal strike by the air controllers. Poli was quoted: "The only illegal strike is an unsuccessful one."

Three days later, on May 7, the 1982 Budget Resolution, the Gramm-Latta version supported by the White House, with projected spending of $689 billion, came to a vote in the House. Assuming that the President's proposed 10 percent a year income tax cut for three years would be approved later, the resolution projected a budget deficit of $31 billion. Inside the Oval Office, the President's Legislative Strategy Group, an inner circle of six created by Baker to meet early each morning around a small table in his office—the power point of this White House—was already estimating that the deficit would be $55 billion, rising to $102.8 billion in 1983, and $151.5 billion in 1984. But those numbers were secret, and every Republican, including Vermont's Jim Jeffords, voted for the bill, as did sixty-three Democrats. It was a tremendous victory for the President, who grandly proclaimed: "When the people speak Washington will now listen . . . let us never forget this historic moment." *The New York Times* was only slightly less celebratory, under the headline: "Wide Support in Setting New Course for Nation." *

On May 12, the Senate voted 70 to 28 for a $700.8 billion version of the same budget with more increases in military spending, and both houses began selecting members of the conference committee that would reconcile differences in the two bills. "A great victory . . . representative democracy at its best," Reagan said. That same day, *Time* magazine completed a national poll that indicated Reagan, too, was at his best. "It's Rightward On" read the magazine's headline over a story that began: "Majorities ranging from 71 percent to 52 percent agreed with the propositions that Reagan had lived up to his campaign promises in six key areas: working effectively with Congress, providing strong leadership in government, providing moral leadership, keeping U.S. defenses strong, getting rid of waste in government and making Americans feel good again."

The rise of national optimism was remarkable, according to the pollsters of Yankelovich, Skelly and White, who had been tracking the same questions for a decade. Forty-five percent of respondents said they believed inflation would be brought under control, compared with 9 percent who had given that answer in April of 1979. A majority of Americans answered that they thought "America was moving in the right direction," compared with only 26 percent in January of 1981. The nation still had twice as many registered Democrats as Republicans, but they were changing their minds, or at least their answers, on a wide range of policy issues. There was only one dark area for conservatives: substantial majorities were opposed to

---

* The regular LSG members, sitting with Baker and Meese, were mostly Baker's men. They included Max Friedersdorf, Richard Darman, Craig Fuller, and David Gergen.

conservative positions on social issues, including abortion, handgun control, and sex education in public schools.

Then, still cheering themselves and their budget wins, the administration briskly stepped off a political cliff. "The Reagan Administration today announced details of a proposal for the first significant reduction in Social Security benefits since the retirement system was adopted 46 years ago," began *The New York Times* front-page report on May 13. The plan was generally designed to protect the 36 million Americans already collecting benefits, but it would reduce payments to future recipients. The principal provision proposed a 31 percent reduction in payments to workers who chose to retire before age sixty-five. The political firestorm around the White House was checked for a few days when news was dominated by reports of the shooting of Pope John Paul II in Vatican Square—including heroic comparisons with the attempted assassination of Reagan—but on May 19, the Republican-controlled Senate voted 96 to 0 for a resolution stating: "The Congress shall not precipitously and unfairly punish early retirees." *

Then the Speaker of the House, Tip O'Neill, appeared: "I have a statement on the Social Security," he said. "A lot of people approaching that age [sixty-two] have either already retired on pensions or have made irreversible plans to retire very soon. These people have been promised substantial Social Security benefits at age sixty-two. I consider it a breach of faith to renege on that promise. For the first time since 1935 people would suffer because they trusted in the Social Security system."

A reporter asked the Speaker whether the President had made a political mistake.

O'Neill knocked that one out of the park: "I'm not talking about politics. I'm talking about decency. It is a rotten thing to do. It is a despicable thing."

Reagan was angry. He felt, with good reason, that O'Neill and other Democratic leaders—"crazy" the President called them in private—had sucked in White House emissaries with talk of a bipartisan solution to Social Security's recurring financial crises. He wanted to

---

* Reagan had been advocating privatization options for Social Security since at least September of 1975. In three syndicated radio broadcasts that month he said: "There was a basic flaw in the design of Social Security. Congress decided to let a government agency collect the worker's contributions, pay out the retirement benefits, and manage the trust fund. . . . That's a cruel joke."

go on television to attack the Democrats, but Baker and Deaver talked him out of that one, good advice considering that congressional Republicans had voted against him, too—for the first time. He scowled and growled around the Oval Office for a day, personally searching his old files to find a 1975 *Barron's* magazine article with the headline: "Memo to Young Workers: The Burdens of Social Security Now Greatly Exceed the Benefits" and sent it to Secretary of Health and Human Resources Richard Schweiker. His cover note said: "Dick, since Soc. Sec. is still with us, thought this piece would be of interest to you. . . . Ron." His scrawled answers with a felt-tip pen to the next day's "Log of Selected House Mail" were uncharacteristically testy:

"Butler Derrick, a conservative South Carolina Democrat, states his opposition to the proposed changes in the Social Security System." On the "Comments" line, Reagan wrote: "Can he do better?"

Ralph Hall, a conservative Texas Democrat, wanted to know the administration's position on the future of the Department of Education. Reagan wrote: "I hope it has none."

James Howard, a New Jersey Democrat, asked about funding to clean up a hazardous waste site called "Burnt Fly Bog." Reagan wrote: "Never heard of it."

Robert Walker, a Pennsylvania Republican, asked for a meeting to discuss greater presidential effort in support of block grants to states. Reagan wrote: "He doesn't have to sell me—I want those block grants as much or more so than he does."

The President calmed down by preparing to go to Rancho del Cielo. He was not going to let the presidency take that from him. He had called in Deaver to say, "Mike, I've been looking at this schedule, and I don't see any ranch time."

"Well, that's right, sir," said Deaver. "Every time you go out there, the press makes a big deal about you being away from Washington, and the cost to the taxpayers of you traveling out to your ranch, and so forth and so on."

Tough. On May 22, the Reagans headed for their helicopter, Marine One, for the short trip to Andrews Air Force Base to board Air Force One for the trip to California. His senior staff was meeting to decide what "The White House" would do and say while the boss was cutting brush and riding far from the madding schedule. The fifteen action items, with assignments for other officials, included:

"7. Regarding nerve gas decision, yachts, infant formula"—he wanted to keep the first, stop taxing the second, and ignore complaints in Africa that letting corporations sell the third was condemning infants to disease and death because of impure local water—"we need to be sensitive to these items cutting against our desire to increase the perception that the President has compassion. . . . 10. President will sign normal paperwork and make normal announcements Monday afternoon for Tuesday press to show activity while in California. Darman collecting the necessary."

Reagan's third news conference, the first since he had been shot, was scheduled for the afternoon of June 16. White House correspondents had been pushing for this one, putting more and more pressure on communications director David Gergen. The questions had just kept piling up as reporters and most everyone else had been watching the President only from afar.

Reagan had his own three-item agenda. The Democrats were using their power in the House to chip away at the Gramm-Latta budget cuts (Stockman estimated that one-fourth of the cuts had been quietly restored in committee), and the president wanted to threaten a new budget-cutting resolution, Gramm-Latta II, "son of Gramm-Latta," he called it, restoring $48 billion of those budget cuts. Then he wanted to push his tax cuts, the 36 percent overall reduction for three years that was still being bounced between the White House and Congress—really between Reagan and O'Neill as they tried to top each other's Irish stories—and he wanted to defend himself on Social Security.

Reagan thought he was ready for his close-up, but his staff was not sure at all about that. "Be dull, Mr. President, be dull," was Meese's regular advice. He sounded like he was begging Reagan. One of his assistants, Edwin Harper, who helped in briefing the President that morning, quoted the advice of others: "Mr. President, we know that you are familiar with all these numbers about Social Security, but we would really urge a simple yes-or-no answer."

"All right," Reagan would say. But he didn't mean it; he had a headful of numbers and statistics he had collected over the years, particularly on Social Security and taxes. The problem, which everyone in on the briefing knew, was that many of those "facts" were not true, even if the President believed them. He cut off the quibbling of his briefers by saying: "Don't worry. I won't behave this way at the press conference. I'll faint, or I'll start a coughing fit."

That morning at the daily senior staff meeting in Baker's office, much of the time was spent going over an opening statement on the budget and tax agenda. Gergen warned the President and the others that most of the questions could be on foreign policy, particularly on reaction to a surprise Israeli bombing raid June 7, which destroyed a nuclear reactor in Iraq. The French-built installation just outside Baghdad was not a power plant, claimed the Israelis, but an almost completed factory capable of being converted to the manufacture of nuclear weapons. The attacking planes were American-built F-4 and F-16 fighter-bombers piloted by Israelis, which was a blatant violation of U.S.-Israel military aid agreements barring the use of American-built weaponry in offensive actions. When he had been told what happened, Reagan said only, "By golly, what do you suppose is behind that?" But he had dutifully signed an order suspending the scheduled delivery of four more F-16 fighters that week. Still, he insisted he could handle questions on the raid or any other foreign policy situations.

It turned out he could not. In all, the President was briefed for less than an hour and a half on the morning of the conference. Gergen reported first that the text of his opening statement—"I am asking Congress today to live up to its original commitment and deliver to my desk before the August recess not one but two bills . . ."—had already been leaked to the press. When Reagan completed the statement, he turned to the reporters, calling first on Dean Reynolds of United Press International, who asked about the reference to communism as "bizarre" in his Notre Dame speech and about events in Poland: "Do the events of the last ten months in Poland constitute the beginning of the end of Soviet domination of Eastern Europe?"

The President did think that—in a speech at the U.S. Military Academy two weeks before he had characterized the Soviet Union as an "evil force that would extinguish the light we've been tending for 6,000 years"—and he answered Reynolds's question on communism with undiplomatic candor: "It's not a normal way of living for human beings. . . . I think we are seeing the beginning cracks, the beginning of the end."

Then came the first of seven questions on Israel's preemptive attack in Iraq. The President's answers were as tangled and confusing as the politics of the Middle East. He could not unravel his own feeling that Israel did the right thing, did what it had to do, but the right thing was illegal under international law—and had already been officially condemned by him and by the State Department. Besides that, he did not like Israeli Prime Minister Menachem Begin, and he was angry and getting angrier about the fact that Begin had gone ahead without notifying him or the United States.*

Two questions later, Reagan appeared confused when he was asked for the United States's reaction to the fact that Israel had not signed the Nuclear Non-Proliferation Treaty and consistently refused to submit to inspections by the International Atomic Energy Agency. "Well," he said slowly, "I haven't given very much thought to that particular question. . . . It is difficult for me to envision Israel as being a threat to its neighbors. It is a nation that from the very beginning has lived under the threat from neighbors that they did not recognize its right to exist as a nation. I'll have to think about that question you asked."

He also muddled the answers to two questions about the use of tactical nuclear missiles to fight an invasion—a so-called contained nuclear war—of Western Europe by the Soviet Union. "I try to be optimistic," he said, "and think that the threat of both sides would keep it from happening, and yet, at the same time, as I say, history seems to be against that, that there comes a moment of desperation when one side tries to get an advantage over the other."

His tax plan was not mentioned until the fourteenth question. Noting that he had modified his income tax cuts in back-and-forth maneuvering with Democrats in Congress, a reporter asked whether he was open to more compromise. "No," was the answer. "The three-year across-the-board spread which I did modify—to the extent of making it 5-10-10 insted of 10-10-10, and which I moved up to October 1st instead of retroactive back through the year in going into effect—was done in an effort to create, as we did with the spending law, a bipartisan package. . . . I can't retreat and I don't think the people want us to. The latest polls show that 79 percent of the people approve of the individual tax cut and approve of it over a three-year span. And that, I think, should be the message to anyone who's elected to office on the Hill."

* "That fellow Begin makes it very hard for us to support Israel," Reagan had said at one meeting. In his diary two days after the raid he wrote of Begin: "I can understand his fear but feel he took the wrong option. He should have told us and the French. We could have done something to remove the threat. . . . Under the law I have no choice but to ask Congress and see if there is a violation of the law regarding use of American produced planes for offensive purposes. Frankly, if Congress should decide that, I'll grant a Presidential waiver. Iraq is technically still at war with Israel and I believe they were preparing to build an atomic bomb." His congressional mail of June 8, less than twenty-four hours after the raid, included a letter from Representative Barney Frank, the Massachusetts Democrat, urging immediate delivery of the four F-16s. On the "Comments" line, Reagan scribbled: "They'll get delivered."

Reynolds rose to cut off the questions—"Thank you, Mr. President"—after a half-hour. But as Reagan turned to leave, Sam Donaldson of ABC News shouted a final question: "Tip O'Neill says you don't understand about the working people, that you have just a bunch of wealthy and selfish advisers."

The President stopped, then said with obvious anger: "Tip O'Neill has said that I don't know anything about the working man. I'm trying to find out about his boyhood, because we didn't live on the wrong side of the railroad tracks, but we lived so close to them we could hear the whistle real loud.

"And I know very much about the working group. I grew up in poverty and got what education I got all by myself and so forth, and I think it is sheer demagoguery to pretend that this economic program which we've submitted is not aimed at helping the great cross-section of people in this country that have been burdened for too long by big government and high taxes."

Then he went back to the Oval Office and resumed what he had been doing before the press conference briefing. He called eight more House members to ask for their votes on the tax bill, now called Conable-Hance after its sponsors, Barber Conable, an upstate New York Republican, and Kent Hance, a conservative Texas Democrat. "We have him," he wrote after talking to Gary Lee, another upstate New York Republican. Next was Billy Tauzin, a Louisiana Democrat: "He's with us—like me he dreams of the day we can get rid of the whole d—n 'Windfall profits tax.' "

The next morning's *New York Times* gave the press conference two front-page headlines: "Reagan Asserts Israel Had Cause to Mistrust Iraq" and "President Demands Tax Cut and Budget Be Passed by August"—that one carried the subhead "Democratic Efforts Described as 'Unconscionable'—O'Neill Is Assailed as Demagogic." The day's lead headline was "U.S. TO SELL WEAPONS TO CHINA IN POLICY REVERSAL," over a story from Beijing reporting that visiting Secretary of State Haig had announced that the President had decided to eliminate a ban on selling "lethal" American weaponry to the Chinese. But what really caught the White House's attention in the *Times* that morning was a column by William Safire, a former writer for and briefer of President Nixon. "The President has been skimping on his preparation, neglecting the black book, relying instead on oral give-and-take with his aides for a couple of hours before press conferences. He thinks he can wing it. Some member of the inner circle with a great sense of security should tell him this is how a democracy tests its leader's range of comprehension, and that he has been flunking the test."

Ignore Safire, advised Richard Wirthlin, the President's pollster, in a memo Reagan read the next day, June 18: "At no time during this administration has naming of foreign policy as the number one national problem risen above 8 percent, instead, the domestic issues of inflation and the economy in general far outpace concern over any other problems, receiving combined attention of consistently over 40 percent of the nation. . . . It would be unwise to allow the press to dictate the agenda for your Administration."

"OK," Reagan wrote in the corner of Wirthlin's memo. Members of the Baker-Meese-Deaver inner circle spent two days chewing that over at morning meetings before deciding to do what they could to keep their man away from reporters.

Reagan's first call the morning after the conference was to Tip O'Neill. He apologized for attacking him. "Old Buddy," said O'Neill, "that's politics—after 6 o'clock we can be friends; but before 6 it's politics." But, in fact, by 6 o'clock most evenings, Reagan's phone calls to Democratic conservatives were steadily chipping away at the power and control of O'Neill and his principal deputy, Majority Leader Wright, an old-style Texas liberal. In mid-June Wright wrote of Reagan in his diary: "His philosophical approach is superficial, overly simplistic and one-dimensional. What he preaches is pure economic pap, glossed over with uplifting homilies and inspirational chatter. Yet so far the guy is making it work. Appalled by what seems to me a lack of depth, I stand in awe nevertheless of his political skill. I am not sure that I have seen its equal."

The memo on top of the President's desk reading that same day was a set of one-page biographies of eighteen possible candidates to succeed Potter Stewart. There were five women on the list—that for a President who had appointed white men to sixty-eight of seventy-two lower court judgeships so far. But candidate Reagan had promised to try to find a woman Supreme Court nominee, an announcement he made two weeks before the election—in fact, on the afternoon of October 14, 1980, the day Wirthlin's tracking polls showed Reagan trailing Carter for the first time and *The New York Times* published a poll showing him running nine points behind Carter among female voters. The age of each of the eighteen candidates was highlighted with a felt-tip pen. What conservatives and most of his staff wanted was to name a conservative who could serve as long as Stewart had. What Reagan wanted was to make history by naming the first woman to the Supreme Court. He sent the list back, saying he wanted a short list of all women.

Five days later, on June 23, correspondents and photographers from the newsmagazine *U.S. News & World Report* were invited into the White House for another "Day in the Life" feature on the President. There was some good news to begin with: The lead headline in the morning's *New York Times* read: "AIR CONTROL STRIKE CANCELLED AS UNION AND U.S. REACH PACT." PATCO's president, Robert Poli, had agreed to submit the government's offer of $40 million in wages and new benefits to the union's members for a vote.

Baker and Deaver told *U.S. News* this would be the busiest day ever for Reagan—the struggle over the budget cuts of Gramm-Latta II was climaxing in Congress—and they were frank to admit they wanted to show that Reagan was fully recovered from his gunshot wound. In fact, the first person the President saw on his way to the Oval Office at 9 A.M. was Tim McCarthy, the Secret Service agent who had taken a bullet for him and was back at work for the first time since March 30. "Welcome back," Reagan said. "How are you feeling?"

Thirty-eight Democrats waited for him at a breakfast meeting in the State Dining Room, where he pushed for budget and tax cuts. They were the first of 239 members of Congress who would meet with the President before 6 P.M. that day. He saw his friend Senator Paul Laxalt of Nevada in mid-afternoon and said, "Oh, this is the worst! I've still got half a day's work to do." Just before 5 P.M., he went into the Rose Garden, took his cards from his pocket, and began, "Where's Paul Findley? Today Paul Findley can celebrate his 60th birthday knowing he's still younger than the President who also happens to be in good health."

There was no reaction. The President looked up and saw 175 teenagers from Republican youth clubs around the country. Wrong cards. An hour later he did get to wish a happy birthday to Findley, a House Republican, one of 190 at a reception in the East Room. One, Margaret Heckler of Massachusetts, asked him to bend down, then whispered in his ear, "A woman for the Court—it's the right moment."

"I'm thinking about it," he said. Indeed. His new list to replace Justice Stewart had just four names, all women, two of them from the original list: Mary Coleman, Chief Justice of the Michigan Supreme Court; Amalya Kearse, a black Court of Appeals judge; Cornelia Kennedy, a district court judge; and Sandra Day O'Connor, an Arizona Court of Appeals judge, appointed two years before by a Democratic governor, Bruce Babbitt. She had been a Stanford Law School classmate of Justice William Rehnquist. In fact, they had dated a couple of times at Stanford.

By 10:30 the next morning the President was on Air Force One, flying to Texas and California for speeches and a long weekend at his ranch. As he left, Richard Darman told him that Max Friedersdorf estimated that they were still twelve votes short on the budget in the House. O'Neill and Wright hoped to eliminate the Gramm-Latta II budget cuts by breaking the bill into five parts, a procedural move designed to divide the Republicans and conservative Democrats backing the bill. In the air and on the ground in Texas and at the Century Park Plaza Hotel in Los Angeles, the President made more than two dozen calls to House members, most of them Democrats being pressured by their leaders to stick with the party line. Reagan carefully wrote out what they said and sent the list back across the country by fax to Darman and Friedersdorf. Next to the name of John Breaux, a Louisiana Democrat, he noted: "I don't know where he is. He's part of the leadership & they had a meeting on the subject this afternoon. But before he was through he was telling me he supported me & wants to help." The notation on Ron Mottl, an Ohio Democrat, was: "Says he's with us. Says he & I are going to be real friends."

It was now one-vote-at-a-time, retail politicking. The President got Breaux's vote by promising to stop opposing sugar beet price supports in Louisiana and by promising him, as he had promised other Democrats, that he would not campaign against his new Democratic friends. "No way," he told Breaux. "I couldn't look myself in the mirror if I went and campaigned against you." On his call sheet for William Boner, a Tennessee Democrat, he wrote: "With us. Assured him I'll remember him come election time." The great persuader in the sky on Air Force One ended each call with the three words "God bless you!"

The next morning, Reagan was making more calls from his nineteenth-floor suite at the Century Plaza. Just before 11 A.M. Pacific time, he was on the line with Senator Robert Dole of Kansas, chairman of the Senate Finance Committee, when Dole said he just got news from the House. Deaver, who was in the suite, heard the President say: "Oh, my God. You've got the news on the House vote. I just can't believe it!" The White House had won; the procedural vote was 217 to 210, with 29 Democrats voting with the Republicans. The final vote on son of Gramm-Latta was 232 to 192.

Downstairs at a lunch of the California Taxpayers' Association, Reagan happily proclaimed: "A great victory . . . the greatest reduction in government spending that has ever been attempted."

The Republican-controlled Senate then passed similar legislation by a vote of 80 to 15. The next morning, Reagan began calling congressmen to thank them. The first call was to Ron Mottl, the Ohio Democrat. Then it was off to Rancho del Cielo for him, with a *New York Times* headline saying: "REAGAN'S AIDES SAY A BALANCED BUDGET IS POSSIBLE BY 1984."

While the President was in the West, Judge O'Connor, considered a moderate conservative when she was a state legislator, came east on June 27 for a secret interview with Attorney General William French Smith at a hotel. Then, on July 1, with the Reagans back, she was interviewed by Bill Clark, the former chief justice of California, now serving as deputy secretary of state. Both men were impressed. Clark walked her over to the White House that day for a talk with Reagan. The conversation began with horses—O'Connor had grown up on a ranch called the Lazy-B, twenty-five miles from the nearest town— then moved on to more serious matters of law and politics, focusing on abortion. She told Reagan she was personally against it but said that the law was the law. Reagan liked her immediately and that was that.

The formal announcement of her nomination was set for July 7. But a couple of days before that, there was a quiet flurry of last-minute opposition from fundamentalist religious leaders and from members of Congress. The president of the National Right-to-Life Committee, Dr. John Willke, was one of dozens of anti-abortion activists who began calling Meese and saying they had proof that O'Connor was pro-abortion. On July 6, Max Friedersdorf reported: "Senator Don Nickles (R-Okla.) and Rep. Henry Hyde (R-Ill.) called this morning to protest the possible appointment of the Connor woman from Arizona to the Supreme Court." Their preferred candidate was Yale Law School professor Robert Bork, fifty-four, a conservative intellectual who served as Solicitor General during the Nixon administration.

An hour later, Meese added three more senators to the list of objectors: Jesse Helms of North Carolina, Strom Thurmond of South

Carolina, and Steve Symms of Idaho. The Reverend Jerry Falwell of the Moral Majority added himself to the list. Evans and Novak filed a column saying that Reagan had been misled into believing Mrs. O'Connor was anti-abortion by "A hurriedly prepared error-filled memo by a young Justice Department lawyer named Kenneth W. Starr."

The President went to the White House press room on the morning of July 7 to make the announcement himself, on live television. Reagan said that after 101 men had served, he was nominating the first woman. When the questions about her record began, he grinned and turned the microphone over to Attorney General Smith. For once he got more support from liberals and the press than from the Republican right, which was still generating calls and telegrams to the White House—messages running better than ten to one against O'Connor. Tip O'Neill said, "This is the best thing he's done since he was inaugurated." *The Washington Post* editorialized: "That the President has gone to the second tier of a state court structure in his search for a female nominee may be less a commentary on Judge O'Connor's qualifications than on a system that, until the quite recent past, kept almost all women lawyers from reaching high places in their chosen profession."

Conservatives, though, went public with their criticisms about her lack of experience and her stands on abortion and the Equal Rights Amendment, but that pretty much ended when Arizona's grand old conservative, Senator Barry Goldwater, got angry when Reverend Falwell preached that "good Christians" should be concerned about the nomination. Responded Goldwater: "Every good Christian ought to kick Falwell right in the ass." Reagan himself was less direct, calling Falwell to say: "Jerry, I am going to put forth a lady on the Supreme Court. You don't know anything about her. Nobody does, but I want you to trust my judgment on this one."

"I'll do that, sir," said Falwell. Within a few days he was calling other Christian conservatives, urging them to back the President. Unlike many politicians, including many conservative Republicans, Reagan was comfortable with the people, like Falwell, who introduced themselves by saying, "I am a Christian. . . ." The President did not go to church regularly—his home church in Los Angeles was Bel Air Presbyterian—but he was a student of the Protestant sects that debated and believed in prophecies that led to a belief in Armageddon and other phenomenal events.

When Mrs. O'Connor walked the halls making courtesy calls in Senate office buildings, women staffers lined the halls, waving and applauding as she passed. When she met with the Senate's Democratic leader, Robert Byrd of West Virginia, he asked whether she could stay a few minutes longer because his wife would like to come over and have a photo taken with Judge O'Connor. After quick visits to Senate offices, thirty-nine of them, the lady from Phoenix easily won over even Helms and Thurmond. She was an idea whose time had come.

During the O'Connor hearings, Smith came to the White House to brief Reagan on proposals to check illegal immigration. The Attorney General wanted to use counterfeit-proof Social Security cards as national identity cards. Cabinet members were nodding in agreement, but one of the President's assistants, economist Martin Anderson, was appalled. He raised his hand. The President said, "Marty?"

"I would like to suggest another way that I think is a lot better," said Anderson. "It's a lot cheaper. It can't be counterfeited. It's very lightweight, and impossible to lose. It's even waterproof. . . . All we have to do is tattoo an identification number on the inside of everybody's arm."

The comparison to Nazi concentration camps drew gasps. But Reagan took it biblically. "Why, it sounds to me that you are talking about the mark of the Beast. That's terrible."

Most of the men in the room did not understand the reference. It was to Revelation 13, verses 16 to 18. No one said anything for some very long moments. Finally, Reagan grinned, looked at Smith, and said: "Maybe we should just brand all the babies."

On July 16, the House approved the administration's military buildup by a vote of 354 to 63, joining the Senate in approving a $136 billion military authorization bill, appropriating $26.4 billion more than was spent the year before. It was the largest single military authorization bill in history and included almost $5 billion for new weaponry, including Trident submarine missiles, the B-1 stealth bomber, Navy F-14 fighters, the M-1 tank, and the MX (Missile Experimental) program initiated by President Carter to develop a new generation of ICBMs, one of the weapons areas where the Soviets had a numerical lead over the United States. There was, however, a problem with those ten-warhead surface-to-surface missiles: There was controversy over where to put them.

Carter had left Reagan with a rail system called "Race Track" that would move missiles from silo to silo along ten thousand miles of rails in Utah and Nevada, shuttling them around each day to foil Soviet targeters. Then the President began a new round of telephone calls and Oval Office meetings with members of Congress, forty-four in one day, thirty-nine the next, most of them, as usual, conservative Democrats from the South. As to the details of the legislation, that was not his real business. Walking by the Cabinet Room the day before, he looked in and saw Secretary of the Treasury Donald Regan presiding over a tax meeting. "Want to join us?" Regan asked.

"Heck, no," said the President. "I'm going to leave this to you experts. I'm not going to get involved in details."

Then came a prime-time television speech, this one on July 27, to rally support for his 25 percent income tax cut over three years. Democratic leadership in the House—Speaker O'Neill and Ways and Means Committee Chairman Daniel Rostenkowski—countered with their own tax-cut bills, skewed more toward people earning less than $50,000 and with the third-year reduction eliminated if budget deficits were declining. The President mocked all that on television on July 27, predicting the budget would soon be in balance, then turning to charts and saying: "The majority leadership claims theirs gives a greater break to the workers than ours, and it does—that is, if you're only planning to live two more years."

The most important difference, actually, was that the White House plan would mandate indexing tax rates after 1984, taking into account the effect of inflation on incomes. "Bracket creep is an insidious tax," he said. "If you earned $10,000 a year in 1972, by 1980 you had to earn $19,700 just to stay even with inflation. But that's before taxes. Come April 15th, you find your tax rates have increased 30 percent. . . . We intend to stop that." Two days later, after the Republican-controlled Senate approved the White House plan by a vote of 89 to 11, the House voted for it by 238 to 195. Forty-eight Democrats voted with the President.

"Political-Economic Turn" was The New York Times headline over twinned "News Analysis" pieces by Hedrick Smith and Leonard Silk. "With stunning victories today, the President has won Congressional approval for the largest budget and tax cuts in modern American history, changes that his partisans have termed 'the Reagan revolution' inviting comparisons to the early New Deal period of Franklin D. Roosevelt," wrote Smith. Silk said: "Ronald Reagan's radical change in United States fiscal policy, aimed at cutting back the role of the Federal Government in the United States economy, has come to pass." *

The fight was over, even though one of the President's essential allies, Senate Leader Howard Baker, proclaimed victory in a nervous way, telling CBS News that making supply-side economics into government orthodoxy was "a riverboat gamble." Reagan, the man who knew when to hold them and when to fold them, was happily about ready to leave town and head for his ranch. Item 4 on the senior staff agenda meeting the next morning, July 31, read: "Period when President is in California (8/6–9/3): There will be no Senior Staff meetings during that period. Staff will be expected to work normal working hours with deputies of operating sections here when the heads of those sections are away. The press operation will shift to California; there will be limited facilities in California for others. Vacations should be scheduled, if possible, during this period." Further down was this item: "Current PATCO situation—guidance and where do we stand?"

That was at breakfast. At noon, Robert Poli, president of the air controllers' union, called a press conference. He announced that PATCO's membership had rejected the administration's $40 million offer—95 percent voted no after the union's executive committee rejected the offer—and then said he was going back to the original union demand of close to $700 million in higher wages, cost-of-living differentials, four-day workweeks, and retirement at 75 percent of pay after twenty years. He wanted immediate raises of $10,000 for all 17,500 controllers, 14,800 of whom were PATCO members. Asked why he thought they could get that, even with an illegal strike, Poli said: "They cannot fly this country's planes without us, and they can't get us to do our jobs if we are in jail or facing excessive fines."

When Secretary of Transportation Drew Lewis responded by saying the government would not raise its June offer, Poli scheduled a strike to begin at 7 A.M., August 3. It began that morning before the President's eight o'clock wake-up call. When he came downstairs, his

---

* Reagan's mastery of Congress, the product of all those phone calls and the television appeals, and invitations to Camp David, was historic. A study prepared for House Minority Leader Robert Michel stated: "Under President Eisenhower, House Republican support varied from 60 percent to 79 percent. During the Nixon Administration, House Republicans voted with him approximately 73 percent of the time from 1969 to 1974. President Ford claimed party unity only 65 percent of the time. The Republican membership of the House has backed Reagan 92 percent. Limiting the average only to budget and tax cut votes, the score is 99 percent."

senior staff was waiting with recommendations for government action. But Reagan had already made up his mind. David Gergen, the communications director, took notes at the meeting quoting him: "Dammit, the law is the law and the law says they cannot strike. They have quit their jobs and they will not be rehired. . . . Government cannot shut down. I don't see any other way. . . . I'm willing to say 48 hours. . . . They have terminated themselves. They're in defiance of the law. . . . Desertion in the face of duty."

The strike also gave Reagan a chance to quote one of his favorite Presidents, budget-balancer Calvin Coolidge. He had put a portrait of the laconic Vermonter in the Oval Office and now he repeated what Coolidge had once said when he was governor of Massachusetts and was asked to reinstate Boston police officers dismissed for striking in 1919: "There is no right to strike against the public safety of anybody, anywhere, at any time." *

The President had written out a statement himself, which he read in the Rose Garden just before 11 A.M., saying:

> Let me read the solemn oath taken by each of these employees:
> "I am not participating in any strike against the Government of the United States or any agency thereof, and I will not so participate while an employee of the government of the United States or any agency thereof."
> It is for this reason I must tell those who failed to report for duty this morning they are in violation of the law and if they do not report for work within 48 hours they have forfeited their job and will be terminated.

Back inside, Reagan said: "I'm sorry, and I'm sorry for them. I certainly take no joy out of this." That was that. Telephone calls and telegrams to the White House that day, thousands of them, supported the President's stand by more than ten to one.

Commentators on television and in newspapers seemed awed by Reagan. *The Washington Post*'s most important columnist, David Broder, summed it up this way: "The message is getting around: Don't mess with his guy. Whatever gets in his way, he tries to break." In the *Philadelphia Inquirer,* Tom Fox wrote: "Ronald Reagan is a cross be-

* Coolidge acted months after the police strike ended. As governor, his only role was to deny the requests of strikers seeking reappointment. He denied all such applications.

tween John F. Kennedy (for style, grace, charm, looks and dash) and Franklin Delano Roosevelt (for political insights and an uncanny reading of contemporary moods)." Lou Cannon of the *Post* was neither surprised nor awed: "While Reagan started out in politics as an aloof celebrity content to soar above the political battlefield, he learned gradually how to focus his personal charm upon the lowly riflemen of politics: the assemblymen and congressmen who have to vote each day and give their constituents a plausible account of their actions."

While the President was having lunch, the Justice Department was collecting injunctions and contempt-of-court orders against the union's leaders around the country. The Federal Aviation Administration began to implement contingency plans drawn up by the Carter administration in January 1980. Thirteen thousand controllers struck on August 3, leaving more than 4,000 of their colleagues, 2,500 supervisors, and 2,000 military controllers in airport towers and traffic control centers. Airlines canceled almost half the day's 14,300 scheduled flights. Secretary of Transportation Drew Lewis said flights would reach 75 percent of normal numbers within three days—a goal that was met—but that it would take a full ten years to train a full workforce to replace the fired controllers.

Lunch was a tough one this day. Ten of Reagan's men, including Vice President Bush, waited for him in the Cabinet Room. David Stockman came with a stack of forty-two-page budget folders. Black books. The first page read: "The long term outlook is grim. We face a minimum budget deficit of $60 billion for each of the next four years."

As dessert was served, sherbet, the budget director began a thirty-minute lecture: "The scent of victory is in the air. But I'm not going to mince words. We're headed for a crash landing on the budget. We're facing potential deficits so big they could wreck the President's entire economic program." There was going to be no balanced budget in 1984, he said, or '85, or '86 . . .

At the moment, Stockman repeated, the deficit estimate for the coming year was $62 billion—almost exactly $20 billion more than Stockman had told the public in a statement eighteen days before—and unless there were hundreds of billions of dollars in budget cuts in the next four years, the annual shortfall was headed for new territory, triple digits. Even if the tax cuts produced 5 percent a year GNP growth, and the President got every spending cut he asked for, the deficit would rise to $81 billion in 1983 and hit $112 billion by 1986. Murray Weidenbaum, the chairman of his Council of Economic Advisers, told the President a dirty little secret about why real numbers had been withheld from both him and the nation: "We didn't want to confuse the tax picture."

In other words, they had kept deficit projections secret until after the tax vote. Reagan, who had seemed disinterested, acting as if he were already on his way to the ranch, suddenly came alive, saying: "Dave, if what you are saying is true, then Tip O'Neill was right all along."

Stockman said one option would be to abandon the balanced-budget goal.

"No," Reagan said. "We can't give up on the balanced budget. Deficit spending is how we got into this mess."

Stockman said that by reducing the defense buildup, now a 9.5 percent increase, to 7 percent a year, spending could be cut 16 percent in 1984 and double that by 1986.

"No," Reagan said. "There must be no perception by anyone in the world that we're backing down an inch on the defense budget. When I was asked during the campaign about what I would do if it came down to a choice between defense and deficits, I always said national security had to come first, and the people applauded every time."

Stockman said that $15 billion to $20 billion per year could be raised by taxes on imported oil, alcohol, and tobacco, and by creating new user fees.

No.

Ed Meese began to talk about how well workforce reductions had worked in Sacramento. Stockman said, as he often had, that the federal budget was different from state budgets: Employee salaries and benefits were a very small part of the federal budget when compared with entitlements and subsidies mandated by law.

Reagan cut Stockman off, saying: "The Federal government's lathered in fat when it comes to employment. We should tell all the agencies, 'To the rear march!' "

After a state dinner that night for President Anwar Sadat of Egypt, the President and his wife were off for their month in California.

Reagan was asked about the PATCO strike when he arrived in California and he answered: "There is no strike. . . . What they did was terminate their own employment by quitting." He had said about the same thing to Drew Lewis before boarding Air Force One. Lewis, who favored terminating the controllers, admitted that he was worried that Reagan's friends with private planes might talk him into giving in to PATCO. Reagan had looked at him strangely and said: "Drew, don't worry about me. When I support someone—and you're right on this strike—I'll continue to support you, and you never have to ask that question again."

CHAPTER 5
AUGUST 13, 1981

THE MORNING FOG WAS SO THICK up at Rancho del Cielo on August 13 that you could not see a horse thirty feet away. That killed Mike Deaver's plan of a picturesque backdrop for the ritual signing of the tax and budget legislation that President Reagan had sold to the country and the Congress. Reagan sat down at a table in front of the porch of the small, unheated stucco ranch house. Dozens of reporters milled about in the mist, waiting for cameramen to figure out how to work in the half-light. Steve Weisman of *The New York Times* asked the President the name of his dog, a collie running around the place. Reagan looked perplexed, then brightened and said what was apparently the first thing that came into his head: "Lassie."

More than a thousand pages of law and tax code, many unnumbered, had been cobbled together so quickly that one provision read, "255-4855," which was the phone number of a Senate clerk named Rita Seymour who had worked on those pages. The President may not have known his dog's name but he had his lines down, saying, with more than a little exaggeration: "These bills that I'm about to sign . . . represent a turnaround of almost half a century of a course this country's been on, and mark an end to the excessive growth in government bureaucracy, government spending, government taxing."

After the signing, the President, in denims and cowboy boots, leaned back, laughed, and took some questions from the reporters who had been driven up the twisting roads to the Reagans' place. There was a lot of joking about ranch life and his wife's preference for Beverly Hills, but the rancher himself seemed to enjoy it and the reporters got interesting answers to a couple of questions. For the first time, he conceded that the budget might not be balanced by 1984. In fact, the new deficit numbers in internal memos were already exceeding Stockman's secret July estimate of $62 billion. The new number was $80 billion, the highest in history.*

Still outside in the fog, when Reagan was asked about arguments between Secretary of State Haig and Secretary of Defense Weinberger, he described how he liked to work:

> The whole Cabinet argues in front of me. That was the system I wanted installed. Instead of the traditional Cabinet meeting with each Cabinet member making a brief report on how things were going in his agency, I wanted this operation where I have the benefit of the thinking of all of them. . . . What we do is have an agenda, and it goes out on the table and the thing is that, when there's been enough discussion and enough argument and I've joined in and I've heard enough, I make the decision.

That was indeed the way it worked when Reagan was interested. More often than not the President did not actually join in discussions. He just listened and doodled—or did not listen and doodled. One memo from Darman on a "Weekly Update" session ended: "If there are any matters on which you would wish to have additional briefing, would you please note the issues or topics here below." The President responded, "Haven't had time to think of any."

Often he had made up his mind before the meeting, but he never said that. Some of the new people working for him were baffled and turned to old Sacramento hands. "He won't think about things that he ought to do," Lyn Nofziger told them. "Somebody has to come along and remind him. 'Hey Mr. President,' or 'Hey Ron . . . ' "

"A Disengaged Presidency," headlined *Newsweek* in an article prepared while Reagan was at the ranch. The magazine used words like "inattention" and "ignorance," quoting an anonymous aide, saying, "He is easily bored, alternately joking and yawning through subjects

---

* Richard Darman later analyzed what happened this way: "Ultimately, the revenue from the enacted program came in at 18.5 percent of GDP. That was one full percentage point below the level put forth in candidate Reagan's September 1980 plan. At the same time, spending stayed up in the 22 to 24 percent range." For most of the postwar period, deficits had been below 2 percent of GDP. The Reagan plan had originally said the 1983 deficit would be zero. But it was actually on its way to 6.3 percent of GDP—a peacetime record that still stands.

that don't interest him. All he wants to do is tell stories about his movie days."

And now and then he dozed at the head of the table. Reagan's management style, considered slothful and uninterested by many hyperactive politicians and political journalists, was beginning to attract the attention of business journals. Ronald Hoff, director of FCB/Corporate, a division of the advertising company Foote, Cone and Belding, wrote in the business pages of *The New York Times:* "Hail to the chief, as executive," which listed Reagan's techniques as a valuable management guide: "For heaven's sake, smile a little" . . . "Let your people know what you stand for—but keep it simple" . . . "When you get a new job, get a fast start. Show people you know precisely where you're going" . . . "Never underestimate the power of a speech" . . . "Use simple words that stir emotions" . . . "Never apologize for what you are" . . . "Never hesitate to pick up the phone and sell somebody your program" . . . "Pour on the praise" . . . "Delegate responsibility to those you trust and don't stew about their decisions."

Reagan was no stewer. When his mind was made up, there was no reason to keep talking. In the first postelection meeting with his staff to talk about the Cabinet, beginning with the Justice Department, Reagan had walked in and said, "Now listen, before we get started, Bill Smith is going to be my attorney general."

"Have you thought about the fact that he has no experience?" someone asked.

"Let me just tell you something, fellas. I have made my decision: he is going to be my attorney general."

When the subject of the deficit (and tax increases to reduce it) came up in a briefing before a press conference, Baker said, "Mr. President, we really ought to leave ourselves an opening."

"No," said Reagan. Meese agreed with Baker. "No," said Reagan. Speakes, who had replaced Brady in the press office, agreed with them, too. "Mr. President, I have written out something here. Maybe this will suit you."

The President read it, then grabbed a pen and scrawled a couple of words. "*This* is what I want to say." Speakes looked at the paper. It said: "NO TAX INCREASE!"

"Got it," said Speakes. "Loud and clear." Like many other people in the White House, Speakes was often afraid of the boss. What *Newsweek* saw as disengagement, the men who worked under Reagan saw as distance above them. He gave them less guidance and more freedom than many wanted, leaving them to worry and wonder. So they tried to reach him or please him in ways great and small. One Friday afternoon, Lesley Stahl, the White House correspondent of CBS News, was sitting with Jim Baker in his large corner office. They stopped talking for a moment as Marine One, the President's helicopter, landed on the lawn behind them. "What time do you have?" Baker asked.

"Five-twenty," she said.

"Oh my God," said Baker. He was pale and flustered; it was the first time Stahl had ever seen him rattled. "Just wait here," he said, jumping up. "I'll be right back."

"What's wrong?"

"I think I may have missed the helicopter. The president's leaving for Camp David any minute. Maybe I can still make it."

He ran out the door.

He came back smiling. "I made it."

"Well, tell me, what was so urgent?" asked Stahl.

"Oh, I didn't have anything special to tell them," said Baker. "I just wanted them to see me standing there as they left for the weekend."

The President's schedule after his ranch press conference read: "The President and the First Lady had lunch." After lunch, the President spent the afternoon chopping wood and clearing brush. That was on the schedule each ranch day, which always began: "The President and the First Lady had breakfast" . . . "The President and the First Lady went riding." As he waited for his wife, he would look over whatever papers had been delivered up the mountain. Not many were. The August 13 package included the usual summaries of letters from members of Congress. The first one, from Representative John Burton, a California Democrat, read: "Urges you to appoint a third party to mediate a settlement in the Professional Air Traffic Controllers Organization dispute."

"Nope," Reagan wrote in the margin. "No way," he wrote next to a plea by Representative William D. Ford, a Michigan Democrat, to appoint a panel of arbitrators to settle the strike.

The next day's *New York Times,* which did not get to Reagan, analyzed the strike in an article by A. H. Raskin, its retired labor columnist, under a two-deck headline: "The Air Strike Is Ominous for Labor . . . Unions May Face a Bitter Era in Both Public and Private Sectors." Douglas Fraser, president of the United Auto Workers, agreed, telling *The Wall Street Journal*: "It's a fair warning to all unions that if they get into a struggle and look to the government for some kind of comfort, they aren't going to get it. Or if government officials intervene, they'll intervene on the side of the employer against the union."

They got the message. So did America. Pollster Wirthlin sent the President a fourteen-page analysis indicating that more than 71 percent of respondents backed the firing of the controllers—and the younger the respondents the more the support.

Meanwhile, back at the ranch, Reagan rode on, so far above it all that CBS was trying to install a telescope, the one used to cover space launchings, on another peak, hoping to catch a glimpse of the Reagans—or their horses. When they finally got it working, the President told his wife he was going to step off the porch and drop to the ground, grabbing his chest. Mrs. Reagan was not amused, neither by the pantomime nor the long lens.

The President's daily package from Washington included his "Recommended Telephone Call" list. One reminded him that August 15 was the birthday of Ann Regan, the wife of Secretary of the Treasury Don Regan. The Secretary was giving a surprise party for her at Mount Vernon in Virginia and hoped the President would call. "Call made," Reagan wrote on the memo when he sent it back.

On Cape Cod, where he was vacationing, Tip O'Neill, two years younger than the President, saw photographs of Reagan chopping wood and decided to try it himself. After fifteen minutes he could barely breathe or walk. The next time he saw Reagan, he made a point of grabbing the presidential biceps. "It's like iron," he told an assistant.

The President came down from his mountaintop and wood-chopping on August 17 for a couple of daytime hours of staff meetings and a Republican fund-raising dinner at the Century Plaza Hotel in Los Angeles. Reagan was asleep in the hotel when Meese called him at 4:23 A.M., August 19, and informed him that five and a half hours earlier—before 11 P.M., August 18, Pacific Daylight Time—two United States F-14s had shot down two Soviet-made Su-22 fighters of the Libyan Air Force over the Mediterranean Sea during American naval maneuvers off the coast of Libya. The leader of that oil-rich country of only four million people, Colonel Muammar el-Qaddafi, unpredictable to a point close to madness, claimed sea and air rights of two hundred miles into the Gulf of Sidra. The United States, declar-

ing that it would continue to be bound only by law and custom specifying that international waters began twelve miles from the national
shores, had warned the Libyans not to interfere with maneuvers in the
gulf. Meese told the President the Libyans fired first. "Good work,"
said Reagan, and went back to sleep.

The timing of the air battle was a surprise but not the combat. The
F-14s were based on the USS *Nimitz* and the aircraft carrier was in the
gulf in deliberate response to Qaddafi's threat to shoot down any
American aircraft that passed what he called "The Line of Death."
Before the United States exercise began, the Navy had raised the question of rules of engagement with the President at a National Security
Council meeting in the Oval Office. Reagan had answered that pilots
were free to shoot back at anyone who fired on them. "What about
'hot pursuit'?" an admiral asked. "Suppose the Libyan planes shoot
at our planes and then flee back into Libyan territory. Do you authorize us to follow them?"

"You can follow them into their own damn hangars if you have
to!" Reagan had said. The quote spread through the Pentagon in
hours.

The Sidewinder missiles that brought down the Libyan jets were
the first shots fired in anger under the new administration. That was
part of the story. The other part, emphasized in most every paper in
the country, was headlined this way in the tabloid *New York Daily
News:* "AIDES LET RON SLEEP ON IT." *Washington Post* White
House correspondent Lee Lescaze wrote: "Meese's decision not to notify Reagan immediately raised once again a question that has popped
to the surface from time to time in the Reagan administration: who is
in command?" In the *Miami News,* cartoonist Don Wright did a
drawing of Reagan in bed on the phone: "World War III? Six hours
ago? No kidding? Well, gee, thanks for calling, Ed."

But Reagan had a quip of his own holstered, and drew it for the
crowd at a Republican fund-raiser in Costa Mesa: "If our planes were
shot down, yes, they'd wake me up right away; if the other fellow's
were shot down, why wake me up?"

On the first day of September, Acting Press Secretary Larry Speakes
(he never got the full title, which Reagan gave permanently to the
crippled James Brady) announced that the President was almost ready
to go back to work. He quoted Reagan as saying of his stay at the
ranch: "I hate to see it come to an end." That was the day *Newsweek*

was quoting "staff members" saying that the boss worked only two or three hours a day even when he was in Washington. James Baker took on the task of rebuttal: "You ought to judge him by the bottom line. . . . The fact of the matter is he's been more effective in the first six or seven months than any President in recent history."

That was true, for better or worse. Unfortunately for Reagan's press managers, that same day, in Los Angeles, the leader of the free world spent an hour with an old cowboy movie buddy, Rex Allen, and with Tony Lama, a celebrity bootmaker who measured the presidential feet for a $1,000 pair. "He acted like there was nothing else in the world he had to do—nothing else on his mind," said Allen, trying to be helpful when questioned by the workaholic White House press corps. A great part of that work was finding people like Allen to interview, instead of actually covering the President. The myth of intimacy appeared on billboards around the country promoting ABC News and its energetic White House correspondent, Sam Donaldson. Under a picture of him standing outside the President's house the copy read: "TO GET MORE ACCURATE COVERAGE OF THE WHITE HOUSE, YOU'D HAVE TO LIVE THERE." More down to earth, Donaldson looked up at the thing and laughed, telling a friend: "Actually, I seldom see Reagan. And quite often when I do see him, it is at such a distance, that I really need to look later at the videotape made with a long lens to take a close look at his face and expressions."

"Reagan Returns" was the lead headline of the News Summary on the President's desk on September 5, his first day back. The first item was from Lee Lescaze and Dan Balz of the *The Washington Post*: "President Reagan returned to the White House Thursday to begin the second chapter of his Presidency, in which new characters and problems promise to be introduced at the same time Reagan does battle to again cut the federal budget. His month-long vacation marked the end of a single-minded and remarkably successful opening chapter. . . . The open question is whether it also marked the end of his honeymoon. Another complication is that Reagan's relaxed Presidential work habits have come in for more open comment than ever before."

The *Chicago Tribune,* more conservative than most Eastern papers, in an editorial titled "Home on the Range," wrote: "If you can't criticize the President for getting too little done despite all the time he puts in, then try criticizing him for putting in so little time despite all he manages to get done. But if the choice is between Carter who put in conscientious 20-hour days with little to show for his efforts and a Reagan who has achieved a series of goals once thought impossible, despite taking things easy and delegating much of his authority, then we opt for the latter."

Disengaged laziness was the conventional wisdom about the seventy-year-old wounded President on the mountaintop. Thus, the country must be being governed by his staff. But a funny thing happened while Reagan was up in the clouds above the Pacific: When the chief wasn't around, his administration began unraveling. No matter what went on inside the White House, there seemed to be no Reagan administration, as well as no Reaganism, without Reagan. Suddenly the vaunted Troika, as it was called, of Baker, Meese, and Deaver were contradicting one another about issues like defense spending and the ever-growing budget deficit. There was squabbling across Washington over Israeli objections to the President's intention to sell $8.5 billion worth of AWACS (Airborne Warning and Control System) electronic surveillance aircraft and other advanced military equipment to Saudi Arabia—giving the Arabs more capacity to see attacking planes or missiles over the horizon, including Israeli planes and missiles.

On Wall Street, stock and bond prices were plunging; money men simply did not believe high interest rates would go down as the national debt grew and grew, and the government made up the gaps by demanding more and more borrowing. The White House was having trouble defending its proclaimed neutrality on the question of racial segregation in South Africa, vetoing United Nations Security Council resolutions condemning apartheid laws. And, in an effort to cut the cost of school lunch programs, someone in the government issued nutritional guidelines declaring that ketchup was a vegetable. That same day it was announced that Nancy Reagan had ordered $209,508 in new White House china, the dinner plates at $900 each.

When *New York Times* correspondent Weisman asked "a top White House official" what should be done to prevent the recurrence of such problems, that anonymous source answered: "Don't let the President go on vacation next year."

The paper's Washington columnist, James Reston, added this: "He wants everybody to work harder and produce more, but takes it easy himself. . . . Unlike Jimmy Carter, he doesn't pretend that he can cook every meal and wash every dish, or stamp out sin; but in the process, he gives the impression that nobody's in charge unless it is Ed Meese, a nice guy nobody elected and nobody knows."

Controversy over the air traffic controller firings survived the summer—not for Reagan but for everybody else—and the "Reagan Returns" summary also noted that the President had stopped at a carpenters' union convention in Chicago on the way home. The reception was friendly enough, but after he left, Charles Manatt, the chairman of the Democratic National Committee, called the Reagan administration a "wrecking crew . . . the most anti-union, anti-labor Administration in Washington since Calvin Coolidge." He also questioned why the President cheered Polish workers for striking illegally and jailed Americans for doing the same thing. The delegates rose to their feet in roars of cheers and applause. However, that same day, according to the *Post*, a Canadian government team flew from Ottawa to Washington to test firsthand the American air traffic system. The pilots reported back that the American system was "working as well as it ever has, if not better."

Reaganomics was another story. By the time the President returned to Washington, Stockman was gloomily telling anyone in the White House who would listen that the budget deficit was now looking like $100 billion or more per year. With help from Baker, the budget director brought the chairman of the Senate Budget Committee, Pete Domenici, into the Oval Office to say: "We can't hide from reality. The balanced budget is long gone. It's the whole economic recovery and Republican future that's now at stake."

The President's final briefing papers for a September 8 meeting on the 1982 budget deficit, prepared by Murray Weidenbaum, chairman of the Council of Economic Advisers, added more numbers to warnings of growing economic troubles: "The financial markets have been deteriorating without interruption since January 23 . . . raising the odds of a severe recession in 1982 if interest rate levels do not abate. . . . The combined FY 1981 deficit will reach record levels of $80 billion. Many private forecasters expect $90 billion. . . . The growing perception that the FY82 deficit is out of control feeds the fundamental belief that the entire economic recovery program does not add up—that the tax cut will mean permanent, huge deficits and renewed inflationary momentum."

None of this had much impact on the President. In frantic rounds of meetings in the White House, with Reagan occasionally at the table, Stockman was saying that if cuts in the entitlement programs—Social Security and Medicare—were off that table as deficit-cutting devices, then only one big thing was left to cut: defense spending.

Secretary of Defense Caspar Weinberger said no. The President said no.

"If it comes down to balancing the budget or defense, the balanced budget will have to give way," Reagan said, not for the first time, in one of those White House meetings. That same day, in the privacy of the White House, he also killed the idea, proposed by Republican congressional leaders, of delaying the effective date of some of the tax cuts he had signed into law just twenty-eight days earlier, saying: "What would people think? We shouldn't even be discussing that idea. . . . Any delay on reducing taxes would be a total retreat and an admission that we were wrong." *

Reagan had long ago mastered the political arts of avoiding self-incrimination: he never admitted mistakes, never admitted changing his mind or his position on an important issue. He scheduled a speech for September 24. Memos and drafts bounced around the White House; the text was changed right up to the day of the address. Editor in chief Reagan took out a proposal to phase out general revenue-sharing payments to state and local governments, writing in the margin: "Left this out. I thought this one coming on the air might set off so much local 'holler.' " During the back-and-forth, Stockman added a marginal note declaring that meeting deficit targets was crucial to the administration's credibility on Wall Street: "No easy way to correct with speeches—need hard action . . . DS."

Words did fail Reagan this time. "We have no choice but to continue down the road to a balanced budget . . . to hold to a steady, firm course," he began. But it was a speech of small things—a 12 percent cut in the budgets of lesser federal agencies that would save less than $8 billion a year, token cuts in defense, some layoffs of government workers by 1984, dismantling the Energy and Education departments, new user fees, and wrong or misleading or missing statistics. A thirteen-page "Fact Sheet" distributed to the press claimed that such

---

* The first Republican to suggest ignoring the deficit in the White House meetings was Dick Cheney, a Republican congressman from Wyoming and former chief of staff in the White House of Gerald Ford. "The White House is going to have to face up to something. This isn't the time to launch a new blood-letting. People aren't convinced it's needed. . . . We've been through seven months of political trauma around here. . . . People are shell-shocked and antsy. You're not going to get a consensus for anything big or meaningful. So I think we have to ride it out a while. See where we are in January. The deficit isn't the worst thing that could happen."

actions would produce a budget deficit of $43.1 billion, just $600 million more than the old $42.5 billion figure—and more than $50 billion less than the real estimates inside the administration.

"Tinkering" was the verdict of *The New York Times* editorial page. "Reagan in Retreat" said the *Baltimore Sun*. On Wall Street, which wanted actions not words on reducing the deficit, the Dow Jones Average dropped 11 points the next day to 824, just about 200 points below where it was shortly after Reagan took office. Was Reagan concerned about that, Sam Donaldson of ABC News shouted at him a couple of days later. "No," he replied. "I don't own any stocks!"

The president scheduled a press conference on October 1, his first since his embarrassing June effort when many of his answers were variations on "I don't know" and he had ended with his I'm-just-a-poor-boy-from-Dixon defense. This time, with Baker and Deaver in charge, was going to be different. Reagan endured hours of mock conferences, the questions asked by a half-dozen aides over two days. Each answer was refined by the group and then the question asked again, and again. Speakes placed budget and welfare facts and figures cards on the podium before reporters were let into the room. He seated "friendlies"—reporters from California's Copley papers, the *Christian Science Monitor,* the *Daily Oklahoman,* and others—in the front two rows to the President's right. "If there's trouble," said Speakes, "just turn right and pick one of them."

Reagan stuck to his script this time, saying: "I will sign no legislation that would 'bust the budget' and violate our commitment to hold down Federal spending." When questions pushed him on why stock prices were dropping, why Wall Street seemed to be rejecting his policies, Reagan turned to his right and called on an RKO Television executive, who asked if he had any plans to go to China. But the gamesmanship of the rehearsals and the "friendlies" was revealed in the first edition of *The Washington Post* in a story by Martin Schram, whose sources were obviously Larry Speakes and the administration's designated leaker, David Gergen. The next time Reagan saw Speakes, he was angry, saying his own spokesman had made him look like a dummy, a famous one: "You made me sound like Charlie McCarthy."

Reagan did make news that night by saying he intended to seek congressional approval of the controversial plan to sell five AWACS and support equipment to Saudi Arabia for $8.5 billion. But under the Arms Export Control Act, majority votes of both houses of Congress could stop the sales. And members were being lobbied hard by American Jewish organizations to do just that, and so was the government of Israel. The House was a lost cause, so Reagan had to win in the Senate—and in the upper house fifty-eight of the one hundred members, led by Senator Robert Packwood of Oregon, a Republican, had already signed pledges to vote against the sale. As far back as April, *The New York Times* wrote in the first of a series of anti-AWACS editorials: "If those Airborne Warning and Control Systems planes the Administration promised to sell to Saudi Arabia were now flown over Capitol Hill, they would send back a very clear message: Cancel this mission."

"AWACS is dead," said White House correspondent Phil Jones of CBS News in the network's post-conference analysis. The Senate Foreign Relations Committee voted 9 to 8 to recommend the full Senate reject the sale. *Time* magazine, published two days before the Senate voted, reported that the President had only forty votes. But Reagan kept at it. He had met or talked with every member of the Senate again and again after returning from California. During the conference he directly warned Israel about its lobbying, saying, "It is not the business of other nations to make United States foreign policy." The *New York Daily News,* the country's largest-circulation newspaper, ran this front-page headline: "Ron to Israel: Butt Out—Raps Jewish anti-AWACS Lobby."

The President was using everything and anything he had. While the roll was being called, Reagan telephoned Senator Larry Pressler, a South Dakota Republican, and Iowa's Roger Jepsen, both of whom had signed the original Packwood petition. Jepsen, a Republican, had been summoned to the White House days before the vote and, after a pleasant chat with Reagan about football, came out and told waiting reporters: "I'm going to vote against AWACS, period." He didn't—and his local paper, the *Des Moines Register,* reported that the White House had organized his financial supporters back home to telephone him and say they would not support him if he did not support the President on this one. "We just took Jepsen and beat his brains out," said an anonymous White House staffer. Another line from the White House to the folks back home was that Jepsen was selling out to "Jewish interests in New York." Working on another switcher, Senator Howell Heflin, an Alabama Democrat, the President himself used an end-of-the-world argument, reminding Heflin that the Bible said

Armageddon would begin in the Middle East and that Russians would be involved.

Finally, the Senate voted late on the afternoon of October 28. The President was in the Oval Office. After talking one last time to Pressler and Jepsen, he began doing what he had been doing since he got his first fan mail as a young actor. He was sitting with a yellow pad and his felt-tip pen, answering letters.

"I'm sitting here waiting out the long afternoon till 5 P.M. when the Senate votes on AWACS," he said in a letter to a friend, George Eccles, in Utah. He picked up a letter from a lady named Dorothy Walton in New York City, who worked him over pretty good, even taking a shot at Mrs. Reagan's fondness for haute couture: "I would feel better if you concentrated more on leading the country—the poor as well as the wealthy—and less on your personal needs, such as long vacations, shorter hours, fashion, parties and being the head of a royal family."

"I'm glad you provided me with a return address so I can respond to your letter . . ." he began. And he wrote that address out for the White House secretaries, who would then file away the handwritten original. He told Mrs. Walton that he faithfully did his reading upstairs in the residence right up "until 'lights out,' " and that Congress was out of session when he was at his ranch. He ended this one: "Thanks again for letting me respond. Sincerely, Ronald Reagan."

The call on the AWACS vote came at 5:20 P.M. The Republican leader of the Senate, Howard Baker of Tennessee, telephoned Reagan to say he had won 52 to 48. "One senator told me," said Baker, almost giddily, " 'you know that man down at the White House could sell refrigerators to an Eskimo.' I said, well I'm glad he could sell AWACS to you." The President left his desk and his letters to go to the press room and talk first about Israel, saying: "Our support for the security of Israel is, of course, undiminished by today's vote. . . . The cause of peace is again on the march in the Middle East."

By November, the economy was officially in recession, "a slight one" declared the President. In fact, nine million Americans were out of work, the largest number since the Great Depression. While Reagan was trying to explain, without much luck, he was blindsided by his boy-genius budget director. Stockman, it turned out, had been having Saturday-morning breakfasts, tape-recorded, with *Washington Post* writer William Greider. The result was a fifty-page *Atlantic*

Monthly article entitled "The Education of David Stockman." The *Post*'s chief economic correspondent, Hobart Rowen, a fervent critic of supply-side economics, summed it up on November 12 by saying: "So you thought 'voodoo economics' was just a George Bush campaign wisecrack about Reagan's policies? . . . Stockman is saying flat out that Reaganomics is a failure, and the economic arguments for it were fraudulent—and he knew it."

Stockman's breakfast conversations included assertions that supply-side economics was nothing more than a polishing of "trickle-down economics," the idea that if the rich get more money, some of it will trickle down to the poor. He had told Greider that the intent of Reaganomics was to use tax reform as a Trojan horse to bring down the top income tax rate, channeling more money to Americans making more than $50,000 a year. "None of us understands what's really going on with all these numbers," Stockman remarked at one point.

That last thought saved Stockman's job, even as he was being likened to Judas in White House meetings. He did know more about the numbers than anyone else, and Baker directed a little pageant that kept the budget director and his calculator in the White House. On November 12, Stockman had lunch with Reagan in the Oval Office. It was the first time he had ever been alone with the President. Before he went in, Baker told him: "My friend . . . your ass is in a sling. All the rest of them want you shit-canned right now. . . . I got you one last chance to save yourself. . . . The menu is humble pie. You're going to to eat every last motherfucking spoonful of it. You're going to be the most contrite son of a bitch."

The President himself was fatherly: "Dave, how do you explain this? You have hurt me. Why?"

Stockman told Reagan his life story, from the family farm to Harvard and Congress, how he became a devoted and energetic disciple of conservative economics, an idealistic follower of the only man who could make a difference in the old politics of dividing the spoils: Ronald Reagan. "Sir, none of that makes a difference now," he said. "One slip and I've ruined it all."

"No, Dave, that isn't what I want. I need your help. . . . I read the whole article. It isn't what they're saying I know, the quotes and all make it look different. I wish you hadn't said them. But you're a victim of sabotage by the press. They're trying to bring you down because of what you have helped us accomplish."

Reagan got up and walked toward his desk, then turned and said:

"Oh, Dave, the fellas think this is getting out of control. They want you to write up a statement explaining all this and go before the press this afternoon. . . . God bless you."

Baker and Deaver had a script waiting. "I am grateful to the President for this second chance," Stockman said in a quavering voice. He had been taken to the woodshed, he said, as if his grandfather had paddled him for using bad words.

Reagan said it again in an interview with Barbara Walters of ABC News: "David Stockman was not the sinner. He was sinned against." In another interview, with Donald Lambro of *The Washington Post,* he seemed to sin himself: "Somewhere along the line, I might be forced to accept more tax increases in order to get the budget cuts we're trying to get." It was the first time he had said something like that. Then the Reagans took off for the ranch on November 23 for a week to celebrate Thanksgiving.

When they returned, Washington was alive with interviews, hints, and rumors that projected deficits had reached the point where the administration was considering new taxes—"revenue enhancements" was the euphemism. By December 13, with a finger in the wind, *The New York Times* ended its lead editorial: "Over the horizon lie some big tax increases—or big troubles."

There were already big troubles in Poland. Tanks were in the streets, as Solidarity members in all parts of the country began strikes in defiance of the martial law that had been declared on December 13—and there were intelligence reports and troop buildups that indicated the Soviet Union might move in to crush the workers and demonstrators everywhere as they had in Hungary and Czechoslovakia in years past. The President went before the press on December 17, his sixth news conference of the year, to urge or warn the Soviets not to try that, and to say he had "No plans to increase taxes in any way." Within fifteen minutes, Larry Speakes appeared in the press room to tell reporters that the President had not meant to rule out "revenue enhancements."

That was familiar give-and-take in the Reagan White House. The staff edited the boss regularly—and the boss did not mind, nor did he pay much attention. Upstairs that night he wrote in his diary: "We who were going to balance the budget face the biggest budget deficit ever. And yet, percentage wise, it will be smaller in relation to GNP. We have reduced Carter's 17 percent spending increase to 9 percent. The recession has added to costs and reduced revenues, so even with the reduction in government size, we have a large deficit. . . . Now my team is pushing for a tax increase to help hold down the deficit. I'm being stubborn . . . I intend to wait and see some results."

As the Polish crisis seized the world's attention, the Israeli Knesset voted 63 to 21 to annex the Golan Heights on its northern border, asserting perpetual sovereignty over Syrian land captured in 1967 and occupied since then. American officials, the President among them, were taken by surprise, and Reagan, with conviction he never felt in the Iraq incident, said: "We do deplore this unilateral action by Israel, which has increased the difficulty of seeking peace in the Middle East." With Secretary of State Haig and Secretary of Defense Weinberger in agreement for once—Haig called in the Israeli ambassador to formally protest and Weinberger called the annexation an illegal and destabilizing move—the United States cast a rare vote formally condemning Israel in the United Nations Security Council. "Boy," said Reagan in private one more time, "Boy, that guy Begin makes it hard for you to be his friend."

A reporter asked whether the annexation made promoting peace in the Middle East more difficult. "Yes," Reagan said, then he laughed and said, "I've come to the conclusion that there is a worldwide plot to make my job more difficult on almost any day that I go to the office."

On December 27, the President and Mrs. Reagan left Washington for a ten-day Christmas vacation. An NBC News "White Paper" that night did a generally positive report on the first Reagan year, ending with this from anchorman Roger Mudd: "There is very little mumbo-jumbo or self-doubt about the President. While he's surrounded by advisors who worry about the economy, there he stands making us feel good. . . . America seems to give him the benefit of the doubt—a growing doubt."

CHAPTER 6

JUNE 8, 1982

RONALD REAGAN NEVER REALLY LIKED TO TRAVEL. For more than twenty years, when he was making speeches for General Electric, he refused to fly, going around the country by train. In his first year and a half as President, he left the United States only twice, for short trips to Canada and Mexico. He spent so little public time on foreign affairs that Dick Cheney, a Republican congressman from Wyoming who had served as chief of staff in the Ford White House, told a friend in this White House: "He just doesn't seem to have the hunger to get into that area. . . . He does what he has to do and that's all."

And often Reagan got it wrong doing what he had to do. In a campaign speech to veterans organizations in Columbus, Ohio, he talked about ongoing arms control negotiations and said: "What is really back of our great attempt to refurbish our military is to strengthen three delegations of Americans, two of which are in Geneva, and one, I believe, still in Switzerland." A classified memo in early October from Secretary of State Haig about covert United States efforts to defeat leftist insurgents in El Salvador used the phrase "members of the FDR," the Spanish acronym for Democratic Revolutionary Front, the political arm of the insurgents. It was returned by Richard Allen of the National Security Council with an angry scrawled note: "How many times must I mention that items like 'FDR' are not household terms for the President? Use an asterisk and explain, dammit!"

On October 15, 1981, speaking to a delegation of newspaper editors from around the country at lunch in the Cabinet Room, the President had been asked whether a "limited exchange" of nuclear weapons was possible. "I don't honestly know," he answered. "I could see where you could have the exchange of tactical weapons against troops in the field without bringing either one of the major powers to pushing the button." Whatever he had meant, the Soviets used that remark to attack him as a criminal ready to fight a nuclear war, and Western European leaders and commentators asked whether the President of the United States was talking about a nuclear war with Europe as the battleground. One clarification followed another until Reagan gave his first major foreign policy speech a month later, on November 18, 1981, two weeks before American and Soviet delegations were scheduled to resume arms control negotiations in Geneva, Switzerland.

Reagan began the speech with his hospital letter to the Soviet leader, Leonid Brezhnev. "May I say," he read, "that there is absolutely no substance to charges that the United States is guilty of imperialism or attempts to impose its will on other countries by use of force." His key proposal was an offer to cancel the deployment in Western Europe, scheduled to begin in late 1983, of 572 new American ground-launched cruise missiles and Pershing II intermediate-range ballistic missiles aimed at the Soviet Union—if the Soviets would dismantle their intermediate-range missiles, already in place and aimed at Western Europe. "Zero Option" was the White House name for that one, an idea that had first been proposed by the Social Democratic Party in West Germany. Reagan made it his own in the speech on national television. He had told Allen that he wanted a one-sentence arms control initiative. This was the sentence: "The United States is prepared to cancel its deployment of Pershing II and ground-launched cruise missiles if the Soviets will dismantle their SS-20, SS-4 and SS-5 missiles."

Six months later, he announced his first grand tour, 10,659 miles in ten days, to begin on June 2, 1982. The President flew to Paris for a three-day economic summit meeting at Versailles with the leaders of five European nations, Japan, and Canada. With the United States officially in a recession since July 1981, with unemployment at 9.5 percent, the worst numbers since early 1941, and with annual deficits projected at more than $100 billion, Reagan's days had been spent fighting for a 1983 budget that was rejected almost immediately by the Republicans in Congress. The White House's internal briefing documents, marked "EXTREMELY CONFIDENTIAL," predicted worse: "The Administration's fiscal program is in danger of pulling apart at the seams. Massive adverse shifts in the budget projections continue. . . . The current services deficits for FY 1983–85 are now in the $160–$200 billion range. . . . The national security build-up programmed for FY 1981–85 now nearly doubles the Vietnam build-up. . . . It should be recognized that our current long-term fiscal policy does not generate the tax resources to finance it even under ideal economic performance."

Panicky budget and tax fights were still the daily business of Washington. Two shooting wars around the world were getting less attention. Iraq had invaded Iran in September 1980. Since Reagan had signed a National Security Directive in June 1981, America's policy—one of the best-kept secrets in Washington—was to aid Iraq: "President Reagan decided that the United States could not afford to lose the war to Iran. . . . The United States would do whatever was necessary and legal to prevent Iraq from losing." In May of 1982, Great Britain had sent an expeditionary force to try to retake the tiny Falkland Islands in the South Atlantic, a British colony occupied by Argentina on April 2, 1982. The United States tried to prevent that one, but ended up reflexively siding with Britain and Prime Minister Margaret Thatcher after British troops landed on May 26. Then, four days after Reagan began his trip, on June 6, Israel invaded Lebanon in an attempt to destroy the Palestine Liberation Organization once and for all—and there was no way America could ignore that one.

The Israeli invasion had come after the shooting of Israel's ambassador, Shlomo Argov, on June 3 on a street in London. But that was only a pretext, and so was the official story that the Israeli Defense Forces intended to go only twenty miles into Lebanon to establish a buffer zone to protect northern Israel from the PLO's long-range Soviet-built ground-to-ground missiles. In fact, Israel's Defense Minister, Ariel Sharon, had had troops and armor ready to break through the border fence with Lebanon for weeks. The Palestinians, led by Yasser Arafat, had more or less taken over southern Lebanon and parts of Beirut after being driven out of Jordan in "Black September" 1970, during a short war that began when the PLO attempted to depose King Hussein.

Lebanon was barely a country anymore, really just 3.5 million people on the verge of destroying themselves in a civil war between Muslim and Maronite Christian militias. The country's 1932 constitution, written when Christians were the country's majority, mandated that the Christians would hold the presidency and more than half of other political offices. But by the 1960s, Muslims were clearly the majority and were fighting to win control of the government. The PLO had taken advantage of the war to take military control of much of the south of the country and most of West Beirut. In 1976, the shaky Christian government of Camille Chamoun had invited the Syrian army into Beirut to end the fighting. In a deal brokered partly by Secretary of State Kissinger, the Syrians, designated the "Arab Deterrent Forces," had some success, brutal success, but then refused to leave, basing seventy thousand troops in the Bekaa Valley, east of Beirut.

For six months, Sharon had been conspiring with Bashir Gemayel, commander of the most powerful Christian militia in Lebanon, who hoped to use the Israelis to drive out both the Palestinians and the Syrians. Their plan was secret and simple: The Israeli Defense Forces, 80,000 soldiers, would race the forty-five miles to Beirut, secure the city, and then allow Gemayel's fighters, the Phalange, to go into the slums and refugee camps of Muslim West Beirut to flush out and kill PLO fighters, an estimated 20,000 men hidden among the 500,000 Palestinians in Lebanon.

President Reagan, who knew little of these things, was still in Paris when the Israelis moved. When he looked at a map of the Middle East, he used two fingers to mark the distance between Israel and Beirut on the mileage scale. "Gosh, they really are close," he said. Such details were not his strong suit, but Reagan was a man who knew what he believed: He had an emotional attachment to the idea of brave little Israel and a sense of fair play. He had, in fact, dispatched a special envoy in May of 1981, Philip Habib, a former ambassador and retired undersecretary of state considered the best negotiator in the Foreign Service, to try to broker an Israel-Lebanon agreement before the Israelis prepared for the invasion.

Reagan was on the road internationally because he wanted to reassure the world, particularly American allies in Western Europe, that he was a man of peace, as he was trying to persuade Americans that the reason for his massive military buildup was to pressure the Soviet Union to negotiate arms control agreements. "Force them to the bargaining table" was the line he had used in the 1980 campaign and that he repeated now, as President. It was a tough sell after decades of Cold War–mongering. He also believed that the United States could strengthen its position—in war or negotiations—by developing defenses against nuclear weapons. That was the idea much discussed among conservative defense intellectuals in *Human Events* and in research papers prepared by the Heritage Foundation—the kind of stuff that Jim Baker and other advisers tried to keep away from their boss. Reagan's thinking on such matters had been revealed in his October 15 interview with newspaper editors after he talked rather casually about using tactical nuclear weapons: "Unlike us, the Soviet Union believes that a nuclear war is possible. And they believe it's winnable. . . . I know that all over the world there's research going on to try and find the defensive weapons against strategic nuclear weapons."

Reagan, as John Kennedy did before him, had begun his thinking about nuclear action by asking for Defense Department estimates of American civilian casualties in an all-out nuclear exchange with the Soviet Union. The number: 150 million dead. That was MAD, the policy of mutual assured destruction. The idea (or the hope) was that projected casualties on both sides would be so high that no leader would ever push the button. Reagan was intrigued by another idea, a nuclear shield scheme being pushed in *Human Events*. Dismissed by the Pentagon and most scientists, it was called "Project High Frontier," a $50 billion missile defense screen using existing missile systems and new laser weapons to intercept Soviet missiles as they were launched or in space before they could hit American missile installations.

He thought about that again in March, when he had become the first President since Eisenhower to actually sit through a war game, a five-day computerized affair in March 1982 code-named "Ivy League." The Defense Department exercise began with Soviet attacks, using conventional weapons, in Europe, Korea, and Southwest Asia. When the President—played by former Secretary of State William Rogers—responded with conventional forces, the Soviets destroyed an American destroyer with a small tactical nuclear missile. "President" Rogers retaliated with small nuclear weapons and later authorized field commanders to use tactical nuclear weapons. The game ended with a Soviet nuclear attack on Washington, killing the "President"—and the United States fought on under the "Vice President." *

As Reagan had shown during the campaign, he was a man who did not give up on simple ideas just because he was told that things were not so simple. In Versailles, he had tried to persuade America's most important allies that better economic numbers would be coming out of the United States one of these days, then added that that was not

---

* President Reagan, like Eisenhower before him, was not allowed to speak or act during the game. The reason, according to NSC officials quoted by Richard C. Halloran in *The New York Times Magazine*: "No President should ever disclose his hand, even in a war game."

going to happen in the Soviet Union. He was convinced that the Soviet Union was inevitably moving toward economic collapse, and that an arms race would hasten that collapse. "They are in very bad shape," he had written in his diary on March 26, 1981, "and if we can cut off their credit they'll have to yell 'uncle' or starve." At Versailles, armed with new CIA statistics showing a 50 percent decline in the growth rate of the Soviet economy over the past thirty years, he argued with some passion that the allies could push Marxism over the edge by reducing trade and aid to the communists.*

That goal had already been secretly defined in a National Security Decision Directive (NSDD 32) that Reagan had signed ten days before leaving for Europe. The new eight-page "National Security Strategy," distributed to only thirty-six people, was backed up by a ninety-five-page document, a National Security Study Directive titled NSSD 1-82, prepared secretly over five months by a team of six men supervised by Haig's deputy, William Clark. The most important writer was a Soviet expert from Harvard, Richard Pipes, who met regularly with the President. If the ninety-five pages could be compressed into two sentences, this would be it: Ronald Reagan's thinking had become the political and military policy of the United States. The President was determined to go on the offensive in the Cold War.†

The President had approved every line and word of the eight-page Decision Directive. "I have carefully reviewed . . ." it began. And then: "Our national security strategy requires development and integration of a set of strategies, including diplomatic and informational, economic/political, and military components." The "global objectives" included:

> To deter military attack by the USSR and its allies against the U.S., its allies, and other important countries across the spectrum of conflict; and to defeat such attack should deterrence fail. . . . To contain and reverse the expansion of Soviet control and military

---

* A Central Intelligence Agency memo to the White House on June 1, 1982, estimated that the growth rate of the Soviet gross national product had decreased from 5.5 and 5.9 percent in the 1950s to 3.7 and 2.7 percent in the 1970s.

† Pipes left the White House to return to Harvard in September 1982. In an exit interview he said: "It was interesting that the way the air controllers' strike was handled impressed the Russians. Seeing a union leader taken away in chains—that surprised them and gave them respect for Reagan. It showed them a man who, when aroused, will go the limit to back up his principles."

presence throughout the world, and to increase the costs of Soviet support and use of proxy, terrorist and subversive forces. . . . To foster, if possible in concert with our allies, restraint in Soviet military spending, discourage Soviet adventurism and weaken the Soviet alliance system by forcing the USSR to bear the brunt of its economic shortcomings.

And then:

In a conflict involving the Soviet Union, the U.S. must plan, in conjunction with its allies, for a successful defense in a global war.

The backup study was punctuated with language Reagan had been using for almost twenty years. But as policy, it was a language separate from the old words of containment and détente. The operative word now, Reagan's word, was "prevail." The final paper sounded like a multisyllabic version of what Reagan had been saying in forgotten campaign speeches and in radio and newspaper commentaries going back as far as 1963: "Contain *and reverse* the expansion of Soviet control and military presence throughout the world" was a key line. And there were specific, if secret, calls for nuclear war–fighting strategies—including civil defense, a form of martial law, and technological defenses against Soviet missiles:

The United States should pursue the development of effective Ballistic Missile Defense technology and preserve the options to modify or withdraw from international agreements that would limit the deployment of a BMD system. . . . Strategic defenses need not be impenetrable to enhance our nuclear strategy. They can still enhance deterrence by increasing both our civil survivability as well as the certainty that sufficient offensive strategic firepower will remain after an attack.

Other sections of the study included such key lines as:

Arms control can complement military forces in support of U.S. objectives and national security. . . .
    In conflicts not involving the USSR, the U.S. will rely primarily upon indigenous forces to protect mutual interests, with U.S. assistance as appropriate. . . .

The legislation governing security assistance is flawed: it is too inflexible and provides for too much congressional micro-management. . . .

Over the longer term, control of space will be decisive in conflict. The military potential of space must be exploited in support of national security objectives. . . . The United States, with its increasing dependence on space-based systems, must maintain the capability to operate in space throughout the conflict spectrum, while denying any enemy the use of space in war. . . . The question is not whether space will be a medium for warfighting, but when, and who will dominate. . . .

The decade of the eighties will pose the greatest challenge to the survival and well-being of the U.S. since World War II. Our response to this challenge could result in a fundamentally different East-West relationship by the end of the decade.

In Versailles, Reagan spoke only of his ideas on economic strategy as a weapon against the Soviet Union. He was well liked there, but not well received. "His summit partners treated with cool contempt his call for significant credit restraints to the Soviet bloc," the conservative columnist William Safire reported back to *The New York Times*. And his partners' constituencies were in the streets denouncing the American President, blaming him for new nuclear missile sites being drilled into the ground of both Eastern and Western Europe. Hundreds of thousands of people came out in Paris, in Rome, and later in Bonn with signs calling for a freeze on production and deployment of nuclear weapons and chants saying "No to Nukes!" and "Out of NATO!"—and the old "Yankee Go Home!" In fact, part of the reason Reagan was away from home was to try to promote his Zero Option arms plan as a way to slow down the "Nuclear Freeze" movement. The goal of antinuclear demonstrations everywhere in Europe was to try to prevent the deployment of the United States's Pershing II and cruise missiles, which Reagan, and Carter before him, wanted in the ground to match Soviet SS-20 intermediate-range missiles already aimed at European targets.

The President's own people, though, made more trouble for him than did the demonstrators. When Secretary of the Treasury Donald Regan was asked by European reporters about his boss's declaration that there was "a balanced budget in sight," Regan paused, chuckled, and answered: "President Reagan is a man of long vision." After that, the President's preference for undisturbed sleep once again became an international issue. Haig, without bothering to wake or tell Reagan, ordered the United States ambassador to the United Nations, Jeane Kirkpatrick, to abstain rather than veto a Security Council resolution calling for an immediate cease-fire in the Falklands war. The cease-fire, opposed by the British, was designed to save Argentina from certain and humiliating surrender to an expeditionary force that sailed eight thousand miles to regain control of the islands (and their eighteen hundred British residents) off the southern tip of South America. It turned out that Kirkpatrick got the order three minutes after casting the veto. Haig had not only ignored the President, he had passed the order through State Department channels rather than use the telephone to save time. The retired general's explanation was: "You don't talk to the company commander when you have a corps and division in between."

Actually, Haig and Kirkpatrick were barely talking to each other under any circumstances. Reagan, a man of manners, was bothered by the way Haig treated the only woman in the Cabinet. At one meeting, the President made that point by walking around the table, which he had never done before, passing by Haig, and then kissed Kirkpatrick on the cheek. Reagan was as confused as anyone about the United Nations veto. Asked about it by reporters who caught him at lunch the next day, he said: "You've caught me a long way from there, let me catch up with it." Kirkpatrick, who could be as prickly as Haig, retaliated in public: "A bunch of amateurs. . . . I believe that the decline of American influence in the United Nations is part of the decline of U.S. influence in the world—and that is a direct reflection of what I see as a persisting U.S. ineptitude in international relations."

On June 7, the President went to Vatican City for a meeting with Pope John Paul II, a man he saw as a partner in his personal war against communism, particularly in Poland. As the former Archbishop of Kracöw, who had also survived a 1981 assassination attempt, talked on about war and peace and freedom, Reagan began yawning, then dozed off. All on television. Back home, CBS News showed the yawns, NBC News the dozing. Inside the Vatican, away from cameras, the story was dramatically different. The President and the Pope, the two most important anti-communist leaders in the world, had agreed to consult and support each other in taking every opportunity to aggravate the obvious cracks in relations between

Poland and the Soviet Union. Together they went over American satellite photos and maps, discussing missile placement on both sides of the old Iron Curtain—and John Paul promised Reagan he would never support the freeze movement. A week after his visit to the Vatican, the President wrote a letter to a friend, John Koehler, saying: "I have had a feeling, particularly in the Pope's visit to Poland, that religion may turn out to be the Soviets' Achilles' heel."

The Reagans slept that night in England, in Windsor Castle, where they were the guests of Queen Elizabeth. The President was up early the next morning, riding eight miles on the castle grounds with the Queen. Prince Philip and Nancy Reagan followed them in a carriage. At noon, Reagan became the first American President to speak to a joint session of both Houses of Parliament, although 195 of the 225 Labour members of Commons boycotted his appearance, in the Royal Gallery of Westminster Palace. Reagan had been thinking about the speech for more than a month, working with speechwriter Anthony Dolan and with conservative thinkers, including columnist George Will, who sometimes doubled as a Reagan adviser and was cabling London with edits and comments before the speech.

Westminster was perfect for a debut on the world stage—a great set and a chance to deliver the big lines he had polished long ago before audiences of businessmen, GE employees, and American voters:

> In an ironic sense Karl Marx was right. We are witnessing today a great revolutionary crisis, a crisis where the demands of the economic order are conflicting directly with those of the political order. But the crisis is happening not in the free, non-Marxist West, but in the home of Marxist-Leninism, the Soviet Union. It is the Soviet Union that runs against history by denying human freedom and dignity to its citizens. It is also in deep economic difficulty. . . . A country which employs one-fifth of its population in agriculture is unable to feed its own people. . . . The decay of the Soviet experiment should come as no surprise to us. Wherever the comparisons have been made between free and closed societies—West Germany and East Germany, Austria and Czechoslovakia, Malaysia and Vietnam—it is the democratic societies that are prosperous. . . . I don't wish to sound overly optimistic, yet the Soviet Union is not immune from the reality of what is going on in the world. . . . What I am describing now is a plan and a hope for the long term—the march of freedom and democracy which will leave Marxist-

Leninism on the ash heap of history as it has left other tyrannies which stifle the freedom and muzzle the self-expression of the people.

The plan Reagan spoke of involved creating government-financed foundations and institutions to promote and expand democracy around the world, sort of a grand and ideological Peace Corps. He was applauded only once during the speech, when he said the British were on the right side of history in the Falklands. The speech was televised live on American television and the anchors and correspondents from Washington and New York quickly dismissed the speech, in the words of ABC's White House correspondent, Sam Donaldson, as "Vintage Reagan," the same old stuff he had heard in the 1980 campaign. "Lovely. Just lovely," said ABC's anchor Frank Reynolds, quoting a member of Commons. "Noncontroversial, inspirational, and well received," said Tom Fenton of CBS News. Bryant Gumbel of NBC News talked of how tired the President looked.

Marvin Kalb, NBC's diplomatic correspondent, was about the only American commentator who sensed the real weight of Reagan's words, saying: "The President is in effect saying, after sixty years in power, the Soviet leadership still has no political legitimacy and he wants to take on the entire communist world."

Correspondent Tom Brokaw interrupted to ask: "Aren't a lot of people going to see this as naive? . . . The President is inviting the Soviets to participate in their own suicide. . . . The Russians are not likely to participate in their own suicide?"

"The Russians are not likely to participate," Kalb answered, then added, "but the President believes, and it is vintage Reagan, that the communist system is dying."

The Americans had heard these things before, and almost never took them seriously. In May of 1975, doing his syndicated radio show, former Governor Reagan had said: "Communism is neither an economic or a political system—it is a form of insanity—a temporary aberration which will one day disappear from the earth because it is contrary to human nature." Campaigning for President in June of 1980, he had told surprised editorial writers of *The Washington Post*: "I think there is every indication and every reason to believe that the Soviet Union cannot increase its production of arms. Right now we're hearing of strikes and labor disputes because people cannot get enough to eat. They've diverted so much to military spending, that they can't provide for their consumers' needs." Almost two years later, in March of 1982, Reagan had shocked Senate Majority Leader Howard Baker by saying: "We must keep the heat on these people. What I want is to bring them to their knees so that they will disarm and let us disarm; but we have got to do it by keeping the heat on. We can do it. We have them on the ropes economically. They are selling rat meat in the markets in Russia today."

But what the British and much of the world heard on June 8 was not vintage Reagan, but President Reagan. Words spoken by the leader of the strongest nation in the world were of a different order than were the campaign speeches of an old actor or a right-wing governor. This was not about balancing the budget or welfare legislation. Peter Jay, a former British ambassador to Washington, told NBC: "The speech was very strong, very striking, and extremely hard line. . . . He seemed almost to be declaring non-military war on the Soviet Union." He paused and added: "If he does mean it, it's very frightening."

David Owen, a former Foreign Minister, was impressed, saying: "Maybe he'll go down as a much better president than any of us are yet prepared to admit." Ray Whitney, the Conservative foreign affairs chairman of the House of Commons, added: "It was a very hard-hitting speech. . . . The U.S. must have a leadership role, that of first among equals."

Reagan had considered hitting harder than that. Until two days before the speech, he and Dolan, students and admirers of Whittaker Chambers, the brilliant American communist who had turned on the party and become a conservative icon, had intended to use a phrase from Chambers's 1952 book, *Witness*: "I see in communism the focus of the concentrated evil of our time." His sophisticated British audience was also enormously impressed that the American could speak so easily without referring to a text. Many had expected a halting, not-too-bright old man. Instead, Reagan was in total command, speaking from behind two rather small panes of bulletproof glass. That's what they thought. Actually the glass panes were a new generation of TelePrompTer. The speaker could see words crawling across the glass; the audience could not. Reagan also had another forensic trick: He mixed and matched contact lenses, wearing one for reading on his left eye and a farsighted one on his right eye to make eye contact with the crowd.

The European trip was also an international debut of sorts for Reagan's new National Security Adviser, William Clark, who had served as deputy secretary of state before replacing Richard Allen early in January. Judge Clark, the most successful of Governor Reagan's chiefs of staff in Sacramento, and then a Reagan appointee as a justice of the California Supreme Court, had no foreign policy experience and was known in Europe as "the nitwit minister." That name and others had been pinned on him by the European press after confirmation hearings in which he could not define "Third World" or "détente," and could not name the Prime Ministers of South Africa and Zimbabwe. It seemed an amazing appointment—Safire wrote, "Clark is living proof that still waters can run shallow"—until it was realized, at least in Washington, that Clark had been positioned to be the buffer between Haig and the White House. "Okay," Haig said to Clark on their first day together. "You run the building, I'll run the world." The retired general had developed into a parody of his mercurial mentor, Henry Kissinger. Like Kissinger, he could not stop himself from raging against his colleagues and bosses in private. Of Clark, Haig said: "He doesn't know his ass from third base." Of Baker: "That son-of-a-bitch is the worst influence I have ever seen in the federal government." And of the President: "His staying power is zilch. He isn't a mean man. He's just stupid."

Indiscreet and volatile, knowledgeable and arrogant, Haig was ever ready to take offense at slights real and imagined. He was despised by Baker and now by Clark, once his appointed friend, but he was essential to them and to Reagan as well—at least during their first year in the White House. Clark, called Reagan's closest friend by those who did not know that the President's only close friend was his wife—it was obvious to many that Mrs. Reagan was often jealous of the time her husband spent alone with Clark—more than made up for his ignorance of the world with his knowledge of and love for the boss. The boss's work habits were mystifying to most of his harddriving men, but Clark knew Reagan's reactive nature: The President responded to what was brought to him, to letters from strangers, anecdotes from *Reader's Digest*, or conservative dogma in *Human Events*. They also were never sure he heard what they told him; the biggest change in Reagan after a year or so in office had been that he was rapidly losing his hearing, which some realized only when he turned the television volume so painfully high they had to leave the room.

For more than a year, Baker, Meese, and Deaver had controlled the day-to-day work of the Oval Office. Allen, a Meese friend, reported to his patron, the most inefficient of the three, and much of his work simply disappeared into Meese's bulging briefcases. So, Allen rarely saw the President and the President rarely was involved in the workings of foreign policy. What Reagan knew about the affairs of the world, beyond his belief in the superiority of America and Americans, came from his casual reading and from Haig's condescending Oval Office lectures and his weekly lunches with Vice President George Bush, who had served as CIA director and as ambassador to China and to the United Nations.

That began to change immediately when Clark, who had been Meese's boss in Sacramento, moved over to the White House. On Clark's first day in the White House, Meese invited him to Baker's morning meeting to review the day's NSC briefing. "No thanks," Clark said. "I'll be reviewing that with the President." His next move was to demand White House passes for NSC staffers, half of whom were allowed only in the Old Executive Office Building across a little street from the offices of the West Wing. Clark, with the same Western conservative values and politics as his hero, immediately began using the one-page, four-paragraph mini-memos that he had created in Sacramento and introduced film or videotape briefings—the CIA was the usual producer for the President's eyes only, replacing its traditional printed biographies of world leaders with mini-documentaries—knowing that Reagan could instantly memorize such material and quote it for years. When he communicated with the President on paper, Clark scrawled only a few words on old three-by-five notecards from Sacramento, marked with the state seal of California. He also sent typed letters and memos to others which ended: "FOR THE PRESIDENT:" Then he signed his own name.

The Clark/Reagan style showed itself in a one-paragraph memo from the new NSC director to the boss regarding a state visit by President Muhammad Zia ul-Haq of Pakistan:

> You mentioned today in the video briefing on Zia that you would like to say a few words about his retarded daughter, Zain, if this were appropriate. We have checked with Ambassador Ronald Spiers who thinks this would be a very touching gesture. . . . I suggest that you inquire after Zain when you meet with President and Mrs. Zia in the evening prior to the State Dinner. Attached is a card with suggested talking points.

With Clark out of the State Department, Haig was on his own, easy prey for Deaver and Baker, who plotted like schoolboys to goad him into destroying himself with Reagan. When Haig attempted unsuccessful shuttle diplomacy to try to prevent the Falklands war, Deaver had tried to trick him into using an Air Force plane without windows for the eleven-hour flights between Washington and Buenos Aires. Haig canceled the trip. On the trip to Europe, Haig found himself in the second cabin behind the Reagans' private compartment. His old seats in the first cabin were occupied by wives Carolyn Deaver and Joan Clark. Then Deaver relegated him to the third helicopter as the entourage moved around. On the trip to Windsor Castle, in a clattering military copter, the Secretary of State was heard to ask: "What am I, a leper?"

The Reagans arrived back in Washington on the evening of June 11. The traveling party was exhausted and a bit testy, particularly about Haig. Clark, who knew the old Sacramento rule—"A happy Nancy means a happy governor"—told one of his assistants, Bud McFarlane: "This situation with Al is very serious. . . . The President has just about reached the end of his rope. And I think Al upset Nancy with some protocol things." The President's mood was not helped the next day when an estimated 700,000 people gathered in New York's Central Park to demonstrate their support for the Nuclear Freeze.

In the far South Atlantic, the British were finishing off the Argentines in their little war over the Falklands. In Lebanon, sixty thousand Israelis, using American planes, tanks, arms, and ammunition, ignored formal United States demands to withdraw and continued to say that the only reason they had gone into Lebanon was to secure a twenty-mile buffer zone to prevent long-range artillery and guerrilla attacks on their northern territories. Within two days they had surrounded Beirut, trapping the Palestinians and several thousand Syrian troops. The Israelis, with the secret cooperation of Gemayel, were becoming, in effect, the new occupiers of Beirut and southern Lebanon. In the United Nations on June 11, Ambassador Kirkpatrick vetoed a Security Council resolution calling for sanctions against Israel if it did not withdraw its troops from Lebanon.

On June 16, Prime Minister Menachem Begin of Israel came to New York to address a special session of the United Nations on disarmament. He called self-defense "the noblest concept." Two-thirds of the General Assembly delegates rose and walked out. Begin's next stop was Washington. There had been some talk that he would not be invited to see and be seen with Reagan. But the President changed his mind and invited the abrasive Mr. Begin after seeing a CIA briefing video that had been prepared for him. It opened with shots of bulldozers burying Jewish concentration camp victims with Begin's voice repeating "Never again. . . . Never again." Then another voice said, "To understand this man, this is all you need to know."

Still, Reagan considered Begin a liar. The Israeli leader had personally promised, in an Oval Office meeting in September of 1981, that he would not lobby against the AWACS sale to Saudi Arabia—and then immediately headed for Capitol Hill to try to persuade Israel's friends in Congress to vote against the sale. Now the issue was deceiving the Americans with regard to Israeli intentions in Lebanon. Secretary of State Haig had met with Defense Minister Sharon only twelve days before the invasion, and many Israelis, rightly or wrongly, took that as American permission to invade. Begin prevailed, as the Israelis often did in such matters, forcing or persuading Reagan to accept the facts on the ground and back the invasion—as he had ended up endorsing the Israeli air attack on the nuclear reactor in Iraq, the bombing of Beirut a year before, and the annexation of the Golan Heights, formerly part of Syria, six months before.

Reagan had been speaking at the economic summit in Versailles when Israeli troops crossed into Lebanon in June. The United States immediately protested, as usual, but the black wisecrack in Versailles was that the big mistake had been not inviting Begin to the summit—because the 1981 Lebanon bombing had begun during the June summit that year in Ottawa. The Israeli takeover of occupied territory in Golan had been announced on December 18, 1981, the day after martial law was declared in Poland, when the world was focused on the possibility of a Soviet invasion. The United States had reacted to that takeover by suspending a new $200 million military aid agreement, granted on top of annual aid of $2.5 billion a year. The new agreement, signed just three weeks before the Lebanon move, supposedly obligated Israel not to use American weaponry for anything other than self-defense and to inform Washington before new military actions.

Begin's response to American surprise and objections was read to the American ambassador in Tel Aviv: "What kind of talk is this 'punishing Israel'? Are we a vassal state of yours? Are we a banana republic? You will not frighten us with punishments." Then Begin added: "The people of Israel have lived for 3,700 years without a memorandum on a cooperation agreement—and we will live without one for another 3,700 years."

In the Oval Office on June 21, the President, using cards prepared by Clark, speaking calmly, told the Prime Minister that the invasion was destroying the hopes for peace that had peaked when President Carter persuaded Egypt and Israel to sign accords at Camp David in 1978. Hostilities around Beirut had to be ended quickly, Reagan said; among other things the terror was eroding American influence in the Arab countries. Begin responded with seething passion, saying there had been no "invasion," only "intervention." It was part of a semantics game the United States State Department played by calling the Israeli blitz not war but "an outburst of violence."

The standoff continued through lunch. The President had planned to end the meal with a toast to Israel and Begin. He decided not to say anything, and even considered not walking out of the White House with Begin. He did walk out. "All of us share a common understanding," he told waiting reporters without saying what that understanding was. The President's jaw was set hard as Begin stood before the usual cameras and began, "My friend . . ." In Beirut, Israeli planes and artillery were bombarding the refugee camps of Palestinians in West Beirut and cutting off the water and electricity. The hardships of the siege had little effect on PLO fighters, who were operating out of the caves under West Beirut, chambers well supplied with food, water, and generators. In Christian East Beirut, where residents had cheered and tossed flowers as the Israelis advanced, life went on at crowded restaurants, nightclubs, and Mediterranean beaches.

"REAGAN BACKS ISRAEL" headlined *The Washington Post* the next morning. "REAGAN AND BEGIN APPEAR IN ACCORD" headlined *The New York Times*. Both papers cited "senior Administration officials." The competing front-page headlines in both papers was over a story reporting that a Washington, D.C., jury had found John Hinckley, the young man who shot the President, crippled his press secretary, and killed a Washington policeman, not guilty by reason of insanity. He was ordered committed to a mental institution.

On top of the President's papers when he walked into the Oval Office on June 25 was a one-page memo from Richard Darman titled "Talking Points—Haig." It began: "Al, after considerable thought about the matter, I have decided to accept your resignation. . . .

"Al, I do this with great personal sadness. I honestly believe we see the world in the same way. . . . I propose to announce this at two o'clock this afternoon. . . . I would characterize this decision as not for reasons of policy difference, but rather for personal matters. Do you agree?"

Haig most certainly did not agree. He had met with the President on Monday, June 21, to talk about the Begin visit, and also to explain why he had sent a cable over the weekend with detailed instructions to the American "special envoy" in Lebanon, Ambassador Habib, when Clark had told him to send it first to Camp David to be "round-tabled" with the President. Before Haig sat down at that meeting, Reagan said: "Al, what would you do if you were general and one of your lower commanders went around you and acted on his own?"

"I'd fire him, Mr. President," replied Haig.

"No, no, I didn't mean that," Reagan said. "But this mustn't happen again. We just can't have a situation where you send messages on your own that are a matter for my decision."

"There was no time for that, Mr. President," said Haig. "It was too urgent." Then he began another recitation about how badly he was being treated and deceived by Baker and Deaver—and now Clark. He was right about the deception. On Wednesday, Clark set up an evening meeting to hear an hour and a half of Haig's complaints.

"You must come to the White House tomorrow and tell all this to the President," Clark said.

"Oh, no!" said Reagan when he was told. "What for? What's this all about?" Clark said he expected Haig to offer to resign. If that happened, he added, a successor should be announced immediately, and handed the President a short list: Weinberger, former Treasury Secretary George Shultz, Senate Majority Leader Howard Baker, and Democratic Senator Henry "Scoop" Jackson.

When Haig met with Reagan on Thursday, he began by saying: "Mr. President, I want you to understand what's going on around you. I simply can no longer operate in this atmosphere. It's too dangerous. It doesn't serve your purposes; it doesn't serve the American people."

The President turned to Darman's June 25 talking points and began: "You know, Al, it's awfully hard for me to give you what you're asking for."

The Secretary reached into his briefcase and pulled out a written list of complaints about what he called "guerrilla" attacks on the prerogatives of his position. There was a letter of resignation in the folder in an envelope that stayed closed.

"This situation is very disturbing," said Reagan.

"It has been disturbing from the first, Mr. President. If it can't be straightened out, then surely you would be better served by another Secretary of State."

Reagan, always reluctant to fire anyone personally, said he wanted to study the gripe list overnight. After Haig left, he told Clark to find Shultz, which Clark had already done.*

But Reagan had still not made up his mind, at least on the timing, telling Clark and Deaver that he wanted to wait until after the congressional elections in November. On Friday morning, he told Clark to draft a letter accepting Haig's resignation. After a lunch meeting with Haig and members of the National Security Council, the President invited the Secretary back into the Oval Office. Reagan stood behind his desk and said: "On that matter that we discussed yesterday, I have reached a conclusion."

He handed the Secretary an unsealed envelope. "Dear Al," the letter began. "It is with the most profound regret that I accept your letter of resignation . . ."

"I'll talk shortly to George Shultz, who is in London," Reagan said. "I'm confident he'll take the post."

Haig asked for some time to compose a resignation letter. He was angry enough to say, "The precipitous way in which you're conducting yourself, Mr. President, means I can't just up and leave, I will have to make it clear publicly . . . that I no longer support your policies and that is the case."

Reagan struck first, going to the White House press room at 3 P.M., while Haig was still working on a resignation letter, and announced the resignation and the nomination of Shultz. He was there for only two minutes and reporters thought he was close to tears. He walked outside where his wife was waiting and boarded a helicopter for Camp David, where he saw Haig on television reading the letter he had written after leaving the President. That night Reagan wrote in his diary: "I'm told it was his fourth rewrite. It was okay. . . . He did say there was a disagreement on foreign policy. Actually, the only disagreement was over whether I made policy or the Secretary of State did."

The Monday memos to the President reported that press reaction

* Clark told me he once asked Reagan about his feelings about firing people. The answer was: "You never shoot your own horse. Your neighbor does it for you."

was positive—Shultz had the country's best résumé, from the U.S. Marine Corps to dean of the Business School at the University of Chicago to three Cabinet-level jobs and the chairmanship of the global Bechtel Corporation—but added: "Conservatives upset . . . Israel and Jewish groups reported very concerned." That concern was over Bechtel's huge construction contracts in Arab countries and the fact that Secretary of Defense Weinberger, who was often critical of Israel, had been president of Bechtel under Shultz. "Direct RR assurances to American Jewish Community may be in order" was part of one memo. There was a bad word, too, from former President Nixon, who regularly advised Reagan on foreign affairs: "Beware of Shultz. If things go wrong, he wasn't part of it or never knew about it."

Meanwhile, there was no budget for fiscal year 1983, which would begin on October 1, 1982. Even while he was in Europe, the President had taken time out to telephone dozens of House members to try to persuade them to vote for a $770 billion budget cobbled together by Republican leaders. The White House's budget, released early in February, had already been laughed out of Congress. Any chance of passage had ended in a forty-minute Cabinet Room confrontation between the President and the Speaker of the House, with aides to each sitting as witnesses. Democratic Majority Leader Wright wrote in his diary that night: "It was the toughest going-over I've ever heard a President subjected to. . . . The Speaker, asked by Reagan to support the budget request, told the President very plainly that Democrats could not acquiesce in good conscience to this passive acceptance of high unemployment and its attendant evils without making every effort to amend such a budget. Reagan's face grew red and he swore, 'God damn it, Tip, we do care about those people.' The Speaker said, 'It's easy to say that you care but you aren't willing to do anything about it.' "

The Republican majority in the Senate unanimously rejected the budget numbers presented to them by Stockman and the Office of Management and Budget. The President's numbers just had not added up, particularly projections of 5.1 percent growth in gross national product and a deficit projection of $91.5 billion—compared with Congressional Budget Office projections of $650 billion in deficits over the next three years. By the beginning of June, a dozen more budgets had been introduced and rejected in the House. There was a growing consensus among Democrats and most Republicans in Congress, in the press, among economists and Wall Street analysts, and in the White House itself: Taxes had to be raised and defense spending cut to somehow reduce those deficits. The Republican chairman of the Senate Finance Committee, Robert Dole of Kansas, an old-fashioned conservative who distrusted most everything about supply-side theory, said he intended to introduce a bill raising taxes to reduce the deficit.

There was one problem with the consensus: Ronald Reagan was not part of it. But he was being surrounded. The President's approval rating, according to the monthly Harris poll, had dropped from 67 to 29 percent positive to 56 to 44 percent negative in eleven months. The Business Roundtable, the most prestigious business group in the country—its members were chief executives of major corporations—urged Congress to delay the 10 percent income tax reduction scheduled to take effect at the beginning of 1983. Reagan's response to that was to tell the National Association of Manufacturers: "I have been a little disappointed lately with some in the business community who have forgotten that feeding more dollars to government is like feeding a stray pup. It just follows you home and and sits on your doorstep asking for more." Then, when Bill Moyers of CBS News did an hour-long documentary called *People Like Us,* about three families hurt by Reaganomics, the President angrily snapped back: "Is it news that some fellow in South Succotash has just been laid off . . . or someone's complaint that the budget cuts are going to hurt their present program?" *The New York Times* published a front-page headline on March 11 saying: "AIDES BATTLE TO CHANGE REAGAN'S MIND ON BUDGET."

The Washington Post's resident Reagan expert, Lou Cannon, wrote, with Lee Lescaze, a series about the declining influence of the White House Troika: Baker, Deaver, and Meese. The third paragraph ended: "Its influence has been reduced by both the rise of lesser aides and the increasing proclivity of the President to do what he wants to do, no matter what his staff is telling him."

The reaction to Reagan's stubbornness or principled intransigence, from conservative loyalists, the *Human Events* crowd, was just the opposite: They treated the President as if he were a prisoner of his staff. A new bumper sticker read: "Let Reagan Be Reagan." The daily press and weekly political magazines, picking up the "disengaged theory," began to question whether Reagan was up to the job—and so did some high-profile Republicans. Senator Robert Packwood of Oregon told the Associated Press of the frustrations of meeting with Reagan to discuss the budget deficit, only to sit there as he veered off into old stories, particularly this one: "You know a person told me yesterday about a young man who went into a grocery store and he had an orange in one hand and a bottle in the other and he paid for the orange with food stamps and he took the change and paid for the vodka. That's what's wrong."

William Safire wrote that the man in the White House was in his "anecdotage." Cannon summed it up well: "More disquieting than Reagan's performance or prospect on any specific issue is a growing suspicion that the President has only a passing acquaintance with some of the most important decisions of his Administration."

The New Republic published a piece by Jack Beatty titled "The President's Mind," writing: "Dumb he may or may not be, but he clearly is not serious. . . . He finds it next to impossible to say anything that is not in some crucial way untrue. It's not a credibility gap, for there is no evidence of cynical or even conscious duplicity. The President is so far out of touch that it amounts to a reality gap."

In fact, Reagan was engaged. His apparent intransigence was being put to use to pull congressional Democrats into joining his campaign against logic. On March 20, he dispatched James Baker to House Speaker Tip O'Neill's home to begin negotiations on a new budget. Baker and Darman were the only Reagan representatives involved at the beginning in a dozen secret meetings over the next five weeks at the homes of Baker and Vice President Bush, at Blair House, in the basement of the White House. Suddenly, budget-making was a secret bipartisan effort. Now O'Neill was being set up, and he knew it. Inside the White House, one Darman memo read: "RR needs to seek to meet with O'Neill and . . . make O'Neill a thoroughly reasonable offer—that O'Neill will nonetheless reject on the grounds that he will not agree to protect the third year of the tax cut."

O'Neill had reasons to go along. Part of it was an old-fashioned sense of duty. A bigger part was fear. He was afraid that Reagan would blame the Democrats for refusing to talk, and he was afraid of the President's personal popularity and his zealous supporters. O'Neill sometimes needed police protection to get through airports because other travelers shouted and cursed at him. "Leave the President alone, you fat bastard!" was one line he told friends about. The secret sessions came to a climax on April 28, when Reagan and a few of his men went to the Capitol and met with O'Neill and his group. There was a ceremonial photograph taken of the President and the

Speaker. O'Neill knew it would be used to make him seem like a co-conspirator in a budget process that was actually controlled by the White House. Reagan's failures would be his failures as well, but if he walked out, the political consequences would be even worse.

The President opened the meeting with an Irish joke. Mary came home after a visit to the doctor and asked her friend Deirdre what "a specimen" was. "Piss in a bottle," said Deirdre. "Well, you can shit in a hat," said Mary. And the fight was on. So it was. "Mr. President, the nation is in a fiscal mess," O'Neill said. "Last year you were going to win on everything you put up. Now the economy is going bad. If we don't have agreement there will be massive deficits. I know you people don't like to hear it, but you're just advocating trickle-down economics. Your program has failed, and you should take the lead in admitting it."

The President, flushed, shot back: "I've read that crap about my program. We haven't thrown anybody out in the snow to die. . . . It has not failed at all. It hasn't even started yet." After three emotional hours, the Speaker asked the President whether he would accept a three-month delay in instituting the final 10 percent reduction in the third year of his 5-10-10 percent income tax reduction. "You can get me to crap a pineapple," said Reagan, "but you can't get me to crap a cactus."

O'Neill met reporters outside the building: "The President offered a raw deal to the Democrats and to the American people. He advocated that we continue his economic program, which has brought hardship to millions." Reagan held his public fire until the next night, when he went on national television to make a speech that had been written before the Capitol meeting. "They," he said, meaning the Democrats, "want more and more spending and more and more taxes. I believe we should have less spending, less taxes and more prosperity." Then he called for bipartisanship—urging viewers to write to their congressmen—and revived old conservative demands for a constitutional amendment that would require a balanced federal budget every year. It was not one of his more successful rallying calls. The Newhouse Newspapers analysis written by Loye Miller began: "President Reagan attacked his own budget Thursday night as if it were a hostile invader from outer space."

On the day Reagan returned from Europe, June 11, the House, which had formally rejected the President's budget in May, finally passed a Republican-sponsored budget of $765.2 billion, with a listed deficit of $99.3 billion. The Congressional Budget Office estimated the actual deficit would be $109.8 billion, a figure ignored by members of both parties. Some of the numbers were just made up. The same thing had happened in the Senate, which passed a $784 billion budget with a listed deficit of $115.8 billion. The final House vote, after agreement in the Senate-House conference, was 210 to 208— with 63 Democrats voting with the majority and 32 Republicans voting against it after five months of debate and after seven other budgets, including Democratic alternatives, had been voted down.

The final budget bill, with cuts in both the Democrats' domestic spending agenda and Reagan's proposed military spending, attempted to show a smaller deficit by including a $99 billion increase in revenues from unspecified new taxes or tax increases over three years. The White House avoided the word "taxes," preferring its old euphemism "revenue enhancers." Whatever the words, the tax cuts and increased defense spending of 1982 were widely blamed for the exploding deficits and deficit projections for the rest of the 1980s, which were panicking Wall Street and Republicans in the Senate. The economy was in deep recession already, the numbers were the worst since the Depression of the 1930s, and indicators of that included the highest unemployment since before World War II and stock prices below 1960s levels.*

Senator Dole's proposals became the Tax Equity and Fiscal Responsibility Act of 1982, meeting the $99 billion mandate by closing some old tax loopholes and increasing taxes on cigarettes, telephone calls, medical expenses, travel, and investment income, and imposing $50 billion of new but pretty well hidden business taxes. "The largest revenue-raising bill ever," said *The New York Times* in its coverage of the Senate debate, an overnight affair that ended with a 50 to 47 vote at 4:48 A.M. on July 23. All 50 "aye" votes were Republicans. Before going home to bed, Dole, whose budget-making partners included Peter Domenici, the chairman of the Senate Budget Committee, and Baker and Stockman in the White House, said: "The future of this economy is now in the hands of Tip O'Neill."

O'Neill responded five days later by orchestrating a House vote to go directly to a House-Senate conference on a final tax bill. With only the Dole bill on the table, the Speaker left it to Reagan to round up enough House votes to pass the thing. The man who had just a year

---

* The actual 1983 deficit, calculated two years later, was $207.8 billion.

before pushed through Congress the largest tax cut in history was cornered. Now he was campaigning on television and in his daily calls to House members for the largest tax increase in history. He did that his way, declaring victory because the Dole bill preserved the final 10 percent personal income tax cut of his 1981 bill. This time, he had to persuade Republican House members, most of whom wanted to vote against the conference bill. O'Neill did not make it easier. The Speaker held back Democratic votes until Reagan lined up his Republicans. He wanted one hundred Republican House votes. It was a tough business. To win the votes of three Republican congressmen from Long Island, the White House had to agree to restore $350 million for new A-10 fighters, planes the Navy said it no longer needed—but Grumman Aircraft, headquartered on the island, did need the contract to stay in business. Reagan also approved a letter from the Republican National Committee to fifty thousand Republican officeholders, candidates, and contributors. The message: "The President has made his decision, and you're either on the team or off the team."

On the afternoon of August 13, Reagan, who had unhappily postponed his summer trip to the ranch, walked into the White House press room and told reporters he would take questions on two subjects, the tax bill and the ongoing Israeli bombing and shelling of Muslim neighborhoods in Beirut. The morning before, during a fourteen-hour Israeli bombardment—Americans counted 220 bombing sorties and 44,000 artillery shots—West Beirut saw the most ferocious of nine weeks of long Israeli barrages and short cease-fires. "Watching the Israeli Air Force smashing Beirut to pieces was like having to stand and watch a man slowly beating a sick dog to death," a *Newsweek* reporter cabled back to New York.

The President had received frantic calls from Philip Habib and from King Fahd of Saudi Arabia, begging him to do something to stop Begin and Sharon. There were more subdued pleas from the new Secretary of State, George Shultz, and from Bill Clark. Then Mike Deaver, who had trouble watching television coverage of the siege, surprised Reagan by saying that he intended to resign over what he saw as United States support for whatever Begin and Sharon did. "I can't be part of this anymore, the bombings, the killing of children," he told Reagan. "It's wrong. And you're the one person on the face of the earth right now who can stop it. All you have to do is tell Begin you want it stopped."

As Reagan told a White House operator to place the call, Shultz said softly to Deaver: "Thank God. I'm glad you had the guts to do that."

The President got through to Begin in the late afternoon, then wrote in his diary that night: "I told Begin it had to stop or our entire future relationship was endangered. I used the word 'Holocaust' deliberately." "Menachem, this is a Holocaust," he had said. "Twenty minutes later," Reagan wrote that night, "he called to tell me he'd ordered an end to the barrage and pleaded for our continued friendship." The Israeli leader also told the President that he had persuaded his cabinet to reduce the authority of Defense Minister Sharon, who had ordered the new attacks. Reagan ended the call by saying, "Menachem, Shalom"—a nice gesture but probably a mistake, giving Begin the impression that Reagan was not as mad as he sounded. After the call Reagan told Deaver: "I didn't know I had that kind of power."

On the night of August 16, the President went on national television to pitch the tax increase. He cited the best economic figures at hand—inflation was down from 12.4 to 7.3 percent on his watch and the Federal Reserve's prime interest rate was down from 21.5 to 14.5 percent—and tried to close the deal by saying: "I had to swallow hard to agree to any revenue increase. You helped us start this economic recovery program last year when you told your representatives you wanted it. You can help again—whether you're a Republican, a Democrat or an independent—by letting them know you want it continued."

Two days later, on August 18, the Senate and House passed a conference bill reducing federal spending by $13.4 billion—cutting the Food Stamp program and reducing cost-of-living pension increases for retired federal employees—as the President and Speaker O'Neill appeared together in the Rose Garden to make a final plea before the tax vote in the House. On August 19, Congress approved the bill, 52 to 47 in the Senate, 226 to 207 in the House—with 103 Republicans voting with liberal and moderate Democrats. The final vote shared front pages with news that the Israeli Knesset had voted to accept proposals, negotiated by Habib in July, to get the PLO out of Lebanon under the supervision and armed protection of a multinational troop force: "Timid Dawn of Peace in Lebanon," said *The New York Times*. Under the agreement, ten thousand PLO fighters, including their leader, Yasser Arafat, would be given safe passage out of the country, under the supervision of American, French, and Italian troops, for resttlement in five Arab countries—Syria, Jordan, Iraq, South Yemen, and Tunisia.

Signing the tax bill the next day, Reagan declared victory: "To even refer to this as a tax increase, I think was wrong. It was an adjustment to the tax cut passed last year." His mastery over Congress was certainly reaffirmed, at least he thought so, but Reaganomics and supply-side economics, too, were suddenly yesterday's news. From the left, a Manhattan congressman named Theodore Weiss said, "We have a budget wrapped in deceit, based on phony figures and erroneous assumptions." From the right, *Human Events* published a front-page analysis by M. Stanton Evans under the headline Reagan most hated: "The Largest Tax Increase in History." Evans calculated the increase in revenues would total $227.7 billion by 1987. But Wall Street was encouraged by the tax bill and the decline in interest rates; new records were set for trading volume, and the Dow Jones Industrial Average showed its largest ever weekly increase, up 81.24 points to 869.29.

The President finally got off to California on August 20, after a Rose Garden statement confirming that he was ordering eight hundred Marines on ships off the Lebanese coast to land in Beirut, along with French and Italian troops, as a temporary Multinational Force (MNF) to help supervise the departure of Palestinian leaders and fighters. "In no case will our troops stay longer than 30 days," he pledged. On the gray morning of August 25, the message of the Commander in Chief could be heard coming from loudspeakers in the port of Beirut, on United States warships, as Marines boarded landing craft less than a mile offshore: "You are about to embark on a mission of great importance to our nation and the free world. . . . You are asked to be once again what Marines have been for more than 200 years—peacekeepers. Your role in the Multinational Force, along with that of your French and Italian counterparts, is crucial to achieving the peace that is so desperately needed in this tortured city. . . . Godspeed, Ronald Reagan."

Among the papers Reagan took to the ranch were forty-three pages of weekly political memos, each marked: "In Strictest Confidence . . . 1982 Election Update." The first paragraph of the first one, all capitalized, read: "IF THE 1982 MIDTERM ELECTIONS WERE HELD ON JUNE 1 INSTEAD OF NOVEMBER 2, REPUBLICANS WOULD LOSE 44 HOUSE SEATS, 5 SENATE SEATS, AND 10 GOVERNORSHIPS."

The memo, written by Richard Beale, director of the White House's Office of Planning and Evaluation, combined numbers from public and private polls:

The President's image as a leader has declined considerably. In late January, his excellent/good rating was 69 percent and his inspiring confidence rating was 56 percent. The rates now stand at 48 percent and 39 percent, respectively.

The mood of the electorate is becoming increasingly pessimistic. . . . There is little reason to hope that economic conditions will improve significantly in the near future. . . . There is only one acceptable way to thwart the pending Democratic victory: the President must continue the highly political schedule through the summer that he initiated in May.

For these and many other reasons, it appears to many that the Reagan Administration may have commenced its demise.

Reagan was not ready for anything like that, of course. He was preparing the most detailed speech on foreign affairs that he had ever given. Since mid-August he had been learning about the daunting intricacies of the Middle East in a unique way: Shultz had assigned four of diplomacy's bright young men—Robert Ames, Nicholas Veliotes, Paul Wolfowitz, and Richard Fairbanks—to produce a drama with each of them playing roles: One was Begin, one Jordan's King Hussein, one President Hosni Mubarak of Egypt. Reagan loved it. Meese told Shultz: "The President was ready for this a year ago, but Al Haig kept the Middle East away from him." On September 1, as the last PLO fighters were removed from Beirut—their families were allowed to stay in refugee camps on West Beirut's southern border—the President traveled down from his ranch to an NBC studio in Burbank to offer a new peace plan in a nationwide prime-time television speech. It was a powerful speech, restating American commitment to the Camp David Accords and then incorporating new ideas worked out by Shultz, Habib, and others.

"I have personally followed and supported Israel's heroic struggle for survival, ever since the founding of the State of Israel 34 years ago. In the pre-1967 borders Israel was barely ten miles wide at its narrowest point. The bulk of Israel's population lived within artillery range of hostile Arabs. I am not about to ask Israel to live that way again.

"The war in Lebanon has demonstrated another reality in the region. The departure of the Palestinians from Beirut dramatizes more than ever the homelessness of the Palestinian people. Palestinians feel strongly that their cause is more than a question of refugees. I agree."

The most controversial provisions of the "Reagan Plan" would be to grant full autonomy to Palestinians on the West Bank and Gaza, in a kind of federation supervised by Jordan, and to freeze the building of Israeli settlements in the West Bank, occupied by Israeli troops since 1967. The speech and Israeli reaction were laid out in four-column headlines on the front pages of *The New York Times* of September 2 and September 3:

REAGAN URGES LINK TO JORDAN
AND SELF-RULE BY PALESTINIANS;
ISRAEL REACTS ANGRILY TO PLAN

"Fresh Start Asked"

President Calls for Halt
to Jewish Settlements
in Occupied Areas

ISRAEL REJECTS REAGAN PLAN
FOR PALESTINIAN SELF-RULE;
TERMS IT 'SERIOUS DANGER'

"Cabinet's Decision"

Settlement of Occupied
Areas to Be Continued
Despite U.S. Appeal

The front-page *Times* analysis on September 3 was by Leslie H. Gelb, a State Department veteran, now a diplomatic correspondent: "In his speech, Mr. Reagan said publicly what presidents and senior American officials have been saying in private meetings and planning papers for 15 years: that the Israelis would have to give up all or most of the territory they captured in the 1967 war and that the Palestinians should have 'full autonomy over their own affairs.' " In Washington, Sam Donaldson, the White House correspondent for ABC News, said, "Begin must be wondering what's going on; the President is firmly becoming a major player in his Administration."

In New York, Alexander Haig, speaking at a dinner of the United Jewish Appeal, said Reagan had made a huge mistake in calling for the end of settlements in the occupied territories. In Israel, Prime Minister Begin was meeting secretly with Sharon and Israel's Christian ally, Bashir Gemayel, who was the only candidate for President of a new Lebanon. The Prime Minister was in despair, telling aides: "We have been betrayed by the Americans. . . . They have stabbed us in the back." He felt betrayed again, this time by Gemayel, who had received $250 million in Israeli military aid over the years and was now scheduled to take office in three weeks, but finally told the Israelis he could not keep a promise to sign a peace treaty because, if he did that, he would surely be killed by Lebanon's Muslims.

On September 5, Begin had another answer for the Americans. He announced that his government was allocating $18.5 million to build ten new West Bank settlements—and it hoped to increase the number of settlers from 34,000 to 100,000 by 1987. Five days after that, on September 10, the last of the MNF troops left Beirut. The Marines sailed for Naples, where they had begun their short mission. On September 14, the day King Hussein of Jordan formally endorsed the Reagan plan, President Gemayel was killed by a four-hundred-pound bomb planted in the headquarters of his Phalange Party. Twenty-four hours later Sharon ordered his troops into West Beirut, as Israeli gunboats and artillery pounded the Muslim quarter. The State Department, under the President's name, called for immediate withdrawal of the Israeli Defense Forces. But the President himself, campaigning for congressional candidates in New Jersey, asserted that the Israelis moved only after attacks by "leftist militias"—to which the State Department was forced to respond: "Even the Israelis are not claiming they were fired on." *

By the end of that day, September 17, the Israelis had control of the entire city and had surrounded but not entered the two largest Palestinian refugee camps, sprawling urban slums called Sabra and Shatila. The Israeli Defense Forces sealed off West Beirut, allowing no foreigners in, and there were soon unconfirmed reports that Christian militias had been allowed into the Muslim camps. In fact, Begin's cabinet had authorized the entry to search for Palestinian fighters hiding among the civilian population.

By the morning of September 18, the reports were confirmed: The Israelis were outside the gates; the Christians were inside for sixty-two hours—from 6 P.M. Thursday to 5 A.M. Saturday—slaughtering

---

* The bomber was later identified as a Syrian agent, Habib Tanouis Sartouni, twenty-six, a Lebanese of Greek Orthodox descent. The Syrians hated Gemayel, and hated even more his many ties to Israel.

the Muslim families left behind by the PLO—and hundreds of people were dead, crumpled in the narrow streets and alleys, shoved into shallow mass graves with arms and legs sticking out, covered over by bulldozed rubble. Television showed mounds of bloody corpses, attacked now by flies and dogs. Newspapers identified the killers as members of two Christian militias, Gemayel's Phalangists and a southern group headed by Major Saad Haddad, armed and supported by Israel and brought to the gates of the camps by IDF trucks. The Israelis also fired hundreds of flares and star-shells over the camps at night to provide light for the militias' work.

"I was horrified to learn . . ." began Reagan's official statement. "All people of decency must share our outrage and revulsion. . . . We strongly opposed Israel's move in West Beirut. . . . We demanded that the Israeli government withdraw its troops from West Beirut." There were anti-Israeli demonstrations all over the world as news of the massacres spread, but the biggest protest march was in Israel itself. In Tel Aviv, 300,000 demonstrators chanted for the resignation of both Sharon and Begin. The leader of the Knesset's opposition, Shimon Peres, said: "We have a sense that underneath the blocks of cement used to cover the bodies of children, women and old men, lie moral ruins." *

On September 21, Amin Gemayel, who, like his brother Bashir before him, had been meeting secretly with Sharon and Israeli foreign minister Yitzhak Shamir, was elected unanimously as the country's new President by Lebanon's Christian-controlled parliament. Then he asked both Israel and Syria to withdraw troops from West Beirut and approve proposals for the Multinational Force peacekeepers to come back to Beirut.

The Marines, twelve hundred lightly armed men sailing from Naples, landed again in Lebanon on September 29. The mission statement said: "U.S. Marine Landing Force in Port of Beirut and/or vicinity of Beirut Airport. . . . Provide security posts at intersections in assigned section of line and major avenues of approach into city of Beirut from south/southeast to deny passage of hostile armed elements in order to provide an environment which will permit LAF [Lebanese Armed Forces] to carry out their responsibilities in city. . . . Commander U.S. Forces will provide air/naval gunfire as required."

The rules of engagement, carried by each Marine on a small white card, were summarized as follows:

* The official Lebanese government count was just under two thousand deaths during the sixty-two-hour rampage.

The mission of the MNF is to keep the peace.... Action taken by U.S. forces ashore in Lebanon will be for self-defense only.... Reprisal or punitive measures will not be initiated.... Commanders are to seek guidance from higher headquarters prior to using armed force, if time and situation allows.... Hostile ground forces which have infiltrated and violated USMNF lines by land, sea or air would be warned that they could not proceed and are in a restricted area. If the intruder force fails to leave, the violation would be reported and guidance requested.... Hostile forces will not be pursued.

"Hostile forces" included the IDF, which had been occupying the airport area. Almost immediately, relations between Israeli and American troops, particularly officers, began to reflect the mistrust separating Habib, Begin, and Sharon. The Israeli commander considered the American diplomat an Arab agent and the American considered the Israeli a liar and a killer. Besides, Begin had ample reason to distrust Sharon, who routinely ignored orders to halt the advance of his troops. Israeli warplanes and patrol craft began harassing the Marines from the moment they left the ships in the harbor. The Americans, in combat gear and flak jackets but with unloaded weapons, were forced to sit in the sun all day on the airport's runways while minesweeping teams tried to clear paths through unexploded cluster bomblets, ordnance Made-in-the-USA—offensive weapons the Israelis had promised not to use in Lebanon. One American, Corporal David Reagan, was killed when one of the bomblets exploded.

Israeli-American relations on the ground reflected the troubles in higher places. That showed—and smelled—when Marines moved into the buildings and offices vacated by Israelis and found desk drawers filled with human excrement, a parting gift from Sharon's men.

Back home, Reagan returned to his campaigning for Republican congressional candidates. The crowds were big and friendly, but the economic numbers were still not good enough. On October 8, the Labor Department announced that the national unemployment rate had reached 10.1 percent—more than 11 million Americans were out of work—the first double-digit jobless figure since 1940. The President's approval rating, as measured by the Gallup poll, had dropped to 42 percent by November.

But there was good news the President could and did emphasize. Interest rates had declined—the Federal Reserve's prime rate was down another couple of points to 12 percent on his watch. Inflation was down as well, from an average of 8.9 percent in Reagan's first year to 5.1 percent in the first nine months of 1982. (The reductions in interest rates and inflation were generally credited to the tight money policies enforced by the Federal Reserve Board, led by a Carter holdover, Paul Volcker.) The recession seemed to be ending, with the gross national product increasing some, wobbling from 2.1 percent in the second quarter of 1982 to 0.8 percent in the third. On the same day, Labor released its monthly numbers, the Dow Jones stock average was up 20.88 points, reaching 986.85, its highest in two years—and finally going back over 1,000 points in mid-October.

The President watched the election returns upstairs in the living quarters, sitting with his wife on one of the red couches they had brought to Washington from their home in Los Angeles. A number of White House aides and their wives were there—the Bakers, the Meeses, the Deavers—along with his pollster, Richard Wirthlin, sitting with a computer and telephones. Reagan was subdued most of the evening—there was a lot of bad news for him—but he still talked to himself and to the television as if there were no one else in the room. "Oh dear, I'm sorry," he said when a network declared that Congresswoman Millicent Fenwick had lost her Senate race in New Jersey. Republican Chic Hecht was announced as a Senate winner in Nevada, defeating a Democratic veteran, Howard Cannon—and Wirthlin spoke up to say a late Reagan visit had turned that race around. The screen showed that Margaret Heckler, the Massachusetts congresswoman, had lost her seat. "Gee, I'm sorry to lose Heckler. She was a good little girl."

Paul Sarbanes, easily reelected as a senator from Maryland, came on the screen, saying, "This was a people's victory."

"What are you talking about? The people lost," said Reagan. "D-E-M no longer stands for 'Democrat.' It stands for 'Demagogue.' "

The final counts the next day showed that the Republicans took a 26-vote loss in the House of Representatives, giving the Democrats a 268 to 167 advantage, when the 98th Congress convened in January of 1983. The President's men barely held their own in the Senate, maintaining their 54 to 46 margin over the Democrats.

In gubernatorial races, the Democrats won 27 of 36, although Reagan woke up pleased to learn that his Democratic successor as governor of California, Edmund "Jerry" Brown, had been defeated in a run for the Senate. By the time the President came downstairs for a short Rose Garden news conference to discuss the results, his staff had already met and distributed talking points: "Press guidance: The coalition remains intact; the President still has the ability to govern. . . . The President's reaction: He is pleased with the results in the Senate. The outcome in the House is roughly what we expected."

That was about the best they could do. Before the election, the President met with the newest American winner of the Nobel Prize for Economics, George Stigler, considered a strong conservative voice, who was escorted into the White House press room and said: "You know we're in a depression now—supply-side economics is a gimmick, a slogan . . ."

He had to be literally pulled away from the podium, still talking.

Economic numbers, except for inflation, which was down to just over 4 percent, were between bad and worse. Unemployment was still over 10 percent. The gross national product, which the White House predicted would rise 4.2 percent in 1982, actually declined by 1.8 percent. Testing the microphone before his weekly radio broadcast, three weeks after the election, Reagan quipped, "Well, the economy is in a hell of a mess"—unfortunately for him the mike was on, for all America to hear. "Requiem for Reaganomics" and "The Failing Presidency" were the headlines over *New York Times* editorials on January 8 and 9. A *Time* magazine poll reported that 70 percent of respondents agreed with the statement. "Reagan represents the rich rather than the average American."

As the new year began, *The Washington Post*'s David Broder wrote: "What we are witnessing this January is not the midpoint in the Reagan presidency, but its phase-out. 'Reaganism,' it is becoming increasingly clear, was a one-year phenomenon, lasting from his nomination in the summer of 1980 to the passage of his first budget and tax bills in the summer of 1981. What has been occurring ever since is an accelerating retreat from Reaganism, a process in which he is more spectator than leader."

"I have some bad news for you," his pollster Richard Wirthlin told the President early in 1983. "Your approval rating is down to 35 percent, the lowest ever." Reagan patted Wirthlin's arm and said: "I know what I can do about that"—he smiled—"I'll go out and get shot again."

CHAPTER 7
MARCH 8, 1983

O NE OF THE CONCLUDING PARAGRAPHS of the long political memo to President Reagan on the upcoming 1982 midterm elections had focused on a single set of numbers collected by his pollster, Richard Wirthlin. Wirthlin concluded that since the 1980 election, a steady 25 percent of American voters agreed with the statement that Ronald Reagan was "Likely to Start an Unnecessary War." The copy continued: "It is essential that during this period the President capture the image of peace through the arms control and summit opportunities. . . . In the short period between from July through October, 1982, the President should focus single-mindedly on (1) arms control, and (2) the summit between himself and Brezhnev. . . . There is every opportunity at the present time that Ronald Reagan could be to arms control what Richard Nixon was to China."

The President knew he had a problem, but he also had a certain contempt for the dons of the American arms control establishment, and for existing treaties limiting—but not reducing—the production and deployment of nuclear missiles. He believed that American negotiators had allowed the Soviet Union to surpass the United States as a nuclear power, and he considered the Soviets to be liars and cheats seeking advantage over the world's democracies. But he also understood that global and domestic politics of peace required the appearance of openness to arms control. By the end of 1982, Reagan had given two arms control speeches, in November 1981 and May 1982, the second one at his alma mater, Eureka College in Illinois. At Eureka, he offered to reopen START (Strategic Arms Reduction Talks) negotiations, which had been put on hold since December 1981 when martial law was declared in Poland.

But those speeches were essentially for public consumption at home and abroad. Polls and politicians' speeches at home and in Europe indicated the American people and America's allies wanted arms control above all.

Reagan's real feelings—"We win, they lose"—were not part of most of his own speeches. Except in the Westminster speech, Reagan's hard inner determination was still deliberately held below the radar of press and public. His real agenda was in a series of secret National Security Decision Directives; there were only twelve copies of the latest and most comprehensive and secret policy directive, NSDD 75, "US Relations with the USSR." That directive, nine single-spaced pages, began with a clarification of the Soviet sections of NSDD 32, the May 1982 directive and attached study that had been circulated to only thirty-six people. NSDD 75 repeated earlier language about reversing Soviet expansionism, then moved on to a second goal of undermining the Soviet system at home:

> To promote, within the narrow limits available to us, the process of change in the Soviet Union toward a more pluralistic political and economic system in which the power of the privileged ruling elite is gradually reduced. The U.S. recognizes that the Soviet aggressiveness has deep roots in the internal system, and that relations with the USSR should therefore take into account whether or not they help to strengthen this system and its capacity to engage in aggression.

NSDD 75 repeated that the United States was unwilling to accept "second place or a deteriorating position" in any area of conventional or nuclear weaponry, then focused on economic and political strategies:

> The U.S. must convey clearly to Moscow that unacceptable behavior will incur costs that would outweigh any gains. At the same time, the U.S. must make clear to the Soviets that genuine restraint in their behavior would create the possibility of an East-West relationship that might bring important benefits for the Soviet Union. . . . Ensure that East-West economic relations do not facilitate the Soviet military buildup. This requires prevention of the transfer of technology and equipment that would make a substantial contribution directly or indirectly to Soviet military power. . . . While Allied support of U.S. overall strategy is essential, the U.S.

may on occasion be forced to act to protect vital interests without Allied support and even in the face of Allied opposition.

In a section titled "The Soviet Empire," the directive stated:

There are a number of important weaknesses and vulnerabilities within the Soviet empire which the U.S. should exploit. The primary U.S. objective in Eastern Europe is to loosen Moscow's hold on the region while promoting the cause of human rights in individual East European countries. The U.S. can advance this objective by carefully discriminating in favor of countries that show relative independence from the USSR in their foreign policy, or show a greater degree of internal liberalization. . . . Afghanistan: The U.S. objective is to keep maximum pressure on Moscow for withdrawal and to ensure that the Soviets' political, military, and other costs remain high while the occupation continues. . . . Cuba: The U.S. must also provide economic and military assistance to states in Central America and the Caribbean Basin threatened by Cuban destabilizing activities.

That, in fact, was already being done. In December of 1981, Reagan had signed a "finding"—the document required to begin clandestine CIA action—that said: "I hereby find that the following operation in a foreign country (including all support necessary to such action) is important to the national security of the United States. . . . Support and conduct paramilitary action against Nicaragua."

The directive on policy toward the Soviets concluded:

The U.S. will remain ready for improved U.S.-Soviet relations if the Soviet Union makes significant changes in policies of concern to it; the burden for any further deterioration in relations must fall squarely on Moscow. The U.S. must not yield to pressures to "take the first step." . . . The interrelated tasks of containing and reversing Soviet expansion and promoting evolutionary change within the Soviet Union itself cannot be accomplished quickly. The coming 5–10 years will be a period of considerable uncertainty in which the Soviets may test U.S. resolve by continuing the kind of aggressive international behavior which the U.S. finds unacceptable.

The Soviets—whose own cables in that spring of 1982 warned that the United States might be preparing for nuclear war—responded in the coolest of tones to Reagan's public overture in the Eureka speech. Premier Leonid Brezhnev, or whoever was acting for him in what appeared to be a shaky old age, did agree to begin negotiations again in Geneva, but questioned whether the Americans were serious. In return, the American President was mightily annoyed at the Russians' tone. Reagan went through Brezhnev's letter, scrawling a few words after each paragraph: "He has to be kidding" . . . "Because they have the most" . . . "It is an apple for an orchard" . . . "He's a barrel of laughs."

Brezhnev, who had been in power for eighteen years, died at the age of seventy-five a week after the 1982 midterm elections. He was replaced by sixty-eight-year-old Yuri Andropov, former head of the KGB, the secret service and secret police of the Soviet Union. Two weeks after that, Reagan pitched his version of "Peace Through Strength" in a national television speech. On one level the speech was little more than a plea for Congress to vote for a $26.4 billion plan to begin production of one hundred MX intercontinental missiles. Having junked Carter's Race Track scheme, the administration wanted to base the missiles in hardened silos in a twenty-square-mile area of Wyoming. The theory this time, called "Dense Pack," was that incoming ICBMs targeted at a small area would destroy each other, and that most of the American MXs would survive to counterstrike. On television, the President called up a phalanx of electronic graphs that indicated, in his words: "Today, in virtually every measure of military power, the Soviet Union enjoys a decided advantage. . . . Follow the red line which is Soviet spending. It's gone up and up and up. . . . The defense share of the United States Federal budget has gone way down. Watch the blue line."

On another level, Reagan laid out his own thinking about war and peace and nuclear weaponry:

> The prevention of conflict and the reduction of weapons are the most important public issues of our time. . . . It is sadly ironic that is these modern times, it still takes weapons to prevent war. I wish it did not. We desire peace. But peace is a goal, not a policy. Lasting peace is what we hope for at the end of our journey. . . . I intend to search for peace along two parallel paths: deterrence and arms reductions. . . . I believe that if we follow prudent policies, the risk of nuclear conflict will be reduced. Certainly, the United States will never use its forces except in response to attack. . . . And if we re-

tain a strong deterrent, the Soviets are exceedingly unlikely to launch an attack.

He ended with a crescendo of American exceptionalism:

I've always believed that this land was set aside in an uncommon way, that a divine plan placed this great continent between the oceans to be found by a people from every corner of the Earth who had a special love of faith, freedom and peace. Let us reaffirm America's destiny of goodness and good will. Let us work for peace and, as we do, let us remember the lines of the famous old hymn: "O God of Love, O King of Peace, make wars throughout the world to cease."

That was the stirring music rising behind an array of statistics showing Soviet military superiority. But most of those numbers were wrong or deliberately misleading. It took two days for a *Washington Post* reporter, Michael Getler, to fact-check the President. In making up the red and blue curves and columns, the President had ignored the 572 Pershing and cruise missiles scheduled to be deployed in Europe beginning before the end of the year, ignored the United States's invulnerable submarine-based missiles, and ignored the bombs and new cruise missiles on American warplanes—almost all of them superior to Russian weaponry in accuracy and in number of warheads carried. He also did not count the nuclear arsenals of America's European allies, England and France.

With the 1982 election over, Congress returned to Washington for an unusual lame-duck session. One item on the agenda was the MX— Reagan now called it the "Peacemaker"—and the House voted 245 to 176 against funding production. Fifty Republicans joined the Democrats in the vote; most of them simply did not believe in Wyoming's Dense Pack. "A grave mistake," said an angry Reagan. "A majority chose to go sleepwalking into the future." But he did not accept the defeat. A stubborn man by nature, he was particularly suited to play and prevail in one of the oldest of Washington games: Weapons systems appropriations were often voted down, but the systems never died. Military research and development always had a life of its own. Forget Wyoming, said Reagan. He would appoint a special commission to recommend a basing plan—and on December 9, by voice vote, the House approved a $2.5 billion appropriation to continue MX development. A week later, the Senate revived the program, voting 70 to 28 to reject a bill eliminating the $988 million production costs. Unnoticed in Washington, that same day in Beirut, the United States Marines confidently expanded its original peacekeeping mission by beginning to train small units of the LAF, the Christian-led Lebanese Armed Forces.

A blizzard hit Washington during the second week of February 1983. The Reagans had to cancel a weekend in Camp David, the presidential retreat in the Catoctin Mountains in Maryland, north of the city. So, Nancy Reagan called O'Bie Shultz, wife of the Secretary of State, and asked the Shultzes over for Saturday night dinner—just the four of them. It was a pleasant evening and Shultz was surprised by the President's apparent openness to ideas about the Soviet Union and China. At one point, the President said that although he had met Leonid Brezhnev in 1973, he had never had a serious conversation with a high official of a communist country. "Do you want to?" asked Shultz.

"Yes," said the President.

Shultz mentioned that he regularly met with the Soviet ambassador, Anatoly Dobrynin, who had first come to Washington when Kennedy was President. He was, in fact, scheduled to meet with him on the coming Tuesday. "I could bring him over for a private chat," he said.

"Great," said Reagan. "But we have to keep this secret. I don't intend to engage in a detailed exchange with Dobrynin, but I do intend to tell him that if Andropov is willing to do business, so am I."

"Anatoly, how would you like to go see the President?" asked Shultz three days later when Dobrynin was shown into his office. The Russian, of course, answered yes. So Shultz said: "Why don't we just go back to my elevator, get in the car, and go over there?"

The President and the ambassador talked for almost two hours, about arms control, about Poland, about Afghanistan, and about human rights, especially about the treatment of Jews in the Soviet Union. Then, surprising both Shultz and Dobrynin, Reagan brought up "The Pentecostals"—six Siberian Christians who had been living in two basement rooms of the United States embassy in Moscow since running past Soviet policemen and guards into the compound in June of 1978. As a radio commentator and syndicated newspaper columnist, ex-Governor Reagan had actively promoted their cause, along with other American conservatives, urging Carter and the State Department to pressure the Soviets to allow them to emigrate. Reagan made clear to Dobrynin that he would consider their release an important small step toward better relations—and that he would not take credit for their release or embarrass the Soviets in any way.

On the other hand, though, this President was not about to change his mind about the Soviets or communism. One of the documents that regularly circulated in Reagan's orderly White House was the "Presidential Speech Planning Schedule," a register of upcoming addresses, ranging from his regular five-minute radio shows every Saturday, which he still usually wrote himself, to the State of the Union address. There were twenty-two appearances on the list spanning February 12 to March 12, 1983. Each listed the date and event, the responsible members of the speechwriting office, and the final draft date. One line read: "Address National Association of Evangelicals. Orlando, Fla. . . . Tony [Dolan], Misty [Church]. . . . Draft 3/3 Thursday."

It was not considered a major foreign policy speech and it was not considered important enough for live national television. The first two-thirds of the seventeen-page speech were attacks on abortion advocates and on groups providing birth control information to teenage girls without parental permission, and about the power of prayer. But when Dolan and the President began working together on the speech in mid-February, Reagan was concerned about religious groups that were endorsing the Nuclear Freeze movement, particularly the Protestants of the National Council of Churches, the National Catholic Bishops Conference, and the Synagogue Council of America. As far as he was concerned the Nuclear Freeze amounted to unilateral disarmament for the United States. He was also offended by the idea of "moral equivalence," the conclusion by some on the left that in many ways democratic capitalism was just as bad as totalitarianism or communism. The President wanted to emphasize his own passions about good and evil. And, finally, he was also greatly influenced by an idea that had been developed by Judge Clark and an NSC staffer named John Lenczowski and presented to him in January as a one-page memo titled "The Truth and the Strength of America's Deterrent," stating, in part:

> The Soviet system depends for its survival on the systematic suppression of the truth. . . . The key element in Soviet assessment is the adversary's strength of moral-political conviction—i.e., his will to use force if necessary to defend his vital interests. In practice, as the Soviets see it, this means the willingness of their opponent to

speak plainly about the nature and goals of communism. . . . The key feature of "Finlandization" is for the target country to censor itself—if not to lie outright, then at least to remain silent. . . . As the Soviets see it, to tell the truth about the USSR is to risk igniting their internal security threat—the threat of mass popular resistance to the ideology, as in Poland. When stating that the Soviets will "lie," "cheat" and "commit any crime" to further their goals, you lifted a partial veil of self-censorship we had imposed on ourselves for some 15 years. Thus, by simply telling the truth, you incalculably strengthened the credibility of our military deterrent.

Reagan thought that way. "I want to remind the Soviets we know what they're up to," he told Clark. Reagan and Dolan began looking again at the tough Whittaker Chambers language of evil the President had eliminated from his Westminster speech nine months earlier.

They decided to put those words into this one. There were a lot of objections in the White House and over at the State Department. More than once communications director Gergen crossed out paragraphs in the Dolan-Reagan versions. But, finally, the cautious types retreated, figuring it was just some good old "Onward Christian Soldiers" stuff for a bunch of ministers. As Air Force One took off for Florida, five thousand protesters were chanting outside the Capitol, encouraging members of the House Foreign Affairs Committee, who then voted 27 to 9 for a resolution calling for "an immediate, mutual and verifiable freeze" on the production and deployment of nuclear weapons. The President, who had spent the morning with twenty-two members of Congress, trying to persuade them to vote for $110 million in military aid for El Salvador, then told the twelve hundred evangelicals convened in Orlando:

And this brings me to my final point today. . . . There is sin and evil in the world. And we are enjoined by Scripture and the Lord Jesus to oppose it with all our might. . . . Yes, let us pray for the salvation of all of those who live in that totalitarian darkness—pray that they will discover the joy of knowing God. But until they do, let us be aware that while they preach the supremacy of the state, declare its omnipotence over individual man, and predict its eventual domination of all peoples on earth, they are the focus of evil in the modern world. . . . In your discussions of the nuclear freeze proposals I urge you to beware the temptation of pride—the temptation to blithely declare yourselves above it all and label both sides equally at fault, to ignore the facts of history and the aggressive impulses of an evil empire, to simply call the arms race a giant misunderstanding and thereby remove yourself from the struggle between right and wrong and good and evil.

The church crowd in Orlando rose as one, cheering on and on as their band *did* play "Onward Christian Soldiers." The next day's reaction was startling. *New York Times* columnist Anthony Lewis said of the speech, "Primitive: that is the only word for it." His colleague Tom Wicker added: "The holy war mentality on either side tends to evoke it on the other; and holy wars are both the hardest to avoid and the least likely to be settled short of one side's annihilation." In *Time* magazine, Hugh Sidey's weekly column on "The Presidency" was headlined: "The Rt. Rev. Ronald Reagan." In *The Washington Post*, historian Henry Steele Commager, the country's most celebrated presidential scholar, was quoted as saying: "It was the worst presidential speech in American history. I've read them all. No other presidential speech has ever so flagrantly allied the government with religion."

The President's speech schedule listed his next nationally televised speech for March 23. The subject was defense, twice over. He had to defend his defense budget, which had become the target of most everyone concerned that federal deficits—now projected in the $200-billion-a-year range—were spinning out of control, even after Reagan proposed and Congress passed a new 5-cents-a-gallon national gasoline tax. The President, who had said in September of 1982 that the only thing that would make him sign new tax bills was "a palace coup," signed the gas tax into law in January of 1983. He had begun to talk about "structural deficits" of $100 billion a year and "structural unemployment" of 6 to 6.5 percent of the workforce. But Reagan now had grander things on his mind than closing the budget gap. He intended once again—for the second time in just two weeks, the third time in nine months—to change the dialogue of war and peace and ideology in the world. He had decided to speak of what he called in his diary "My dream."

He had dreamed, he wrote, of a world he had imagined for years, a world free of the fear of nuclear attack. Some who knew him would trace the dream back to a time before there were nuclear weapons, to 1940, when he had played "Brass Bancroft" in a science fiction film, *Murder in the Air*, involving a device called the Inertia Projector, which could shoot rockets and bombers out of the air—a shield to protect all the United States. In the film, the actor playing the Chief of Naval Operations says of the Inertia Projector: "It not only makes the United States invulnerable in war—but in so doing promises to become the greatest force for world peace ever discovered."

Wherever and whenever Reagan absorbed the idea of invulnerable missile defense, he had been talking for more than ten years about his moral disgust over the theory of mutual assured destruction—the idea that the countries with nuclear weapons would never use them because their land and cities would be destroyed by other nuclear powers. He had often compared it to two cowboys at a bar holding their guns against each other's head. One of his favorite lines was: "Look, every weapon has resulted in a defense—the sword, then the shield."

Reagan, the *Human Events* reader, was still fascinated by High Frontier, the missile defense scheme financed by the Heritage Foundation. At the beginning of 1983, *Human Events* had published a five-page interview with General Daniel Graham, who had been director of the Defense Intelligence Agency from 1974 to 1976, and who had formed High Frontier Incorporated early in 1981. He outlined a series of space umbrellas using 432 satellites to spot and target missiles as they left the ground, shooting many of them out of the sky with high-speed pellets. The proposed system—Graham and Heritage costed it out at $15 billion, less than hardening old silos for the MX missile—would not get every missile, but the uncertainty about how many it would get could deter an attacker.

All of that was in Reagan's mind when the Joint Chiefs of Staff had come to the Oval Office for their quarterly report just before Christmas in 1982. During that session, the President had asked, rather casually, or at least seemingly so: "What if we began to move away from our total reliance on offense to deter a nuclear attack and moved toward a relatively greater reliance on defense?" After the Chiefs returned to the Pentagon, one of them, Admiral James Watkins, the Chief of Naval Operations, called Judge Clark to ask: "Is he serious?"

Watkins had already thought a good deal about missile defenses, considered and rejected many as not feasible, but believed that new technologies might make possible what had never been before. Clark's deputy, a retired Marine lieutenant colonel named Robert "Bud" Mc-Farlane, had done some research of his own and was also championing missile defense, but for a different reason. He thought the idea itself would be a bargaining chip in ongoing United States–Soviet Union arms control negotiations—that we could get something for nothing. McFarlane briefed Reagan on all that before his February 11, 1983, meeting with the Chiefs. General John Vessey, the chairman, did the talking, but he repeated something Watkins had said as they prepared the briefing at the Pentagon: "Wouldn't it be better to protect the American people rather than avenge them?"

"Exactly," said Reagan, who was obviously excited.

"Mr. President," said McFarlane. "What the Admiral is saying is that we may be able to move in our lifetimes from reliance on offense toward defense."

"I understand," said the President. "That's what I want to do."

That night, in his diary, Reagan wrote: "What if we were to tell the world that we want to protect our people not avenge them; that we are going to embark on a program of research to come up with a defensive weapon that could make nuclear weapons obsolete?"

The Chiefs and most of Reagan's people left the February meeting thinking that they had been part of secret discussions that could go on for months, even years. That was not what Reagan was thinking. Working with a draft from McFarlane and his deputy, Admiral John Poindexter, Reagan the writer took over. The man of imagination. His secret draft was called "MX plus," a page or so in his own handwriting that would be tacked onto the end of his speech about the defense budget and the MX missile. Like another speech add-on, President Lyndon Johnson's 1968 declaration that he would not seek reelection, "MX plus" was not reviewed or vetted by the bureaucracies of State, Defense, or CIA. Secretary of State Shultz only learned about Reagan's intentions on Monday morning. Vice President Bush learned what the President planned to say when his chief of staff, Admiral Daniel Murphy, rushed into his office and said: "We've got to take this out! If we go off half-cocked on this idea, we're going to bring on the biggest arms race that the world has ever seen!" Bush agreed, but did nothing. Shultz's first reaction was similar: "This is lunacy." He did go to the White House to try to talk the President out of saying anything. He failed, but he did persuade Reagan to add a phrase saying that the research and development would be done within the restrictions of the 1972 Anti-Ballistic Missile Treaty. Only a couple dozen people knew the President was going to say something about missile defense, and few of them knew what he was going to say as he went on the air at 8 P.M. that night, March 23.

The President began the speech by saying that his $239 billion in defense requests had already been "trimmed to the limits of safety," then he went on to a recitation of numbers defining a massive Soviet increase in defense spending—including the modernization of missile guidance systems, the old Soviet weakness. And he accused communists far and near—Soviets and Cubans—of beginning the construction of a military base and airfield in Grenada, a small Caribbean island of 110,000 people ninety miles off the coast of Venezuela. "Grenada doesn't even have an air force," he said. "Who is it intended for?" He moved on then to what had been the original ending of the speech, saying:

> The calls for cutting back the defense budget come in nice, simple arithmetic. They're the same kind of talk that led the democracies to neglect their defenses in the 1930's and invited the tragedy of World War II. We must not let that grim chapter of history repeat itself through apathy or neglect. . . . That is why I'm speaking to you tonight—to urge you to tell your Senators and Congressmen that you know we must continue to restore our military strength.

He spoke of commitment to the control of existing nuclear weapons and then shifted to his new message:

> In recent months, my advisers, including in particular the Joint Chiefs of Staff, have underscored the necessity to break out of a future that relies solely on offensive retaliation for our security. . . . Wouldn't it be better to save lives than to avenge them? . . . After close consultation with my advisers, including the Joint Chiefs of Staff, I believe there is a way. Let me share with you a vision of the future which offers hope. . . . What if free people could live secure in the knowledge that their security did not rest upon the threat of instant U.S. retaliation to deter a Soviet attack, that we could intercept and destroy strategic ballistic missiles before they reached our own soil or that of our allies? . . .
>
> I call upon the scientific community in our country, those who gave us nuclear weapons, to turn their great talents now to the cause of mankind and world peace, to give us the means of rendering these nuclear weapons impotent and obsolete. . . . Our only purpose—one all people share—is to search for ways to reduce the danger of nuclear war. My fellow Americans, tonight we're launching an effort which holds the promise of changing the course of human history.

The telephone calls to the White House set new records, and 948 of the first 1,136 callers supported the President and his idea.

Among Reagan's men, many as surprised as any other viewers, the scramble was on to catch up to the President's parade. Vice President Bush told CBS News: "What this offers is hope—hope that you won't have to kill people, hope that you can get to total arms reduction." Secretary of Defense Weinberger, who was at a NATO conference in Lisbon when he learned of "MX Plus," had frantically called the White House asking that the antimissile idea be dropped or the speech postponed so that allies and congressional supporters could be informed. The answer was no; the television time had already been reserved. The next morning, interviewed by ABC News defense correspondent John McWethy, Weinberger attacked opponents of the idea, then said: "I think we are going to have to raise our sights considerably above mere fiscal thinking."

On the other side, House Speaker O'Neill told the network, "The President went a little far, to be truthful . . . this kind of Buck Rogers style last night."

Editorial judgments around the country were generally negative— or worse. It was treated as a joke, called "Star Wars" after the popular science fiction films. "Video-Game Vision," said *Time;* its cover showed Reagan in front of old drawings of Buck Rogers, a science fiction hero of 1930s comic books and movies. Among the word images in newspapers were: "Fantasy Death Ray gun" . . . "Razzle-Dazzle" . . . "Sophisticated nonsense." "A pipe dream," said *The New York Times.* The *Chicago Tribune* said: "President Reagan used an old debater's trick. If you're losing an argument, change the subject. . . . Having trouble justifying the largest peacetime buildup in American history, Reagan tried to distract his audience by talking of exotic new defensive weapons. For all his efforts to achieve Churchillian heights, Reagan's speech was irrelevant to the prosaic issues involved in writing a defense budget." The *Miami Herald* made the same point, then added: "Mr. Reagan's military spending would perpetuate annual Federal budget deficits of about $200 billion. That endangers the U.S. and world economies. A threat to the U.S. economy is as great a menace to national security as is the Soviet military. Both threats must be countered simultaneously. Balanced judgments are required."

As for the President, he was thrilled—"I felt good," he wrote in his diary—and he dictated his excitement in a memo to himself that became a nine-page secret decision memo, NSDD 85, stating: "I direct the development of an intensive effort to define a long term research and development program aimed at an ultimate goal of eliminating the threat posed by nuclear ballistic missiles. These actions will be carried out in a manner consistent with our obligations under the ABM treaty and recognizing the need for close consultation with our allies."

"Close consultation" and "careful consultation" were both mentioned in the speech, though neither had happened. This was Reagan, the man of imagination. Our allies were as astonished, flabbergasted really, as were our adversaries. In Moscow, where American words were routinely answered only after days or weeks of secret consultations, Soviet officials took to the airwaves immediately, claiming Reagan was violating the Anti-Ballisitic Missile Treaty signed by President Richard Nixon in 1972. *Pravda* and other Soviet journals charged that the Americans intended to take weaponry to a new level—"cosmic war technology that can give the other side a first-strike capability"— and that Reagan's real goal was military domination of the world. The President's response to that was: "I didn't expect them to cheer."

A week after the speech, during an Oval Office interview with six reporters, the President again startled the world. He was asked about all the editorials arguing that missile defense programs would destabilize the balance of power (or terror) between the United States and the Soviet Union, and he began by saying he had read those interviews, collected by the press office and published in the White House News Summary—"Quite irresponsible," he said—and then added:

> If a defensive weapon could be found and developed that would reduce the utility of these [missiles] or maybe even make them obsolete, then whenever that time came, a President of the United States would be able to say, "Now, we both have the deterrent, the missiles—as we had in the past—but now this other thing has altered this." He could offer to give that same defensive weapon to them to prove that there was no longer any need for keeping those missiles.

Give the Soviets the missile defense system? Yes. "If this thing works, we can give it to the Soviets, too," Reagan told Mike Deaver. Lou Cannon speculated that the whole thing might be another Reagan idea from the movies, specifically from a film called *The Day the Earth Stood Still*. In that one, made in 1951, an alien tries to halt earthly arms races by sharing weapons information with everyone around the globe. Then, on the same day he proposed weapons-sharing, the President told a meeting of European diplomats that he had ordered American arms control negotiators in Geneva to drop Zero Option demands for the time being and see if it was possible to negotiate an interim agreement eliminating some Soviet SS-20s and reduce the planned deployment of American Pershing IIs.

Two days after the President's missile defense speech, March 25, *The New York Times* carried five busy Washington headlines across its front page:

Aides Urged Reagan to Postpone
Antimissile Ideas for More Study

$165 BILLION PLAN
ON SOCIAL SECURITY
PASSES IN CONGRESS

Israelis Reported
To Balk at Plan
For Withdrawal

ACTING E.P.A. CHIEF
IS SAID TO BE READY
TO QUIT POST TODAY

SENATE COMMITTEE
CALLS FOR HALVING
NEW SALVADOR AID

The national security community was leaking all over the capital city, with various officials making sure that reporters and each other knew they had had nothing to do with the President's big surprise. "Strategic experts within the administration were not given an opportunity to review the proposal before he made his speech," reported Les Gelb of *The New York Times*.

The Social Security story was the climax of months of intensive and bipartisan work to pump more money into the system and take less out before July 1, the date when the program would be technically bankrupt. The heavy lifting had been done by a temporary National Commission on Social Security Reform—with members appointed by both the President and Speaker O'Neill—charged with restoring public faith in the government's old-age insurance trust and, not incidentally, taking the pressure off politicians of both parties living in fear of tens of millions of Americans expecting monthly government checks when they retired. But Reagan controlled the process more than people knew. The chairman he appointed, a conservative economist named Alan Greenspan, was secretly coming to the White House to confer with the President and his men. The President's briefing memo for one such meeting, written by Dick Darman, said: "For obvious reasons the fact and subject of this meeting are being kept *Confidential*. . . . Your legislative strategists believe that it would be extremely difficult (close to impossible) to pass legislation that goes beyond what the Commission majority recommends. It is therefore extremely important to try to get the Commission to move toward a satisfactory set of recommendations. . . . There is only one month in which to try to influence the commission. Your guidance is therefore essential for Greenspan—as soon as possible."

Finally, between ten minutes before midnight on March 24 and 2 A.M. on March 25, the House approved the commission plan by a 243 to 102 vote and the Senate did the same by a 58 to 14 vote. Despite the rhetoric of denial from both sides in Washington, the Social Security Reform Act was a huge and enduring tax increase, raising the FICA payroll tax from 6.7 percent of individual income to 7.65 percent by 1990, raising the retirement age from sixty-five to sixty-seven over the coming forty years, delaying cost-of-living increases to retirees, and forcing future government employees to give up separate plans and contribute to the trust fund.

Meanwhile, in Lebanon, Israeli and Syrian troops and a few thousand Palestinian fighters were still refusing to leave the country. American-led negotiations were going nowhere. U.S. Marines, twelve hundred of them, were responsible for security in South Beirut, the area around the Beirut airport, which often meant confrontation with soldiers of the Israel Defense Forces, who were used to roaming the Muslim sectors of the city at will and using tanks and cannons to blast away buildings or cars that got in their way. The IDF was refusing to leave the city until the Syrians were gone and the beleaguered Lebanese Christian government signed a peace treaty recognizing Israel's sovereignty.

On March 18, 1983, Secretary of Defense Weinberger had released an official letter written to him by General Robert Barrow, the Marine Corps Commandant, which detailed incidents of Israeli harassment of U.S. peacekeepers "timed, orchestrated and executed for obtuse Israeli political purposes." Barrow said that Israelis had fired at or near American soldiers at least three times. In the most publicized of hundreds of incidents, three Israeli tanks tried to pass through a Marine checkpoint and were blocked by Captain Charles Johnson, who twice aimed his pistol at Israeli tank commanders as their cannons lowered to target him. "If you come through," said Johnson, "it will be over my dead body."

In Washington, Weinberger and Reagan praised Captain Johnson, but the Israeli tanks were back the next night, crashing through the airport, saying they had lost their way. That same week, American-Israeli relations got a little worse, too, as former Presidents Jimmy Carter and Gerald Ford, in a joint article in America's most popular magazine, *Reader's Digest,* wrote that the major obstacle to peace in the region was Israel's settlement policy, saying: "The evidence is convincing to the Arab world and beyond that Israeli leaders have simply chosen to seize these lands and hold them by force." As for Israeli politics, it was often obtuse to outsiders, particularly after Defense Minister Ariel Sharon resigned on February 11, the day the Israeli cabinet endorsed a judicial commission conclusion that Sharon "bears personal responsibility" and Prime Minister Menachem Begin bore "indirect responsibility" for the massacres of thirteen hundred Palestinians at the Sabra and Shatila refugee camps. Two days later, Sharon was back in the cabinet, as a minister without portfolio.*

Resignations under fire were also happening in Reagan's Washington. On March 19, after weeks of denying he would, the President accepted the resignations of his administrator of the Environmental Protection Agency, Anne McGill Burford, and most of her senior staff. For six months the agency—under orders from the President—had refused to give congressional investigators documents regarding political influence in the management and funding of programs to clean up toxic waste sites around the country. It was the usual Washington scandal—charges, denials, leaks, White House claims of "executive privilege," a citation for contempt of Congress, talk of cover-up, and finally, evidence of paper-shredding—except for one thing: Reagan's stubborn refusal to get it over with by firing the EPA director. Until twelve days before the end, the President insisted that Burford had his full confidence and could keep her job as long as she

---

* The Israelis stayed in Lebanon for more than twenty years, withdrawing from Beirut in September of 1983, but continuing to occupy the southern part of the country until 2004.

wanted it. In case anyone was confused about the President's attitudes, he deflected questions about Burford at his March 11 press conference with a smile and a line: "There is environmental extremism. I don't think they'll be happy until the White House looks like a bird's nest."

The press had already taken to pounding the Reagan environmental record. On March 13, Andrea Mitchell on the *NBC Nightly News* had summed it up this way:

> President Reagan said at his last press conference that the EPA has a splendid record. That splendid record includes: 1. Delaying the the cleanup of toxic dumps. . . . 2. Withholding information on Dioxin levels from residents. . . . 3. Budget cuts of more than 30 percent. . . . 4. Personnel cuts of 12 percent. This is exactly what candidate Reagan promised in 1980, less regulation. He also blamed pollution on trees and volcanoes.

Reporters were also on the case of Secretary of the Interior James Watt, another target of environmentalists, a tough conservative from Wyoming with a habit of saying the wrong thing at the wrong time. He compared himself to Jews in Nazi concentration camps, saying that he was being persecuted as an evangelical Christian. Like many of those Reagan appointed as federal regulators, Watt had spent his professional life fighting the regulations he was now called on to enforce. He was a former legal counsel of the United States Chamber of Commerce and a fierce advocate of deregulation to allow oil-drilling off California and mining in wilderness areas. As Burford was leaving, Watt was announcing that rock bands would be barred from performing at the annual Interior-sponsored July 4th celebrations on the Mall, which stretches from the Washington Monument to the Lincoln Memorial. The idea, he said, was to keep away the "wrong element," to make the party "patriotic and family-friendly." Who was he banning? "The Beach Boys," he said. He wanted to replace them with the U.S. Army Band and Wayne Newton, the Las Vegas star.

The Beach Boys? *Surfin' USA*. Nancy Reagan loved the Beach Boys.

Things had gotten touchy between the President and the press after the 1982 elections. In January, Reagan had called in senior staff to say: "I've had it up to my keister with leaks. Do something!"

The chore was turned over to communications director David Gergen. There was a bit of irony there because reporters sometimes referred to him as "Assistant to *The New York Times* for Communications." Gergen produced a twelve-point guidance memo. The principal guideline ordered White House staffers to route all calls from reporters to Gergen, who would then select a designated answerer and provide guidance on what to say and, more importantly, what not to say. A separate memo, approved personally by the President and distributed on March 19, required thousands of government employees to sign secrecy agreements and to submit to lie detector tests if they were suspected of breaking those agreements.

Gergen's orders were ignored more often than not, particularly after he lost a small battle of wits with Helen Thomas, the veteran United Press International White House correspondent, who said: "David, this happens in every White House at this point in time. When the press stories start turning bad, you all put out gag rules." Then, three days later, Reagan himself came to the press room, an encounter reported by Cannon in the *Post:* "His attempt to demonstrate that he is firmly in control and fully knowledgeable about the policies of his administration was marred by his reference to Paul Nitze, his chief arms negotiator, as 'Ed Nitze.' "

The lie detector tests, recommended by Judge Clark, did not last much longer than it took Secretary of State Shultz to get over to the White House and say: "If you strap me up, I'm out of here." Baker, no great fan of Clark's, added: "But what about the Vice President? Are you going to strap him up too?" Reagan got on the phone and said, "Bill, you should not have brought that in here to me."

The March 25 headlines on congressional opposition to sending more military aid to El Salvador by redirecting aid earmarked for other countries reflected an ongoing struggle. Reagan was listening to his CIA director, William J. Casey, the tough New York attorney who had managed his 1980 campaign, who was telling him what he wanted to hear, and what he himself believed about Soviet vulnerability around the world. "Mr. President, we have an historic opportunity," said Casey. "We can do serious damage to them." The two old men—Casey was just two years younger than Reagan and mumbled so badly that Reagan often did not understand what he said even when he was wearing a hearing aid—had been determined since the first weeks of the administration to gain control of events in Central America, particularly in El Salvador, Nicaragua, and Guatemala.

The official story at the end of 1981, when the President had secretly signed off on covert action in Nicaragua, was that all the United

States was trying to do was interdict arms shipments from Nicaragua to leftist insurgents trying to overthrow El Salvador's government. And many in Congress were determined to try to stop what they saw as something like another Vietnam. Twice in the same week that Reagan made his missile defense speech—he was now calling it the "Strategic Defense Initiative"—the President spent the hour before bedtime thinking about Central America. He put down these thoughts in his diary: "Meeting re: El Salvador. We must step up aid or we're going to lose this one" . . . "Tomorrow we start trying to convince Congress we must have more money for El Salvador. We have an entire plan for bolstering government forces. This is one we must win" . . . "Those in Congress who are dribbling out about one-quarter of what we ask for and need. They'd like to keep enough money in the game while El Salvador bleeds to death. Then they'll call it my plan and we've lost Central America" . . . "If the Soviets win in Central America, we lose in Geneva and every place else."

There was indeed blood everywhere in Central America, the thin band of land joining Mexico and South America, the land where American troops had invaded or intervened at least sixty-nine times since 1850. Leftist guerrillas were trying to overthrow the brutal business-military oligarchy in El Salvador, their dirtiest work often done by extreme right-wing death squads, some of them military men out of uniform, accused of murdering thousands of peasants. When the American ambassador, Deane Hinton, who had been sent in as the tough guy at the beginning of the Reagan administration, was indiscreet enough to condemn the brutality of government security forces at a luncheon of the San Salvador Chamber of Commerce, he was immediately ordered by the White House to never do that again. Ten weeks later the State Department officially certified to Congress that the country was making progress on human rights problems, a dubious assertion but a legal prerequisite for continuing American military assistance.

At the same time, at Reagan's urging, the CIA was recruiting and training insurgents, the contras, and spending millions of dollars to try to destabilize the Marxist Sandinista government in Nicaragua, which was providing support for Salvadoran insurgents. As part of that effort, the United States was paying the government of Honduras to establish contra bases on their side of the Nicaraguan border. Reagan was also trying to help another brutal regime, the military rulers of Guatemala. Even one of the most populist conservative newspapers in the country, the *New York Daily News,* editorialized in early April: "The Reagan administration deplores attempts by the Soviet Union to impose Marxism in Central America. But it seems to be playing the same kind of game in Nicaragua's aid to anti-government elements in El Salvador and supporting a rebel movement in Nicaragua. That puts us in the same boat as Moscow and Havana, and flies in the face of our stated goal of democracy and respect for human rights throughout Central America."

The President's plan was laid out in NSDD 17, "National Security Decision Directive on Cuba and Central America," which Reagan had signed off on early in 1982. The most specific provision was the allocation of $19 million to recruit and train the five-hundred-man contra force operating along Nicaragua's border with Honduras. That was followed by a series of secret findings and decision memos ordering the use of military and intelligence funds for covert action from Guatemala to Grenada, the small Caribbean island off Venezuela, fifteen hundred miles south of Florida.

But O'Neill and House Democrats, who knew nothing of NSDD 17, had a plan, too. In November of 1982, *Newsweek* had reported that the American ambassador to Honduras, John Negroponte, was overseeing the training of Nicaraguan guerrillas inside Honduras. That news enraged Representative Edward Boland of Massachusetts, an O'Neill man who was chairman of the House Select Intelligence Committee. Boland had never been informed of covert actions there, and he reacted by introducing the first of a series of "Boland Amendments," regulating and later prohibiting the allocation of Defense Department and CIA funds "for the purpose of overthrowing the government of Nicaragua." Soon enough, with Reagan's blessing, Clark at the National Security Council and CIA Director Casey were looking for even more secret ways to fund one side or another in the bloody wars of Latin America. So, of course, was Reagan. At one angry meeting with O'Neill, Reagan said: "The Sandinistas have openly proclaimed communism in their country and their support of Marxist revolutions throughout Central America. . . . They're killing and torturing people! Now what the hell does Congress expect me to do about that?"

The President was convinced that all the left-wing movements in Central America—insurgents in El Salvador and Guatemala and the Sandinista government, which was recognized as legitimate by the United Nations—were a direct threat to the United States. He was forever repeating a phony "Lenin quote": "First we will take Eastern Europe, then we will organize the hordes of Asia . . . then we will move on to Latin America; once we have Latin America we won't have to take the United States, the last bastion of capitalism, because it will fall into our outstretched hands like overripe fruit."

Reagan was, in fact, concerned enough about Latin America that he had made a brief tour of the continent and of Central America at the end of 1982. The trip had its moments: He raised a glass to toast "The President of Bolivia" as he looked into the eyes of the President of Brazil, and he came back saying it was interesting to discover that the Latin countries were different from one another. But there were more serious mistakes in judgment. Guatemala was one. After meeting with that country's dictator, President José Efraín Ríos Montt, one of the most brutal men in a brutal region—the meeting was actually in a hangar at an airbase in Honduras—Reagan came out to speak to American reporters, saying: "I know that President Ríos Montt is a man of great integrity and commitment. . . . I have assured the President that the United States is committed to support his efforts to restore democracy and to address the root causes of this violent insurgency."

The root causes were well known: An estimated 200,000 Guatemalans, men, women, and children, most of them Mayan Indians, had been killed in twenty years of ongoing civil war, tens of thousands of them in the nine months since Ríos Montt, a former general who made himself the leader of his own evangelical sect, "The Church of the Word," had been installed by the military in a coup specifically approved of by the United States in the backup papers of NSDD 17. Then, in a series of scorched-earth campaigns, Ríos Montt's army had totally destroyed more than four hundred villages in the country's interior.

On the flight back to Washington, Reagan was in a good mood and came back to the press cabin. He was immediately asked whether the fact that Ríos Montt had scheduled an election in the coming year was reason enough to resume military aid to the country—aid that had been suspended since 1974 because of widespread and obvious human rights abuses. "I frankly think they've been getting a bad deal. You know he was elected president in 1974 and was never allowed to take office. . . . I'm inclined to believe they've been getting a bum rap."

In other words, he liked the man. Within a month, the United States was once again selling military equipment to Guatemala, though Congress was still blocking outright aid. But Clark's shop, the National Security Council, was trying to find ways around congressional restrictions. Three months later, in early April, the President sent his ambassador-at-large, Vernon Walters, to Guatemala City, carrying a letter signed by Reagan, but written by a Marine officer on Clark's staff, Lieutenant Colonel Oliver North, to be read to Ríos Montt. "I have dispatched Ambassador Walters for the specific purpose of reassuring you of our continued support for you personally and your programs to counter the guerrilla threat which you are so valiantly confronting," the letter began. "We are committed to assisting that effort in any way we can." But then it continued: "You must recognize that my ability to respond to your needs in the short term is limited by a lack of Congressionally authorized funding. We will attempt, however, to provide some assistance on an urgent basis to meet your highest priority requirements."

An additional note from Clark, read to Ríos Montt, said that Reagan did not believe Congress would approve open transfers of military equipment until Guatemala arrested officers accused of ordering the murder of four Americans working in the country for the U.S. Agency for International Development.

The murders were also brought up in a meeting between Ríos Montt and the American ambassador, Frederic L. Chapin, who reported back to the State Department in a cable saying: "The President [Ríos Montt] launched into a philosophical discussion to say that the United States should recognize that it was impossible to maintain control over all members of the Armed Forces in Guatemala or of the civilian administration. . . . If the United States found him an inconvenient President we should simply remove him. We had the power to do so and it would be easy."

The primary focus, though, remained on El Salvador. More than twenty officials in the White House, the State and Defense Departments, and intelligence agencies made themselves available, on background, to brief Les Gelb of *The New York Times,* who presented their viewpoint in a long front-page story under the headline "U.S. Aides See Need for Big Effort to Avert Rebel Victory in Salvador." One paragraph began, "The Reagan Administration, unable to win and unwilling to lose, is playing for time."

By April 18, 1983, the President, against all advice inside the White House, had decided he wanted to address a joint session of Congress to press his case for more United States aid and involvement in Central America. He was working on drafts with speechwriter Aram Bakshian and NSC staffers on the morning of the eighteenth. One of the lines they were refining was: "Our military forces are back on their feet and standing tall." Then Deaver rushed into his office with bad news from Lebanon.

The President went straight to the press room. "Let me begin with a brief statement. . . . Our embassy in Beirut was a target this morning of a vicious terrorist bombing. This cowardly act has claimed a number of killed and wounded." A suicide bomber had driven a car up to the entrance of the embassy and detonated at least two thousand pounds of dynamite, bringing down five stories of the building. The final death count reached sixty-two, seventeen of them Americans. (It was never announced, but among the victims were Robert Ames, the CIA's chief Middle East analyst and a participant in Secretary of State Shultz's war-gaming, and eight other CIA operatives.) More than one hundred others were badly injured. Reagan said the United States would rededicate its efforts to bring peace and democracy to Lebanon and the entire Middle East.

But in Beirut, Marines were standing on shifting sands, ready to duck as Muslim militias in the Shiite slums around the airport—"Khomeiniville" Marines called those neighborhoods—moved closer and closer to the American lines and to the stations where Marines were training Lebanese Armed Forces units. And most of those Marines had no bullets in their guns or were bound by rules of engagement that may have made sense in Washington but left those Marines in real danger in Lebanon. After the embassy bombing, the Marines guarding the ruins and new American offices in the nearby British embassy were issued blue cards with revised rules allowing them to fire on vehicles approaching their positions at high speed. The rest of the Marine force, back at the airport, was bound by the old rules, including: "When on post, mobile or foot patrol, keep a loaded magazine in the weapon, weapons will be on safe, with no round in the chamber. . . . Do not chamber a round unless told to do so by a commissioned officer or unless you must act in immediate self-defense where deadly force is authorized."

On the morning of April 27, the President flew up to New York to speak at the annual convention of the American Newspaper Association, using the occasion to boast a bit: "There's economic recovery. Pretty soon they won't be calling it Reaganomics anymore. . . . Auto production is up 40 percent in the last quarter over the same quarter a year ago; new home sales in February were up by 49 percent; building permits were up in March by 79 percent. . . . Consumer confidence has had its best monthly gain in nine years. . . . We now have the lowest prime rate in four and a half years. And inflation for the last six months is averaging one-half of one percent." During a question-and-answer period, when the subject turned to Central America, the President told the crowd to tune in at 8 P.M.

The speech to Congress was modeled on President Truman's address to a joint session on March 12, 1947, the speech that introduced the "Truman Doctrine," beginning: "The United States has received from the Greek government an urgent appeal for financial and economic assistance. . . . That assistance is imperative if Greece is to survive as a free nation. I do not believe that the American people and the Congress wish to turn a deaf ear to the appeal."

Reagan quoted Truman extensively, repeating his words about the American stake in Europe—"I believe that it must be the policy of the United States to support free peoples who are resisting attempted subjugation" was one phrase he used—then applied those same words to El Salvador, Honduras, Guatemala, Costa Rica, and Nicaragua:

Too many have thought of Central America as just that place way down below Mexico that can't possibly constitute a threat to our well-being. And that's why I've asked for this session. . . . El Salvador is nearer to Texas than Texas is to Massachusetts. Nicaragua is just as close to Miami, San Antonio, San Diego, and Tucson as those cities are to Washington. . . .

The people of El Salvador are earning their freedom. . . . Yes, there are still major problems regarding human rights, the criminal justice system and violence against non-combatants. . . . The Sandinista revolution in Nicaragua turned out to be just an exchange of one set of autocratic rulers for another and the people still have no democratic rights and more poverty. . . . It is the ultimate in hypocrisy for the unelected Nicaraguan government to charge that we seek their overthrow, when they're doing everything they can to bring down the elected government of El Salvador. . . . What I'm asking for is prompt congressional approval for the full reprogramming of the funds for key current economic and security programs so that the people of Central America can hold the line against externally supported aggression. . . . The total amount requested for aid to all of Central America in 1984 is about $600 million. That's less than one-tenth of what Americans will spend this year on coin-operated video games. . . .

The national security of all the Americas is at stake in Central America. If we cannot defend ourselves there, we cannot expect to prevail elsewhere. Our credibility would collapse, our alliances would crumble, and the safety of our homeland would be put in jeopardy.

Reagan was interrupted by applause only three times, once when he pledged never to send American troops to those countries. The speech was not a success. Instant analysis on the three networks was bolder and more negative than usual. On NBC News, anchor John Chancellor said: "In the past 27 months the U.S. has spent $700 million on El Salvador. This may have kept the place from falling apart completely, but it hasn't produced much progress." James Wooten of ABC News was caustic: "I think he made his case, if you accept his premises. And his premises were that the contras in Nicaragua are not die-hard supporters of Somoza. If you accept his premise that it is Nicaragua that is threatening Honduras. If you accept his premise that it is Nicaragua that is really fueling the El Salvador rebellion. If you accept all these premises, then he made his case. I'm not sure Congress or the country is ready to accept those premises." After a day of reflection, the *Boston Globe* editorialized: "Can Americans in the 1980s still be dazzled by patriotic theatrics, fooled by misleading recitations of events and historical analogies, impressed by superficial calls for 'bipartisan' unity and jerked into line by Red Scare oratory? . . . Have we grown enough through experiences as different as losing the Vietnam War and seeing the Third World anew through Peace Corps eyes to understand that it *is* possible for the United States to get ahead of the curve of history if we want to?"

The conservative columnist James J. Kilpatrick, a friend of Reagan's, attacked from another direction: "If the danger is as great as the President implied . . . why not send in our troops?"

The answer was that most Americans, and most members of Congress, did not believe the danger was that great. The seven countries of Central America, including Panama and Belize, had a combined total population of about 25 million, 75,000 untrained soldiers, and per capita income in the $500-a-year range—most of El Salvador's wealth was held by fourteen families—and painful histories of native genocide, civil war, military rule, and foreign exploitation. More often than not, the exploiter was the United States and its corporations. Senator Christopher Dodd of Connecticut, who gave the official Democratic response to the President's speech, made a couple of those points and added some description from a recent trip to El Salvador: "I know about the morticians who travel the streets each morning to collect the bodies of those summarily dispatched the night before by Salvadoran security forces—gangland style—the victim on bended knee, thumbs wired behind the back, a bullet through the brain."

The minutes of the White House senior staff meeting the next morning noted that Dodd had been given the President's text one and a half hours before delivery, then stated: "It was suggested that, in the future, we consider not distributing advance copies of the speech."

The next morning the President was on his way to Houston to make a fund-raising speech for Senator John Tower. During the day he stopped at a drug and alcohol rehabilitation center to promote "Just Say No!," Mrs. Reagan's high profile campaign against drug use. He told the small crowd there that the smartest thing they could do was take care of their bodies. "When you get along to where I am, you find out taking care of that machinery sure pays off when you can still tie your shoes and pull on your own socks without sitting down"—he stopped and grinned—"and do a lot of things that are much more enjoyable than that."

Los Angeles Times reporter George Skelton turned to Mike Deaver—they had been fraternity brothers in college—and asked: "Was he talking about sex?"

"Ask him," Deaver answered.

On Air Force One, he did. "I've got to ask a seventy-two-year-old president . . ."

"Yeah?" said Reagan, grinning again.

" . . . if you still have an active sex life?"

Reagan laughed. "This is a subject I think I'll stay away from."

Skelton persisted, asking if he felt physically different than he did ten or twenty years before. Reagan laughed again. And said: "Well, George, in many ways I feel better."

CHAPTER 8

SEPTEMBER 5, 1983

AT 1:55 A.M. ON AUGUST 29, 1983, President Reagan was wakened by the telephone at his ranch. Bill Clark told him that two Marines had been killed and fourteen wounded in Beirut by artillery and mortar shells fired at American positions from the Shouf Mountains, southeast of the city. Beirut was a battleground again, as more than ten thousand soldiers of the LAF, the official Lebanese army, moved into two poor Muslim neighborhoods in West Beirut in an attempt to clear out the masked gunners of the Shiite Amal militia—"Amal" means "hope" in Arabic—and other local war gangs who had taken over those areas. Larry Speakes, the President's spokesman, ever sensitive to questions about his boss's work and sleep habits, told reporters down the mountain at the Santa Barbara Biltmore Hotel that the call to the ranch was made exactly one hour and six minutes after the incident.

The Marine peacekeepers, the 24th Marine Amphibious Unit, had first been fired on by artillery in July. It had been officially announced in both Beirut and Washington that the shots were meant for Israeli or Muslim militia positions. But, in fact, the Americans at the Beirut airport were becoming targets—and had been since they began training LAF units. The danger to the Americans had been building since Secretary of State Shultz had announced that Israel and the Lebanese government had agreed to a treaty—the May 17 Agreement—that all foreign troops would leave Lebanon within the next few months, and that Lebanon would become the second Arab country (after Egypt) to recognize the sovereignty of Israel. The agreement, though, was nothing more than paper because secret caveats said that Israeli troops would not leave until Syrian forces did and Shultz had already been told in Damascus that the Syrians had no intention of leaving. The Syrian soldiers were not as well trained or equipped as the Israelis and the Americans, but there were more of them and they had some relatively sophisticated Soviet weaponry. That same day, May 17, President Reagan held a press conference in Washington and rather casually misstated the mission of the MNF, the peacekeepers from the United States, France, and Italy. Asked how long the MNF was staying in Beirut, he had answered: "Well, you have to remember what the multinational forces went in there for. The multinational forces are there to help the new Government of Lebanon maintain order until it can organize its military and its police and assume control over its own borders and its own internal security." In effect, he had taken sides in an ongoing civil war, standing with the Christians against the country's Muslim militias.

Peacekeepers no more, the Marines dug deeper into the sand of Beirut and began joint patrols with LAF units in the Shiite Muslim neighborhoods, driving through mean streets decorated with posters of the Ayatollah Khomeini. Still, the summer had been relatively quiet—until mid-August. By then, on some days more than one hundred artillery and mortar shells were incoming. The Americans, encamped on the flatlands of the Beirut airport, were perfect targets for Muslim artillery and rockets firing from the mountains. The Reagan plan for a Jordan-administered West Bank was dead after Yasser Arafat announced that the PLO would refuse to allow Jordan's King Hussein to negotiate for them, dooming one more American peace plan. It was a bad time for United States foreign policy. Soviet Foreign Minister Andrei Gromyko had announced that the Soviet Union was rejecting President Reagan's call for an interim agreement on medium-range missiles in Europe.

The Israelis were already anxious to get their troops away from Beirut—in Tel Aviv and Jerusalem the Israeli Defense Forces invasion was being compared to Vietnam. Talks and shuttle diplomacy were cheap, but nothing good was happening on the ground, at least in Beirut. In Washington, Clark, who seemed to be in charge of Reagan's foreign policy, had secretly tried to reopen negotiations with Syrian President Hafez al-Assad, sending his deputy, McFarlane, on a secret three-day trip to Damascus along with the Saudi ambassador to the United States, Prince Bandar bin Sultan.

At the same time, Clark, with some help from United Nations Ambassador Jeane Kirkpatrick, seemed to be changing the American mission in Central America. He had presided over the firings of Ambassador Hinton in El Salvador and Thomas Enders, the assistant secretary for Latin America. The White House wanted men who thought like the Commander in Chief, who had taken to calling contras "freedom fighters." On July 12, the President had signed a secret "Covert Action Finding on Nicaragua," superseding a more limited December 1981 finding. The new finding concluded: "Support and conduct covert activities including paramilitary activities designed to . . . facilitate the efforts by democratic Nicaraguan leaders to restore the original principles of political pluralism, non-alignment, a mixed economy and free elections to the Nicaraguan revolution. Work with foreign governments and organizations as appropriate to carry out the program." In public, Reagan continued to insist that the American goal in Nicaragua and the rest of Central America was simply to prevent the Sandinista government from organizing shipments of Soviet arms and equipment to the leftist guerrillas in the hills and jungles of El Salvador. But contra leaders, told they would be provided funds and enough equipment and training in Honduras for a force of twelve thousand men, began talking openly about overthrowing the Sandinista government.

That kind of covert war was not legal, according to some in the Pentagon. "Despite our desire to support CIA initiatives within Central America, we are nonetheless constrained in the method of this support by statutory restrictions," wrote the Defense Department's general counsel, William Howard Taft IV, in a "Top Secret" memo to his boss, Secretary Weinberger. But, by the end of the summer, enough support was reaching the contras to allow units of several hundred men at a time to attack villages and outposts in the north of Nicaragua—and none of that had anything to do with El Salvador or weapons interdiction. General John Vessey, chairman of the Joint Chiefs, noted Taft's objections and sent the other service Chiefs this memo: "Anticipate a new Presidential Finding, scheduled to be issued in mid-September, will provide necessary authority." That finding, intended to further expand and escalate the contra insurgency, was still in preparation. The key provision read: "Provide training support and guidance to Nicaragua resistance forces . . . in order to hamper arms trafficking through Nicaragua, support indigenous resistance efforts and pressure the Sandinistas. . . . Arms and other support will be provided to Nicaraguan paramilitary forces operating inside Nicaragua. . . . Instructors will train these forces. . . . $19 million is included in the Fiscal Year 1984 CIA budget for this program. Additional funding requirements, to be determined by developments in the area, could be as much as $14 million."

Meanwhile in the Middle East, when Habib resigned after more than two years of frustrating negotiations, Reagan immediately announced that he would be replaced by McFarlane. It was only then that Shultz learned of McFarlane's trip with Prince Bandar. He stormed into the Oval Office to confront the President about McFarlane and about the fact that no one had informed him in advance of naval maneuvers planned to begin in September and go on for six months off both the Pacific and Caribbean coasts of Nicaragua. "You can't do this to me. You've totally undermined me," said the Secretary of State. "To do this behind our backs. . . . You don't need me as Secretary of State if this is the way things are being conducted. And I don't want to be your Secretary of State. . . . Bill Clark seems to want the job because he's trying to run everything."

Reagan was badly shaken by the idea that he could lose another Secretary of State little more than a year after forcing Haig out. He refused Shultz's resignation. The Secretary came away from his Oval Office visit with the impression that the President had not known about the McFarlane trip before he named him to replace Habib as his special envoy. Clark, who was in the Oval Office when Shultz angrily threatened to leave, called the Secretary later to say there was a misunderstanding. The next call, that evening, was from the President himself, inviting Shultz and his wife over for another informal dinner upstairs.

Shultz and Mrs. Reagan connected at dinner that night. He thought Clark was incompetent, another guy from California in over his head. He also thought the naval maneuvers off Nicaragua, pushed by Clark, amounted to a blockade, an act of war. Nancy thought that Clark was making her husband look like a right-wing warmonger. She called the Secretary of State a couple of days later and said she thought Clark should be fired. They were conspirators now, even as Clark's influence seemed to be at a peak. That week's edition of *Time* featured Clark's face on the cover and the line "Clark Takes Charge." An inside story on Shultz was under the headline "Disappearing Act at Foggy Bottom." Shultz declined comment. He was a gifted bureaucratic warrior and now he had reason to believe that his rival was finished. It was just a matter of time.

Six separate armies were fighting each other in Lebanon as McFarlane took that portfolio. Thomas Friedman of *The New York Times* reported: "Palestinian guerrilla factions fought with each other and with the Lebanese army in the central Bekaa, the eastern valley. Israeli troops battled with Syrians in the southern Bekaa, and other Israelis clashed near Sidon with Phalangist Christian militias, whom they are trying to evict from southern Lebanon."

A seventh militia was forming as well, operating out of the Shouf. The Syrians were supplying arms to the National Salvation Front, a force that included Sunni Muslims, anti-Gemayel Christians, and fighters of the Druse, a one-thousand-year-old ascetic and secretive Islamic sect of 250,000 people centered in those mountains. The Druse were mobilizing because they wanted to beat back any attempt by the Lebanese army to move into the mountains to take over Israeli positions. The Israelis were preparing to move south to create an occupied buffer zone along the Awali River, seventeen miles south of Beirut and twenty-eight miles north of their own border. The Druse leader, Walid Jumblatt, became the first militia commander to publicly declare that United States Marines were "enemy forces," because American-trained LAF units were preparing to move into the mountains when the Israelis left.

In a final irony, while the White House and the Secretary of State were publicly calling for IDF withdrawal under the May 17 agreement, the same American officials, including the President, were secretly trying to persuade the Israelis not to leave the mountains. The 5,600 relatively lightly armed MNF troops, including the Marines, were obviously incapable of replacing the 38,000 Israeli occupiers keeping the Lebanese from attacking each other.

"A RETREAT BY ISRAEL" was the headline over a *New York Times* analysis on September 4, when the IDF began to abandon its Shouf positions. After fifteen months of fighting, the Israeli army had accomplished little more than it had won on the first day, when the IDF crossed the Alawi to drive the PLO north and create a buffer zone. In the end, the PLO terrorists they displaced were being replaced with new ones from a group calling itself Hezbollah, or "Party of God," created or bolstered by three hundred to five hundred Iranians who had slipped into Beirut and southern Lebanon under the fog of war. Iran was also the focus of several stories in the international press—including the respected French newspaper *Liberation* and *Time* magazine—reporting that the Israelis were secretly selling the Iranian government American weaponry and ammunition to use in its bloody war against Iraq. The Israelis were also secretly shipping captured PLO weapons to the contras in Nicaragua and Honduras. But even as American officials in Baghdad were assuring Iraqi leader Saddam Hussein that the stories were not true, and as Israeli Prime Minister Menachem Begin, exhausted and depressed over the death of his wife, announced that he was resigning, the Middle East was still a sideshow in Washington. Even back on July 22, when McFarlane's appointment as the new special envoy was announced, *The New York Times* tucked his picture under a two-column lead headline:

REAGAN PLANS RISE
IN MILITARY MOVES
IN LATIN AMERICA

LINK TO WAR GAMES

A Possible Quarantine of
Nicaragua Reported
To Be Prepared

Three days later, the President held a thirty-three-minute prime-time press conference. Twenty-five of those minutes were taken up by questions about Central America. He began with controlled anger, complaining about press coverage of military action and actions south of the border: "There's been entirely too much attention to the efforts that we're making to provide that security shield and not nearly enough to the other elements of our policy. . . . For every $1 that we provide for security assistance to that region, we provide $3 for economic and human development. . . ." A pause. Then: "Now Helen."

"Mr. President, you complain of too much attention," said Helen Thomas of UPI, the senior wire service reporter. "How can the people ignore two battleship groups, thousands of combat troops going to Honduras, it is said the covert funding of 10,000 Nicaraguan rebels? . . . They're unprecedented—to last six months? The polls show that the American people are not for them, and they fear it may lead to war. And my question is remembering the lessons of Vietnam, does this bother you? Do they have any say?"

"There is no comparison to Vietnam and there's not going to be anything like that," Reagan replied. It was not one of his better performances, but he did slide by some of the questions by bringing up the "Kissinger Commission," a bipartisan group led by former Secretary of State Henry Kissinger, announced on July 18, with a mandate to report back to the President on long-range policy in Central America. In the short range, the President lost a new friend when President Ríos Montt of Guatemala was overthrown in a military coup after seventeen months in power. Few Americans seemed to care, which was another reason that Reagan wanted the help of an old adversary. Kissinger's stature might help Americans hear Reagan's constant alarms. The President had been stunned by a *New York Times*/CBS News poll reporting: "Only 25 percent of those surveyed knew that the Administration supports the Government of El Salvador, only 13 percent know that it sides with the insurgents in Nicaragua and only 8 percent know both alignments."

Trying to boost those numbers kept Reagan in Washington and away from the ranch for an extra two weeks. Even then, he came back from California for a day on August 15 to repay a political debt by speaking to the Veterans of Foreign Wars convention in New Orleans. James Baker and others had argued against the speech, annoyed that Senator John Glenn of Ohio, an announced Democratic candidate for President, would be speaking the same day. But the VFW had been the only national veterans group to endorse Reagan in 1980. He wanted to thank them again. And they thanked him by setting up a fund to provide nonmilitary aid—food and medicine—for the contras. No matter how often Congress voted against his little war, Reagan was determined to keep his freedom fighters going. Despite the nibbling away of appropriations for the "covert" operations, the President left town in much better political shape than he had been the year before. Congress had rejected his budget again, approving a compromise version raising taxes by more than $74 billion over three years—the deficit forecast for 1984 was $179 billion—but both the Senate and House had let the MX missile live on, approving the manufacture of one hundred of the weapons to be placed in hardened silos. Poll numbers and national economic numbers were both going his way after months of bad news: The gross national product was growing at more than 9 percent, inflation was down to 3.5 percent, unemployment was still above 9 percent but seemed to be dropping rapidly, and mortgage interest rates had dropped from 17 to 13 percent. A *Washington Post*/ABC News poll showed the President's approval rating at 53 percent, the highest in eighteen months.

The Marines killed in Beirut on August 29—Staff Sergeant Alexander Ortega and Lieutenant George Losey—were the first American combat deaths since the United States withdrew from Vietnam in 1973. The Department of Defense announced that they had been killed in "crossfire," asserting that Americans were not being targeted. Administration spokesmen insisted day after day that the Marines were neither "combatants" nor "targets." The wording was significant because of the War Powers Resolution of 1973. At the end of the Vietnam War, a war never declared by Congress, the House and Senate passed legislation requiring the President to notify the Congress whenever American troops were in a combat situation—and that he must withdraw those troops within sixty days unless he had specific authorization from both houses. Marines being shot at in Beirut were "frosted," to use their slang, by Washington's word battles, because they were being reminded every day that they were in combat.

That same weekend, more than 200,000 people, black and white, gathered on the Mall to commemorate the twentieth anniversary of Martin Luther King's "I Have a Dream" speech to a crowd of the same size. The President was at his ranch, but the White House leaked a story saying that he was reconsidering his opposition to making King's birthday a national holiday. Conservative groups, opposed to the holiday, scheduled a "Blacks for Reagan" rally at the Lincoln Memorial on August 31. Seven people showed up.

The next day, September 1, the President was awakened again in California. The time was 7:10 A.M. and the caller was Meese telling him that a Korean airliner with 269 people aboard, one of them an American congressman, had disappeared over the Soviet Union. Secretary of State Shultz was dealing with the Soviets—and with the CIA—and was not sure what to believe from either of them. The Soviets were obviously lying. A deputy ambassador, Oleg Sokolov, came over to State from the Soviet embassy—Ambassador Dobrynin was hurrying back to the United States from a vacation at home—to say that the flight, KAL 007, had been warned that it had intruded in Soviet airspace and was last tracked over the Sea of Japan. "That is what they told me to tell you," said the Russian, who must have known the Americans already knew the plane had been shot down by a Soviet fighter plane. Shultz did know that. Intelligence briefers had information from secret American tracking stations. But he doubted those briefers were telling him the whole story. "They have no compunctions about fooling you," he told an assistant.

At 10:45 that morning, after talking again with the President, Shultz met reporters and was surprisingly specific in revealing the information gathered at Japanese installations by the CIA and the Defense Intelligence Agency:

At 1400 hours Greenwich Mean Time yesterday, a Korean Airlines Boeing 747 enroute from New York to Seoul, Korea, departed Anchorage, Alaska. Two hundred sixty-nine passengers and crew were on board, including Congressman Lawrence P. McDonald. . . .

The aircraft strayed into Soviet airspace over the Kamchatka Peninsula and over the Sea of Okhotsk and over the Sakhalin Islands. The Soviets tracked the commercial airliner for some two and a half hours. A Soviet plane reported visual contact with the aircraft at 1812 hours. The Soviet plane, we know, was in constant contact with its ground control. . . . At 1826 hours the Soviet pilot reported that he had fired a missile and the target was destroyed. At 1838 hours the Korean plane disappeared from the radar screen. . . . The United States reacts with revulsion to this attack. Loss of life appears heavy. We can see no excuse whatever for this appalling act.

After two days, the Soviets admitted shooting down the 747, declaring that the KAL plane was a spy plane for the United States, testing Soviet radar and air defense systems in restricted airspace over important military installations. Standard air maps of that part of the Soviet Union carried a blue-bordered warning: "Aircraft infringing upon non-free flying territory may be fired on without warning." There was also some speculation that the eight Soviet fighters in the air were confused because an American RC-135 reconnaissance plane had briefly flown near KAL 007 over open ocean two hours before the Korean plane went down—remotely possible, but the American surveillance plane was half the size of the Korean 747 and was already in its hangar in Alaska when KAL 007 was shot down. Even before the Soviets admitted shooting down the airliner, Secretary of State Shultz directed an impressive information war, telling his men early on, "This is not a U.S.-Soviet problem, it's a Soviets versus the world problem." Reagan's spokesman heard that in private and used it in the next press briefing, attributing it to the President. Neither Reagan nor Shultz complained.

The world held its breath. Reagan was still an anti-communist cowboy to many. French President François Mitterrand told an interviewer that he thought the world was as close to war as it had been during the Cuban Missile Crisis in 1962. Pope John Paul II said much the same. In Washington, Reagan's conservative friends were restless—Representative McDonald, a Georgia Democrat, was the national chairman of the far-right John Birch Society—and columnist George Will spoke for many when he said: "The administration is pathetic when it says this proves the President's words have been right all along. We didn't elect a dictionary. We elected a President and it's time for him to act." The *Manchester Union Leader* in New Hampshire, possibly the most conservative daily newspaper in the country, said editorially: "If someone had told us, three years ago, that the Russians could blow a civilian airliner out of the skies—and not face one whit of retaliation from a Ronald Reagan administration, we would have called that crazy. It is crazy. It is insane. It is exactly what happened."

They misunderstood their man: The conservative ideologue was only one among the old actor's many faces. Reagan preferred word wars. "We've got to protect against overreaction," he told Clark before an NSC meeting. "Vengeance isn't the name of the game." At 8 P.M. on September 5, Reagan went on national television from the Oval Office. The draft of the speech he had edited in the morning read: "My fellow Americans, I am coming before you tonight about a matter that continues to weigh heavily on our minds . . ." He crossed out those last ten words and wrote in . . . "the Korean airline massacre."

The President used strong words in condemning the Soviet action: "savagery" . . . "murderous" . . . "monstrous" . . . "an act of barbarism, born of a society which wantonly disregards individual rights and the value of human life." The most dramatic moments of the speech came when he introduced tapes of the air-to-ground radio transmissions of the Soviet fighters scrambled, that night as the Korean plane overflew Soviet territory for more than two hours, including the voice of "pilot 805," the pilot of the Su-15, as he fired two rockets at KAL 007. Translations were shown on the screen as the pilot spoke and the President listened:

"The A.N.O. (air navigation lights) are burning. The strobe light is flashing."
  "Roger, I'm at 7500, course 230."
  "I am closing on the target."
  "I have executed the launch."

"The target is destroyed."

"I am breaking off attack."

American deeds were more moderate than Reagan's words. The President announced a confusing list of wrist-slaps, actions that included continuing the ban on Soviet Aeroflot commercial flights to the United States, imposed by President Carter after the Red Army troops invaded Afghanistan in 1979, and a suspension of the negotiations on opening new consulates in Kiev and New York. He demanded an accounting and an apology to the world—the Soviets still had not admitted downing KAL 007—and reparations for the families of the passengers, sixty-one of them Americans. But he had decided not to end grain sales to the Soviets or suspend upcoming arms control negotiations in Geneva. He seemed to have won the night as surprised television commentators praised his moderation: "This was a more temperate President in dealing with the Soviet Union," said Tom Brokaw of NBC News.

But he lost the morning. The count of telephone calls to the White House went against Reagan for the first time, with 308 callers praising the speech and 489 demanding stronger action, right up to bombing Moscow. In an odd turn, Larry Speakes dismissed the number of negative calls as part of a right-wing campaign to make the President look bad. Then he recommended to Baker and Gergen that in the future the White House should use the Office of Public Liaison and the Republican National Committee to organize callers supporting the President to make sure that positive calls would always outweigh negative ones. At the same time, *The New York Times* lead editorial said: "What has been so admirable about President Reagan's performance so far is his insistence on arguing from the evidence and tailoring his actions to the problem at hand."

The *Times*'s lead story on September 7 was under the headline:

MOSCOW CONCEDES
A SOVIET FIGHTER
DOWNED AIRLINER

Government Statement

Citing an Investigation, It Says
The Pilot 'Could Not Know'
Target Was a Civil Plane

The off-lead headline was:

> ### Druse Take Key Mountain Town
> ### After Heavy Fighting in Lebanon
>
> ### Fierce Battles Continue Near Beirut's Airport
>
> ### 2 More U.S. Marines Killed and 3 Wounded

The Marines were being shelled around the clock by artillery, rockets, and mortar fire coming from the Shouf Mountains, where the Druse, LAF, and Christian militias were all trying to take over abandoned Israeli positions. The Americans seemed to be caught on the wrong side of the civil war. "Some Marines 'Feel Helpless' " headlined the *Times* on September 7. But the White House continued to maintain that those Americans crouched behind sandbags were not in combat.

The President himself made a show of announcing that ships with two thousand more Marines were steaming toward Lebanon, along with the world's last surviving battleship, the USS *New Jersey*, a forty-one-year-old World War II veteran refitted in 1982 at a cost of $326 million. "I've had the strange feeling that I'm back on the set filming *Hellcats of the Navy*," said Reagan as he sent the *New Jersey* off to the Mediterranean.

On September 10, the President signed NSDD 103, "Strategy for Lebanon," making official his earlier statements about the mission of the Marines:

> Our objectives in Lebanon remain: (a) to restore the sovereignty of the Government of Lebanon throughout its territory, (b) obtaining the complete withdrawal of all foreign forces, and (c) ensuring the security of Lebanon's borders, especially the northern border of Israel. In support of our objectives, the mission of the U.S. contingent in the Multi-national Force is to support the Government of Lebanon in deterring hostilities by maintaining an active presence in the Greater Beirut area.

That night, McFarlane, staying at the American ambassador's house in the foothills of the Shouf, watched the fire in the sky as the LAF's best unit, the American-trained Eighth Brigade, and the Muslims—Sunnis and Shiites, Palestinians, Syrians, and Iranians working together—fought for hours over one of the positions abandoned by the Israelis, a town called Suq-al-Gharb. The fighting was only three miles from the residence. A mortar shell landed near the swimming pool of the courtyard. The President's special representative ended the night in a shelter the size of a closet. The next day, September 11, he sent a FLASH cable to Washington, saying:

> There is a serious threat of a decisive military defeat which could involve the fall of the Government of Lebanon within twenty-four hours. Last night's battle was waged within five kilometers of the Presidential Palace. For those at the State Department, this would correlate to an enemy attacking from Capitol Hill. This is an action message. A second attack against the same Lebanese Armed Forces unit is expected this evening. Ammunition and morale are very low and raise the serious possibility that an enemy brigade . . . will break through and penetrate the Beirut perimeter. In short, tonight we could be in enemy lines.

Clark, Shultz, and Weinberger trooped into the Oval Office, with the Secretary of Defense saying the Marines did not back what he called "The sky-is-falling cable." The Marine commander on the ground, Colonel Timothy Geraghty, thought McFarlane's request for naval gunfire would bring the United States into the war as full partners of the Christians—and that a lot of his Marines would die on the losing side of a civil war. "We'll be slaughtered down here," Geraghty yelled at one of McFarlane's assistants. But Clark and Shultz won the morning in Washington. The President signed an amendment to NSDD 103 giving permission for American commanders to aid the LAF in the mountains: "Assistance for this specific objective may include naval gun fire support and, if deemed necessary, tactical air strikes, but shall exclude ground forces."

The colonel, who believed the Eighth Brigade could hold the town, won the night. The firing began again at dusk—mortar rounds were again hitting the American compound—but Geraghty refused McFarlane's requests to call in the Navy and its big guns. McFarlane telephoned his boss, Judge Clark, saying: "Our basic strategy is on the line here. . . . Even if Cap Weinberger will not endorse my conclusions regarding the political process we've set in motion here, which Assad is trying to destroy, you do face the undeniable reality that

Americans are also under fire and the existing rules of engagement provide authority for returning fire."

McFarlane won the week. In an opening salvo on September 16, the frigate *John Rodgers* fired 60 five-inch rounds in support of the LAF, trying to destroy Druse positions in the Shouf. The United States was in the war; certainly the Marines in Beirut were. But Washington was another world. With his men pinned down on flat ground in bunkers and trenches, the Commandant of the Marine Corps, General Paul Kelley, appeared before a congressional committee to say: "There is not a significant danger at this time to our Marines . . . no evidence that any of the rocket or artillery fire has been specifically directed against Marines."

That was the White House line, opposed by Weinberger, who was angry at the obvious mission creep drawing the Marines into a civil war. The President's priority was different; he wanted to avoid triggering the War Powers Act of 1973. Invoking the law, Reagan said more than once, would send "extremely dangerous signals . . . to Syria and the Soviet Union."

On September 19, as Muslim tanks moved toward LAF positions in Suq-al-Gharb, Colonel Geraghty requested Navy fire. The *Rodgers,* the cruiser *Virginia,* and the destroyer *Bowen* began dropping 338 five-inch rounds on Muslim positions in the mountains in direct support of the LAF. A dozen Marines and U.S. Army officers were in the Shouf with the LAF, choosing targets for the ship. In the air, Navy F-4 Tomcats and larger carrier-based aircraft circled over the sea and the mountains but did not attack.

But KAL 007 was bigger news than that. In New York, United Nations debates continued, with an overwhelming majority of countries standing with South Korea and the United States against the Soviets. But there was criticism of a State Department ruling that the Aeroflot flight carrying Soviet Foreign Minister Andrei Gromyko to New York had to land at a military base rather than Kennedy Airport. An American delegate, Charles Lichtenstein, responded by saying that if diplomats did not like the United States role as host country, they should move the United Nations to another country. "The United States strongly encourages such member states seriously to consider removing themselves and this organization from the soil of the United States," said Lichtenstein. "The members of the U.S. mission to the United States will be down at dockside waving you a fond farewell as you sail into the sunset."

White House spokesmen quickly tried to play the thing down—"a personal opinion" was the guidance in a press office memo—until a reporter asked the President what he thought. Without guidance, Reagan said: "I think that the gentleman who spoke the other day had the hearty approval of most people in America in his suggestion that we weren't asking anyone to leave, but if they chose to leave, good-bye." Then the Senate by 66 to 23 voted to cut United Nations funding by 20 percent immediately, with reductions rising to 50 percent in three years.

As for the American shelling of Suq-al-Gharb, White House spokesman Speakes once again called it self-defense, then added, perhaps in absolute ignorance of what was actually happening: "The shelling out of the mountains is not directed at U.S. troops or diplomats and for that reason, U.S. personnel are not in a situation of imminent hostilities."

"Imminent hostilities" was part of the language of the War Powers Act. The next day, September 20, a day the U.S. ambassador's residence was hit by artillery and a Navy F-14 Tomcat was fired on from West Beirut, the administration worked out a compromise with the Congress on War Powers. The Marines were authorized to stay in Beirut for eighteen additional months. The fight between Congress and the President had been about Washington, not Lebanon. As they voted, Senate liberals declared their support for American troops and the mission. House Speaker O'Neill declared: "It would be unwise for the United States to ever cut and run." The vote seemed to end a tense debate over the war-making powers of the President and Congress, but Reagan started it all over again by doing one thing and saying another, a tactic he regularly used: "I do not and cannot cede any of the authority vested in me under the Constitution as President and as Commander-in-Chief of United States Armed Forces."

Some comic relief was provided the same day, by Secretary of the Interior Watt, who finally went too far with a nasty joke during a speech to the U.S. Chamber of Commerce. Forced by congressional action to appoint a commission to study the leasing of federal land in North Dakota to coal-mining companies, he cracked: "I appointed five members . . . I have a woman, two blacks, a Jew and a cripple."

On September 21, the President invited regional editors in for a question-and-answer session at the White House. Most of the questions were about Lebanon, but one editor asked: "Yesterday the

Philippine president, President Marcos, said that if you cancelled your trip to the Philippines that would be 'a slap in the face.' "

"There are no plans to change the trip," Reagan said. But pressure to cancel the November visit had been building since the assassination of Benigno Aquino as he was led off a plane from the United States on August 21. Aquino, a fifty-year-old member of the Senate until President Ferdinand Marcos declared martial law in 1972, was considered the most popular opposition leader in the country. For the past three years, he had been in self-exile in Boston, but had decided to return home because he believed that Marcos, not in the best of health at sixty-five, was losing his grip on the power he had exercised since taking over in 1965. As several thousand supporters waited for him in the terminal, Aquino was escorted off the China Airways plane by three uniformed soldiers and taken down a stairway off the jetway. When he stepped onto the tarmac, he was shot in the back of the head by a man in a mechanic's uniform—then the assassin was killed by the soldiers.*

The President considered Marcos a friend and a kindred anti-communist soul. The Reagans had stayed with the Marcos family at the Malacanang Palace in Manila four times, the first in 1969, when he was governor of California. President Nixon sent the Reagans to the Philippines, the first trip overseas for either of them in twenty years. The governor's job there was to represent the United States at the opening of a Culture Center on Manila Bay, a project sponsored by Marcos's flamboyant wife, Imelda. A signed photograph of the Marcoses held a place of honor on top of the unused grand piano in the Reagans' Pacific Palisades home. The United States and the Philippines had an intertwined history, which included occupation after the Spanish-American War. "Our little brown brothers" was the phrase used in those days. "A very special relationship," Secretary of State Shultz had said in a toast in Manila in late June. Earlier, in another toast, Vice President Bush had said: "We love you for your adherence to democratic principles and to the democratic process." In addition

---

* On October 3, Mike Deaver was dispatched to Manila to hand-deliver a letter from Reagan to Marcos canceling the trip: "I want you to know I've always had confidence in your ability to handle things. . . . Now, however, a new problem has arisen which is going to force us to postpone the entire trip to your beautiful country. . . . We had planned our trip for November on the assumption that Congress would have ended its work but they will be in session through November. . . . We both look forward to seeing you when a mutually acceptable date can be set."

to substantial foreign aid, the United States was paying $900 million in rent to the Philippine government for two of its largest military bases, Clark Air Base and the Subic Bay naval base. Besides all that, Aquino, in exile and teaching at Harvard, had been critical of Reagan, saying: "Americans taught us for fifty years to love freedom. . . . But America does not really appreciate the values of democracy. America is only standing for a strategic interest—this happened in Iran, it happened in Nicaragua. It's happened everywhere."

After Aquino was killed, Reagan met with Shultz, but the subject quickly shifted to Lebanon, where American ships were firing hundreds of shells into the Shouf. Both men were determined to stand fast, seeing the situation not as a civil war but as part of the worldwide battle against communism. "Are we going to let the Syrians and the Soviets take over?" asked Reagan. CIA reports he received detailed $2 billion in Soviet military aid to Syria and counted seven thousand Soviet trainers in that country. "Are we just going to let it happen?"

On September 25, after McFarlane had spent a good part of the day with Assad in Damascus, he returned to the residence, where his wife, Jonny, was also staying. There had been ferocious little firefights all day between the Marines at the airport and Amal Shiite militias firing from buildings a hundred yards away in the slums of a neighborhood called Hay-es-Salaam. That was the place Marines called "Khomeiniville," dirty streets where posters of the Iranian ayatollah decorated walls all around. Fighting began again in the mountains that night and shells were once again landing in the American ambassador's compound. McFarlane went to a telephone. His wife asked whom he was calling and he said, "Jim." She knew that meant their minister, Dr. James Macdonnell, at St. Mark Presbyterian Church outside Washington. It was Sunday and Macdonnell interrupted his sermon to take the call.

"Jim, I really need your help. We've got a shot at a ceasefire here in Lebanon that will go one way or the other within 24 hours. Could I ask you to pray for it and ask the congregation to join in?"

"Let's go for a swim," he said to Jonny. They swept away shrapnel near the pool and dove in. "I think it's going to be all right."

Assad and Gemayel did agree to a cease-fire the next day. It lasted, more or less, for a couple of days.

Two more Marines were killed in action and several more wounded during the first two weeks of October. A lot more Amal warriors were killed as junior officers began unofficially rewriting the rules of engagement to let their men fire at any bad guys they could get in their sights. On October 8, in the President's weekly radio address, was another escalation in rhetoric: "Can the United States or the free world stand by and see the Middle East incorporated into the Soviet bloc?"

A French soldier had also been killed and French warplanes were attacking mountain positions in retaliation. In Washington, where the President had approved the decision in NSDD 103, only Weinberger continued to argue against the engagement. At a National Security Council meeting on October 18, the Defense Secretary maintained again that the Marines should be immediately removed to the ships offshore. He repeated that the Joint Chiefs of Staff agreed—and, once again, he lost that argument. Reagan ignored him. The next day two more Marines were killed by Amal snipers firing from Khomeiniville. That made six and the President personally called each of their families. Colonel Geraghty came within seconds of being killed. Just after his jeep passed a parked white Mercedes-Benz, the car exploded. It was the first time the Americans had seen a car bomb.

Colonel Geraghty did not talk about it, but he blamed Bud McFarlane personally for the new dangers his men were facing. But, in fact, Clark and McFarlane believed they were only following orders from the President. "Something's got to be done," Reagan had said almost a month earlier, on September 11. It was a Sunday and the President spent the day going over road maps of Lebanon, carefully marking out the positions of a dozen groups of troops and militias, choosing targets that he was told had to be hit to save the Lebanese army and the country's Christians.

That night he had begun his diary entry: "Troops obviously PLO and Syrian have launched a new attack against the Lebanese Army. Our problem is do we expand our mission to aid the Lebanese army with artillery and air support? This could be seen as putting us in the war."

He ended that entry: "I've called for use of Navy fire power and air strikes if needed."

In fact, the Marines had been in a war for weeks, even if most of the time they were prohibited from using most of their weapons. And the Navy, firing from afar, had been killing Muslims in the mountains since the second week in September.

On October 13, Bill Clark abruptly resigned as National Security Adviser. In fact, no one knew he had resigned until the President, taking questions after a speech to a Christian women's group, praised Clark as a "God-fearing Westerner," and then casually announced that Clark was replacing Watt as Secretary of the Interior. The move stunned political Washington, which had no notion of the collusion between Nancy Reagan and George Shultz to push out Clark. The wife who wanted her husband to be seen as a peacemaker thought Clark was too much of a warrior; Shultz thought he was too ignorant of foreign affairs. Baker and Deaver also had reasons to get Clark out. Baker wanted the NSC job and Deaver wanted to be chief of staff. Reagan approved the three-way switch and the announcement was scheduled for 4 P.M. on October 14. Walking to a one o'clock meeting with Clark, Reagan told him of the Baker-Deaver moves. "Can we talk before you announce that?" Clark said. Then Clark called Meese, Weinberger, and Casey, who were also unaware of what was about to happen. The four hawks faced off with their boss in Clark's small office. They attacked Baker, calling him "our leaker-in-charge" and saying that the appointment of a pragmatist would signal the world that the administration was going soft on the Soviets.

The President called in Baker and Deaver, and told them there would be no announcement yet. "The fellas have a real problem with this," Reagan began. "I want to think about it over the weekend." He wrote in his diary that night: "Jim took it well but Mike was pretty upset." On Monday, back from Camp David, the President announced that McFarlane would replace Clark at NSC.

On October 19, the one thousandth day of the Reagan presidency, a fourteen-page "Memorandum for Administration Spokesman" circulated in the White House and the Washington outposts of the executive branch. The highlights were the drop of the inflation rate to 2.6 percent, a drop in the prime interest rate to 11 percent, a quarterly 7.9 percent growth in gross national product, and the creation of 300,000 new jobs in the past month. Unmentioned were an unemployment rate stuck at 10 percent and a $195 billion deficit for the fiscal year.

That evening Reagan held his twentieth news conference, the first one since the end of July. He opened with a statement declaring economic victory. The questions focused on foreign policy, particularly in Lebanon, and on the fact that Reagan had reversed his opposition to creating a national holiday in honor of Martin Luther King. As he had done on War Powers questions, he wanted to have it both ways. He said he would sign the bill authorizing the holiday, but when a reporter asked about his reaction to charges by Senator Jesse Helms of North Carolina that King was a communist or a communist sympathizer, the President said: "We'll know in about 35 years, won't we?" That was roughly when the Federal Bureau of Investigation was scheduled to release classified records of their long surveillance of the civil rights leader.

Reagan avoided most of the questions about the risks facing the Marines on the flat, sandy plain of the Beirut airport. One reporter asked whether he saw parallels between the Marine deployment and the surrounded French army that had been almost destroyed at Dien Bien Phu in 1954 when the Vietnamese fired on their position from surrounding hills. "No," said Reagan, asserting that the Marines were being fired on from the flats as well as from the hills, then added: "Maybe the French in that terrible defeat didn't have a *New Jersey* sitting offshore as we do."

On October 21, the President flew to the Augusta National Golf Club in Georgia for a weekend of golf with Secretary of State Shultz, Secretary of the Treasury Donald Regan, and a former senator from New Jersey, Nicholas Brady. He was awakened just before 4 A.M. by McFarlane, who then came to the "Eisenhower Cottage," the six-room house the former President used on his regular Augusta trips, where the Reagans were staying. In his pajamas and robe, Reagan listened as Shultz and McFarlane briefed him on events, not in Lebanon but in Grenada. The Prime Minister there, Maurice Bishop, an anti-American Marxist who had seized power in a 1979 coup, had apparently been killed the day before by a group of harder-line communists in another coup. The island, said McFarlane, was in chaos and the one thousand or so Americans there, including 250 students at the St. George's School of Medicine, might be in danger. The NSC had already worked out an arrangement encouraging the Organisation of Eastern Caribbean States, a two-year-old alliance of six island countries with fewer than one thousand troops of their own, to invite United States troops to intervene militarily—and that invitation, a bit of legalistic cover, had just been cabled to Vice President Bush in Washington.

It was an opportunity the President had been thinking about for months. As far back as February, as Bishop's government publicly proclaimed that the United States was preparing to invade the island, the White House had begun quietly sounding out the Senate Intelligence Committee about undermining Bishop's government. The idea died because important senators had declared they would not support the plan. As in Central America, the National Security Council then prepared "Top Secret" covert plans, incorporated in NSDD 105, which Reagan had signed on October 4, to use the CIA to destabilize both the Bishop government and the island's tiny economy. With that authorization, an NSC "Pre-crisis Group," headed by McFarlane's new deputy, Rear Admiral John Poindexter, monitored events on Grenada at weekly meetings. An estimated 110,000 people lived on the 133-square-mile island, the smallest independent country in the Western Hemisphere. The President's interest, as he had broadcast six months earlier, was focused on the new ten-thousand-foot airport runway being constructed with the help of several hundred Cuban workers on the southern tip of the island. Bishop had claimed that the strip was for jumbo tourist jets; the CIA said it was to handle Soviet military aircraft.

After hearing out Shultz and McFarlane at Augusta, the President said, "Do it."

McFarlane called Bush and the President took the phone, saying: "OK George, tell Mrs. Charles"—Prime Minister Eugenia Charles of Dominica was chairperson of the OECS—"that we recognize the problem, we'll be glad to respond."

Then he went back to bed. In Washington, an NSC team headed by Constantine Menges and Oliver North was drawing up NSDD 110 authorizing military action against Grenada. A ten-ship flotilla, which had left Norfolk, Virginia, on October 18, sailing east in a protective circle around the aircraft carrier *Independence,* had already shifted course from east to south and suspended radio transmission. The nineteen hundred Marines on those ships, the 22nd Marine Amphibious Unit, were being transported to Lebanon to relieve the 24th MAU in the first week of November. Only their officers knew what was happening as the ships turned toward the lower Caribbean: "Urgent Fury." That was the code name for the mission to rescue the medical students and take control of Grenada. What was urgent aboard the ships was finding maps of the island. The men of the hour were a Navy commander and a British Royal Marine observer. The Navy man had recently vacationed on Grenada and the British Marine had once sailed around the island.

Reagan slept for only an hour more after ordering the Grenada operation, then he got up to play golf. At the sixteenth hole, Secret Service agents ran across the green to surround the President—and then put him in an armored limousine. An armed man had smashed his pickup truck through a gate and taken over the pro shop, holding seven hostages there, including two White House staffers. He wanted to talk to the President. Back in his cottage, Reagan called the shop five times, each time saying "This is Ronald Reagan." Each time the man hung up, saying he had to see the President in person. That was not going to happen, but the Reagans were confined to their cottage until the hostage-taker gave up peacefully. The Reagans went to bed at 10 P.M.

At 2:27 A.M. in Augusta, the President's phone rang. It was McFarlane. "Mr. President, I have bad news . . ." he began. At 6:22 A.M. Sunday in Beirut, a suicide bomber in a truck carrying six tons of high explosives encased in canisters of flammable gas had crashed through the guardpost, an eight-foot-high plywood kiosk surrounded by a four-foot-high sandbag wall—the Marine guards had no bullets in their rifles—roared into the interior floor-to-roof lobby of the four-story Marine barracks at the Beirut airport, and stopped. The driver then blew up his truck. The steel-reinforced concrete building lifted off its foundation, then collapsed on itself and on the 350 Marines sleeping in converted offices inside the building. Dozens, probably hundreds, of young Americans were dead under the rubble. Rockets and shells stored inside the building were firing off in the heat. There were unattached hands, arms, legs, and heads on top of the broken concrete of the building. Seismic readings indicated it was the largest nonnuclear device ever recorded. Two minutes later, another suicide bomb exploded at French MNF headquarters two miles away. More than half the 110 men sleeping there were believed dead in the rubble.

CHAPTER 9

FEBRUARY 26, 1984

PRESIDENT REAGAN FLEW FROM AUGUSTA BACK to Washington at first light on the morning of October 23, 1983. It was already midday in Europe, another day of massive protests against the deployment of new American intermediate-range missiles in West Germany. More than a million people were in the streets of London, Rome, Vienna, and other cities across the continent. But the grim conversations aboard Air Force One focused on Beirut. Arriving at a National Security Council meeting, Reagan sat for two hours, from 8:40 to 10:40 A.M., being handed one cable after another recording the Marine death toll until it passed two hundred. "This is an obvious attempt to run us out of Lebanon," he said more than once. "The first thing I want to do is find out who did it and go after them with everything we've got."

A public statement was released by the White House press office saying: "Those who sponsor these outrages believe they can intimidate the Government of Lebanon, its people, and their friends in the international community. They are wrong. We will not yield to international terrorism." In a cable that night to President Gemayel, Reagan wrote: "This vicious attack will not cause the United States to weaken its resolve. . . . We will not be intimidated." *

The next day, Monday, October 24, the President was more specific as he took questions from regional television correspondents: "The option we cannot consider is withdrawing while the mission still remains. . . . We have vital interests in Lebanon. . . . Peace in Lebanon is key. It is central to our credibility on a global scale."

---

* The final American death toll in the Beirut bombing was 241. The French lost 58 men in the simultaneous bombing of their Beirut headquarters.

Meanwhile, the American flotilla continued its detour to Grenada. A short CBS News report of the ships' Sunday night activity was not followed up by other news organizations. The secret was holding well enough, at least in the United States. By the end of the day, however, Cuban radio had begun reporting on American ship movements, and officials in Barbados reported that fifty United States Marines had flown in on military transports and then left immediately on helicopters. *The Washington Post* played that news on page fourteen the next morning, as the White House and the Pentagon were being questioned by news organizations about whether anything was being done to protect Americans on Grenada. Actually, the United States ambassador to Barbados, Milan Bish, unaware of everything going on in Washington, was negotiating with the Cunard Line to charter a cruise ship—*The Countess*—to evacuate Americans from Grenada, particularly the medical students at St. George's University. The *Post* also reported in a separate story, on page four, that Navy ships that had been bound for Lebanon were on station near Grenada. But a page-one map and story in *The New York Times* reported those same ships loaded with Marines were now in the Atlantic headed for Lebanon. The big stories in Washington were still the Beirut body count and questions about overall Middle East strategy—and the impact on Reagan and his future.

The President was meeting that morning with members of the National Security Council and the chairman of the Joint Chiefs of Staff, General John Vessey, for sketchy briefings on the invasion of Grenada. He was not paying much attention to them—at least that's how it seemed. When they were about to leave, Reagan asked Vessey: "What did you say the number of troops was?"

Vessey gave him the number.

"Double it," said the President.

"Excuse me, sir? Why?"

"Because if Jimmy Carter had used eighteen helicopters for Desert One instead of nine"—the catastrophic hostage rescue mission in Iran—"you'd be briefing him now instead of me."

In another part of the White House, Speakes was asked by Bill Plante of CBS News about the Cuban reports that an invasion of Grenada was imminent. Speakes went to the new deputy national security adviser, John Poindexter, who lied to him. Speakes came back and told Plante, "That's preposterous! Don't go with that."

So there were no Grenada stories on television that night. Lebanon was the lead on the *CBS Evening News*. Tom Fenton, reporting that the number of Marines in Beirut had grown to eighteen hundred, said: "The Marines rely on the inexperienced Lebanese army to check vehicles. Today, all kinds of vehicles were being waved right through without the slightest verification. . . . The question remains: What are the Marines doing in Beirut? They're here to prop up a government that still controls only a part of Beirut and none of the rest of the country, and are being told to do it sitting at the Beirut airport, where they become prime targets." On ABC's *World News Tonight,* Richard Threlkeld was even harsher: "Tennyson would have understood it. Theirs not to reason why, theirs but to do and die."

Later that night, five congressional leaders were driven, secretly and separately, to the Old Executive Office Building. They were walked through empty corridors and offices to the White House residence, where they were met by the President, Cabinet members, and the Joint Chiefs of Staff. They expected to be briefed on Lebanon. Instead, in a ninety-minute meeting, Reagan told them the Marines, the 22nd Marine Amphibious Unit, were about to land in Grenada. Speaker O'Neill, who was sitting next to Reagan, said: "You are informing us, not asking us."

"Yes," Reagan said. The Speaker touched Reagan's arm reassuringly several times as the President talked about the medical students, the airport, Cuban workers and soldiers, and Soviet advisers. Then Reagan told a story about Filipinos greeting Americans on the beaches near the end of World War II, waving flags and throwing flowers. That sounded like an old movie to O'Neill, but Reagan said he thought that would happen in Grenada. And in Beirut, too. He added: "I can see the day, not too many weeks from now when the Lebanese people will be standing at the shore, waving and cheering our Marines when they depart." At one point the President left the room to take a very angry telephone call from Prime Minister Margaret Thatcher in London. She had just learned of the invasion plans—Grenada was a former British colony and still a member of the Commonwealth—and demanded that the Americans pull back. At points, the hard-of-hearing President had to pull the phone away from his ear as the Prime Minister let him know what she thought of the American plans.

When Reagan came back, O'Neill banged the table in front of him at one point and said with passion: "Mr. President you are going to have to tell America why Americans are in Lebanon!" Reagan was taken aback by the vehemence, but before he could respond, the Republican Senate Majority Leader, Howard Baker, said: "Mr. President, he's not being critical. He's one of your strongest supporters. . . . He's trying to give you the facts of life." As the meeting broke up, O'Neill reached for Reagan's arm one more time and said: "Good luck!" The Speaker thought staying in Lebanon was a blunder, a tragic one, but the next day, in the most emotional performance any of his Democrats had ever seen, O'Neill told a closed caucus that this was no time to undermine the President, ending with a call for "patriotism over partisanship."

More than two thousand miles to the south, Marine company commanders, flown by helicopter to the cruiser USS *Trenton,* were being read the mission statement by Lieutenant Colonel Ray Smith:

> Conduct amphibious/helo landing to secure Pearls Airfield and Grenville in order to assist in the peaceful evacuation of US and foreign nationals. We will neutralize the Grenadian Army, evacuate the American citizens and restore peace to the country. . . . Seize the populated areas before any significant resistance can be mounted. I'm concerned about the strength of Cuban forces on the island. Some intelligence reports list them as regulars, and there is a Cuban ship in port, the *Vietnam Heroico.*

Smith paused, puffed on a cigar, and said: "I don't want anyone talking to the press. I want all the Marines to treat the Grenadians with respect and tell them we're here to help them." He paused. "Tell your Marines we're going to attack a communist country and this time we're going to kick some ass!"

The next morning's *New York Times* still showed the 22nd Marine Amphibious Unit out in the Atlantic. Five of the seven front-page stories focused on the Beirut bombing and its aftermath. "The devastating bomb blast in Lebanon has left President Reagan a man under siege, tested politically and personally more severely than at any other time in his tenure," wrote Hedrick Smith in a front-page *Times* analysis. "He looked exhausted, emotionally drained, even old for the first time in his Presidency when he stepped from his helicopter at the White House Sunday morning."

On Tuesday morning, Reagan looked better. At 9 A.M., correspondents were alerted that the President would be coming to the White House press room. He arrived with a black woman no one there had ever seen before. "Early this morning forces from six Caribbean democracies and the United States began a landing or landings on the island of Grenada in the Eastern Caribbean," the President announced. "The United States' objectives are clear: to protect our own citizens, to facilitate the evacuation of those who want to leave, and to help in the restoration of democratic institutions in Grenada." Then he said, "I'm very proud to present to you the Chairman of the Organisation of Eastern Caribbean States and the Prime Minister of Dominica, Prime Minister Eugenia Charles."

A reporter asked Mrs. Charles: "Do you think the United States has the right to invade another country to change its government?"

"I don't think it's an invasion," she began. "This is a question of our asking for support. We are one region. Grenada is kith and kin . . . part and parcel of us."

Reagan added that the United States action, which began with helicopter and parachute landings at 4 A.M. Washington time, was justified because of a mutual support treaty signed when the British gave the island countries their independence in 1974. That was a stretch—the OECS was American inspired—and the President made a couple of other mistakes in the press room. Caribbean troops—including units from two countries not part of OECS, Jamaica and Barbados—were not part of the invasion; they would be flown in after Americans had taken the island. And he was wrong when he announced that St. George's School of Medicine had been secured as the invasion's first priority.

Three hundred and fifty Army Rangers, flown from Savannah, Georgia, parachuted onto the ten-thousand-foot runway still under construction south of St. George's city, taking heavy fire from the ground, and evacuated 130 American students. Then they learned that the medical school had two campuses on the island and that two hundred more Americans might be in danger four miles away. Ground troops were not able to break through lines manned by Cuban fighters and the second campus was not taken until thirty hours later with helicopter landings. All the students were safe, but five Rangers were killed in those operations.

It was a long day for Reagan. He ended it with a nineteen-minute telephone conversation with one of his more important foreign policy advisers, former President Richard Nixon. And he made up with Prime Minister Thatcher in a ten-minute "Ron" and "Margaret" conversation. "If I were there, Margaret, I'd throw my hat in the door before I came in." It ended when she said she had to get back to Parliament, saying, "It's a bit tricky there." Reagan said: "All right. Go get 'em. Eat 'em alive."

The next morning's *New York Times* carried a three-deck headline across the six columns on top of the front page:

> 1,900 U.S. TROOPS, WITH CARIBBEAN ALLIES,
> INVADE GRENADA AND FIGHT LEFTIST UNITS;
> MOSCOW PROTESTS; BRITISH ARE CRITICAL

There were five Grenada stories and a large map of the island under the headline; the other two front-page stories, with single-column headlines, were about Lebanon. One reported that the death toll in the Beirut bombing had reached 216, with 20 or 30 Marines still missing. The other was about the funeral of one of the Marines in Connecticut. Though reinforcements were not announced in Washington, the number of Americans in the Grenada force rose to 7,600 the first day—1,800 Marines from the 22nd MAU, 700 Army Rangers flown in from the United States, almost 100 Navy SEALs with their own small boats, and 5,000 paratroopers from the 82nd Airborne Division. The original number of paratroopers, 1,600, was increased after some fierce resistance persuaded commanders that there might be 1,000 or more trained Cuban soldiers on the island, along with 2,000 Grenadian troops. The NSC passed a radio message from General Jack Merritt, the Joint Chiefs' man on the scene, to the President at 9 P.M.: "It appears that Cuban workers were actually soldiers. . . . We may be in for a longer fight than planned."

A few Democrats in Congress noted the newsplay with quotes such as this from Senator Lawton Chiles of Florida: "One day we've got the numbers of Marine deaths which shocked us all, the next day we find we're invading Grenada. Are we looking for a war we can win?" But Speaker O'Neill responded quite differently, saying: "It is no time for the press of America or we in public life to be critical of our government when our Marines and Rangers are down there."

Walter Mondale, Jimmy Carter's Vice President and now the front-runner in national polls among the Democrats who might run against Reagan in 1984, emphasized what he called the "considerable dispute" over whether any Americans in Grenada were actually in danger, saying: "If American citizens were not in danger, how can we justify the invasion under international law?" The founder and president of St. George's School of Medicine, which served students rejected by medical schools at home, a Long Island businessman named Charles Modica, reinforced that argument, saying there was no threat to his students and that the new government in Grenada was allowing foreigners to leave.*

In fact, as the students were returning on Air Force planes, the White House press office confirmed Cuban reports that two days before the invasion the self-proclaimed government of Grenada, calling itself the Revolutionary Military Council, had indeed officially offered to allow American planes in to evacuate all American citizens who wanted to leave. The United States never responded. Those arguments ended in a single moment on national television: The first student back in the United States, Jeff Geller of Woodridge, New York, came running down the stairway of a rescue plane, an Air Force C-141 that landed in Charleston, South Carolina, kneeled and kissed the ground, letting out a whoop of joy at being home. Jean Joel of Albany, New York, followed him and said: "I don't think there's any more beautiful sight than the United States. And the Rangers who arrived to save us."

The happy students were all that Americans, including the President, saw on their televisions that first day. There were no television cameras and no reporters on Grenada. The military had sealed off the island. When Navy pilots spotted and buzzed a small boat chartered by NBC News, a patrol boat was sent to turn the NBC crew back to wherever it came from. The sailors were under orders from the commander of the Grenada Task Force, Admiral Joseph Metcalf III, to blow the boat out of the water if it continued toward the island. Three American reporters already on the island, from *The Washington Post, Newsday,* and the *Miami Herald,* along with a British writer, were seized by Marines and flown to the USS *Guam*—"For their own safety," announced the Pentagon—where they were held and prohibited from calling office or home.

Three hundred and twenty-five correspondents congregated—"crazed" was *The Washington Post*'s description of them—in Bridgetown, Barbados, watching U.S. planes and helicopters take over the airport there. When photographers tried to photograph landings and takeoffs, Barbadan soldiers grabbed their film and cameras, stripping

---

* Modica changed his mind two days later, saying: "I was given new information I was not aware of. . . . I feel Mr. Reagan was justified in making the decision he made."

several American photographers naked to search for hidden film cans. Officials from the United States embassy tried to tear notebooks out of reporters' hands.

American journalists were reduced to covering the little war by repeating Pentagon handouts and what they heard from ham radio operators on the invaded island 150 miles away. Their most reliable source was the enemy, Radio Havana, which was reporting the action from Grenada. After two days of that, an Army captain named Dean Chamberlain appeared with a mimeographed release covering two days of action—the entire war, really. It said: "Between Oct. 25 and Oct. 27, all major military objectives on the island of Grenada are secured. . . . Our forces have been well received by a friendly populous [sic]."

Finally, the military began taking small press pools, a half-dozen or so reporters and photographers at a time, by helicopter to Grenada, where they were given guided tours and brought back to Bridgetown to brief colleagues—after the day's newspaper and television deadlines. "This action raises the suspicion that the Reagan administration did not want independent observers on the scene, but sought to shape the news flow to Americans," the *Los Angeles Times* said in an oddly understated editorial. In the White House, the communications director, David Gergen, sent James Baker a memo saying: "Military-Press Dialogue: It would take some of the sting out of current bitterness if someone like Secretary Weinberger were to call in the heads of major press organizations." Baker answered, "Do nothing." Weinberger said, "No."

White House reporters were asking Speakes whether he intended to resign after being lied to by Poindexter and passing along the lie to CBS. He said, "No." He loved the job too much. He blamed Baker for his troubles, convinced that the chief of staff had ordered the NSC deputy to lie. He sent a sad memo to Baker, Meese, Deaver, and McFarlane when he learned of the invasion—Baker told him about it after it began—saying: "I was given virtually no information regarding the Grenada action—either before or after. What I was given yesterday was grossly misleading. In today's briefing my credibility was called into serious question. I can take that. That's what I am paid to do. More seriously, the Reagan administration was accused of lying or deliberately misleading the public. This we cannot stand." Secretary of State Shultz could. Asked about banning reporters, he told *The Washington Post,* "Reporters are always against us and so they're always seeking to report something that's going to screw things up."

The President—happy to hear that Grenadians were calling him "Uncle Reagan"—went on prime-time television on October 27. He spoke just two hours after the military declared it controlled all military positions on the island, to talk about both Grenada and Lebanon. Reagan was at his best, switching back and forth between narrative and patriotism and idealism, ending with passion and prayer:

> This past Sunday, at 22 minutes after six, Beirut time, with dawn just breaking, a truck, looking like a lot of other vehicles in the city, approached the airport on a busy main road. . . . Why are we there? Well the answer is straightforward: to help bring peace to Lebanon and stability to the Middle East. . . . The multinational force was attacked precisely because it is doing the job it was sent to do in Beirut. It is accomplishing its mission. . . . Brave young men have been taken from us. Many others have been grievously wounded. Are we to tell them their sacrifice was wasteful? We must not strip every ounce of meaning and purpose from their courageous sacrifice.

Then he switched countries, talking of the confrontation of Marxists on Grenada:

> A crowd of citizens appeared before Bishop's home, freed him, and escorted him toward the headquarters of the military council. They were fired upon. A number, including some children, were killed, and Bishop was seized. He and several members of his cabinet were subsequently executed, and a 24-hour, shoot-to-kill curfew was put in effect. Grenada was without a government. . . . One thousand of our citizens on Grenada, 800 of them students. . . . Concerned that they'd be harmed or held as hostages, I ordered a flotilla of ships. . . . I will not ask you to pray for the dead, because they're safe in God's loving arms and beyond need of our prayers. I would like to ask all of you—wherever you may be in this blessed land—to pray for those wounded young men and pray for the bereaved families of those who gave their lives for our freedom. God bless you, and God bless America.

Most of those passages, including the ending, had been written by Reagan himself, crossing out his speechwriters' more ponderous prose. In his last editing of the speech, the President added a couple of phrases, tying the "presence" in Beirut and the small war in the Caribbean to the great cause of his life, fighting monolithic communism: "The events in Lebanon and Grenada, though oceans apart, are closely related. . . . Grenada, we were told, was a friendly island paradise for tourism. Well, it wasn't. It was a Soviet-Cuba colony being readied as a major military bastion to export terrorism and undermine democracy. We got there just in time."

The immediate reaction to the speech was all a President could hope for—and what Reagan confidently expected. "I have an idea that this may go down as one of the President's strongest, more effective speechs," said Dan Rather, beginning the post-speech analysis on CBS stations. A quickie poll of 250 people questioned before and after watching the speech was broadcast on ABC News's *Nightline* program. Before the speech, 50 percent of those folks said they approved of Reagan's handling of Lebanon; after the speech, 80 percent said they approved. As for Grenada, 64 percent of respondents said they approved before the speech, a number that jumped to 84 percent afterward. The White House received more than double the calls, 4,592, than had come in after any previous Reagan speech—4,272 were positive.

Congressional reaction was also over the top. "Fantastic. Best ever," said Senator William Cohen, a Maine Republican. "Good speech. Marvelous communicator," said Senator Slade Gorton, a Washington Republican. But he added a caveat: "On Grenada, I'm 100 percent, but the President's wrong on Lebanon." Senator Sam Nunn, a Georgia Democrat, nodded as Gorton spoke.

Later polls of larger numbers of Americans, conducted during the last days of October, also indicated there was a difference between support for military action and for Reagan as President. A *Newsweek* before-and-after survey showed a seven-point rise in the number of respondents who approved of Reagan's Lebanon decisions, and 53 percent approval of the Grenada invasion. But overall approval for Reagan actually dropped from 53 percent in September to 48 percent after the speech. Only 44 percent answered "yes" when asked if they wanted Reagan to run for reelection. In a similar *New York Times*/CBS News before-and-after poll, only 34 percent said they believed he handled crises wisely and 52 percent said he used military force too quickly.

As the fog of the sixty-hour war cleared, new numbers gave some indication of the size of the operation: 19 Americans died and 115 were wounded; the number of Cubans on the island was 784 and 29 were killed and more than 600 captured; there were 30 Soviets on the island and they were confined to their embassy during the action; there was no reliable estimate of Grenadian soldiers and civilians killed, although the number was certainly less than 100. At least 18 of those deaths (and 115 wounded) were victims of a mistake that the American military denied for a week. A Navy A-4 had mistakenly bombed a wing of the island's mental hospital. On October 30, the President called Secretary of Defense Weinberger and told him to allow unescorted reporters into Grenada.

Partly because of the tensions between the Pentagon and the press, the White House quickly put forth a tremendous effort into justifying the invasion. Soldiers and Marines on Grenada were dispatched to search government offices and homes for documents confirming the Soviet-Cuban connection. Units were also sent out to search for weapons indicating a military buildup on the little island. On November 1, the State Department's Bureau of Intelligence and Research sent the President a secret analysis titled "Grenada: What the Captured Documents Prove." It began:

> Documents captured show that East Bloc countries had plans to provide Grenada with far more war material than its 1,500-man army could use. They also confirm that the late Prime Minister Bishop's New Jewel Movement party was in fact a hardline Marxist-Leninist party dominated by radicals who eliminated Bishop because he was 'too bourgeois.' . . . Documents show that Soviet, Cuban and North Korean involvement in the militarization of the island was on a relatively large scale. The three Soviet agreements—covering the period 1980 to 1985—provided for delivery of $25.8 million in weapons, ammunition, uniforms, trucks and other logistical equipment. Another $12 million in war material were to be supplied per an agreement with North Korea, signed in April.

The memo, which catalogued more than sixty items, including training agreements with the Red Army and lengthy handwritten minutes of New Jewel leadership meetings, concluded that the military aid would supply an army of six thousand men, but that there was so far no evidence that Soviet or Cuban troops would be part of that larger military. Also: "No evidence has yet been found that the Soviets or Cubans were playing a direct role in the island's power struggle." In fact, one of the more intriguing finds was a letter from Fidel Castro to the Grenadian Central Committee on October 15—

two days after Bishop's arrest, four days before his execution—in which the Cuban dictator sounded more like a political science professor than a puppeteer, predicting that the coup against Bishop would bring disaster to the island.

Reagan initialed the memo and ordered the captured documents released to members of Congress and to the press, which was done two days later. At the same time, he authorized a Defense Department plan to fly captured Cuban equipment—two armored personnel carriers, twelve antiaircraft guns, 291 submachine guns, 6,330 rifles, and 5.6 million rounds of ammunition—to Andrews Air Force Base outside Washington, where they were displayed in a hangar for members of Congress and the press.

Another White House memo on November 1, this one from Gergen, quoted an observation by Theodore H. White, the author of the *Making of the President* series of books: "If Reagan has the troops out of there in six weeks, he'll be a hero. If not, you will see the support fade." The President signed on to that, too, and early November polls did indeed show him as a hero. When it was obvious that the little war was won and American troops were leaving Grenada, a *USA Today* survey reported that the President's lead over possible Democratic candidates in the 1984 election had increased from 3 to 19 percent against Senator John Glenn and from 9 to 27 percent over former Vice President Walter Mondale.

One victim of the tragedy in Lebanon and the triumph in Grenada was Tip O'Neill—or, more specifically, the personal relationship between O'Neill and Reagan. After sitting with Reagan and wishing him luck, O'Neill had told an assistant, "I'll have plenty to say when this thing is over." And he did. The day after the President's October 27 speech, O'Neill, the partisan turned patriot, decided the war was over and won—and that he was free to say what he apparently believed all along. He literally erupted at a press briefing focused on the ongoing debate over when, where, and how to apply the War Powers Act. "We can't go with gunboat diplomacy," he said. "The Marines did a tremendous job down there, but we can't continue that route—going into Nicaragua and places like that. His policy is wrong and frightening. . . . To be perfectly truthful, he frightens me, I think he was looking for a reason to go there and he found the opportunity last week." A couple of days later, O'Neill made it personal, calling the President "lazy and short-sighted" in an interview with James Reston of *The New York Times*. He added that he hoped Reagan would not run for reelection. "He should go home, his wife can be queen of Beverly Hills."

O'Neill cut closer than he knew. Mrs. Reagan was trying to persuade her husband not to run in 1984. Policy was not part of her thinking, she was simply worried—"petrified" was her word—that he would be shot at again or that the job would break his health. Bill Clark was also urging Reagan not to seek reelection and he was worrying about health as well: He thought the President was slipping, both physically and mentally.*

What O'Neill was losing, more and more often, was his temper. "They hoodwinked me," he grumbled later, when someone asked him why he was so mad. He had felt that way almost every time he dealt with Reagan, particularly on tax issues. He thought the President always grabbed a little bit more after a deal was made. The President, who had once negotiated contracts as president of the Screen Actors Guild, considered himself a shrewd bargainer. O'Neill agreed with that, and he did not like it one bit. But Reagan won again. On November 9, after meeting with a bipartisan House fact-finding commission that had spent four days in the Caribbean, O'Neill stood with them and agreed with their conclusion that the invasion was justified. Then he added: "But he better not try this again."

Actually, Grenada was already off the President's desk. On the morning of November 14, a gigantic United States Air Force C-141 Starlifter landed clumsily and secretly at Greenham Common, a former Royal Air Force base now used by the Americans, fifty miles west of London. Its cargo was wrapped in tarpaulins. That afternoon, Britain's Defense Secretary, Michael Heseltine, rose in the House of Commons to say: "I have to inform the House that earlier today the first cruise missiles were delivered by air." Howls of protest—"Shame! Shame!"—came from surprised Labour members. "Hear! Hear!" called Conservative members. The Labour leader, Neil Kinnock, stood to call Prime Minister Thatcher "a lackey of the Americans."

The American nuclear-tipped missiles were the first of 572 Tomahawk cruise missiles and Pershing II intermediate-range (1,000 to 1,500 miles) missiles to arrive in Europe and to be aimed at the Soviet Union. Two hundred and forty Soviet less-accurate SS-20s, with three nuclear warheads on each one, were already aimed at the capitals of

---

* Reagan, ignoring the arguments of his wife, did announce four days later that he would seek reelection in November.

Western Europe. After more than four years years of massive Nuclear Freeze demonstrations, parliamentary votes, and failed arms control negotiations with the Soviets, the first sixteen of the new weapons systems, approved by President Carter and the countries of the North Atlantic Treaty Organization in 1979, were scheduled to be operational before the end of the year.

Events followed with a certain predictability: New demonstrations began in England. The Soviets offered to dismantle half of their intermediate-range missiles if the Americans would stop the deployment in Britain, West Germany, and Italy. Reagan turned down the offer. The West German parliament, after a thirteen-hour debate, voted 286 to 226 to accept 104 U.S. missiles on its territory. Twelve hours later, the Soviets, who had been hoping that the fact of ongoing negotiations might influence the West German vote, walked out of the two-year-old medium-range force talks in Geneva, Switzerland. "They'll be back," said a Reagan administration spokesman, Assistant Secretary of Defense Richard Perle. "They'll be back because the world expects the United States and Soviet Union to bend every effort to achieve an agreement."

Indeed. "Negotiations" and "peace" sometimes seemed synonyms in the nuclear age. Opening ABC's *World News Tonight* one Thursday evening, Peter Jennings caught that, saying: "For the first time in twenty years, all the major U.S.-Soviet arms negotiations are now either cancelled or in limbo. Not a very comforting thought." That was an urgent problem for Reagan, whose greatest political weakness both at home and abroad was his old image as a trigger-happy anticommunist ideologue willing to risk war to have his way. In fact, British public opinion, or polls of public opinion, had indicated that 48 percent of British respondents favored missile deployment, with 38 percent opposed, but those numbers almost exactly reversed themselves after the Grenada invasion. Post-Grenada almost two-thirds of British respondents said they believed Reagan's policies made nuclear war more likely than it had been in the past.

The Marines of Grenada were back at sea in the Atlantic, leaving U.S. Army and Caribbean troops as an occupying force. By then, President Reagan had named a new special representative for the Middle East, Donald Rumsfeld, a former congressman and Secretary of Defense, who was taking leave from his position as president of a pharmaceutical firm, G. D. Searle—and sixty more people had been killed, twenty-nine of them Israeli soldiers, when a truck bomb crashed into

IDF headquarters in Tyre, south of the Awali River. The loudspeakers of the USS *Fort Snelling* carried a message from the President, timed for the 208th anniversary of the founding of the Corps:

> To 22nd MAU: Although you have scarcely cleaned off the sand of Grenada where you were magnificent, you will now shortly relieve 24th MAU in Beirut. Once there you will assume the key role in our efforts to bring peace to Lebanon. You have proven without doubt that you are up to the task as our very best. Godspeed . . . Semper Fidelis, Ronald Reagan.

The Marines were off the coast of Lebanon on the evening of November 16, the day Reagan approved an air strike on the headquarters of two Shiite groups, both closely connected to Iranian intelligence and based five miles from the Syrian border. This was to be the retaliatory strike for the Beirut Marine bombing. The strike never happened. Secretary of Defense Weinberger, determined to get Americans out of Lebanon, refused to issue the orders to the Sixth Fleet. McFarlane, whose NSC staff had selected the target with the Central Intelligence Agency, was outraged. He told Weinberger: "The President isn't going to understand this, Cap. . . . You saw how strongly he felt about this."

"I'll be glad to talk to him," the Secretary replied. "I thought it was the wrong thing to do."

McFarlane went to the President, saying: "You approved this operation, and Cap decided not to carry it out. The credibility of the United States in Damascus just went to zero."

"Gosh, that's really disappointing," Reagan told him. "That's terrible. We should have blown the daylights out of them."

McFarlane realized he was losing the President, and that Reagan was not going to call Weinberger. Perhaps he was afraid his Secretary of Defense would quit, or he just wanted to avoid confrontation with the one official who wanted to get out of Lebanon, who never wanted to be there in the first place. Perhaps Reagan himself had already decided to get out. There was no public comment from the White House that day or the next as Israeli and French jets bombed and strafed Shiite positions in the city of Baalbek, forty miles east of Beirut, in separate raids, killing dozens of Islamic Amal militiamen and their Iranian trainers.

In Paris and Tel Aviv, announcements were made that the strikes were in retaliation for the truck-bomb attacks of October 23 and November 4. Two days later, in a news analysis in the *Washington Times,* a conservative newspaper with excellent access to the administration, White House correspondent Jeremiah O'Leary, wrote: "The Reagan Administration has not retaliated for the bomb killing of 239 U.S. servicemen by Moslem extremists primarily because of the effect such an action might have on the 1984 elections and President Reagan's chances for a second term, according to senior U.S. officials." *

On the sea off Beirut, where the American commitment had gradually escalated from 1,200 to 2,000 Marines, the 22nd MAU was ready to disembark the next morning and march to the Beirut airport. Officers selected two films to be shown to the men on board that night: *Conan the Barbarian* with Arnold Schwarzenegger and *First Blood* with Sylvester Stallone.

Some of the Marines who had already done a tour in Beirut were shocked by what they found when they landed on November 17. The Marines at the airport were living underground, moving from bunker to bunker in deep trenches. Seabee bulldozers were being used to bury a hundred Sea-Land cargo containers. Covered with sandbags and dirt, they were called "living bunkers." "Mole City," said a returning officer. Marines, under fire most every night, were ordered to tie one of their dog tags—identity tags—into their boot laces so that they could be identified if they were decapitated. The patrols in the city that Reagan had referred to three weeks before had just about ended. Too dangerous. Thanksgiving dinner, with decent hot food for a change, was served to the Marines a day early because of concerns that militias were planning to move against the Marines on the holiday. American flights over Muslim-controlled territory had became more dangerous, too, as Syrian antiaircraft positions fired on Navy reconnaissance jets for the first time on December 2. This time the United States did retaliate.

Two days after the incident, at dawn on December 4, twenty-eight Navy fighter-bombers from the aircraft carriers *Independence* and *John F. Kennedy* attacked Syrian antiaircraft positions, some of which

---

* There was never any official American retaliation for the bombing of the Marine barracks. According to McFarlane: "The CIA had tracked the source of the bombing to a Shia Muslim commando unit known as the Husayni Suicide Forces, led by Abu Haydar Musawi, a radical Shia Muslim who had broken away from the mainline Amal organization in 1982 and formed the more radical Islamic Amal. The group was put under the command of Iranian Revolutionary Guards in June 1983. If the Iranians didn't plan and launch the attack, they were witting conspirators to it. And the Iranians were allied with Syria."

were equipped with the most advanced Soviet SA-5 surface-to-air missiles and believed to be manned by Soviet gunners. "Very successful action," declared the Department of Defense. But two of the Navy planes were shot down, one pilot was killed, and one crewman was captured by the Syrians.* That afternoon, for more than four hours, the Beirut airport was shelled from the Shouf Mountains, and U.S. ships fired into the mountains. Eight Marines were killed in the barrage. The President, who had personally authorized the American air strike, returned to the White House that Sunday from Camp David saying, "Our mission remains what it was: to help stabilize the situation in Beirut until all the foreign forces can be withdrawn and the government of Lebanon can take over the authority of its own territory."

"How long can this go on?" asked NBC News anchor Tom Brokaw at the beginning of the next night's newscast. "Beirut, a city that already is slowly bleeding to death, was bloody again today." Democrats were critical. "We have a trigger-happy President with a simplistic and paranoid worldview, leading the nation toward a nuclear collision that could end us all," said Senator Alan Cranston of California. A few Republicans were beginning to speak out as well. Barry Goldwater, Reagan's political godfather, said: "I think the President ought to bring everybody in Lebanon who is in American uniform back, and do it now, because we're headed for war." Three former CIA directors—Stansfield Turner, James Schlesinger, and William Colby—urged the President to move the troops away from the airport before it was too late. Newspaper editorials were savage: "We have to get out of Lebanon, now," said the *New York Daily News*; "Toying with Catastrophe," said the *Philadelphia Inquirer*. The *Baltimore Sun* said, "Our Marines went to Lebanon 16 months ago to keep the peace. Finding no peace, they joined the war. That, in a nutshell . . ."

Huge dump trucks and new three-foot-high concrete barriers were placed around the White House fences after the CIA indicated that

---

* The captured airman, Navy Lieutenant Robert Goodman, was in a Syrian jail for a month before being released to the Reverend Jesse Jackson, the civil rights leader who was running for the Democratic nomination to oppose President Reagan. The President refused to see Jackson before his very unofficial mission to Damascus. But when Jackson succeeded, Reagan invited Goodman and Jackson to the White House. He had a simple answer for the White House staffers and other Republicans who reminded him of Jackson's attacks on his record, saying: "You don't quarrel with success. . . . If that guy could get him out and we couldn't more power to him."

there was a chance Muslim extremists intended to target the President's house in the kind of suicide attacks plaguing Lebanon and Israel. In fact, the first trucks had moved into position during a two-day late November visit by Israel's Prime Minister, Yitzhak Shamir, who had replaced Begin in September 1983. During that visit the two countries had tied themselves together more closely than ever, as strategic allies against Syria and the Soviet Union. The U.S.-Israeli alliance in Lebanon was made official in two secret NSDDs. Number 111, signed by Reagan on October 28, specified: "The Rules of Engagement . . . changes should allow support to Lebanese Armed Forces. . . ." Number 115, signed on November 26, called for "a more mature strategic relationship with the Government of Israel . . . enhance and deepen our strategic relationship with the Government of Israel." The face-offs between Marines and Israeli soldiers in Beirut were long forgotten as Reagan and Shamir concluded one agreement after another—most secret, some unwritten—beginning with an American write-off of more than $1.7 billion of Israeli debt and formation of a joint military commission to coordinate action and policy in the Middle East. One compact involved the resumption of sales of cluster bomb artillery shells to Israel—sales banned since July of 1982 because the Israelis had used the shells in Beirut neighborhoods—if Shamir promised not to use them again against civilians.

Then, on December 6, in the worst terrorist attack in five years, a suicide bomber on a Jerusalem bus killed four Israelis and wounded forty-three others. Five days later, nine people were killed in Kuwait when suicide truck bombs collapsed the American embassy and blew out the front of the French embassy. The President's Morning Intelligence Briefing four days later identified the driver killed in the bombing of the American embassy as "An Iraqi national . . . with the Shiite group Islamic Jihad and possibly controlled directly from Iran." *Time* magazine's headline on that story was: "The Shadow of Terrorism—Under attack overseas, Americans now worry: Can it happen at home?" President Reagan threw out one of his uncheckable statistics: "As many as a thousand kamikaze terrorists are being trained in Iran alone."

The Department of Defense's report on the bombing of Marine headquarters—called the Long Report for commission chairman Admiral Robert Long—was released at the same time. The key sentences of the 166-page document blamed Colonel Geraghty and his commanders for not anticipating the terrorist threat, but blamed unnamed higher-ups for the dangerous politics of the mission: "The investigation revealed a lack of systematic and aggressive chain of command attention to antiterrorist security measures. . . . In the eyes of the factional militias, the Marines had become pro-Israel, pro-Phalange and anti-Muslim." The highest higher-up, the Commander in Chief, ready to leave for a Christmas holiday at his ranch, appeared unexpectedly in the White House press room before the report was released. He took the blame himself, echoing President Kennedy's accepting responsibility for the disastrous Bay of Pigs invasion of Cuba in 1961.

"The local commanders on the ground have already suffered quite enough," said Reagan. "If there is to be blame, it properly rests here in this office and with this President. And I accept responsibility for the bad as well as the good."

As Reagan wrapped up the meeting, a reporter asked, "What do you want for Christmas?"

"What do I want for Christmas? You know what I'm going to say."

"What?"

"Peace."

There was no peace in Beirut. On December 21, two car bombs exploded, at a French command post and outside a hotel bar. Nineteen people were killed. The last Marine patrol into Khomeiniville, on the next to last day of 1983, was led by a lieutenant named Charles Dalgleish. The Marines were stopped by men of Amal, the Shiite militia, carrying machine guns. "Why do you invade our country and rape our women?" one asked.

"We came here to help," Dalgleish said.

"Amal will win this war," the gunman said. "Kill all the Marines and Christians!"

The loudspeakers atop the mosques of Khomeiniville were blasting out the same messages day after day: "All Americans must die, they are vermin, infidels, unbelieving filth. This is holy war." Marines on guard, prohibited from firing unless they were fired upon, shouted back: "Fuck you, Assholes!" . . . "Fuck Allah!" And in tribute to the big guns of the battleship *New Jersey*, which fired 1,900-pound shells from its 16-inch guns into the Shouf Mountains for the first time on December 14, the shouting Marines added: "Suck the big 16-inches."

Amal and the other militias, both Shiite and Sunni, were also threatening to kill Muslims serving in the 27,000-man Lebanese army, telling them to desert or their families would be killed. The LAF desertion rate rose to something like 50 percent, and the deserters took their American uniforms and weapons with them to give to the militias. In two December appearances, the President said of the LAF: "We have helped train the Lebanese Army, and it's a very capable force. We have armed it. . . . It is a very good military force."

As the Marines made their last regular patrols through the Shiite slums of Beirut—they were being shot at regularly in broken streets choked with rubble and flowing with sewage—Speaker O'Neill announced that he was calling a conference of Democratic leaders to discuss Lebanon. He made it clear that he was rethinking the eighteen-month extension in Marine deployment he had argued for earlier in 1983. Then, on January 25, 1984, the day of Reagan's fourth State of the Union address, O'Neill confronted Reagan face-to-face in private. "Every time I talk to you, you say things are going well," he said. "But there's nothing but deterioration over there."

The State of the Union speech that night focused on tax reform. But that focus was fuzzy—so fuzzy that congressional Democrats began laughing at the President when he said: "Let us go forward with an historic reform for fairness, simplicity and incentives for growth. . . . I am asking Secretary Don Regan for a plan for action to simplify the entire tax code. . . . I've asked for specific recommendations, consistent with those objectives, to be presented to me by December 1984. . . ." *After* the November election. That was what started the laughing.

"Did I say something funny?" the President said, looking a bit confused. Sort of. It was not as funny as it was obviously political. Jim Baker had come up with the idea of a study as a way to avoid talking about deficits and taxes for the rest of the campaign year. The chief of staff was worried that the Democrats planned to make tax reform their issue, building on legislation introduced in 1982 by Senator Bill Bradley of New Jersey, a Democrat who first made his name as a basketball star, for Princeton and then for the professional New York Knicks. The Bradley Fair Tax Plan was a complicated way to make personal income taxes simple, with only three brackets—14, 26, and 30 percent—and far fewer deductions and credits.*

When the laughing stopped, the President switched to foreign affairs. He said: "We are making progress in Lebanon. We must not be

---

* Reagan and Bradley both began thinking about taxes and tax reform for the same reason. They were both stars who made a lot of money when they were young. The President hated paying 90 percent taxes on some of his movie earnings and Bradley referred to himself as a "depreciable asset" because his high-earning basketball years would inevitably end as he got older and slower.

driven from our objectives for peace in Lebanon by state-sponsored terrorism." In the end, the speech was a long election-year pep talk with rhetorical flag-waving that climaxed with the words "America is back—standing tall!"

"Retreating tall," wrote one of the President's most important supporters, columnist George Will. A special Pentagon commission reported that desertions had reduced the Lebanese Armed Forces to between a third to half the size it was when the Americans landed. The president of the American University of Beirut, Malcolm Kerr, was murdered by a gunman in the hallway outside his office. A pro-Iranian organization called Islamic Jihad, in calls to news organizations, claimed responsibility, saying: "We also vow that not a single American or Frenchman will remain on this soil." On February 1, the House Democrats agreed on a resolution calling for "the prompt and orderly withdrawal" of Marines from Beirut. It had no legal power and the President reacted by saying, "I'm not going to pay any attention to it." Reagan was burning mad about the criticism of O'Neill and other Democrats—and Republicans, including three congressional leaders, House Minority Leader Robert Michel and one of his whips, Dick Cheney of Wyoming, and Senator Trent Lott of Mississippi—but the President waited for his chance to get back at O'Neill personally. It came in an interview with editors of *The Wall Street Journal* on February 3. The paper's Washington editor, Albert Hunt, asked about O'Neill's remarks. The President snapped back: "He may be ready to surrender, but I'm not."

The Speaker retaliated with his own Irish anger, saying things Presidents rarely hear: "The deaths of the U.S. Marines are the responsibility of the President of the United States. He is looking for a scapegoat. The deaths lie on him and the defeat in Lebanon lies on him and him alone."

The cheapest shot, though, was Reagan's. He had already decided, on February 1, to withdraw the Marines from the hell of the Beirut airport, before he attacked O'Neill as a quitter. The White House continued to talk tough as the situation in Beirut got worse—and so did some news at home. On February 5, Muslims, led by Prime Minister Shafik al-Wazzan, quit the Gemayel cabinet. The Lebanese government, all Christians now, was doomed. But the State Department responded by announcing that the President fully intended to continue full participation in the Multinational Force—even as the White House and the Pentagon planned withdrawal.

That same day, numbers released by the Congressional Budget Office quantified the dirty little secret of Reaganomics: The increases in interest costs on the ballooning budget deficts ($47.4 billion interest payments in the 1985 budget alone) were greater than all the Reagan reductions in health, education, welfare, and social programs ($39.6 billion in 1985). The conservative President who'd made a career of attacking liberals for "tax and spend" policies was practicing a politics of "borrow and spend." Later in the day, while the President was at the ranch, far away from cameras, his spokesman, Deputy Press Secretary Speakes, distributed a written statement—the President did not want history to have videotape of him withdrawing—which began: "Even before the latest outbreak of violence, we had been considering ways of reconcentrating our forces and the nature of our support in order to take the initiative away from the terrorists. Far from deterring us . . . recent events only confirm the importance of the decisive new steps I want to outline." The statement said there would be more naval activity and accelerated training and equipping of the LAF. "Third, in conjunction with these steps, I have asked Secretary of Defense Weinberger to present me with a plan for redeployment of the Marines from Beirut Airport to their ships offshore." *

The last American unit to leave, Lieutenant Dalgleish's platoon, camped on the Beirut beach as February 25, 1984, dawned. Behind them, Shiite militiamen moved into the buildings and bunkers abandoned by the Marines. As the platoon waited for the landing craft that would take them away, Dalgleish wondered whether it was like this when the Crusaders left Beirut for the last time on July 31, 1291. In Washington, military sources leaked data showing that the big guns of the battleship *New Jersey* had been generally ineffective in hitting military targets, and the President was giving his weekly radio address, from Camp David this day, which began: "From the early days of the colonies, prayer in school was practiced and revered. . . ."

---

* Shultz wrote of the "redeployment": "The reality of our departure turned out to be far different from my earlier redeployment plan, which the president approved. Our troops left in a rush amid ridicule from the French and utter disappointment and despair from the Lebanese government. The Italians left as they saw us departing. The French stayed until the end of March, saying that their peacekeeping mission was no longer possible in what was basically a civil war, supported, in effect, by Syria. They left with their flags flying and a band playing. I liked their style. And the dignity of their departure made an impact, too. I knew then that our staying power under pressure would come into question time and again—and not just in the Middle East. In all, the MNF had lost 343 men; the United States, 264; France, 77; and Italy, 2."

CHAPTER 10
NOVEMBER 6, 1984

I N ITS LAST ISSUE OF 1983, *Time* magazine published its "Man of the
Year" cover story about the person who had been most influential
over the past twelve months, for good or for evil. This time it was
"Men of the Year": President Ronald Reagan and Soviet Premier Yuri
Andropov. The cover art showed them standing back-to-back, sym-
bolizing the depth of bad relations between the United States and the
Soviet Union. There seemed to be no communication between the superpowers after three years of Reagan-style anti-communism—and
White House polls and secret United States Information Agency reports showed that people around the world generally blamed Reagan
for that. He was still seen as a dangerous man, ready for war and hostile to arms control negotiations, the symbol of superpower restraint.

On January 16, 1984, on the eve of a thirty-five-nation European
disarmament conference in Stockholm, Sweden, the President went
on television from the White House to speak of Soviet-American relations. He spent most of the half-hour blaming aggressive Soviet
weapons programs and territorial ambitions for the ending or suspension of arms talks and for most of the shooting wars around the
planet:

> Over the last ten years, the Soviets devoted twice as much of their
> gross national product to military expenditures as the United
> States. . . . I have openly expressed my view of the Soviet system. I
> don't know why this should come as a surprise to Soviet leaders
> who've never shied away from expressing their view of our system.
> But that doesn't mean that we can't deal with each other. . . . We
> don't refuse to talk when the Soviets call us imperialist aggressors

and worse, or because they cling to the fantasy of a communist triumph over democracy. . . . Reducing the risk of war, especially nuclear war, is priority number one. . . . Our policy toward the Soviet Union is credible deterrence, peaceful competition, and constructive cooperation.

Reagan was beginning to flirt with détente. The President ended with a flight of imagination he had added to the text in longhand:

Just suppose with me for a moment that an Ivan and Anya could find themselves, oh, say, in a waiting room, or sharing a shelter from the rain or a storm with a Jim and Sally. Would they then debate the differences between their respective governments? Or would they find themselves comparing notes about their children and what each other did for a living? . . . And as they went their separate ways, maybe Anya would be saying to Ivan, "Wasn't she nice? She also teaches music." Or Jim would be telling Sally what Ivan did or didn't like about his boss. They might even have decided that they were all going to dinner some evening soon.

The Soviet response to the speech came the next day from Foreign Minister Andrei Gromyko, in a Moscow meeting with American ambassador Arthur Hartman. The veteran diplomat stated that the Kremlin's problem with the Reagan administration was that Washington was refusing to acknowledge his government's legitimacy. More formally, speaking a few days later in Stockholm, Gromyko characterized Reagan's ideas as: "Maniacal plans . . . criminal and dishonest methods . . . pathological obsession."

On February 10, three days after Reagan announced the redeployment of the American Marines in Lebanon, the Soviets announced that Andropov had died the day before. He had served just fifteen months as Premier. He was sixty-nine years old, four years younger than Reagan, and had not appeared in public for more than four months. The Kremlin had been telling the world that their leader had only a bad cold. The new number one in Moscow was Konstantin Chernenko, another old man, born seven months after Reagan. The first question the President had to deal with was whether to attend the funeral in Moscow. Abandoning his "Gosh . . . Gee Whiz" persona for a moment, Reagan told Jack Matlock, the NSC's Soviet expert, that he was not going anywhere: "I don't want to honor that prick."

If the President was discouraged by the events in Stockholm or Moscow or Beirut, it was not obvious on February 20, when he embarked on one of his sentimental journeys to the heartland. After Notre Dame, Eureka College, and his hometown of Dixon, Illinois, this time it was Des Moines, where he had been a sportscaster at WHO radio from 1933 to 1937, before he left for Hollywood to become a movie star. The visit was on the day of the Iowa presidential caucuses, the first contest of the race to choose the Democratic candidate who would oppose Reagan in November. Sitting in his old chair, talking with the station's sports director, Jim Zabel, who had been there for forty years, the President was charming, warm, and funny. It was hard not to like him in one of his favorite roles, local boy makes good—remembering names, places, and stories. "Melba King . . . B. J. Palmer . . . Curly Waddel . . . Ed Reimers . . . Pete McArthur . . ."—the names rolled out as if it had all happened yesterday. Zabel even brought up the fact that young Reagan had once won a Wheaties Sportscaster of the Year award. The chat produced a glimmer of insight into the way his mind worked, particularly when it came to truth telling and stretching.

"Out at Birdland Park, they were having the Olympic tryouts out there, the AAU for the Olympic team," said the President. "And we were feeding network—going to feed the NBC network, and that was really tops. . . . Some of the Olympic officials got in an argument, and I was on the air for 30 minutes, nationwide—and they did not run off one single swimming event. . . . I think I described every drop of water in the pool."

Zabel asked him about one of his favorite stories, the day he was broadcasting a Chicago Cubs–St. Louis Cardinals game and the Western Union ticker to Des Moines stopped transmitting the play-by-play in the ninth inning, leaving him to make up the action:

> They had to abbreviate things down, like in would come the paper, and it would say, "Out 4-3." Well, that meant out from second base to first base, that meant it had to be a grounder. So, you'd take it and you'd say, "And Dean comes out of the windup and here comes the pitch, and it's a hard hit grounder down toward second base, So-and-so going over, picks it up, flips over to first, just in time . . ."
>
> But the thing you're talking about was the time . . . It was Dizzy Dean on the mound and I had Billy Jurges at the plate. . . . Here comes this slip of paper and it says, "The wires have gone dead,"

and I knew in the ninth inning if I suddenly said, "Well, we'll have a little interlude of music until we get back connected to the ball-park," we'd lose every listener—they'd all turn on some of those other stations. So I thought, "There's only one thing that doesn't get in the scorebooks: foul ball. So I had Jurges foul one and then foul another. And then I had him foul one that missed being a homerun by a foot. Then I described two kids down back of third base that were in a fight for the ball that went into the stands there. I'm begin-ning to set a world record for somebody standing at the plate and hitting successive fouls. . . . I was beginning to sweat a little, be-cause I knew that if I told them we'd lost the wire they'd know I hadn't been telling the truth.

When the wire came back, it turned out that, in real life back in Chicago, Jurges had popped up to the infield on the first pitch. But they wouldn't know that in Des Moines, unless they bought the next day's newspapers. Listening to the wire-down story for the hundredth time, Reagan's man Lyn Nofziger said: "Truth is not the same thing to him as to you and me. If Ronald Reagan tells a story three times it be-comes true, at least to him."

"How does it feel to be back in Des Moines?" Zabel asked Reagan.

"Oh, great . . . Give me another seven and a half minutes and I'd be so far down nostalgia lane. . . . I always had in mind a listener out there, and I thought I was painting a word picture."

"Well, you gave them a lot of pictures, Mr. President. A thrill to have you here at WHO today."

If Reagan's latest Cold War rhetoric painted a confusing picture— his words and attitude were clearer than his intentions—that may have been an accurate portrait of American foreign policy. In a final memo before the January 16 speech, communications director David Gergen, who was leaving the administration, had laid out a page of specific suggestions for the President's future speeches on domestic policy. On foreign policy, he was reduced to writing: "To strengthen prospects for peace: we need X, Y, and Z." Many in the informal busi-ness of Sovietology thought that the reason there were few specifics was that the President was essentially playing a waiting game and that his approach to negotiations on arms and other issues was for public consumption at home and abroad. Internal White House documents talked of potential economic crisis in the Soviet Union by the late 1980s, of forcing the Soviets to invest more on arms production to counter American talk of missile defense, and of raising Soviet costs in Afghanistan by supplying more sophisticated weapons to Muslim insurgents fighting the Red Army. Then there was the matter of how long another old man in the Kremlin would last.

In one of a series of memos to the President before a review of Soviet policy, McFarlane wrote: "We must stress in public your call for dialogue and your desire to reduce tensions and solve problems. . . . You must be in a position by late summer or fall to make clear that this is their fault not yours. . . . Your reelection is of strategic importance for the United States." In another memo, the NSC director wrote: "Some in Congress are interested in inviting a delegation of Supreme Soviet members this year. This could be a way for us to meet possible successors to Chernenko such as Gorbachev"—naming the youngest member of the Politburo, Mikhail Gorbachev, fifty-two, a lawyer considered an expert on agriculture.*

Gergen's position was abolished, leading to a new White House structure with Richard Darman adding supervision of the speechwriters to his Baker-driven domain. Ironically, the internal rap on Gergen in the leak-obsessed White House was that he just talked too much to too many reporters. But so did Darman. The *National Journal,* the most serious of Washington journals, in a January 28 article by Dick Kirschten on Gergen's departure caught an eternal White House truth that sometimes seemed lost on Reagan: "Administration leaks to the press have often had as much to do with trying to sway the President's decisions as with selling them." The more distant a President, the more his men used newspapers and television to get his attention. There was room for a new speechwriter and the chief of the speech group, Bentley Elliot, wanted to hire a woman, but he had to get the President's personal permission because of her current job.

"I am interviewing a young woman named Peggy Noonan, with very strong writing skills and conservative convictions," Elliot began a February 20 memo to the President. "The rub is that she is Dan Rather's radio writer. I've read through his scripts and can assure you that the radio Dan Rather bears little resemblance to his left-wing TV twin. . . . By the way, I worked at CBS on my first job, and that's when I first saw the light."

The note came back to Elliot with: "OK. RR."

---

* *Time* magazine would later, in April, say of Gorbachev, previously identified only as an Andropov protégé: "Unusually well traveled for a Soviet leader, he has been to Canada, France and West Germany. His foreign hosts have found him to be open and informed."

As Reagan reminisced in Des Moines, former Vice President Walter Mondale was winning the state's Democratic caucuses, getting 45 percent of the vote against seven opponents. Senator Gary Hart of Colorado finished second with just 15 percent, surprising analysts, who thought Senator John Glenn was the only possible threat to Mondale's nomination. The next contest was eight days later in the New Hampshire primary. On the eve of that vote, a *New York Times/CBS News* poll showed Mondale with the largest lead ever recorded nationally, 57 percent, to 8 percent for Jesse Jackson and 7 percent each for Hart and Glenn. "Mondale: Going for a Knockout" was *Time* magazine's headline. But Hart won easily, getting 41 percent of the New Hampshire vote versus 29 percent for Mondale. The White House, like most of the country, had no sense of Hart except that he was forty-seven years old, more than twenty-five years younger than the President, and was billing himself as a "New Ideas" candidate. Reagan had called himself that in the 1980 campaign.

The White House was geared up to run against Mondale, a conventional liberal from Minnesota, with strong union support and the advantages and disadvantages of having served as Jimmy Carter's Vice President. Among the stack of campaign memos on James Baker's conference table were one from pollster Richard Wirthlin and the designated campaign manager, Ed Rollins, and one from Morton Blackwell, an important conservative activist.

The seven-page Blackwell memo focused on the concerns of conservative groups. His principal recommendations were laid out in a first section titled "Church-State Relationship: The Civil Rights Issue of the 1980s." He urged the President to identify closely with Christian groups protesting any government regulation of church-sponsored schools or mandatory Social Security taxation of church employees." Also: "Introduce packages of appropriate legislation to deal with dial-a-porn, cable pornography, and unclear Federal standards." The thirty-three-page Wirthlin-Rollins memo, "The GOP Presidential Coalition of 1984," was an impressively complex document that attempted to divide the electorate geographically, economically, ideologically, and religiously. One chart divided voters three ways:

Reagan has now:

High income voters across all groups including union families and Catholics; educated Catholics and educated Southern whites with low-to-moderate incomes; Middle class Northern Protestants and middle class Southern whites; Younger non-union voters (This support is probably soft); Non-union men, North, South and Catholic.

No clear trend beyond party vote: Educated Northern Protestants with low-to-moderate incomes; Catholics who are middle-class, middle-aged, or in the industrial Middle West; Northeastern WASPs; Northern women—WASP, Catholic, and union; Lower-end Southern whites.

Voting against Reagan:

Northern union voters with low-to-moderate incomes; Lower-end, non-union, northern WASPs; Blacks.

Wirthlin's polls also consistently showed Reagan's appeal to voters who considered themselves religious, and he reached out to them: "I urge the Senate to reaffirm that voluntary prayer in school is indeed a basic right of our people, and I hope the House will follow suit," he said in an opening statement before taking questions at a news conference on February 22. There were no questions about that. Eleven of the sixteen questions were about Lebanon and the Middle East—and three of the others questioned whether Reagan was too lazy to be President. It sounded like this:

"Has the United States lost credibility in the region? Has Syria won?" . . . "You also said you weren't going to cut and run even though there's widespread perception that that's what we're doing." . . . "Can you say to those parents, now that you've withdrawn the marines to the ships, why more than 260 young men died there?" . . . "Would you accept a resignation from George Shultz, who, some people feel, has failed in this policy?" . . . "And what's your response to people who ask . . . whether in fact you are really running things and whether you are a full-time President?" . . . "Sir, Walter Mondale says you're intellectually lazy and you're forgetful— so forgetful that he says you're providing leadership by amnesia. What do you say to that?"

To that Reagan said: "I'm surprised he knew what the word meant."

It was not a happy evening. The President was on the defensive from beginning to end. He defended Shultz—"I think he has done a splendid job"—and angrily defended himself, saying, "We're not bugging out; we're just going to a little more defensive position." About his work habits, Reagan replied: "They don't know what they're talking about. . . . Presidents, I've learned, don't take vacations. They just get a change of scenery."

Reagan also had to defend himself against continuing criticism of the federal deficit, estimated at almost $190 billion in fiscal year 1984. Unfortunately, the most prominently placed critic of Reaganomics was the chairman of his own Council of Economic Advisers, Martin Feldstein, a forty-three-year-old conservative Harvard professor appointed in the summer of 1982. A hard worker who ignored the social life of his Georgetown neighbors, Feldstein was a stranger in a strange town, unknown before the fall of 1983, when he had begun saying that the deficit was obviously a result of Reagan's tax cuts and increased military spending. "There is no avoiding the need to either raise taxes or cut spending," he had said in a November speech. "It is only a question of when." By mid-December, Feldstein was saying, "The longer the large deficits are expected to persist, the greater will be the damage and the risk to our economy." Early in February, he had lectured a group of economics reporters about deficits and taxes: "We can't grow ourselves out of these deficits. And if we don't deal with them, we can't have the kind of economic recovery we want. . . . We're going to have to have additional tax revenue, we're going to have to trim back on the size of defense authorizations, and we're going to have to have domestic spending cuts."

Except for the bit about cutting domestic spending, the professor was calling out that the President had no clothes. The transcripts of Feldstein's remarks to reporters were on Jim Baker's desk before noon—and the chief of staff's first move was to order Feldstein to cancel a scheduled appearance on ABC News's *This Week with David Brinkley*. Baker sat Feldstein down and spelled out the rules. In the Reagan White House you follow the President's talking points or you don't talk. There were at least three things never to be talked about: the ballooning deficit, the growing problem of homeless people living in city doorways or on the streets, and AIDS (acquired immunodeficiency syndrome), a deadly new blood-transmitted viral desease that was primarily striking down young men, particularly homosexuals and drug users who shared contaminated needles. The victims were not the most sympathetic of Americans, particularly in the White House.

The President himself had never used the word "AIDS" in public.

The disease, which had been identified early in Reagan's first term, had killed more than four thousand Americans by 1984. Millions more were infected according to Reagan's own surgeon general, Dr. C. Everett Koop, a burly Philadelphia pediatrician, a religious conservative known as one of the country's leading opponents of abortion. Koop had begun speaking out about the dangers of AIDS and the need for sex education to slow the spread of the disease. He was speaking out because he could not speak inside. He had never had a conversation with the President and there was little chance he would, because his way was being blocked by Baker and others, particularly another zealous evangelical, Gary Bauer, Reagan's domestic policy adviser. Koop, a popular figure whose blue uniform and whaler's beard made him look like an old-fashioned sailor caught in the wrong century, was lobbying for major public health research and putting together government literature about the ways the disease was being transmitted—ways that included sexual practices. When he pressed Bauer to speak to Reagan, he was told that he had to change the way he spoke and wrote.

"Like what?" Koop asked.

"Well, like stop using words like condom and penis and vagina and rectum."

The doctor refused to do that. "They hate gays," he told friends. "I suspect they're saying, 'Mr. President, AIDS is something you don't have to worry about . . . after all, it only affects homosexuals, it only affects drug abusers, it affects sexually promiscuous people, Mr. President. These are not your people.' . . . Some of them actually told me, to my face, that I was leading the children of America down the garden path to immorality."

Reagan also avoided using the word "homeless" in public. One of his very few mentions came during an appearance on ABC's *Good Morning America*. The host, David Hartman, brought up the subject and the President knocked it down, saying, "One problem we've had, even in the best of times. And that is the people who are sleeping on the grates; the homeless who are homeless, you might say, by choice." But the deficit story line was set—partly because Reagan had made a career of attacking liberals as budget-busting debt lovers. *Time* magazine put Feldstein on the cover of its March 5 issue under the headline "THAT MONSTER DEFICIT: America's Economic Black Hole." The story inside began: "In many ways the President of the U.S. could not ask for a better election-year economy. Unemployment is falling (to 7.7 percent), sales and profits are surging, investment is perking, inflation seems under control. After presiding over a deep recession, Ronald Reagan can now boast of having engineered one of the most stunning economic turnarounds in U.S. history. But if the economy is going up, why do so many feel so down about it? . . . The answer to all of the above: the Federal deficit."

The first quote in the *Time* piece was from Thomas Johnson, president of Chemical Bank in New York: "Everyone wants to feel good. . . . But we are working on borrowed money and borrowed time." The last word was reserved for America's most famous car salesman, Lee Iacocca, chairman of the Chrysler Corporation: "It is a scandal. I don't know what they're on down in Washington. It's wacko time."

The President, of course, was blaming Congress, his favorite big spenders, but then the nonpartisan Congressional Budget Office declared one more time that the reason for the triple-digit annual deficits was the expensive combination of Reagan's tax-cutting and military buildup, and offered a new number: Without the Reagan tax cuts and defense increases, the federal budget would be heading toward an $11 billion surplus by 1989. Feldstein's standing in the White House was expressed in a clumsy way as Larry Speakes made fun of him in press briefings by deliberately mangling the pronunciation of his name, shifting back and forth between "Feld-steen" and "Feld-stine." By mid-March, the President was in rhetorical retreat on deficits or, rather, negotiations with Senate Majority Leader Howard Baker and other Republican "deficit hawks" in Congress. He agreed finally to a vague three-year deficit-reduction package that would increase federal taxes on liquor, tobacco, telephone service, and diesel fuel—small and relatively painless but certainly not Reaganesque—and included a decrease in defense spending.*

March, in fact, was a cruel month for the White House. Ed Meese, whom Reagan nominated for Attorney General on February 3— signaling the victory of the Baker-Deaver-Darman team inside the White House—was being embarrassed by dripping revelations about his personal finances. It was tacky stuff—help on mortgages, interest-free loans to his wife from friends and government appointees—but it focused attention briefly on the fact that more than forty of the President's appointees had been forced to resign because of conflicts of in-

---

* Feldstein announced his retirement and returned to Harvard on May 9, 1984.

terest that might be common in the upper reaches of American business but were against the law in government.*

In Lebanon, on March 16 there was a cease-fire, the 180th since 1975. But on that day, the first secretary of the American embassy's political section, William Buckley, was kidnapped by a carload of gunmen who knew that the diplomatic title was a cover for Buckley's real job. He was the CIA station chief. Two days before that the man Reagan thought was the key to his Middle East peace plans, King Hussein of Jordan, had surprised the White House with a stinging attack on the United States's role in that part of the world. In an interview with *The New York Times,* Hussein said: "I now realize that principles mean nothing to the United States. Short-term issues, particularly in election years, prevail. We see things in the following way. Israel is on our land. It is there by virtue of American moral and political support to the point where the U.S. is succumbing to Israeli dictates. You obviously have made your choice and your choice is Israel. Therefore, there is no hope of achieving anything."

In Washington, the President reacted angrily by pulling back legislation to allow the sale of American weaponry, especially shoulder-held Stinger antiaircraft missiles, to Jordan and to Saudi Arabia.

On March 30, the final fifteen of the twenty-five United States Navy ships off Lebanon sailed away. The White House announced: "Foreign policy interests in Lebanon have not changed. . . . The United States has not abandoned Lebanon." Four days later, during a televised news conference, the President himself moved away from taking blame for what had happened in Beirut, saying: "A debate as public as was conducted here, raging, with Congress demanding, 'Oh, take our, bring our men home, take them away'—all this can do is stimulate the terrorists and urge them on to further attacks, because they see a possibility of success in getting the force out which is keeping them from having their way."

Democrats in Congress responded in anger, led by Speaker O'Neill, saying: "Despicable. This is the qualms of a guilty conscience." Senator Alan Cranston of California added: "To suggest we should not debate policy is to suggest a dictatorship."

That same day, final results in the party's New York primary made

---

* The Meese Senate hearings and investigations, including the appointment of a special prosecutor, took more than a year. He was finally confirmed by a 63 to 31 vote on February 23, 1985, after the special prosecutor, Jacob Stein, reported that he may have used bad judgment but had committed no crime.

it certain that the Democrats' 1984 presidential candidate would be former Vice President Mondale, who had survived Gary Hart's early wins in New England. Mondale won 45 percent of the New York vote to 27 percent for Hart and 26 percent for the Reverend Jesse Jackson, who was establishing himself as a new power in the Democratic Party. So, Reagan and Mondale were the story, as written on April 26 by the columnist Joseph Kraft, who emphasized the embarrassment and the dangers of revelations that the CIA was mining Nicaraguan harbors and that twelve foreign ships had already been damaged: "Fritz Mondale did more than score a big win. . . . He moved back into contention with Ronald Reagan. For the president, having peaked with the Grenada invasion last fall, is now stumbling badly. . . . All the worst suspicions about the president and his foreign policy have been revived. The nightmare of entering an endless and unjust war, inadvertently and without allied support, comes alive again. The country has the sensation once more of big lies in high places."

National polls seemed to confirm that judgment. A *New York Times*/CBS News poll in late April reported that two out of three respondents disapproved of United States policy in Central America, and only 13 percent approved of the mining of Nicaragua's harbors. The mining had begun in February, but was only made public early in March after it was reported by Nicaraguan radio. It became an issue, or at least a topic of public discussion in Washington, only after it was reported in the *Times* on March 15 just before the polling began. On April 6, *The Wall Street Journal* revealed that the mining was not a contra operation at all; CIA agents were running it, supervising and training Latin American mercenaries to lay the mines from small speedboats. The American agents, based in Honduras, had also commanded mercenaries—the term of art was UCLA, "Unilaterally Controlled Latino Assets"—who had blown up fuel tanks, destroying 3.2 million gallons of fuel in the port of Corinto on October 10, 1983. But the press did not know that the President, both verbally and then in a formal finding authorizing covert action in Central America, had specifically approved the mining during two NSC meetings in January.

None of those actions, or others, were reported to Congress. When the mining became public, Senator Daniel Patrick Moynihan, a New York Democrat, resigned as vice chairman of the Senate Select Committee on Intelligence to protest the deliberate misleading of the committee. Senator Barry Goldwater, the seventy-five-year-old symbol of

Republican conservatism, was even angrier, writing a letter to CIA Director William Casey, an old friend, that was remarkable for its language:

> I am pissed off. . . . The President has asked us to back his foreign policy. Bill, how can we back his foreign policy when we don't know what the hell he's doing? Lebanon, yes, we all knew he sent troops over there. But mine the harbors of Nicaragua? This is an act violating international law. It is an act of war. For the life of me, I don't see how we are going to explain it.

Another member of the Intelligence Commmittee, Republican David Durenberger of Minnesota, already considered something of a loose cannon in party ranks, added: "There is no use in our meeting with Bill Casey. None of us believe him. The cavalier, almost arrogant way he has treated us as individuals has turned the whole committee against him." Casey did whatever explaining he did in the Oval Office. But no one was ever sure what Casey was saying to the President—literally, because his mumbling got worse when it suited his purposes. In the Oval Office, he would sit on the side of the President's desk, leaning toward Reagan. "The mumbling leading the deaf," said one of the President's men. Even Reagan laughed about it. Before one Casey visit he jokingly asked McFarlane, "Who's going to interpret?" Jim Baker, who was not amused, sitting in on one meeting, shook his head and whispered to McFarlane: "God knows what he just approved." *

Kraft had concluded his column by referring to the political impact of the administration's Central American lies: "So the Democrats have a chance. . . . Mondale looks like the candidate. On the issues he is well-placed to challenge Reagan. But on the personal side he has yet to show the humorous, self-deprecating qualities . . . [that] can work against the soft-shoe routines of the old stager in the White House."

The April 26 Kraft column demonstrated the problem the Washington press corps was having with Reagan. A few days later, in *The New York Times Magazine,* Steven Weisman, the paper's chief White

---

* In fact, Casey had informed the full committee in secret testimony, saying: "Mines have been placed in the Pacific harbor of Corinto and the Atlantic harbor of El Bluff, as well as the oil terminal at Puerto Sandino." Casey was asked no questions about what he said, one sentence in eighty-four pages of transcript. Apparently it was one of those committee moments, not uncommon, when most senators were somewhere else and the ones who were in their seats were not paying attention.

House correspondent, wrote a seven-thousand-word exercise in journalistic exasperation, calling the President "Teflon Man":

> One of the most astonishing features of Ronald Reagan's political
> success is that, whether or not they agree with him and his policies,
> Americans *like* him. . . . He has committed untold public bloopers
> and been caught in dozens of factual mistakes and misrepresenta-
> tions. He has presided over the worst recession since the Great De-
> pression. The abortive mission in Beirut cost 265 American lives,
> and there has been a sharp escalation in United States military in-
> volvement in Central America. An extraordinary number of Mr.
> Reagan's political appointees have come under fire, with many
> forced to resign, because of ethical or legal conflicts. Yet . . . noth-
> ing sticks to him.

Finally, a third voice, Hugh Sidey of *Time,* weighed in with his
thoughts, challenging Weisman while making some of the same
points:

> The United States desperately wants its Presidents to succeed. Too
> often political critics measure a President against perfection. The
> public does not. Voters, after all, must choose a warm body rather
> than an ideal. . . . Reagan has made many blunders, from his tax
> and budget formulas to his press conference fictions to the tragedy
> in Lebanon, on through his insensitivity to blacks and women and
> the shady dealings of a host of his aides. Yet these so far simply do
> not outweigh the reductions in interest rates and inflation, dealing
> with the striking air traffic controllers, restraining government
> spending, enhancing American power, emplacing new NATO mis-
> siles and fighting in Grenada.
>
> Washington, which often seems to substitute a box score for a
> mind, has trouble realizing that much weight is also given in the
> presidency to optimism, good cheer, obvious enjoyment of the job,
> grace, personal kindness, decisiveness, boldness, individuality and
> other rather misty elements. They add up to leadership, which is al-
> ways imperfect but nevertheless creates a national momentum and
> vitality. The Teflon tag does not really explain the political struggle
> that is going on.

On the day Weisman's article was published, the President was in
Shanghai, ending a tour of China—signing trade and cultural agree-

ments—with a visit to Fudan University, where he told students a bit about his former life and how it served him as President: "You'd be surprised how much being a good actor pays off." The students applauded but Chinese leaders were not as impressed. Not only did Reagan fall asleep during the formal welcoming banquet in Beijing's Great Hall of the People, he dozed off in a private meeting as Premier Deng Xiaoping was laying out China's position on the future of Taiwan. When that meeting was over, Deng turned to an aide and said, "Did he understand anything I said?"

On April 11, a "Sense of the Senate" resolution sponsored by Edward Kennedy condemning the Nicaraguan mining passed by a vote of 84 to 12, with 42 Republicans defying their President to vote with the Democrats. For three years, both houses of Congress had tried to have it both ways on Reagan's wars in Central America, usually giving the White House about half the funding it asked for to support the government of El Salvador against leftist insurgents and to support contra insurgents against the government of Nicaragua. The 1984 appropriation for contra aid had been capped at $24 million, exactly half of what Casey and Reagan had requested.

After the mining fiasco—the International Court of Justice in The Hague ruled it illegal aggression—the Congress was tilting toward cutting off all funding for the contras. On May 9, two days after the White House's favored candidate, Christian Democrat José Napoleon Duarte, won 54 percent of the vote to become President of El Salvador, Reagan turned to television for his fourth prime-time speech on Central America, trying one more time to rouse people and rally Congress:

> The defense policy of the United States is based on a simple premise: We don't start wars. We will never be the aggressor. We maintain our strength in order to deter and defend against aggression. . . . We help our friends defend themselves.
>
>   Central America . . . is so close: San Salvador is closer to Houston, Texas, than Houston is to Washington, D.C. It's at our doorstep, and it's become the stage for a bold attempt by the Soviet Union, Cuba and Nicaragua to install communism by force throughout the hemisphere . . . to destabilize the entire region and eventually move chaos and anarchy toward the American border. . . .
>
>   The Sandinista rule is a Communist reign of terror. The role that

Cuba has long performed for the Soviet Union is now also being played by the Sandinistas. They have become Cuba's Cubans. . . . Many who fought alongside the Sandinistas saw their revolution betrayed. . . . Thousands who fought with the Sandinistas have taken up arms against them and are now called the contras. They are freedom fighters.

The President repeated some of the language of the Kissinger Commission, the bipartisan commission on Central America, which recommended a five-year, $90 billion package of military, economic, and humanitarian aid for the region. The President called the Sandinistas anti-Catholic and anti-Semitic and asserted that a communist takeover in Central America would lead to millions of poor and uneducated refugees trying to get into the United States. He closed with questions and some vivid imagery:

> The simple questions are: Will we support freedom in this hemisphere or not? Will we defend our vital interests in this hemisphere? Will we act while there is still time? . . . As I talk to you tonight, there are young Salvadoran soldiers in the field facing the terrorists and guerrillas in El Salvador with the clips in their rifles the only ammunition they have. . . . This is no way to support friends, particularly when supporting them is supporting ourselves. . . . It's up to all of us—the administration, you as citizens, and your representatives in Congress.

Newspapers and television broadcasts the next morning led with the news from Moscow that the Soviets were withdrawing from the 1984 Summer Olympics in Los Angeles, interpreting it as another sign that Soviet-American relations had reached a new low. Reporters in El Salvador reported that there was no ammunition shortage in the field—and they were backed up by Salvadoran officials. But Duarte's election and Reagan's words checked the flight of the Congress away from El Salvador. Many members disagreed with the facts as the President had presented them, but they were not willing to risk being accused in an election year of "losing" El Salvador.

By a 212 to 208 vote—56 Democrats sided with the President—the House approved a White House request for $170 million in new military aid for El Salvador. More importantly, the legislation did not tie the aid to any improvement in the country's human rights record, ignoring investigations by agencies such as Amnesty International, which had issued a thirty-eight-page report stating that a significant number of the forty thousand civilians killed during the five years of civil war had been murdered by government forces. Death squads, often soldiers in civilian clothes, were littering the country with mutilated bodies.*

In San Salvador, the Republican Nationalist Alliance, the extreme rightist party called ARENA, lavishly financed by large landowners whose families had controlled the country for centuries, and the party usually associated with the savage death squads, claimed that the election had been stolen from them—by the Americans. "It is the CIA that won the election, and not the Christian Democrats," said an ARENA spokesman. Certainly the CIA was there, spending perhaps $2 million on the election. The same charges were made in Washington by ARENA supporters led by Senator Jesse Helms of North Carolina, who angrily charged: "We"—meaning the CIA—"did everything but stuff the ballot boxes."

Whatever the CIA's involvement, the election was the freest in El Salvador's bloody history. Duarte was an impressive man, a civil engineer educated at the University of Notre Dame, courageous and apparently honest, a patriot who had been jailed, beaten, and exiled for years after he began winning elections. He was the country's most visible reformer. On May 22, Duarte spent eleven hours roaming the halls of Congress, urging members to vote for another aid package— "Don't leave me standing alone"—this one for $62 million in emergency military aid. "He's our kind of man," said Representative Clarence Long of Maryland, one of Reagan's severest critics on Latin American questions. Tip O'Neill, who said he was still opposed to military aid to El Salvador, was as impressed as everyone else, saying: "We're not going to send him back empty-handed."

An hour after approving the El Salvador aid by a vote of 267 to

---

* Oliver North of the NSC staff, who had guided Kissinger Commission members on quick trips to Central America, was delegated to write a rebuttal of the Amnesty International report. "The accusation," he wrote in a memo to McFarlane, "that it is 'the authorities themselves' who perpetrate the murders cannot be proved by *anyone*." He argued that Amnesty had made no attempt to investigate killings by leftist rebels. The situation in El Salvador was dramatized when a plot to assassinate the United States ambassador, Thomas Pickering, was uncovered and the White House sent General Vernon Walters to the country on May 18, 1984, to personally warn ARENA leader Roberto D'Aubuisson—called a "pathological killer" by one American ambassador—of severe consequences if anything happened to Pickering. Senator Helms called the charge "an absolute falsehood." Perhaps, but I visited Pickering in that period and his office and others could be sealed off by bulletproof panels and steel bars at the touch of a switch if the building was penetrated by "hostiles" of any kind.

254, the House voted 241 to 174 to cut off all aid to the contras in Nicaragua, specifically $21 million already approved by the Senate. After some parliamentary maneuvering, the Senate also cut off the contra aid, although Republican leaders vowed to overturn that one.

On the day of the House vote, May 22, the question of the funding came up during the President's news conference. Andrea Mitchell of NBC News posed a long question that began: "Mr. President, there have been reports that the administration has gone around Congress and continued to increase military and intelligence activities in Central America by channeling money through accounting tactics, tricks of accounting through the Pentagon to the CIA?"

"Andrea, we've followed no procedures that are any different from what has been done in past administrations, nor have we done anything without the knowledge of Congress."

Truth be told, and it was not, she did not know the half of it. Since late March, when it had become obvious that Congress was not going to provide any more funding for the contra war, the administration, from the President down to McFarlane's assistants, Admiral Poindexter and Lieutenant Colonel North, had been coming up with one secret plan after another to finance the jungle war against the leaders of one of the smallest and poorest countries in the Western Hemisphere. The President had pulled McFarlane aside after one Oval Office meeting and said: "Bud, I want to do whatever you have to do to help these people keep body and soul together. Do everything you can."

In fact, Casey and McFarlane had already begun exploring private funding of the contra war by wealthy anti-communist activists. At the same time they were looking for ways to get equipment, weapons, ammunition, and secret funding from American allies, particularly South Africa, Israel, and Saudi Arabia. Two days after those House votes, McFarlane sat in the living room of the Virginia mansion of Prince Bandar, the Saudi ambassador to the United States, and his companion on his secret 1983 mission to the Middle East. McFarlane began this mission by telling Bandar that the only real threat to Reagan's reelection was trouble in Central America when the money ran out.

"I believe," Bandar said, "that His Majesty, King Fahd, would understand the importance of this to both of us, and to President Reagan." How much?

"About a million dollars a month."

Prince Bandar called McFarlane a week later, asking where to send the money for the rest of the year. McFarlane gave him the number of a Miami account used by Adolfo Calero, the political director of the Nicaragua Democratic Front. The first millions were delivered after Memorial Day weekend. On Saturday, with most members of Congress out of town, the White House had announced that two Air Force tankers and crews were being dispatched to Saudi Arabia to give the country air-refueling capacity. On Sunday there was another White House announcement, an emergency sale of four hundred Stinger ground-to-air missiles and two hundred launchers would be delivered to Saudi Arabia within seventy-two hours. The "emergency"—using the word avoided a thirty-day delay in which Congress could have voided the sale—was that both Iran and Iraq, at war for almost four years, were attacking foreign oil tankers in the Persian Gulf.

After the weekend, on May 29, McFarlane slipped a note about the Saudis' contra contributions into the President's morning briefing book. On the back of the note Reagan wrote, "Mum's the word," and sent it back to McFarlane. At a Pentagon meeting a couple of weeks after that, both Shultz and Weinberger said they were getting reports of new actions by the contras and asked McFarlane what was happening. "You don't want to know," he said. They nodded and left it at that.

The President left Washington on June 1 for a ten-day trip to Europe. The business at hand was in London, the tenth annual Economic Summit of the leaders of "The Seven," the leading industrial nations. Under the deft direction of Mike Deaver, it was nostalgia at the highest level that was fed back to the United States on live television. Millions of Americans awoke on June 3 to see their President on NBC's *Today* and the other network morning shows as he visited Ballyporeen in Tipperary County, Ireland, the village where Reagans lived before his great-grandfather emigrated to the United States. Great-grandson Reagan was charming, looking up family names in local church records as 1,800 reporters and cameramen crowded out the 350 residents of the village—then saying: "From what I'm told we were a poor family. . . . Today I come back to you as a descendant of people who are buried here in paupers' graves. Perhaps this is God's way. . . . Well, the Reagans roamed to America, but now we're back."

There were anti-Reagan demonstrators wherever the President went, including thousands in the streets of Dublin marching under the banner "Reagan's Policies Spell Death For Millions." But the greatest tension in the trip was not about peace and war but about television. Mike Deaver's office and the Elysée Palace, France's White House, were at cross-purposes over the timing of events. The American image maestro wanted the President to speak at a site where American troops had landed on D-Day, June 6, 1944, at about 1 P.M. local time, so that he would appear live again on the morning shows back home. The Elysée protested that Reagan should not speak before 4 P.M., the time he was scheduled to be officially greeted by French President François Mitterrand. On the beach, Reagan's Secret Service detail was arguing with French security men, who were insisting that only one Secret Service agent could go onto Utah Beach and the cliff called Pointe du Hoc with the President.

"You didn't say that in 1944," snapped the head of the American detail, Joseph Petro. The Americans won both arguments, and the President spoke at Pointe du Hoc, an amazing spot, a Normandy green moonscape of artillery craters and bunkers, a kind of windy museum that the French had preserved as it had been forty years before. It was there that 225 American Rangers tried to scale the cliffs from the sea to disable German artillery. Only 90 of the Rangers were fighting by the next day. Sixty-two of those survivors sat in front of the President. Old men. Reagan told their story, then said: "These are the boys of Pointe du Hoc. These are the men who took the cliffs. These are the champions who helped free a continent."

There was not a dry eye on the cliff, or in millions of American kitchens. After that the morning shows shifted to the news of the last Democratic presidential primaries in New Jersey, California, and three other states and said that Walter Mondale had officially won enough delegates to become Reagan's opponent in November.

Back home, the President convened a meeting of the National Security Council on the afternoon of June 24. The subject again was Central America; the purpose was extraordinary—to figure out how to pay for military actions turned down by Congress. Eighteen people crowded into the Situation Room, including Vice President Bush, Shultz, Weinberger, Casey, United Nations Ambassador Jeane Kirkpatrick, General John Vessey, chairman of the Joint Chiefs of Staff, and McFarlane and his deputy, Poindexter. The meeting was scheduled for an hour but lasted two. McFarlane spoke first: "The purpose of this meeting is to focus on the political, economic and military situation . . ." But what they talked about was focused on finding ways to get military aid to the anti-Sandinista contras in Nicaragua.

"At the moment CIA has $250,000 left; about half of that is being kept to hold U.S. personnel in Honduras and Costa Rica so that we can help immediately in the event that a continuing resolution makes more money available," McFarlane continued. "Our warehouses have arms and ammunition which can hold till August . . . need about $3 million to get by for the next three months. . . . We estimate that about half will retreat into Honduras and Costa Rica in some disarray, and we have to provide humanitarian assistance to help these individuals. . . ."

Weinberger argued for more pressure on congressional Democrats, saying: "We need to hold them accountable for not providing the resources needed to defend democracy."

Reagan spoke then for the first time, almost a half-hour into the meeting, saying: "How can we get that support from Congress? We have to be more active. With respect to your differences on negotiating, our participation is important from that standpoint, to get support from Congress."

The differences were, as usual, between Weinberger and Shultz. The Defense Secretary said the United States had to avoid a bilateral negotiation with Nicaragua. The Secretary of State responded: "I think Cap's characterization of what we are trying to do is inaccurate and unfair."

The President repeated that negotiations—like negotiations with the Soviets—were necessary for domestic reasons: "If we are just talking about negotiations with Nicaragua, that is so far-fetched to imagine that a communist government like that would make any reasonable deal with us, but if it is to get Congress to support the anti-Sandinistas, then that can be helpful."

"We must require the Democrats to stand up and be counted," interjected Kirkpatrick. "We should consider using the anti-Sandinistas elsewhere for the time being, for example in El Salvador, to help defend against the coming guerrilla offensive."

"I would like to get money for the contras also," said Shultz, dismissing Kirkpatrick by saying the Democrats were already on the record against that idea. "But another lawyer, Jim Baker, told me that if we go out and try to get money from third countries, it is an impeachable offense."

Casey and Weinberger attacked Shultz, saying he knew Baker had said that before he had been briefed on the details of the solicitations. "You heard him say that, George," said Casey, speaking quite clearly.

"Baker should realize that the United States would not be spending the money for the anti-Sandinista program," said Weinberger. "It is merely helping the anti-Sandinistas obtain the money from other sources."

Reagan then said: "The contra funding is like the MX spending. It will keep the pressure on Nicaragua. . . .

"We must obtain the funds to help those freedom fighters. We need to make sure that our friends know they can rely on us."

No decisions were made. McFarlane closed by saying it would be unwise to give anyone formal authority to seek third-party support—though he was doing that himself with the Saudis—and added: "I certainly hope none of this discussion will be made public in any way."

The President nodded. "If such a story gets out, we'll all be hanging by our thumbs in front of the White House until we find out who did it."

Outside the Situation Room that day, Poindexter's assistant, Oliver North, was going ahead with other money-raising, writing in his day-book: "Bank Acct # . . . No one in our government can be aware."

Reagan met with all his speechwriters after that, which was something he rarely did, even though he was writing less and less of his own material as the years went on, and doing a fraction of the editing he once did. He seemed surprised to see a woman he had never met. It was Peggy Noonan, the one who had written for Dan Rather. As everyone got up to leave after a half-hour, he took her hand and said, "You know a while ago I wanted to call you about something, but . . ."

It was obvious he did not remember. Ben Elliot, who had hired her, said, "Peggy wrote the Pointe du Hoc speech, Mr. President."

"That's it. That was wonderful, it was like 'Flanders Fields.' I read it upstairs, and when I read something I like to look up at the corner to see the name, and I saw 'Noonan.' I meant to call you."

The next day, July 18, at the Democratic National Convention in San Francisco, former Vice President Mondale accepted the nomination and named as his running mate New York Representative Geraldine Ferraro, the first woman to be chosen by either major party for Vice President. Mondale emphasized two themes in his acceptance speech, the chill in Soviet-American relations and the ballooning federal deficit, saying: "Why? Why? Why can't we meet in summit conferences with the Soviet Union each year? . . . By the end of my first term I will reduce the Reagan budget deficit by two-thirds. . . . It must be done. Mr. Reagan will raise taxes and so will I. He won't tell you. I just did."

That was for the future. In the present, on the day before, with front pages and nightly newscasts focusing on the Democratic convention, the President had signed HR-4170, the Budget Reduction Act of 1984. The new law, which Congress and the White House had been negotiating all year, increased federal taxes by more than $50 billion over five years and mandated $11 billion in spending cuts. "This is a down payment on the deficit this year," the President had been repeating as the Democratic House and Republican Senate hammered out agreements to once again raise taxes on liquor and cigarettes, close a range of corporate loopholes, and extend excise taxes on telephone calls. The spending savings were almost all effected by capping physicians' Medicare fees. The President referred to none of this in the one-paragraph press release that reported the signing. His single comment was to register a complaint about powers given to the Comptroller General, who reported to Congress rather than to the White House.

On July 24, the President held his twenty-sixth televised press conference. Four of the first six questions were about taxes and deficits. Reagan had tried to defuse the tax questions raised by Mondale six days before in San Francisco with an opening statement saying one more time that he favored a constitutional amendment mandating a balanced budget. That didn't work. The first question was: "Will you now flatly rule out the possibility of seeking a tax increase next year if you're reelected?" *

"Yes."

That was his answer. And he intended to stick to it. A four-page campaign memo was on Jim Baker's desk, titled "The Tax Issue—Historical Parallels." It began:

Presidential candidates have walked down a path similar to ours three times in this century. All three won. Of the three parallels the clearest of all is the 1916 Hughes-Wilson contest. . . . Wilson's slogan was "He kept us out of war." Wilson was the "peace candi-

---

* President Carter had held more than twice as many conferences, 59 of them, during his first twenty-four months in the White House. Reagan did 175 press interviews during those first forty-four months, compared with Carter's 65 question-and-answer sessions with groups of reporters and 46 one-on-one interviews.

date." . . . A month after his second inauguration, the United States was at war. But the pragmatist looks at the bottom line: who won and who lost. . . . Imagine what would have happened if Wilson had found it necessary to equivocate on his fundamental issue of "peace"? . . . He would have lost. The goal is re-election. That's the big picture. Everything else is small-picture. . . . People want to believe. . . . Taxes are a big picture issue. If we want to win—and win big—we need to keep the contrast between the President and Mondale sharp and clear. . . . The exigencies of the election force us to solemnly swear that Walter Mondale is the tax-increase candidate and Ronald Reagan is the no-tax-increase candidate. We need to hold that posture through November 6. After that we can always do as Wilson, Roosevelt and Johnson did.

For his part, Baker cautioned against any absolutes, writing out Reagan talking points: "RR formulation on taxes: (a.) Don't say *will* balance budget—Want to, but need tools—line item veto, Balanced Budget Amendment. (b.) Don't say NEVER on tax ques—Say: I want to cut, not raise."

Whatever happened with the tax issue, Reagan still had to deal with his "peace" problem himself. In his monthly memo, his pollster, Richard Wirthlin, reported: "A disturbing plurality of Americans continue to feel that the world is less safe than it was four years ago." While the President was running a dozen points ahead of Mondale in horse-race polling, and was getting better and better ratings on his handling of the economy, Wirthlin reported that there was a twenty-eight-point difference on the question of who was "more likely to start an unnecessary war"—28 percent more thought Reagan was the dangerous one on that question. There were two sore points in the backup data: Reagan's policy in Central America, and the fact that the Soviets and the Americans were still not talking to each other about nuclear arms control.

Reagan was feeling the pressure. In Ireland, on the way to the London economic summit, he had been asked about Soviet-American relations and had answered: "I know that the relations are bad right now. . . . Sure, they're unhappy. They're unhappy because they see that we're preparing to defend ourselves if need be." Then, during the summit, Canada's Prime Minister, Pierre Trudeau, said, "For Heaven's sake, Ron, do a bit more." Reagan, who insisted on being called by his first name by other nations' leaders, took off his reading glasses and snapped back: "Damn it, Pierre, what do you want me to do? We'll go sit with empty chairs to get those guys back to the table." Then, after he returned to Washington and briefed the Republican leaders of Congress, Senator Howard Baker told the President: "Let's just get together and talk about the world situation because we've got to figure out some way not to blow each other up." Senator Charles Percy, the Republican chairman of the Senate Foreign Relations Committee, added: "It's been five years since we met with our chief adversaries."

Reagan was greatly annoyed, but there was a campaign on and he shifted his rhetoric smoothly. *Time* magazine caught the change in a cover story that began: "Exit Ronald Reagan, rough rider. . . . Enter Reagan the statesman, man of peace and reason, holding out an olive branch to the Kremlin: 'I am willing to meet and talk anytime. . . . The door is open, we're standing in the doorway, seeing if anyone's coming up the steps.' . . . Reagan's softer line was not aimed so much at Moscow as to the American electorate."

No one was coming. The Soviets were not even coming to the 1984 Olympics in Los Angeles, retaliation for the American boycott of the 1980 Moscow Olympics after the Soviet invasion of Afghanistan. In reporting that, *Time* had used the headline: "Behind the Bear's Angry Growl. What the Soviets really want is to get rid of Ronald Reagan." As if to confirm that, the new Soviet leader, Konstantin Chernenko, said that same week: "[The Reagan Administration] has chosen terrorism as a method of conducting affairs with other states and peoples." Superpower matters were not helped much, either, by a Reagan joke heard by the whole world. Testing the microphone before his weekly radio address, this one live from the ranch, the President said: "My fellow Americans, I am pleased to tell you I just signed legislation which outlaws Russia forever. The bombing will begin in five minutes." He chuckled. The technicians laughed—until they realized the microphone was on.

The Reagans had decided to spend a month up there, inviting the press in for just one day in August—and the President seemed out of it, unable to answer a simple question about weapons in space. "Doing everything we can," his wife whispered. "Doing everything we can," Reagan said.

That was the month of "U.S.A.! . . . U.S.A.! . . . U.S.A.!" The chant began as the United States won medal after medal at the

Olympic Games in Los Angeles—triumphs made easier by the absence of Soviet runners and gymnasts, East German track stars and swimmers, and the athletes of thirteen other boycotting communist countries. By the end of the games, opened and closed by the President, the United States had won eighty-three gold medals, beating the record eighty gold won by the Soviet Union in the 1980 Moscow Olympics—the one that President Carter had ordered boycotted by the United States because of Afghanistan. The roaring American chauvinism and television coverage in Los Angeles were officially protested by the International Olympic Committee, which complained that ABC Sports television, which owned the television rights to the games, focused almost totally on American athletes.

"U.S.A.! . . . U.S.A.! . . . U.S.A.!" The same chant rocked Dallas as the Republican National Convention opened there a week after the end of the Olympics. This time the winner was Reagan, who read the Democrats out of the script, declaring his Republicans "America's Party . . . the party of the future."

"America is back and standing tall . . ." he began. "With our beloved nation at peace, we're in the midst of a springtime of hope for America. Greatness lies ahead of us. Holding the Olympic games here in the United States began defining the promise of this season. The world will beat a path to our door; and no one will be able to hold America back; and the future will be ours!"

"U.S.A! . . . U.S.A.! . . . U.S.A.!" chanted the 2,235 delegates. Their average annual income was $50,000, and almost all of them were white, 75 percent of them Protestant. "U.S.A.! . . ."

"Miss Liberty's torch. Her heart is full; her door is still golden, her future bright. She has arms big enough to comfort and strong enough to support, for the strength in her arms is the strength of her people. She will carry on in the eighties, unafraid, unashamed and unsurpassed."

"U.S.A.! . . . U.S.A.! . . . U.S.A.!"

The campaign itself did not take much of Reagan's time that night. He was able to lay it out in a few sentences:

"Our opponents began this campaign hoping that America has a poor memory. Well, let's take them on a little stroll down memory lane. Let's remind them of how a 4.8 percent inflation rate in 1976 became back-to-back years of double-digit inflation. . . . And while we have our friends down memory lane, maybe they'd like to recall a gimmick they designed for their 1976 campaign. . . . Adding the un-employment rate and inflation rates, they got what they called a mis-ery index. In '76 it came to 12.5 percent. They declared the incumbent had no right to seek reelection with that kind of misery index. Well, four years ago, in the 1980 election, they didn't mention the the mis-ery index, possibly because it was over 20 percent. And do you know something? They won't mention it in this election either. It's down to 11.6 and dropping. . . . In the four years before we took office, coun-try after country fell under the Soviet yoke. Since January of 1981, not one inch of soil has fallen to the communists."

"U.S.A.! . . . U.S.A.! . . . U.S.A.! . . ."

The flags waved, the band played patriotic airs, and Reagan, run-ning for President for the fourth time, was enjoying his last campaign. He went to the United Nations to call for a twenty-year arms control "framework," and then met for three hours with Soviet Foreign Minister Andrei Gromyko, an event the White House promoted as evidence of ongoing superpower dialogue.

Still, there were a few bad moments in the President's sunny morn-ing campaign. On September 1, the Sandinistas shot down a contra helicopter attacking a government military base, killing two Ameri-cans, the first known to die in Nicaragua. "Volunteers," said the White House and the CIA. But it soon became clear the men were CIA mercenaries. The agency said they were paid by donations from cor-porations and by individuals giving money in the name of freedom. On September 20, twenty-three people, two of them American sol-diers, were killed when a suicide truck bomber drove up to the new United States embassy in East Beirut and detonated four hundred pounds of dynamite in the truck. Two weeks later, four acknowledged CIA operatives died in a plane crash in El Salvador.

Then the Associated Press got its hands on a CIA manual being used by the contras: forty-four pages of instructions on political assas-sination, blackmail of ordinary citizens, organizing mob violence, and techniques for blowing up buildings. The administration said the pages were only part of an early draft, but contra leaders, no longer paid directly by the United States government, told a different story. "No, no, no, that is not true," said Edgar Chamorro, director of the Nicaraguan Democratic Force. "There was only one draft. . . . We do believe in the assassination of tyrants. We have killed people in cold blood." Meanwhile, the Nicaraguan Marxists, the government, as-serted that they were ready to sign a treaty proposed by the Contadora Group—the governments of Colombia, Mexico, Panama, and Venezuela—for a Central American peace, elections, and the end of foreign support of insurgent groups. The White House objected, saying that there were not enough verification and control mechanisms in the treaty.

In reacting to the embassy bombing across the world in Lebanon, the President's talent with everyday language betrayed him. Asked why there had been delays in installing barriers and other security measures after the bombing that killed sixty-three people in April of 1983, he said: "Anyone who's ever had their kitchen done over knows that it never gets done as soon as you wish it would."

Democrats running for office jumped on those words, accusing Reagan of trivializing the bombing. He tried to shift the blame by saying the security delays were caused by Democratic cuts in the intelligence budgets of the 1970s. He forwarded a request to the Congress for $110 million in supplemental appropriations to begin upgrades in the security of embassies around the world. At the same time, he gave different answers at different times when asked about the fact that his Secretary of State was regularly talking in public about preventive and preemptive action against possible terrorism. Shultz was, in fact, articulating part of a secret National Security Decision Directive, signed by the President on April 3. NSDD 138 stated: "Whenever we have evidence that a state is mounting or intends to conduct an act of terrorism against us, we have a responsibility to take measures to protect our citizens, property and interests." That was only part of it, though. The directive authorized the training of Green Beret and Navy SEAL teams to try to rescue William Buckley, the CIA station chief being held hostage in Beirut, specifically authorizing "killing." The word "assassination" was avoided because assassinations, which the CIA narrowly defined as eliminating heads of state, were first barred by President Ford in a 1975 directive and reaffirmed by Reagan in a 1981 Executive Order, numbered 12333: "No person employed by or acting on behalf of the United States government shall engage in, or conspire to engage in, assassination."

Shultz, the Cabinet member who most consistently argued for military action, was allied with CIA Director Casey, who was desperate to free Buckley. The President was with them in private, but was stumbling in public because it was not an issue he wanted projected in his reelection campaign. So the Secretary of State was doing the talking: "When—and how—should we take preventative or preemptive action against known terrorist groups? What evidence do we insist upon before taking such steps?" he had asked in an April speech. "It is time to think long, hard and seriously about more active means of defense—about defense through appropriate preventative or preemptive actions against terrorists before they strike," he said in June. In October, he added: "We may never have the kind of evidence that can stand up in an American court of law. But we cannot allow ourselves to become the Hamlet of nations, worrying endlessly over whether and how to respond."

The President and Mondale debated for the first time on October 17 in Louisville, Kentucky. The subject of the ninety-minute show was domestic issues. The President seemed vague and hesitant, defensive on a range of issues, sometimes not finishing his sentences. Mondale was crisp and energetic, pushing the line that the President was ill-informed or not informed at all about what his administration was actually doing. He lectured the President: "It's the toughest job on earth, and you must master the facts and insist that things that must be done are done" . . . "A President must see it like it is" . . . "I am reminded a little bit of what Will Rogers once said about Herbert Hoover, 'It's not what he doesn't know that bothers me; it's what he knows for sure that just ain't so.' "

The President tried a line that had worked for him in the 1980 debate, deflecting charges by shaking his head and saying, "There you go again." He said it again, but Mondale was waiting: "You said it when President Carter said that you were going to cut Medicare. . . . And what did you do after the election? You went out and tried to cut $20 billion out of Medicare."

"I'm all confused now . . ." Reagan said at one point. For the first time, people began to talk openly about his age, to say that maybe he really was not in command of his own government. The White House responded by issuing a statement signed by the Navy physician who had supervised his last full medical examination: "Mr. Reagan is a mentally alert, robust man who appears younger than his stated age." The seventy-three-year-old president, obviously angry, remarked of his fifty-six-year-old opponent: "If I'd had as much make-up as he did I would have looked younger, too."

However he looked, Reagan's polls and other surveys indicated that his strongest constituency was young people. A *New York Times*/CBS News poll taken the day of the Louisville debate showed Reagan ahead of Mondale by better than two to one among voters between the ages of eighteen and twenty-four. Those numbers changed a bit after Mondale's debate victory, but only by a couple of points. The Democrat had missed the point, perhaps deliberately. One of Mondale's advisers, a Harvard economist named Robert Reich, speaking privately before the debate, saw clearly what was happening: "Reagan has presided over a triumph of ideas. . . . They shifted the burden of truth onto government." Afterward, David Rosenbaum of *The New York Times* elaborated on that point: "More than any other President in more than fifty years, Ronald Reagan has changed the terms of the national debate over domestic policy. . . . As a consequence, the debate over the last four years has been over which Federal aid programs to cut rather than which to expand, over which civil rights rules to limit rather than which to enlarge, and over which natural resources to develop rather than which to protect." *

Reagan and Mondale debated again on October 21 in Kansas City, Missouri. The subject was foreign affairs. Mondale came out swinging, charging that the United States had been "humiliated" in Lebanon and "embarrassed" by the Nicaraguan murder manual:

> The bottom line of national strength is that the President must be in command, he must lead. And when a President doesn't know that submarine missiles are not recallable, says that 70 percent of our strategic forces are conventional, discovers three years into his administration that our arms control efforts have failed because he didn't know that most Soviet missiles were on land—these are things a President must know to command. . . . Who's in charge? Who's handling these matters? That's my main point.

Reagan, better prepared this time, answered: "I know it will come as a surprise to Mr. Mondale, but I am in charge." Still, he blundered, or dissembled, when he tried to explain the manual. The President said there were only twelve copies of the version that discussed assassination. The CIA conceded the next day that there were thousands in print. One of the questioners, Henry Trewhitt of the *Baltimore Sun,* asked whether Mondale's command attacks were essentially questions about the President's age. Reagan was waiting for that and came

---

* "You make those kids seem more complicated than they are," Senator Daniel Evans of Washington, a former college president, told me at the time. "They've only known two presidents, Jimmy Carter and Ronald Reagan. They voted for the one who didn't fail."

back with a line: "I want you to know that also I will not make age an issue in this campaign. I am not going to exploit, for political purposes, my opponent's youth and inexperience." *

Mondale laughed as hard as everyone else in the auditorium, but Reagan had won the night. On November 5, the Associated Press reported that Reagan had won the endorsement of 218 major newspapers compared with only 69 for Mondale. On November 6, the President was reelected in one of the great landslide victories in American history, carrying forty-nine states—Mondale carried only the District of Columbia and his home state of Minnesota—and winning the popular vote by 53,426,357 to 36,930,923. It was one of the two most important elections of the twentieth-century—the other being Franklin D. Roosevelt's 1932 victory—according to contemporary studies by two prominent political scientists, Thomas Cavanaugh and James Sundquist. They pointed out that for thirty years up to September 1984, Gallup polls consistently reported that roughly 45 percent of Americans identified themselves as Democrats, while 30 percent said they were Republicans. By the end of the ten-week Reagan-Mondale campaign, Gallup reported that equal numbers of respondents identified themselves as Democrats and Republicans.

---

* A British study of Reagan's debate performances in 1980 (against Carter) and 1984 (against Mondale), as recorded by Lord David Owen, a physician who served as foreign minister of Great Britain, and published as part of a book titled *Ailing Leaders in Power 1914–1994*, Hugh L'Etang, Royal Society of Medicine Press, 1995 (pp. 55–56), concluded: "Whereas in 1980 Reagan's answers were clear and his sentences well formed and understandable, and if necessary corrected, by 1984 there were more grave errors and his replies were at times so muddled they could not be understood. Furthermore there were no paragrammatic errors in the Carter debate, but an average of one every 220 words in the first Mondale debate and one in every 290 words in the second. Pauses occurred less than once in a thousand words in 1980 but five times more often in 1984 and there was a 9-percent slowing in Reagan's speech." Psychologist Brian Butterworth, one of the authors, concluded in 1987 that President Reagan had early senile dementia, which is not Alzheimer's disease. Detailed medical records at the Mayo Clinic in the summer of 1990, after Reagan suffered a bad fall from a horse and had brain surgery, showed no indications of impending Alzheimer's.

CHAPTER 11
MARCH 11, 1985

A S SOON AS PRESIDENT REAGAN WON REELECTION, the White House announced that the President was considering the resumption of diplomatic relations with the government of Saddam Hussein in Iraq. The countries had not exchanged ambassadors since 1967, when Baghdad severed diplomatic ties because of United States support of Israel in the Six-Day War against Arab countries. Until late 1982, the United States had officially labeled Iraq as a terrorist nation. As late as November of 1983, classified State Department documents declared: "Iraq has acquired a CW [Chemical Warfare] production capability, primarily from Western firms, including a U.S. foreign subsidy . . . now there appears to be almost daily use of CW." Deadly poison gas, according to intelligence agencies reporting to the National Security Council, were being used against Iranian soldiers and against Iraqi towns believed to be resisting Saddam's dictatorial rule.

On November 25, Deputy Premier Tariq Aziz was welcomed at the White House, and before the day was over diplomatic relations had been reinstated. The new arrangement followed the outlines of a "Secret/Sensitive" October 7, 1983, State Department memorandum on the war that had begun in 1980 when Iraq invaded Iran. "Iran-Iraq War: Analysis of Possible U.S. Shift from Position of Strict Neutrality" concluded: "The qualified tilt [toward Iraq] which we have in fact practiced for more than a year is again being ratcheted one notch higher. . . . This further tilt toward Iraq would, we believe . . . support our objective of avoiding Iraq's collapse before revolutionary Iran without going so far as to alarm Israel."

For almost two years, operating under the President's personal orders, the United States had been providing Iraq with billions of dollars in cash, credit, weapons, advice, and classified satellite intelligence on Iranian troop movements. The United States also supplied Iraq with cluster bombs adapted for use on the country's Soviet- and French-manufactured aircraft. In a program called "Bear Spares," the CIA facilitated (and paid for) the transfer of captured Soviet ammunition and parts from Afghanistan and Nicaragua—and from Egyptian stocks.

Donald Rumsfeld, the President's special envoy to the Middle East, had traveled twice to Baghdad to negotiate the secret American alliance with Saddam. On December 20, 1983, Rumsfeld had met separately with Aziz and Saddam to discuss a new relationship. The chemical weapons were unmentioned in official documents of the trip, but secret "Talking Points" stated: "A major objective of the meeting with Saddam is to initiate a dialogue and establish personal rapport. In that meeting, Rumsfeld will want to emphasize his close relationship with President Reagan and the President's interest in regional issues. . . . The USG [United States Government] recognizes Iraq's current disadvantage in a war of attrition, since Iran has access to the Persian Gulf and Iraq does not, and would regard any major reversal of Iraq's fortunes as a strategic defeat for the West. . . . This requires diplomatic and economic pressures as well as a military potential."

Rumsfeld then returned to Baghdad in March of 1984. On that trip he stopped first in Israel, where the government had now accepted the American contention that Iran was a greater threat to the Jewish state than was Iraq. Israeli Foreign Minister Yitzhak Shamir gave Rumsfeld a letter to deliver to Saddam Hussein stating that Israel was willing to provide secret assistance in the war against Iran. Meeting with Aziz in Baghdad before he met with Saddam, Rumsfeld offered the letter to the deputy premier. Aziz stepped back and pulled his hands away without touching the letter. "I would be executed on the spot," he told Rumsfeld, "if I read that letter or tried to give it to Saddam."

Rumsfeld reported back to Reagan, and on April 5, 1984, the President signed NSDD 139, specifying that only six copies would be printed, stating: "The Secretary of State, in coordination with the Secretary of Defense and the Director of Central Intelligence, will prepare a plan of action designed to avert an Iraqi collapse. . . ."

Early in January 1985, as the newly elected President prepared for his second Inauguration, Reagan received a five-page memo titled "A

New Approach for the Second Term" from Richard Nixon. "A President in his second term, even after a landslide, has a much briefer honeymoon and a less effective mandate than after his first election," began Nixon, who certainly knew what he was talking about. He wrote about his own second-term troubles and those of Franklin Roosevelt, Dwight Eisenhower, and Lyndon Johnson:

> Personal loyalty among politicians is rare. As far as most Senators and Congressmen are concerned, they are loyal to the President only to the extent he can do something for them or something to them. A President who can't run for reelection will therefore get support only if his *policies* are politically popular. . . . If the second term is not to fall victim to the disaster-prone pattern which has plagued previous landslide winners, action must be taken on three fronts: new men, new ideas and new drive. . . . What is required is to give the new Administration a sense of purpose and drive toward great new goals rather than being satisfied with continuing the policies of the past, even though they have just received an overwhelming vote of approval. . . . What he should recognize is that he will have won on his own. He will owe his victory to *no one* and *everyone*.

Nixon's words, underlined, annotated, and debated inside the Oval Office, and upstairs in the living quarters as well, pumped up Reagan with lines like: "The President has already won his place in history as the leader who demonstrated that conservative policies produce prosperity and who restored the American people's faith in themselves. . . . He can become the preeminent post–World War II foreign policy leader by establishing a new, less dangerous relationship with the Soviet Union."

Nixon's memo was a significant part of the pressure for some kind of arms control talks, any kind, really, that had been building around the world after the Soviets walked away from negotiations in Geneva in November of 1983. Presidents and Prime Ministers around the world, congressional leaders, editorial writers, half of Reagan's Cabinet led by his Secretary of State, and his wife, too, were making the point over and over again that the world just felt better when the nuclear superpowers were at least talking to each other.

There was, however, a powerful faction, led by Secretary of Defense Weinberger and one of his assistants, Richard Perle, and CIA director Casey, who thought there was nothing to talk about with what they still called the Evil Empire, even if the President had moderated his rhetoric during 1984. But a return to negotiations had become more likely each day as Reagan campaigned as the peacemaker. Inside Washington, Shultz was prevailing more often by periodically threatening to quit. In Moscow, leaders were worried by the possibilities of the Strategic Defense Initiative. "The Soviets are afraid that U.S. computer wizardry and advances in laser and particle-beam research will leave them far behind in a space arms race," reported *Time* magazine from Moscow.

At the end of the year the Kremlin's number two man, Mikhail Gorbachev, traveled to London for meetings with Prime Minister Thatcher. "I like Mr. Gorbachev," she cabled Reagan. "We can do business with him." But Gorbachev's business included pushing the Soviet line and he said: "It is especially important to avoid the transfer of the arms race to outer space. If it is not done, then it would be unreal to hope to stop the nuclear arms race." Finally, after an exchange of letters between Reagan and Soviet General Secretary Chernenko, it was announced that Secretary of State Shultz and Foreign Minister Gromyko would meet on January 7 in Geneva.

The get-together was only to talk about talks—topics and dates—but the three American television networks immediately dispatched their anchormen and the hosts of their morning shows to Switzerland to stand outside the gates of the American and Soviet missions, along with more than a thousand other journalists, to speculate on what might be happening inside. Journalists interviewed each other in live reports as the networks back in New York and Washington showed animated videos, supplied by the Department of Defense, of wonderful American satellites covering North America and shooting down Soviet missiles. The conventional wisdom, as articulated by NBC News anchorman Tom Brokaw, was: "There is every indication that it is the Soviet Union's concern about Star Wars that brought them back to the bargaining table."

Indeed, one of the things happening as Gromyko and Shultz met for more than six hours inside was a calculation of the balance of nuclear strength of the superpowers and Gromyko's insistence that the Kremlin had a fundamentally different view of SDI than Reagan did, saying: "SDI is not defensive. If you develop a shield against ICBMs, you could launch a first strike." But after two days Shultz was able to call Washington and tell his boss: "We have an agreement. . . . We'll begin new negotiations." *

On Shultz's first day in Geneva, Baker and Deaver had gone into the Oval Office with the Secretary of the Treasury, Don Regan. Deaver had already told the President that he was leaving to make some money in public relations and lobbying. Now he had other news: Baker and Regan wanted to trade jobs. The President did not seem surprised. He hardly seemed interested. That shocked Regan, a tough executive who thought the government could be managed the way he had once managed Merrill Lynch. After a few minutes of conversation, mostly about the Christmas and New Year's holidays, Reagan said it sounded like a good idea to him and said he would announce the swap the next day. The meeting was over within twenty minutes, even as Regan continued to say he knew the President needed time to think it over, talk it over. In fact, he already had done that with Deaver and with his wife.

The idea had first come up when Regan and Baker had argued just after the election over a leak of a Regan Cabinet briefing, in which the Treasury Secretary said he thought the Federal Reserve Board's restriction of money supply was slowing the economic growth that had so much to do with Reagan's landslide. Regan treated Baker to one of his favorite lines: "Fuck you and the horse you rode in on." Then he slammed down the phone. He dictated a resignation letter and had a messenger take it over to the Oval Office. The President immediately called him, full of flattery, telling Regan, "You're the only friend I have left around here." He told Baker to walk over to Treasury and calm Regan down. Mission accomplished, Baker stayed for lunch in the Secretary's private dining room. Regan said: "You know what's wrong with you, Baker? You're tired. You're fed up. You want to get out but you don't know how."

Baker did know how, or at least he knew what he wanted. He wanted a top Cabinet post. He wanted a résumé that might make him President one day. But State and Defense were taken and so was Justice. The President had resubmitted Meese's nomination as Attorney

* At the beginning of 1985, according to the RAND Corporation, the military think tank created by the United States Air Force, this was the lineup of superpower nuclear warheads: intercontinental ballistic missiles: United States—2,132, USSR—5,800; submarine-launched missiles: U.S.—5,728, USSR—2,500; long-range bombers: U.S.—3,280, USSR—400; intermediate-range missiles: U.S.—100, USSR—1,358.

General when the special counsel investigating his tangled finances had cleared him of possible criminal action.

"We ought to swap jobs," said Regan.

"Watch out," said Baker. "I may just take you up on that."

And he did. Knowing the workings of the White House, upstairs and downstairs, Baker brought in Deaver. Then Deaver talked to Nancy Reagan, whose interests focused on her husband's health, safety, and image and on the service and loyalty of the men around him. When the news got out that the old Troika of Meese, Baker, and Deaver were all moving out, Bill Clark made some moves toward coming back from the Interior Department to the White House. Mrs. Reagan, through Deaver, let it be known that perhaps it was time for Clark to go home to California, which he did. Of the original thirteen Cabinet members, only four were sitting in the same chairs in 1985: Weinberger, Malcolm Baldridge at Commerce, and Samuel Pierce at Housing and Urban Development. (Labor Secretary Raymond Donovan, a former construction company president, was on leave, the defendant in a criminal case in New Jersey.)*

Reagan's second inaugural parade was canceled because of the weather; the temperature in Washington was just nine degrees Fahrenheit with twenty-mile-per-hour winds whipping light snow through the streets on January 20, 1985, no day for a Southern Californian. The President took his oath in a one-minute ceremony in the grand foyer of the White House.

Both *The New York Times* and *The Washington Post* published front-page stories that day on Reagan's possible place in history. Hedrick Smith of the *Times* was tentative, writing: "His aggressive buildup of the nation's arsenal has set the stage to test the Reagan thesis that successful arms control can be achieved only when the United States bargains from a position of strength. Already Mr. Reagan has turned to that as his first priority, and most politicians say that achieving a major arms agreement with the Soviet Union would secure him an important place in history, but failure to strike any accord in his eight years in office could be damaging. . . . On the domestic side, Mr. Reagan's 25 percent cut in income tax rates and his costly military buildup now require another major assault on budget deficits that have soared." David Gergen, out of the White House

---

* Donovan was tried in 1986 on charges of fraud and grand larceny. On May 25, 1987, he was acquitted of all charges. The trial lasted ten months; the jury deliberated less than ten hours.

now, was candid and damaging: "I'm not clear whether the fire is still there."

In the *Post*, Robert Kaiser began by writing, "Will marble tablets record: 'He cut the growth rate of federal spending'? Will our grandchildren recall in song and verse: 'He conquered Grenada'? No, Reagan's specific accomplishments don't yet look like the stuff of history." But then he went on to say there was indeed something Rooseveltian about Reagan's undeniable restoration of American confidence. "Wouldn't he love to be remembered as the President who put the unhappy, divisive '60s and '70s behind us." Kaiser quoted William Leuchtenburg, an FDR biographer from the University of North Carolina, saying: "You could write the diplomatic history of the 20th century and leave Reagan out at this point." But he also added: "Of course, if Reaganomics continues to bring prosperity—if all the prognosticators of economic doom are proven wrong—then Reagan's historical reputation will be golden. He'll be forgiven for failing to balance the budget if it turns out that the big deficits don't have the bad consequences so many people, including, for years, Ronald Reagan, have contended."

The Reagans made the best of the day, appearing at the Capital Center in Landover, Maryland, before the fifty-seven bands that would have been marching down Pennsylvania Avenue if the day had been warmer. Mrs. Reagan gave them a moment to remember, leaving the microphone after saying a few nice words but not mentioning her husband, then rushing back to say: "I was supposed to introduce my roommate who happens to be my husband who happens to be the President of the United States." The President gave his inaugural address in the crowded Rotunda of the Capitol. He talked of history with more gloss than weight: "Let history say of us: 'These were golden years—when the American revolution was reborn, when freedom gained new life, and America reached for her best.' " The weather just did in everyone, including the speaker, who concluded: "We stand again at the steps of this symbol of democracy—well, we would be standing at the steps if it hadn't got so cold."

In the next two weeks, Reagan did sound warmer, even fiery once or twice, cheering some, provoking others. "A new danger we see in Central America is support being given to the Sandinistas by Colonel Qaddafi's Libya, the P.L.O. and most recently, the Ayatollah Khomeini," he told a meeting of dubious legislators from Latin America. He accused the leaders of unnamed black organizations of twisting his record to make sure their constituencies remained hostile to his administration. For the first time the President, speaking from the Oval Office, his voice heard from a temporary loudspeaker system in front of the Supreme Court, cheered on seventy thousand anti-abortion demonstrators. Their march past the Court building was on January 22, the twelfth anniversary of the court's decision on *Roe v. Wade*, the decision essentially legalizing abortion. "I feel a great sense of solidarity with all of you," Reagan declared. "The momentum is with us."

With the election behind him, Reagan could again speak out on social issues that divided Americans, beginning with abortion, and he realized that, as is often the case, technology was moving faster than legislation and the decisions of judges. "For the first time, through the new technique of real-time ultrasound imaging, we're able to see with our own eyes . . . the abortion of a twelve-week old unborn child. . . . If every member of Congress could see this film of an early abortion, the Congress would move quickly to end the tragedy of abortion. And I pray that they will." Then he agreed to allow the twenty-eight-minute film, titled *Silent Scream,* to be shown to an invited audience in the White House theater. The connection between the President's words—or leadership—and actions in the lower reaches of his administration was demonstrated by the fact that as he spoke, appointed officers of VISTA (Volunteers in Service to America) were sending letters to anti-abortion groups encouraging them to apply to the agency and to anti-poverty agencies for federal funding.*

"Tonight we can take pride in 25 straight months of growth, the strongest in 34 years; a three-year inflation rate of 3.9 percent, the lowest in 17 years; and 7.3 million new jobs in two years," said the President in his fifth State of the Union speech before a joint session of Congress on February 6. He declared a "Second American Revolution," but the ideas were pretty much what he had been saying all along: "Of all the changes that have swept America the past four years, none brings greater promise than our rediscovery of the values of faith, freedom, family, work, and neighborhood." And, though Republicans in Congress, led by the new Senate Majority Leader, Robert Dole of Kansas, had been urging him to cut military spending as a

---

* Reagan obviously knew the power of film. The narration of *Silent Scream* included such lines as: "The abortionist will attempt to crush the head with this instrument in this manner and remove the head piecemeal from the uterus." Critics claimed that the sonogram images had been manipulated, slowed down and speeded up to give the impression of great pain to the fetus. But whatever the medical facts, Reagan's endorsement of the film guaranteed heavy media coverage and enormous political impact.

way of reducing record budget deficits, Reagan gave that subject only a short paragraph: "There are some who say that growth initiatives must await final action on deficit reductions. Well, the best way to reduce deficits is through economic growth." *

As the President spoke, the deficit was more than 5 percent of the gross national product, and more than 15 percent of the 1985 budget was earmarked to pay interest on the national debt. But both the people and the President were getting used to numbers once unprecedented, including a projected $200 billion deficit for the year. The *National Journal* reported on the new budget figures under the headline: "REAGAN BUDGET PURSUES HIS POLITICAL GOALS, LETS CONGRESS FRET ABOUT BOTTOM LINE. In ruling out tax increases and steep defense cuts to reduce the deficit, the President is forcing Congress to deal with the budget his way and on his terms." As usual, Reagan found simple words and vivid imagery to make his point in briefing his new Cabinet on the budget: "We came here to dam the river. Let's start throwing in the rocks."

There were more words than rocks around, but Reagan was having it both ways. The *National Journal* remarked: "It is now almost a foregone conclusion that Reagan will get spending cuts of large magnitude, although perhaps not the ones he has proposed. He has already won on the second count, taxes. The third, defense, is the only real battle for him, and there is a good chance that he can win. If he does, his campaign to realign national priorities will have scored a major victory."

Every once in a while things did not go according to the leatherbound schedule (or script) placed on the President's desk each morning. Reagan came down one morning and began the day with a telephone call to William Schroeder, a man newly famous after doctors had connected him to a permanent mechanical heart. Television cameras were rolled into his room in Louisville, Kentucky, for a telephone call from the President, who asked how he was doing.

---

* The deficit issue was splitting the majority party, not an unusual thing in the second term of even the most popular Presidents. Representative Newt Gingrich of Georgia, leader of a group of young conservatives in the House, told me during the Republican National Convention: "Dole is nothing more than a tax collector for the welfare state." Dole then told me that "your little friend," meaning Gingrich, was going to be in trouble when we all got back to "the real world," meaning Washington. Another conservative Republican, Representative Dick Cheney of Wyoming, said: "If Congress is not successful in reducing the deficit, the United States will soon be paying a quarter of a trillion dollars in interest on the Federal debt, which will drive up interest rates and throw us into a recession."

Schroeder said: "Not too well. I've got a Social Security problem. I filed in March of 1984 for Social Security and I'm getting the runaround. I'm not getting anything at all . . ."

"What? Wait a minute, I'm having trouble hearing you. This has to do with Social Security?"

"Yes, sir."

"Well, I'll get on it . . ."

"Thank you, Mr. President . . ."

The next morning, a Social Security official flew to Louisville with a $324 check for Schroeder. "Got a problem," said Morton Dean of CBS News, on the scene. "Call the nice man in the White House. Operators are standing by."

On Nicaragua, the nice man was still not getting his way. Democrats in Congress had stopped funding the White House's surrogate war in the jungle, but the President managed to carry on. The National Security Council was having some success in trying to solicit money and arms around the world—from Israel, South Africa, Chile, Portugal, South Korea, Taiwan, and Brunei, among others—and since January had been routing mortars, grenades, and ammunition through Guatemala to the contras in Honduras and inside Nicaragua. A March 25 memo to McFarlane from Colonel North, who was running the day-to-day arms business, was titled "Guatemalan Aid to the Nicaraguan Resistance": "Attached at Tab 1 is a memo from you to Secretaries Shultz and Weinberger, Director Casey, and General Vessey asking for their views on increased U.S. assistance to Guatemala. . . . The real purpose of your memo is to find a way by which we can compensate the Guatemalans for the extraordinary assistance they are providing the Nicaraguan freedom fighters."

Some of the money for arms was coming in from private citizens, an effort helped along by two White House employees, Pat Buchanan and speechwriter Peggy Noonan, who provided the President and Oliver North with lists of "highly patriotic" gentlemen. But there was a price for such help. The price was meeting the President, according to a March 5 memo to North from a public relations executive named Edie Fraser, who wrote: "Ollie. Very Imp. Two people who want to give major contribs i.e. 300,000 and up if they might have one 'quiet' meeting with the President." That request went into the Oval Office. Reagan said, "Yes."

In public, Reagan escalated his rhetoric again, admitting in effect what he had often denied, that the real goal of the United States was to overthrow the Sandinista government. At the annual dinner of the Conservative Political Action Conference, he said: "They are our brothers, these freedom fighters. . . . You know who they are fighting and why. They are the moral equal of our Founding Fathers and the brave men and women of the French Resistance. We cannot turn away from them for the struggle here is not right versus left; it is right versus wrong."

On March 11, the day before the Geneva arms control negotiations were scheduled to reconvene, Reagan was awakened at 4 A.M. by a telephone call from McFarlane and told that Konstantin Chernenko had died and once more the Soviets were choosing a new leader. Within five hours, the Kremlin announced that Chernenko would be succeeded by fifty-four-year-old Mikhail Gorbachev, a child during "The Great Patriotic War" of the 1940s, the first Soviet leader with no memories of Stalinist terror, the first Soviet leader with a college education. In his acceptance speech, Gorbachev said: "I promise you, comrades, to do my utmost to faithfully serve our party, our people and the great Leninist cause. . . . We are to achieve a decisive turn in transferring the national economy to the tracks of intensive development. We are bound to attain within the briefest period the most advanced scientific and technical positions, the highest world level in the productivity of social labor . . . a real and major reduction in arms stockpiles, and not the development of ever-new weapons systems, be it in space or on earth."

Gorbachev assumed office on the day the Soviet Union and the United States negotiators in Geneva resumed arms control talks, meeting in a room built for wedding receptions above a large lamp store. The Americans, who had leased the room, had a view of Lake Geneva. The Soviets on the other side of the table faced a wall of sports prints by the American illustrator LeRoy Neiman.

President Reagan, meanwhile, was in Bethesda, Maryland, for his annual physical examination at the Naval Medical Center there. His blood pressure was recorded as 130 over 74, remarkably good for a man his age, and lower than it had been a year before. He came out of the hospital talking about the same issue he talked about on the way in, urging congressional approval of $1.5 billion in funding to build twenty-one more MX missiles. His argument was simple. Calling it "a vote for peace," he asserted that the threat of new American weapons had brought the Soviets back to Geneva, and if arms control talks failed, he would blame members of Congress who opposed him. One who did, Representative Barney Frank of Massachusetts, responded: "We used to be told the MX was needed because we weren't having talks with the Russians. Now we're told we need it because we are having talks with the Russians. I'll predict that if we ever have successful negotiations, we'll be told that we need it because we used to have talks with the Russians." But Reagan won again. This time it was 55 to 45 in the Senate, 219 to 213 in the House.

Vice President Bush carried a letter from Reagan to Gorbachev, presenting it to the new leader after Chernenko's March funeral. "I would like you to visit me in Washington at your earliest convenient opportunity," wrote the President, who had always wanted to personally show a communist leader the way "ordinary" Americans—Sally and Jim—lived and worked. "I recognize that arriving at an early answer may not be possible. But I want you to know that I look forward to a meeting that could yield results of benefit to both our countries."

Gorbachev responded within two weeks, practically return mail in the business of summitry, discussing arms control at some length but ending: "I would like to say that we deem improvement of relations between the USSR and the USA to be not only extremely necessary, but possible, too. . . . I have a positive attitude to the idea you expressed about holding a personal meeting between us . . . a meeting to search for mutual understanding on the basis of equality. . . . Let us agree that we shall return again to the question of the time and place for the meeting."

That was on March 24. Reagan responded on April 4: "I look forward to meeting you personally at a mutually convenient time. Let me close by affirming the value I place on our correspondence. . . . I hope we can continue to speak frankly in future letters." The letters flew back and forth; some of them repeated old charges, old grievances, and diplomatically veiled threats. The new Soviet leader picked up the phrase "Star Wars" and, both publicly and privately, attacked it each time as the beginning of a new arms race. In speeches to officials at home he often sounded like a very old-fashioned Marxist, attacking "the ruling circles of the U.S.A." But finally Reagan and Gorbachev agreed to meet in November, in Geneva.

The President went to his ranch early in April for a ten-day Easter break. He returned to Washington on April 15 and immediately began another charge up Capitol Hill to try again to persuade legislators to resume funding for the contra war in Nicaragua. His strategy this time was a variation on the words that had worked in winning the votes to continue building MX missiles. He surrounded himself with a bipartisan squad of hawks—former Defense Secretary James Schlesinger, President Carter's NSC director, Zbigniew Brzezinski, and retiring U.N. ambassador Jeane Kirkpatrick—and declared that this war was necessary to win peace: "A vote against this proposal is a vote against peace. I'm asking Congress to give this peace initiative and democracy a chance. I'm asking Congress to work with me to stem the flood of refugees, the threat of hostile forces on our borders, and the loss of faith in America's commitments around the world." What he wanted from Congress was an emergency appropriation of $14 million for the contras.

His first night back in Washington, Reagan spoke at a fund-raising dinner, organized by Oliver North, that raised $220,000 for the Nicaragua Refugee Fund, closing with a passionate plea: "We cannot have the United States walk away from one of the greatest moral challenges in postwar history. . . . We will fight on. We will win this struggle for peace. . . . *Viva Nicaragua Libre!*"

After the dinner, Reagan met privately with two of the donors who had promised $300,000 for a "quiet" moment with the President. All that, most of it arranged by Colonel North, was part of a secret $750,000 plan coordinated from the White House, one of several operations designed to deceive the Congress about the true amount of contra funding. In February, the chairman of the House Intelligence Committee, Representative Lee Hamilton of Indiana, had discovered that the chief contra lobbyist in Washington, Arturo Cruz Sr., was being paid $7,000 a month by the CIA. When Hamilton complained privately to the White House, Colonel North shifted Cruz to a secret account funded by Saudi Arabia. Another account was used to pay $50,000 to a retired British officer named David Walker, who planned the March 6 bombing of a Sandinista ammunition depot. In all, since U.S. government funding had been cut off by Congress in May of 1984, North's secret accounts indicated that $17,145,594 worth of ammunition and other military supplies had been provided to the contras, most of it shipped, using falsified papers, through Honduras and Guatemala. And North was urging McFarlane to find a way to reward the Guatemalans with shipments of United States weaponry.

North's arguments were not subtle. Like McFarlane, he had served with the Marines in Vietnam, and they shared stories and feelings about bad times there when men in the field, the end of the supply line, were short of weapons, ammunition, and food—and he would remind McFarlane of those shortages when he was trying to get money or authority to resupply the contras. "Bud, when our grand-children are fighting communists coming across the border from Mexico," he would say, "we'll think back to this moment and you'll know it was you who didn't have the backbone to stand up for our country and do what was right." It worked, sometimes. McFarlane knew North was a zealot, using words like "traitor" and "coward" about people who disagreed with him—some folks at the NSC thought he was just plain crazy—but he also had the energy and ded-ication to make things happen, one way or another.*

There was also the NSC "Fallback Plan for the Nicaraguan Resis-tance," written by North and approved by McFarlane, to be used if the President could not win congressional approval of more aid. Basi-cally, the NSC wanted the President to go on television to solicit more private donors willing to finance the contras: "Send your check or money order to Nicaraguan Freedom Fighters, PO Box 1776, Gettys-burg, PA." That one never got off the ground, but North did find sev-eral big donors, including Ross Perot, a Texas businessman who contributed $200,000 to a North account, but who wanted it used not for the contras but to buy freedom for American hostages in Lebanon. North was also able to begin conversations that led to do-nations of $470,000 from Texas billionaire Nelson Bunker Hunt and $65,000 from Joseph Coors of the Colorado beer family.

All of that was separate, of course, from the public part of the Nicaragua planning. The President's formal request for the $14 mil-lion classified as "humanitarian aid" was thrown off-track when con-troversy erupted over the planning for a presidential trip to Europe in May. While Reagan was still at the ranch, a White House press release announced that one of his stops after the world Economic Summit in Bonn, West Germany, would be a wreath-laying ceremony at a mili-tary cemetery in a town called Bitburg. The visit was called a "recon-ciliation event" on the President's schedule, but Jewish groups around the world and the press at home were not reconciled to the idea of a President honoring German soldiers who had fought American sol-diers at the Battle of the Bulge, a battle in which the Americans took seventy thousand casualties. The town was in the parliamentary dis-

---

* In 1974, when North was commanding a Marine training battalion in Okinawa, he was re-lieved of duty and treated for three weeks at Bethesda Naval Hospital. According to some pub-lished reports he had been discovered running around naked with a U.S. pistol, babbling incoherently and threatening to kill himself. The incident disappeared from his service record.

trict represented by Chancellor Helmut Kohl, who was facing crucial regional elections. The President had promised in November to do what he could for Kohl, a reward for his unwavering support for the siting of new American missiles in Europe. There was another complication: The White House had said that the President had decided against a visit to Dachau, site of a Nazi concentration camp near Munich. Within days, Mike Deaver, getting ready to leave Reagan's staff, was on his way to Germany. The image-maker was going to figure out how to make the cemetery visit short and, a rare thing in his work, untelegenic.

On April 16, five prominent Republican Jews opposed to the Bitburg visit were invited to the White House for a 1:15 meeting with Don Regan, with Ed Rollins, who wanted the visit canceled, and with Pat Buchanan, who did not. Richard Fox, a Philadelphia builder, sitting next to Buchanan, noticed he was writing a single sentence over and over on a yellow pad: "Succumbing to the pressure of the Jews." Then Rollins slipped Fox the statement that the President intended to make at 2 P.M. It said that the President would not buckle to any pressure, that he had promised Chancellor Kohl that he was going to Bitburg and he was going to keep that promise.

"Come on, let's quit bullshitting each other," Fox interrupted. "Is the President going out at two to make this announcement?"

He was and he did. Later that day, it was reported that Bitburg contained the graves not only of eighteen hundred ordinary German soldiers, but that forty-seven of the Germans buried there had been members of the murderous SS, the most elite and vicious of Nazi units. One of the graves commemorated SS Staff Sergeant Otto Franz Begel, awarded the German Cross for killing ten Americans in one day, a day in which at least seventy captured Americans were executed and tossed into a shallow mass grave. The next day the President met with editors of regional newspapers. The session was scheduled to promote his ideas of war and peace in Nicaragua. But the questions that made headlines were once again about Bitburg, with Reagan repeating he would never "cave in": "I think that there is nothing wrong with visiting that cemetery where those young men are victims of Nazism also, even though they were fighting in the German uniform, drafted into service to carry out the hateful wishes of the Nazis. They were victims, just as surely as the victims in the concentration camps."

"DON'T COMMEMORATE BUTCHERS" was the headline on

the editorial page of the *Denver Post* the next morning. Its language was typical of pages around the country: "It is tempting, 40 years after a war, to try to heal the wounds, to admit there was guilt on both sides, and to see that all sides had innocent victims. But we weren't fighting for world conquest. Our soldiers buried in Europe fought to liberate the continent from Nazidom. Why honor those who killed them?"

"The press has the bit in their teeth and they're stirring up as much trouble as they can," Reagan had written in his diary the night before. Later that morning, the White House announced that the President had spoken by telephone with Chancellor Kohl and that a stop had been added to his schedule. He would visit a concentration camp, Bergen-Belsen, the place where the young Jewish diarist Anne Frank had been killed.

On April 19, Elie Wiesel, the concentration camp survivor who coined the word "Holocaust" and was chairman of the official United States Holocaust Memorial Committee, came to the White House to receive a Congressional Gold Medal. "Elie," said the President, "we present you with this medal as an expression of gratitude for your life's work."

"This medal is not mine alone," Weisel responded. "It belongs to all those who remember what SS killers have done to their victims." He remembered being liberated by American soldiers at Buchenwald, he praised Reagan for his efforts on behalf of Jews in the Soviet Union, and then he continued:

> I am convinced, as you have told us earlier when we spoke that you were not aware of the presence of SS graves in the Bitburg cemetery. . . . May I, Mr. President, if it is possible at all, implore you to do something else, to find a way, to find another way, another site. That place, Mr. President, is not your place. Your place is with the victims of the SS. . . . The issue here is not politics but good and evil. And we must never confuse them, for I have seen the SS at work, and I have seen their victims. They were my friends. They were my parents. . . . Fathers being beaten to death; mothers watched their children die of hunger. . . . Terror, fear, isolation, torture, gas chambers, flames—flames rising to the heavens.

The setting gave the words great drama, great power. This was the Roosevelt Room of the White House. The President was sitting five feet from Wiesel.

"My Dreyfus case," Reagan wrote in his diary that night. "The call [from Kohl] came. . . . He told me my remarks about the dead soldiers being victims of Nazism as the Jews in the Holocaust were, had been well received in Germany. He was emphatic that to cancel the cemetery now would be a disaster in his country and an insult to the German people. I told him I would not cancel. While I was on the phone to Kohl, the VP was in the room with our gang hearing my end of the call. He wrote me this note: 'Mr. President, I was very proud of your stand. If I can absorb some heat, send me into battle—it's not easy, but you are right!!' "

A couple of days later, Reagan wrote: "The press is still chewing on the Bitburg business. I'll just keep on praying." The following night he continued: "I'm worried about Nancy. She's uptight about the situation and nothing I can say can wind her down. I'll pray about that too."

The President was blaming the press. The press was often blaming the new White House staff, particularly chief of staff Regan, and also the new communications director, Patrick Buchanan. Both liked to play the tough guy. On the nightly newscasts, Regan was shown repeatedly ordering the President around, or so it seemed. In one bit of video repeated again and again, Regan was heard saying, "Better speed it up." The President seemed confused, saying, "Oh! . . . Okay." Regan reacted to news that 82 of 100 senators and 257 House members had signed anti-Bitburg petitions by saying: "We are going to Bitburg, period." The new chief of staff seemed to be equating himself with the President. It was a trait not appreciated by other staffers, nor by the President's wife.

Mrs. Reagan was frantic about the disastrous public relations of the trip and about the danger that her husband could get killed over this. She had Deaver call her astrologer to choose the times the President would be safest during his German moves—and the Bitburg schedule was changed one more time after Quigley said flight schedules were putting Reagan in starry danger zones. When Deaver protested, Mrs. Reagan shouted at him: "We're talking about my husband's life." *

Regan had taken to referring to the President as "the chairman of the board" and himself as "the chief executive officer." White House

---

* The fact that the Reagans consulted astrologers—Deaver called Quigley "Madame Zorro"— and made decisions based on their readings of the stars became known in 1988, when Donald Regan revealed it in his memoir, *For the Record.*

reporters, and some staffers, called the men Regan brought with him to the White House "the mice." Except for Buchanan, they followed the chief's orders not to talk to reporters. There were questions inside as well—and some frankness mixed with the usual flattery. In a memo to the chief, the new Cabinet secretary, Alfred Kingon, one of Regan's men, wrote: "I have become distressed at the process of scheduling the President's time. The election is over. . . . The campaign we are in now is for the President's place in history, and that calls for a much different strategy. Coupling the above with the fact that Mrs. Reagan apparently wants a lightening of the schedule, I am proposing more substance and less PR. Where is the time for the wise counsel with his new chief of staff or other senior aides and Cabinet members?"

On Nicaragua, Reagan seemed to be losing the debate, at least on television—and perhaps in Congress—despite "White Propaganda," a secret public relations operation run by a Washington company financed by $440,000 from the State Department's Office of Public Diplomacy. The company, International Business Communications, had reported to Buchanan in an "Eyes Only" memo in mid-March, offering examples of its work, particularly anti-Sandinista op-ed pieces placed in *The Wall Street Journal, The New York Times,* and *The Washington Post.* But the Sandinista government was doing the same thing, perhaps more effectively. Network cameras and correspondents were waiting in Managua for members of Congress, who were being escorted by bus to schools and medical clinics in the countryside, where they were greeted by peasants telling them their lives were better than they had been during the decades of the American-backed dictatorship of the Somozas. In the capital, the Sandinista leader Daniel Ortega entertained them with stories of his parents being tortured and of being forced to wear a bag over his head during one of his own years in prison.

April 23 was practically Nicaragua day in Washington. As hundreds of anti-contra demonstrators blocked the Pennsylvania Avenue gates to the White House, the President invited Democratic senators to come in the back way to listen again to his version of the story as rhetoric on both sides got nastier for Washington cameras and correspondents. Inside, administration briefers were using aerial photographs showing baseball diamonds around Managua, saying the fields proved that large numbers of Cubans were there. That night

NBC anchorman Tom Brokaw, just back from Nicaragua, pointed out that baseball was the country's national sport, learned from United States Marines during more than twenty years of occupation beginning in the 1920s. In fact, the most famous man in the country was not Ortega but a local boy made good, Dennis Martinez, a Baltimore Orioles pitcher.

Democratic Senator John Kerry of Massachusetts came out of the White House after the briefings to say: "The real issue here is the government of the United States. . . . Is this administration going to overthrow the government of the Sandinistas no matter what they do? That's what's at stake."

On television, Kerry and other Democrats were played against Defense Secretary Weinberger, who said: "For the life of me, I can't understand why a communist regime in Nicaragua has so much support in Congress." Then House Speaker O'Neill weighed in again: "The President of the United States, and I hate to say this, but I don't think he's going to be happy until he has troops, our boys, in Central America." Senator Goldwater attacked the Democrats: "It isn't a question of $14 million for food or butter or guns. It's a question of who's going to run the foreign policy of this country." During the House debate on the $14 million, Representative David Bonior of Michigan rose to say: "We are being asked to embrace as freedom fighters paramilitary forces who burn homes, destroy crops, who murder, who torture, who rape and kidnap innocent civilians." Henry Hyde, an Illinois Republican, answered: "So they'll die, and they'll die hungry and without shoes on. . . . Someday our children are going to ask, 'How and why did you let it happen?' "

The President announced that same day that he would not allow any of the $14 million in contra aid to be used for military purposes, endorsed a cease-fire, and reversed himself on his opposition to direct American-Nicaraguan negotiations. With that, the Senate then approved the aid package by a vote of 53 to 46. Four hours later, the House voted 248 to 180 to kill the whole thing. The next day, both the Republicans and Democrats in the House proposed substitute packages that would funnel the $14 million to Nicaraguan refugees in other countries. In the end, the substitutes were killed by a 303 to 120 vote, with angry Republicans withdrawing their votes from the compromises. One Republican leader, Representative Dick Cheney, embellished a reputation for sarcasm, mocking "humanitarian" aid:

"Got a problem with the communist government in Nicaragua? Are they censoring the press? Why, we'll give a donation to the International Red Cross."

That night, the President changed the subject, going on television to talk about the federal budget and federal deficits, calling on Americans to send in cards and letters in support of a Republican budget, stitched together by Senate Majority Leader Dole and Finance Committee chairman Pete Domenici. It was not his budget; that one had been dismissed months before by the leaders of both parties in both houses as fiscal 1986 deficit estimates climbed to more than $200 billion. "The President's address followed the central theme of four years in office—a shift in federal priorities away from domestic spending and toward defense while cutting taxes," reported David Hoffman and Helen Dewar of *The Washington Post*. "It also followed past themes in laying all the blame for the record peacetime deficits of his Presidency on domestic programs."

"Can he win this time?" asked Lesley Stahl during a CBS News instant analysis after the President's address. "Only a fool would bet against Ronald Reagan. . . . But there are three things that are different this time. . . . A lot of mainline powerful groups are going to write the same kind of letters against what he wants. Senior citizens, farmers and education groups. Secondly, Ronald Reagan before has always stuck to one issue at a time. These days he has many high-order priorities: Nicaragua, the budget. . . . The third thing is he lost on Nicaragua today. Even at the White House, they're saying that cannot help but have a spillover effect."

The spillover effect was shaking the President of Honduras, Roberto Suazo Córdova, whose government had stopped a shipment of arms to the contras on the day after the vote. McFarlane reacted in a memo to the President on April 25: "It is imperative that you make clear the Executive Branch's political commitment to maintaining pressure on the Sandinistas, regardless of what action Congress takes. . . . President Suazo will need some overt and concrete sign of this commitment. . . . Two actions which would signal our commitment are: impose a trade embargo . . . downgrade diplomatic relations."

Reagan offered money. He telephoned Suazo, then told McFarlane in a note: "Expressed his support of *me* and his belief we must continue to oppose communism. Will call his commanders . . . to deliver the armaments." Suazo had also asked the President for $15 million in emergency aid to his country. Five days later, Reagan did sign off on $4.5 million in new money for Honduras, aid channeled through the CIA.

As the President took off for the Bonn summit on April 30—the House was voting 390 to 26 to urge him not to visit Bitburg—the White House declared a national emergency and announced it was abrogating a twenty-seven-year-old friendship treaty with Nicaragua, and that it would impose a total embargo on imports, exports, and travel between the United States and that Central American country. Ortega, a poor student of American political attitudes, was aglow with praise for the Democrats of the United States—and then two days later appeared in Moscow with Gorbachev. He won promises of trade and aid from the Soviet leader. The next day the House and Senate passed unanimous resolutions condemning the Sandinista government.

Reagan was greeted by huge and cheering crowds everywhere in Germany. At one stop, ten thousand teenagers, who had rehearsed for weeks, sang "The Star-Spangled Banner" in perfect phonetic English. "You have won the hearts of all Germany by standing firm," said a grateful Chancellor Kohl as they approached the town of Bitburg. The President responded by saying all the criticism had bothered him not a bit—though he told the Chancellor it had bothered his wife— and that he was too old to worry about what the newspapers were saying. The cemetery visit on May 5 was anticlimactic, which was the way Deaver had planned it. With all three American networks covering the day live, Reagan went first to the camp at Bergen-Belsen, saying, "Never again! I promise you we will never forget."

At Bitburg, the President never touched the wreath, which was laid down by two generals who had opposed each other forty years ago, United States General Matthew Ridgway, ninety-one years old, and Wehrmacht General Johannes Steinhoff. The path Reagan and Kohl took through the cemetery was anti-Deaverism planned by Deaver himself. Usually he choreographed camera angles to show Reagan at work, but this time the faces of the President and the Chancellor were hidden behind trees and hedges. The President never looked at a grave. A bugler played "Taps." The entire ceremony took eight minutes. Then Reagan ended the day at the U.S. Air Force base a mile from the cemetery—more than half Bitburg's population of 23,000 were Americans—and said: "Our gesture of reconciliation with the German people today in no way minimizes our love and honor for those who fought and died for our country."

"Mission Accomplished," said the President when he returned home on May 10. Few agreed with that. After the Bitburg visit, Thomas Friedman of *The New York Times,* reporting from Jerusalem, began: "Israeli leaders across the political spectrum expressed anger and bitterness over President Reagan's visit to the military cemetery . . . language rarely heard here in reference to an American president." The *Times* the next day, reporting on speeches marking the fortieth anniversary of VE Day, the end of World War II in Europe, headlined a sharp exchange between the leaders of the two countries that contributed the most to crushing Adolf Hitler and Nazism. "PRESIDENT ACCUSES SOVIET OF THREAT TO ARMS STABILITY" was the headline over a speech by Reagan to the European Parliament in Strasbourg, France—a speech in which he was booed and jeered by leftist members from several countries and by chants of "Nicaragua! . . . Nicaragua!" "GORBACHEV SAYS U.S. POLICY GROWS MORE 'BELLICOSE' " was the headline over the report of the Soviet leader's VE Day speech in Moscow.

Those speeches marked the first public confrontation between Reagan and Gorbachev. Even as each celebrated the Soviet-American partnership against the Nazis, they sharply raised their levels of rhetorical hostility. "We see similar Soviet efforts to profit from and stimulate regional conflicts in Central America" was a Reagan line that triggered jeering in Strasbourg. After showing that film, NBC News switched to Tom Brokaw reporting on the Gorbachev speech to an audience of World War II veterans, telling viewers: "Gorbachev used some of the harshest anti-American rhetoric heard in Moscow in years."

Returning home, the President finally focused on the tax reform he had vaguely endorsed the year before in his 1984 State of the Union message as Democrats laughed. Safely reelected—Mondale never brought up tax reform in the campaign—Reagan had again mentioned "tax simplification" in his fifth State of the Union message, calling it part of a "Second American Revolution." But all he said about his reform plan was that it would include a top individual rate of 35 percent and be revenue-neutral, meaning that overall tax revenues would remain the same. Then, just before leaving for Europe on May 28, he had declared a "Second American Revolution" one more time in a rousing twenty-minute national television speech. It was a speech that sounded like a younger Reagan, or the young Tom Sawyer he sometimes saw when he looked back, filled with words and phrases that resonated in the spoken music of America:

I'd like to speak to you tonight about our future, about a great historic effort to give the words "freedom," "fairness," and "hope" new meaning and power. . . . Death and taxes may be inevitable, but unjust taxes are not . . . taxation without representation is tyranny. . . . One simple straightforward message to the entire nation: America, go for it! . . . Will our proposal help you? You bet it will! . . . To young Americans: Why not set out with your friends on the path of adventure and try to start your own business? Follow in the footsteps of those two college students who launched one of America's great computer firms from the garage behind their house. . . . There is one group of losers in our tax plan—those individuals and corporations who are not paying their fair share or, for that matter, any share. From now on, they shall pay a minimum tax. No more free rides! . . . Comparing the distance between the present system and our proposal is like comparing the distance between a Model T and the space shuttle. And I should know—I've seen both." *

The Reagan reform may not have been revolutionary, but it was ambitious. His plan, released in a forty-six-page book, cleverly combined free market capitalism and traditional American populism to attack progressive taxation. As he had when he was General Electric's spokesman in the 1950s, he characterized such taxation as a creation of Karl Marx. Now he called for whittling down the fourteen tax brackets created by his 1981 tax cut (brackets ranging from 11 to 50 percent), to just three brackets: 15 percent, 25 percent, and a top bracket of 35 percent for individual earnings of more than $70,000 a year. The personal deduction allowed for each taxpayer and dependents would increase from $960 to $2,000, but those same taxpayers would lose $38 billion a year because deductions for state and local taxes paid would be eliminated. The top rate for capital gains or investment income would be reduced from 20 to 17.5 percent. The plan would also create something called Individual Retirement Accounts, IRAs, allowing taxpayers to save income that would not be taxed until they retired. In all, Reagan said, taxes on individuals would decrease by about 6 percent, while major corporations would pay about

---

* In 1939, William Hewlett and David Packard, two Stanford engineers, went into business in a rented garage five years after their graduation. Beginning with instrumentation equipment bought by the Walt Disney Company in making the film *Fantasia*, the two men built a high-tech empire over the years.

25 percent more with the elimination of a wide range of tax code in-centives and deductions—even as the top tax rate paid by corpora-tions would decrease from 46 to 33 percent.

There was a Democratic response to that speech, delivered by the chairman of the House Ways and Means Committee, Dan Ros-tenkowski, the big, bluff model of a working-class Chicago politician. He made it clear to reporters that he did not intend to fight Reagan. Instead, he welcomed the President to what he considered Democratic territory: "Trying to tax people fairly: That's been the historic Demo-cratic commitment. . . . But this time there's been a difference in the push for tax reform. This time it's a Republican president who's buck-ing his party's tradition as protectors of big business and the wealthy. His words and feelings go back to Roosevelt and Truman and Ken-nedy. But the commitment comes from Ronald Reagan. And that's so important and so welcome."

"Jesus," Reagan said as he watched Rostenkowski from the Roo-sevelt Room next to the Oval Office. "He's got me with Truman and Kennedy on this." So he did, but what "Rosty," as he was called, was trying to do was to take over the writing of the bill.

At 8 A.M. the next morning, May 30, hundreds of lawyers and lob-byists lined up at the Government Printing Office waiting to pay $18 for the text of the proposal—each looking to see what the effect of Reagan's changes would be on their companies and clients. Someone quickly figured out that the reform would save $28,000 on the Rea-gans' own joint return. The President laughed when that was brought up by Bill Plante of CBS News. "I think that just points out for every-one how advantageous the new tax system is," said Reagan.

"Even for the middle class?" asked Plante, after economists figured out that Americans earning more than $1 million a year would save 11 percent in income taxes, but those earning between $30,000 and $50,000 would save only 6.6 percent. "They don't save that much," Plante said.

"Well," Reagan chuckled. "They also don't pay as much."

On ABC News, the conservative columnist George Will character-ized the plan as the Republicans' boldest attempt to become the party of the "common man" rather than of country club members. "I know this is a conservative era, but conservatism in America is the prayerful belief that it is time to cut my neighbor's benefits."

"How long do you think it will take to get reform through?" asked anchor Peter Jennings.

"Till 1989," Will answered. "The first year of a first term of a new president."

The old President, as usual, turned the details over to others. The new Secretary of the Treasury, Jim Baker, and his sharp deputy, Richard Darman, worked the plan for the White House while Rosty's Democrats worked away in congressional committee rooms. Reagan's attention shifted back to foreign affairs and he won a surprisingly sudden victory: The Senate and then the House voted to end the ban on aid to the contra scheming and fighting to overthrow the government of Nicaragua. Actually, President Ortega of Nicaragua once again seemed to have had more to do with the changing mood of Washington than did the telephone calls and Capitol Hill visits of the President of the United States. Ortega's splashy visits to Moscow and other communist capitals were humiliating enraged antiwar Democrats. The White House capitalized on that anger by openly, if anonymously, promoting "humanitarian aid" by leaking newspaper stories that the White House was considering an American invasion if the contras went broke and disbanded. On June 6, the Republican-controlled Senate voted 55 to 42 to provide $38 million to be distributed to the rebels by the CIA for "non-military" use. Then, on June 12, the Democratically controlled House, which had barred all aid in April, voted 248 to 184 to distribute $27 million in humanitarian aid to the contras and also voted 232 to 196 to repeal its three-year-old ban on cooperation between intelligence agencies and the Nicaraguan rebels.

After a relatively rough spring, the President seemed to be setting the agenda again. On June 10, he played the host at an unusual White House party, a midday reception for new Republicans, more than 150 men and women, all politicians who had switched parties, including three members of Congress, Senator Phil Gramm and Representatives Andy Ireland and Robert Stump. Most were state legislators, mostly from the South, doing what Reagan himself had in 1964 after years as a Democrat. "Let the other party have the entrenched interests and the power-brokers and the special interest politics. . . . We just have the people," the President proclaimed. Then he said with a triumphant laugh: "I don't normally read *The New York Times* for fun, but there it was on the front page: 'About the same number of people now identify themselves as Republicans as call themselves Democrats.' Remember when they called us the minority party? How sweet it is! . . . Welcome aboard. Welcome home!"

Reagan was wakened before 7 A.M. on June 14—the White House

was continuing to announce all early risings—and told that at least two gunmen had hijacked Trans World Airlines Flight 847, en route from Athens to Rome, with 104 Americans and 49 other passengers aboard. The hijackers identified themselves as members of Islamic Jihad, claiming they were the same terrorist organization that had bombed the American embassy and the Marine barracks in Beirut in 1983. The plane, a Boeing 727, appeared over the Beirut airport. The pilot radioed for permission to land.

"You have not permission to land Beirut airport. It's up to you and the hijackers to go on," said the control tower.

"Beirut, the hijacker has pulled the pin on his hand grenade," said the TWA pilot, John Testrake, ". . . and is ready to blow up the aircraft."

The people in the tower relented: "Understand you are landing without permission. . . . OK sir. Land. Land quietly. Land quietly."

That was not to be. The words were soon being broadcast around the world. After refueling, the jet took off again, appearing above Algeria's Houari Boumédienne Airport at 2:45 A.M. New York time. Again the plane took off for Beirut. The pilot's words on final approach were: "He just killed a passenger! He just killed a passenger!"

"You see," broadcast the hijacker in the cockpit. "You see. You now believe. There will be another in five minutes."

"They are beating the passengers!" said the pilot. "They are beating the passengers."

The President, who was at Camp David, was given that news at 2:20 A.M. on Saturday, June 15. By breakfast time he had received the first two-page "Status Report on the TWA Hijacking" from the Secretary of State, including: "One still unidentified American was shot through the back of the head. . . . The TWA team in Algiers reports that the hijackers are requesting $10–$15 million, the release of 700 prisoners in Israel." Those prisoners, according to backup documents sent to the President, were Lebanese Shiite Muslims held since the 1982 Israeli invasion of Lebanon. Israel's Defense Minister, Yitzhak Rabin, had announced in April that they were to be released as the IDF withdrew troops from southern Lebanon.

Reagan's first statement, issued as he returned to the White House on Sunday morning, was not couched in diplomatic language. It was addressed to the hijackers: "For their own safety, they better turn these people loose." Larry Speakes issued a statement asserting: "We do not make concessions to terrorists and we do not encourage others to make concessions." Later, the President repeated the same words.

In Beirut, the hijackers opened the front door of the plane and dumped the body of the murdered American onto the tarmac, a Navy diver named Robert Stethem. The hijackers had released passengers in Algiers and released fifty-three women in Beirut. But ten more terrorists boarded the plane there. There were still at least thirty-three hostages aboard, the three-man flight crew and thirty men, most of them American. The hijackers were running up the aisles shouting "New Jersey! . . . New Jersey!" No one understood that what they meant was not the state but the battleship that had fired into the hills around Beirut two years earlier. They claimed that Stethem must have been part of American anti-Shiite operations in the city. In exchange for the crew's lives, the hijackers were demanding the release of those hundreds of Shiite prisoners in Israeli prisons. The next day, the passengers were turned over to Nabih Berri, one of the most powerful men in the chaos of Lebanon, an American-trained lawyer who commanded the Shiite Amal militia, the fighters who had taken over the Beirut airport when American Marines were moved offshore in February of 1984. The freed hijackers disappeared inside the slums the Marines had called Khomeiniville.

The world watched, galvanized by live television footage and then photographs of the TWA pilot, John Testrake, leaning out the cockpit window with a hijacker holding a .45-caliber pistol next to his head. "Captain," yelled Charles Glass of ABC News, standing below the nose of the plane, "many people in America are calling for some kind of rescue operation, or some kind of retaliation . . . have any thoughts on that?"

"We'd all be dead men if they did because we're continually surrounded."

"That captain is quite a guy, absolutely unruffled," wrote the President in his diary that night. Mrs. Reagan said they would have to cancel the ten-day vacation at the ranch scheduled around the upcoming July 4 weekend. Reagan said no, and so did his men. The order of the day was "Business as usual." He was determined not to be seen as Jimmy Carter had been, suspending the presidency day after day, week after week, then month after month because Americans were being held hostage in Iran. Night after night, the television networks replayed Reagan's criticisms of President Carter's inaction during the 444-day Iranian hostage crisis, often replaying a Reagan statement on his first full day in office, January 21, 1981: "Let terrorists be aware that when the rules of international behavior are violated, our policy will be one of swift and effective retribution." But, the anchormen intoned, there had been no retribution when the American embassy was bombed in Beirut, nor when 241 Marines were killed by another bomb there. "The Reagan administration, which has been long on talk and short on action when it comes to international terrorism . . ." began Tom Brokaw, opening the *NBC Nightly News.*

Talks between Berri and President Hafez al-Assad of Syria on one side, and the White House and the Israelis on the other, went on day after day. On the fifth day, the President announced that he was canceling his vacation to concentrate on winning the release of the TWA hostages and the seven other Americans kidnapped in Beirut over the past fifteen months. There was no more talk of retribution, just of the effort to save lives, and to save face on all sides. Berri did not want to be seen as giving in to the Americans; Reagan and the Israelis were trying to protect their public policies of never giving in to terrorist demands. It was a tricky business, with the Americans and Israelis often at odds over who would be seen as backing down on their no-concessions policies. The President recorded his version of what was happening in his diary:

> The demand is still for the Shiites held in Israel. These are people the Israelis intend to release in a few weeks, but they are unwilling to let it appear that they are giving in to hijackers' demands. . . . The price is the release of 760 Shiites. Israel is publicly saying they will—but the U.S. at the highest level of govt. must ask them to do it. This of course means that me—not they, would be violating our policy of not negotiating with terrorists. . . . The Israelis are not being helpful. They have gone public with the statement that they would release their prisoners if we asked them to. Well, we can't do that . . . loused things up by establishing a linkage we insist does not exist. . . . I've urged that we approach Assad of Syria to go to Berri and tell him that he can be a hero by releasing our people or he can be stubborn and we will begin some actions such as closing down the Beirut airport, closing Lebanon's harbors etc., until he releases our people. This is all being staffed out now. . . . The Israelis are already planning to begin returning their prisoners. We want linkage between what they are doing and the release of the hostages. Berri released one today because of a heart condition.

We are really optimistic. I've just learned that Berri owns a couple of markets and some oil stations here in the U.S. We might consider that a pressure point. . . . Qaddafi is talking to Iran and Syria about a joint terrorist war against us. . . . Having breakfast in bed, we turned on the TV. There were our hostages still in Beirut, not in Damascus. Apparently neither Mr. Berri or Assad could spring the missing four from the bastardly Hizballah.

On July 1, after seventeen tense days, with the last of the hostages released in Damascus and flown to West Germany, Reagan wrote: "Awoke with the knowledge that our people were in Wiesbaden at our air base there. Nancy and I plan to meet their plane here. . . . I phoned Assad to thank him. . . . He got a little feisty and suggested I was threatening to invade Lebanon. I told him nothing of the kind but we were going to do everything we could to bring the murderers of our young men to justice. . . . We know the identity of the two hijackers who murdered Robbie Stethem. The problem is how do we get them for trial in the U.S. All in all, it's frustrating even though we are overjoyed at our success in getting the hostages back."

Reagan ended that journal entry by stating his determination to find a way to bring home the seven kidnapped Americans still hidden somewhere in the broken buildings and basements of Beirut. Like any diarist, the President was sometimes writing about the way he wished things had happened, rather than admitting that he had indeed negotiated with the terrorists—and that his men were doing the same thing with Iranians and anyone else who might bring about the release of the kidnapped Americans. Two days after the release of the hijacked passengers, an Israeli official, David Kimche, the director general of the Foreign Ministry, came to the White House to meet with McFarlane to sound out the Americans on improved relations with the Iranian government, emphasizing that important Iranians had been helpful in the TWA 847 negotiations, telling the American that the price would almost certainly be providing weaponry, ammunition, and replacement parts for the American war matériel the Khomeini government inherited from the Shah. McFarlane, who knew the Israelis were already selling arms to Iran, promised to take the idea to the President.

After Beirut and the killing of four U.S. Marines and two American businessmen in El Salvador on June 20, the Reagan administration was obsessed with terrorism, and Reagan himself was obsessed with hostages, particularly after meeting with the families of the TWA victims and the seven kidnapped Americans still being held somewhere in Beirut. A *New York Times* analysis of Reagan's actions in the past weeks began: "By establishing as his 'primary goal' the safe return of American hostages held in Lebanon, President Reagan has turned to a policy of restraint along the lines followed by Jimmy Carter in the Iranian hostage crisis. . . . Mr. Reagan finds himself relying on an approach that he criticized as a Presidential candidate in 1980 and that he promised to change immediately upon being sworn into office in 1981."

At a press conference while the passengers were still being held, Reagan had sounded like a man who had come to understand that all answers were not so simple. Asked whether the United States could still protect its own citizens around the world, he had said: "Those people, I think, are jumping to conclusions and don't realize what the situation is. But I'm as frustrated as anyone. I've pounded a few walls myself, when I'm alone, about this. It is frustrating. But, as I say, you have to be able to pinpoint the enemy. You can't just start shooting without having someone in your gunsights."

When it was over, after weeks of dealing and wheeling, the President put on his elegant and straight-faced mask of state and declared: "The United States gives terrorists no rewards and no guarantees. We make no concessions, we make no deals." His job approval rating, measured in weekly *Washington Post*/ABC News polls, jumped 5 points to a near-record 67 percent.

On July 2, the President and Mrs. Reagan went out to Andrews Air Force Base in Maryland to welcome thirty of the hijacked passengers. While he was there, the White House released a statement saying that the President would meet officially with a Soviet leader for the first time. He and Mikhail Gorbachev would spend two days together in Geneva in late November. But it would not be a real summit meeting, they emphasized. "Our expectations are not great at all," an unnamed "senior official" told reporters. "Its main purpose will be to engage the new Soviet leadership and for each side to have a better understanding of the other."

CHAPTER 12
NOVEMBER 16, 1985

On July 12, President Reagan traveled to Bethesda Naval Center for routine surgery, the removal of a small benign polyp in his lower colon detected during his annual physical examination in March. In the days before the scheduled operation, considered routine for a man his age, he made a florid speech about international terrorism to the American Bar Association. He denounced five countries as terrorist states—Iran, Libya, North Korea, Cuba, and Nicaragua—calling them "The new international version of Murder, Incorporated." He continued: "All of these states are united by one simple criminal phenomenon—their fanatical hatred of the United States, our people, our way of life, our international stature. . . . The American people are not—I repeat, not—going to tolerate intimidation, terror and outright acts of war against this nation and its people. And we are not going to tolerate these attacks from outlaw states run by the strangest collection of misfits, Looney Tunes and squalid criminals since the advent of the Third Reich. . . . We must act together, or unilaterally if necessary, to insure that terrorists have no sanctuary—anywhere." The words were tempered, however, by the reality of the moment. There were six countries in the first drafts of the speech, but Syria was dropped from the list because that country had played a role in the release of the TWA 847 hostages.

Reagan also issued a statement praising David Stockman, who was leaving the Office of Management and Budget—"future OMB directors will be measured against the standard of your performance"—after almost five years trying to reduce deficit spending, five years during which the federal deficit increased by $762.6 billion, more than three-quarters of a trillion dollars. Stockman, as always, was candid—in private. At a closed meeting with the board of the New York Stock Exchange—he had accepted a job with Salomon Brothers on Wall Street—the budget director said: "We are violating badly, even wantonly, the cardinal rule of sound public finance: governments must extract from the people in taxes what they dispense in benefits, services and protections. Perhaps not every year—but certainly over an intermediate period of time. . . . If the Securities and Exchange Commission had jurisdiction over the executive and legislative branches, many of us would be in jail."

His final words in public were more tempered and may have summed up a political reality of the Reagan years: "It is very clear to me, after five years, that the spending cut episode is over, we've had a referendum on what we want in the budget and what we don't. What's left, most people want. And we're going to have to raise taxes to pay for it."

At Bethesda, the President's little operation suddenly loomed large. Doctors performing a colonoscopy discovered a second polyp, higher and bigger than the first one, and possibly precancerous. The surgery would now be a major abdominal operation. "Let me be the one to tell him," said Mrs. Reagan after the doctors told her about the polyp.

She sat by him on the bed in the recovery room. "Why is everybody so quiet?" Reagan asked in a slurry voice. "They found something in there . . ." she said. "They think they better operate tomorrow."

"You mean," he said, "that the bad news is that I don't get to eat supper tonight?"

That was it. Just before noon on July 14, as Reagan was going under general anesthesia for the three-hour operation—two feet of his intestine around the polyp were removed—Vice President Bush became "Acting President" under a letter signed by the President before he was taken into the operating room. Almost eight hours later, at 7:22 P.M., the President was able to sign a letter reclaiming his authority. Then he looked up and said, "I feel fit as a fiddle."

Not quite. *The New York Times* front-page headline of July 16 crossed four columns:

> REAGAN'S DOCTORS FIND CANCER
> IN TUMOR BUT REPORT REMOVAL
> LEAVES HIS CHANCES EXCELLENT

"The President has cancer," Dr. Steven Rosenberg announced, after discussing the biopsy results with the Reagans. He said there was a better then 50 percent chance that cancer cells had not spread beyond the malignant polyp. The President's reaction was more optimistic: "Well, I'm glad that that's all out." He began insisting that the doctor was wrong in saying "has cancer," that he should be saying "had cancer"—because now it was gone. Mrs. Reagan and the physicians spoke of a spectacular recovery; one doctor said he had the insides of a forty-year-old man. Once again Americans were hearing about Ronald Reagan, the cheerful, the indestructible. A *Washington Times* cartoonist, Bill Garner, caught that in a drawing showing a nurse and doctor looking down from a hospital window. "Somebody get down there and stop that clown from chopping wood before he disturbs the President!" says the nurse. The doctor says: "Good Heavens— That *is* the President!"

Reagan was making jokes, waving from his window, reading Western novels and a biography of Calvin Coolidge, as Don Regan bustled about the hospital and the White House, trailed by his own little entourage, as if he were the Acting President. Regan proclaimed on everything from budget deficits to world peace while Mrs. Reagan— visibly annoyed by the chief of staff's performance—and Vice President Bush handled ceremonial duties. One of Bush's appearances was to announce the winner of a NASA competititon to select a schoolteacher to become the first American civilian in space. Christa McAuliffe, a thirty-six-year-old social sciences teacher at Concord High School in New Hampshire, was chosen to be part of the crew of a January flight of the space shuttle *Challenger.* A week after that ceremony, one of the three engines of the *Challenger* failed as the shuttle lifted off from its Florida base at Cape Canaveral, preventing it from reaching its planned orbit, but NASA officials quickly dismissed the failure as not serious enough to abort the mission.*

On July 17, the doctors were beginning to take postoperative tubes out of the President. That night, in his diary, Reagan wrote: "Miracle of miracles. I had my first food by mouth. A cup of tea. The doctor says maybe he'll take the feeding tube out tomorrow. . . . Some strange soundings are coming from some Iranians. Bud M. will be here tomorrow to talk about it. It could be a breakthrough on getting our seven kidnap victims back. Evidently the Iranian economy is disintegrating fast under the strain of war."

---

* The Coolidge book was *From These Hills: The Vermont Years of Calvin Coolidge* by Jane Curtis and Will Curtis with Frank Lieberman.

McFarlane had been telling Don Regan that he had urgent information for the President. He tried to bring Reagan up to date on arms control talks with the Soviets. Then he went on to the news he considered urgent. He reported on the visit from David Kimche, the director general of Israel's Foreign Ministry, who said he was representing the country's Prime Minister, Shimon Peres. He repeated Kimche's claims that the Israelis had been supplying American-made arms to Iran— the army there depended on United States equipment originally sold to the Shah—and were in contact with Iranian emissaries, who claimed to be connected to moderate groups concerned about what would happen after the death of Ayatollah Khomeini, who was eighty-five years old. The Iranian "moderates," or the man who claimed to represent them, an exiled merchant named Manucher Ghorbanifar, wanted better relations with the United States and said that perhaps the Iranians could demonstrate their influence and intentions by arranging the release of one or more of the seven American hostages held by Shiites in Beirut. In return, they were interested in buying American antitank weapons, as a signal that the scheme had the approval of the highest levels of the U.S. government. They particularly wanted wire-guided shoulder-held TOW anti-tank missiles. At the mention of hostages, Reagan sat up straighter and began asking questions.

"What do you think?" the President asked McFarlane. The National Security Adviser said he thought the scheme was worth talking about, without any commitment. The arms-selling was probably illegal, said McFarlane, who did not actually know the people he was dealing with. "I'm not put off by the idea," the President said. "Tell them again we want to talk with them, we want to exchange ideas, and we'll work toward the day when our confidence with each other can grow."

The President was in the hospital for seven days. The last thing he did before returning to the White House on July 20 was to sit down at a small table outside his room to give his weekly Saturday radio address. "There's something I wanted to say. . . . First ladies aren't elected, and they don't receive a salary [but] in my book, they've all been heroes. Abigail Adams helped invent America. Dolley Madison helped protect it. Eleanor Roosevelt was FDR's eyes and ears. And Nancy Reagan is my everything. . . . I say for myself, but also on behalf of the nation, thank you, partner, thanks for everything. By the way, are you doing anything this evening?"

There were two thousand federal employees on the back lawn of the White House to cheer the President as he walked into the White House. One of the first people he saw on the ground floor after he walked in was McFarlane. Reagan motioned him over to say: "Get the guys together to talk about that matter you mentioned at the hospital."

McFarlane called a series of National Security Planning Group meetings. Secretary of Defense Weinberger was unequivocally against dealing with the Iranians, from the start and under any circumstance. Secretary of State Shultz, who had been informed of the Kimche initiative before McFarlane went to the hospital—and had essentially approved McFarlane's visit—now said: "I think this is a very bad idea." CIA director Casey was ready to go ahead, even though Ghorbanifar had failed CIA polygraph tests and was listed as a known liar in an official agency "fabricator notice." Vice President Bush and Don Regan tried to avoid committing themselves. The President, just out of the hospital, called McFarlane at home one night during these secret debates. "Bud, I've been thinking about this Israeli thing," he said. "Couldn't you use some imagination and try to find a way to make it work?" *

"Mr. President, your Secretary of State and Secretary of Defense were against this."

"I know, but I look at it differently. I want to find a way to do this."

Four days later, on August 2, McFarlane met again with Kimche, saying that "the guys"—Reagan and his national security team—had doubts about the position and power of the Iranians. The Israeli's response was: "Okay. What if *we* ship these weapons? . . . If we do it, can we buy new weapons from you?"

"I'll get an official response for you," said McFarlane. He asked the President, who answered: "Good. Get the guys together."

* On July 13, 1985, while the President was still in the operating room in Bethesda, McFarlane sent Shultz, who was traveling in Australia, a six-page memo in a sealed envelope marked "Must be opened by the Secretary only." The text included: "This message . . . concerns a proposal by an Iranian official endorsed by the Government of Israel. . . . The short term dimension concerns the seven hostages; the long term dimension involves the establishment of a private dialogue with Iranian officials on the broader relation. . . . The Iranians stated that they were very confident that they could achieve the release of the seven Americans held hostage in Lebanon. But in exchange they would need to show some gain. They sought specifically the delivery from Israel of 100 TOW missiles." The Secretary of State replied the next day: "Please have following messages typed on plain bond and hand carried to Bud: I agree with you that we should make a tentative show of interest without commitment. . . . In other words, we are willing to listen and seriously consider any statement on this topic they may wish to initiate. I do think it important that you make clear to the emissary that you and I are in close contact and agreement."

Two days after that, Reagan was back at Bethesda, where doctors removed a growing, irritated red splotch on the side of his nose. That, too, turned out to be cancerous. But nothing was said until three days later, when television cameras showed the redness and scraping, and the press office finally conceded it was skin cancer. In his diary, Reagan, the boy who used to say he could live on popcorn, the lifeguard and movie star who always had the best tan, wrote in his diary: "First I had to give up popcorn"—because it irritated his vulnerable intestines—"and now sunbathing." They were among his very favorite things, but Reagan was a disciplined man who followed doctors' orders. Finally, on August 10, the doctors gave him the okay to travel to California for a twenty-three-day stay at Rancho del Cielo. One evening there, the Reagans turned on CBS News and saw pictures of themselves walking along a ridge, holding hands. The network had its telescope camera working again, on a hill closer to the clouds, almost three miles away. Mrs. Reagan was sure they could be watched through the windows, too.

As Reagan mended on his mountaintop, on August 20, sixteen wooden crates, each containing six TOW missiles, were loaded onto a chartered DC-8 in the military section of Ben Gurion International Airport near Tel Aviv. Four hours later, the plane was being unloaded at Mehrabad International Airport in Tehran. Meanwhile, Lieutenant Colonel North, traveling under a fake Irish passport issued in the name of William P. Goode, was in Europe making preparations for the simultaneous release of the seven American hostages. But there was no release. Ghorbanifar, who was on the chartered DC-8, said the reason was that the Revolutionary Guards, who were not part of the three-country secret deal, had taken the missiles. Now he said that four hundred more missiles would have to be shipped to free the hostages.

"I'm back and rarin' to go," the President said as he returned to Washington after Labor Day. But no one seemed to notice. All the talk inside the Beltway—the eight-lane highway that circles the District of Columbia—seemed to be about Mikhail Gorbachev. The Russian's determined face was on the cover of *Time* magazine over words from his first interview with Americans: "The situation today is highly complex, very tense. I would even go so far to say it is explosive."

The interview, in Moscow, with *Time*'s senior editors, was his first with American journalists. He put on quite a show, extraordinary

1

In his inaugural address, President Ronald Reagan attacked the government he was taking over: "In this present crisis, government is not the solution, government is the problem." His pollster reminded him there could be trouble ahead: "You can expect to be pictured as a simplistic and untried lightweight (Dumb), a person who consciously misuses facts to overblow his own record (Deceptive) and one who would be too anxious to engage our country in a nuclear holocaust (Dangerous)." The oldest man ever elected, he had heard it all. Stubborn and set in old-fashioned ways, he and his wife, Nancy, settled in by themselves, watching television or old movies together above the Oval Office.

Reagan came to office with four simple goals: (1) reducing taxes and deficits, thus reducing the power and size of the federal government; (2) rebuilding the American military; (3) confronting communism around the world; (4) restoring American patriotism and pride. He began by trying to win over Congress to cut taxes, meeting with his principal partisan adversary, Speaker of the House Thomas ("Tip") O'Neill (*top, second from left*), along with House minority leader Robert Michel (*top, left*), and Senate Republican leader Howard Baker (*top, right*). In the White House, his point man was David Stockman (*above, center, and at right*), a bright and arrogant thirty-four-year-old congressman he appointed Director of the Office of Management and Budget.

3

4

5

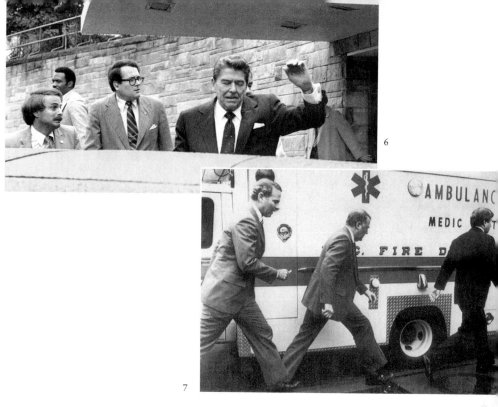

6

7

On his seventieth day as President, Reagan was shot leaving a speech at the Washington Hilton hotel by a young man named John Hinckley. Aides James A. Baker III, Edwin Meese III, and Larry Speakes rushed to George Washington Hospital. "Oh my God, we've lost him," said the chief of his Secret Service detail. The President, giving the performance of a lifetime, had walked into the hospital before collapsing. Back at the White House, in the Situation Room under the building, Secretary of State Alexander Haig (*standing below television*) and others argued over who was in charge.

8

9

10

Reagan left management of the White House to platoons of assistants. "He treats us all the same, as hired help," said James Baker of the first-term Troika, who, along with Ed Meese and Michael Deaver (*above left*), made up the most successful of the management teams. They were all replaced by Don Regan (*above right*), the arrogant former Treasury Secretary who boasted that he made 85 percent of the President's decisions. Reagan's job was on television and on the road, selling his programs. But after he was shot in 1981, he almost never worked crowds again, seeing and speaking to people from the inside of an armored limousine surrounded by Secret Service agents.

11

"Reagan changed national security advisers like underwear," said one of his men. His first team included Secretary of State Alexander Haig (*top, center*) and National Security Council director Richard Allen (*top, left*). Both were gone within eighteen months, replaced by one old pro, Secretary of State George Shultz, and one California neophyte, Judge William Clark (*right*), a conservative ideologue dubbed "the nitwit minister" by Europeans. Shultz stayed for six years; Clark was gone in one, replaced by a quiet former Marine colonel, Robert ("Bud") McFarlane. In October 1983, McFarlane and Shultz (*below, left and center*) awoke Reagan to discuss invading the tiny Caribbean island of Grenada.

McFarlane resigned as National Security Adviser in May 1985, after apparently suffering a nervous breakdown. He was replaced by his assistant, Rear Admiral John Poindexter (*above, right*), a reclusive man almost unknown inside (or outside) the White House. Most of the President's men did not know that the President had secretly ordered covert wars and hostage negotiations, managed by McFarlane and then by Poindexter and a staffer, Marine Lt. Col. Oliver North. Some of those orders came through Central Intelligence Agency director William Casey (*below*), who mumbled almost incoherently when it suited his purposes. Before one Casey visit Reagan jokingly asked McFarlane, "Who's going to interpret?" James Baker, who was not amused, sat in on one meeting, and when he saw the President nod, said: "God knows what he just approved."

The President's cavalier ignorance of foreign policy caught up with him in Beirut, where U.S. Marines were part of an international peace-keeping force. Reagan carelessly declared their mission was to train the Lebanese Army, a Christian-led force allied with Israel against a half-dozen Muslim militias. On October 23, a Muslim suicide bomber drove a truck of explosives into the lightly guarded Marine barracks at the Beirut Airport, destroyed the building, and killed 241 Americans (*above*). Coincidentally, Reagan had decided to divert Marine reinforcements headed toward Beirut to launch an invasion of the tiny Caribbean island of Grenada run by feuding Marxists (*below*). Several hundred American medical students were rescued, kissing the ground as they came home—and most Americans chose to celebrate triumph in Grenada rather than mourn slaughter in Lebanon.

In Nicaragua, four American-funded contras (*above*) were killed in an ambush by a squad of Sandinista soldiers. Reagan's secret foreign policy began to unravel in October 1986, when a CIA plane supplying contra insurgents was shot down. There was one survivor, a Wisconsin man named Eugene Hasenfus, captured by the Sandinistas (*below*). "There is no [United States] government connection," said Reagan of the incident. But, of course, there was. Reagan had the NSC secretly avoid congressional antiwar mandates by soliciting funding from foreign countries, most notably Saudi Arabia and Brunei, and private donors, calling the contras the "moral equivalent" of America's Founding Fathers.

21

22

Oliver North (*above left*) was in Frankfurt, Germany, with an American arms merchant, retired Air Force general Richard Secord (*below, right*), negotiating the sale of American weapons to Iran in exchange for American hostages held in Beirut when he heard of Hasenfus's capture. He immediately flew back to the White House to begin shredding records showing that profits from the arms sales were being used to illegally fund the Nicaraguan opposition. Foreign publications revealed the White House plots, leading to the resignation of National Security Adviser Poindexter (*above right*) and the firing of North, beginning years of investigations and congressional hearings. On the day he fired North, the President called him and told him he was a "national hero," saying his story could make a good movie.

23

24

25

In June 1982, Reagan electrified the world with tough talk to British members of Parliament (*top*). Disregarding the niceties of détente and coexistence, he said: "The march of freedom and democracy . . . will leave Marxism-Leninism on the ash heap of history." Back home, at a convention of evangelical Christians, he called the Soviet Union "the focus of evil in the modern world." Later, he won the respect of skeptical foreign leaders, particularly President François Mitterrand of France (*above, center*), a socialist, and Germany's Christian Democratic Chancellor Helmut Kohl (*above, left*), who stood by him as anti-American demonstrations swept Europe. The President repaid Kohl by visiting a cemetery (*at right*, accompanied by General Matthew Ridgeway) that included the graves of members of German SS units.

26

President Reagan's special ally and conservative soulmate was Prime Minister Margaret Thatcher of Great Britain. "Margaret" and "Ron" talked regularly, though his aides remember more than one conversation in which his contribution was: "Yes, Margaret . . . No, Margaret . . . I know, Margaret, but we think . . . Yes . . . Yes." Most importantly, she told Reagan that he could "do business" with the new leader of the Soviet Union, Mikhail Gorbachev. In the White House, the special relationships were between Reagan and Secretary of State Shultz (*below, right*), and Reagan and Secretary of Defense Caspar Weinberger (*below, left*). But the two men, shown here at Reagan's 1985 State of the Union address, despised each other, and one often walked out of meetings when the other was speaking.

The most important political relationship of the late twentieth century began in a boathouse in Geneva on November 19, 1985 (*above*). President Reagan and General Secretary Gorbachev did not agree on anything more than that they would meet again. But it was obvious that they liked each other's style. Eleven months later they came together in a marathon negotiating session (*below*) in Reykjavik, Iceland, on nuclear arms cutbacks that ended in frustration and anger on both sides. But it was the frankest Soviet-American dialogue of the Cold War. "We saw their bottom line and they saw ours," said Jack Matlock (*sitting against the wall*), Reagan's chief Soviet adviser. Gorbachev later said: "From the top of the hill you can see a long way, and we went to the top of the hill at Reykjavik."

31

32

Reagan was a man of words, understanding they were often more important than deeds. He considered speeches the most important part of his job. In France on the fortieth anniversary of the D-Day landing (*top*), he talked to the old men who had been the American boys who landed there under withering fire on June 6, 1944. In Germany in 1987, he stood in front of the Brandenburg Gate (*above*) separating East and West Germany and demanded of Gorbachev: "Tear down this wall!" At Moscow State University in 1988, standing beneath a huge bust of Lenin, he praised the applauding students as the builders of a new society.

33

34

"Stop the car!" Gorbachev ordered as he drove along Connecticut Avenue on his way to meet with Reagan in Washington, D.C., in December 1987. He stepped out into crowds of shocked Americans, waving and shaking hands as pedestrians cheered. Jack Matlock thought it was the moment the Cold War ended: "It was not the Manichean world he had grown up studying. He saw that the Americans didn't hate him." Reagan, watching on television, said: "Wait until next summer and he sees what I do with his people." He was as good as his word, greeting smiling, cheering Russians on Moscow streets and in Red Square outside the Kremlin.

35

Reagan, worried about his standing with women voters in 1980, promised to appoint the first woman to the Supreme Court. It was a promise he kept, nominating Sandra Day O'Connor, a likable Arizona Appeals Court Judge. She became part of Reagan's undisputed legacy: changing the balance of the Federal court system. He appointed more than half the district court judges in the country by the time he left office. He appointed William Rehnquist (*upper left*), a relatively young associate justice appointed by President Nixon, as Chief Justice, then nominated two more justices to the highest court, Antonin Scalia (*lower left*) and Anthony Kennedy (*below*). All conservatives, all lifetime appointments.

37

38

39

Reagan and Gorbachev became friends and they changed each other and the world. When the two had walked in Red Square, an American reporter had called out: "Do you still think you're in an evil empire, Mr. President?" "No." "Why not?" "I was talking about another time in another era." A few minutes later, the President threw an arm around Gorbachev's shoulder as they walked along like a couple of guys coming off the field after the big game.

compared with the style of his predecessors. The rhetoric was frightening—"Relations between our two countries are continuing to deteriorate, the arms race is intensifying"—but the editors agreed that the rhetorician was charming and laughed easily. Like Reagan.

At one point, Gorbachev said that all Reagan seemed interested in was "a new campaign of hatred." He said he doubted the American had any intention of negotiating seriously in Geneva. "It looks as if the stage is being set for a bout of some kind between political 'supergladiators,' " the Russian said. "We must not allow things to go so far as confrontation between our countries. . . . The Soviet Union is preparing very serious proposals, regardless of what some of Reagan's advisers to the right or to the left—if I am correct he does not have any advisers to the left—regardless of what any of his advisers try to sell to him."

What was this? Jokes from a Soviet leader? At another point, he invoked the name of a *Washington Post* columnist, quoting Mary Mc-Grory as saying that it had been so long since Soviets and Americans had talked to each other that Americans would be thrilled by an exchange of ballet troupes. Then this, the supreme leader of the world's godless communists, saying: "Surely God on high has not refused to give us enough wisdom to find ways to bring us an improvement in relations between the two great nations on earth, nations on whom depends the very destiny of civilization." The God bit was excised from the Russian-language version of the interview circulated in the Soviet Union.

As Reagan prepared for his journey to the summit, he was thrown on the defensive by Congress. From the day he took office, he had threatened to veto legislation imposing economic sanctions on South Africa unless it altered its apartheid racial policies, instead championing a policy he called "constructive engagement." In fact, on August 27, in a radio interview, he had asserted, "South African reformers have eliminated the segregation we once had in our own country." Then, on September 10, facing certain defeat on a Senate resolution demanding the sanctions, he reversed himself, ordering the sanctions he had been threatening to veto by signing executive orders banning both loans to South Africa as well as the sale of advanced technical equipment to the country's military and security services. A day later, Reagan reversed administration policy on trade, abandoning threats to veto "protectionist" legislation, and offering to work with the Congress on crafting legislation to restrict the "unfair trade practices" of Japan, Korea, Brazil, the countries of the European Union, and others running huge surpluses in trade with the United States. "In so doing," David Hoffman, the White House correspondent of *The Washington Post*, wrote in a News Analysis, "Reagan followed a common pattern of his Presidency, holding out to the very last before retreating when threatened with certain defeat."

The opening statement of Reagan's September 17 press conference, his first since returning from his cancer operation and California recuperation, focused on those trade issues, but eleven of the first thirteen questions were about the Soviets and Gorbachev.

"On the summit, sir, British Prime Minister Margaret Thatcher met Mr. Gorbachev and said, 'I like Mr. Gorbachev. We can do business together.' . . ."

"Well," said the President, "I wasn't planning on giving him a friendship ring or anything. . . . It isn't necessary that we love or even like each other. It's only necessary that we are willing to recognize that for the good of the people we represent, on this side of the ocean and over there, that everyone will be better off if we can come to some decisions about the threat of war."

Chris Wallace of NBC News, a reporter with a reputation for getting along with the Reagans, asked: "Some people believe the Soviets are winning the propaganda war leading up to the summit, that Mr. Gorbachev, in recent days, has made a number of proposals for test moratoria, for a chemical free zone in Europe, while the U.S. is testing an antisatellite weapon, and we learned today a test of a component of SDI. With them talking peace, while we're testing weapons of war, is Mr. Gorbachev beating you at your own game?"

"Well, I'm not engaged in a propaganda game . . ." the President began. "He can practice any tactics he wants. . . . We're going to meet and, and we're seriously going to discuss the matters that I've just mentioned here."

Reagan's tone did not change even when the subjects did: "Mr. President, members of your own party in Congress have failed to follow your leadership on two key policies—South Africa and trade." . . . "Mr. President, Bishop Tutu called you a racist." * . . .

---

* Episcopal Bishop Desmond Tutu, among the most important of South Africa's anti-apartheid leaders and winner of the Nobel Peace Prize for 1984, said of Reagan: "He doesn't care two beans about black people in South Africa. I don't think he cares at all. And that's why I call him a crypto-racist. I think I should call him a racist, pure and simple."

"Mr. President, the nation's best known AIDS scientist says the time has come now to boost existing research into what he called a minor moonshot program to attack this AIDS epidemic which has struck fear into the nation's health workers."

The risk to nurses and doctors forced Reagan to begin talking about, or just mentioning the epidemic. The President recited figures from the budget of the federal Centers for Disease Control in Atlanta. "Yes, there's no question about the seriousness of this and the need to find an answer." In his answer, he said "AIDS" for the first time in public. There was a second question about AIDS. Michael Putzel of the Associated Press asked the President, if he had young children, would he allow them to go to school if a classmate had the disease—a situation that had become an issue in New York City. Reagan avoided a direct answer. He also avoided saying "AIDS" two weeks later, when an old Hollywood friend, actor Rock Hudson, became the first celebrity to die of the disease.

For the first time in the President's thirty-two press conferences there were that day no questions or mentions of Iran. But neither the press nor the people knew American weapons were being distributed to Iranian troops. The President had given the nod to a second DC-8 flight three days before, this one delivering 408 TOW missiles to Tabriz airport in the northwest of Iran. A few hours after the delivery, the Israeli contact, Kimche, called McFarlane and told him the Iranians were reneging on the deal to release all the hostages in Beirut. They would release one. McFarlane's choice. "Buckley," he said. The CIA station chief. Ghorbanifar said that Buckley was too ill to be moved. (In fact, he had died on June 3.) McFarlane then chose the Reverend Benjamin Weir, a Presbyterian missionary who had been kidnapped in May of 1984. He had been held the longest and, not incidentally, his wife, a critic of American policy in the Middle East, was making a lot of bad noise in the press about the White House. The next day, September 15, Weir was found wandering outside the shell of the bombed-out United States embassy in West Beirut. He was flown to Cyprus and then on to a naval hospital in Virginia. The White House remained silent, hoping for more releases. Finally, on September 18, the day after the news conference, at the end of a long speech about tax reform in Concord, New Hampshire, Reagan said: "I'm pleased to inform you. . . . That Reverend Benjamin Weir, who was held hostage for 18 months in Lebanon, has now been released. I talked with Reverend Weir on Air Force One this morning. And I'm happy for him and his family. But I will not be satisfied and will not cease our efforts until all our hostages, the other six, are released."

White House reporters pressed Ed Djerejian, the assistant press secretary, who repeated the announcement later in Washington, about whether any ransom had been paid or any deals made. The press aide had asked the same questions of Oliver North, who had lied to him. So Djerejian responded: "The United States government has made no deal." Reverend Weir was the focus of television news for only one night, September 19, and he delivered the message his kidnappers had asked him to: "They have one demand, namely the release of 17 prisoners being held in Kuwait. Though they do not want to harm anyone, they will go so far as to proceed to execute the six hostages if their demand is not met."

The President was watching the news upstairs in the family quarters. Downstairs, his staff repeated the standard White House line that under no circumstances would the government negotiate with terrorists or pressure other governments to meet terrorist demands. Regan and McFarlane were determined to keep hostage families away from the President. They had made what they considered a big mistake back in June when they scheduled a meeting in a Chicago high school between Reagan and the families of many of the TWA hostages. That session went well enough until the brother of one of the seven long-term hostages, Father Lawrence Martin Jenco, a Catholic priest kidnapped that January, confronted the President. "Why won't you at least try to negotiate?" he demanded. Attempting to answer their rapid-fire questions, Reagan's voice began to crack and Regan practically pushed him out of the room as the Jencos followed.

"Stop those motherfuckers!" called one of Reagan's men, William Henkel. The President, pulled into a small office, was not angry; in fact, quite the opposite. He said: "It's an awful thing these parents and loved ones have to live with."

It was a time of awful news. On October 7, a Monday, a two-sentence "FLASH" message from the United States ambassador in Cairo, Nicholas Veliotes, stated that an Italian cruise ship, the *Achille Lauro*, had been hijacked by armed men in the Mediterranean Sea off the coast of Egypt. It was just after 10 A.M. in Washington when the President got the word from George Shultz. Though the first reports indicated that there were 72 Americans among the 755 passengers, it was not known how many of them had gone ashore for a daylong tour of Alexandria and Cairo. The initial White House reaction was to maintain the "business as usual" mode, to keep the President out of one more complicated hostage crisis.

The first CIA report to the White House summarized the situation: "The ship . . . has broken radio contact with shore. The terrorists have claimed that they killed two US citizen passengers, a male and female. The ship's captain told Cypriot authorities everyone on board is in good health. . . . The 7–12 hijackers believed aboard the ship claim to be members of the Front for the Liberation of Palestine . . . relatively small Abu Abbas wing, closely associated with PLO Chairman Arafat."

One of the first messages tracked in a separate State Department situation room was a radio transmission from the ship saying that the hijackers, Palestinians, were demanding the release of fifty prisoners from Israeli jails, and would kill Americans first if any rescue mission were attempted. United States planes and ships joined Egyptian and Italian craft and vessels following the *Achille Lauro* as it moved north toward the Syrian port of Tartus. American rescue teams, Navy SEALs, were flown into the area, but the principal United States efforts were requests to Syria and other eastern Mediterranean countries not to allow the ship to dock—the idea was not to have a repeat of TWA 847 when the hostages were dispersed through a city.

Those appeals (and threats) worked. Syrian officials turned the ship away, as did the Greek and Turkish governments of the divided island of Cyprus. By the next day, October 8, the ship was headed south toward Port Said in Egypt, at the head of the Suez Canal. By radio, the hijackers were negotiating with Egyptian officials and two Palestinian leaders on land, one of them Abu Abbas, who was one of the most wanted men in the world because of his bloody career as a terrorist.

As Americans monitored the ship-to-shore conversations—in which the hijackers called Abbas "commander"—it seemed apparent that both the Italians and the Egyptians were willing to give the hijackers safe passage out of Egypt if they surrendered at Port Said and if all the passengers and crew, more than four hundred of them, had not been harmed. That was not true. It was based on an earlier transmission by the captain of the ship, Gerardo de Rosa, who spoke as an AK-47 was pressed against his head. At 11 A.M. Washington time, the Americans were notified of the surrender. Five hours later, Ambassador Nicholas Veliotes was allowed onto the *Achille Lauro* and learned that Leon Klinghoffer, a sixty-nine-year-old New Yorker in a wheelchair, had been shot twice and thrown into the sea off Tartus. Witnesses said that he had bit one of the terrorists after the man slapped a woman.*

Both the Americans and the Italians demanded that Hosni Mubarak, the Egyptian President, cancel the "safe passage" deal. Mubarak said it was too late, the Palestinians were no longer in Egypt. Somehow, perhaps from Israeli intelligence, perhaps from Mubarak himself, the Americans learned that that was not true. The four terrorists and Abbas were at the Cairo airport, waiting for a chartered EgyptAir Boeing 737 to take them to the Palestine Liberation Organization's new headquarters in Tunisia.

The President was flying to Deerfield, Illinois, for another speech on tax reform, reading a *Washington Times* editorial headlined "Fish or Cut Bait, Mr. President!"—an editorial arguing that conservatives everywhere were questioning their leader's commitment and courage. In Chicago, McFarlane told him that back in Washington a group of NSC and State Department people—Admiral Poindexter, Oliver North, and Morton Abramowitz at State—thought there might be a chance to intercept the EgyptAir plane and force it to land in Europe, where Americans could get their hands on the Palestinian hijackers. "Go ahead!" said Reagan.

The President was on Air Force One, headed back to Washington, when the Egyptian 737 took off over the Mediterranean at 4:15 P.M. Washington time. Shortly after that, a ham radio operator was able to listen in on a telephone conversation from Air Force One to Weinberger. The Defense Secretary talked about the difficulty of forcing down the Egyptian plane and the President responded: "I don't care what it takes, I want that plane down in friendly territory." Six Navy F-14 Tomcats, from the carrier USS *Saratoga,* were already in the air, along with two E2-C Hawkeye radar planes. They received the order to go after the 737 at 4:37 P.M. They saw it at 5:30. Four Tomcats surrounded the passenger jet and one of the Hawkeye pilots radioed the

* During their trial in Italy, the four hijackers testified that it was never their intention to try to take over the *Achille Lauro.* They said that they had planned to leave the ship at Ashdod in Israel and mount an operation to avenge an Israeli air attack on PLO headquarters on October 2 in Tunis. More than fifty people had been killed in the raid. Reagan's public support for the attack—"Self-defense is always justified"—had triggered anti-American protests in Tunisia. The hijackers' plans changed, however, when a waiter on the Italian ship discovered them cleaning weapons in their cabin. There was real concern during the crisis that the actual target of the terrorists had been a Norwegian cruise ship, the *Royal Viking Sky,* which was in the same area of the Mediterranean. One of the passengers aboard that ship was Maureen Reagan, the President's older daughter.

Egyptian pilot: "EgyptAir 2483. Be aware you are being escorted by F-14s. You are to land immediately at Sigonella."

The 737 and its escorts arrived over Sigonella, a NATO base in Sicily, a few minutes after 6:30 P.M. American troops and a plane were already on the ground, waiting to take the Palestinians to the United States to be tried for the murder of Klinghoffer. But the Italians refused permission for the 737 to land. The plane and its escorts circled as Italian F-104s rose to join the aerial ballet. Weinberger, against the mission from the beginning, called his Italian counterpart, Giovanni Spadolini, who was furious about the American violations of international law and Italian sovereignty. Spadolini said no. So Reagan called Italy's Prime Minister, Bettino Craxi. State Department and White House situation rooms then reported: "Agreement has been reached between President and PM Craxi: six Palestinians (four hijackers plus two officials who had accompanied from Cairo) would be held, prosecuted by Italy. Craxi also agreed that USG should submit ASAP requests for extradition."

The 737, with the Palestinians looking out its windows, came down at 7:15 P.M. and was immediately surrounded by dozens of American soldiers. Then the Americans were surrounded by hundreds of Italian soldiers. Rifles were at the ready on both sides. The next call was from Secretary of State Shultz to his counterpart, Giulio Andreotti. "They will stand trial in Italy," said Andreotti. Shultz's legal adviser, Abraham Sofaer, told him the Italians were right; the United States authority at the base extended only to NATO affairs. The Americans lowered their guns. The next morning, when Poindexter arrived at the Oval Office with McFarlane for the President's daily national security briefing, Reagan stood up behind his desk and snapped a salute, saying: "Admiral, I salute the Navy!"

The President was euphoric, and so was the nation. "WE GOT 'EM" was the headline across USA Today. "Thank God we finally won one," said New York's Democratic senator, Daniel Patrick Moynihan. As Commander in Chief, Reagan sent an open message to American military units in the Mediterranean area: "You have my gratitude and the appreciation of all your countrymen. Best of all you have sent a message to terrorists everywhere: 'You can run, but you can't hide.' " American polls showed President Reagan's approval ratings jumping from the mid-50s to almost 70 percent.

The American cheers did not travel well. "Please, no more gloating," cabled Ambassador Veliotes from Cairo. Old allies praised the

United States and the President for political decisiveness and military execution. "All law-abiding people will have to support the U.S. action," commented the newspaper *Sueddeutsche* in Munich. But other governments and papers around the world were calling Reagan "the cowboy" and the Americans "pirates" for violating international treaties by forcing down the Egyptian plane. "An action of the jungle" commented the left-wing *Trouw* in Brussels. France's left-wing but pro-American *Libération* had it both ways: "The bad guys were punished without a shot. The cowboy chose the right moment to impose morals over right. . . . But this military victory ends in a true diplomatic defeat."

There were anti-American demonstrations in Paris, Rome, and Brussels and in all Arab and communist capitals. Some officials and commentators compared the interception with the Soviet destruction of KAL 007. In Cairo, the newspaper *al-Akhbar,* closely tied to the government, editorialized: "The gun in the hands of the cowboy is not a guarantee for ever-lasting victory, particularly since his enemies are everyday increasing." President Mubarak expressed public outrage: "I am deeply wounded. It was an act of American piracy. . . . We had not expected this attack from a friend." Veliotes hand-delivered a note of explanation from Reagan to Mubarak, but the Egyptian leader refused to open it.

In Italy, Prime Minister Craxi's five-party coalition government collapsed. His actions, which included allowing Abbas to leave Italy on a mysterious charter flight to Yugoslavia and then on to safety in Iraq, seemed to please no one. Parties and newspapers of the left accused him of being a "lapdog" of the Americans. His Defense Minister, Spadolini, refused to attend cabinet meetings because he believed Craxi consistently took pro-Palestinian positions to buy protection from Arab terrorism. On October 17, Spadolini pulled the twenty-nine members of his Republican Party out of the coalition supporting Craxi, a Socialist, and the Prime Minister resigned after twenty-six months in office, the second longest tenure in Italy's volatile politics since the end of World War II.*

On the evening of November 14, President Reagan went on national television to say: "My fellow Americans . . . In 36 hours I will

---

* Craxi was back in power eight days later. Abu Abbas was finally seized by United States troops on April 15, 2003, in Baghdad after American troops captured the city during the Second Gulf War. He had been sentenced in absentia to life in prison in an Italian court. Two of the hijackers were also sentenced to life, one to thirty years, and one to five months.

be leaving for Geneva for the first meeting between an American President and a Soviet leader in six years. . . . So tonight I want to share with you my hopes and tell you why I am going. . . . My mission stated simply, is a mission for peace."

It was a short speech for the occasion, and a pretty corny one, too: a Reagan speech. The President had spent day after day gently building up his knowledge of the Soviet Union—not of communism, a subject he knew all he wanted to know about, but of the ordinary life of people there, and of the life that had produced the power and character of the younger man who now led world communism. He understood what the CIA told him:

"Gorbachev by all accounts has a greater measure of self-confidence, even arrogance, than recent Soviet leaders about his ability to revitalize the Soviet system, deal effectively with foreign leaders, and restore credibility to Soviet diplomacy. . . . It is Gorbachev's unorthodox charismatic leadership style that most clearly sets him apart and captures the spirit of the regime he is now assembling."

The summit would be about control of the weapons of death that threatened both sides of the superpower struggle, but the President's speech that night was romantic, Jim and Sally, Ivan and Anya all over again:

> Imagine how much good we could accomplish, how the cause of peace would be served, if more individuals and families from our respective countries could come to know each other in a personal way. For example if Soviet youth could attend American schools and universities, they could learn that the spirit of freedom rules our land . . . they would learn that we are all God's children with much in common. Imagine if people in our nation could see and hear the Bolshoi Ballet again while Soviet citizens could see and hear groups like the Beach Boys, and how about Soviet children watching *Sesame Street*.

The President left Washington on the morning of November 16. He arrived in Geneva that evening, two days before the Russian leader, the time his physicians said he needed to avoid the fatigues of jet lag.

CHAPTER 13

NOVEMBER 19, 1985

"IT'S READY, SET, GORBACHEV!" said Dan Rather, opening the *CBS Evening News* on November 18, live from Geneva. On the *NBC Nightly News,* also live from Geneva, NBC anchor Tom Brokaw announced: "This long-awaited summit between Ronald Reagan and Mikhail Gorbachev is now less than twelve hours away." ABC's Peter Jennings, live from Geneva, said: "It is already Tuesday morning here in this Swiss city, and there is a mood of expectation."

"The Super-Summit" United Press International called it, the first meeting of the American and Soviet leaders since President Carter and Leonid Brezhnev in June of 1979. It was certainly a Super Story, covered from most every angle by more than three thousand reporters and hundreds of spokesmen and public relations officers from around the world, like the Olympics, with breathless accounts of events and incidents great and small, cold and warm. Brokaw ended his newscast that night, the day Gorbachev arrived: "The issues here are, of course, monumental. A lot of people believe the future of the world is at stake, but along with those larger matters, President Reagan is dealing with—well, a few smaller ones. A little boy whose parents own the mansion where the Reagans are staying left the President a note asking him to look after the fish in his bedroom. Mr. Reagan is following his instructions."

Inside that mansion, Maison de Saussure, the home of both the goldfish and Prince Karim Aga Khan, Reagan was in debate with Jack Matlock, the State Department's ranking Soviet expert. Speaking in Russian, Matlock played Gorbachev in a dress rehearsal complete with interpreters to make sure the President was not thrown by the bilingual conversations scheduled for the next day. Reagan was enjoying it, comparing the dialogue to watching a foreign movie with subtitles. An actor would speak for five minutes and up would pop the words, "That's fine." He had been learning his lines—and what they meant—since June. Matlock, assisted by Morton Abramowitz of State and Robert Gates of the CIA, was the President's tutor, professor of what the State Department called "Soviet Union 101," twenty-four ten-page papers, one or two a week, along with lunches with experts and interpreters of Soviet and Russian policies and politics. Reagan made his usual clutch of mistakes, telling his briefers that he knew the key to Russian life was that the language had no word for "freedom." It did, of course: *svoboda*.

But he was learning. He watched hours of videotape of Gorbachev and his men, and was impressed when the State Department's Intelligence and Research unit told him that Gorbachev himself had watched every foot of video coverage of a recent trip to Leningrad before deciding what would be shown on Soviet television. CIA director William Casey traveled to London to personally debrief Soviet defectors, including Oleg Gordievsky, a former Soviet intelligence (KGB) station chief—and then reported back to the President. Casey said Gordievsky said the Soviets were open to serious negotiation, but that they believed Reagan was planning attacks on Cuba and on the Soviet Union itself. The President also talked for hours with Suzanne Massie, a writer of popular histories of Russia, and, upstairs with his wife, watched Soviet films, including *Moscow Does Not Believe in Tears,* a bittersweet romantic comedy that won the foreign language film Oscar at the 1981 Academy Awards. He understood, instinctively, that Gorbachev and his wife, Raisa, who had earned a doctorate in political theory, were both sensitive to Western views that the Soviet Union was a huge but backward country—which happened to be what Reagan himself believed. And, as always, Reagan was receiving personal guidance from former President Nixon.

The first joint announcement to the press assembled in Geneva was that there would be no announcements. A cone of silence descended over the actual words between the two leaders, producing the usual spectacle of reporters interviewing each other and telling fish stories supplied by spokesmen. And there were the leakers. For weeks, the Soviets had been leaking stories that Gorbachev was ready to consider a 50 percent reduction in his country's fleet of land-based nuclear missiles. One response to those leaks was a "secret" letter to Reagan from Secretary of Defense Weinberger—generally believed to be the Secretary's attempt to sabotage the summit—which appeared in *The New York Times,* arguing that the Soviets were routinely violating previous arms control agreements and that the United States should be doing the same thing. McFarlane, off the record, leaked to reporters that the letter leaker was the Secretary himself. He considered the letter treason and said, off the record, that the leaker should be in jail.*

As he waited for Gorbachev's arrival, the President reviewed a five-page memo he had dictated and edited just before leaving Washington. His notes to himself made it clear that he was ready for a new phase in both the Cold War and his presidency. His thoughts included these:

"I believe Gorbachev is a highly intelligent leader totally dedicated to traditional Soviet goals. He will be a formidable negotiator. . . . He is dependent on the Soviet communist hierarchy and will be out to prove to them his strength and dedication. . . . He will wish to reduce the burden of defense spending that is stagnating the Soviet economy . . . [that] could contribute to his opposition to SDI since he doesn't want to face the cost of competing with us."

Then he offered himself some advice: "How about just hanging back until we get some of the things we want instead of giving consideration up front to what they want? . . . Let there be no talk of winners and losers. Even if we think we won, to say so would set us back in view of their inherent inferiority complex." He also emphasized that he wanted to set a schedule of future meetings: "We should set up a process to avoid war and settling our differences in the future."

Gorbachev, on arrival, was surprisingly candid about his agenda: "You ask what changes in the world economy could be of benefit to the Soviet Union. First of all, an end to the arms race. We would prefer to use every ruble that today goes for defense to meet civilian, peaceful needs. . . . On the other hand, if billions and billions of dollars had already been spent on SDI research, then nobody is going to stop because all that money has been invested. And then, once space weapons are deployed, once they are in space then no one could control that process."

The candor of the man from Moscow was producing rock star treatment in the Western press, but Gorbachev was playing a weak hand, according to one American commentator: "Americans, from

---

* Matlock's take on Weinberger was more direct. He said he once heard the Defense Secretary say: "If Congress sees us negotiating, they'll cut my budget."

President Reagan on down, have become so hung up on the image of Soviet leader Mikhail Gorbachev that we are in danger of forgetting that substantively it is the Soviet Union, not the United States, that is on the defensive on the dominant issue of our times, arms control. . . . It is Gorbachev who is having a fine time these days waving to the crowds from the back of limousines, but it is Reagan who is in the driver's seat as both men start down the road to Geneva. Reagan has what former President Nixon has called 'the ultimate bargaining chip' in the Strategic Defense Initiative because whether the system works or not, developing it would break the Soviet economy long before it would break the American one."

The President's briefing packages emphasized the point. The longest CIA study, "Gorbachev's Economic Agenda," began: "Gorbachev still faces an economy that cannot simultaneously maintain rapid growth in defense spending, satisfy demand for greater quantity and variety of consumer goods and services, invest the amounts required for economic modernization and expansion, and continue to support client-state economies." The State Department's Intelligence and Research operation produced a somewhat similar paper titled "USSR: A Society in Trouble." The National Intelligence Estimate, combining data for military and civilian agencies, began: "The Soviet Union is a far less healthy society than either its leadership or its population wishes it to be, and a parody of its official values of social progress, public welfare and popular optimism."

Reagan had believed exactly that with certainty and passion for more than thirty years. He had never seen the Soviet Union, but he was a faithful reader of conservative journals and books that consistently characterized communism as a utopian dream that had failed and the USSR as a poor and unjust country governed by men who held power by fear and force. An Evil Empire. There was, though, an irony in hawkish conservative thinking, and Gorbachev cleverly mocked that in one of the Geneva meetings. "To substantiate increased military spending, all they do in the U.S. is talk about the fantastic achievements of the U.S.S.R. in technology," he said. "When they need an excuse for prohibitive measures, they portray us as a country of yokels."

Reagan had been a spokesman for the hawks of American conservatism for decades and he still read those journals, even as his public rhetoric moderated. Ten days before leaving for Geneva, he had invited a group of SDI advocates, led by Edward Teller, the scientist often credited with leading the development of the hydrogen bomb, to the White House to talk about the summit. One of them, a cocky twenty-seven-year-old *Wall Street Journal* editorial writer named Gregory Fossedal, said: "I've had made a special model of Mikhail Gorbachev for you to study before the summit." He handed the President a plastic model of Darth Vader, the villain of the film *Star Wars*.

"You know they really are an evil empire," said Reagan. "I've never had any regrets or retractions about that." In his diary, he added: "Gorbachev is adamant we must cave in on SDI. Well, this will be a case of an irresistible force meeting an immovable object."

The night before he was to meet Gorbachev, Reagan wrote in his diary: "Lord, I hope I'm ready." But the next morning began badly. "Oh, Lordy," Reagan exclaimed when he went to feed the fish left in his charge. One was dead. He told Don Regan to dispatch the Secret Service into the city to find a fish that looked like the dear departed.

The leaders met for the first time the next morning at Villa Fleur d'Eau, a lakeside château. It was gray and cold, European weather, perfect for an old John Kennedy trick. As the Soviet leader, the younger man, stepped out of his limousine in overcoat, scarf, and hat, Reagan bounded down the stairs without coat or hat. Round one to the American, reported the world's news-starved press. The principals, with only interpreters present, were scheduled to talk for fifteen minutes—really seven or eight minutes because of translation time—but they remained together for more than an hour. Reagan, officially the host, dominated the session, mainly because he was determined not to begin with the details of arms, but with the realities of mistrust. The official American Memorandum of Conversation recorded this:

"The President said that the two of them would talk about many things, including arms, in the main meeting, but he wondered if the primary aim between them should not be to eliminate the suspicions. . . . Countries do not have mistrust of each other because of arms, but rather countries build up their arms because of the mistrust between them. . . . The President expressed the hope that in the meetings the two sides could get to the sources of the suspicions."

Gorbachev began by talking about arms and agreements, but he emphasized that what was necessary to relieve world fears of Soviet-American military confrontations was "political will at the highest levels." He continued: "The Soviet people and the leadership of the Soviet Union recognized the role of the United States in the world, and wished it no harm. They realized that international relations could not be built on a desire to harm American interests." Before they left the room to begin a plenary session with aides, Gorbachev surprised Reagan by saying that Soviet scientists had concluded that there was high probability of a major earthquake in California within the next three years—as bad as 7.5 on the Richter scale—and were eager to share that information with the Americans. Perhaps most importantly, Reagan told Matlock, one of nine Americans at the plenary session, "You're right. I did like him."

Gorbachev spoke first at the larger meeting, but he led from weakness. Matlock, for one, was stunned by the defensiveness of the Soviet leader as he spoke of trade, and of Americans who believed the Soviet Union was crippled by economic problems. Reagan, of course, was the leader of that crowd—though Gorbachev did not mention that. The official notes recorded: "The President had said . . . the task before us is strengthening confidence . . . for example trade and economic relations can be helpful. . . . The Soviets know of some studies in United States think tanks in which the United States ruling class indicates its view that the Soviet economy is in a perilous state. Therefore it would be good to push the Soviet Union into an arms race. . . . If the United States thinks that by saying these things, Gorbachev is showing weakness, then this will all come to nothing."

President Reagan responded by laying out his view of history after World War II: "When that war ended, the Americans were the only ones whose industry had not been bombed and who had not sustained great losses. The Americans were the only ones who had a weapon of great devastation, the nuclear weapon. . . . The United States began making proposals to the Soviet Union and the world about sharing nuclear technology and doing away with the weapons. The United States was willing to give it up. Most of the time the United States did not get cooperation from Gorbachev's predecessors."

Now, Reagan continued, an expansionist Soviet Union and its surrogates were on the move militarily in Afghanistan, Ethiopia, Angola, and Yemen. "The President," the notes continued, "stat[ed] that he was setting all of this as the basis for American concern and distrust. . . . Maybe the Soviets did not want war but it seemed to want to get its way. . . . If the two sides just get in bargaining over a particular type of weapon we will just go on trying to keep advantages. But if we can go on the basis of *trust,* then those mountains of weapons will disappear quickly as we will be confident that they are not needed."

This was Reagan's utopian view, but he was not finished. The notes, still quoting Reagan, shifted to the subject of SDI:

> Gorbachev had said that the United States had indicated an interest in achieving a first strike capability by having an anti-missile shield. . . . The United States had a research program. The Soviet Union had the same kind of program. The United States has some hope that it might be possible. If both sides continue their research and come up with such a system then they should sit down and make it available to everyone so no one would have fear of a nuclear strike. If we could come up with a shield and share it, then nobody would worry about the madman. He didn't even want to call this a weapon; it was a defensive system. . . . It is the sincerest desire of the United States to eliminate suspicion.

After lunch, it was again Gorbachev's chance—and his voice rose as he tried to rebut Reagan point by point. Matlock's notes described his presentation:

> You mentioned Afghanistan, Angola, even Yemen. We can agree that hotbeds of conflict do cause problems in our relationship. But we cannot agree with your view of their cause, because you feel USSR "expansionism" is responsible. This is either a delusion or deliberate distortion. . . . You overemphasize the power of the Soviet Union. We are categorically opposed to impose solutions from the outside. However, we are against counterrevolution, and support the struggle for liberation—some wanted to crush the revolutions in the US, France and the USSR. . . . We have no secret plans for world domination. Regional problems are due to the struggle evolving over many stages. . . . We support a settlement in Afghanistan, a political settlement under the United Nations, if you help us. You accuse us of deploying troops but you work against us. You want our troops there, the longer the better. . . . You are now trying to assure that no agreements are violated. But twenty years ago you had four times Soviet power. Soviet leadership had to offset your advantage, so that it would not be possible for you to manipulate us. You would have had to take steps just as we did to establish parity. The negotiations began as we approached parity. . . . Scholars tell us

any shield can be pierced. SDI will not save us, so why is SDI necessary? It only makes sense if it is to defend against a *retaliatory*
strike. Weinberger has said that if the USSR had such a defense first,
it would be bad. If we go first, you feel it would be bad for the
world, feeding mistrust. We can't believe your rationale. . . . We
will build up to smash your shield.

Reagan took the floor, repeating "mistrust" again. He went back to
World War II, condemning the Soviets for not allowing American
bombers to land and refuel in the Soviet Union. He attacked Soviet intentions and actions in Vietnam, in Cambodia, in Afghanistan, in
Nicaragua. He said: "All this is behind the mistrust." *

The Soviets were surprised by the personal force of the older man.
One of the Russians in the room, Sergei Tarasenko, an assistant to the
new Soviet Foreign Minister Eduard Shevardnadze, a Gorbachev
friend, had been briefed to expect the President to be inattentive, wandering, dependent on his four-by-six cards, but it was not like that.
"He was unattentive when the subject didn't interest him. He let it go.
But as soon as Shevardnadze or Gorbachev touched some point of interest to the president he immediately came out with an extremely
good, spontaneous delivery. He would deliver a good piece, strong on
conviction, strong on facts, emotionally charged. He was another guy
immediately."

Gorbachev as well saw two Reagans. He did not appreciate the
President's sanctimonious little lectures on American superiority.
"Mr. President, you are not a prosecutor, I am not the accused," he interrupted at one point. "You are not a teacher. I am not a student."
But the Soviet leader had a sense of humor and he laughed lustily at
Reagan's oft- and well-told jokes. The first one that scored was about
an old Russian lady who got into the Kremlin and told Gorbachev,
"In America, I could go into the White House and say to Reagan, 'I
don't like the way you're running the country.' " Gorbachev (in the
joke) answered, "Why, my dear, you can do the same thing in the Soviet Union. You can come up to my office *anytime*, and say, 'I don't
like the way Reagan's running his country.' "

Finally, the real, and serious, Gorbachev asked: "What are we to
say to our negotiators?"

---

* Reagan was wrong about the refueling, which he quickly learned. The Soviet deputy foreign
minister, George Kornienko, immediately told Shultz that during the war he had been stationed
at a Soviet base built to refuel American bombers.

"We could give them guidelines that call for 50 percent reductions leading to parity for all," Reagan answered. "Instruct them to go forward."

"What about the objective announced in January—no arms race in space," asked Gorbachev. "What about that goal?"

"I don't see the defensive shield as an arms race in space. It's a means to eliminate weapons."

The room was hot, in more ways than one. "Why don't we go for a walk?" Reagan asked.

It was 3:45 P.M. in Geneva—9:45 A.M., November 19, in New York. The television network morning shows were over. The big three had pictures, but no words from the participants. "They talked!" had been the first words from Dan Rather. But he did not know what they said. Jesse Jackson, who had paid his own way to Geneva, did what he did best, filling the news vacuum, this time by confronting Gorbachev in the lobby of the Soviet mission and badgering him about the treatment of Jews and other minorities in the Soviet Union, a smooth maneuver designed to soften charges of anti-Semitism left over from his 1984 presidential campaign in New York, the place he famously called "Hymietown." Reagan's spokesman, Larry Speakes, was another press draw, but he said only that he was playing by an old rule: "Those who talk don't know what's going on, and those who know what's going on won't talk."

Speakes then proved what he had said. Afraid that Reagan might not be a match for Gorbachev, the spokesman assigned an assistant, Mark Weinberg, to draft quotes that would make the President look good. One of the phonies attributed to the President made all the network news shows that night and probably a majority of the world's newspapers. "The President's best statement came off camera," reported Chris Wallace of NBC. " 'There is much that divides us, but I believe the world breathes easier because we are talking here together.' " *

Reagan and Gorbachev walked to a pool house at the shore of Lake Geneva. The break had been planned by Bill Henkel, the new Mike Deaver, and approved by Mrs. Reagan. The two men talked about

---

* The manufacture of that quote and others only became known after Speakes left the White House in 1987 and wrote a book called *Speaking Out: The Reagan Presidency from Inside the White House.* The uproar over making up Reagan quotes—not an uncommon phenomenon in that White House—cost him his new job as the vice president of public affairs for the Wall Street firm of Merrill Lynch.

Reagan's movies as they walked into the cold wind from the lake. The President made it clear that he was annoyed that a Soviet official, Georgi Arbatov, director of the Institute of the United States and Canada, had once dismissed him as just an actor in B films. He said he had done some A movies, particularly *Kings Row*. Gorbachev surprised him by saying he had seen it and liked it. He should have, since, in Marxist analysis, it was a dark film about American hypocrisy and class conflict, in which Reagan played a rich young man deliberately destroyed after he married a girl from the wrong side of the tracks in small-town America.

As they walked into the pool house, Reagan slowed for a moment and offered a line, probably rehearsed, probably sincere. At least Gorbachev took it as sincere: "Mr. General Secretary, here we are, two men born in obscure rural hamlets, both poor and from humble beginnings. Now we are the leaders of our countries, and probably the only two men who can start World War III, and possibly the only two men . . . who can bring peace to the world."

In the small house by the lake, with their interpreters, they settled into easy chairs before a fireplace with a welcome roaring fire set by Henkel. As Gorbachev rubbed his hands in front of the fire, Reagan handed him a couple of pages typed in Russian, an outline of a sweeping nuclear arms control agreement. "Just a seed," he emphasized. Gorbachev read for several minutes. They began to talk, they began to argue. Whatever else it was, it was a real conversation between two men who appeared to accept each other's sincerity. The pool house conversation lasted for a little more than an hour. The American paper included an overall 50 percent cut in nuclear weapons, but Gorbachev pointed out that there was more than a little vagueness about what kinds of weapons and delivery systems would be included—and then, once more, there was the question of shield weapons and research. The Memorandum of Conversation included:

> With some emotion Gorbachev appealed to the President as follows: If the two sides were indeed searching for a way to end the arms race and to begin to deal seriously with disarmament, then what would be the purpose of deploying a weapon that is as yet unknown and unpredictable? . . . People would not be in a position to determine what it was that would be placed into space and would surely regard it as an additional threat, thereby creating crisis situations. . . .

The President asked Gorbachev to remember that these were not weapons that kill people or destroy cities. . . . He would also urge Gorbachev to remember that we were talking about something that was not yet known, and that if it were known, that would still be years away. Why then should we sit here in the meanwhile with mountains of weapons on each side?

Gorbachev countered by suggesting that they announce to the world that President Reagan and General Secretary Gorbachev had declared firmly in official statements that both countries would refrain from research, development, testing and deployment of space weapons. . . . Thus they could implement the idea of open laboratories and at the same time begin the process of 50 percent reductions in offensive arms?

The President said . . . We certainly have no intention of putting something into space that would threaten people on earth. . . . In 1926 in this city of Geneva, all of the countries that had participated in World War I had reached an agreement not to use poison gas. Nevertheless, all had kept their gas masks.

Gorbachev said that to a certain extent he could understand the President on a human level; he could understand that the idea of strategic defense had captivated the President's imagination. However, as a political leader he could not possibly agree. . . .

The President recognized that both of them had made some strong statements and that it would be difficult for either of them to reverse direction. . . . Our people look to the sky and think of what might happen if missiles suddenly appear. . . . We believe that the idea of having a defense against nuclear missiles involved a great deal of faith and belief. When he said we, he meant most of mankind.

Gorbachev said . . . If SDI were actually implemented, then layer after layer of offensive weapons, Soviet as well as U.S., would appear in space and only God himself would know what they were . . . and God provides information very selectively.

So it ended. Walking back to the villa, Reagan asked Gorbachev to come to the United States. The Russian agreed immediately and invited Reagan to Moscow. The President's men were surprised, but the President was not. Dobrynin had let the Americans know that if Gorbachev were asked to visit, he would come. At dinner that night, at the Soviet mission in Geneva, the General Secretary announced the exchange of visits to applause all around.

Reagan toasted the forty-third anniversary of the Soviet counterattack against the German armies besieging Stalingrad. Good research there. There was obvious rapport between the two leaders, a bit of coolness between their wives—Raisa Gorbachev had degrees in political theory and preferred to be called "Dr."—but the Gorbachevs were delightful hosts, talking about long driving trips through France and Italy when they were younger and no one knew who they were. They both talked about the popularity of American playwrights in the Soviet Union, particularly Tennessee Williams and Edward Albee, disagreeing about whether Elizabeth Taylor was better in the film of *Who's Afraid of Virginia Woolf?* than the Russian actress currently playing the role onstage in Moscow.

Mrs. Gorbachev told of taking a granddaughter to see an ancient palace in the Crimea and learning that the ruler was said to have two hundred wives—and the girl later asked her grandfather why he did not have more. He had told the girl he had enough trouble handling one.

In his final toast, the General Secretary cited the Bible, and later Reagan told his wife that Gorbachev had told him Raisa was an atheist, but that his mother had often read the Bible to him when he was a boy in the village of Privolnoye. Reagan responded with a quote he said was from the 16th Book of Acts: "We are all of one blood regardless of where we live on the Earth." *

As the First Couples talked, lesser American and Soviet negotiators worked through the night, beginning the drafting of a final summit statement. Their problem was the same as that of the three thousand reporters: The negotiating teams might know more of what was actually happening, but so far it did not amount to much beyond a certain male bonding between the principals.

In the morning, on November 20, the leaders again met alone with their translators. The talk went round and round about human rights in both countries, with Reagan taking most of the time and asking for the release or consideration of release for individuals and families that had come to his attention in various ways. Gorbachev replied that he believed most of those cases were being publicized by anti-Soviet groups, but that he would check into them. Then he said that he was tired of hearing such things from a country where women made

---

* Acts 17:26, in the King James Version of the Bible, says: "And hath made of one blood all nations of men for to dwell on all the face of the earth, and hath determined the times before appointed, and the bounds of their habitation."

only 60 percent of men's pay for the same jobs, that he knew that was American law. "No, no," said Reagan. "The law says there can be no discrimination, but that there are people with personal prejudices."

"You're wrong about how much power a President has—" Reagan said, but Gorbachev cut him off without waiting for the translation. The American interpreter, Dimitry Zarechnak, was shocked. He had been told the Russian understood no English. He concluded that Reagan was repeating himself enough that Gorbachev knew where he was going.

The morning's plenary session was at the Soviet mission. Once more, Gorbachev went after SDI, according to the official notes:

"Gorbachev told the President that he had recently observed to a Soviet scientist that he could see no reason why the President should be committed to SDI . . . interested in further exacerbating U.S.-Soviet relations. The scientist said that she had done research into the matter and found the explanation: SDI would produce $600 billion to a trillion dollars in new military expenditures. That was the reason."

"That's a fantasy," said Reagan.

"No," said Gorbachev. "It's emotional. . . . It's one man's dream. . . . There are dreams of peace and there are realities."

The Soviet leader was becoming more emotional himself, interrupting the President, asking why he would not believe him when he said the Soviet Union would never attack first. Three times he interrupted, repeating that same question. Then he said he could not believe promises that the United States would share SDI technology—that it did not even share technology with its allies. Finally, according to the notes: "The President wants to catch the 'Firebird' of SDI by using the U.S. technological advantage. There would be disillusionment, but it would come too late, as the 'infernal train' would already be moving."

"No one even knows whether it will work," Reagan said. "The effort is designed to find out if it's possible."

Gorbachev ended by saying it was obvious that the United States was committed to development, to testing, to deployment of space weapons. "The Soviet Union," he said, "would have to base their policy on that fact."

That meeting broke for lunch at 12:40. "Are you getting along?" an American reporter shouted to Reagan. The President called back: "You can see that, can't you?"

The Reagans hosted the dinner at the Maison de Saussure that night as squads of their aides hammered out a final statement for the closing ceremony. In his toast, the President nodded to Gorbachev and repeated a Thomas Paine quote he often used: "We have it in our power to start the world over again."

"We have started something. . . . To dialogue and cooperation!" responded Gorbachev.

The President went upstairs at 10:30 that night. His entourage was fighting over the wording of his closing speech until past 4:30 A.M. Geneva time. Matlock and Bud McFarlane were trying to wait out two conservative speechwriters—Pat Buchanan and Peggy Noonan—who were punctuating Reagan's closing remarks with anti-Soviet rhetoric and disparaging comments about Gorbachev. There were still three of those comments in the text when it was given to the President. He handed the speech back to Buchanan with the three sentences crossed out. "Pat, this has been a good meeting," he said. "I think I can work with this guy. I can't just keep poking him in the eye."

Reagan went back upstairs for a final task. He wrote out a note and laid it next to the aquarium:

Dear Friends,
   I put the white half dome in the tank according to the directions and fed them with 2 good pinches morning and night from the big food container. Now and then I added some of the colored flakes from the small container. Lights on in the morning and out at night. On Tuesday I found one of your fish dead in the bottom of the tank. I don't know what could have happened but I added 2 new ones (same kind). I hope this was alright. Thanks for letting us live in your lovely home.
                         Ronald Reagan

NBC's coverage of the closing began with Chris Wallace standing in front of the stage at Geneva's International Press Center. With Reagan and Gorbachev seated above him, the correspondent began: "When the President and Soviet leader arrived for today's ceremony they were all smiles, but it was soon apparent their summit had produced few concrete results."

The statement was a basket of small agreements on such things as cultural exchanges, civil air safety procedures, and new consulates. The key paragraphs included: "They agreed to accelerate the work . . . to prevent an arms race in space and to terminate it on earth . . . including the principle of 50 percent reductions in the nuclear arms of the U.S. and USSR appropriately applied."

"Appropriately applied" was a code phrase for later interpretation and negotiation, or stalemate. As the two leaders stood side by side, their national flags behind them, Reagan leaned over to Gorbachev and whispered: "I bet the hard-liners in both our countries are bleeding while we shake hands."

The General Secretary spoke first, saying: "We have to be realistic and straightforward and, therefore, the solving of the most important problems concerning the arms race and increasing hopes of peace, we didn't succeed at reaching in this meeting. . . . However the President and I have agreed that this work of seeking mutually acceptable decisions for these questions will continue."

Reagan said: "I came to Geneva to seek a fresh start in relations between the United States and the Soviet Union, and we have done this. . . . I'm convinced that we are headed in the right direction."

People loved it, at least Americans did. The President returned to Washington on November 22 and went straight to the Capitol to report to a cheering joint session of Congress. A quick CBS News poll indicated that 83 percent of respondents approved of Reagan's summit performance. Fifty-seven percent agreed with the questionnaire statement that Gorbachev was "a new kind of Soviet leader."

So did the President. As soon as he returned home, Reagan telephoned former President Nixon for what amounted to a debriefing, and one of things he told Nixon was that he thought the leader of atheistic world communism, on some level, believed in God.

That night he wrote in his diary: "I haven't gotten such a reception since I was shot."

CHAPTER 14
JANUARY 28, 1986

H E CHANGES THEM LIKE HE CHANGES HIS UNDERWEAR" was the private comment of Larry Speakes about the appointment of Admiral John Poindexter as director of the National Security Council. On December 4, 1985, Poindexter became the fourth NSC chief in less than five years, replacing Bud McFarlane, who had slipped a letter of resignation into the President's daily security briefing that morning. McFarlane was a strange man, "bone-tired," he said. He may have been over his head in trying to manage the complicated rivalries and manipulation that surrounded the Oval Office. A retired Marine lieutenant colonel (and son of a Texas congressman), he had risen to high station in the apparatus of three administrations, one more young military man who came in as a White House Fellow and made an impression by working hard and saying, "Yes sir!" But he was ground down in the incessant struggles between this administration's heavyweights, Secretary of State Shultz and Secretary of Defense Weinberger.

Or, some thought, he was squeezed out because the President would not choose between Shultz and Weinberger. In one of his first meetings with the two secretaries, McFarlane watched tight-lipped, his usual expression, as Weinberger began a lecture on defense requirements and Shultz stood up, walked to a doorway, turned around, and said: "You know it's pointless to try to do business with you, Cap. You don't analyze things. You take stances. If you're going to govern, you have to listen and analyze to figure out the right thing to do. But you don't ever do that, Cap."

Some who worked with him believed that McFarlane, who was forty-seven years old, was having a nervous breakdown. Despite the most stoic of faces, he was seething with frustration and insecurity over his inability to deal with Reagan in the same way his older colleagues did, or to initiate the creative bursts or solid options of his former NSC bosses, Henry Kissinger and Brent Scowcroft. Perhaps his problem was that the President did not really care who was NSC director; they were just staff, hired hands. McFarlane happened to be the available man when his boss, Bill Clark, was worn down in the same way. As number two, McFarlane was hardworking and diligent, experienced and outwardly unflappable—most of the people he worked with knew nothing of the hostage games being played in Beirut, Jerusalem, and Tehran, or the details of the covert Central American wars he was running with his hard-charging deputy, Oliver North. His reputation peaked as he helped prepare Reagan for the Geneva summit. "Taking Charge" was the headline of a *New York Times Magazine* profile of him on May 26, 1985. The author was Leslie Gelb, the paper's national security correspondent, who wrote: "Within the last few months, McFarlane has suddenly emerged as a powerhouse in the formulation of Administration foreign and defense policy."

In Gelb's piece, McFarlane described Reagan's decision-making this way: "Well, the President has a clear sense of a goal. . . . He says 'Go figure out a way to do that.' So, we'll have an NSC meeting or two, usually preceded by work done under the guidance of Assistant Secretaries of State. We get up a paper and we send the paper to the President and he digests that and then we have a couple of morning oral briefings."

The briefings, fifteen minutes long, were followed by full NSC meetings—225 of them compared with 86 over the same time period when Nixon was President—which were really seminars for Reagan, who sometimes never spoke at all. "Then," said McFarlane, "I come back to him and say, 'Well, here's what you can do and here's another way.' And he signs the directive." He described the directives, circulated within the administration's foreign policy hierarchy: "The strategy will be thus and so. Here are your fallback options, and here's who I want to be in charge. . . ."

That was the theory. The reality, more often than not, was stalemate as Shultz and Weinberger were often inclined to interpret the directives according to their own predilections—and McFarlane did not have the clout to challenge them or the confidence to complain to the President. If he had, Reagan would have told him what he had told

Matlock: "Don't worry about it. Cap wants to be Secretary of State, but he'd be a disaster. Shultz wants Cap fired, but I'm not going to do that."

McFarlane was a marked man after the *Times*'s journalistic coronation. Whoever was out to get McFarlane—most people thought it was chief of staff Regan trying to cut him down to size—began by spreading rumors that he was having an affair with NBC News White House correspondent Andrea Mitchell. True or not, the rumors, published without names in the Sunday supplement magazine *Parade,* were pushing McFarlane close to the edge. Shultz took note of the rumors in a nasty way when Mitchell asked the Secretary a tough question at a news conference and he answered: "When we make our decision, I'm sure you'll be the first to know." Regan, quick with grudges and temper, had never forgiven McFarlane for informing the President of the death of Soviet leader Konstantin Chernenko in the early hours of March 11 without first calling him. "The Chief," as Regan liked to be called, was embarrassed later that morning when he walked into the Oval Office and was mystified when Reagan said: "Boy, isn't this something?"

"This is outrageous," Regan yelled at McFarlane. "You don't seem to realize you work for me."

"No, I don't. I work for the President. . . ."

"The hell you do! You work for me and everything you do will come through me or you'll be out of here."

Now, he was out, replaced by his deputy. Admiral Poindexter, who had rarely appeared in public, was introduced in the press room by Reagan. The first question, from Sam Donaldson of ABC News, was, "Admiral, will we ever see you again?"

"Maybe," Poindexter answered.

Before leaving the building, McFarlane went to the President to give him a final briefing on arms-for-hostage maneuvers going on with Iran and Israel. "You should know, Mr. President, that this is not working," he said. "Our hopes at the beginning of this were that we were talking with Iranian politicians said to have a political agenda. It has ended up that we are talking to arms merchants. . . . I think you ought to review this matter once again."

"Okay. Get the guys together." That night, in his diary, Reagan wrote: "NSC briefing—probably Bud's last—subject our undercover effort to free our last 5 hostages—complex undertaking with only a few in on it—won't even write in this diary what we were up to."

Poindexter, in his first Oval Office briefing as National Security Adviser, on December 5, gave the President more details. His briefing notes included: "Hostages—1 to Tehran 22—2." Meaning that one shipment of arms to Tehran on December 22 would result in the release of two hostages.

On December 7, McFarlane came back to the White House residence and laid out the series of events that had begun late in the spring, when the Israelis had come to him talking of contacts with "moderate" Iranians. Shultz and Weinberger, in agreement this time, urged the President to walk away from the deals. The President disagreed: "The way I look at it, we're trying to reach opponents of Khomeini. . . . We're not dealing with terrorists." When Weinberger said there were legal problems with these schemes, Reagan answered: "The American people will never forgive me if I don't get those hostages out over a legal question."

Then McFarlane suggested that he go to London to size up Manucher Ghorbanifar and the other merchants and go-betweens who claimed they were brokering the deal with Tehran.

"Go ahead," said Reagan.

When Shultz and Weinberger voiced objections that same day, the President cut them off, saying: "It's the same thing as if one of my children were kidnapped and there was a demand for ransom; sure, I don't believe in ransom because it leads to more kidnapping. But if I find out there's someone with access to the kidnappers and can get my child back without doing anything for the kidnapper, I'd sure do that. And it would be perfectly fitting for me to reward that individual if he got my child back. That's not paying ransom to kidnappers."

In his diary that night, the President wrote: "[A] complex plan which could return our five hostages. . . . It calls for Israel selling some weapons to Iran. As they are delivered in installments by air, our hostages will be released. The weapons will go to moderate leaders in the army who are essential if there is to be a change to a more stable government. . . . George Shultz, Cap and Don are opposed. . . . Bud is flying to London where the Israelis and Iranian agents are. Britain has no embargo on selling to Iran."

McFarlane, traveling with Oliver North, arrived in London on December 8. Three Israelis—Kimche and two arms dealers, Al Schwimmer and Yakov Nimrodi—were with Ghorbanifar in an apartment owned by Schwimmer. A retired American Air Force general, Richard Secord, was there as well. McFarlane said he was under instructions from the White House and was ready to break off all talks unless Iranian political figures came forward for secret negotiations. "Until that time," he concluded, "we have no interest in transferring arms, and cannot encourage others to do so."

The Iranian exploded, shouting: "Are you crazy? . . . My contacts are desperate people! . . . They must first get strong and take power! . . . Then we think about all this nice political science. . . . The hell with the hostages! Let the Hezbollah kill them!"

Mc Farlane stood. "I don't believe we have anything more to talk about," he said.

North followed his former boss out, but McFarlane now wondered which side his former assistant was on. He thought North may have briefed Ghorbanifar before the meeting. The hostage line sounded too perfect, as if it had been crafted for its impact on the President. On the flight back, North told McFarlane he thought he had made a mistake. What he did not tell McFarlane, as he had told Israeli Ministry of Defense contacts a month before, was that he intended to divert profits from the missile sales to the contras still fighting in Nicaragua.

On December 9, in the Oval Office, McFarlane advised the President to shut down the hostage operation. "Bud's right, Mr. President," said Weinberger. Vice President Bush, who rarely spoke at such meetings, did this time, agreeing with McFarlane: "It's what I've been saying all along."

"I'm sorry to hear this," Reagan said, as McFarlane told the story of the London trip. "I think this has real promise."

"It's risky," said CIA director Casey. "But most things worth doing are."

That night, Reagan wrote in his diary: "Bud is back. . . . His meeting with the Iranians did not achieve its purpose, which was to free our hostages first and then we'd supply the weapons. Their top man said he believed that if he took that proposal to the terrorists they would kill our people." The next night, December 10, after more meetings, Reagan wrote: "Go between turns out to be a devious character. Our plan regarding the hostages is a 'no go.' " That's what he wrote—and what he told Shultz and Weinberger—but McFarlane came away with the specific impression that the President wanted him and others to keep trying to find a way to make it happen.

Most of his December 10 diary entry was was about budget meetings and tax reform, specifically a spending-cap scheme devised by three senators: "Spent most of our time on the Gramm Rudman

Hollings bill which later in the day I found had made its way out of the conference. Not as good as we would have wanted but still a bill I'll have to sign. Some of the time we talked about tax reform."

The Democrats of Dan Rostenkowski's Ways and Means Committee were finishing up drafting their tax reform legislation—and it was theirs because House Republicans had been more or less excluded from the process. In fact, most of the Republicans had little enthusiasm for tax reform anyway, and most were angry at the White House and Treasury for dealing with the Democrats. Secretary of the Treasury Baker's strategy from the beginning was to let Rostenkowski and House Democrats craft their version of tax reform and then, in the Republican Senate, recast it as Reagan tax reform. So Baker and Darman and a Regan assistant, Dennis Thomas, were pretty much ignoring the Republicans as they made deals with Rosty and the Democrats.

The President, still postoperative and still exhausted after the summit, was not dealing with much of anything. He had objections to the House plan, beginning with the fact that the Democrats had written in a 38 percent top rate on personal income and 36 percent on corporate income. He wanted 35 percent and 33 percent. He also wanted a personal exemption of $2,000 for each taxpayer and dependent, an amount Republicans considered pro-family. But Reagan seemed unaware of the effect his words, or lack of them, were having. The marginalized House Republicans were on the edge of revolt. On December 3, only five of the thirteen Republicans on Ways and Means voted for the tax reform bill that had been hammered out after the weeks of consultations and deals, miscalculations and misunderstandings that marked the Baker-Rostenkowski negotiations. Then the Republican House Caucus, all 182 Republicans in the House, voted overwhelmingly against supporting the Democratic bill. Rostenkowski and other Democrats predicted tax reform would die on the House floor unless the President rounded up his angry Republicans. The White House responded with a couple of mild statements crafted by Don Regan: "The President is committed to keeping tax revision alive in Congress. . . . The President believes that the legislative process must be allowed to go forward."

Hearing that, even Baker concluded that the President did not much care what happened. The chairman of the Republican Conference, Representative Jack Kemp of New York, said: "The hard truth is that the Democratic bill is anti-family, anti-growth and anti-investment." Outside the committee rooms, lobbyists representing bankers, oil and gas companies, home builders, and most every other industry were pressuring their Republican friends to vote down reform. Finally, in his weekly radio address, Reagan displayed a little more energy: "I hope the House will vote yes next week and allow the Senate to consider, debate, and to improve this important measure."

That did not happen. On December 11, the House rule required to allow a final vote on the Rostenkowski reform was defeated by a vote of 223 to 202. Only fourteen Republicans voted for the rule; 164 Republicans, organized and led by the party's Whip, Representative Trent Lott of Mississippi, voted no. The President was stunned. So was Senator Bradley, the New Jersey Democrat who had started the move toward tax reform. He called his friend Kemp, another famous athlete turned politician, to ask what was happening on the Republican side. Kemp said: "We're just trying to get the President's attention."

They got it. The word was that tax reform was dead—Rostenkowski said Reagan was the killer—and that maybe the President was, too. The "Inside Politics" column of the *National Journal* headlined what everyone else with a typewriter was saying: "Reagan Being Viewed as Irrelevant Lame Duck."

Baker was dispatched to talk to Speaker O'Neill on how to get a second vote. "This is your bill, this was your idea," O'Neill told him. "Now you've got to produce the votes for it." Fifty Republican votes, he said—then he'd consider a new vote. And he gave them a deadline: 8 P.M. on December 16.

There was only one way to go and that might not work. The President himself went to the Capitol for a closed meeting with the Republicans at 2 P.M. on December 16. He came into an angry room. Lott and other leaders were still pressing for "no" votes, using Reagan's own words about vetoes against him. Kemp introduced the President: "All of us revere your leadership. The vote on the rule last week, in the view of some of us, prevented a choice presented by the Democrats— between a bad tax bill or no tax bill."

Reagan began by telling them he had just been at Andrews Air Force Base, attending services for 248 young men, soldiers of the 101st Airborne Division returning from international peacekeeping duties in the Middle East, who died together in a plane crash as they took off after a refueling stop in Gander, Newfoundland, on December 12. His voice choked as he asked for a moment of silent prayer.

Standing in the back, Lott felt the anger draining from the room.

He knew he would lose and the President would win. Several congressmen did rise to complain about the way they were being treated, particularly by Don Regan and Dick Darman. They attacked the personal exemptions and antibusiness provisions. Then Representative Henry Hyde of Illinois, one of the most articulate opponents of the bill, said: "Mr. President, if you say you'll fight for the $2,000 exemption, the rate reduction, effective dates, and a lower capital-gains rate, I don't need a letter. I'll vote for it."

It was almost over. For the rest of the day, Republican representatives called the White House, trading votes for new roads and help for old industries. One wanted Baker to campaign in his district. They got what they wanted. So did the President. The rule was passed the next day by a vote of 258 to 168—with 70 Republican "yes" votes. Then H.R. 3838, the Ways and Means tax reform bill, a Democratic bill forced by a Republican President, was passed by a voice vote.

On December 20, the Senate and the House, weary and frustrated, adjourned the unpredictable and essentially unproductive first session of the 99th Congress. "The worst I have seen," said Senator Robert Byrd of West Virginia, who had seen thirty-three of them. The adjournment was ten weeks later than originally scheduled, but then everything the Congress intended to do in 1985 was late, half-done, or undone. A good deal of that happened (or did not happen) because the President had spent most of the fall studying for the Geneva summit. Also, he had lost his budget director; whatever his faults, David Stockman knew which numbers were real and which were fabrications. He was, after all, the official fabricator. And it was obvious that Don Regan talked a good fight—and seemed to be photographed every day whispering in the President's good ear—but he was no Jim Baker.

The Gramm-Rudman-Hollings legislation that the President had written about on December 10—officially titled "Balanced Budget and Emergency Deficit Control Act of 1985"—was the written climax of another year of rising deficits and endless talk about annual revenue-spending gaps climbing above $200 billion. Instead of actually cutting costs or raising taxes, Congress passed and the President signed G-R-H, a piece of legislative wishful thinking intended to produce a balanced budget by 1991 through mandatory across-the-board budget cuts or selective cuts in programs like national defense. The law was named after the three sponsoring senators, Phil Gramm, the Democrat-turned-Republican from Texas; Warren Rudman, a

New Hampshire Republican; and Ernest Hollings, a South Carolina Democrat. It was left to the second session of the 99th, convening in January, to work on the specific details of how this was to be done.

"According to Democrats, the real purpose of Gramm-Rudman-Hollings is to force the President to choose between punishing cuts in his Pentagon budget or a long-resisted boost in tax revenues," editorialized the *Baltimore Sun*. "According to Republicans, the bill would give the President the leverage needed to crunch federal and domestic programs down to the size he always intended. What's especially striking is that these views pass each other in the dark, with no one knowing which or either will prevail. That's what happens, we suppose, when you have government by blindfold."

The editorial page of the *Philadelphia Inquirer* put it this way: "This bill is designed to fool the voters into thinking that Congress fixed the deficits, without forcing actual recorded votes or cutting specific programs. At its least harmful then, Gramm-Rudman is no more than an order by Congress to itself to end the deficits—later."

The passage of Gramm-Rudman-Hollings shared the front pages and news broadcasts with two other stories that had been building for months. The *Los Angeles Times* reported that on November 1, the President, greatly upset about a series of arrests of American military personnel as paid agents of foreign countries—the Soviet Union, China, and Israel—had for the second time secretly signed an order authorizing lie detector tests for government employees. At the same time, in Manila, the widow of the murdered opposition leader, Benigno Aquino, announced that she intended to run for president of the Philippines in the February election called by President Marcos.

The new polygraph order was much broader than the short-lived document Reagan had signed in March of 1982 to try to stop high-level leaks to the press. That one was canceled almost immediately when Vice President Bush and Jim Baker said they would resign rather than submit to tests. The new one covered ten thousand employees, including Cabinet members. When Secretary of State Shultz returned to the United States from NATO meetings in December he was asked by reporters whether he "would" submit to polygraph testing.

"Once," he answered.

"Once?" said Don Oberdorfer of *The Washington Post*.

"Once. The minute in this government I'm told that I'm not trusted is the day I leave."

The President announced that Cabinet members would be exempt from testing.

As for Mrs. Corazon Aquino, called "Cory," the President made it clear that his loyalties were to Marcos, a man he considered a friend— and a war hero. In August of 1982, during a state visit, the President had toasted the Marcoses: "In World War II Filipinos and Americans fought and died together. And you, yourself, Mr. President, played an unforgettably heroic part in that conflict."

Indeed, Marcos said he did, claiming to have led a guerrilla unit called Maharlika—"Noble Men" in Tagalog—in running battles against Japanese occupiers from 1942 to 1944. The President had been told by American officers that a 1948 U.S. Army investigation had concluded that the unit never existed, and that Marcos's claims were "fraudulent and absurd." Still, Reagan believed. When reporters questioned White House staffers about that, one, guaranteed anonymity, cracked: "The old man is confusing Marcos with Robert Taylor in the movie *Bataan.*" But Reagan did realize that Marcos had problems, and he had dispatched Senator Paul Laxalt of Nevada, his closest friend in Congress, in late October of 1985 to urge Marcos to focus on communist insurgents fighting government troops on far-away islands in the archipelago rather than on political opponents in Manila. Marcos told Laxalt that reports of unrest were greatly exaggerated, but he also told Laxalt that he intended to move up by a year national elections scheduled for 1987.

With the election set for February 7, 1986, candidate Aquino, fifty-three years old, a graduate of the College of Mount Saint Vincent in Riverdale, New York, who had never been in politics, sat for an interview with *The New York Times* in Manila on December 15. "The only thing I can really offer the Filipino people is my sincerity," she told reporter Seth Mydans and the *Times*'s editor, A. M. Rosenthal. "What on earth do I know about being President?"

Rosenthal was not impressed. In mid-January, at a dinner with the President and Mrs. Reagan, he said: "Mrs. Aquino is an empty-headed housewife with no positions. . . . She is a dazed, vacant woman." George Shultz and other State Department people told the President that seemed a bit exaggerated, but Shultz saw that Reagan believed it. The President was still loyal to Marcos and he was most worried that political unrest in the Philippines might benefit communist insurgents. In meetings, Reagan compared Marcos with the Shah of Iran, and he believed that the Shah had fallen because he had been abandoned by the United States. After one Oval Office meeting alone with Reagan, Secretary Shultz was stopped in the hallway by NSC director Poindexter, who was holding a newspaper with the headline "State Dept. Assails Marcos."

"The President doesn't want that," Poindexter said.

Shultz answered: "If we say we're for free elections, we're accused of assailing Marcos. Those charges can't be allowed to stop us."

The White House was not a happy place as 1985 came to an end. There seemed to be a loss of national momentum, a wilted Congress, the 248 deaths in Newfoundland, holiday killings in European airports, and new waves of terrorism and fear. Nineteen people, four of them Americans, had been killed in bloody terrorist attacks inside the Rome and Vienna international airports on December 27. The President and Mrs. Reagan met the families of the young men and women killed in Newfoundland at a service in Houston and then walked into the crowd, hugging parents and widows, their grief transmitted, repeated, and magnified on live television.

There was a new hierarchical meanness around the Oval Office as Don Regan and his men patrolled the halls with, it seemed, a bad word for everyone. "Regan introduced a new stamp to be banged on official papers, "NOTED BY DTR," in eighteen-point headline type, more than double the size of the ten-point type of the stamp marked "The President has seen," which had been used for more than twenty years. The only upbeat news as the year ended was day-by-day photo coverage of the space training of Christa McAuliffe, the New Hampshire schoolteacher who had been chosen to go into space on the *Challenger* mission scheduled for January 28.

The President's sixth State of the Union message, scheduled for the night of the twenty-eighth, was in preparation and memos from Regan's men ricocheted around the building: "This speech doesn't read like a Ronald Reagan speech" . . . "It's not punchy" . . . "It mushes down" . . . "There's something about this draft that doesn't hang together" . . . "Where's the challenge" . . . "Isn't there a way to beef up?" . . . "Is this really RR philosophy?"

Then the speechwriters learned that Regan's staff had written a draft of their own—"in crayon," thought Peggy Noonan when she saw it. Among the phrases in it were: "We cannot perpetuate these problems no longer" . . . "Rather than looking to the past, we must look to the future" . . . "Many of the programs that exist today were literally created in the 1930s to the 1960s, while others are oriented to the problems as they existed then."

Finally, a few days before the speech, the chief speechwriter, Bentley Elliot, shot back: "Those of you who authored the 'Regan comments'—i.e., substitute draft—you have done a great disservice to the President." One of the arguments was over whether the President would say "AIDS." Sometimes it was in the drafts, sometimes it was not. The Public Health Service had reported that AIDS deaths had gone from one in 1978, to 151 in 1981, and 1,145 in 1983. The projected figure by 1999 was 179,000. Surgeon General Dr. Koop had been ordered not to bring up the subject in speeches or television appearances. Then, suddenly, in January of 1986 Koop was told: "You're in the State of the Union." The President wanted to emphasize that federal spending on AIDS research, which had been $5.5 million in the fiscal year 1982, would reach almost $400 million by the end of 1986. At the last Domestic Policy Council meeting of 1985, Ed Meese had presided over a discussion of the disease's rapid spread and, according to the minutes, "A general discussion about AIDS followed with the President noting that several eminent medical scientists suggested that individual responsibility for one's behavior is a key factor in the struggle against AIDS. He asked whether federal agencies have AIDS screening programs." After that speechwriters told the surgeon general that the President was tired of being accused of ignoring the disease because most of the victims were homosexuals or drug users, ready targets of the Moral Majority and other religious fundamentalists. So, they said, Reagan was going to call on Koop for a national study, but they also warned him to stay away from anything that suggested sex education or the use of condoms.

On the day of the speech, January 28, as usual, the President invited in television anchormen and commentators to discuss what he would be saying and what they would be interpreting and analyzing later that night. They were being briefed on the text by Don Regan in the Roosevelt Room, then would lunch with the President. In the Oval Office, Reagan was talking with Larry Speakes about what he thought the anchors might be asking him at lunch. Suddenly, his door burst open, and Vice President Bush came in, followed closely by the new NSC director, John Poindexter, and Pat Buchanan. Bush began to speak, but he was interrupted by Buchanan saying: "Sir, the *Challenger* just blew up!"

"Oh, no!" the President said, dropping his face into his right hand.

The men rushed to the television set in the small private office off the Oval Office—and watched what all America was watching: Smoke and debris falling from ten miles up in the sky filled the screen. The audience included America's children, called together in the country's schools to watch six veteran astronauts and Christa McAuliffe rocket into space on an exceptionally cold Florida morning. Karna Small, the NSC's principal spokesperson, took notes as Reagan watched and then answered questions from the reporters who were there for the State of the Union briefing.

"What can you say? It's a horrible thing. I can't rid myself of the thought of the sacrifice of the families of the people on board. I'm sure all America is more than saddened."

Somebody asked whether it had been wise to have a citizen, the teacher, McAuliffe, on board. "They're all citizens," Small wrote as Reagan talked. "That is the last frontier, the most important, the space program has been most successful. We've become so confident that this comes as such a shock."

What can we tell the children?

"Pioneers have always given their lives on the frontier. The problem is that it's more of a shock to all as we see it happening, not just hear something miles away—but we must make it clear that life goes on. . . . I can't put out of my mind her husband and children—the others knew they were in a hazardous occupation. . . . But here, your heart goes out to them."

Small's notes went to Peggy Noonan. The speechwriter was already working on what the President would say, though he did not want to speak until a search confirmed the obvious, that the *Challenger* seven were all dead.

"Ladies and gentlemen, I had planned to speak to you tonight on the State of the Union, but the events of earlier today have led me to change those plans," he began on national television at 5 P.M. He looked stricken. Noonan thought he looked lost as he read her words and his in an address that lasted less than five minutes. It ended:

We're still pioneers. . . . The *Challenger* crew were pulling us into the future, and we'll continue to follow them. . . . We'll continue our quest in space. There will be more shuttle flights, and more shuttle crews and, yes, more volunteers, more civilians, more teachers in space. Nothing ends here. . . . We will never forget them, nor the last time we saw them, this morning as they prepared for their journey and waved goodbye and "slipped the surly bonds of earth" to "touch the face of God."

He was afraid he had done badly. He was wrong. The calls, the mail, the telegrams to the White House broke all records. The last lines, particularly, touched people profoundly. They had been written in 1940 in a poem "High Flight" by an American pilot named John Magee, who flew for the Royal Canadian Air Force. He was nineteen when he was killed, and had written the verse on the back of an envelope he had sent to his parents. Reagan knew the poem; it had been carried through World War II by another pilot, this one in the United States Air Force—another actor, his friend Tyrone Power.

The President finally gave his State of the Union message on February 4. There was no Koop, no mention of AIDS. Not long after that, Regan ordered Buchanan to tell Elliot he was finished. None of the writers knew exactly why or whether Reagan knew what was happening. Probably not, they agreed. When he was ushered into the Oval Office for a formal goodbye handshake photo, Elliot said, "Mr. President, I hope you know I was fired."

Reagan stepped back and said, "Oh." Then he smiled for the camera. But he obviously did know about the AIDS debate inside the White House. On the day after the delayed State of the Union, he went over to the Health and Human Services building for a little pep talk and a few jokes to welcome a new HHS Secretary, Dr. Otis Bowen. He surprised most everyone there by saying: "One of our highest public health priorities is going to be continuing to find a cure for AIDS. . . . I'm asking the Surgeon General to prepare a major report to the American people on AIDS."

That was just two days before the election in the Philippines. Mrs. Aquino told a rally of more than one million people: "As the old dictator lurks in his palace with his dwindling band of cronies and his false medals for comfort, I warn him: Do not cheat the people on Friday."

The voting began on February 7, one day after the United States Air Force dispatched a plane to Port-au-Prince, Haiti, to pick up that poor country's President, Jean-Claude Duvalier, and fly him and his family to exile in France, in the hope that the end of twenty-eight years of Duvalier dictatorship, established by his father, would end two bloody months of anti-government demonstrations. The results in the Philippines, which, like Haiti, was once occupied by United States Marines, were less definitive, with both President Marcos and Cory Aquino claiming victory. International observers, from nineteen countries, reported that there was widespread fraud and violence—by the government and the army. Marcos had immediately claimed victory and the vote-counting quickly slowed and then stopped as election workers complained that ballots were being destroyed and computer results fabricated. One Marcos critic, the former governor of Antique, Evelio Javier, was chased down and killed by six masked gunmen in the town square of San Jose de Buenavista. Witnesses said the killers escaped in a government jeep. The leaders of the official American team of twenty observers, Senator Richard Lugar of Indiana and Representative John Murtha of Pennsylvania, reported government fraud to Reagan when they returned to Washington on February 11. Lugar estimated that Aquino had actually won more than 70 percent of the vote, but the President created a furor in both countries that night, declaring in a news conference that the United States was neutral. Questioned on fraud and violence, he added: "It could be that all of that was occurring on both sides." Reporters did not like his deceptive answers that night and the President did not like the tone of the questions. Walking away from the microphone, he could be heard clearly saying, "sons of bitches."

By the end of that day, the American ambassador in Manila, Stephen Bosworth, had called on Mrs. Aquino to emphasize that the Americans would not automatically side with Marcos. Then he cabled the State Department: "The bottom line is inescapable: Mrs. Aquino would have won if there was even a minimally fair count. The opposition therefore will not accept the National Assembly proclamation of a Marcos victory. . . . The election has effectively cost Ferdinand Marcos his remaining political legitimacy and credibility."

Still not ready to accept that, Reagan called Ambassador Philip Habib out of retirement one more time to travel to the Philippines for another official assessment. Then two important senators, Republican Robert Dole and Democrat Sam Nunn of Georgia, called on the President to cut off aid to the Philippines if there was indeed fraud by the Marcos forces. Shultz called Reagan to emphasize that there was no evidence of fraud on the opposition side. He sensed that the President did not or would not believe him. When an assistant secretary of state, Michael Armacost, began angrily shouting about Reagan, Shultz cut him off, saying: "The President is the President. He has strong views; that is how he got to be President."

On February 15, the National Assembly in Manila declared that Marcos had won with 53.8 percent of the vote, including one precinct vote recorded as thirteen thousand for Marcos to zero for Aquino. Few believed that, but the most important rejection came from the Roman Catholic bishops of the country, who unanimously denounced the election as the most fraudulent in Philippine history. The White House moved by inches, issuing a statement that began: "It has already become evident, sadly, that the elections were marred by widespread fraud and violence largely perpetuated by the ruling party."

In the Philippines, the regime was mobilizing the army, while the opposition was mobilizing crowds in the streets. In the early morning hours of Sunday, February 23, in Manila, Marcos's troops moved, but they were blocked by the crowds and refused to use their weapons. Ambassador Bosworth cabled Shultz, telling him that Marcos had told him he would leave office only if he were asked to personally by President Reagan. The President was at Camp David and he returned to the White House that afternoon to meet Shultz and Habib. "The Marcos era has ended," Habib told the President. At 6:45 P.M., Reagan issued a public statement warning the Marcos government that the United States would consider ending aid to the country if troops fired on civilians—the same threat made by Congress ten days before—and approved a private message to be delivered to Marcos through diplomatic channels: The time had come to begin the transition of power.

In his diary that night, Reagan wrote: "All we can do is send the message . . . and pray."

The next day, as Marcos and Aquino held separate presidential "inauguration" ceremonies in Manila, there was a public declaration from the White House: "Attempts to prolong the life of the present regime are futile."

That night's diary entry read: "The situation in the Philippines is deteriorating. . . . I was approving statements for delivery to the President, pleading for no violence. Then a call from Nancy—what to say to Imelda Marcos who was calling her? . . . I was told Paul Laxalt, George Shultz, John Poindexter and Don R. were coming in about

Paul's call to Marcos. We've agreed that he should be told I'm recommending he step down and we'll take the lead in negotiating his safety and offering him sanctuary in the U.S. . . . Wound up the day in the dentist's chair. Time for inspection. I passed." *

The next day, February 26, Marcos fled to Clark Air Force Base, a U.S. Air Force base eighty miles from Manila. He asked the Americans for passage to his home in northern Luzon. In the diary, Reagan wrote: "We are ordering our ambassador and others to contact Aquino to see if we could persuade her to accept his staying in the islands. . . . We learned she wasn't going to do that. He incidentally is quite ill and is bedridden at Clark. By evening, we learned his party had left by medivac plane for Guam." He was carried to a U.S. C-141 Starlifter on a stretcher.

So, the Marcoses were on American territory, on their way to Hawaii, with an entourage of eighty-nine aides and servants and twenty-two crates of documents, currency, gold bars, and jewelry, the portable assets of a fortune worth hundreds of millions of dollars, millions somehow acquired on Marcos's salary of $5,700 a year. Investigators around the world were combing bank and real estate records; they found that the couple had at least $800 million in Swiss bank accounts and owned Manhattan real estate worth more than $250 million. Hundreds of thousands of Filipinos surged into the streets and lanes of the country's cities and villages, cheering and throwing firecrackers in celebration. Television crews allowed into the Malacanang Palace filmed the living quarters to show what was left behind, including six thousand pairs of Mrs. Marcos's shoes.

It was a snowy day in Washington and when Shultz arrived at the White House that morning, he saw the President throwing snowballs at photographers, who were ducking, laughing, and shooting. Stomping his feet, Reagan came in through the French doors, flushed and happy, until Shultz said the time had come to recognize an Aquino government. Don Regan appeared, saying, "Wait a minute! How can we say she is president? She hasn't won an election or been ratified by the National Assembly." The President agreed. But by 10 A.M.—emphasizing that the whole world was watching—the Secretary of State won the day, walking over to the press room to announce: "The

---

* Mrs. Reagan told Mrs. Marcos that the most important American objective was to avoid violence and bloodshed, and that the United States would provide safe haven for her family.

President is pleased with the peaceful transition to a new government in the Philippines. . . . The United States extends recognition to this new Government headed by President Aquino."

Most everywhere in the Philippines citizens were celebrating, hundreds of thousands, perhaps millions of them, waving yellow banners of "People Power." It was not much different in the United States; Americans had followed the four-day revolution on network television. *Time* magazine led its cover story on the Aquino ascension by saying: "Try not to forget what you saw last week. . . . The rich were in the streets with the poor, a whole country up in flowers. . . . Not since 18th-century France have Americans approved so heartily of a rebellion."

Knowing little of Reagan's hesitation and ambivalence about siding with Aquino against Marcos until the final hours of the four-day bloodless revolution in the Philippines, the press in America and around the world almost unanimously praised a new Reagan, a statesman, a man who appeared to learn and grow under pressure—rather than one who only reacted to events he could not control. Newspaper editorials told that story:

"The President's earlier equivocations—his obvious reluctance to break with an ally who has preserved U.S. military bases in the Philippines—serve to make his new stand even more dramatic. . . . For a politician who once criticized Carter for turning his back on the Shah, Reagan has come a long way," wrote the *Baltimore Sun*. The *Detroit News* said: "The Reagan administration appears to have handled the tactical situation brilliantly. . . . Twice in a month—first in the case of 'Baby Doc' Duvalier of Haiti—the Administration has acted as a facilitator of change when the leader of a friendly country overstayed his welcome." *Newsday* on Long Island added: "It has been a good month for democracy: two vicious and corrupt dictators—Marcos and Duvalier—have both been removed. . . . The Reagan administration deserves credit. . . . Is it possible that the U.S. government has finally learned how to shed its ties with repressive governments?"

Perhaps more surprisingly, *Quotidien* in France said: "Reagan acted intelligently and showed that he was able to adapt himself to the situation and get the best out of it for his country." In Italy, *La Stampa* said: "It seems incredible that it took President Reagan, after so many progressive presidents, to revolutionize American strategies, to discover that America's ideas can be more effective than its weapons." In West Germany, *Volksblatt* speculated that the American example might heighten the moral pressure on the Soviet Union to find a peaceful solution in Afghanistan.

The thoughts, or fantasies, of editorial writers that Reagan had fundamentally changed had a shorter shelf life than their editorials. On the morning after that triumphant day in Manila, the President went to Congress one more time looking for a renewal of military aid to the contras in Nicaragua—$100 million this time, with $70 million of that earmarked for military use. Five days later, the President met with his "freedom fighters," four contra leaders. He came out of the private meeting with some new tough talk: "I've asked for $100 million and we'll fight for it . . . you can't stop tanks and gunships with bandages and bedrolls. Defeat for the contras would mean another Cuba on the mainland of North America. . . . It would mean consolidation of a privileged sanctuary for terrorists and subversives just two days driving time from Harlingen, Texas."

The next day Reagan added: "If the Sandinistas are allowed to consolidate their hold on Nicaragua, we'll have a home away from home for Muammar Qaddafi, Arafat and the Ayatollah. . . . If we don't want the map of Central America covered in a sea of red, eventually lapping at our own borders, we must act now." Then he said that if Congress turned down the request, we should expect vast waves of refugees moving north toward the borders of the United States. His aides briefed reporters, saying that if the money was supplied, nineteen thousand new contras would join the six thousand scattered along the Nicaragua-Honduras border. One aide, not interested in anonymity, communications director Pat Buchanan, wrote an op-ed piece in *The Washington Post* saying: "With the vote on contra aid, the Democratic party will reveal whether it stands with Ronald Reagan and the resistance, or Daniel Ortega and the communists."

On March 20, three days after another Reagan prime-time television speech calling on viewers to pressure their representatives on aid to the contras, the House rejected the $100 million by a vote of 222 to 210. Members of Congress simply reflected the fact that their constituents, most Americans, did not see Nicaragua as a threat to freedom or their own lives. News organization polls taken after Reagan's speech indicated that only one-third of respondents favored more aid to the contras.

The strength of the Congress was also the weakness of the Congress. While a President might be able to alert and persuade the American people—lead!—change hearts and minds—Congress was both privileged and condemned to track public opinion more closely. And the White House had many more chances to deceive people or the Congress in pursuit of its goals in the national interest, perceived or distorted. Neither the public nor any legislators knew that the President, on January 17, had signed a secret intelligence finding authorizing the sale of weapons to Iran that ended: "Because of the extreme sensitivity of this project, it is recommended that you exercise your statutory prerogative to withhold notification of the Finding to the Congressional oversight committees." At the bottom of the finding, which was written by Oliver North, Admiral Poindexter wrote: "Orally briefed to President, present were Vice President, Don Regan. . . ."

Plans to transport the weapons were being worked out on the third floor of the Old Executive Office Building by Lieutenant Colonel North, with the consent of his boss, Admiral Poindexter, who kept the only copy of the President's finding in his office safe. The two of them were also diligently working to find secret (and illegal) funding for the contra war in Nicaragua. "Release of American Hostages in Beirut" was the title of the five-page "Top Secret" memo North was preparing for the approval of Poindexter and the President. The memo recounted the nine-month secret history of the Iran-hostage negotiations, including meetings with Ghorbanifar in Washington on April 3, which were supposed to climax on April 20 in Tehran. The schedule laid out in the memo had Bud McFarlane meeting there with Ali Akbar Hashemi Rafsanjani, leader of Iran's parliament, and consummating a deal in which the Iranians would receive $3.65 million worth of Hawk missile parts from Israel. They would pay $17 million into a Swiss account controlled by the government of Israel, and $15 million of that would be transferred to private American accounts set up by North. Then $3.65 million of the $15 million would go through CIA accounts to the Pentagon to send replacement missiles and parts to the Israelis. And the Iranians would show their gratitude by effecting the release of five American hostages in Beirut.

The numbers never exactly added up, but there would certainly be profit for someone. Near the end of the memo, North wrote this paragraph:

Residual funds from this transaction are allocated as follows:
$2 million will be used to purchase replacement TOWs for the

original 50 percent sold by Israel to Iran for the release of Benjamin Weir. . . .

$12 million will be used to purchase critically needed supplies for the Nicaraguan Democratic Resistance Forces.

The idea was that one American adversary, Iran, would finance an insurgency against another American adversary, Nicaragua. "Neat," said North. It was also a violation of several laws. The memo ended:

RECOMMENDATION

That the President approve the structure depicted above.

Despite his most bellicose public words on Nicaragua in a long time, Reagan was actually focusing on Libya for the better part of each day—and had been doing that since the December 27 shootings of Americans and others at the Rome and Vienna airports. Intelligence agencies in the United States and its allies had "irrefutable evidence"—Reagan's words—that Libya's Colonel Qaddafi was behind those terrorist attacks. (United States intelligence agencies informed the President that the attacks had been planned by a Palestinian, Abu Nidal, who lived in Libya and operated terrorist training camps there.) In response, on January 7, the President had ended all economic ties to Libya and ordered all Americans in the country—an estimated one thousand to fifteen hundred—to leave, warning that if they stayed they would face legal penalties when they did return. That could have been a warning of military retaliation, but the White House denied such actions were being considered.

That was not true. The President ordered the Sixth Fleet to once again conduct maneuvers in the Gulf of Sidra, inside Qaddafi's Line of Death along the coast of Libya. He wanted a repeat of the maneuvers that had led to air combat and the shooting down of two Libyan jets in 1981. And he wanted assurances about a possible Soviet military response—"Could this lead us into trouble?" he asked the chairman of the Joint Chiefs of Staff, Admiral William Crowe—but his military men were confident that action in the Mediterranean would not trigger a Soviet response. "All right," the President said. "Let's do it."

As he had just before the Grenada invasion, the President called congressional leaders of both parties to a secret White House meeting.

After briefings on evidence of Libyan sponsorship of the Berlin explosion and military plans for hitting Libya, he said, perhaps disingenuously: "I am not presenting you with a fait accompli. We will decide in this meeting whether to proceed. . . . I would like to ask if any of you believe we should cancel the operation, which I can do by placing a call from this telephone. Please raise your hands if you think we should cancel." No hands were raised. "Thank you all," he said.

But then the operation was postponed; the Navy wanted to wait until a third aircraft carrier group could be moved into position with the two already available over the horizon north of Libya. The delay gave the United States time to try to line up allies if a decision were made to strike targets inside Libya. The answer everywhere was no, an answer not unrelated to the amount of Libyan oil imported by European countries. Even Margaret Thatcher urged the President and his men not to hit Libya, a strike she considered only revenge, a violation of international law that might lead to the kind of troubles that Reagan wanted to avoid. Bold rhetoric aside, Reagan proved to be a far more cautious man than he had been three years earlier in Lebanon. Believing that some of the several thousand Soviet troops and technicians in Libya were manning the coastal surface-to-air emplacements, the United States embassy in Moscow provided the Kremlin with day-to-day details of the maneuvers and of the danger that they could escalate into combat once again—and that the United States was anxious to avoid Soviet casualties.

An armada was ready in mid-March—showing the flag of a cautious leader. America's overwhelming force included more than fifteen thousand men. Dozens of Navy A-7 attack fighters were flying overhead as three of the forty-five American warships assigned to "Operation Prairie Fire" crossed the Line of Death on the afternoon of March 24. Libyan shore batteries responded quickly, firing at least six SA-5 surface-to-air missiles at the jets, but missed by miles. The Libyans continued to fire into the evening without hitting anything. Reagan was informed of all that during his regular 9 A.M. security briefing by Poindexter. A few hours later, a U.S. A-6 Intruder from the carrier *America* sank a Libyan patrol boat approaching the U.S. fleet. The order of engagement specified that no Libyan vessel would be allowed to come within forty miles of the carriers. An hour after that, a little after 10 P.M., two A-7s from the carrier *Saratoga* disabled the radars controlling the Libyan missiles. Two more flew another raid three hours later, hitting the radars again and firing at launch pads. A

Soviet communications ship in the harbor near the sites was lit up like a Christmas tree, apparently to alert American pilots to stay away. Another Libyan patrol boat was destroyed the next morning, before the American exercise was ended during the afternoon of March 27. There were no American casualties during the operation. In Tripoli, Libyan officials reported fifty-six deaths.

With the President having left for ten days at the ranch, the White House press room became a war room. Larry Speakes issued twice-daily briefings on the action off Libya, interspersing them with reports of a raid on contra bases inside Honduras by Nicaraguan troops. There was a political edge to his statements. One, on March 25, began: "Within 48 hours of the House rejection of aid to the Nicaraguan resistance, Sandinista military units crossed into Honduras in a large-scale effort to attack United Nicaraguan Opposition and Nicaraguan Democratic Forces camps, training centers and hospitals. . . . The numbers are up to 1,500 Nicaraguan military troops. . . . The President of Honduras has requested that the United States provide urgent military assistance." The President of the United States was sounding urgent as well. After a *New York Times*/CBS News poll indicated that respondents opposed more military aid to the contras by 62 to 28 percent, Reagan said: "The Sandinista government is not a duly elected chosen government. It's a gang that took over by force."

Reagan stopped in New Orleans on his way to California to speak at a Republican fund-raiser, and reporters caught up with him for a minute at the airport there. "Mr. President," one called, "are you hyping up these stories about troops in Honduras?"

"What?" Reagan said.

"Are you hyping up those stories—"

"The White House is giving you the truth, as I think all of us know."

Not even close. Honduras initially denied there had been any attack, because admitting an attack was admitting there were American-financed contra bases inside Honduras, something the Hondurans had always denied. A spokesman for the country's President, José Azcona Hoyo, said: "We believe this is part of the publicity campaign of the Reagan administration to get $100 million for the counterrevolutionaries."

There were screaming calls from the State Department to Tegucigalpa. William Walker, a deputy to the assistant secretary of state, Elliott Abrams, telephoned the U.S. embassy, saying: "You've got to get the Hondurans to declare there was an incursion." The American ambassador, John Ferch, sick with the flu, pulled on three sweaters and a bathrobe and went to Azcona's home. The Honduran President stopped arguing when he was told that Reagan was immediately signing off on emergency military assistance to Honduras to hold off the Sandinistas: "Presidential Determination No. 86-8. . . . I hereby authorize the furnishing of up to $20,000,000 in defense articles from the stocks of the Department of Defense for military education and training to Honduras . . . under the Foreign Assistance Act of 1961."

Azcona told his office to do whatever the Americans wanted, then headed for the beach and a Holy Week vacation. In fact, no Honduran soldier was within five miles of a Nicaraguan; what fighting there was involved the contras and their American advisers.

Whatever was actually happening along the Honduran border—apparently nothing more than a routine anti-contra raid by several hundred Sandinista soldiers—the Senate voted 53 to 47 that night to approve the President's request for $100 million more in contra aid. Senator Patrick Leahy of Vermont, a Democrat, joked that perhaps President Ortega of Nicaragua was a secret White House lobbyist who did something stupid every time Congress was ready to cut off the contras—this time it was sending troops into Honduras, other times it was taking trips to Moscow or Havana to star at anti-American rallies. The Senate approved the same package, containing $70 million in military aid that had been rejected by the House on March 10. The President's job now was to talk the Democrat-controlled House into voting one more time. What no one in Congress knew was that deliveries of weapons and ammunition to the contras—financed by the Iranian purchases of American missiles—were delivered to the Tegucigalpa airport that week.

The President was at his ranch on April 5 when he took a call from Admiral Poindexter saying that a bomb had exploded at 1:50 A.M. local time at a discotheque in West Berlin, a place called La Belle Club, popular with American soldiers stationed in the city. One American, an Army sergeant, was dead and sixty other men and women were injured. Electronic surveillance of the Libyan embassy during Operation Prairie Fire had picked up multiple messages from Tripoli urging quick retaliation against "American targets." Then, on April 4, an intercepted message from East Berlin read: "Tripoli will be happy when you see the headlines tomorrow."

That headline, in *The New York Times,* was:

2 KILLED, 155 HURT
IN BOMB EXPLOSION
AT CLUB IN BERLIN

Libyan Role Is Suspected

Reagan was back in the White House on April 7, listening more than speaking, at daily National Security Council meetings beginning that day to plan retaliation from the sky against Libya, plotting targets on maps and reconnaisance photos to weave a noose to drop on Qaddafi himself. The President was fascinated by CIA presentations on the personality of the Arab leader, who had seized power in 1969 and run a flamboyant dictatorship since then. Told that Qaddafi used makeup and was said to wear women's clothes and high heels, the President said: "Maybe we could stop the terror by letting him into Nancy's closet."

On April 9, he held a prime-time news conference, beginning by pitching, as always, for budget-cutting and then for military aid for the contras. But the questions concentrated on terrorism. Reagan got the reporters' attention by calling Qaddafi "the mad dog of the Middle East." Chris Wallace of NBC News asked him about that language. Reagan grinned and said: "You know I never used that term before, 'Mad dog,' but I saw one of you using it on television and I thought it sounded good."

The next day, newspapers and television reported that the American carrier groups in the Mediterranean were once again steaming toward Libya, reports that enraged the President, who considered the descriptions of ship movements tantamount to treason.

The Americans struck at 2 A.M. local time on April 15, hitting at least five targets. Eighteen F-111 bombers flew a circuitous, seven-hour, three-thousand-mile route from bases in England—refueling four times in the air after being denied the use of French and Italian airspace—and attacked three targets in Tripoli. At the same time, Navy jets from the carriers *America* and *Coral Sea* attacked two targets hundreds of miles to the east, near the city of Benghazi. The targets were all classified as miltary, but one load of bombs tore up a rich neighborhood in Tripoli, killing civilians and damaging the French embassy. Five of the F-111s returned to their bases because of mechanical trouble and one was shot down or crashed, killing two crewmen. The Tripoli-area targets included the Libyan Army's El Azizia barracks, where Colonel Qaddafi often stayed overnight. That night he was there, sleeping in the elaborate desert tent he favored. There were early reports that he had been killed, but those turned out to be untrue, although two of his sons, three and four years old, were seriously wounded, and a fifteen-month-old infant, said to be his adopted daughter, Hana, was killed.

Two hours after the raids, at 9 P.M. Washington time, the President went on national television with the military details and then said: "We have done what we had to do. If necessary, we shall do it again. Before Qaddafi seized power in 1969, the people of Libya had been friends of the United States. And I'm sure that today most Libyans are disgusted that this man has made their country a synonym for barbarians around the world. . . . He counted on America to be passive. He counted wrong."

Most of the world condemned the American attack, at least publicly. In France, which had just expelled two Libyan diplomats plotting to bomb the American embassy, the conservative daily *Figaro* reasoned: "For Europe, Qaddafi is not worth a rupture with the Islamic world." Among governments only Great Britain, which had privately advised against the action; Canada; and Israel issued statements of support. But the story at home was completely different. Polls by all the major news operations showed American approval of the raid at 70 percent and more. The President's approval rate in a Gallup poll jumped to 68 percent, matching the high figure recorded after he was shot in 1981.

"He asked for it. And he got it," said the *Dallas Morning News* of Qaddafi. *The New York Times* effected a more judicious tone: "Even the most scrupulous citizen can only approve and applaud the American attacks on Libya. . . . If there were such a thing as due process in the court of world opinion, the United States has prosecuted and punished him carefully, proportionately and justly." There was, though, a word of caution from the *Milwaukee Sentinel*: "The U.S. cannot fight a world war against terrorism by itself."

A week later, on April 21, the Library of Congress held a big-name symposium on the presidency, and one of the biggest names there, a man routinely attacked by Ronald Reagan over the years, former Secretary of State Henry Kissinger, said: "You ask yourself 'How did it ever occur to anybody that Reagan should be governor, much less

President?' On the other hand, you have to say also that a man who dominated California for eight years, and now dominates the American political process for five and a half years, as he has, cannot be a trivial figure. It is perfectly possible history will judge Reagan as a most significant President."

CHAPTER 15

JUNE 17, 1986

P RESIDENT REAGAN'S THIRTY-SIXTH NEWS CONFERENCE was held in Tokyo on May 7, 1986, after a World Economic Summit in the Japanese capital. A reporter asked: "Mr. President, while you've been here, you've been losing ground in the Senate. . . . The Senate tax committee has approved a plan that . . . does quite a few things that you said you're not for?"

"Well," said Reagan, "let them just wait 'til the old man gets home," as the reporters began laughing, "and see what happens to 'em."

Actually the old man had to take care of some tax reform business before he left for home. In Washington that same day, Senator Robert Packwood of Oregon, the Republican chairman of the Senate Finance Committee, was ready to call the committee vote on the Senate version of the tax reform bill passed the year before in the House after the President ended the little revolt of Republicans there. The chairman had sentenced the twenty members of his committee to six months of very hard labor before he felt confident that he had enough votes to bring the bill to the floor. Now, to be sure, he wanted a statement from the President indicating that there were no more veto threats. Richard Darman, who had stayed in Washington to work the bill while Baker was in Tokyo, had been back and forth by telephone until he got that statement, a bureaucratic-sounding paragraph with Reagan's name on it. The official version concluded: "We congratulate you and the distinguished members of the Senate Finance Committee, for your bold tax-reform proposal."

"The President knows how to steal a headline 10,000 miles away," said Senator Bradley, the Democratic committee member who could take a huge amount of credit after his five years of reform efforts. In Tokyo, as the committee prepared to go on record—Packwood thought he might have as many as sixteen votes—Reagan was more quotable and more positive.

"Well, there are a few things in there I've got some questions about, but I haven't had time to really study in depth," he said. "I think that, very likely, I can find myself supporting the Senate committee's version. I hope it comes to the floor."

The committee vote, which surprised Packwood, was unanimous, 20 to 0. "A miracle," he said. The full Senate passed its tax reform bill, a version of simplified tax law that was 1,489 pages long, by a vote of 97 to 3. "This is a great day for America," began the President's official reaction. "The score is taxpayers, 1; special interests, nothing. . . . The Senate gathered an overwhelming consensus for tax reform with lower, flatter rates. Fifteen and 27 percent rates for individuals and a 33 percent top rate for corporations were the magic numbers that swept aside the opposition of the special interests. . . . Now the Senate and House committees under the leadership of the chairmen, Bob Packwood and Dan Rostenkowski, will meet to hammer out their differences."

There were real differences between the House and Senate versions, beginning with the number of individual income brackets—four in the House bill and two in the Senate bill—but no one doubted now what most everyone had doubted only a few weeks before: There was going to be a significantly, even radically different United States Tax Code. Even the business lobbyists who had been courting or threatening their Republican Senate friends to kill reform were now voicing support for the Senate version, because it raised corporate taxes by $100 billion while the House version raised them $140 billion. And none of this, the most important tax changes since withholding was introduced during World War II, would have happened if Ronald Reagan had not been President. Reagan did not understand many of the details of the code, past, present, or proposed. He was presiding now over a transfer of tax burdens from individuals to corporations when only three years before he had told a business group that he could see "no justification" whatever for taxing corporations at all. Of course, he also repeatedly said there was no justification for deficit spending as the national debt was doubling under the eyes of his Roosevelt Room portrait of Calvin Coolidge, his budget-balancing hero.

There was more. While the Senate debated tax reform, the President had been campaigning to revive aid to the contras of Nicaragua. As he was flying from Jakarta, Indonesia, to Tokyo on May 2, Reagan had called his latest NSC director, Admiral Poindexter, into his cabin on Air Force One to talk about messages to the White House from CIA director Casey like this one on April 23: "Either we get funding for the contras to implement the policy or scrap our present policy and move ahead with final alternatives . . . embargo, blockade or direct military action." Then Reagan told Poindexter: "Look, I don't want to pull out our support for the contras for any reason. . . . If we can't move the contra package by June 9, I want to figure out a way to take action unilaterally to provide assistance."

Back in Washington, Reagan publicly requested that he be allowed to address the House of Representatives to plead his case. No President had ever addressed one house of Congress, and Speaker O'Neill refused the request as Reagan knew he would, then he used the refusal as the reason to schedule an address to the nation. Declaring that Nicaragua was becoming a Soviet beachhead and invoking words of Harry Truman and Abraham Lincoln, he said: "The Nicaraguan people have chosen to fight for their freedom. Now we Americans must also choose. Do we want to be the first elected U.S. officials to put our borders at risk? . . . Give them, give me, your support." He was also working the phones again, concentrating on twenty House members, most of them Democrats. All of them had voted against his $100 million contra aid package; their "no" votes were the difference when the package was defeated in March by a vote of 222 to 210.

"Mission Accomplished" . . . "Mission Accomplished" . . . "Mission Accomplished" the President wrote at the bottom of each call slip. On June 25, the day after the Senate voted on tax reform, the House voted again on the $100 million contra package. This time the President won. The new vote was 221 ayes and 209 nays.

As Kissinger had a couple of months before, skeptical journalists, the ones who had been calling the President a lame duck and irrelevant in December, were trying to figure out how this congenial and seemingly disengaged "old man" could again and again bend so many of his fellows to his will.

"THE REAGAN LEGACY," a cover article in The New York Times Magazine of June 22, 1986, by one of the paper's White House correspondents, Bernard Weinraub, was part of the newest conventional wisdom: "It is clear that his impact, like Franklin D. Roosevelt's, rests in large part on restoring the primacy of the Presidency as an institution, after nearly two decades of White House disarray marked by Vietnam, Watergate and the hostages in Iran." The first affirming quote after that statement was from one of Reagan's most powerful critics, Senator Edward Kennedy, who said: "He has contributed a spirit of good will and grace to the Presidency and American life generally and turned the Presidency into a vigorous and forceful instrument of national policy." The next one was from the most articulate of contemporary Democrats, Governor Mario Cuomo of New York, who said: "By his personal conduct when he's shot, when he's told he has cancer, when he goes to Normandy— the way he's comported himself has been a moral instruction to my children."

The Reagan impact had rearranged American politics, said both critics and supporters. He not only strengthened conservatism, he institutionalized many of the ideas that had been promoted, often without visible effect, by political thinkers of the right, including Russell Kirk, James Burnham, and William F. Buckley. He had opened the political process to the Christian fundamentalists and evangelicals of the so-called Religious Right. Hugh Heclo, a professor of government at Harvard, said: "The economic, as opposed to the social face of Reagan's individualism, can easily be portrayed as playing to the most rationalized forms of selfishness. . . . The economic losers are not victims, just incompetents." He added: "Reagan made it clear you don't have to be hyperactive to be President, to have an answer to every question. He seems to make the job manageable." Charles O. Jones, the former president of the American Political Science Association, called Roosevelt and Reagan "the bookend presidents," saying: "One pushed in the direction of more government, and trying to make the system work. This one is trying to make it work in the sense of less government. They're both radical, but in totally different directions." *

---

* Three months later, Michael Barone of *The Washington Post* referred to the Reagan-Roosevelt connection in a column on September 17, 1986: "His intellectual processes had always been intuitive rather than logical. He often thought lazily and superficially. But he felt profoundly. Some observers . . . condemned his oversimplifications and felt that portentous decisions were precariously reared on idiotic anecdotes. But the individual case was really more often the symbol rather than the source of his conclusion; it was the short-cut way to put over a vast amount of feeling, imagination and sympathy which the President himself could neither articulate nor understand, but which had a plunging accuracy of their own." Barone then revealed that those words were written about Franklin D. Roosevelt, by one of his more fervent admirers, historian Arthur Schlesinger.

In his article, Weinraub concluded that wherever Reagan ranked historically, he was sure to have one potent legacy in the works and words of his judges. He might end up appointing half of the 761-member federal judiciary—all with lifetime tenure. So far, according to a study in the *Journal of the American Bar Association* in 1985, the Reagan judges were a new breed: younger, richer, and more political than the nominees of previous modern Presidents. Better than one in ten Reagan judges were under forty (a couple of them just thirty-one years old) compared with one in fifty under President Carter; one in four were millionaires compared with one in ten under Carter; 97 percent of trial judges and every appellate judge had been active Republicans.

During the week the magazine appeared, Chief Justice Warren Burger, who was seventy-eight, announced his retirement after seventeen years on the Supreme Court. He had come over to the Oval Office in late May to tell the President that he intended to work full-time in his capacity as the chairman of planning for national celebrations of the bicentennial of the writing of the Constitution. Reagan's eyes had glazed a bit as Burger droned on about the importance of the celebration, but he had come alive when he realized that Burger was quitting.

It was a golden moment for American conservatives. Attorney General Meese, finally confirmed in February of 1985 after ten months of debate, was in charge of the search for a new Chief Justice and he quickly settled on Associate Justice William Rehnquist, a Nixon appointee, because he thought Democrats would have a difficult time denying confirmation to a justice who had already served fourteen years, most of them as a minority of one among nine liberals and moderates. The choice to replace him was a little less automatic, and the President had to choose between Antonin Scalia, a former law professor on the Court of Appeals, and another Court of Appeals judge and former law professor, Robert Bork. That choice was made when Reagan, proud of having appointed the first woman justice, was told that Scalia, a child of immigrants, would be the first Italian-American on the nation's highest court. He announced the nominations on June 17.

"More Vigor for the Right" was the headline over *The New York Times*'s front-page "News Analysis" the next day, reporting general agreement that Rehnquist, sixty-one, and Scalia, fifty, would be more conservative than any other members of the Court, and that both were men of powerful legal intellect. That was a problem for some. *The Washington Post*'s lead editorial the next day said: "Both men have, in our opinion, demonstrated an alarming insensitivity to civil liberties and the Bill of Rights." In Dallas, the conservative *Morning News* cheered: "If this means the Supreme Court will be taking more care to interpret the laws rather than make them, that's an auspicious beginning." But the *Dallas Times Herald* said: "To many people . . . this will be seen as the fulfillment of the President's dream to reshape the federal judiciary along more conservative lines. One can only hope it doesn't turn out to be a nightmare for the American people."

On the same day, in her office in the Old Executive Office Building next to the White House, Peggy Noonan was sitting for an exit interview, part of a National Archives project. She was quitting as one of the President's six speechwriters, after being recommended by communications director Buchanan and vetoed by chief of staff Regan as head of that department. She began by describing what she found after she was hired in April of 1984:

> I was astonished at first. . . . I was shocked that we didn't meet with the President, by the lack of input, and shocked that the speeches were so widely staffed. My speeches would be sent out to about a hundred people within the administration and they would all get to comment and put in their opinions. . . . Sometimes secretaries would rewrite sentences. . . . Dick Darman had the final say on a speech, now I came here assuming the president did, but it was really Dick. Jim Baker, of course, had input, and he said "I don't like that section" and it was out. No appeal. . . . Mike Deaver. Those three guys. . . . Darman was something special. He appreciated literature. Government draws activist, not literate people. I was astonished by his authority and power. I was appreciative of his protection.

In the first four years, as Darman liked to say, the strategic, political, and philosophic tensions of the administration were worked out in the preparation of the President's speeches. The words were both policy and marching orders. But by the fifth year, the President, who was regularly reminding staffers that he had once upon a time written his own speeches, had said about all he had to say. Except for editing a final draft of important addresses, Reagan's days as his own writer were pretty much ended. That June day in 1986, Noonan said:

> Speechwriters make policy by writing words. In this administration, you have real conservatives who believe in Ronald Reagan. . . .

That type butts heads with the folks who are pushing other agendas. Executive Office types and West Wingers there to advance their own careers. . . . I would call it the difference between the true believers and the pragmatists. . . . There is also a void left by the President's disinterest. In the absence of such involvement from the President there's all sorts of jockeying, movement and decision-making from the staff members around him. This made a bubbling pot, and Don Regan tries to take the pot off the fire, and it didn't work so well. Conflict is good. We wind up with this sterile sloganeering about the freedom fighters fighting for democracy and we're going to back them up, just sound-bites. They're big on sound-bites here.

Finally, as she left, Noonan said: "We went in to meet with the President about six months ago. . . . I stood immediately to his right and looked at him, aware of his hearing aid and being touched by the tentative way he listens, and you never get the sense that he hears every word. I was surprised by his bigness and fitness, but also his frailty. I understood that he was aging. The lion in winter."

The frailty and the aging were also noticed by another woman, Lesley Stahl of CBS News. Leaving the White House beat to take over *Face the Nation,* the network's Sunday talk show, Stahl, along with her husband, Aaron Latham, a writer, and their eight-year-old daughter, Taylor, were invited into the Oval Office by Larry Speakes for a farewell photograph. She was stunned by how Reagan looked. "Oh, my God," she thought. He looked shriveled to her. His skin was like paper, his hands dotted with age spots, bleeding into each other. She thought she could almost look through him, seeing the sunlight outside. His eyes seemed milky and she wasn't sure he actually knew who she was. "This is Lesley Stahl," Speakes was bellowing. "Of CBS."

"He's gone," she thought. "I'm going to have to go out on that lawn and tell a camera the President of the United States is a doddering space cadet."

Trying to make a connection, Stahl said: "When I covered Jimmy Carter, Taylor used to tell everyone that the president worked for her mommy. But from the day you moved in here, she began saying, 'My mommy works for the president.' "

Reagan did not react. Speakes shouted: "Sir, Lesley's husband, Aaron, writes for Hollywood. He's a screenwriter out there. Wrote a couple pictures for John Travolta."

The President came alive. His eyes cleared. He pulled Latham aside and walked him over to a couch. They sat down and Reagan, animated, began to talk about an idea for a White House movie. After a few minutes, Speakes walked over and said: "Sir, it's time for them to leave." Reagan waved him away. Latham, a very shy man, was entranced and engaged by the vigor of the old actor. Finally, after ten more minutes of movie talk, Speakes was able to move the three of them out. Suddenly, Reagan followed them into the hall. "Taylor, Taylor!" he called. "Taylor, I can't let you leave without telling you the truth." She was looking up at that tall, robust figure. "Taylor, I worked for your mother too."

As Reagan headed for New York and a dazzling July 4 rededicating and reopening of the Statue of Liberty after two years of renovation—a grand celebration under fireworks filling the night sky over the harbor—he was presented with some dramatic reminders of why Presidents yearn and scheme to control the Supreme Court. On July 3, by 6 to 3 votes, ruling in two separate cases, the justices endorsed the use of affirmative action to cure past discrimination in public and private workplaces. The decision undid much of six years of work by the President and his Justice Department, which had argued that only individuals who had been identified as having personally suffered because of racial or gender discrimination by employers should be entitled to legal relief. In these cases, involving New York policemen and Cleveland firefighters, the administration had argued that numeric race-conscious employment goals were "morally wrong." They lost. The decision, written by Justice William Brennan, asserted that such goals were appropriate in cases of "persistent or egregious discrimination." Then, five days later—after a busy Court session in which the justices had ruled against the administration in cases that involved restricting abortion rights, voting rights, and Social Security disability benefits—the Court voted 7 to 2 to void the principal provision of the Gramm-Rudman-Hollings bill that was supposed to reduce federal spending and deficits.

As seen from the Justice Department, Brennan, an energetic and persuasive jurist appointed by President Eisenhower, was a principal factor in that string of defeats. "There is no individual in this country, on or off the Court, who has had a more profound and sustained impact on public policy in the United States over the past 27 years," said one memo to the President during the secret deliberations after Burger had told Reagan he was retiring. In those meetings, Meese pressed the argument that Rehnquist could control Brennan and the rest of the

Court as Burger had not. In fact, the Gramm-Rudman decision was written by Burger himself, his last case.

As spectacular as the New York July 4 ceremony was, the President had hoped for one more event. He had wanted to have a freed hostage there, Father Lawrence Martin Jenco, the fifty-one-year-old priest who had been the director of Catholic Relief Services in Beirut before being kidnapped and held for nineteen months. The hostage negotiations and arms sales had seemed close to some kind of interim resolution in late June. In May, the President had approved a very brave or very foolish McFarlane mission to Tehran, supposedly for a meeting with the speaker of the Iranian Parliament, Akbar Hashemi Rafsanjani, the secret rendezvous mentioned in North's NSC memo listing schedules and details implementing the January 17 presidential finding authorizing secret arms sales to Iran. McFarlane and North, with false Irish passports, along with a CIA technical team and an Israeli official, had flown from Israel into Tehran airport on May 25. Their plane, an unmarked white Boeing 707 flown by Americans, carried a pallet of HAWK missile parts demanded (and paid for) by the Iranians as part of the price for the meeting. Eleven more pallets were loaded in Tel Aviv, for delivery when the four remaining American hostages would be released in Beirut. McFarlane expected to be met by Speaker Rafsanjani and an official delegation when they landed at 9 A.M.

There was no one waiting for them. They sat in the terminal for two hours. Then McFarlane confronted airport officials, angrily shouting: "We are emissaries of Ronald Reagan. . . ." If we are not out of Iran by a designated time, U.S. Rapid Deployment Forces in the Persian Gulf are ready to rescue us. Finally, Ghorbanifar, the ubiquitous middleman, drove them in an old car to what had once been the Tehran Hilton. McFarlane asked when he would see the Speaker and the Prime Minister, the men North had told him would be waiting. "What?" said Ghorbanifar. "Well . . ."

No one but bureaucrats, junior ones at that, appeared for two days. McFarlane had trouble getting over the fact that one of them told him he had been a cobbler before the revolution. Also, the Iranians had boarded the plane and taken the HAWK parts—something that was supposed to happen only after the release of hostages. The junior officials wanted to know where the rest of the shipment was. After two days, a more assured emissary arrived, saying he was a member of Rafsanjani's staff. McFarlane labored through a night with him, trying to work something out, but the Iranians had to leave for instructions. McFarlane did the same by a CIA radio channel to Poindexter at the White House. Twice, Reagan himself had come on the line to talk about Iranian demands that included Israeli withdrawal from southern Lebanon and the Golan Heights. Talking to Poindexter again, McFarlane asked whether he was free to negotiate a new deal. Poindexter talked to the President and came back with a common Reagan message. No orders, just: "Bud's the man on the scene. . . . He should do what he thinks is right."

McFarlane left for Tel Aviv and then home on May 28, telling his Iranian contacts that there were going to be no more deals until all four of the hostages remaining in Lebanon were released. McFarlane was discouraged—so far, more than twenty-five hundred TOW missiles had been sent to Iran and only one hostage had been released—but as far as North was concerned it was all worth it. On the trip back, he told his old boss for the first time that, after all, much of the money the Iranians had already paid was now being used in Central America. In Washington, Reagan, who had monitored McFarlane's radio transmissions, wrote in his diary: "It was a heart breaking disappointment for all of us."

McFarlane had gone directly to the White House when he returned on May 29, and told Reagan that it would be a mistake and a waste to continue dealing with the Iranians. Let them make the first move. Perhaps they did. Perhaps that was why Jenco was released on July 25. The President himself saw it that way, writing in his diary: "This release of Jenco is a delayed step in a plan we've been working on for months. It gives us hope the rest of the plan will take place." *

Casey and Poindexter advised Reagan to authorize the shipment of the eleven pallets of HAWK parts, still in a hangar in Tel Aviv, to Iran as a demonstration of gratitude or goodwill. Reagan agreed on August 3. "Back on the roller coaster," said the President.

All of this was secret, of course. An editorial in the *Newark Star-Ledger,* in New Jersey, which was echoed in other newspapers around the country, was reprinted in the President's daily News Summary. It could be considered a tribute to White House secret-keeping: "Father Jenco's release and the free world's long, trying experience with ex-

---

* In his autobiography, President Reagan wrote: "We were *not* trading arms for hostages. None of the arms we had shipped to Iran had gone to the terrorists who kidnapped our citizens." After Jenco's release, three more Americans—Frank Reed, Joseph Cicippio, and Edward Tracy—were kidnapped and held in Beirut.

tremism prove that the only way to deal with the ordeal of terrorism is not to deal with the terrorists."

On September 17, Rehnquist was confirmed by the Senate, but it was a struggle. Rehnquist's problem was not his judicial record. What hurt him were questions about his candor. Witnesses appeared to swear that as a young lawyer in Arizona, he had worked with teams of Republicans who questioned and harassed black and Hispanic voters outside polling places, demanding that they prove they could read, asking if they had criminal records, trying to discourage them from going inside and voting. He was also hurt by legal records showing that, in 1963 in Arizona and again in 1974 in Vermont, he had bought houses with restrictive covenants, one barring resale to any "Negro," the second to "any member of the Hebrew race." Senator Kennedy prefaced his vote against Rehnquist by saying, "He is too extreme on race, too extreme on women's rights, too extreme on freedom of speech, too extreme on separation of church and state, too extreme to be Chief Justice."

The case against him had been summed up on the *CBS Evening News* on August 5 by commentator Bill Moyers, a Texan and a former assistant to President Lyndon Johnson: "When I was growing up, the arguments that blacks should remain second-class citizens were often made by men with first-class minds—men steeped in Blackstone, the classics, and the founding fathers—they were dazzling in defense of segregation, but they were blind. . . . We've come a long way since then, but not with the help of William Rehnquist. It is still a struggle, this quest for equal rights, and now we're about to get a Chief Justice who never believed in it in the first place, opposed it along the way, and for all his learning and intellect is no friend of it today." Thirty-three senators from both parties voted against his confirmation, the most who had ever opposed a nominee for Chief Justice. Then, Antonin Scalia, just as conservative, was confirmed by unanimous vote.

The Prime Minister of Israel, Shimon Peres, happened to be in Washington that day, September 17. At the White House, he asked Reagan whether there was going to be a 1986 summit with Gorbachev. The President said he was not sure. The President and the General Secretary had exchanged letters and more statements on arms control problems since the Geneva summit—and its closing promise of a Washington summit in 1986. Two weeks into 1986, just eight weeks after the Geneva summit, Gorbachev had proposed in one of the letters—and made it public—that the superpowers eliminate all nuclear weapons by the year 2000. A bold thought, but one that was dismissed as propaganda by most American officials. There was one exception, the President, who responded in private, "Why wait until 2000?" He was ready to go, eager for the next summit in the United States, perhaps in June. "A world free from nuclear weapons" was a phrase that suddenly popped up in Reagan-Gorbachev correspondence. But Shultz and Shevardnadze had been unable to make much progress in their discussions on weaponry and summitry. Whatever the principals were saying in public, Reagan's subordinates were dismissing the idea as a ploy that would maximize the threat of the Soviets' edge in troop numbers, tanks, and other conventional arms—there was still no date set for a 1986 meeting.

Reagan saw summits as negotiating sessions. He loved the give-and-take and he was good at it, going back to his days as president of the Screen Actors Guild, when he hammered out agreements with studio executives. But Gorbachev, he told Peres, was more a traditionalist, preferring summits to be public ratifications of agreements worked out in advance. Besides, the Soviet leader was preoccupied and on the defensive because of continuing economic struggle and decline at home and a nuclear disaster, the meltdown of a reactor at a place called Chernobyl in the Ukraine on April 26. The burning reactor had not only spewed radioactive clouds first over the Soviet Union, and then over Eastern and Western Europe, the accident served as a deadly reminder of the old and rusty infrastructure of the communist countries. The Kremlin had begun admitting to two deaths in the accident, but the number was climbing into the hundreds. More than 135,000 people were evacuated and contaminated topsoil was being scraped off an area of one thousand square miles.*

---

* A Reagan assistant, Martin Anderson, said of his boss's style: "In 1984 Meg Greenfield, editor of the editorial page of *The Washington Post,* wrote an essay for *Newsweek* in which she explored the question of 'How Does Reagan Decide?' A liberal Democrat, she is one of the more astute political analysts in Washington, and she observed something that even many of Reagan's closest conservative supporters failed to understand—that he makes decisions like a labor negotiator for a workers' union. Greenfield summed up part of his style this way, ' . . . the long waiting out of the adversary, the immobility meanwhile, the refusal to give anything until the last moment, the willingness—nonetheless—finally to yield to superior pressure or force or particular circumstance on almost everything, but only with something to show in return and only if the final deal can be interpreted as furthering the original Reagan objective.' " A Russian note-taker who watched Reagan closely in two summits told Jack Matlock that the American reminded him of an old lion, lazily watching an antelope on the horizon, taking no interest, dozing a bit. He doesn't move when the antelope stops only ten feet away, that's too far. At eight feet, the lion suddenly comes to life!—Reagan, the negotiator, suddenly fills the room.

"Our hearts go out to those Soviet citizens who have been affected by the tragedy," Reagan wrote to Gorbachev in one of his letters, the letters in which they had talked of another summit and in which both took to using the phrase "arms reductions" instead of the old "arms control."

The other problem between the superpowers was Nicholas Daniloff, a Moscow correspondent for *U.S. News & World Report* magazine. On August 23, the FBI had arrested a Soviet employee of the United Nations Secretariat named Gennady Zakharov, charging him with attempting to recruit an American employee of a defense contractor to spy for the Soviets. The employee had gone to the FBI. The FBI moved in at a subway station in Queens, New York, as Zakharov exchanged envelopes with the American, one containing cash, the other classified documents. It was the usual Cold War spy gamesmanship—with a couple of differences. At the time, five Americans were jailed or on trial for attempting to pass secrets to the communists, and Zakharov, as an employee of the U.N. rather than his government, did not have diplomatic immunity. If he had immunity, he would have been deported rather than arrested. Jack Matlock, the NSC Soviet expert, warned the White House that an American would be seized for a prisoner trade. A week later, Daniloff was the American.

On September 4, the President had sent a cable to the Kremlin, saying: "I can give you my personal assurance that Mr. Daniloff has no connection whatever with the U.S. Government. If you have been informed otherwise, you have been misinformed." *

Gorbachev responded within twenty-four hours: "Regarding the question you raised. . . . As was reported to me by the competent authorities, Daniloff had for a long time been engaged in impermissible activities damaging to the state interests of the USSR. . . . We should not permit the use of questions of such kind to lead to the detriment of Soviet-American relations."

Reagan was furious. He wrote in his diary: "Word came the Soviets

---

* In fact, as Secretary of State Shultz told the President, Daniloff may have violated Soviet law by delivering envelopes from Soviet citizens, left in his mailbox in a Moscow apartment building, to the American embassy, where officers turned over at least one to the CIA. He had also mailed copies of Soviet documents marked "Secret" to the office of *U.S. News & World Report* in Washington. The magazine's editor, David Gergen, the former White House communications director, gave those copies to Shultz when Daniloff was arrested. The CIA had also used Daniloff's name in messages to at least one Soviet dissenter. "The CIA has compromised Daniloff," said Shultz, angrily, during White House discussions.

were going to officially charge Daniloff with espionage. Gorbachev's response to my letter was arrogant. . . . I'm mad as hell."

He was. Over the next two weeks, the "Daniloff Affair," as it was being called, was about the only thing he wrote about in the diary:

"Sept. 9—If it's possible we'll do something of an exchange but only if they'll release some dissidents like [Andrei] Sakharov. Once we have him back, I propose we kick a half a hundred of their UN KGB agents out of the country." . . . "Sept. 10—I think it's very important to get our guy out of their jail and away from that four hours a day interrogation." . . . "Sept. 12—We have agreed to turn Zakhgarov [sic] over to the Soviet ambassador pending trial if they will deliver Daniloff to our ambassador. This does not mean a trade. Their man is a spy caught red-handed and Daniloff is a hostage." . . . "Sept. 18—Gorbachev has gone on TV to declare our man is definitely a spy. . . . Gen. Sec. of UN has stated our action in ordering 25 UN Soviet staff out of the country is against UN charter. He'd better be careful, if we cut off UN allowance they might be out of business."

Soviet Foreign Minister Shevardnadze arrived in Washington the next day with a letter from Gorbachev. When he reached the Oval Office, he discovered he had left the envelope at the Soviet embassy, and a couple of his men were sent to get it. When they arrived back inside the White House with the letter, they were stopped by Secret Service agents, who said: "We don't allow KGB agents inside the Oval Office." There was a shouting match until, finally, the Soviet messengers were allowed to slip the letter to the President's translator through a slightly opened door.

"The U.S. side has unduly dramatized that [Zakharov and Daniloff] incident," Gorbachev wrote. "It is as if a pretext was deliberately sought to aggravate Soviet-American relations and to increase tension. One has to conclude that, in effect, no start has been made in implementing the agreements we reached in Geneva." Reagan grew angrier as he read those lines. He underlined them. In six pages, Gorbachev reviewed past letters and several public statements by both sides on anti-missile defenses, medium-range missiles in Europe, and American nuclear testing, concluding: "There has been no movement on these issues. . . . They will lead nowhere unless you and I intervene personally. I have an idea, Mr. President, that in the very near future and setting aside all other matters, we have a quick one-on-one meeting, let us say in Iceland or London, maybe just for one day, to engage in a strictly confidential, private and frank discussion . . . that would result in instructions to our respective agencies to draft agreements on two or three very specific questions, which you and I could sign during my visit to the United States."

"I opted for Iceland," Reagan wrote in his diary that night: "I'm agreeable to that but made it plain we wanted Daniloff returned to us before anything took place. I let the Foreign Minister know I was angry and I resented their charges that Daniloff was a spy after I had personally given my word. . . . I told him they couldn't understand the importance that we place on the individual because they don't have any such feeling."

Daniloff was allowed to leave Moscow on September 29—and Zakharov was sent home from New York. The Soviets also agreed to allow a prominent dissident, Yuri Orlov, held in a Siberian labor camp for most of the past twelve years, to leave the country. The release of Orlov and his wife was announced the next morning by Secretary Shultz, who came to the White House briefing room. As Shultz spoke, Reagan walked in behind him and said: "I am pleased to announce that General Secretary Gorbachev and I will meet October 11th and 12th in Reykjavik, Iceland. . . . That will take place in the context of preparations for the General Secretary's visit to the United States, which was agreed to at Geneva in November of '85." *

"This is not a summit," Reagan remarked at one point. "I have no way of knowing what the outcome will be."

"The Soviets blinked?" asked a reporter, referring to a line the President had thrown out as he boarded Air Force One after a Republican campaign rally in Kansas City the day before. Reagan answered more diplomatically this time: "I shouldn't have said that."

In fact, conservatives were complaining that Reagan had done the blinking, that he had swapped a spy for a hostage. "A Humiliation for the President" was the headline on the editorial page of the *San Diego Union*. "Justice is not served when a purse-snatcher flings down the purse and escapes," said the *Washington Times* in an editorial. "George Shultz is a complete sellout and Ronald Reagan is behaving like a damn fool"—that was the verdict on the day's events by Howard Phillips, president of an important right-wing group, the Conservative Caucus. It was all on the news that night, of course. NBC anchorman Tom Brokaw began: "What we seem to have tonight

* Reykjavik was chosen because it is equidistant from Moscow and Washington, a five-and-a-half-hour flight from either capital.

is a summit that is not a summit, after a deal that was not a deal, for a swap that was not a swap."

As he was preparing for the Iceland trip, the President lost his Republican troops in the Senate. The issue was the imposition of economic sanctions on South Africa as punishment for apartheid. From the day he took office, he had held off liberal demands for action against South Africa's brutal racial segregation. "Constructive engagement" was his name for the idea that the United States could do more to change South Africa as a friend of the country's ruling whites than as an opponent. But his time ran out—the House had already voted for sanctions—because nothing seemed to be changing in the country but its level of violence and suppression of the black majority. He sent Secretary Shultz and other administration heavyweights to the Capitol with a final argument, or plea, that overriding his veto would weaken him during his summit meeting with Gorbachev. It was not enough, nor was the South African government's threat to cut off its wheat purchases from American farmers. On October 3, thirty-one Senate Republicans joined with all the Democrats to override Reagan's veto of sanctions by a vote of 78 to 21, 11 votes more than the two-thirds required.

Two days later, on Sunday, October 5, five days before Reagan was to leave Washington for Reykjavik, an unmarked cargo plane was reported missing in Central America. It had been shot down by a lost Sandinista patrol waiting for supplies of food and ammunition. The twenty-six soldiers had been eating monkey meat in the jungle thirty miles north of Nicaragua's border with Costa Rica. The plane, an old American C-123, roared over them, flying low. A nineteen-year-old Nicaraguan soldier named José Fernando Corales grabbed a SAM-7, a Soviet shoulder-fired surface-to-air missile launcher, and its heat-seeking missile flew into the plane's right engine. There was fire, a side door opened, and a man with a parachute managed to jump out as the plane dipped before going into a last dive. The soldiers found three dead men in the wreckage, along with pallets of AK-47 automatic rifles, 100,000 rounds of ammunition, boots, and other supplies. They also found flight records and crew logs indicating that the plane had already delivered 123,000 pounds of weaponry to the contras as part of an air supply operation. In the wallet of the dead pilot, they found the business card of Robert Owen of the National Security Council, a deputy to Oliver North.

It took the Sandinistas more than a day to find the survivor hiding in an abandoned peasant's hut. His name was Eugene Hasenfus, a forty-five-year-old ex-Marine from Marinette, Wisconsin. His job, paying $3,000 a month, was to muscle the pallets out of the plane near hidden contra bases and camps. He told his captors that he was working for the CIA on an operation that he had been told was run from the White House. He had, he told interrogators, been on more than fifty supply flights from an airbase at Ilopango in El Salvador, and that his boss was Joseph Fernandez, the CIA station chief in Costa Rica. When he was informed of the crash, Fernandez sent a cable to Washington saying: "Situation requires that we do necessary damage control." *

In Washington, on October 7, Shultz, who had been briefed by assistant secretary Elliott Abrams, told reporters: "There was no connection with the U.S. Government at all."

Poindexter briefed the President at 9 A.M. the next day. "We don't know exactly who it was," said the National Security Adviser. "But I think you should be careful about denying any U.S. role." Very careful. In the building next door, the Old Executive Office Building, Oliver North and his secretary, Fawn Hall, were shredding documents as fast as they could. He had been in Frankfurt, Germany, for yet another meeting with arms dealers and Iranian go-betweens, the most important of them, one who presented himself as Ali Hashemi Bahramani, a nephew of Rafsanjani. North had gone to Frankfurt with a Bible inscribed by the President as a gift for the powerful Iranian Speaker. Reagan signed under a verse, Galatians 3:8: "And the Scriptures seeing that God would justify the Gentiles by faith, preached the Gospel beforehand to Abraham, saying, 'All nations shall be blessed in you . . . ' " North was his usual lying self, caught on a hidden tape recorder this time. Among the tales he told was this: "I flew up to Camp David to talk to the President and I showed him the list of required weapons. 'Why are you thinking so small?' . . . I was sitting across the table—and he said: 'For someone who has seen as much war as you, North, you should understand that I want to end that war on terms that are acceptable to Iran. I don't want to simply help, go out, and kill more Iranian youngsters. What about the two

---

* Oliver North later testified that it was a government operation because he ran it himself— "I was the government connection"—but that the plane was owned by Richard Secord, the retired Air Force general who had become an American arms merchant, and Hasenfus was paid by Secord.

million people without homes?' . . . He banged the table, 'I want to end this war!' "

Never happened. Colonel North had never been alone with President Reagan, never briefed him, never was at Camp David with him.

Then North heard that Hasenfus's plane had been shot down and that he was a prisoner. He flew back to Washington, knowing that his secret webs were about to unravel, and the shredding began. The irony of it all was that the C-123 flight would have been one of the last privately financed operations—paid for by the Saudis and rich American donors—because the President was about to sign the $100 million contra aid package passed by the Congress in June.

An hour after he was briefed on the capture of Hasenfus, the President made a short statement about budget negotiations in Congress. A reporter asked him whether the government was involved in operations over Nicaragua. "I'm glad you asked that," he replied. "Absolutely not. While they're American citizens, there is no government connection with that at all. . . . We've been aware that there are private groups and private citizens that have been trying to help the contras—to that extent—but we did not know the particulars of what they were doing."

Reagan was in Reykjavik when the Nicaragua government put Hasenfus in front of microphones and television cameras to repeat in public what he had said during interrogation: "Two Cuban naturalized Americans that work for the CIA did most of the coordination for the flights and oversaw all of our housing, transportation, also refueling and some flight plans. . . . We would be flying into Honduras to an airbase called Aguacate and there we would load up on small arms and ammunition and fly into Nicaragua. There it would be dropped to the contras."

CHAPTER 16
OCTOBER 12, 1986

GENERAL SECRETARY GORBACHEV ARRIVED IN REYKJAVIK on October 10, a day after Reagan. The President was staying in one of the rented apartments that served as both the American embassy and the home of the ambassador, alternating briefings and naps. He was walking by a television set, broadcasting a special feed by CNN, as the Soviet leader's plane landed. He watched Gorbachev stepping out of the plane and talking about his hopes to build a safer world. Reagan scowled and told the television set: "When you stop trying to take over the world, then maybe we can do some business."

There was something almost telepathic about the President's words. A few days earlier, at a secret Politburo meeting in Moscow, Gorbachev had ridiculed draft position papers by his experts, saying: "If we are still trying to conquer the entire world, then let's discuss how to defeat the Americans in the arms race. But then we can forget all we have said about our new policies. . . . We have to realize that if our proposals imply weakening U.S. security, then there won't be any agreement. If we don't back down on some specific, maybe even important issues, we will lose in the end. We will be drawn into an arms race that we cannot manage."

When the television cameras in Reykjavik showed Raisa Gorbachev standing behind her husband, Reagan's jaw set in a harder line. Nancy Reagan had remained in Washington—this after all was supposed to be a one-day working session—and they had been told Mrs. Gorbachev would stay home as well. Both leaders were men who performed best when their wives were around. Gorbachev, in fact, had rejected the first Reykjavik schedule his staff prepared, saying, "You have reserved no time for me to consult with my wife."

The President, expecting something like a pre-summit planning meeting, had been preparing for only a week. He was surprised when he saw the size of the Soviet leader's bulging briefcase. Something was up. It was unlikely that he was carrying position papers on human rights or Afghanistan. Was it possible he was coming with serious new arms control proposals?

He was. The Soviet leader, in the Politburo meetings and for weeks before at his Black Sea *dacha,* had been pushing his aides toward more and more dramatic proposals. One of his men, Anatoly Chernyaev, sent Gorbachev a cover note at one point, saying: "The main goal of Reykjavik, if I understood you correctly . . . is to sweep Reagan off his feet with our bold, even risky approach to the central problem of world politics."

Much of the American intelligence on that subject pointed in that direction. The final CIA briefing included: "Gorbachev's strategy requires keeping a lid on current defense spending in order to modernize the economy and allow it to compete more successfully with the U.S. over the long haul." Former President Nixon had also reported back to Reagan along those lines after meetings in late July with Gorbachev in Moscow. Interesting, but the Americans still did not expect much to happen in Iceland. The State Department's "Concept Paper" concluded: "Working meetings to prepare for Gorbachev's visit to the United States."

Gorbachev had also been asking questions of Nixon, and of French president François Mitterrand, who had been with Reagan in New York on July 4 for the rededication of France's great gift to the United States, the Statue of Liberty. Nixon told Gorbachev that whatever he thought of Reagan's "disengaged" style, the President viewed the relationship with the Soviet Union as a personal responsibility. Aides and advisers might come and go, he said, but Reagan was a confident man of great common sense and he was the one making the decisions.

Gorbachev told Mitterrand that he was convinced that what Reagan feared most was modern economic development in the Soviet Union. He described the American President in Marxist terms, that whatever his personality he would act as a tool of the so-called military-industrial complex. Mitterrand, who knew more than a little about such Marxist theory, told the Russian he was wrong. The French leader, who liked Reagan but opposed SDI and many other Reagan ideas, told Gorbachev: "Not withstanding his political past, Reagan had the intuition that the current tension must be ended. He is not a machine. He likes to laugh and more than the others is influenced by the language of peace." Then he warned Gorbachev that he would get nowhere if he tried to persuade Reagan to give up on SDI.*

That was not advice Gorbachev wanted to hear. Like Reagan, like most successful political leaders, the Soviet leader had the egoistic confidence that one-on-one he would always prevail. He would persuade Reagan. That's why he was in Reykjavik. Reagan thought the same thing. That's why he was in Reykjavik. It was going to be all work and no play.

There was no place to play. Gorbachev slept on a Russian ship in the harbor. The meetings of the wills were held in an official government guesthouse, Hofdi House, a modest white stucco building overlooking Reykjavik harbor, once used as the residence of the British ambassador. It was said to be haunted and the house was sold back to the government of Iceland when one ambassador complained of night noises, doors opening and closing for no reason, and pictures falling off the walls. The landscape was lava swirls and ridges, so forbidding that American astronauts had come there to practice before moon shots.

The leaders sat down across a table in a back corner conference room, once the house's dining room, facing the water, with only interpreters and note-takers at 10:40 on Saturday morning. Upstairs, their staffs, men who knew each other's names and jobs but had never met, sat and waited—and talked. For almost an hour, Gorbachev and Reagan repeated the ideas and proposals and frustrations that they had harbored since Geneva; the Russian, bouncing with energy, sure he

---

* Their politics were very different, but Mitterrand liked and admired Reagan. In a 1985 interview with Marguerite Duras, the novelist and a woman of the left, the French President said: "Reagan is a man of common sense, gracious and pleasant. He communicates through jokes, by telling ultra-California stories, by speaking mainly about California and the Bible. He has two religions: free enterprise and God—the Christian God. . . . He is not a man who dwells on concepts, yet he has ideas and clings to them. It is no small achievement to lead a country of 250 million. . . . I feel sympathy for Reagan as a man, less sympathy for his policies." The conversation continued, including these exchanges: DURAS: "I think he is the incarnation of a kind of primal, almost archaic power. He governs less with his intellect than with common sense. But I approve of this. And he doesn't look for anything more than the approval of the American people." MITTERRAND: "But Ronald Reagan is not only President of the United States. He is head of the most powerful empire in the world." DURAS: "Good for us! Thanks be to God! It is funny, he displays the same defiance toward the Soviet Union as would an old member of a European Communist party. All of a sudden, he recognized what kind of people Russians are, and he will never turn his back on this knowledge. That's it—the great virtue of simplicity. You may be slow, but when you learn something, it's forever."

was making history, did most of the talking. Then they were joined by Shultz and Shevardnadze. As if on cue, Gorbachev began to talk of new thinking—*perestroika* in Russian. "Bold" was a word he repeated as he laid out a prepared arms reduction schedule. He rolled over Reagan's attempts to talk of dates for a Washington summit or of human rights and other issues between the superpowers. Matlock took notes for the American side, beginning with: "Gorbachev indicated that . . . the mutual ultimate aim was total elimination of nuclear weapons. . . . This stemmed from what had been agreed upon in Geneva, i.e., that a nuclear war must never be fought."

Finally, Gorbachev handed the President a summary (in English) of his proposals, written as a directive from the leaders to their foreign ministers, directing them to prepare agreements based on these provisions, ready, the draft concluded, "to be signed in Washington during the General Secretary's visit to the United States. . . ."

1. Strategic arms. An agreement on a 50 percent reduction in the strategic offensive weapons of the Soviet Union and the United States. . . . All types of strategic offensive weapons, including heavy missiles, will be subject to reduction within specified limits. A solution will also be found to the problem of limiting the deployment of sea-based, long-range cruise missiles. . . .

2. Medium-range missiles. An agreement on the complete elimination of Soviet and US medium-range missiles in Europe, without taking the nuclear potentials of France and England into account . . . separate talks will be started on Soviet and American medium-range systems in Asia. . . . *

3. The Treaty on the Limitation of Anti-Ballistic Missile (ABM) Systems. An agreement pledging not to use their right to withdraw from this treaty for 10 years and to strictly abide by all of its provisions throughout that period. The testing of all space-based elements of anti-ballistic missile defenses in space will be prohibited.

Then they broke for lunch. The Americans were astonished and excited. Most of them, anyway. "They're coming our way," said Shultz. Paul Nitze, the Americans' most experienced negotiator, still formidable at the age of seventy-nine, said this was far and away the best pro-

---

* Ignoring French and British missiles was a concession opposed by many Soviet officials and military men. Gorbachev's response to the objections was: "Don't be ridiculous. We are never going to be attacked by France or England."

posal the Soviets had ever made. The Defense Department's man, assistant secretary Richard Perle, who many thought was there to do his best to resist any proposal, said he was impressed. Reagan was the holdout. The Americans crowded into "The Bubble," the plastic room within a room inside the embassy, a sealed place safe from electronic bugs and eavesdropping, and the President said: "He's got a lot of proposals, but I'm afraid he's going after SDI."

It was Reagan's turn when they returned. His pockets were filled with index cards, mostly numbers and descriptions of the weapons nomenclature he had never mastered. Once he spilled a small pile onto the floor and Gorbachev helped pick them up. The American note-taker—Thomas Simons replaced Matlock—began: "The President recalled that Gorbachev had presented him with a paper that morning. He had not yet had a chance to digest it, and he would like to read Gorbachev a paper here, which had some suggestions at the end."

The President, consulting his cards, went into as much detail as Gorbachev had. He argued that the United States was not trying to eliminate the ABM Treaty. He wanted, he said, to expand it: "Some new provisions would take precedence over certain provisions of the ABM Treaty. . . . You have suggested that our defense might be used to attack the Soviet Union. I can assure you that it is not being developed for that purpose. . . . We are even prepared to share the benefits of strategic defense. We will agree now to a treaty committing to do so in conjunction with the elimination of ballistic missiles."

Gorbachev's first question was whether the President agreed with the proposal of a 50 percent reduction in strategic missiles.

"Yes."

"So . . ." said Gorbachev, looking away from the translators, addressing Reagan. "So, let us agree to eliminate all the types the Soviet Union and the U.S. have by 50 percent: land-based, sea-launched and those carried by strategic bombers. . . . If we proceed to reduce it by 50 percent across the board, we will reduce the level of strategic confrontation . . . cut it in half."

Reagan said he was interested: "This should be taken up by the experts . . ."

"This is not a matter for experts," Gorbachev snapped. He passed the sheet of numbers he was holding across to Reagan. "This is not a matter for experts," he said again. "Here's the data. Let's cut it in half. Otherwise it goes back to Karpov and Kampelman." (Victor Karpov and Max Kampelman were two of the Soviet and American negotiators.) "And that's *kasha* forever!—porridge forever!"

Reagan did not engage. "The idea is interesting," he said, but he asked for trust in himself and faith in America. The notes read: "The President recalled the time, after World War II, when we were the only ones to have nuclear weapons. We could have dictated to the world, but we did not. . . . When he was growing up—a little before Gorbachev—there had been rules of warfare that protected noncombatants, civilians. 'Wouldn't it be great if we could make the world as safe today as it was then?' Some of his own delegation later kidded among themselves that the boss's true ambition was to turn the clock back to the 1920s and the small-town life he remembered. Or imagined. The American notes continued: "All the U.S. is saying is that in addition to the missiles covered by this treaty, here is something bigger we want the world to have. . . . With the progress we are making we do not need ten years. We do not think it will take that long. Progress is being made."

Not as much progress as Reagan believed. Kampelman and other American "experts" were furious at Weinberger because the Defense Secretary had told Reagan back in Washington that SDI could be deployed within six months—a ludicrous idea that the President seemed to believe.

"Sharing?" Gorbachev interrupted Reagan a couple of times, again surprising the Americans with his candor—"We're not in a press conference, there's no reason to speak in banalities." He said that the Soviet Union did not currently fear development of a three-level SDI system and would not match it. Could not match it. "The Soviet response will not be symmetrical, but asymmetrical," he said. "The U.S. has money and could do things the Soviets could not." Then he added: "Excuse me, Mr. President, but I cannot take your idea of sharing SDI seriously. You are not willing to share with us oil well equipment, digitally guided machine tools, or even milking machines. Sharing SDI would provoke a second American revolution! Let's be realistic."

The President stuck with the idea of experts, suggesting that the men upstairs meet that night to try to mold Saturday's words into a Sunday-morning agreement. He and Gorbachev were scheduled to leave after lunch, and Raisa Gorbachev was providing a bit of diversion for the two thousand reporters besieging Reykjavik during a blackout of negotiation news. Correspondents surrounding Hofdi

House and in press centers scattered around the city of 87,000 hardy souls were almost completely unaware of the astonishing events overwhelming the tired, excited people in that building.

The "experts," divided into two groups, began work at 8 P.M. on Saturday. Nitze led the American arms control group, and Assistant Secretary of State Rozanne Ridgway led the group working on human rights and regional conflict issues. Their Soviet equivalents were Marshal Sergei Akhromeyev, chief of the Soviets' General Staff, and Alexander Bessmertnykh, head of the Soviet Foreign Ministry's American department. The presence of Akhromeyev at a summit for the first time was interpreted by the Americans as a sign that Gorbachev's political problems at home were not with the Politburo but with the military, which was concerned that their new General Secretary was moving too fast to reach accommodation.

If that was true, his counterpart on the American side was the Defense Department's Richard Perle, representing the view of Secretary Weinberger and the Joint Chiefs of Staff, who worried that Reagan was several concepts ahead of the United States military. The groups worked through the night all over Hofdi House—Perle and Robert Linhard, an Air Force colonel assigned to the National Security Council for the past five years, set up their office on a board over a bathtub in one of the house's two bathrooms—finally emerging into the cold outside at 6:30 A.M. For the Americans it was just in time to send their luggage to Air Force One and backup planes for the scheduled midday trip home.

Nitze's team of negotiators came to Reagan's room before breakfast, saying that they had made more progress on the idea of controlling strategic weapons in the past ten hours than in the previous ten years. Reagan seemed euphoric downstairs at breakfast, saying: "Literally a miracle is happening."

Just outside that inner circle, Larry Speakes, the President's spokesman, was waiting to be told what he could pass on to reporters. He knew no specifics, but he could feel the hope. He began to cry, thinking he was present at the creation of a new world. The press, though, knew nothing. Back home, the Sunday *New York Times* printed a front-page "News Analysis" by Leslie Gelb, possibly the best-informed journalist waiting in Reykjavik, under the headline "A Quest for Compromise." Neither he nor any other reporters knew that Soviets and Americans were talking about actually eliminating classes of nuclear weapons, interacting in ways they never had before—as if Gorbachev's intensity and Reagan's imagination had changed national characters in a separate universe by the bay. Gelb's conclusion was from a different place: "To officials on both sides, the principal test of the meetings is whether Mr. Reagan and Mr. Gorbachev will agree to meet again in the next several months in the United States."

The first subjects on the table at Hofdi House Sunday morning were INF middle-range missiles in Europe and in the Asian reaches of the Soviet Union. There was a good deal of back-and-forth, essentially because the Soviets were determined to keep some INF—intermediate-range nuclear forces—missiles in Asia. Finally they agreed on eliminating Soviet and American missiles in Europe. It was an amazing result, what Reagan had called the Zero Option during the ten-year political struggle by both the Carter and Reagan administrations to install cruise missiles and updated Pershing missiles in Western Europe to match Soviet SS-20s west of the Ural Mountains. As for the Soviet missiles east of the Urals, in Asia, they agreed that one hundred could remain and the Americans would be allowed to install one hundred on their own territory, presumably in Alaska.

The INF talk was so positive that Shultz ordered his assistant secretary, Roz Ridgway, to begin calling foreign ministers in Western Europe, in the countries where Pershing and cruise missiles were deployed, to inform them that a U.S.-Soviet deal was close: Those missiles were going to be removed. The happy confusion at Reykjavik was moving so quickly that no Americans thought to tell the President that with the INF missiles gone from both sides, the Soviet Union would have overwhelming regional superiority in conventional forces. Its troops and tanks and artillery massed or pointed at the borders of West Germany, Belgium, the Netherlands, and Italy.

The principals turned to the ABM treaty. Both sides knew that the conversation was really about SDI. The notes recorded:

The President replied that the U.S. had no intention of violating the ABM treaty. It had never done so, even though, as the Soviets knew, it believed the Soviet Union had. . . . With respect to SDI, the President recalled that he had made a pledge to the American people that SDI would contribute to disarmament and peace and not be an offensive weapon. . . . It would be a threat to no one. . . . He could not retreat from that pledge. . . . The President did not see why SDI could not be part of the ABM Treaty.

Gorbachev said he understood all that, and offered a political argument: "Research would continue, and this would show that SDI was alive. . . . There could be mock-ups, even testing in laboratories. Such efforts would ensure against the appearance of a nuclear madman of the type the President often mentioned."

"No, it would not," said Reagan. "Such a regime did not give protection; it limited protection. Why the hell should the world have to live for another ten years under the threat of nuclear weapons if we have decided to eliminate them?"

Gorbachev responded to say that it was time for the United States to move toward Soviet positions. "There is an American expression," he said. " 'It takes two to tango'. . . . Was the President prepared to dance?"

Shevardnadze said that the Americans had to understand that the Soviet proposals were a package: The 50 percent cuts in heavy weaponry, the INF cuts, the restrictions on testing were all linked to the ABM moves.

"Are we going to leave here with nothing?" asked Reagan.

"Yes," said Gorbachev. "Let's go home. We've accomplished nothing."

But they talked some more, this time about human rights issues, and Gorbachev then suggested that they keep talking rather than go home. "Okay," said Reagan. The meetings would continue after lunch. Shultz and Shevardnadze, and their "experts," continued talking and scribbling. Even after the President and the General Secretary left, there was a heroic magnetism around the table, a sense that history was being made in that room, that people everywhere would remember these days. Shevardnadze turned to Kampelman, the American negotiator, and said: "You're a creative person—can't you think of something?" Then, to Nitze, he said: "You're so experienced, can't you come up with something?"

The Americans did—just about a hundred words written out by Linhard and Perle, who had shared the bathroom office all night:

Both sides would agree to confine themselves to research, development and testing which is permitted by the ABM Treaty, for a period of 5 years, through 1991, during which time a 50 percent reduction of strategic nuclear arsenals would be achieved. This being done, both sides will continue the pace of reductions with re-

spect to all remaining ballistic missiles with the goal of the elimination of all ballistic missiles by the end of a second 5-year period. . . .
At the end of the 10-year period, with all offensive ballistic missiles
eliminated, either side would be free to introduce defenses.*

That paragraph, approved by both Nitze and Kampelman, would
commit the superpowers to destroy more than four thousand missiles
and almost twenty thousand nuclear warheads. The Russians talked
among themselves for a while, then Shevardnadze said he was not
sure Gorbachev would accept the last sentence.

Reagan returned to Hofdi House at 3:20 P.M. He read the American
draft and liked it: "He gets his precious ABM Treaty, and we get all his
ballistic missiles. And after that we can deploy SDI."

"Can this be done?" he asked Perle, who said, "Yes."

"Are you for it?"

Perle answered yes again. But then he added: "Of course there's no
way the program [SDI] can be seen through to a successful conclusion
if we accept the restraints Gorbachev has in mind."

The President turned to Regan and said: "If we agree to the Gorbachev limitations, won't we be doing that simply so we can leave
here with an agreement?" Perle, who was there as Weinberger's surrogate—his true mission to block any broad agreement—was sure he
had won the day.

Then Gorbachev returned. He had already talked with Shevardnadze about the American draft and approved a Soviet paragraph. It
had two critical differences. The phrase "strategic offensive arms"
was used instead of "offensive ballistic missiles"—a rewording that
would mandate the destruction of nuclear bombs and cruise missiles.
And a sentence was added in the ABM Treaty section: "The testing in
space of all space components of anti-ballistic missile defense is prohibited, except research and testing conducted in laboratories."

---

* The plan to eliminate all ballistic missiles—ICBMs and SLBMs—was a secret proposal by Secretary of Defense Weinberger at a meeting with the President on June 12, 1986. Weinberger was
generally opposed to arms control proposals, but was interested in taking advantage of the fact
that ICBMs were more important to the Soviet Union than to the United States, which had more
submarine-based missiles and cruise missiles. At the time, according to the Arms Control Association, the Soviets had 9,540 warheads on 1,398 ICBMs and 3,120 submarine launchers, compared with 7,740 U.S. warheads on 1,008 ICBMs and 640 submarine launchers. In addition, the
Soviets had 3,250 warheads on 980 bombers, while the U.S. had 4,836 warheads carried by 553
bombers. The Soviets had 1,535 intermediate-range warheads on 553 launchers, and the U.S.
had 572 intermediate-range missiles on 224 launchers. (The French and British had a combined
total of 194 warheads.)

The General Secretary went on and, as the American notes recorded: "The Soviet proposal was intended to assure that today's ABM Treaty is confirmed and strengthened, with secure obligations that for ten years it will not be gone around, and that there will be no deployment of systems in space, as we go through deep reductions in the elimination of offensive weapons."

"Isn't it necessary," Reagan responded, "to pledge something to assure a defense against someone who might come along and want to redevelop nuclear missiles?"

"Why should we create other problems," Gorbachev responded, ". . . that leave one side in doubt about reducing nuclear weapons while the other side retains them in the guise of defensive weapons?"

"If the Soviets feel that strongly about strengthening the ABM Treaty, why didn't they get rid of the Krasnoyarsk radar and the whole defense structure you've built around Moscow?" said Reagan. "You have a big defense structure and we have none." *

Then the President switched gears: "Look, we're very close to an agreement. . . . Ten years from now I'll be a very old man. . . . You and I will come to Iceland and bring the last missile from each country. We'll give a tremendous party for the whole world. . . . I'd say, 'Hello, Mikhail.' You'd say, 'Ron, is it you?' "

"I don't know if I'll live ten years," said Gorbachev, "especially after negotiating with you, you're sapping all my energy."

"Well, I'm counting on living that long," Reagan said.

Gorbachev laughed. "You're past the dangerous period, you're going to live to be a hundred . . ."

"Not if I have to worry every day about being hit by a Soviet missile . . ."

"We just agreed to eliminate them."

Then Reagan had an idea: "We obviously have a different interpretation of the ABM Treaty and we have had for a long time. Let's just say we'll take this up in Washington when you come."

"No," Gorbachev said. "It's a package." He repeated what he had said a few minutes before: "If we agree on deep reductions in nuclear weapons, we need confidence the ABM Treaty will be observed during the process."

Gorbachev seemed to think he was going to get that package. The

---

* The United States considered that a Soviet radar complex, built in 1983 at Krasnoyarsk, deep in Siberia, was part of a national missile-tracking system that violated the Anti-Ballistic Missile Treaty, signed by both countries in 1972.

session broke at 4:30 P.M. so the backup teams could work on clarifying the language of "missiles" and "weapons" and "arms." During a brief break, the Soviet leader was so excited he could not sit still. Linhard and Perle went back to their bathroom desk to try to reword the package. Gorbachev stood up, then sat down, then went into a different room with Shevardnadze and said: "Everything could be decided right now."

Donald Regan, the President's chief of staff, pulled his boss aside and told him there were suggestions of continuing the meetings for another day. Reagan just said, "Oh, shit!" He had already called home and told his wife that things were going very well and he would be there for a late dinner—and none of his men were about to argue about that.

The two leaders returned to the table at 5:30 P.M. They began with new American language. The notes began:

"Gorbachev asked again whether the language on laboratory testing had been omitted on purpose.

"The President confirmed that it had been left out on purpose."

Then the two men began to go around again on the wording, trying to top each other with examples of their dedication to arms reduction. It was not about paper anymore, they were both flying in worlds of their own imaginations. Finally, the President said: "We would be reducing all nuclear weapons—cruise missiles, battlefield weapons, sub-launched and the like. It would be fine with me if we eliminated all nuclear weapons."

"We can do that," said Gorbachev. "We can eliminate them."

Suddenly, George Shultz interrupted them: "Let's do it!"

They got back on the subject of laboratory-only testing of SDI. After Gorbachev said he needed the word "laboratory" in the agreement, Reagan said: "What the hell difference does it make. . . . We can be proud of what we've done. We may not build SDI in the end; it might be too expensive. But I promised the American people that I would not give up on it. . . . I can't confine work to the laboratory."

"I can't do that," said Gorbachev.

"I can't give in," said Reagan. "I have a problem you don't have. If they criticize you, they go to jail—"

Gorbachev interrupted that one, saying: "You should read what's being said about me in our newspapers."

The notes went on: "The President continued that the people who were the most outspoken critics of the Soviet Union over the years"—

he mentioned his favorite paper, *Human Events*—"the so-called right wing, and esteemed journalists, who were the first to criticize him."

"They're kicking my brains out," Reagan said.

Gorbachev said he had done all he could, had said all he had to say.

"It's a question of one word," said Reagan. "This should not be turned down over a word."

"It's not a question of a word, it's a question of principle," Gorbachev responded. "If I let go on the testing of space weapons, I couldn't return to Moscow. . . . They call me a *durak,* a dummy."

"I'm asking you for a favor," said Reagan. "You're refusing me a favor."

"If you came to me and said things were hard for American farmers and asked me to buy American grain, I would understand. . . . But this is not an acceptable request."

Reagan said he believed the Soviet Union was violating the ABM Treaty already. "I don't talk about that much. . . . I'll say nothing outside this room. But we should not stop because of one word. I'm asking you to change your mind as a favor to me, so hopefully we can go out and bring peace to the world."

"I can't do it," said Gorbachev. "But if we could agree to ban research in space, I'd sign in two minutes."

The notes end: "At that point the President stood, and both leaders gathered up their papers and left the room. As they stood together before departing, glaring, Gorbachev tried to soften the moment by asking the President to pass on his regards to Nancy Reagan. . . . Since Gorbachev was officially the 'host' of the meeting, the President departed first from the site."

They stepped out into a cold rain. Chilled staff members and reporters, with no idea of what had happened, were in something of a frenzy. Assistant Press Secretary James Kuhn rushed up to Reagan to ask about a joint statement. "No statement," Reagan snapped, his emphasis on the first word. Blinding lights flashed into the bleakness as the American television networks went to live coverage. Reagan would not look at Gorbachev and reporters overheard the Russian saying: "I'm sorry it didn't work out. I don't know what else I could have done."

"You could have said 'Yes,' " Reagan said. He still avoided looking at Gorbachev.

The President pushed into his limousine, sitting next to Shultz. "Goddamnit!" he said, then looked away from the window and the television lights. He went back to the American ambassador's apartment to rest before heading home. Poindexter was there.

"Mr. President," he said, "we've got to clear up this business about you agreeing to eliminate all nuclear weapons."

"John, I did agree to that."

"No, you couldn't have."

"John, I was there and I did."

Reagan was not interested in talking, and Shultz was dispatched to the auditorium of the press center to tell the American story. Glassy-eyed with fatigue, the Secretary used the word "disappointed" a half-dozen times.

"No one who attended the summit, or watched the Secretary's televised news conference to the end," wrote David Ottaway of *The Washington Post*, "is likely to forget the sense of almost grief etched across Shultz's usually expressionless face." Sam Donaldson of ABC News was more graphic, telling viewers: "Shultz looks like his dog has just been run over by a truck."

There was gloom and confusion aboard Air Force One as the plane headed home. On the ground, Gorbachev was still talking, holding a press conference in Reykjavik that lasted almost an hour and a half. The President's men knew that the American correspondents aboard had already filed their stories. They had written and dictated while Reagan traveled thirty miles to a NATO base at Keflavik for a pep talk to three thousand American soldiers and airmen. The theme of those stories, as Matlock wrote across his notepad, was: "FAILURE!"

The only man around the President who was smiling was his old social friend, the ever-cheerful Charles Wick, director of the United States Information Service. "Ronnie, you just won the Cold War," he said. "They admitted they can't compete. They don't have the money to fight the dollar."

No one said anything, until Reagan looked up: "I hope you're right. . . ."

Donald Regan was staring at Reagan, who seemed inert. He had already told his wife that he thought the President was failing mentally. But, physically, he was still as strong as a horse and could go one-on-one for hours with a younger man in his prime. The salesman in Regan suddenly took over. The man who rose to the top of Merrill Lynch by persuading people to buy stocks and bonds said: "We can't go home this way, like a team that lost the World Series." Switching sports metaphors, he said administration spokesmen should say that their team went ninety-nine yards down the field and there was no shame in not making that last yard. The chief spokesman, Speakes, pulled out a stack of Air Force One stationery and began to prepare a media plan, a crusade against FAILURE. Shultz would be sent to the editorial boards of *The New York Times, The Wall Street Journal,* and *The Washington Post*; Buchanan would do *Good Morning America*; Ken Adelman, director of the Arms Control and Disarmament Agency, would go on the *Today* show; Nitze got *The CBS Morning News*. Speakes laid out ninety-three media shots, all to declare victory. The line was: Reagan stood up to the Soviets! It began with Poindexter, who usually avoided the press, going back to brief the pool reporters on Air Force One. He kneeled down with his elbows on the low press table, puffing his pipe as the correspondents leaned forward, listening to him laying out the case that the Soviets were accepting American proposals until Gorbachev ruined everything because of his intransigence and ignorance on SDI. Hugh Sidey of *Time* magazine wrote a single-spaced four-page "Pool Report" for the reporters traveling on a backup plane:

> Somber, weary but eager to explain the perplexing events in Reykjavik, Poindexter talked for an hour and twenty minutes. . . . He was tieless, stubble on his face, but he stated at the outset that the story was so complex and difficult to understand. "We really did not expect to get agreements," the Admiral explained. "We felt the best we could do was focus the issues for agreements to be negotiated later. . . . It was the U.S. intent to negotiate a complete test ban ONLY when the two sides had reached the point of complete elimination of nuclear missiles."

He went through classes and subclasses of weapons and launchers to the point that Sidey, just as tired as Poindexter, wrote, "I am frankly a little hazy here . . . would advise further checking." Then, toward the end, the columnist continued:

> "The meeting did not end in bitterness," insisted Poindexter. "There was a sadness on our part." . . . At this point our source went on background. . . . Maybe, our source suggests, Gorbachev has a political problem, being so far out on a limb now he cannot yield on SDI. The rhetoric may have gotten out ahead of reality, says our man. . . . Back on the record: "We're not going to give up," he

declared. "We are going to find some way to preserve SDI and still have reductions in nuclear weapons. Both sides need to reflect on what happened."

He ended grandly, saying this summit was a turning point in reducing the dangers of the nuclear age. "Wow!" said Regan, watching the reporters scribbling on. "A star is born."

The real stars went on national television in two nations on Monday evening, October 13. Reagan spoke less than twenty-four hours after he arrived back in the White House for a very late dinner with his wife. From the Oval Office, the President blamed the Soviets for the collapse of the instant summit, but he repeated his invitation to Gorbachev for an American summit. He was generally upbeat, saying: "We made progress in Iceland. . . . We offered the complete elimination of all ballistic missiles—Soviet and American—from the face of the earth by 1996. . . . SDI is America's security guarantee if the Soviets should—as they have done too often in the past—fail to comply with their solemn commitments. While we parted company with this American offer still on the table, we are closer than ever before to agreements that could lead to a safer world without nuclear weapons."

Meanwhile, in Moscow, General Secretary Gorbachev was telling the Soviet people: "A turn in world history failed to take place, although it was possible. . . . Standing within one or two or three steps of a decision that could become historic for the entire nuclear-technological age, we were unable to take those steps." And he blamed Reagan: "I did all I could, but only a madman could go ahead with arms control while the United States was developing a space weapons system." The next morning, though, he was blunt and angry during a secret Kremlin meeting with sixteen Politburo members, perhaps telling them what he thought they wanted to hear: "As far as Reagan was concerned we have to wage a struggle in Reykjavik not only with the class enemy but also with a representative of it characterized by extreme primitivism, caveman appearance, and intellectual impotence. . . . When Reagan bid farewell to me, he could not bring himself to look into my eyes." His language was tough with his own men, but less so around the world, and he told his comrades: "After Reykjavik we collected more scores in our favor than after Geneva. In a way, we traded sides with the Americans. Before we usually lagged behind them in promoting our information for consumption in the outer world. We were late in giving interviews, conducting press conferences. This process should be developed further. Reykjavik must become a new beginning for our propaganda. It should acquire a more aggressive character."

In his speech, as always, Reagan tried to simplify language and concepts, carefully spelling out the meaning of the acronyms ABM and SDI. But even after the speech, there was confusion about what had happened in the small dining room of Hofdi House—and great concern about what concessions the President had made when he was alone with Gorbachev or when the two of them were alone with their foreign ministers. The words "ballistic," "strategic," "missiles," and "weapons" were thrown around so casually in two languages that no one was sure what they meant behind the guarded doors of Iceland's haunted house.

Headlines on the front pages of *The New York Times* over the next two weeks chronicled the statements, leaks, and misunderstandings as officials in Washington and Moscow tried to write (or rewrite) the history of those extraordinary days in Iceland. The *Times*'s post-summit coverage kicked off with an October 15 "News Analysis" under the headline "Summit Puzzles Linger." The same day's *Washington Post* claimed to have unraveled part of the puzzle. Haynes Johnson wrote of the 1940 Reagan film *Murder in the Air* and its "inertia projector." "There it is, presidential biographers," wrote Johnson. "Substitute particle beam for inertia projector and missiles for planes, and you have President Reagan launching the Strategic Defense Initiative."

The *Times* headlines continued:

October 18:   Shultz Details Reagan's Arms Bid
                    At Iceland to Clarify U.S. Position

October 23:   Gorbachev Says
                    U.S. Is Twisting
                    Iceland Results

October 24:   U.S. SAYS 2 LEADERS
                    SPOKE OF GIVING UP
                    ALL NUCLEAR ARMS

                    Seeks to Clarify Summit

October 26:   REAGAN IS QUOTED
BY SOVIET ON END
OF ALL ATOM ARMS

October 27:   U.S. SAYS RUSSIANS
VIOLATE DIPLOMACY
BY QUOTING TALKS

October 28:   U.S. OFFICIAL BACKS
MOSCOW'S VERSION
OF REAGAN STAND

It was not only the press that was befuddled about what Reagan
had been thinking. Publicly, Henry Kissinger was on the *NBC Nightly
News* saying: "When one side suddenly springs a major plan on
the other and expects it to be negotiated in 36 hours, that's preposterous and outrageous." A former Secretary of Defense, James
Schlesinger, spoke for much of the country's national security establishment, writing: "For a generation, the security of the Western
world has rested on nuclear deterrence. Its goal has been not only to
deter nuclear attack but also massive conventional assault from the
East. . . . The American position at Reykjavik seems to have reflected
no understanding of these simple fundamentals." Calling SDI nothing but a distant hope, Schlesinger concluded that the idea itself
probably did more to protect the United States than it ever could in
the future, because Reagan's stubborn and dreamy fixation saved him
from decimating the country's nuclear arsenal. Prime Minister
Thatcher was also badly shaken by Reagan's performance at Reykjavik. She came to Camp David after the summit to persuade Reagan
to issue a joint statement reaffirming his commitment to the modernization of Great Britain's nuclear force. Her political future was on the
line, she told him, because her opposition, the Labour Party, was
against nuclear weapons on British soil and Labour spokesmen were
beginning to say that they, not Thatcher, stood with Reagan and the
Americans.

On the last day of October, in the Situation Room of the White
House, the chairman of the Joint Chiefs of Staff, Admiral William
Crowe, sure he would be fired for what he was about to do, read a
four-page statement listing the dangers and costs of eliminating ballistic missiles, reminding everyone in the room that missiles were cheap,

that replacing them with planes and men would mean a 12 percent annual increase in military spending. He looked at Reagan as he read his last paragraph, ending with: "Mr. President, we have concluded that the proposal to eliminate all ballistic missiles within ten years time would pose high risks to the security of the nation."

Reagan nodded and began talking about his visit to the NATO base at Keflavik, saying it reminded him of how much he loved the young men and women defending the frontiers of freedom. "I really love the U.S. military. . . . Everywhere I go I tell people how proud I am of our armed forces. . . . I am constantly trying to get the country to recognize and understand the true value of our military."

Americans, at least poll respondents, decided that Reagan had done great, as they almost always did when American and Soviet leaders talked and shook hands. All the major public-opinion polls indicated that Americans supported the President's summit performance by better than three to one. In a *Wall Street Journal*/NBC News national poll, the count was 71 percent favorable to just 16 percent negative. Inside the White House, pollster Richard Wirthlin told the President his overall approval rating had jumped from 64 to 73 percent, a record high. Interestingly, and despite Gorbachev's diatribe before the Politburo, Reagan received passing marks, too, from some of his adversaries.

The most influential adviser in Gorbachev's inner circle, Alexander Yakovlev, who had studied in the United States and served ten years as the Soviet ambassador to Canada, was surprised by Reagan in action, saying: "I saw his human hesitation about what decision to make, and it seems to me he wasn't acting. I saw his internal hesitation, his batting back and forth in his mind what to do. . . . He was interested in universal nuclear disarmament. I saw that his professional ability to put on an act somehow wavered. He could be seen from a different angle as a human being and a politician." The Soviet chief of staff, Marshal Akhromeyev, who Matlock believed was there to guarantee that Gorbachev understood the positions of the Soviet military, greatly impressed most of the Americans. And he was impressed, too, saying: "I am an eyewitness to the fact that all these proposals were made in all seriousness. This was a great moral breakthrough in our relations, when the sides were able to look far into the future." Reading and listening to the Soviet reaction before briefing Reagan, Matlock began to think that something had happened that was more important than anything on paper: "We saw their bottom line and they saw ours." *

In the middle of the summit replays, the President clearly did have something to celebrate at home. The Senate and House versions of his Tax Reform Act of 1986 had finally been reconciled. On October 22, with the United States Marine Band playing patriotic tunes, he signed the 879-page bill. Many of those pages were filled with the deductions and loopholes he intended to eliminate—it was hardly the "Second American Revolution" he had promised in January of 1985—but it did mandate a gradual change to two brackets of individual tax rates, 15 percent and 28 percent, and a single corporate rate of 34 percent. On the same day, the Treasury Department announced that the fiscal 1986 federal deficit was $220.7 billion, the highest in the country's history.

On November 3, the front-page news in Washington was the release of an American hostage in Beirut, David Jacobsen, the director of the American University Hospital. He was the third hostage whose release had been purchased by arms. He was let go three days after a shipment of another five hundred TOW missiles to Iran, part of the deal negotiated by North in Frankfurt a month earlier. That left six more hidden somewhere in the city as kidnappings were happening faster than releases. The fifth paragraph of the Jacobsen story in *The New York Times* read: "There was also a report in a Beirut publication that is usually well informed on Iranian affairs that said the United States had sent spare parts and ammunition for American-built fighter planes and tanks that Iran bought from the United States before the fall of Shah Mohammad Riza Pahlevi in 1979. The report was denied by the State Department."

The Beirut story, in a weekly magazine called *Al-Shirra,* began a very bad forty-eight hours for the White House. November 4 was

---

* Gorbachev agreed with that in later years. In an interview for the television series *American Experience* he said: "The process that was eventually started and that brought that about . . . one treaty and further treaties . . . Reykjavik is really the top of the hill. And from that top, we saw a great deal." Gorbachev visited George Shultz at Stanford University after they were both out of power. Shultz remembered the conversation: "I said to him, When you entered office and when I entered office, the Cold War could not have been colder, and when we left, it was basically over. What do you think was the turning point? And he said, without any hesitation, just like that, he said 'Reykjavik.' And I said, Why?, expecting him to talk about missiles and stuff like that. He said, 'Because for the first time the two leaders really had a deep conversation about everything. We really exchanged views, and not just about peripheral things, about the central things, and that was what was important about Reykjavik.' "

election day. The President's pollster, Richard Wirthlin, had been warning him since the campaign kicked off in September that it would be a rough one. "Americans increasingly believe that the period of economic recovery may be ending," Wirthlin reported to the boss, who was as personally popular as he had been for almost four years. "Only one in four people (27%) say the economy has improved in the past year. This represents the lowest proportion of economic optimists in three and a half years." Reagan thought he could make SDI the issue, making peace-through-strength speeches in twenty-two states. "Don't make me a six-year President" was his mantra. But by midnight election night it was obvious that the Republicans had lost control of the Senate. Exit polls pointed to two factors: "Reagan Democrats"—working-class Democrats who had voted for the President twice—had gone back to their party and its candidates, and black voters in the South had come out in greater than usual numbers to vote against Reagan's Republicans. Of the thirty-four senators up for reelection, twenty-two were Republicans, nineteen of whom had been swept into office in the 1980 Reagan landslide—and seven of the nineteen were defeated in states where the economy lagged behind national growth rates. The new count was fifty-five Democrats and forty-five Republicans. Analysts speculated or pontificated one more time that this was finally the end of the Reagan Revolution. One of them, a Republican consultant, was quoted as saying: "The President had no new agenda and the voters got tired hearing him campaign against Jimmy Carter again." There was only one nonelection story on the front page of the *Times* that day. The headline read:

Iran Says McFarlane and 4 Others
Went to Teheran on a Secret Trip

The story was based on a statement in Tehran by the Speaker Rafsanjani, the man McFarlane had waited for day after day. The White House refused to comment. There was no White House comment again the next day as newspapers across the country reported that the McFarlane trip appeared to be part of secret arms-for-hostages swaps. "Fanciful stuff, mostly fiction," said McFarlane after reporters tracked him down giving a speech in Highland Heights, Ohio. The President himself finally commented, saying there was "no foundation" for the story: "We will never pay off terrorists because that only encourages more of it."

Then, on November 8, the lead story of *The New York Times* was headlined:

REAGAN APPROVED
IRANIAN CONTACTS,
OFFICIALS REPORT

Secret Approaches Sought to
Improve Relations and to
Help Free Hostages

The hunt was on. Reporters questioned Secretary of State Shultz, who was headed for arms control talks in Vienna. "I'm not going into all that," he said. "The story is being handled by the White House." The White House was on the move as well. The President was in Los Angeles. Pool reporters caught him as he boarded Air Force One for the trip back to Washington. "Is it true? Did we trade arms for hostages?" Reagan first tried to ignore them, but finally snapped, "No comment." In his diary, on November 12, he wrote: "This whole irresponsible press bilge about hostages and Iran has gotten totally out of hand. The media looks like it's trying to create another Watergate."

CHAPTER 17
NOVEMBER 25, 1986

O N NOVEMBER 10, the President called an Oval Office meeting. Vice President Bush, Chief of Staff Regan, Shultz, back from Vienna, Weinberger, Casey, Attorney General Meese, and Poindexter were all there. The official note-taker was Alton G. Keel, one of Poindexter's deputies. This was official, the first meeting to discuss the legal and political implications of the extraordinary arms shipments to Iran. Casey, for one, had already told Oliver North he should get a criminal lawyer. Everyone there, except for the President, was taking his own notes, the surest sign of crisis in the capital. Reagan opened the meeting, which was unusual, and he did most of the talking, which was more unusual. Poindexter droned through a chronology that began with the President's finding of January 17, 1986, authorizing arms sales by the United States to Iran. Most of what he said was inaccurate, including the fact that no mention was made of American-approved deliveries of TOW and HAWK missiles from Israeli stocks to Iran on August 20, 1985, September 15, 1985, and November 18, 1985. Then Reagan took over again and repeated that the point of the meeting was to agree on a White House statement.

Don Regan, who was taking extensive notes as well, recorded exchanges that indicated that neither Shultz nor Weinberger had known of the presidential finding.

President: We must say something but not much.

Poindexter: If we go with this we end our Iranian contacts.

Regan: We must get statement out now, we are being attacked, and we are being hurt. Losing credibility.

President: Must say something because I'm being held out to dry. Have not dealt with terrorists, don't know who they are. This is long range Iranian policy. No further speculation or answers so as not to endanger hostages. We won't pay any money or give anything to terrorists.

Poindexter: Say less about what we are doing, more about what we are not doing.

Weinberger: Be careful of Rafsanjani + Israel + blackmail. What we say will be repudiated.

Shultz: We are saying only what we did and know has happened. . . . Finding was not known to me from Jan to Nov—amazing. . . .

President: Support Pres' policy but say nothing else due to danger to hostages.

Shultz: Support Iran long range policy of contact—No support for weapons for hostages.

"We have not dealt directly with terrorists, no bargaining, no ransom," Reagan said several times. "We don't talk TOWs, don't talk specifics, avoid specifics," he said twice, according to Keel's notes. In his notes, Regan also wrote: *"President:* 'Terrorists have not profited. We let . . . Iranians by supplying and they influenced. No benefits to terrorists. We were working with moderates, hoping in future to be able to influence Iran after Khomeini dies.' "

"It is ransom," Shultz responded, annoying the President.

Then Reagan said that good contacts had been made in Iran and the affair should be put in the context of United States neutrality in the war between Iran and Iraq, that we wanted no winner. "This helps Iran," he said, "which was weaker."

Actually, Iran was stronger and the United States had been supplying substantial amounts of matériel and intelligence since 1983 to keep the Iraqis going, and to keep its President, Saddam Hussein, in power. But then little was said in the meeting that was actually true. At one point, Meese interjected, "We didn't sell. Israel sold."

According to Regan's notes, the meeting ended with the President laying out an official response: "We have not dealt directly with terrorists, no bargaining, no ransom. Some things we can't discuss because of long-term considerations of people with whom we have been talking about the future of Iran." That was translated and abridged to an official statement: "Our policy of not making concessions to terrorists remains intact."

Washington was in heat. "We face a grave communications problem over this Iranian/Hostage issue," Pat Buchanan wrote in a memo to Don Regan on November 12. "I realize this is all being held extremely tight, for obviously good reasons, but we have already witnessed some jubilant assaults upon Ronald Reagan's reputation for principle—from his enemies—and some bitter assaults from some of his friends. . . . We are fortunate Congress is out."

The President decided to go on television the next night. He began:

> I know you've been reading, seeing, and hearing a lot of stories the past several days. [He attributed them to "unnamed" sources.] Well, now you're going to hear the facts from a White House source, and you know my name. . . . The charge has been made that the United States has shipped weapons to Iran as ransom payment for the release of American hostages in Lebanon, that the United States undercut its allies and secretly violated American policy against trafficking with terrorists. Those charges are utterly false. The United States has not made concessions to those who hold our people captive in Lebanon. And we will not. . . . All these reports are quite exciting, but as far as we're concerned, not one of them is true. . . .
>
> For eighteen months now we have had underway a secret diplomatic initiative to Iran. . . . During the course of our secret discussion, I authorized the transfer of small amounts of defensive weapons and spare parts for defensive systems to Iran. My purpose was to convince Tehran that our negotiators were acting with my authority, to send a signal . . . these modest deliveries, taken together, could easily fit into a small single cargo plane.

That was not true, nor was most of the rest of the speech truthful. Reagan said the real purpose of the secret moves was: "To help preserve Iran's independence from Soviet domination; to bring an honorable end to the bloody Iran-Iraq war; to halt the export of subversion and terrorism in the region." He said that he had personally ordered McFarlane's secret trip to Tehran, comparing it to Henry Kissinger's secret trip to Beijing in 1972 to prepare for the visit of President Nixon to that country later in the year.

This time, words failed Reagan. The first national poll after the speech, by ABC News, reported that only 22 percent of respondents approved of the President's stated policy of sending arms to Iran to improve relations. A second question asked about trading arms for hostages, and approval dropped to 17 percent. Later polls were worse: Americans believed the President was lying to them. A national poll by the *Los Angeles Times,* three days later, reported that only 14 percent of respondents believed the White House was not trading arms for hostages. The day that poll was published, Nixon telephoned Reagan and told him that he had to admit the whole thing was a mistake.

That was never Reagan's style. He was a politician willing to compromise when he had to, but he was a man who rarely admitted it. He believed what he said because he had said it.

Over the weekend of November 16, administration officials seemed to be everywhere, trying to defend the Iran operation and their President—with decidedly mixed results. Don Regan produced the quote of the day on Saturday, telling *The New York Times*: "Some of us are like a shovel brigade that follows a parade down Main Street cleaning up"—bragging about how well the White House had done in turning the Reykjavik summit into a public relations triumph. "I don't say we'll be able to do it four times in a row, but here we go again, we're trying." On Sunday, Shultz was the star, a reluctant one. Assigned to appear on *Face the Nation,* the CBS News program hosted by Lesley Stahl, he was asked: "Will there be any more arms shipments to Iran, either directly by our government or through any third parties?"

"It's certainly against our policy," Shultz said.

"That's not an answer," Stahl replied. "Why won't you answer the question directly? I'll ask it again. Will there be any more arms shipments to Iran?"

"I would certainly say, as far as I'm concerned, no."

"Do you have the authority to speak for the entire administration?"

"No."

The show ended. Stahl was the first to speak: "I need a drink."

"I never should have come on," said Shultz.

CIA director Casey wrote a note to Reagan saying Shultz had to be fired for disloyalty. That was leaked of course, and the President had to respond: "I'm not firing anybody." That did not stop half the Congress and all the press from speculating about who would have to go: Regan, Shultz, or Poindexter. Then the President announced that he would tell the Iran story himself once again, this time at a press conference on November 19. Shultz, in a stronger position now, briefed him that day, saying, "We have been deceived and lied to. . . . You have to watch out about saying no arms for hostages."

"You're telling me things I don't know," Reagan replied.

"Mr. President," said the Secretary of State, "if I'm telling you something you don't know—and I don't know very much—something is wrong here. . . . Our credibility is shot. We've taken refuge in tricky technicalities of language to avoid confronting the reality that we lied to the American people. We have been dealing with some of the sleaziest international characters around."

The President scheduled a press conference, confident that he could explain away such talk. The first question, from Helen Thomas of United Press International, set the tone: "How would you assess the credibility of your own administration in the light of the prolonged deception of Congress and the public in terms of your secret dealings with Iran, the disinformation, the trading of Zakharov for Daniloff?"

It went from there to worse. The questions were hostile and so was the President, telling the reporters: "You've disappointed me . . . suggesting that I sound defensive up here. I don't feel that I have anything to defend about at all. . . . I don't think a mistake was made. It was a high-risk gamble that, as I've said, I believe the circumstances warranted." Whatever had been done in secret, Reagan made a string of public factual mistakes that night, saying that the arms shipped could fit in one plane, saying that the United States had nothing to do with Israeli arms shipments, saying that the TOW missiles were small, shoulder-fired weapons, when in fact they were ground-to-ground missile launchers the size of small cannons. One question referred to a confirmation by Don Regan that Israel was involved in the sales. Reagan said: "I never heard Mr. Regan say that and I'll ask him about that." After the conference, the White House issued a statement that began: "There may be some misunderstanding of one of my answers tonight. There was a third country [Israel] involved in our secret project with Iran."

Don Regan and Ronald Reagan got along well, two old Irishmen who had made their way in the world and loved telling and hearing jokes. But almost no one else liked Regan, beginning with Mrs. Reagan, who said she had little antennae that traced the words and deeds of anyone she thought had their own agenda rather than Ronnie's welfare in mind. She blamed the chief of staff when the Iran performances fell flat. Actually, she didn't need antennae; Regan had at least twice hung up on her when she had telephoned to say her husband needed more rest. She was the leader of a band that was playing "Regan must go." It was a big band. Not only did Regan hang up on the First Lady, he also practically never answered calls from congressmen or senators. Within the bipartisan bonds of elected officials, a different breed from appointed overseers, there were men and women waiting to kick Don Regan on the way down.

As the President was speaking to the press and the nation, there was a party of sorts going on the third floor of the Old Executive Office Building. "A shredding party," said Oliver North, the host. Along with an assistant, Robert Earl, and his twenty-seven-year-old secretary, Fawn Hall, whose mother, Wilma Hall, was McFarlane's secretary, North was systematically destroying stacks of documents, one of them over two feet high when the work began. The three went to work after North had received a telephone call from the Justice Department informing him that department attorneys were planning to look through his files. Attorney General Meese, who had been ordered by Reagan to make a preliminary investigation into the Iran scheming, had just received information indicating that there might be a connection between the Iranian affair and contra funding. That information came in a telephone call from Abraham Sofaer, the State Department's chief counsel, who had been looking into both the Iran arms shipments and the case of Eugene Hasenfus, the American who had been shot down over Nicaragua.

On November 15, Hasenfus had been sentenced to thirty years in jail by a Nicaraguan court, and one fact that had come out during his short trial was that his C-123 was owned by a corporation called Southern Air Transport. The company, created and owned by the CIA until 1973, owned the planes that had been used to move weaponry to Iran. "Something is going on," Sofaer told one of Meese's deputies. The Attorney General himself was already focusing on the gross differences between the cost of all the missiles sent to Iran (approximately $12 million) and the prices paid by the Iranians (which may have totaled as much as $42 million). No one ever worked out all the numbers, much less traced what happened to the "profits." *

The shredding at the Executive Office Building continued through the weekend of November 22–23 and on Monday and Tuesday as

---

* Hasenfus was pardoned and released by the Nicaraguans on December 17, 1986, after serving only a month of his sentence.

well—even after a Justice Department team headed by William Brad-ford Reynolds was in North's offices inspecting documents. The shredder broke down twice. The first time, North called the White House Crisis Management Center, which sent over a man to fix the paper-choked machine. The next time, North just took papers over to the White House Situation Room and used the big machine there to rip up memos and other papers. Hall also went over to the White House, going to "System 4," the NSC's locked master file in the White House. She retyped four of those documents, changing dates and names and eliminating incriminating words and para-graphs. With North dictating, she reduced one four-page memo to a single page, going back into the White House and slipping the new versions into the central files. Nearby, in his White House office, Poindexter opened the safe, then destroyed the signed copy—the only copy—of the President's December 5, 1985, finding, the postdated document designed to make earlier shipments of HAWK parts to Iran appear to be legal. It also specified that the weaponry was ransom paid to free hostages.

But, at the end of the day on November 23, Sunday, while the President was at Camp David, the Justice Department searchers did find a copy of the April 4, 1986, North memo to Poindexter, the "diversion memo," the document that proved the Iran-contra con-nection.

On Monday morning, after the President's return from Camp David, he presided over a two-hour meeting about the Iranian sales and he got into an argument with Shultz, who continued to make the point that he had been against the operation from the beginning. It was not until 4:30 that afternoon that Meese and Regan came into the Oval Office to tell Reagan about the diversion memo discovered the day before. That night, in his diary, the President wrote: "After the meeting in the Situation Room, Ed M. and Don R. told me of a smok-ing gun. On one of the arms shipments the Iranians had paid Israel a higher purchase price than we were getting. The Israelis put the differ-ence in a secret bank account. Then our Colonel North (N.S.C.) gave the money to the 'Contras' . . . North didn't tell me about this. Worst of all, John P. found out about it and didn't tell me. This may call for resignations."

So it did, but the shredding continued as the resigning began. When she left the office the next day, Tuesday, Fawn Hall stuffed some pa-pers into her boots and the back of her dress to get them out of the building before more Justice Department investigators arrived. But it was too late; the investigators had shown the diversion memo to Meese.

Poindexter, after talking with Meese and Regan, went to the Oval Office and said: "Mr. President, I assume that you are aware of the paper that Ed Meese has found that reveals a plan to transfer funds to the contras. I was generally aware of the plan and I would like to submit my resignation to give you the necessary latitude to do whatever you need to do." He shook hands with the President and left. Reagan and Meese headed for the press office, where the President asserted that information generated by the Meese inquiry made him realize that he had never been fully informed about the Iranian operation. The Attorney General—called Inspector Clouseau behind his back after the comic detective in the *Pink Panther* film—came to the White House and stood with Reagan in the press room as the President announced that his fourth National Security Adviser would be leaving. "Although not directly involved, Admiral John Poindexter has asked to be relieved of his duties," said Reagan. "Lieutenant Colonel Oliver North has been relieved of his duties."

North learned he was finished on television, watching the President's unscheduled appearance in the press room. A reporter there called to Reagan, as he turned to leave: "Did you make a mistake in sending arms to Tehran, sir?" Reagan was annoyed but he answered: "No, and I'm not taking any more questions." Meese then stepped up and publicly revealed for the first time that as much as $30 million of the money paid by Iranians had ended up in numbered Swiss bank accounts, which may have been controlled by contra leaders.*

The three top leaders of the United Nicaraguan Opposition—Adolfo Calero, Alfonso Robelo, and Arturo Cruz—immediately denied that. "The administration is in disarray," Vice President Bush wrote that night in the diary he kept. "Cover up. Who knew what and when." But whatever the Vice President thought, the President still admired the swashbuckling North. He was not bothered by the fact that North had lied and lied about one-on-one Oval Office meetings. White House operators found the colonel in a Washington hotel room

---

* In his final report, Lawrence Walsh, the special prosecutor appointed to do the criminal investigation of Iran-contra, wrote: "Meese was conducting the November 21–24 investigation as 'counsellor and friend' to the President, not as the nation's chief law enforcement officer. Independent counsel concluded that he was not so much searching for the truth . . . as he was building a case of deniability for his client-in-fact, President Reagan."

with his co-conspirator, Richard Secord—so Reagan could thank him for all he had done. "You're an American hero," said the President as North stood at attention, saluting the phone. He also told the man he had just fired on national television that his story would make a good movie.

Mrs. Reagan did not agree. That night she saw Oliver North on television, being asked if he planned to seek immunity from criminal prosecution. "Immunity," he said. "If I had immunity, I wouldn't have this bad cold."

"Not funny, sonny!" she said to the set.

On the NBC Nightly News, after anchorman Tom Brokaw and correspondents reviewed the startling news of the day, Brokaw concluded with an interview with Henry Kissinger. "Is it conceivable," the anchorman asked, "that this operation could have been carried out by a single Marine Lt. Colonel . . . ?

"No," said Kissinger. "It is not conceivable to me."

The next day, November 26, the President announced the appointment of a "Special Review Board" to review the role and performance of the National Security Council. The chairman was John Tower, a former Republican senator from Texas. The other two members were former secretary of state and former senator Edmund Muskie, a Democrat, and General Brent Scowcroft, who had served as NSC director under President Ford. Then, before leaving for a five-day Thanksgiving break in California, Reagan did an angry telephone interview with Time magazine's Hugh Sidey, praising North for what he had done and blaming the press for the scandal:

> I have to say there is bitter bile in my throat these days. What is driving me up the wall is that this wasn't a failure until the press got a tip from that rag in Beirut and began to play it up. I told them that publicity could destroy this, that it could get people killed. They then went right on. This whole thing boils down to a great irresponsibility on the part of the press. The press has to take responsibility for what they have done. . . . Lieutenant Colonel North was involved in all our operations: the Achille Lauro, Libya. He has a fine record. He is a national hero. My only criticism is that I wasn't told everything.

The lead story of Time took the Kissinger line: "Reagan and Meese were asking the nation to believe something that seemed flat-out incredible: that Ollie North, a furtive, 43-year-old member of the NSC staff who operated out of an office across the street from the White House, had arranged the contra scam without the knowledge of the State Department, the CIA, the Joint Chiefs of Staff, the White House chief of staff or anyone in authority except his boss, Poindexter, who did nothing to stop him. . . . This disaster throws a pitiless light on the way the President does his job, confirming the worst fears of both his friends and his critics." An editorial in the *Philadelphia Daily News* was as pitiless, saying: "Reagan has surrounded himself with second-rate minds. His own, at least, is fronted by a first-rate presentation."

On the President's first day back at his desk, December 1, the morning's *New York Times* reported that its polling indicated his national approval rating had dropped 26 points in a month, from 67 percent at the beginning of November to 41 percent on November 30. A *Wall Street Journal*/NBC News poll reported that only 28 percent of respondents approved of the President's handling of foreign policy, down from 51 percent in October.

The capital city was already in full Watergate mode, with columnists and commentators debating all day in print and all evening on television whether the shipment of arms to Iran and diversion of the proceeds to underwrite the Nicaraguan contras was similar or dissimilar to the burglary and cover-up scandals that had brought down President Nixon. Certainly the daily coverage of December and the leaks that fed it were similar, if not identical, to the press performances of 1973 and 1974. Appropriately enough, one of the first of the stories—a follow-the-money tale in *The Washington Post* on the morning of December 2—was written by Bob Woodward, a Watergate press hero.

He reported that six months before, on May 23, North had solicited $2 million more from the Texas billionaire Ross Perot for deposit to a Crédit Suisse Bank account in Zurich, Switzerland (number 386-430-22-1)—an account in the name of Lake Resources, Inc. Just as Perot had been preparing to telex the funds, he was called by North and asked to send it in cash to Cyprus by courier, which he did. That afternoon, December 1, former NSC director McFarlane testified in secret for six hours before the Senate Select Intelligence Committee, which produced *The New York Times* headline: "EX-AIDE TO REAGAN IS SAID TO LINK HIM TO EARLY IRAN SALE." NBC News reported that burglars had recently broken into the office of Robert White, the ambassador to El Salvador who had been fired in the first days of the Reagan presidency. Both North and Poindexter were reported to have invoked the Fifth Amendment privilege against self-incrimination rather than answer the Senate committee's questions. The Israeli government confirmed the relationship between North and Israeli counterterrorism officials. Following the money, the *Los Angeles Times* reported that Assistant Secretary of State Elliott Abrams, an enthusiastic contra supporter, had gone to London and solicited $10 million from the government of Brunei, the rich little oil sultanate on the island of Borneo, and that the money was added to one of the Swiss accounts tied to contra aid. That was the transaction Abrams had denied in congressional testimony eleven days before. And that was also the day that both the Senate and House voted to create special Watergate-style investigating committees for this new scandal. Most bizarrely, on the day after the Abrams revelations, in Tehran Speaker Rafsanjani held a press conference to denounce the American press and Congress for unfairly attacking President Reagan, saying: "Yes, he did something foolish sending McFarlane to Iran, but he was probably just duped by arms dealers." Abrams was then called back before the committee for a tongue-lashing by Senator Thomas Eagleton, a Missouri Democrat: "Had you been under oath that's perjury. That's slammer time."

"You've heard my testimony," Abrams responded.

"I've heard it," Eagleton said. "And I want to puke."

The White House responded as well as it could. The President said he would not oppose the appointment of a special Iran-contra prosecutor, and announced the appointment of Frank Carlucci, who had served as deputy secretary of defense and deputy CIA director, as his fifth National Security Adviser. "Savvy and well-schooled in the substantive issues," editorialized *The Washington Post*. The capital's conservative paper, the *Washington Times*, quoted a prominent right-wing activist and fund-raiser, Richard Viguerie, saying: "This signals the end of the Reagan revolution. . . . He has totally capitulated to the Washington Establishment."

The editor of *The Washington Post*, Benjamin Bradlee, sort of confirmed that, saying: "Yes, this is the most fun we've had since Watergate." That prompted Pat Buchanan, a Watergate veteran back in the White House as communications director, to write a *Post* op-ed column criticizing Bradlee, but really going after congressional Republicans who were calling for investigations: "Is this how they repay the leader who has done more for the Republican Party than any American since Theodore Roosevelt, who brought us back from Watergate?"

Buchanan's essay was published as the administration began to aggressively rally 'round the President. Four White House speechwriters—Anthony Dolan, Peter Robinson, Josh Gilder, and Clark Judge submitted drafts of "Remarks for Administration Surrogates" on December 9. Their lines, circulated throughout the executive departments and to the friendliest members of Congress, included:

It was the President—not the Congress or the media—who revealed that funds had been diverted to the contras. . . . As Secretary Shultz said the other day: "There is no Constitutional crisis; to the contrary, our system of Government is working well.". . . The President has taken the lead in disclosing what's wrong and setting things right. His personal qualities of candor and honesty have never been more apparent. . . . A cover-up, never. . . . No American involved in the Iranian controversy profited by so much as a penny. . . . That's taken leadership. That's taken a man who stands taller than any president we've had in generations. That's why I'm so proud today to serve with Ronald Reagan. . . . When it comes to Iran, there's no question that mistakes were made lower down in the Administration, but the President's purposes were courageous, even noble. And I say more power to him.

Another set of "White House Talking Points" were prepared at the same time in question-and-answer pages, including: "Question 9. Why doesn't the President order Oliver North and John Poindexter to stop 'taking the Fifth Amendment' and tell the truth?"

"Answer: Because the President is sworn to uphold the Constitution and they are exercising a Constitutional right."

Other papers provided guidance for dealing with the press: "Question 3. Is this another Watergate?"

"Answer: Absolutely not . . . There is one striking similarity, however: The Left's interest in bringing down another President. . . . There is a whole new generation of reporters out there who missed their chance 12 years ago to win a Pulitzer Prize."

In the editing, that one included a marginal comment: "Who is picking this fight? Us or the Press? Can't we stay on the high ground—must we grovel in the slime with the Press whores?"

On December 10, in full Marine uniform, ribbons, and medals, Oliver North appeared before the first public session of the House committee investigating the Iran operations. The chairman, Representative Lee Hamilton of Indiana, asked: "Colonel North, did you make the decision to put the proceeds of the arms sales to Iran into an account for the use of the contras?" North answered: "Mr. Hamilton, on the advice of counsel I respectfully and regretfully decline to answer the question based on my constitutional rights." He answered every other question the same way. The same thing happened when the committee questioned Admiral Poindexter and Richard Secord, the retired Air Force general who had worked unofficially with North to handle the transportation of weapons to Iran.

The press was alive now, part of the process after years of accepting without much serious question great communications from the man in the Oval Office. On one day, December 15, the front page of *The New York Times* reported that North and Secord personally controlled Swiss accounts, that a Saudi arms merchant named Adnan Khashoggi was part of the money chain, and that a Massachusetts paper, the *Lowell Sun*, was reporting that North was diverting some of the funds into the campaigns of congressmen who supported the contras. The next day, President Reagan urged the congressional committees headed by Representative Hamilton and Senator Daniel Inouye, a Hawaii Democrat, to offer "use immunity" to North and Poindexter in return for their testimony—that is, nothing they said could be used against them in criminal prosecutions. The committees lost the chance to question a third major figure in the covert operations when CIA director Casey collapsed in his office on December 15, the day before he was scheduled to testify. The seventy-three-year-old director was rushed to Georgetown Hospital after his arms and legs went into violent spasms. Brain seizures. Chief of Staff Regan replaced Casey as a witness, secretly testifying that the President never approved arms sales from Israeli stockpiles to the Iranians, a direct contradiction of earlier sworn testimony by McFarlane that the President knew of and personally approved the Israel-to-Iran deal in August of 1985.

Finally, on December 19, the investigation took a new turn when a panel of three judges named by Meese selected a special prosecutor—"Independent Counsel" was the official title—charged with unraveling the legal implications of the eighteen months of arms trades, cash diversions, and lies upon lies. Their choice was Lawrence Walsh, a seventy-four-year-old retired federal judge who had once served as president of the American Bar Association. He was a Republican and he admired the job Reagan had been doing. Still, he had a secret reservation, an interesting one: Walsh thought Reagan's refusal to campaign enthusiastically for President Ford in 1976 had cost Ford the election. He thought Reagan had betrayed the party and its nominee because he wanted the presidency for himself.

Except for the President's thirty-minute State of the Union message, his sixth on January 27—he spoke of balancing the federal budget as he presented the first one of more than a trillion dollars—Reagan was barely visible in early 1987. "Virtual seclusion" was the phrase used by *The Wall Street Journal*. Part of that was health, part strategy. The health part was, as always, the business of the President's wife. Returning from California after a New Year's holiday, the President went once more to Bethesda Naval Hospital, this time for relatively minor prostate surgery—there was no cancer—and his wife, ever protective, wanted him to follow doctors' orders. That is, take a full six weeks for recuperation. The strategy part was staying away from microphones and cameras to avoid talking in public about Iran and the contras. The idea was to distance himself from the press frenzy as his top assistants went from one hearing to another, generally contradicting one another about what the President knew, and when he knew it. On the day before his State of the Union speech, the President had met for the first time with the Tower Commission. The secret session lasted more than seventy minutes, with the questioning focused on whether Reagan had authorized arms shipments from Israel to Iran in 1985. He insisted he had trouble remembering details like that, but finally answered "Yes."

On January 29, the first official report on Iran-contra, a sixty-five-page document released by the Senate Select Committee, one of seven ongoing official investigations, emphasized the President's personal concern for hostages held in Beirut and said that, in reality, the Iran operation was a straightforward arms-for-hostages deal. It stated that President Reagan had indeed approved every significant move involving Iran. The report also revealed for the first time that the National Security Council, over CIA objections, had provided military intelligence to the Iranian government, including satellite photographs of Iraqi positions before the Iranians' most successful attack, the taking of Fao, a port near the Kuwaiti border, in February of 1986.* As far as the profits from arms sales, the report said it could trace only part of the money involved, although it did identify numbered accounts in Switzerland and the Cayman Islands—and reported that significant amounts were controlled by Richard Secord.

The New York Times report on the contents of the document, the paper's lead story, began: "WASHINGTON, Jan. 29—A report on the Iran-contra affair made public today by the Senate Intelligence Committee portrays Reagan Administration officials as regularly deceiving one another, as well as Congress, about major elements of the operation."

The document listed dozens of lies Reagan's men told one another, including: McFarlane lied to Shultz about the role of Michael Ledeen, a middle man in American-Israeli dealings; McFarlane lied to a Senate committee about his knowledge of the role of the Iranian middleman, Manucher Ghorbanifar; U.S. officials lied about the cargoes American planes were carrying; North told CIA officials that Reagan had signed a finding that never existed; Poindexter lied to Charles Price, the United States ambassador in London, denying reports that Ghorbanifar had backing in Washington; Poindexter and Casey lied to Shultz, telling him the Iran operation had ended months before it actually did.

Three days after the report was issued, Casey, gravely ill in the hospital after his brain surgery to remove a cancerous tumor, resigned as CIA director.

Five days later, McFarlane attempted suicide. He had become more and more depressed as Shultz and Weinberger denied they knew anything about the operations he had worked on with them, and as Poindexter and North continued to refuse to talk about their roles in eighteen months of double-dealing and betrayal. Then, watching the State of the Union address, McFarlane waited for the President to acknowledge real responsibility for what had gone on. He was sure that would happen. In his years with Reagan, he had come to see the President as different from the smaller men around him. His Reagan was

---

* American intelligence agencies regularly claimed that photographs and other material supplied to both Iran and Iraq were "doctored" to prevent either side from winning the eight-year war (September 1980 to August 1988). And as for discouraging hostage-taking: three more Americans and a British hostage negotiator, Terry Waite, were seized that same week. This time, the administration response was a presidential statement: "Our government has regularly warned American citizens against travel to Lebanon. . . . Americans who ignored this warning clearly did so at their own risk and their own responsibility."

larger than life, a man with an innate personal sense of the heroic, a man in touch with destiny. But that was not the Reagan he saw on television. The President had comfortably slipped past responsibility and talked only about putting this unpleasantness behind him.

McFarlane felt abandoned. He thought he was the only one willing to talk and willing to tell the truth. He was alone. On the night of February 8, 1987, the forty-nine-year-old former National Security Adviser systematically wrote and distributed letters to be found after his death and just as systematically began taking one Valium pill after another. He took more than thirty, washing each one down with some wine. He then went upstairs to bed, to die. His wife, Jonny, awoke in the early morning hours, but could not wake him. She telephoned a friend who was a physician, then called 911. Her unconscious husband was taken to Bethesda Naval Hospital in an ambulance. He came back to consciousness at 8 A.M., February 10—two hours before he had been scheduled to testify again before the Tower Commission.

CHAPTER 18
JUNE 12, 1987

I N EARLY FEBRUARY 1987, the President asked for a second meeting with the Tower Commission, and Senator Tower, Muskie, and Scowcroft came to the White House on February 11. Reagan wanted to change his story about whether he had authorized the first shipment of American weapons and parts from Israel to Iran. Three weeks earlier, he had told the three commissioners that he had known about, and ordered, the shipment in the summer of 1985—as Bud McFarlane had told the commission under oath. Now, he said, he had talked with his chief of staff, Don Regan, and agreed with Regan's testimony that he did not know of the shipment until early 1986. No recording or official note-taking was allowed, but news of the President's shifting testimony leaked to the press within an hour after the seventy-five-minute session.

Reagan also used the sessions to try to influence the language of the forthcoming Tower report about decision-making in his White House. He worked from a three-page, seventeen-section "Talking Points" memo. "My management style has always been to choose good people, to establish clear policies and directions, and to provide those I have appointed with the authority to make the subordinate and secondary decisions to carry out my policies," the memo said. "I think this approach has worked very well. . . . But this approach also assumes that the policies I approve will be carried out in a manner which is coordinated with all the relevant members of my Administration. . . . It also assumes that when I establish policies and general directions I am able to do so with the best available information. . . . In the case of Iran the implementation was carried forward without the continuing involvement of those in my administration who might have questioned certain of the steps that were taken."

His case was made: No one told me. But the President's performance frightened the three commissioners. Except for reciting his talking points, he was vague and seemed confused. And the recitation produced the worst moment of all. Across the memo, White House counsel Peter Wallison had written another reminder in clear longhand: "On the issue of the TOW shipment in August 1985 in discussing this matter with me . . . you said that you were surprised to learn that the Israelis had shipped the arms. If that is your recollection, and if the question comes up at the Tower Board meeting, you might want to say that you were surprised."

Tower did raise the question. Reagan picked up the memo and began, saying: "If the question comes up at the Tower meeting, you might want to say that you were surprised . . ."

Reagan's know-nothing case was a tough sell. "God, it was just terrible," said Wallison, who sat with the President during the questioning. The President's spokesman, Larry Speakes, who was leaving the administration, tried to make the case that Sunday on CBS News's *Face the Nation,* but he got tangled up in contradictions when he was asked how involved the President really was in critical decision-making and he answered: "Any whispers by people who come out of the White House about Ronald Reagan not being involved and on top of the job and there for the final two years is hogwash. But Iran is a different question. The President set a good policy in motion. He thought he had good people carrying it out and those people misserved the President."

The moderator, Lesley Stahl, asked the question that engaged Washington each day and every day: "Nancy Reagan. How powerful is she really?"

Speakes answered: "She makes her viewpoint known and her judgments are very, very good."

The Washington Post, in a feature article later that week by Donnie Radcliffe, put it more directly, beginning with this lead: "Nancy Reagan's campaign to oust Donald T. Regan as White House chief of staff is portrayed by friends and other sources as a struggle to rescue Ronald Reagan's presidency, and to protect his honor, his health and his place in history." The *Post* quoted, anonymously, "one friend" who said of the forthcoming Tower report: "She said she didn't care what the report said. She just wanted it to come out so Ronnie could talk about it"—with her. There was a pattern to Mrs. Reagan's personal campaigns, most of them involving White House personnel: She told her husband whom she trusted and whom she did not. Sometimes he answered or did what she advised, sometimes he did not. Sometimes he said, "That's enough, Nancy, I understand." During the campaign to get rid of Regan, he was heard saying to his wife, "Get off my goddamn back!" He was, she said, a very stubborn man. When that happened she took to the phone, calling friends and staffers for hours or days, for weeks if she thought something was important, trying to persuade them, asking them to push her husband in her direction. Sometimes they did, sometimes they did not.

Having her way with Regan was not quick or easy. At one point she persuaded Deaver and Stuart Spencer, his old California campaign consultant, to talk to her husband. "You have to make a bold move," said Deaver to the President. "The media is not going to let you go on. You have to get rid of somebody, because you've got to do something that says, 'This is an action I'm taking and I'm gonna go on.' "

"I'll be damned if I'm going to throw someone overboard to save my own ass," the President said.

"It's not your ass, Mr. President. It's the country's ass."

As for her day-to-day role, Mrs. Reagan once told a reporter she liked, Chris Wallace of NBC News, "I think I'm aware of people who are trying to take advantage of my husband—who are trying to end-run him lots of times—who are trying to use him—I'm very aware of that."

"More aware than he is?" Wallace asked.

"Uh-huh," she said. ". . . I try to stop them."

On February 18, the reporter who knew the Reagans longest and best, Lou Cannon of *The Washington Post,* made it all but official, writing: "The First Lady is no longer speaking to Regan." Washington, at least the part of the city attached to the White House, was obsessed with this subject. William Safire of *The New York Times* wrote: "President Reagan is being weakened and made to appear wimpish by the political interference of his wife."

"The Myth of the Decisive President" was the headline over another of Cannon's columns: "[This is a] sad commentary about Reagan's inability to control the White House or deal with complex foreign policy programs." By then, the Tower Commission was completing its work, interviewing McFarlane in his hospital room on February 20 and poring over hundreds of computer messages between the former NSC director and Poindexter and North, who corresponded regularly on a White House internal e-mail system called PROFS, which had been installed in 1982. The commission only discovered the existence of the system two weeks before its report was due. By then, worried that investigators might find the e-mail, Poindexter had deleted 5,012 of his 5,062 messages and North had deleted 750 of 758. Some, but not all, of that correspondence was found saved on the building's mainframe computer located in the basement.

In two days of hospital interviews, McFarlane was asked repeatedly about the difference between Reagan's two answers as to whether he had approved the first Israeli project. He said: "The President did agree to the project on August 8, 1985 . . . I did spell it out. I said, 'Mr. President, what's involved here is the sale by Israel and ultimately them coming to us to buy replacements.' And he said: 'Yes I understand that.' And I said: 'Do you understand, of course, now that George and Cap are very much opposed to this and they have very good reasons?' And he said: 'Yes, I do, but I draw a difference between our dealing with people that are not terrorists and shipping arms to terrorists. And I'm willing to defend that.' And he even said something like: 'I will be glad to take the heat for that.' "

Later, on February 20, the President, probably aware of what McFarlane had just said, wrote a letter in longhand to Tower: "I'm afraid that I let myself be influenced by others' recollections, not my own. . . . The only honest answer is to state that try as I might, I cannot recall anything whatsoever about whether I approved a replenishment of Israeli stocks around August of 1985. My answer therefore and the simple truth is, 'I don't remember—period.' "

On February 25, Tower, Muskie, and Scowcroft came to the Oval Office again to brief the President on their findings, telling him that they had concluded that the Iranian transactions were never anything more than arms-for-hostages deals. When Reagan protested, Scowcroft said that no other conclusion was possible, the intent was clear on the day in May of 1986 when General Secord and a plane full of missiles waited on a runway in Israel, waiting for word that hostages had been released. "Yes," said Reagan finally, "if the plane was waiting there to receive word on the hostages, the arms are loaded up, then it was arms for hostages."

The Tower Commission Report was released the next day, February 26. *The New York Times* devoted all of its front page and eleven inside pages to the report under a six-column headline:

INQUIRY FINDS REAGAN AND CHIEF ADVISERS
RESPONSIBLE FOR 'CHAOS' IN IRAN ARMS DEALS

Regan Also Blamed

Tower Panel Portrays the President as Remote and Confused Man

Tower said at a press conference releasing the report: "The President clearly did not understand the nature of this operation, who was involved and what was happening." Former Senator Muskie then read specific items uncovered during the ninety-day investigation, including, almost word-for-word, the President's February 11 statements about his management style—adding that assistants, including the chief of staff and Cabinet members, had a special obligation to inform and explain operations to the President. Muskie, who served as Secretary of State under President Carter, was the only Democrat on the panel, but he joined the two Republicans in giving Reagan the benefit of most doubts, accepting the unwritten imperative that whatever had happened, the President and the presidency should be protected. "Knowing his style," said Muskie, "they [staff and Cabinet members] should have been particularly mindful of the need for special attention to the measures in which this arms sales initiative developed and proceeded."

Scowcroft, an Air Force general and former National Security Adviser, followed the line in different words when the three commissioners met the press: "The problem at the heart was one of people, not of process. It was not that the structure was faulty, it is that the structure was not used."

The "people," as defined in the 288-page report, was everyone up to the President, from the autocratic chief of staff, Don Regan, who acted as if he were a prime minister rather than a hired hand, down to the super-patriot Oliver North. Secretary of State Shultz and Secretary of Defense Weinberger were criticized for their determination to distance themselves from what they obviously knew was happening, but the heaviest hammer fell on Regan, who was assigned "primary responsibility for the chaos that descended on the White House." Former CIA director Bill Casey, who died on May 6, also came in for his share of criticism. One immediate result of the report was the withdrawal of the President's nomination of the agency's deputy director,

Robert Gates, as Casey's successor. The report indicated that Gates had signed off on phony intelligence estimates regarding Iran.

Admiral Poindexter, too, was criticized, but he had already resigned, going back to a comfortable command in the Navy. The electronic chatter between Poindexter, North, and McFarlane, the PROFS e-mail discovered in the final days of the Tower investigation, showed pretty convincingly that they saw themselves as a secret cell within the government. The messages also showed that after McFarlane's resignation on December 4, 1985, a White House computer was installed in his home, secretly and illegally.

The messages clicked back and forth and around among the three secretive Naval Academy graduates:

North to Poindexter, regarding threats being made to officials of the government of Costa Rica of retribution by the United States if they revealed the locations of secret CIA airstrips in that country: "I recognize that I was well beyond my charter in dealing with a head of state this way and making threats/offers that may be impossible to deliver."

Poindexter to North: "You did the right thing."

McFarlane to North: "If the world only knew how many times you have kept a semblance of integrity and gumption to U.S. policy, they would make you Secretary of State. But they can't know and would complain if they did—such is the state of democracy in the late 20th Century."

Poindexter to North: "Do not let anyone know you are in London or that you are going there."

North to Poindexter: "I have no idea what Don Regan does or does not know re: my private US [fund-raising] operation but the President obviously knows why he has been meeting with several selected people to thank them for their 'support for Democracy' in Central America."

Poindexter to North: "Don Regan knows very little of your operation and that is just as well."

At one point, North suggested that the President be briefed on the Iran operation, along with Shultz, Weinberger, and Casey. Poindexter wrote back immediately: "I don't want a meeting with RR, Shultz, Weinberger and Casey."

Bob Woodward, who was working on a book about covert CIA operations, wrote in *The Washington Post* on February 27: "North secretly ran the contra war from the White House throughout 1985 and 1986, during Congress' ban on direct U.S. assistance. . . . North had his own set of private benefactors, including an unidentified foreign official who contributed a total of $25 million. A reliable source identified that source as Saudi King Fahd. Some of the donors solicited by North"—including King Fahd—"had been personally thanked by Reagan at the White House." The almost religious status the NSC conspirators gave themselves and their operations was shown by the way North described what he thought about being pushed out of the White House. North said: "The Eighth Beatitude says, 'Blessed are those who are persecuted for righteousness' sake, for theirs is the Kingdom of Heaven.' "

As for the money, more than $33 million was missing. "It's disappeared into a black hole, so to speak," said Tower. "We don't know that the contras ever got it or material purchased by it."

That was one of the answers commission members offered as they fanned out on the Sunday-morning television shows on March 2. The seventy-six-year-old President's health, energy, and focus were at the center of much of the questioning. "What about his grasp of reality?" asked Lesley Stahl of *Face the Nation*. Muskie answered: "He was definite in what he remembered and what he didn't. But what he didn't astonished us . . . to have the President not focusing and not recalling these significant occasions is worrisome." On the more raucous *The McLaughlin Group,* hosted by a former Nixon political assistant, John McLaughlin, guest journalists were asked for a one-word evaluation of the Reagan presidency. They answered: "Henpecked" . . . "Newsworthy" . . . "Struggling" . . . "Almost dead in the water" . . . "Automatic pilot." A *New York Times*/CBS News poll confirmed that the President's overall approval rating was in free-fall, dropping ten points to 42 percent—down from 69 percent when the Iran arms sales were first revealed.

Don Regan's day did not go well. On the afternoon that the Tower Report was issued, Vice President Bush asked Regan to come to his office, which was next door in the West Wing. "I've just had lunch with the President," said Bush. "He asked me to find out what your plans are about leaving."

"What's the matter?" snapped Regan, his color and voice rising. "Isn't he man enough to ask me that question himself?"

"I know it's rough . . ."

"After two years as chief of staff and four years as Treasury Secretary, I'm being fired like a shoe clerk. I'm bitter, George, and you can tell that to the President."

As Regan calmed down, Bush asked him about the President's schedule after the release of the Tower Report.

"That's in the hands of an astrologer in San Francisco, George."

The Vice President looked mystified. Regan poured out his frustrations about the woman Mrs. Reagan called "My friend," Joan Quigley.

"Good God," said Bush.

Warming up with a vengeance, Regan told the Vice President that he had to keep color-coded calendars of good days and bad days, all based on Quigley's reading of the stars. He pulled out a slip of paper, calculating which dates were good and bad for dealing with the Tower Report:

"Feb. 20–26 be careful . . . March 7–14 bad period . . . March 10–14 no outside activity . . . March 12–19 no trips exposure . . . March 19–25 no public exposure . . . March 16 very bad . . . March 21 no . . . March 27 no . . . April 3 careful . . ."

And so it went. Bush did not ask if the President knew this. Regan had never asked, keeping the secret even from his own staff. Finally Regan said he would leave in four days, on Monday, March 2, so he could have a dignified hearing as the excitement over the Tower Report faded. In fact, Regan was already doing exit interviews with *Time* magazine and *The New York Times*. Bush went back to the Oval Office and told the President, who wrote in his diary that night: "My prayers have been answered." One more time, he did not have to do the deed himself. He had already offered the job to one of the most popular men in Washington, former Senator Howard Baker of Tennessee. Practicing law now, and considering a run for the Republican nomination for President in 1988, Baker was asked to come to the White House. He was walking toward the Oval Office and saw the President standing by himself in the hallway. Without any formality, the President said, "Howard, I have to have a new chief of staff, and I want you to be it."

"All right," Baker said.

Within hours, the Baker ascendancy was on CNN. Regan did not know that. He was with two *Time* reporters, Barret Seaman and David Beckwith, talking about his accomplishments. Frank Carlucci, who had replaced Poindexter as National Security Adviser, saw the report and rushed over to Regan's office, walking in as the two *Time* correspondents left. Cursing the world—Regan dictated a fourteen-word letter: "I hereby resign as chief of staff to the President of the United States." Then he put on his coat.

"You have to tell the President," said Carlucci, placing a call to the Oval Office. Reagan called back and urged Regan to stay until Monday for a joint appearance with Baker. "I'm sorry," Regan said, his voice cracking. "I won't be here anymore. . . . I deserved better treatment than this. I'm through." Then he was gone. Meese called Baker at his law office, saying: "Howard, I think you better get over to the White House. There's no one in charge."

When Baker got to the White House, he talked first to Regan's mice. The words they used to describe Reagan were "inattentive, inept, and lazy." As they saw it, Don Regan had been running the country. They told Baker he should read the Twenty-fifth Amendment on presidential incapacity because he might have to use it. The next morning, after meeting with his own people, Baker brought them in to the Oval Office and introduced them to the President. They were really there, though, to watch Reagan and see whether he was okay. For Reagan, here was a new audience and he performed. He was funny, quick, charming, and concerned about the country. Baker decided the mice had it all wrong.

The President's television speech on the Tower Report was set for the evening of March 4, a good Quigley day. In the morning he announced his next nominee to be CIA director, William Webster, the director of the FBI. Reporters cornered Reagan at the announcement and he let off some of his own steam about stories on his wife's power and influence, saying: "The idea that she is involved in governmental decisions and so forth and all of this, and being a kind of dragon lady—there is nothing to that. . . . That is fiction, and I think it's despicable fiction. A lot of people ought to be ashamed of themselves."

The speech, which lasted only twelve minutes, was written by Landon Parvin, who usually wrote for Mrs. Reagan. After saying he had remained silent for so long on Iran-contra because he had not wanted to speak before he knew more about what had happened, the President said: "Let's start with the part that is most controversial. A few months ago, I told the American people that I did not trade arms for hostages. My heart and my best intentions still tell me that's true, but the facts and the evidence tell me it is not. . . . There are reasons why this happened, but no excuses. It was a mistake."

Reagan talked about the personnel changes, beginning with Baker and Carlucci, and with new regulations and record-keeping procedures at the NSC, which was a way to explain away his own fogginess before the Tower Commission and to disregard the wholesale trashing of NSC documents: "One thing still upsetting me, however, is that no one kept proper records of meetings or decisions. This led to my failure to recollect whether I approved an arms shipment before or after the fact. I did approve it; I just can't say specifically when. Well, rest assured, there's plenty of record keeping now going on at 1600 Pennsylvania Avenue."

On the contra side of Iran-contra, the President had little to say: "The Tower Commission wasn't able to find out what happened to the money, so the facts will be left to the continuing investigations of the court-appointed Independent Counsel and the two Congressional investigating committees. I'm confident the truth will come out." As for himself, Reagan offered some of his patented colloquial wisdom: "What should happen when you make a mistake is this: You take your knocks, you learn your lessons, and then you move on." A cartoon by Steve Kelley in the *San Diego Union* showed a battered Reagan walking past a John Tower figure toward a guy with a mallet marked "Congressional Probes," then moving on to another marked "Special Prosecutor," ready to knock him with a baseball bat. *Time* magazine put it this way: "As televised congressional hearings get underway next month and Special Prosecutor Lawrence Walsh prepares possible indictments against former White House officials, the Administration could be hard pressed to find a subject that will compete for the public's attention. An arms treaty with the Soviet Union, signed at a summit conference in the U.S. with Gorbachev undoubtedly represents Reagan's best opportunity to surmount his difficulties and crown his tenure in the White House."

Polls taken after the speech showed that Reagan's approval rating had bounced back up a few points, which made it a pretty good speech. And there was pretty good feeling in the White House the next morning, along with empty offices that had been used by Regan and his mice. And the President had decided to stop talking to the press for a while, clutching his throat and saying, "I've lost my voice."

Actually, his voice seemed to be about all he had left. "A despon-

dent and demoralized man," he was called on the editorial page of
The New York Times. After six years of political insurrection, Presi-
dent Reagan was being forced to turn his administration over to old
Washington hands led by such professionals as Baker, Carlucci, and
Webster, a former federal judge who had run the FBI since 1978, and
George Shultz. William Schneider of the American Enterprise Insti-
tute, writing in the *National Journal* of March 14, was one of the few
commentators who immediately recognized what had happened.
Under the headline "The Establishment Gets Its Revenge," he wrote:
"The Tower Commission, acting as the executive committee of the
Washington power elite, reproached the Reagan Administration with
the strongest term of disapproval in the Establishment's vocabulary: It
called the Iran arms initiative 'a very unprofessional operation.'. . .
Gone are the true believers, Poindexter, McFarlane and North, who
saw the world in black and white. Also gone are the Reagan loyalists,
Casey and Regan, whose mission in government was to 'Let Reagan
be Reagan.' Unlike their predecessors, they do not depend on Reagan
for their legitimacy." *

In another indication that the insiders were back inside, the Senate
and House committees investigating Iran-contra announced that they
would combine their efforts into a single operation and would begin
public hearings on May 5. That deal, an unusual one, was made possible by the Democratic election victories of 1986. The joint chairmen
were both Democrats, Senator Daniel Inouye of Hawaii and Representative Lee Hamilton of Indiana.

The President faced the press at a news conference for the first time
in four months on March 19, the day the Reagans' loyal friend Mike
Deaver was indicted by a federal court on five counts of perjury involving the lobbying business he set up after leaving the White House
in 1985. But Deaver was yesterday. The questions of the day focused
on the Tower Report and its aftermath.

The President repeated much of what he had said in the past. The
closest he came to satisfying the press's appetite for apology and admission of guilt came early on in answer to two questions. He was

---

* Schneider, who noted that Howard Baker, who had been calling for tax increases since leaving
the Senate in 1984, had also enraged Reagan conservatives by successfully pushing for congressional approval of the treaty turning the Panama Canal over to Panamanian control during the
Carter administration. The writer may have gone over the top when he said in the *National
Journal* commentary: "The Presidency, in fact, looks as if it will be left in the hands of two re-
gents, Baker and Nancy Reagan. They will set the White House agenda, just as Colonel Edward
House and Edith Wilson did after President Wilson had a stroke."

asked whether North was correct in saying, in an e-mail, that the President had knowingly met with private citizens contributing money to the contras in Nicaragua. He answered that he did meet with them, but thought all they were doing was buying television spots to influence Congress. On the Iranian initiative Reagan was asked: "If you had to do it all over again, sir, would you do it again?" He answered: "No, I would not go down that same road again. I will keep my eyes open for any opportunity again for improving relations. And we will continue to explore every legitimate means to get our hostages back."

As April began, the President left the White House, beginning what amounted to a campaign to show he was still the man in charge, the man with a plan. Before the College of Physicians in Philadelphia, he gave his first speech on AIDS, telling fifteen hundred doctors that he considered it to be "Public Health Enemy No. 1." He declared that government-financed progress toward a cure was being made faster than similar drives in the past against polio and hepatitis. It was an awkward speech and afterward in answer to questions, the White House confirmed that the President had never spoken to his Surgeon General, Koop, who had been issuing alarming monthly reports on the spread of the disease for more than five years. In Philadelphia, Reagan asserted that "prevention" was better than "cure." He seemed to be trying to walk a fine political line drawn between Dr. Koop, who was publicly advocating more sex education in schools, and his Secretary of Education, William Bennett, who was telling conservative audiences that government had no business providing sex information to children. Reagan's compromise was: "The Federal role must be to give educators accurate information about the disease. How that information is used must be up to schools and parents, not government." Avoiding the words "sex" or "condoms," he concluded: "AIDS information cannot be what some call 'value neutral.' After all, when it comes to preventing AIDS, don't medicine and morality teach the same thing?"

Koop was among the unsatisfied, saying: "We can no longer afford to side-step frank, open discussions about sexual practices, heterosexual or homosexual." Dr. Neil Schram, head of the Los Angeles AIDS Task Force, was angrier, saying: "Until the Reagan Administration realizes that the government's responsibility is saving lives and not saving souls, we will continue to see the virus spread through the society." A local paper, the *Philadelphia Daily News,* editorialized: "Ronald Reagan finally uttered the word AIDS. The President is so frightened of the moralizing crazies who back him that he couldn't bring himself to say anything intelligent. . . . Nancy probably hasn't gotten around to telling him the stork didn't bring Ron Jr."

Returning to Washington, the President stayed on Air Force One at Andrews Air Force Base for almost a half-hour. He was calling members of Congress—Democrats mostly—urging them to vote to support his veto of an $88 billion highway construction bill. He made a trip to the Capitol, his seventh in six years, the next day to meet for ninety minutes with a number of Republican senators—"I beg you to vote with me on this," he told one of them, Thad Cochran of Mississippi. But the magic was not there this time. Needing to prevent a two-thirds vote in each house, he lost 350 to 73 in the House and by one vote in the Senate, 67 to 33. Thirteen Republican senators voted with the Democrats; they had to choose between the President who called the bill a budget-buster and more roads and jobs back home, and they chose the roads and jobs. It was the old politics as usual. Representative Arthur Ravenel, a South Carolina Republican, summarized the voting: "Reagan ain't gonna be running in 1988, but I am."

The lame-duck President—that status was emphasized when it was reported that rich friends had bought the Reagans a $2.5 million Bel Air house for their return to Los Angeles—did not seem to have much of a future with the 100th Congress. The House had already and almost unanimously rejected Reagan's 1988 budget on arrival—it won just twenty-seven votes—and Republicans quickly decided not to propose an alternate plan. The Democrats were back in control on Capitol Hill, and their proposed budget included $18 billion in new taxes to cut some of a projected deficit of more than $130 billion. But Reagan, taking off for a California vacation on April 10, with a new staff he didn't know, was looking a little more like himself.

"The President walks, talks and gives speeches," wrote Cannon in the *Post*. "Sometimes, he even approaches reporters and answers questions." On the day Reagan left for the ranch, he wrote a friendly letter to Gorbachev—hand-delivered in Moscow by Secretary Shultz. There was a recognition on both sides that the futures of the old President and the younger Soviet leader were linked. To keep walking and talking, Reagan needed some kind of foreign policy triumph, and Gorbachev, trying to push domestic economic and political changes against great and entrenched opposition all around him, needed a success abroad to build a constituency for change at home.

"Together we can make a difference in the future course of world events," the President wrote to the Soviet leader. "Let us pray that you and I can continue our dialogue." A twenty-three-page State Department Intelligence Research Report the President carried to California stated: "Gorbachev more clearly than ever has committed himself personally to an agenda of measured change. . . . The Gorbachev regime is driven by the twin realizations that unless the Soviet Union modernizes economically, it will fall further and further behind as a great power, and that it cannot modernize without significant adjustments of long-standing political habits and practices. . . . Breathtaking change has occurred in some Soviet positions on arms control, and Gorbachev now appears serious about pushing a delinked intermediate-range nuclear forces (INF) agreement." The secret American report also emphasized that Gorbachev might need a shared triumph with Reagan before he could heal what he called "the running sore," the Soviets' ongoing and draining seven-year war and occupation in Afghanistan. That adventure was going badly, particularly after Reagan secretly authorized the shipment of seventy-five Stinger missiles to the Afghan mujahideen. The shoulder-fired ground-to-air heat-seeking missiles were forcing Soviet planes and helicopters to fly too high for effective ground-support action.

On April 16, Shultz flew to California to report on his conversations with Gorbachev. The General Secretary, Shultz said, had repackaged a number of arms control proposals by both countries over the years, offering a plan for the removal of all medium- and intermediate-range (six hundred to three thousand miles) nuclear missiles in Europe, an old idea the Soviets made new by adding on the elimination of shorter-range missiles (three hundred to six hundred miles). But it was an idea that frightened European leaders—as it had when it was discussed in Reykjavik—because of the two-to-one Soviet superiority in battlefield missiles, essentially nuclear artillery, and the 2.5-to-1 Warsaw Pact superiority over NATO in troops, tanks, and guns between the Ural Mountains and the Atlantic Ocean.

Reagan asked about the prospects for a summit with Gorbachev in the United States before the end of the year. The Secretary of State said that Gorbachev offered no commitment, saying only that the reason to come would be to sign an arms agreement. The President then talked, as he often did, of another of his many dreams: the faith that if a communist leader came to the United States he would be changed by the sights and sounds of American prosperity and happiness, Reagan's America. "I often fantasize about taking Soviet leaders in a helicopter and flying around," he said. "I'd just kind of let them choose where we go, so it wouldn't look like a planned tour, and be able to point down and say, 'Yeah, those are houses down there. Yeah, that house with a trailer and a boat in the driveway—that's a working man in America. Yes, he lives in that house. He has that boat. He drives that car to work.' They could not show me comparable things in their country."

The whole idea greatly cheered Reagan, who invited the press gathered in Santa Barbara up to his ranch for a short news conference with Shultz. The President said: "I look forward to and I hope we can have a summit . . . and that Mr. Gorbachev and I can complete an historic agreement on East-West relations."

The congressional Iran-contra hearings—conducted by fifteen senators and eleven representatives, began on Tuesday, May 5. Staffers of the joint committee had already conducted 300 interviews, issued 140 subpeonas, and scrutinized more than 100,000 documents. At the same time, the separate investigations of independent counsel Lawrence Walsh—there was tension between the operations because Walsh's criminal cases could be hampered when suspects were granted congressional immunity to testify—had already gotten one guilty plea that involved the President: A conservative fund-raiser, Carl "Spitz" Channell, pleaded guilty to conspiracy. He was the agent who had brought private contra donors—he raised several million dollars while Congress was refusing military aid—into the Oval Office for thank-you handshakes and pep talks from the President himself. "God bless you all," the President had said to them. "There are thousands of young men and women in Nicaragua waiting to join the contras. Only they don't have the money and arms and the equipment to take them on board. So we know what our job is."

Ironically, although the joint committee chairman, Senator Inouye, said on Sunday television that he believed Reagan knew of the diversion of funds to the contras, the hearings were not the big story of the day. Television and newspapers focused on another senator, Gary Hart of Colorado. The front-runner, in polls, for the 1988 Democratic presidential nomination, Hart was the target of a *Miami Herald* stakeout of his Capitol Hill home the weekend before, surveillance that led to stories that he spent that weekend indoors with a twenty-nine-old actress-model from Miami named Donna Rice. Then a photograph surfaced of Miss Rice seated on Hart's lap on the deck of a cabin cruiser in the Bahamas. The name of the boat was *Monkey Business*. Hart dropped out of the race within a week.

Back at the White House, the President announced that he would not watch the hearings, which were being televised nationally. Most of his information came from two briefing documents delivered to him each morning. A summary of each day's proceedings was being prepared by the new White House counsel, a former law partner of Howard Baker, Arthur Culvahouse, and his staff, who were sitting in on each session. At the same time, the President's new press spokesman, Marlin Fitzwater, who had worked for Vice President Bush before Speakes resigned, was preparing to distribute a presidential response to each day's testimony.

The first Culvahouse memo to Reagan included:

> Secord stated that the administration "approved" of his conduct and that he personally meet with Messrs. Casey (three times on the air supply operation), North and McFarlane. . . . Secord testified that he was approached by Oliver North in the summer of 1984 about providing advice and assistance to the contras. . . . In 1984 and February of 1985, at Oliver North's request, Secord asked for contributions to the contras from "a foreign official" (Saudi)—and you subsequently met with the King in February, 1985. The Saudi Arabia government has consistently denied any contribution to the contras. . . . You have refrained from discussing your conversation with the King.
>
> Secord also provided an accounting of the disposition of the $30 million of Iranian weapons payments that he had handled: "Purchase price—$12 million; Hakim's Swiss account—$8 million; to contras—$3.5 million; transport expenses—$3 million; miscellaneous expenses—$1 million; cannot account for at this time—$2.5 million."

Fitzwater's first press memo was essentially a tip sheet for Reagan, providing him with answers to seven questions raised by Secord, printing past Reagan quotes and one-sentence summaries of the President's positions, including:

> "*Private Fundraising*—He knew about money going for arms and humanitarian aid, from news accounts primarily." . . . "*Presidential Testimony*—He has not been asked and the question remains open." . . . "*Iran Arms Diversion*—He had no knowledge of the di-

version." ... "*Third Countries—Arms*—He knew other countries were giving money for the contras, but he did not *solicit* it or know how it would be used." ... "*Third Country—Humanitarian*—The law authorized third country solicitation for humanitarian aid; of course the President knew." ... "*Channell Fundraising*—He was thanking them for television ads and had no knowledge of other purposes."

The press focused on Secord's dealings with the CIA. "Casey asked me how much money was needed. . . . I said it would take about $10 million. And he said, '$10 million. $10 million' and then he mentioned a country which he thought might be willing to donate this kind of money. But then he said, 'But I can't approach them. . . . But you can.' "

Secord came back for a second day of testimony on Wednesday, May 6. The question that dominated the committee session, as reported in the Fitzwater memo, was: "Did Ollie North tell the President, as Secord suggested, that the Ayatollah's money had gone to support the contras?" The Culvahouse memo to the President reported that North had met with him thirty-three times, mostly at ceremonial functions and never with fewer than three other people present. North also spoke with the President on the telephone on only two occasions: a conference call with other NSC personnel and the provisional president of El Salvador, Álvaro Alfredo Magaña Borja, on March 27, 1984, and the goodbye call to the motel room in Vienna, Virginia, on November 25, 1986. Secord was in the room with North on the second call, which lasted less than two minutes. North, he testified, said: "Mr. President, I'm sorry it had to end this way, I was trying to serve you the best way I knew how, Mr. President."

Reagan responded, as he had in public, that he still thought North was a hero. Then he added: "Your story would make a hell of a movie someday." Fitzwater's memo of the day ended: "Our response is: We are confident that we are aware of every contact between the President and Ollie North . . . the President said he was unaware of the diversion of funds." And, in fact, after the next day's testimony, Culvahouse told Reagan: "Secord stated that he had no personal knowledge of what the President had been told."

The next witness was McFarlane, and his opening testimony, on May 11, was reported to the President by Culvahouse: "McFarlane learned of the diversion returning home from the Tehran trip but did not tell the President. He assumed that North had Presidential approval. McFarlane also testified that on November 18 or 19, 1986, North specifically told him that he [North] had received authority to divert residual funds from the Iran arms sales to the contras. However, McFarlane did not ask nor was he told by whom such authority was given."

In his testimony, McFarlane told it this way:

"Ollie, it was approved, wasn't it?"

"Yes, Bud, it was approved. You know I wouldn't do anything that wasn't approved."

Perhaps North was joking. He was certainly lying. But another slapstick story surfaced while McFarlane was facing the cameras. The $10 million donation squeezed out of the Sultan of Brunei had disappeared—for almost a year. Elliott Abrams, who had solicited the money in London, had transposed two digits in giving the Sultan instructions on how to transfer the money—a prefix "386" became "368"—and it had ended up in the wrong Credit Suisse account. In August of 1986, the money appeared in the numbered account of a shipping company owner, who immediately withdrew it and purchased a certificate of deposit in another bank. Then it came out that on September 19, 1986, a day the Reagans left for Camp David, North and Secord had given a midnight tour of the White House to three Iranians, one identified as a nephew of Rafsanjani, to try to show that they did indeed represent the President himself. There was one other embarrassing detail that day, May 13. The President said he had looked at his diary again and it indicated that he had indeed talked with King Fahd about Saudi contributions to the contras—he said the King brought up the subject—and that the Saudis immediately doubled their monthly contributions from $1 million to $2 million.

On May 18, the congressional hearings were knocked off the front pages again, this time by news that a U.S. Navy guided-missile frigate, the USS *Stark,* had been hit by one or two missiles fired by Iraqi jets. The *Stark,* steaming in the Persian Gulf, one of dozens of U.S. Navy ships posted there to keep open oil shipping lanes during the long Iraq-Iran War, had been struck by a sea-skimming Exocet missile or missiles, fired by one or more French-made Iraqi Mirage fighter-bombers. At least three Americans were dead, according to early reports. That number increased to more than thirty-five within hours. "An unintentional accident," said Saddam Hussein, the President of Iraq, in a cable to the White House. The President was in Chattanooga, Tennessee, speaking to high school students. His first reaction was to say: "From now on, if aircraft approach any of our ships in a way that appears hostile, there is one order of battle—defend yourselves. Defend American lives." But, talking to reporters later, Reagan said that he had accepted an Iraqi apology. "The villian in this piece really is Iran." He blamed the Iranians for refusing to negotiate an end to the war that had begun six years ago with an Iraqi attack.

As the press, particularly television, played up the *Stark* attack and a Washington debate on the American role in the Gulf, a series of Iran-contra witnesses testified about their contributions to the contras through Colonel North and Carl Channell. Ellen Garwood, an eighty-four-year-old Dallas heiress and a generous contributor to conservative causes, put up $65,000 to buy a helicopter dubbed the *Lady Ellen,* then gave as much as $3 million more. Joseph Coors had asked CIA director Casey how he could help and had been referred to North, and contributed $65,000 for a light cargo plane. William O'Boyle, a New York businessman, gave $160,000 for two small planes. Adolfo Calero, a contra leader, also testified, opening personal bank records indicating that he received more than $33 million from foreign governments, principally Saudi Arabia, and private contributors, spending $19 million for arms and approximately $14 million for other equipment and maintenance.

Calero also said that he gave some of the money to North, including $90,000 in traveler's checks, checks that could be traced, showing that at least $2,500 of that money was used by the colonel to buy snow tires, gasoline, groceries, and family gifts. Then Albert Hakim said he had deposited $200,000 of missile sale profits into a Swiss bank account in North's name, telling the colonel's wife, Betsy, that the money and a $2 million life insurance policy were there for her children if anything happened to her husband. Robert Owen, a $50,000-a-year State Department consultant who served as a courier for North, called the boss "B.G.," saying that was his office nickname, "Blood and Guts."

The Culvahouse White House summary of the Hakim testimony focused on the anger of Senator Inouye and others over the businessman's access to secure parts of the White House and his transfer of funds to the North family:

"Chairman Inouye was upset by Hakim's disclosures that private individuals without security clearances were allowed to share in foreign policy secrets and attend meetings in the Situation Room . . . and that Secord and North 'committed the United States government to defend Iran against the Russians and depose the leader of Iraq.' . . . Several committee members concluded that Hakim must have intended to 'compromise' North. Rep. [Michael] De Wine suggested that Hakim wanted to have North 'in his hip pocket.' Hakim denied these allegations and said such characterizations ignored his human attachment to North. . . . Hakim observed that he could not have entered the Situation Room and attended meetings in the White House without high-level approval. After the affair became public, Hakim believed he should have been supported by the President."

Lewis Tambs was next. He had become United States ambassador to Costa Rica in July of 1985. He said his principal job was to help the contras set up military operations in southern Nicaragua and that he reported to "RIG," the Restricted Interagency Group, which consisted of North, Assistant Secretary of State Elliot Abrams, and Alan Fiers, head of the CIA's Central America Task Force.

Abrams was the next witness, on June 3, and he was a combative one. He admitted that he had made false or misleading statements in his previous appearances before congressional committees to discuss Iran-contra. He had lied when he said he had never solicited money for the contras, admitting now that in August of 1986 he had solicited $10 million from the Sultan of Brunei in London, the $10 million that had ended up in a Swiss businessman's account. Why did you lie about that? he was asked. "We had promised the government of Brunei confidentiality." He admitted that his statements after the capture of Eugene Hasenfus—"I can tell you there was no government involvement in this flight"—were not true. That one he blamed on other officials who had lied to him. "Every one of those statements—public and private—was completely honest and completely wrong."

Abrams denied that he had ever talked to Ambassador Tambs about aiding the contras in southern Nicaragua. One of the last of the committee members to question Abrams, Representative Jack Brooks, a Texas Democrat, ended his questioning in exasperation: "You've been very patiently telling us that you don't know about this, you don't know about that, you weren't informed, you weren't authorized to tell the truth. That's the wildest story I ever heard. . . . You're either extremely incompetent, or you're still deceiving us with semantics." Brooks was one of the many committee members publicly demanding that Abrams be fired for misleading the Congress. Secretary of State Shultz responded to that: "Elliott Abrams has my full and complete confidence. . . . He's done a sensational job." *

As Abrams completed his first day of testimony, on June 3, the President left Washington for a nine-day European tour. After almost a month of testimony, a *Wall Street Journal*/NBC News poll indicated that two-thirds of respondents believed Reagan was lying about how much he knew about Iran-contra. But more than half approved of the job he was doing as President. A *Washington Post*/ABC News poll a week later had similar numbers: 69 percent thought Reagan was lying, but his overall job approval was recorded as 53 percent.

The President's first stop abroad was Venice. It was time for another annual Economic Summit, and Reagan had just made economic news by not reappointing Paul Volcker as chairman of the Federal Reserve Board, replacing him with a more conservative economist, Alan Greenspan, chairman of the Council of Economic Advisers under President Ford. "MARKETS SURPRISED" was a *New York Times* front-page headline as the value of stocks, bonds, and the dollar all dropped. For a rather dour and often controversial figure, Volcker was leaving, after eight years, in what amounted to showers of glory, a rare thing in his business. "Anti-Inflation Legacy" read the line over the paper's "News Analysis" by Peter T. Kilborn: "With real success, he battled the gyrations of the dollar, the crises over Latin American debt and the collapse of the Continental Illinois National Bank. . . . In subduing the inflation that reached levels of 12 and 13 percent, Mr. Volcker's achievement probably exceeds that of any of his predecessors. Inflation so menaced the economy then that critics on both the left and the right praise him for his improvement far more than they fault him for the toll he extracted—the highest interest rates since the Civil War and a recession that was longer and deeper than economists with their hindsight say was necessary." *The Wall Street Journal*'s Paul Blustein added: "Greenspan faces a daunting challenge in proving to the financial markets that he is a worthy replacement."

Reagan and Volcker, who had been appointed by President Carter

---

* On August 5, 1987, in a closed committee session, Alan Fiers testified to the committee that he, Abrams, and North did, in fact, work together on resupplying the contras, which he had avoided admitting in earlier Senate testimony. He said he was "taken aback" when Abrams denied American involvement, but he did not say anything to contradict Abrams or other officials. "I was a member of the team," he said on August 5. "I was a member of the administration team. I wasn't going to break ranks with the team." In three hundred pages of testimony, Fiers also said that he knew some contra units were involved in cocaine smuggling.

in 1979, had quite a run together in bad times and good. The giant Fed chairman—he was six feet eight inches tall—had broken the inflation that destroyed Carter's presidency by brutally using the intricate and mostly mysterious powers of the Board to regulate money supply. Less money meant less inflation. It also meant hard times, particularly in 1982, for tens of millions of Americans and tens of thousands of American businesses. But it worked. Reagan took the credit and he deserved it—at least he deserved a lot of it. He stood by, or behind, Volcker when almost every other elected politician in the country— left, right, and center—was crying for relief. Reagan, in his own words, "stayed the course."

Inflation had dropped to 5 percent by 1983, when he reappointed Volcker. By 1987, the economy was a different kind of organism than it had been when Reagan took office. Individual income taxes were lower; the top rate was down from 70 to 33 percent. Interest rates were back in single digits and unemployment had dropped to 6.1 percent, the lowest number in eight years. But even though each year after 1981 the Congress and the President had conspired to raise taxes and fees by more than $80 billion a year—usually calling it "tax reform" or "closing loopholes"—economic expansion was being financed not by greater savings and new investment but by budget deficits averaging $172 billion a year, doubling the national debt in just six years.*

The world was changing. The President was boasting that 18 million new jobs had been created on his watch, but many of those were women or teenagers pushing into the workplace for temporary or insecure service jobs. Many Americans were running in place as manufacturing jobs moved out of the cities and then out of the country, creating trade deficits that made the United States a debtor nation for the first time in almost a century. The rich were getting richer and there were more of them, a trend helped along by a rising stock market—the Dow Jones Industrial Average topped 2,000 for the first time on January 8, 1987, and had increased another 20 percent since then.

* The 1981 income tax cut, by 1985, had the effect of reducing government revenue by 18.6 percent of gross domestic product. Then, using 1985 figures, the 1982 Tax Equity and Fiscal Responsibility Act and the Highway Revenue Act had the effect of increasing government revenue by 6.8 percent. The 1983 Social Security Amendments had the effect of increasing 1985 revenues by 1.2 percent. The 1984 Deficit Reduction Act had the effect of increasing 1985 revenues by 1.2 percent in 1985, increasing to 2.6 percent in 1988. The 1985 Consolidated Omnibus Budget Reconciliation Act increased revenues by 0.1 percent in 1986, rising to 0.3 percent in 1988. The 1986 Tax Reform Act increased revenues by 2.3 percent in 1986. The 1987 Omnibus Reconciliation Act increased revenues by 1.0 percent in 1988. In total, those increases amounted to raising annual tax revenue by 12.2 percent of GDP.

And there were more poor people, too; one in five American children were living in poverty, statistically, 25 percent more than in 1980. Some of the poor were invisible no more, they were homeless, living on the streets—and Reagan occasionally made fun of them. Reagan was hardly the only reason for such changes, but he and his ideas were a very important part of great changes in the distribution of income and wealth in the United States. According to the Census Bureau, from 1965 to 1980, the income of the poorest fifth of Americans increased by 6.5 percent, while the income of the wealthiest fifth dropped proportionately by 10 percent. In the 1980s, the share of the poorest fifth fell by 11.6 percent, while the top fifth gained 19 percent. Politically, Reagan repealed Lyndon Johnson's "Great Society"—and chipped away, too, at the New Deal of Franklin D. Roosevelt.

On June 9, as Congress prepared to recess for two weeks, the Iran-contra hearings ended their first round; it was announced that Poindexter and North would be summoned and questioned later in July. In the last days of the first round, it was revealed that General Secord had used $200,000 from one of the Swiss bank accounts to buy himself a small plane, a Porsche, and two weeks at a weight-reduction clinic—and had spent another $15,000 to pay for an electronic security fence and system installed in May of 1986 at North's home in Virginia. Fawn Hall, making her second appearance, was the last witness before adjournment. The twenty-seven-year-old secretary said: "There are times when you have to go above the written law."

The presidential entourage headed for Berlin to participate in the celebration of the city's 750th birthday. Reagan wanted to give a speech there, a speech to compete with President Kennedy's *"Ich bin ein Berliner"* speech in 1963. He wanted to talk about tearing down the Berlin Wall, erected by the East Germans in August 1961. At that time, more than two thousand people a day, the young and the educated, were escaping communism by simply taking subways or walking across the border that separated Soviet-occupied East Berlin from West Berlin, the half of the city occupied since the end of World War II by the Americans, the French, and the British. Not everyone agreed with the boss, beginning with Chief of Staff Howard Baker, who argued that it was unpresidential, that words were not going to bring the wall tumbling down. In one of the final meetings before the June 12 speech, speechwriter Peter Robinson, who spent three weeks working and reworking the line, reconstructed the conversation between the President and his men:

"Now, I'm the President, aren't I?"

"Yes, sir!"

"So I get to decide?"

"Yes, sir!"

"Well, then the line stays in."

The line Reagan and Robinson settled on was: "Mr. Gorbachev, tear down this wall."

The President's men, promising a major foreign policy address, wanted him to stand in front of the 196-year-old Brandenburg Gate, once the very center of the city, now just the most prominent sight along the wall that divided the city. The towering gate was actually on the other side of the wall, in East Berlin, and the West Germans resisted holding a rally there, thinking the idea was just gimmicky, too provocative, and perhaps too dangerous. But Chancellor Helmut Kohl still owed something to Reagan for Bitburg and the Americans prevailed. The President stood on a platform a hundred yards from the wall with the gate behind him and his back shielded by huge panes of bulletproof glass. The speech itself was actually not very important. *The New York Times* played it on page three, noting that the President had used three German phrases. The best one was from an old song, *Ich hab noch einen koffer in Berlin*: "I still have a suitcase in Berlin." But, as for news, the only new proposal he made concerned cooperation between the international airports on either side of the city. Then, halfway through the text, Reagan said:

"We hear much from Moscow about a new policy of reform and openness. Are these the beginnings of profound changes in the Soviet state? Or, are they token gestures? . . . There is one sign the Soviets can make that would be unmistakable, that would advance dramatically the cause of freedom and peace. General Secretary Gorbachev, if you seek peace, if you seek prosperity for the Soviet Union and Eastern Europe, if you seek liberalization: Come here to this gate! Mr. Gorbachev, open this gate! Mr. Gorbachev, tear down this wall!"

Reagan was shouting, which he rarely did. There was real anger in his voice. The speech was page three as news, but the moment was forever, played again and again and again on television all over the world. "Mr. Gorbachev, tear down this wall!" *

---

* The *Times* did put a photograph of Reagan and Kohl together on the front page of its June 13 edition. The caption began: "Reagan calls on Gorbachev to tear down the Berlin Wall."

CHAPTER 19

JULY 7, 1987

THE JOINT HOUSE-SENATE COMMITTEE investigating the Iran-contra affair, which had held a second round of public hearings for four days, from June 22 to June 25, scheduled its interrogation of Lieutenant Colonel Oliver North to begin on July 7. He had evaded public testimony for seven months by invoking Fifth Amendment protection and bargaining for immunity from criminal prosecution in exchange for his testimony. In the June hearings, he had been accused of being both a thief and a compulsive liar. A retired CIA security expert, Glenn Robinette, testified that North had falsified and backdated bills and letters, after his removal from the White House, to make it appear that he had paid for the $15,000 home security system installed in 1986. Actually, the system was paid for from one of General Richard Secord's Swiss bank accounts. Assistant Attorney General Charles J. Cooper, in charge of the Justice Department investigation, had testified that North, National Security Adviser Poindexter, and CIA Director Casey had conspired to prepare false testimony to Congress about the November 1985 shipment of missiles from Israel to Iran.

"Would you believe Oliver North under oath?" asked Representative Louis Stokes of Ohio.

"No," Cooper had responded on June 26. "I would not."

One occasional viewer went out of his way to tell reporters that he did not like the way the hearings were going. On the day after Cooper's testimony, the President said: "I think the spotlight has been growing so dim in recent days that when you get a mile and a half from the Potomac River, there are an awful lot of people who have gone back to their favorite television shows. And I don't blame them."

The next day, June 28, *The New York Times* ran a two-thousand-word front-page story beginning under the headline: "Reagan's Ability to Lead Nation at a Low, Critics and Friends Say." The piece, by the paper's two White House correspondents, Bernard Weinraub and Gerald Boyd, quoted sources, both anonymous and named, saying that Reagan seemed depressed, particularly by polls indicating the public no longer believed what he was telling them, and that he no longer trusted his own staff after reading and watching the revelations of Iran-contra.

> Aides said that the President did not bounce back, as the White House has publicly asserted, from his most recent surgery, on the prostate gland last January. And more than ever he is showing signs of his 76 years, so much so that his memory lapses and rambling discourse are no longer a source of friendly jokes, but one of concern, friends say. . . . Public signs are emerging. At a recent news conference, for instance, the President was unable to remember the name of the United Nations Security Council.

The memory lapses he joked about, walking into the White House physician's office and saying to Dr. Lawrence Mohr: "I have three things to tell you. The first is that I seem to be having a little trouble with my memory. I can't remember the other two." Dr. Mohr laughed, but like most physicians, he considered such jokes a sign of real anxiety over the plagues of aging.

But Reagan was still the old lion described by the Soviets at Reykjavik, ready to come alive when prey came close. And he did roar to life the day *The Times* story appeared. Howard Baker received a call that morning from Supreme Court Justice Lewis Powell. The seventy-nine-year-old Nixon appointee, who had served fifteen years and had cast the deciding votes against administration positions and policy on several important cases, particularly on abortion and affirmative action, told Baker to inform the President that he intended to retire. The White House produced releases and leaks about careful study and studious selection processes, but in fact, Reagan had long ago made up his mind who would be his next choice: Judge Robert Bork of the U.S. Court of Appeals in the District of Columbia. The President had wanted to appoint Bork in the past, but had been talked out of it.

Bork was smart and qualified, a former professor at Yale Law

School, a former Solicitor General of the United States. But he was also an ideologue without the political gift of suffering fools. He was better at making enemies, including many black leaders who considered him a racist because of some of his writings and opinions. There were also those who hated him because as Solicitor General, the number three person in the Justice Department in 1973, he had carried out President Nixon's "Saturday Night Massacre" orders to fire Archibald Cox, the special prosecutor in the Watergate cases. The number one and two men in the Justice Department, Attorney General Elliot Richardson and Deputy Attorney General William Ruckelshaus had resigned rather than sign the order. Reagan announced Bork's nomination on July 1, saying, "He is widely regarded as the most prominent and intellectually powerful advocate of judicial restraint in the country." Then both the President and his nominee said they would take no questions until confirmation hearings began in the fall.

So the battle began without them. For the opposition, Senator Edward Kennedy responded to the nomination: "Bork's America is a land in which women would be forced into back-alley abortions, blacks would sit at segregated lunch counters, rogue police could break down citizens' doors in midnight raids, school children could not be taught about evolution, writers and artists could be censored at the whim of the government and the doors of the federal courts would be shut on the fingers of millions of citizens for whom the judiciary is—and is often the only—protector of the individual rights that are at the heart of our democracy."

The *Baltimore Evening Sun* defined the coming struggle: "Reagan could search the country and not turn up a candidate who promises to generate more acrimony than Bork. Why? Because Bork combines (1) Impeccable credentials which would make it exceedingly difficult for the Senate to reject and (2) a rigid ideology which would make it exceedingly difficult for the Senate to accept."

On Tuesday, July 7, Oliver North, in uniform and decorations, made his first appearance before the Iran-contra committee. The Culvahouse memo to the President, who had repeatedly said he was too busy to watch beginning-to-end national television coverage, came with a cover note saying: "LtCol North repeatedly stated that he had no direct or indirect knowledge that the President was aware of the diversion of funds, although he *assumed* Presidential approval. North resumes his testimony at 9 A.M. It is anticipated that he will testify *at least* through Friday." The memo reported: "Lt. Col. North testified that he briefed his superiors and had their approval for all his actions. He believed the President was aware of the diversion, but he never discussed diversion with the President and does not know of anyone who did so, and he never saw a document that discussed diversion and bore an indication that the President had seen it."

That was lawyer talk, deniability for the President—so far. In a different language, the press and television focused on new information and on style. The new: North said he had directed five "diversion" memos to Reagan but had no idea whether they had gotten to him before copies were shredded; he said Attorney General Meese was in the room during one of the November 1986 sessions in which North and Poindexter were trying to construct a false chronology of Iran-contra events designed to shield presidential deeds and words; he said he had seen a signed presidential finding authorizing arms-for-hostages deals with the Iranians.

The big story, though, was North himself. With his lawyer, an experienced criminal defense attorney named Brendan Sullivan, North had used his months of public silence to negotiate some surprisingly generous ground rules. He had won "use immunity," which meant his public testimony could not be used against him in Walsh's criminal prosecutions, and that the committee and its attorneys were limited in some lines of questioning on possible criminal behavior. In any case, the committee seemed underprepared, because it was so anxious to hear public testimony (rather than recitations of the Fifth Amendment) that it had not compelled North to submit to private interrogation before his public appearance. His fervent distortions seemed to take his questioners by surprise. North was also accorded two more significant privileges. He could interrupt questioning and statements by committee members and attorneys. More importantly, he could not be interrupted. The concessions gave him the chance to actually control the interrogation, deflecting lines of questioning that he didn't like with long patriotic pep talks, Reaganesque sermonettes on duty, honor, and country. He did that often and well. Television viewers were drawn to his good-guy stories of bad guys out there in the jungles of evil. "First of all, I'm not in the habit of questioning my superiors," he testified at one point. "I saluted smartly and charged up the hill. That's what Lt. Colonels are supposed to do. I have no problem with that."

"What we saw today was political theater," John Chancellor commented on the NBC Nightly News. "Well, this critic says the star was a terrific witness. It's only the first day of the show, but it's beginning to look good for North."

The President had told North in his telephone call of November 25 that one day his story would make a good movie. It was already looking like a terrific television miniseries. When he was younger, Ronald Reagan might have been cast as Ollie North, the patriot, the hero, all based on a true story—even if it were a true story of lies and deception in places high and low. It was hard, that first day, to resist North's medals, two Silver Stars and a Purple Heart, his boyish grin, and his delight in his own use of candor as a substitute for truth. Asked about the lies he told in negotiating with the Iranians, he said: "There is great deception practiced in the conduct of covert operations. They are essentially a lie. We make every effort to deceive the enemy. . . . Bald-faced lies. I would have offered the Iranians a free trip to Disneyland if we could have gotten Americans home for it."

The next day's Culvahouse summary for the President began: "Perhaps the most noteworthy aspect of Lt. Col. North's often dramatic statements was his assertion that Secretary Shultz (as well as Messrs. Casey, McFarlane and Poindexter) knew about North's contra resupply efforts." It also reported that North testified that Assistant Secretary of State Abrams and Attorney General Meese knew more about his operations than they were admitting to investigators.

Much of the Wednesday testimony concerned lying to Congress, as the memo recorded: "North admitted that he participated in providing false written statements over McFarlane's signature in response to Congressional inquiries in 1985 about the NSC's role in providing assistance to the contras. He also testified that he misled Congress in the summer of 1986 in a face-to-face briefing with Chairman Hamilton and other members of the House Intelligence Committee. He stated that he informed Poindexter about the thrust of this briefing, and Poindexter congratulated North on a job 'well done.' "

When chief counsel to the House members of the committee characterized North as lying to "elected representatives of the people," the colonel snapped: "The President was elected by the people, too." Then he asserted his job was advancing the President's agenda. North said: "I want you to know that lying doesn't come easy to me, but we have to weigh in the difference between lies and lives."

One section of the Wednesday memo was titled "Testimony About North's Alleged Misuse of Funds." North was angry when he was asked about his use of traveler's checks to buy snow tires and other personal items, saying: "I often used my own paycheck for contra expenses. . . . Every single penny on the checks that you saw that came to me was used to pay any operational expenses on the scene or to reimburse myself. I never took a penny that didn't belong to me." He said he kept a ledger of monies owed him, but said he shredded it on orders from the late CIA director, William Casey. "He told me, specifically," North testified, "get rid of things, get rid of that book because that book has in it the names of everybody—just get rid of it and clean things up. And I did so." Asked about the $15,000 security system at his home, North said he was in danger from the Palestinian terrorist Abu Nidal because of his role in the *Achille Lauro* operation. He said: "I'll be glad to meet Abu Nidal on equal terms anywhere in the world. Okay. There's an even deal for him. But I am not willing to let my wife and four children meet Abu Nidal or his organization this week on his terms. . . . I also suggest to you that it was General Secord, first of all—thank you, General Secord. And second of all—you guys ought to write him a check because the government should have done it to begin with."

That night, anchor Tom Brokaw began the *NBC Nightly News* by saying: "The most popular soap opera on television this week is the Iran-contra inquiry—starring Lt. Col. Oliver North." Daytime television viewing was up 10 percent. "He is a star, a new national folk hero," said Brokaw. On the *CBS Evening News,* correspondent Bob Schieffer reported on an "Ollie North craze," with T-shirts and other memorabilia featuring pictures of North. *Newsweek* and *Time* put him on their covers. *Newsweek* compared him to Jimmy Stewart in the film *Mr. Smith Goes to Washington. Time* reported that its polling showed that 84 percent of respondents said they believed that North's activities had been sanctioned by higher-ups. Empty rooms in the Capitol were being filled with flowers and telegrams sent to North from all over the country. Capitol guards were trying to turn away people who came with personal checks they wanted delivered to a North defense fund. " 'Olliemania' Sweeps USA" was the front-page headline of *USA Today.* The newspaper also published results of a special "Hot Line" it set up for popular comment: 52,804 callers said North was an honest man who should be given a medal; 1,572 called him a liar who should be in jail.

The *New York Daily News,* usually a reliable voice of populist conservatism, was with the minority. Editors there had no use for the new folk hero, headlining an editorial "North's Brazen Lies." The copy read, in part: "People who believe more than 10 consecutive words of what Lt. Col. Oliver North swore to yesterday have a treat in store. Any morning now, they will see the Tooth Fairy leading the Easter Bunny down a garden path, gently, lest they disturb the grazing unicorns. . . . Unless all those unicorns are blocking your view, it's just plain obvious how deeply, broadly, casually North was lying under oath."

By Thursday, the third day of the questioning, 60 million people were watching the hearings on television. One of them was Reagan. The White House, which had been declaring each day that the President was otherwise occupied, now announced that he was following the hearings—"very closely" . . . "he was fully aware."

The witness, famous now, was allowed an opening statement each day, another negotiated privilege. Culvahouse's memo to the President on the third day's testimony began: "Lt. Col. North read an opening statement in which he praised the President's political and foreign policy leadership." Later, the memo reported: "While admitting he had lied to Congress, North unequivocally asserted that he was not now lying to protect the President. . . . North testified that he was shredding documents in the office on November 22, 1986, even as Justice Department lawyers examined other documents there. North admitted that one of the reasons he shredded was to prevent the Attorney General's staff from seeing politically damaging documents."

Asked how he could continue shredding with investigators ten feet away, he said: "They were working on their projects. I was working on mine. . . . They were sitting in my office and the shredder was right outside and I walked out and shredded documents. They could hear it." Asked if he considered that illegal or wrong, he said, smiling: "That's why the Government of the United States gave me a shredder." *

North was the star of television's Sunday morning political shows, not as a guest, but as the subject. A number of questions asked of committee members cited a *New York Times*/CBS News poll report-

---

* After the July 10, 1987, session, the Justice Department denied any shredding was done in the presence of Justice attorneys. During the Iran-contra hearings, Attorney General Meese had his own problems with Congress. He was testifying before a Senate committee concerned about his $55,000 investment in a Bronx, New York, company, Wedtech, which was being investigated for cheating the government on arms contracts. There were also a number of serious gaps in the financial disclosure statements he had filed when he entered government. Finally, another member of Reagan's original Troika, Michael Deaver, was scheduled to go to trial on perjury charges stemming from his lobbying for foreign governments after leaving the White House.

ing that 62 percent of respondents believed the colonel was telling the truth, but 56 percent thought Reagan was lying. He was, on television, out-Reaganing Reagan. "North is obviously a persuasive, magnetic individual. . . . I think most Americans are taken by his personality," said Senator George Mitchell of Maine, a ranking Democrat. A Republican, Orrin Hatch of Utah, said: "I think what you have here is a good Marine. . . . He's taken on 26 members of Congress, some of the best attorneys in the country, in four of the toughest days of testimony I've ever seen, and I tell you, I think he's come out pretty well. He's come off candid and I think most Americans are proud that we have people like that who are willing to fight for our country." Eleanor Clift of *Newsweek,* appearing on *The McLaughlin Group,* added: "He's Rocky, Rambo, Patton and the boy next door all wrapped up in one."

On Monday morning, the fifth day, North offered a final surprise. He said that Manucher Ghorbanifar, the first middle man in the Iranian initiative, had offered him a $1 million bribe to speed up deliveries of weapons to Iran, but that he had rejected the money. His six-day miniseries ended with lectures from the senators and representatives on their own Americanism. As *The New York Times* reported it in a lead story by R. W. Apple Jr.: "The Congressional committee investigating the Iran-contra affair reached out today, in full view of a national television audience, and tried to take back control of their hearings from the man who so dramatically dominated them last week. Legislators from both parties seemed determined to show that they had thought just as deeply about the conflicts between the executive and the legislative branches and about patriotism, freedom and democracy as had the Marine officer who lectured them."

Many of his interrogators simply preferred focusing on North's patriotic daring rather than his obvious lies and lawbreaking. Hatch's response was fairly typical: "I don't want you prosecuted. I don't. I don't think many people in America do."

But the questioning of North did not end with a whimper. The House chairman, Lee Hamilton, said in his closing statement: "I am impressed that the policy was driven by a series of lies: lies to Iranians, lies to the CIA, lies to the Attorney General, lies to our friends and allies, lies to the Congress, lies to the American people. To uphold our Constitution requires not the exceptional work of the few, but the confidence and trust and the work of the many."

Chairman Inouye, a World War II veteran who lost his right arm in combat, began his final statement saying that the United States Code of Military Justice prohibits military men and women from following unlawful orders. "The principle was so important," he continued, "that we, the Government of the United States, proposed that it be internationally applied in the Nuremberg trials."

Brendan Sullivan angrily interrupted: "Mr. Chairman, I find this offensive. . . . To make reference to the Nuremberg [war crimes] trials, I find to be personally and professionally distasteful. Mr. Chairman, why don't you listen to the American people? There are 20,000 telegrams in our room outside that came in this morning."

The Republican vice chairman, Senator Warren Rudman of New Hampshire, then interrupted Sullivan, saying that some of those telegrams and some pro-North rallies around the country had attacked Inouye and his heritage as a Japanese-American. "He holds the nation's second highest award for distinguished service,"—Inouye won the Distinguished Service Cross as a combat infantryman in Italy—"he is one of the greatest men I have ever known. . . . Ethnic slurs have no place in America."

But North had the last word. "I fully agree, Mr. Rudman."

On July 14, the committee recalled McFarlane to rebut North. McFarlane did just that, saying: "His testimony that I permitted with knowledge the creation of a separate, clandestine and far-reaching network of private operations that involved private profits and to be concealed even from other members of the executive branch—this is untrue." . . . "Colonel North testified that I directed that White House chronologies be altered. This is not true." . . . "Colonel North testified that he and Director Casey had agreed upon a full service operation to support the contras using non-appropriated funds. I never heard of any such full service operation." . . . "The hiring of third parties to sell arms, things like that—went over the line from advice to an operational role. And that was not authorized." But he closed by adding: "I don't think Colonel North would ever make a deliberate misstatement or lie."

The next day, Vice Admiral Poindexter began his testimony. He wore civilian clothes and puffed his pipe, a man as gray as North was colorful, but just as defiant. The man who had finished first in his class at the Naval Academy and was said to have a photographic memory answered 184 questions by saying "I don't recall" or "I don't remember." On the diversion of Iranian funds to the Nicaraguan contras, however, he was more direct: "I was convinced that I understood the

President's thinking on this and that if I had taken it to him, that he would have approved it."

"So," said Arthur Liman, counsel to the Senate committee, "you did not tell the President?"

"I did not. The buck stops here. I made the decision. I felt that I had the authority to do it. I was convinced that the President would, in the end, think it was a good idea. But I didn't want him to be associated with the decision."

The President's summary of the day began: "Poindexter found the concept no different from the support for the contras from private individuals. Poindexter made a conscious decision not to tell the President in an effort to 'insulate' the President from politically volatile consequences and to provide the President with 'deniability.' . . . Poindexter testified that the President signed, probably on December 5, 1985, a finding that the CIA had prepared to ratify its involvement in the November, 1985 Israeli arms shipment to Iran. . . . He destroyed the original, the only copy of the finding on November 21, 1986."

Of that memo, confirming the Iranian dealings were straight arms-for-hostages—with no suggestion of "improved relations" or "moderate elements"—Poindexter said: "I thought it was a significant political embarrassment for the President and I wanted to protect him from possible disclosure of this."

Poindexter completed his testimony on July 21, sticking to his story that Iran-contra responsibility stopped with him—an arrogant claim that a Republican representive, Michael DeWine of Ohio, said amounted to placing himself between President Reagan and the American people. On a factual matter, Poindexter did say that he could not recall the five "diversion" memos mentioned by North: "I frankly don't think those existed." As his last day ended, he said secrecy was necessary to protect White House operations from a Congress that leaked and a press that deliberately distorted the facts, and added that he tried to cut out the State Department as well because he did not trust Secretary Shultz. As far as he was concerned, using one of his favorite expressions, Shultz was a "CYA" guy—that is, "Cover Your Ass." Hamilton attacked him and North as well for, at best, usurping the President's powers by withholding information from him, whatever the reasons. "If the President did not know what you did, he should have," said the co-chairman. Poindexter did not reply to that, but closed saying: "I leave this hearing with my head held high. . . . I don't have any regrets for anything I did. I think the actions I took were in the long-term interest of the country and I am not going to change my mind, and I'm not going to be apologetic about it."

USA Today's lead on his testimony was: "The admiral fell on his sword, saving the President." The performances of the vice admiral and the lieutenant colonel were different in style and substance. Poindexter, it seemed, had accomplished what he had set out to do: protect the President. North had set out to protect and project himself—and by the end of his performance national polls indicated that more than 80 percent of respondents said they believed what he had to say. Whatever he said. As the hearings ended, *The Washington Post* revisited North's contention, during his interrogation, that he had been forced to lie to Congress because leaks from Capitol Hill endangered American lives. The example he used involved the *Achille Lauro* hijacking back in October of 1985. The leaked stories in question were in *Newsweek,* which revealed its source in the issue dated July 27. Its anonymous source, said the magazine, was Oliver North.

The President chose August 12, seven days after the Iran-contra committee ended its public hearings, to finally comment on what America had been seeing and hearing for eleven weeks. During those weeks, he had been pretty much invisible in Washington, though he did make some out-of-town trips—to Florida, Connecticut, Indiana, and Wisconsin—to talk about domestic matters, usually the federal budget and its deficits. All that while, he said he was waiting for the hearings to end. The television show had ended on August 3; the last two weeks had been taken up with a parade of Cabinet members complaining that they were lied to for more than a year by the White House, the NSC, the CIA, and each other. Secretary of State Shultz, appearing on July 23, said he had threatened to quit three times because of the lying in the White House and the CIA, producing a four-column lead headline in the *New York Times*:

SHULTZ ANGRILY TELLS INQUIRY
CASEY AND OTHERS DECEIVED HIM
REPEATEDLY OVER IRAN DEALINGS

TALE OF DUPLICITY

On July 29, Attorney General Meese, whose tricky financial dealings were the subject of a separate federal investigation, was the witness. The next morning's lead headline in the *Times* was:

MEESE SAYS NORTH
LIED EITHER TO HIM
OR TO COMMITTEE

On July 30, it was former chief of staff Regan. The headline in the same place was:

REGAN TESTIFIES
REAGAN FELT IRAN
'SNOOKERED' HIM

On August 1, the last witness, Secretary of Defense Weinberger, said he was told the Iran operation was over when it was not, producing a three-column lead headline:

WEINBERGER SAYS
HE FELT HE'D ENDED
THE IRAN DEALINGS

"The story has now been told," said Senator Inouye. "It is a chilling story of deceit and duplicity and the arrogant disregard of the rule of law. It is a story of how a great nation betrayed the principles that made it great."

The President, who had said "I'm not going to comment until the hearings are over—and then you won't be able to shut me up," spoke for only eighteen minutes on the night of August 12. And only seven minutes were on Iran-contra:

These past nine months have been confusing and painful ones for the country. . . . The image—the reality—of Americans in chains, deprived of their freedom and families so far from home, burdened my thoughts. And this was a mistake. . . . I was stubborn in my pursuit of a policy that went astray. . . . Colonel North and Admiral Poindexter believed they were doing what I would have wanted done—keeping the democratic resistance alive in Nicaragua. . . . I was aware that the resistance was receiving funds directly from third countries and from private efforts, and I endorsed those endeavors whole-heartedly; but—let me put this in capital letters—I did not know about the diversion of funds. . . . Yet the buck does not stop with Admiral Poindexter, as he stated in his testimony; it stops with me. The admiral testified that he wanted to protect me; yet no President should ever be protected from the truth. No operation is so secret it must be kept from the commander-in-chief. I had the right, the obligation to make my own decision.' *

Then he started what amounted to a second and longer speech, saying: "Let me tell you where I'm going to put my heart and my energies for the remainder of my term." He said he would seek peace in Nicaragua, he would sign the intermediate-range missile treaty with the Soviets, he would win Bork's confirmation, and he would win passage of a constitutional balanced budget amendment. The little list was a faint echo of the four goals he had brought to Washington more than six years ago. He ended, a bit sadly: "My fellow Americans, I have a year and a half before I have to clean out this desk. I'm not about to let the dust and cobwebs settle on the furniture in this office or on me."

Not everyone was sure about the cobwebs. *The Wall Street Journal* published a long front-page article that day by Gerald F. Seib and Ellen Hume under the headline "Visibly Aged and Hurt by Hearings, Reagan Tries Hard to Rebound": "Clearly the trauma of the past nine months has taken its toll. The 76-year-old Reagan has aged visibly, he lacks the vigor and passion he once displayed, and he regularly lapses into long discourses about his days as Governor of California. Thus the central question is whether Mr. Reagan still possesses the personal and political strength to keep his administration from sliding into impotence."

The *Journal* also quoted Brent Scowcroft: "He's lost all his clout with Congress. They're not afraid of him anymore." After the speech he flew off for a twenty-five-day vacation at the ranch, marking 374 days, more than a year, that the Reagans had spent in California since he took office in 1981.

The four new goals articulated on August 12—a couple were actually old—were a mixed batch. Victory in Nicaragua had been replaced by "peace" because five Central American countries, under the leadership of President Oscar Arias Sánchez of Costa Rica, had signed

---

* An ABC News quickie poll with 612 respondents indicated that only 46 percent of respondents were satisfied by the President's explanation; 57 percent said they believed he knew about the diversion of funds from the Iran sales to the contras.

a regional treaty five days before with guidelines to seek the end of warfare in Nicaragua, El Salvador, Guatemala, and Honduras. The struggle to confirm Bork in the Senate was a possible loser. "I think Bork's only a little better than 50-50," the Republican leader, Senator Dole, had told the President before the speech. And the balanced budget amendment was a perennial loser.

But still, there were rising hopes around the world that the Soviet Union and the United States were headed toward an intermediate-range missile agreement and a Washington summit meeting between Reagan and Gorbachev. In early July, CIA assessments sent to the White House had reported that the Soviet leader had made great progress in solidifying his party leadership, but that making good on his promises of economic improvement at home were linked to better relations and new agreements with the United States and other Western countries. In a twenty-four-page Intelligence Assessment titled "Gorbachev: Steering the USSR Into the 1990s," agency analysts concluded:

> In the scenario that gives Gorbachev the greatest scope for action, the USSR reaches an agreement with the United States that reduces strategic offensive forces and defers testing of a space-based ABM (Anti-Ballistic Missile) until the 21st century (although a further weakening of Congressional and popular support for the US administration's defense programs would serve much the same purpose). The agreements in turn help to pave the way for a substantial increase in East-West economic relations, including liberal credits and a rising number of joint ventures. Eastern Europe shares the revival of commercial relations, reducing the economic burden in the Soviet Union of supporting East European living standards. Finally, Gorbachev succeeds in solidifying a friendly regime in Kabul that is able to reduce the scale of Afghan resistance to a tolerable level.
>
> A realization of this scenario or major elements of it would give the leadership *peredyshka* (breathing space) necessary to keep rising military budgets from choking off reconstruction of the economy. . . . Less tangible but possibly just as important would be the impact of foreign policy successes on Gorbachev's authority in the party.

There were ironies within ironies in the entangling relations between the General Secretary and the President. Reagan had been right from the start in his simple or simplistic conclusions that the Soviet Union's fatal flaws were economic, and that those weaknesses could be exploited to bring the system down. But now he and a Soviet leader needed each other to cover their own political failings: Gorbachev needed his *peredyshka;* Reagan needed foreign policy triumphs to reverse the drift of his last two years in office. On July 22, former President Nixon reported to the White House on his recent meeting with Gorbachev. As summarized for Howard Baker, Nixon said: "Regarding the INF agreement, he said he had advised Gorbachev to deal seriously with the President because 'if he waits to deal with his successor and negotiates a deal with him that RR doesn't like, RR has more than enough popularity in the country to kill it.' He also told Gorbachev that it would take at least two years to come to an agreement with a new president."

Whatever his reasoning, Gorbachev had made his move the same day that Nixon was offering his thoughts. He announced in Moscow that he was dropping his Reykjavik demand that his military be allowed to keep one hundred intermediate-range nuclear missiles in Soviet Asia—east of the Urals—as part of any treaty eliminating missiles in Europe. In effect, Gorbachev said he was prepared to accept the American "Double Zero" position—first proposed by Reagan in 1981 and quickly dismissed by the arms control establishment in Geneva and other treaty-making places—for an agreement to destroy *all* intermediate-range and medium-range missiles. There was at least one more problem. There were seventy-two Pershing IA short-range missiles in West Germany, old weapons scheduled for renovation and upgrades that would make them capable of hitting Soviet targets thirteen minutes after launch. The United States owned and controlled the warheads but the missiles themselves were owned by the West Germans.

On August 26, West German chancellor Helmut Kohl announced that if the Americans and the Soviets reached an agreement in Geneva on eliminating missiles in Europe, the West German government would destroy the seventy-two Pershings. "What I want," said Kohl, "is to help the American President to successfully conclude the Geneva arms talks." The American President then came down from the mountaintop of Rancho del Cielo to give a speech on Soviet-American relations to a Town Hall of California meeting in Los Angeles. He praised Kohl and then said: "We're near an historic agreement that could eliminate a whole class of missiles. . . . We can wrap up an agreement on intermediate-range nuclear missiles promptly." In Moscow, Gennady Gerasimov, the government's foreign policy spokesman, praised Kohl as well, and said: "The situation has obviously changed for the better . . . there is a realistic chance of an agreement now."

Events were in the saddle. On September 18, in Washington, Secretary Shultz and Soviet foreign minister Shevardnadze completed work on a tentative draft agreement to scrap 1,015 missiles, with ranges from three hundred to three thousand miles, deployed in Europe and Asia. Their agreement proposed destroying 332 American missiles in West Germany, Great Britain, Italy, and Belgium, while the Soviets would destroy 512 missiles aimed at Western Europe and another 117 aimed at China and Japan. The next day Reagan and Shultz met the press with an announcement that produced a decked headline across the six-column front page of the *Times*:

REAGAN AND GORBACHEV TO MEET THIS YEAR
TO SIGN MISSILE PACT, NOW NEARLY COMPLETE

Five weeks later, Secretary of State Shultz was in Moscow working on the INF Treaty and summit plans with Foreign Minister Shevardnadze. On the morning of October 23, Shultz, along with Carlucci and Jack Matlock, the new American ambassador, met with Gorbachev in St. Catherine's Hall in the Kremlin. The main purpose of the session was to set the date and the conditions of the Washington summit, but things went badly. The Soviet leader seemed distracted and hostile, complaining about the time it was taking to work out the treaty, asking what was the point of all these meetings. He refused to set a date for the trip to Washington. Back at Spasso House, the home of the American ambassador, Shultz went into the building's soundproof telephone setup and called the President. "Something's happened," he said of Gorbachev. "He isn't as cocky, like a boxer who's never been knocked down. This boxer has been hit." Then Shultz went into a press conference and said the summit was off.

The Secretary of State was right. Something had happened: Gorbachev had been confronted and criticized at a Central Committee meeting by one of his protégés, Boris Yeltsin, who had been the Communist Party chief in Sverdlovsk before Gorbachev brought him to Moscow as chairman of the Central Committee. On October 21, at a closed meeting of party leaders, Yeltsin had accused Gorbachev of moving too slowly on economic reforms, of spending his time roaming the world and building a personality cult. It took the Americans more than a week to get information on what had happened. By then Yeltsin had been stripped of his party positions and forced to offer a formal apology in the party newspaper, *Pravda*, saying: "One of my most characteristic personal traits, ambition, has manifested itself lately. I tried to control it but, regrettably, without success. I am very guilty before the city party committee, the Politburo and certainly before Mikhail Sergeyevich Gorbachev."

On the afternoon of October 30, the President surprised reporters by coming into the press briefing room in the White House, flanked by Shultz and Shevardnadze: "Mr. Shevardnadze has presented a letter to me from General Secretary Gorbachev, who has accepted my invitation to come to Washington for a summit beginning on December 7. At that time we expect to sign an agreement eliminating the entire class of U.S. and Soviet intermediate-range nuclear forces, or INF." He said that Shultz and Shevardnadze and each country's arms negotiators were working on an agreement to reduce strategic offensive arms (long-range weapons) by 50 percent. "We agreed to work toward such an agreement, which I hope to sign during a visit to Moscow next year."

CHAPTER 20
OCTOBER 19, 1987

THE CONFIRMATION HEARINGS OF JUDGE ROBERT BORK began on September 15, almost three months after he was nominated for the Supreme Court by President Reagan—live and in color on national television. "This is the main event of this Congress," said the Republican leader, Senator Bob Dole. It was the main event at the White House, too. The President's first event when he returned to the White House on September 8 had been a little rally of his senior people in the East Room. After a joke or two, he said: "We face no more important task then securing the confirmation to the Supreme Court of Judge Robert Bork. Well, we all know that since his nomination, Judge Bork has come under attack for being some kind of right-wing ideologue. We also know those charges are wrong."

Right-wing and wrong were in the eyes of the beholders. The chairman of the Senate Judiciary Committee, Joseph Biden of Delaware, had already come out against Bork, saying that he believed the judge's goal was to turn back thirty years of liberal social legislation. Before the hearings began, a long list of organizations had been scouring Bork's writings and his Appeals Court decisions to find the right (or wrong) words to use in statements, newspaper advertisements signed by columns of supporters and detractors, and even television commercials for and against the sixty-year-old jurist. Gregory Peck, more famous as an actor than Reagan had been, was the voice of a $200,000 anti-Bork commercial campaign on television, saying such things as: "He defended poll taxes and literacy tests which kept many Americans from voting. He opposed the civil rights law that ended 'Whites Only' signs at lunch counters." The American Conservative Union responded with ads declaring: "He is probably the greatest legal scholar of our time—probably the most qualified nominee within the last 50 years."

It was not hard for the opposition to find ammunition. Bork was a rumpled, genial man who loved to talk and loved to write. In 1963, he had written an article in *The New Republic* opposing civil rights laws requiring hotels and restaurants to serve black people, saying such laws would curtail "the freedom of the individual to choose with whom he will deal." He later changed that view—"I was in my libertarian phase, wild with ideas"—but he was as provocative on other legal issues, opposing "one-man, one-vote" legislation, then saying "freedom of speech" should apply only to "political speech." On abortion rights, Bork said the fundamental Supreme Court decision, *Roe v. Wade* in 1973, was "wrongly decided . . . and unconstitutional." To that he added: "I don't think abortion is any of the court's business. I just don't think there is anything in the Constitution about it."

When he was a professor at Yale, students had called his antitrust class "Pro-Trust"—and then lined up for his classes to hear his dazzling lectures, arguing that the whole idea of antitrust was based on "intellectual errors." He was fond of using words like "absurd" and "unprincipled," not always a good idea in confirmation hearings. His opponents matched that rhetoric. "He believes the highest right in the society is for the majority to impose its moral views on the minority," said Ira Glasser, the executive director of the American Civil Libertires Union. "Had he been around in the 18th century, he would have been against adding the Bill of Rights to the Constitution." The American Bar Association gave Bork its highest rating for potential justices, "Well Qualified," but four of the fifteen members on the evaluation committee gave him the association's lowest rating, "Not Qualified."

There were more than two dozen television cameras pointed at Bork on September 15 as he was introduced to the Judiciary Committee panel by former President Gerald Ford. On NBC News, Tom Brokaw said: "The nomination of Robert Bork is a struggle for the philosophical soul of the U.S. Supreme Court. It is a test of Ronald Reagan's political power in the closing days of his administration." It was not great television, at least as defined by Tom Shales, the television critic of *The Washington Post*: "Talk about your pillow fights. . . . Slow going. That hothead liberal Biden was so sweet and polite to that wildcat conservative Bork that a ballyhooed sparring session came off more like a waltz." Perhaps, but it was Bork who was danc-ing slowly backward.

The nominee began by saying: "My philosophy is neither liberal nor conservative. . . ." He asked the committee to understand that there was a difference between words written for magazines or lec-tures to students and court decisions that changed lives, picking win-ners and losers. "It is a more serious thing altogether," he said, "to ignore or overturn a previous decision. . . . In a classroom, nobody gets hurt. In a courtroom somebody always gets hurt." He knew the difference, he said. Senators from both parties questioned that, focus-ing at one point on Bork's written criticism of a Connecticut decision overturning an old law banning the use of contraceptives by married couples. "Does the majority have the right to tell a couple that they can't use birth control?" Biden asked. Bork's answer was: "All I have done is point out that the right of privacy . . . was a free-floating right that was not derived in a principled fashion from constitutional mate-rials. That's all I've done."

That was enough. He was whipsawed for five days, as he stated that his views were flexible, that he had changed his mind on many things over the years. "Where is the predictability of Judge Bork?" asked Senator Arlen Specter, a Pennsylvania Republican, citing a list of "significant, pronounced shifts in positions" over the years and since his nomination.

"I've been getting criticism because I never change my mind," Bork said after three days. "And now I'm getting it because I changed my mind."

On the last day, Senator Robert Packwood of Oregon became the first Republican to say he would vote against the President's nominee because he did not trust his answers on abortion issues. When he was asked about that the President said: "I don't think I better say what I think of that." Reagan began to call in senators one at a time, making it personal, asking them to help him, to win one more for the Gipper. "I'd call it arm-twisting, pretty vigorous, too," said Howell Heflin, a conservative Alabama Democrat and former chief justice of that state's supreme court. The retired Chief Justice of the United States, Warren Burger, was recruited to appear before the committee to praise Bork, but on the same day former President Jimmy Carter char-acterized Bork's civil rights views as "particularly obnoxious." Rea-gan was angry about that. When Sam Donaldson shouted a question

during a Rose Garden ceremony honoring high school principals—
"Will Bork fall in committee?"—the President snapped: "Over my
dead body."

The President was in an unusually testy mood, particularly after
reading a wave of newspaper analyses saying that one reason Bork
was in trouble was that Reagan was happily riding his California
trails for almost a month while liberal groups were organizing anti-
Bork campaigns. Speaking at a Republican State Committee meeting
in New Jersey, he looked up from his text and ad-libbed a few angry
lines about the Bork vote: "The process of appointing and confirming
judges is being turned into a political joke. And if I have to appoint
another one, I'll try to find one they'd object to just as much as they
did to this one." In an odd interview with Arnaud de Borchgrave, the
editor of the *Washington Times,* he talked about communist influence
in the press and in Congress: "There is a disinformation campaign
worldwide and that campaign is very sophisticated, very successful,
including a great many in the media and in the press in America. . . .
And on Capitol Hill, too." Reagan spoke with regret of the loss of
House and Senate "Un-American activities" committees to investigate members of Congress and the press who were suspected or accused of having communist connections or leanings. "Now," he said,
"they've done away with those committees, that shows the success of
what the Soviets were able to do in this country."

But it was too late for the old tricks, the telephone talks, and the
twisted arms that had worked so well for Reagan in the past. It was a
painful reminder that as personally popular as he remained, Reagan
was still a lame duck. On October 6, the Judiciary Committee voted
9 to 5 against recommending Bork's confirmation. Specter voted
against the judge. Heflin, deciding on the last day, voted with the majority. It was over. Bork would have no chance in the full Senate and
the President was expected to withdraw the nomination. Or, more
likely, Bork was expected to stand down. But both fought on. The
President declared: "His opponents have made this a political contest
using tactics and distortions that I think are deplorable. . . . I am not
going to withdraw this nomination." Bork appeared at the White
House and said that as a matter of principle he intended to demand
that the entire Senate vote on his nomination. It was a bad couple of
days all around for the administration. In New York, the Dow Jones
Industrial Average, which had been climbing since August of 1982
and hit a record high of 2,641 on October 2, had dropped 91 points

on October 5 and then dropped a record 91.55 points, a 3.47 percent drop, to 2,551 on October 7.

The full Senate vote on the nomination of Judge Bork was scheduled for later in the month, but that was soon a below-the-fold story on the front pages of the nation's newspapers. There was new top-of-the-page news: the possibility of peace in Central America, or of war in the Persian Gulf, and, most of all, as the Dow Jones averages lurched up and down, fear of a stock market crash or a depression.

The hopes of peace in Nicaragua and El Salvador focused on a cease-fire scheduled for November 7, part of the five-nation peace agreement brokered by President Arias of Costa Rica in August. In mid-October, as the White House was lobbying for another $270 million in aid for the contras, Arias was awarded the Nobel Peace Prize for his efforts in ending the wars and insurrections of Central America. At the same time, in the Persian Gulf, Americans and Iranians were exchanging fire as forty ships of the United States Navy began escorting eleven Kuwaiti oil tankers temporarily flying American flags—a legal device called "reflagging" that allowed the Navy to use force in protecting the tankers through the dangers of the Gulf and the Strait of Hormuz on their way to European and Japanese ports.

On October 16, a day when an American-flagged (and American-owned) tanker, the *Sea Isle City,* had been hit by an Iranian missile, wounding eighteen crewmen, the Dow Jones index dropped 108 points, a record. The theories of the day tended to focus on debt; perhaps the week's total decline of 235 points was a reaction to the continuing rise of government, corporate, and personal borrowing—including credit card accounts and home equity loans—that could lead to higher interest rates. *Time* magazine calculated the total of public, business, and private debt was $8 trillion, twice the gross national product, and that Americans were borrowing twice as much money per capita than they had through the end of the 1970s. Or perhaps it was the trade deficit, particularly with Japan, of more than $150 billion a year. There were also concerns about the failure of a couple of banks and dozens of savings and loan associations. And there was fear of war and higher oil prices. As always, no one was sure. Investing, it seemed, was more a matter of emotion and psychology than of logic or science.

The President's only reaction the next day was an answer to a shouted question from one of the reporters who caught up with him as he returned to the White House after visiting his wife at Bethesda

Naval Hospital, where she had been operated on that day for breast cancer. He had not held a press conference in Washington since March and reporters were getting more rambunctious when they actually had a chance to see him. "What do you think of the stock market, Mr. President, what do you think of the stock market?" Reagan answered: "Well, they tell me it's just a correction."

On Monday, October 19, the Dow Jones index lost 508 points, a 22.6 percent drop, to 1,738.74. The percentage loss was almost double that of October 28, 1929, the day of the stock market crash that ended the Roaring Twenties and preceded the Great Depression of the 1930s. The White House issued a three-paragraph statement, read by Marlin Fitzwater: "The President has watched today with concern the continuing drop in the stock market. He directed members of his administration to consult with the Chairmen of the Federal Reserve, the Securities and Exchange Commission, the New York Stock Exchange, the Chicago Commodities and Futures Exchanges, and leaders of the investment community. Those consultations confirm our view that the underlying economy remains sound."

That evening, reporters caught Reagan at the South Portico of the White House when he left the building to go to Bethesda to visit Mrs. Reagan. "Mr. President," a reporter asked, "are we headed for another great crash?"

"I only have one thing to say," Reagan called out. "I think everyone's a little puzzled, and I don't know what meaning it might have because all the business indices are up. . . . Maybe it's some people seeing a chance to grab some profit, I don't know." Someone slipped in a question about the destruction of three Iranian oil platforms, shelled for hours by American destroyers in retaliation for the missile attack on the *Sea Isle City*. "What's your message to Khomeini?"

Another reporter joked, "Invest in our stock market?"

Reagan's answer was: "If I really gave it to you, you wouldn't be able to print it. . . . I've got to go to the hospital."

Overnight polling, on the President's desk the morning of Wednesday, October 20, included a note titled "Stated Reasons for Stock Market Decline." The list began: "Lack of leadership in Washington . . . budget deficit . . . trade deficit . . . declining bond market (worldwide) . . . computer-programmed trading." It ended with: "Stock market overvalued relative to recent economic growth." That day's *Washington Post* analysis by John Berry blamed the President himself: "For months, the huge, stubborn U.S. trade deficit and the Federal government's budget deficit have cast a shadow over the nation's financial markets. The shadow fell first on the bond market last spring. Since late March, the value of some long-term U.S. Government bonds has dropped about 30 percent. . . . To many financial market participants, the existence of the towering deficits underscores the fact that the Federal government, and the nation as a whole, are living beyond their means."

Reporters spotted the President again that evening as he headed for Bethesda. This time, however, there was no shouting because Reagan had a five-paragraph statement that he read to them. It began: "I guess you all know now that the market closed up 102.27. . . ." He ended by saying that he was directing aides to meet with congressional leaders to forge a budget deficit reduction package. "Our citizens should not panic. And I have great confidence in the future."

He answered four questions. The first was "Are you willing to compromise on taxes?"

"I'm willing to look at whatever proposal they might have."

The second question seemed to be asking the President whether he was actually in charge here. "Are you willing to personally—personally—sit down with Democrats at an economic summit?"

"I don't know whether that's necessary or whether we would do it with some of our people."

A reporter began a question by asserting that the President had never submitted a balanced budget to Congress. Reagan answered angrily: "No, because I said from the beginning . . . that there was one way you could balance the budget now in one year. . . . I have never gotten a budget that I asked for, even though the law says I must submit it to Congress. And the Congress is responsible for the deficit."

The South Portico Q-and-A's resumed at the same time on Thursday. "I've got two statements to make today. Yes, both happy. You know about the market. It closed up 186 and some fraction. . . . More than half the loss has already been regained." The Dow Jones index was back to 2,027. "But the most important of today's news is, at 9:15 A.M., tomorrow morning, I will leave here to go out and pick up Nancy and bring her home." Then he announced he would hold a press conference that night, October 22, the first in the White House in more than seven months.

At exactly 8 P.M.—"Cue the President"—Reagan walked purposefully up the red-carpeted hallway to the East Room, to the podium facing rows of reporters, tense and angry men and women, most of whom felt they had been pushed around and manipulated for months as Reagan tried to avoid the questions raised by Iran-contra and various other messes.

"Well," he said, with a grin, "it seems like just yesterday . . ."

Laughter swept the room. Ronald Reagan was back in town. It was almost impossible not to like the man.

The opening statement was about the stock market—the Dow Jones was falling again, 77 points that day—and the federal budget. "First," he began, "I will meet with the bipartisan leadership of Congress to arrange a procedure for deficit reduction. . . . I'm putting everything on the table with the exception of Social Security. . . . I'm creating a task force that over the next thirty to sixty days will examine the stock market procedures and make recommendations on any necessary changes."

There were questions about the Bork vote in the Senate, scheduled for the next day, and about AIDS. But most of the half-hour was about stocks and the deficit, and about the danger of war in the Persian Gulf. The occasion was friendly enough, but the President's performance was far from his best. He mangled references to the new Gramm-Rudman-Hollings deficit-reduction bill, which he had signed less than a month earlier after it was rewritten in Congress to change the key provisions ruled unconstitutional by the Supreme Court. He was defensive in expressing confidence in the economy and blaming Democrats for everything that seemed to be going wrong, beginning with the national debt and the troubles in the stock market.

> I believe this expansion we are having is largely due to the tax cuts we implemented early in our administration—but for all this time the percentage of revenues is about—well, it's about 19 percent every year of the gross national product. Now the gross national product has been increasing in size quite sizably. So that if we are getting revenues that are still 19 percent of that larger gross national product than the smaller, it would indicate that the revenues are sufficient. But the problem is that the deficit is—or should I say, wait a minute, the spending I should say of gross national product—forgive me—the spending is roughly 23 percent to 24 percent, so that is what is increasing while revenues are staying proportionately the same and what would be the proper amount we should be taking from the private sector.

Finally someone asked: "Are you still against tax increases?"

"They'll find out when I sit down there," he answered.

As for the Persian Gulf, Reagan said: "We're not there to start a war. And we're there to protect neutral nations' shipping in international waters. . . . They on the other hand—the irrationality of the Iranians—they have taken to attacking. . . . We've said that if attacked, why, we're going to defend ourselves. . . . And I don't think there's anything to panic about."

The New York Times coverage of the news conference, by R. W. Apple Jr., was harsh and negative: "In a bid to calm the frenzy in the world's financial markets, President Reagan announced . . ." The second paragraph began: "Fighting to restore his fading reputation for leadership, and with it credibility for his hard-pressed Administration, the President conceded . . ."

Garbled sentences and forgetful moments of the kind heard that night were becoming more common. And so was press speculation about the President's age and aging. Even the Associated Press, normally more evenhanded than the *Times* and other important news organizations, sent out a story based on interviews about the President's memory, saying: "Like many Americans, particularly as they get older, President Reagan sometimes has trouble remembering what he wants to say. Some say it's getting worse. . . . Reagan himself said in a recent interview he felt 'desperate' because he couldn't remember a senator's name."

The Bork nomination was rejected by the Senate, 58 to 42, the biggest vote against a nominee in history. The number on Wall Street was zero. The Dow Jones average was up less than one-half of one percent. Four days later, on Monday, October 27, as the President and congressional leaders met in the White House to begin their deficit-reduction discussions, the Dow Jones dropped 157 points to 1,724, losing 8 percent of its total value. On Tuesday, it gained back 55 points. Numbers seemed to be running the government of the United States. Official Washington was clocking the Dow Jones minute by minute and adjusting their rhetoric up and down with the index. *The New York Times* coverage of the deficit-reduction talks this day began: "Eager not to disappoint the financial markets . . ."

After listening to some arguments inside the White House, Reagan announced his next nominee for the Supreme Court on October 29. His chief of staff, Howard Baker, was campaigning for Anthony Kennedy, a fifty-year-old federal judge with twelve years on the bench in Sacramento, California—a moderate conservative by all accounts. But Attorney General Meese had a candidate most notable for his youth, Judge Douglas Ginsburg, who had served on the Court of Appeals in the District of Columbia for the past year. Ginsburg, who was forty-one, had taught at Harvard Law School and served in the Justice Department under Meese. His written work consisted of thirteen Appeals Court decisions. In other words, he was the anti-Bork, no one would read every thought he had ever had. He lasted nine days. He was a great favorite of conservative senators led by Jesse Helms of North Carolina, but Ginsburg asked the President to withdraw the nomination forty-eight hours after confirming a National Public Radio report that he had used marijuana occasionally in the 1960s and 1970s—an admission that embarrassed his conservative sponsors and once again bolstered Meese's image as a champion of sloppy work habits. One of the conservative senators backing off his strong support for Ginsburg, Orrin Hatch of Utah, had an angry reaction: "It's about time for Ronald Reagan to take charge of his White House."

Perhaps Meese was distracted. He was testifying before a grand jury at the U.S. District Courthouse for the fifth time on conflict-of-interest investigations of his personal finances and investments in companies seeking government help. That was on the sixth floor. On the second floor, Michael Deaver was on trial for perjury. On the fourth floor, Oliver North was taking the Fifth Amendment on all questions asked by another grand jury, this one investigating possible criminal charges involving his Iran-contra operations.

On November 11, the President nominated Judge Anthony Kennedy for the Supreme Court. "He stopped going for the home run and tried for the political equivalent of a clean single," reported *Time* magazine. It was a day for important personnel decisions. Secretary of Defense Weinberger had told Reagan that he wanted to resign to spend more time with his wife, Jane, who was suffering from both cancer and arthritis. The President quickly decided on National Security Adviser Frank Carlucci to replace him. The new director of the NSC, Reagan's sixth, would be Carlucci's deputy, Army Lieutenant General Colin Powell, the first black man to serve in that position. The professionals, the pragmatists—Shultz, Carlucci, Powell—had taken over, walking where Haig, Weinberger, Richard Allen, and Bill Clark trod. The Reagan administration that had invaded official Washington was officially a thing of the past, as many thought Reagan was. "The Reagan Revolution has been assimilated," said the President's former communications director, the blunt Pat Buchanan. "The spirit of compromise is in the air. The theme is, 'Let's go up and compromise one for the Gipper.' "

The report of the congressional committees investigating Iran-contra was scheduled for release on November 18. On November 16, the President's counsel, Arthur Culvahouse, as he had during the forty days of committee hearings, sent Reagan a summary. This one was ten pages long. It began: "The majority report reaches harsh conclusions . . ."

The harshest conclusion, according to the memo: "The ultimate responsibility for the events in the Iran/Contra affair must rest with the President. If the President did not know what his national security advisers were doing, he should have." Other conclusions emphasized in the memo included: "The report adds considerable detail to the public record regarding operations of so-called 'Enterprise' (the group of companies and individuals assisting in the arms sales to Iran and in the Contra resupply operations). The 'Enterprise' was allegedly run by Maj. General (Ret.) Richard Secord and naturalized American citizen Albert Hakim, under the direction of Lt. Col. Oliver North. . . . The report concludes that the 'Enterprise' received approximately $16.1 million in profits from the Iran arms sales by marking up the price charged to Iran over the price paid to the U.S. Government . . . approximately $3.8 million was 'diverted' from the arms proceeds to the freedom fighters." In total, the "Enterprise" had raised at least $48 million, and spent approximately $35.8 million. Somebody had made a lot of money. Culvahouse also informed the President that one of the 450-page report's conclusions was: "The President has not yet condemned activities of former members of his staff who lied, shredded documents and covered up their actions." *

The committees' report, which the President did not read, was released forty-eight hours later. It described the Enterprise as a secret mini-government operating out of the White House with its own little air force of six planes and hidden airstrips, boats, weapons, ware-

---

* Eighteen members of the joint committees, including three Republican senators, signed the majority report. Eight House Republicans on the committees, led by Representative Dick Cheney of Wyoming, issued a 150-page minority report, which concluded: "There were mistakes in judgment, and nothing more. There was no constitutional crisis, no systematic disrespect for the 'rule of law,' no grand conspiracy, and no Administration-wide dishonesty or cover-up."

houses, safe houses, communications centers, and Swiss bank accounts. A key paragraph read:

> The common ingredients of the Iran and Contra policies were secrecy, deception and disdain for the law. A small group of senior officials believed that they alone knew what was right. They viewed knowledge of their actions by others in the Government as a threat to their objectives. They told neither the Secretary of State, the Congress nor the American people of their actions. When exposure was threatened, they destroyed official documents and lied to Cabinet officials, to the public and to elected representatives in Congress. They testified that they even withheld key facts from the President. . . . Nevertheless, the ultimate responsibility for the events in the Iran-Contra Affair must rest with the President.

The President did not bother to comment on it. Sam Donaldson hollered a question at him as he crossed from the Oval Office to the Old Executive Office Building, asking him what he thought of the report: "You don't want to know," said Reagan. Then the White House issued a five-paragraph statement that included: "This new report reflects the subjective opinions in not even the unanimous judgment of the committee. . . . The President did not violate any laws. . . . The American people have had the opportunity to make their own judgments, and it serves no purpose for us to argue with the opinions of the committee members. . . . We are moving on."

That was that. The damage to Reagan's presidency had already been done over the full year since the revelation of the arms sales to Iran. One of television's favorite commentators, Norman Ornstein of the American Enterprise Institute, said: "The report today is an aftershock." Senator Inouye had the next-to-last words: "They ran a government outside government. They conducted a secret foreign policy and concealed it through a concerted campaign of dishonesty and deception. And when the affair began to unravel, they attempted to cover over their deeds." The last word would be left to Lawrence Walsh, the special prosecutor investigating possible criminal behavior, especially by North and Poindexter.

With no President to show or quote, Iran-contra disappeared in a day. Literally. The space and time of November 19 were filled with news that the Dow Jones had lost 44 points on rumors and guesses that the budget negotiators in Washington were not close to agreement. But a deal of sorts was announced on November 20, presented with complicated and misleading charts and explanations on revenues and expenditures. Faced that day with the budget-reduction deadlines of the renovated Gramm-Rudman-Hollings law, White House and congressional negotiators announced that they had a plan to reduce the deficit by $30 billion. Under G-R-H, as the President called it, the 1988 budget would have been reduced by across-the-board spending cuts of $23 billion, with half of that coming from the Department of Defense. The negotiated deal, which would have to be approved by Congress, was not much more than an outline. It would take $5 billion from the Defense Department, $6.6 billion from domestic spending, a onetime $6.6 billion from selling assets, and $9.6 billion in unspecified new tax revenues.

News organizations dutifully called Walter Mondale to talk about his 1984 prediction that the President would have to raise taxes to reduce deficits. Even Prime Minister Thatcher became part of the negotiations, issuing a statement in London saying that Reagan should follow her example in raising taxes to cut budget deficits. "Make cuts," she said, "sufficient to restore confidence, clearly and decisively."

There was still no confidence restored on the stock market, as the Dow Jones averages remained stuck in the 1,800 range, just above the level after the crash of October 19. And Central American peace talks seemed bogged down as well. It was not the best of times in the White House upstairs or down. Four days after Mrs. Reagan returned after her breast cancer operation, her mother, Edith Davis, died in Arizona. The news was delivered to the President by his official physician, Dr. John Hutton. He went upstairs to tell his wife, who was lying on her bed, talking to her son, Ronald Jr., on the telephone when the President walked in. "What's wrong?" she said, but he could not seem to speak. Then, using her stepfather's first name, he said: "Edie's with Loyal."

Downstairs there were piles of negative newspaper and magazine clippings outside the President's office. One of them was the *National Journal*, featuring a piece by William Schneider headlined: "Reagan Now Viewed as an Irrelevant President." The text focused on the President's 1984 "Morning in America" reelection, which Schneider characterized as a campaign without an agenda other than winning. Using poll data, he wrote: "After Reagan did the two things he was elected to do in 1980—curb inflation and restore the nation's sense of military security—the public lost interest in his agenda." And so, it seemed, he did, too. "Since November 4, 1986"—the day Republicans lost control of the Senate—"no one in Washington has been afraid of Ronald Reagan."

The politician who was doing really well in American polls was the man on his way to the United States to sign the missile treaty completed in Geneva on November 24 by Shultz and Shevardnadze. "Gorbachev's a Hit with the American Public" headlined *The New York Times,* reporting that only 16 percent of respondents to the *Times*/CBS News poll had an unfavorable view of Gorbachev. The Soviet leader's favorable rating was 38 percent, with the rest saying they had not yet made up their minds. A *Washington Post*/ABC News poll and a *Wall Street Journal*/NBC News poll both showed Gorbachev with approval ratings of more than 50 percent, only a little lower than Reagan's. One result in the *Times*/CBS poll dramatized the change in Reagan's standing after Iran-contra: 45 percent of respondents said they were worried that the "elderly" President of the United States would make too many compromises, would give too much to the "younger and more energetic" Gorbachev.*

Downstairs in the White House, though, the memos and analysis coming to the President in the Oval Office had quite a different view of the man from Moscow. "Summits are moments of high expectations," read a long memo from Richard Perle, who had just left the Defense Department. "People everywhere want desperately to believe that the burden of defending our democracy will be lessened by the Treaty that you and Gorbachev will sign. I have read that your pollster, Richard Wirthlin, has urged you to take as your summit theme the view that the INF Treaty is but a first step leading to a new era in relations with the Soviet Union. I hope Mr. President that you reject that advice. I urge you, instead, to remind the millions who watch you put pen to paper on Tuesday afternoon, that however much we may wish it otherwise, the defense of freedom will require strength and sacrifice."

Robert Gates, back as the CIA's Soviet expert after his nomination as director was withdrawn, wrote the agency's principal briefing: "Gorbachev's Gameplan: The Long View":

---

* By comparison, when Premier Nikita Khrushchev visited the United States during the presidency of Dwight Eisenhower, his favorable ratings never reached 10 percent among American respondents.

The enduring element of foreign policy—even under Gorbachev—is the continuing extraordinary scope and sweep of Soviet military modernization and weapons research and development. Despite Soviet rhetoric, we see no lessening of their weapons production. And, further, Soviet research on new, exotic weapons such as lasers and their own version of SDI continues apace. . . . The third element of Gorbachev's foreign policy is continued protection of Soviet clients in the Third World. Under Gorbachev, the Soviets and Cubans are now providing more than a billion dollars a year in economic and military aid to Nicaragua. And of course, Cuba gets about five billion dollars in Soviet support each year. At a time of economic stress at home, these commitments speak volumes about Soviet priorities.

In the final days before the December 7 opening of the summit, both Gorbachev and Reagan had busily worked to set the context. On December 2, the Soviet leader did a one-hour interview with Tom Brokaw of NBC News, asking: "Why can't we be allies? We were allies at one time, why can't we be allies now? . . . I have to smile when I hear that the security of the United States is being threatened by the Sandinista regime. That's not serious."

The President flew to Jacksonville, Florida, for a question-and-answer session with high school students. He told them: "While talking friendship, the Soviets worked even faster on the largest military build-up in world history. They stepped up their aggression around the world. . . . The simple people of Afghanistan pose no threat to Soviet territory."

Then, on December 3, Reagan sat down for a half-hour with the three network anchormen, Brokaw, Rather, and Jennings, and Bernard Shaw, the anchor of CNN. Rather put the President on the defensive by quoting the *Times*/CBS poll and asking: "What assurances can you give—how can you convince Americans that you have the command of the kind of complex information that's necessary here?—not to have this young, energetic, intelligent, tough Marxist-Leninist eat you and us up?"

Reagan's answer was six years old: "Well, I haven't changed from the time I made a speech about an evil empire."

The same sort of questions were asked by television correspondents when the President was going into a meeting with the Joint Chiefs of

Staff in mid-afternoon on December 7, just before Gorbachev's arrival.

"Are you up to going one-on-one with Mr. Gorbachev?"

"What's that?"

"Are you up to going one-on-one with Mr. Gorbachev? Feeling spunky?"

The plane carrying the Gorbachevs, an Aeroflot Ilyushin 62, landed at Andrews Air Force Base at 5:30 P.M. The Reagans watched on television as the Soviet leader and his wife walked along a magenta carpet to a huge bouquet of microphones. "We are hoping to hear some new words," said the General Secretary. The Reagans went to light the national Christmas tree. The flagpoles around the White House grounds were flying the red hammer-and-sickle flags of the Soviet Union. After the lights came on, reporters were shouting again to the President.

"Do you have some new words for Gorbachev?" one said.

"He'll hear them in the morning," Reagan answered.

CHAPTER 21

DECEMBER 8, 1987

THE HEAVY BLACK RUSSIAN ZIL LIMOUSINE carrying the General Secretary of the Communist Party of the Union of Soviet Socialist Republics arrived at the White House gate at 10 A.M. on Tuesday, December 7, 1987. Inside the building, the President of the United States's valet helped him into his overcoat. His wife refolded his white scarf, kissed him, wiped a bit of lipstick from his face, and whispered: "Knock 'em dead."

Cannons roared twenty-one times and trumpets blared fanfares, the two leaders spoke briefly for microphones and cameras, then went inside to the Oval Office. They indulged shouting reporters and encroaching photographers, and it was almost 11 A.M. before they finally sat down, once more together in front of a blazing fireplace. There were really only a few minutes for conversation, because Gorbachev was returning to the Soviet embassy for lunch and meetings, and the INF treaty signing was scheduled for 1:45 P.M. The time was chosen by Joan Quigley, Mrs. Reagan's astrologer, although no one on the White House staff knew anything about that.

The President had decided to speak first about the issue that most annoyed Gorbachev: human rights and religion in the Soviet Union. He urged the Soviet leader to allow more Jews to leave the Soviet Union. Gorbachev responded to that Reagan style as he had before, with some anger: "I'm not on trial here. I'm not a defendant and you're not my judge." He said he knew the United States had its own immigration problems, talking about quotas and armed guards along the border with Mexico. That short confrontation ended with Reagan saying: "There's a big difference between wanting in and wanting out."

With 250 invited guests looking on in the East Room, Reagan and Gorbachev signed the 80-page treaty calling for the destruction of 1,752 Soviet missiles and 859 American weapons. The missiles accounted for just 4 percent of the two countries' nuclear arsenals, but that did not detract from the drama of the moment. There was a sense that this was a beginning, not an end. Page after page, each paragraph, each word a tribute to the energy and diligence of negotiators laboring for years in the dull quiet of Geneva, working out details of destruction and inspection of the process. "Front section, minute nuclear warhead device and guidance elements, shall be crushed or flattened." . . . "A portion of the launcher chassis, at least 0.78 meters in length, shall be cut off at or near the rear axle" . . . "Inspectors carrying out inspection activities pursuant to paragraph 6 of Article XI shall be allowed to travel within 50 kilometers from the inspection site with permission of the in-country escort. Such travel shall be taken solely as a leisure activity." There was a 73-page annex to the treaty recording the locations of each missile site, a document kept secret by American demand.

Each man had spoken briefly before taking pen in hand. Gorbachev quoted Ralph Waldo Emerson: "The reward of a thing well done is to have done it." Reagan surprised no one by repeating his favorite Russian expression, taught to him originally by Suzanne Massie: "Doveryai no Proveryai," "Trust but Verify." Gorbachev sort of rolled his eyes and got a laugh when he said, "You say that every time we meet."

The two leaders and more than thirty of their staffers then crowded into the Cabinet Room. Reagan was holding the glow of the moment, happy and unfocused. This meeting, closed to the press, was anticlimactic. The President had already done his close-up. But Gorbachev was all business now, working from a small handwritten notebook, taking over the room, saying it was time to move on to discussions of chemical weapons and even the thinning of troop concentrations that could lead to quick escalation of military tensions in places like the Fulda Gap between East and West Germany, where Soviet and NATO troops had faced each other for the past forty years. He spoke for fifteen minutes, listing points he wanted put into the closing statement of the summit. He said that the Soviets were already destroying chemical weapons and facilities, while the Americans had resumed manufacture of such weapons. He also said, as the official minutes recorded: "The United States was still proposing verification only of state facilities. That would include all the Soviet Union's, but not all the U.S.'s."

The Americans in the room waited for Reagan to respond. But the President seemed to be having trouble focusing and, finally, Secretary of State Shultz spoke up, offering an American rebuttal to some of Gorbachev's points. Reagan's only comment was that any country with a fertilizer plant could make chemical weapons. Later, as Gorbachev and Shultz went on, the President said that there was, in America, a legacy of mistrust because of past Soviet expansionism, and that his decisions had to be ratified by the Senate. Gorbachev took over again, as recorded: "Compared to American expansionism, the Soviet side's was a small child. And the Supreme Soviet is even larger than the Senate . . . 2,000 members. . . . It [raised] many questions. There was the question of why the Soviets had been so generous toward the Americans. They were eliminating four times as many missiles. . . . It was not easy to make the first step toward disarmament. People asked how it was possible to have disarmament with the U.S. when the Soviet Union was ringed with U.S. bases. People asked how Gorbachev could bow down to the U.S."

It went on, with Reagan making short comments about supporting Gorbachev's rhetoric and policies of glasnost—"openness." The notes continued: "Gorbachev could assure the President and his colleagues that the Soviet side would be moving ahead toward democratization. That was, if the American side would permit them to do so. He asked the American side to let the Soviet side do it their way."

Then Reagan told a long joke about a professor talking to an American student who had not decided what he wanted to do and the American said he hadn't decided yet. He asked a Russian student and the Russian replied: "They haven't told me yet."

Shultz interrupted again, saying to Gorbachev that perhaps the time had come to turn over the problems he had raised to working groups. The meeting broke up and Gorbachev headed back to the Soviet embassy for tea with an eclectic group of sixty well-known Americans, from Henry Kissinger and Billy Graham to Joyce Carol Oates and Yoko Ono. Graham called him a great preacher. Actor Paul Newman called him a great performer.

Back in the White House, they were worried about the performance of another old actor. Shultz, Powell, and Howard Baker confronted Reagan about his silence and confusion in the Cabinet Room meeting. "That was terrible," said the Secretary of State. Howard

Baker said: "We can't let this happen again, let Gorbachev get away with something like that."

The President nodded, saying: "I better go home and do my homework. Mikhail has all those details. What can we do?"

"Don't do that. Just get some rest," Shultz said. "Colin [Powell] will work up new talking points for your cards." They agreed that there would be no more crowded meetings. Reagan would stick to the Oval Office and its adjoining study.

Dinner was more fun for everybody, or at least almost everybody. Nancy Reagan and Raisa Gorbachev, two women of important influence with their husbands, both impressive public performers, did not get along with each other. "We missed you at Reykjavik," said Mrs. Gorbachev, as soon as they were alone. "I was told the women weren't invited," responded Mrs. Reagan. There were serious moments during the banquet. Richard Perle, in private business now, was seated with the Reagans and the Gorbachevs and decided not to do small talk, instead asking the General Secretary whether he or anyone else in Moscow knew how much the Soviet Union actually spent on defense and national security. "I know," said Gorbachev, adding that it was a state secret. Very secret. Whatever the actual number, it was, in terms of percentage of gross national product, a multiple of American spending. It was the number that made the Soviet Union and the Soviet economy vulnerable to Reagan's increased American spending and development of new systems, beginning with SDI.

"Let me give you my estimate," said Perle. "Twenty-five percent of your Gross National Product." (The official CIA estimate was 16 percent.) Whatever the secret number, Gorbachev just smiled and passed on to other things. At the next table, Secretary of State Shultz was seated near Marshal Akhromeyev, the Soviet military chief he had first met at Reykjavik, and was stunned when the old man, a hero many times over, said: "My country is in trouble, and I am fighting with Mikhail Sergeyevich to save it. That is why we made such a lopsided deal on INF, and that is why we want to get along with you. We want to restructure ourselves and be part of the modern world. We cannot continue to be isolated."

It was, in all, a great and surprising night. Van Cliburn, the American pianist who had become famous twenty years before by winning an international competition in Moscow, played a rousing version of "Moscow Nights," and suddenly the Russians, led by the Gorbachevs, stood up clapping and singing along. As they sang and camaraderie seemed to fill the room, columnist George Will, a friend of the Reagans, whispered to Admiral Crowe, the chairman of the Joint Chiefs of Staff, Akhromeyev's American equivalent: "That song just cost you 200 ships."

The next morning, Wednesday, Reagan and Gorbachev met for ten minutes with only their interpreters in the President's small study next to the Oval Office. The President began by asking Gorbachev to sign a baseball. Joe DiMaggio, the great star of the New York Yankees in the 1940s and 1950s, had been at the dinner but had not had the chance to ask for the General Secretary's autograph. Then he reached into his desk drawer for the cards Powell had produced, his talking points. Reagan said he would like to come to Moscow for a fourth summit in early summer—assuming there would be agreements to sign on arms control and other issues. The American interpreter's memorandum of the conversation continued:

> Gorbachev said that in his conversation with Mrs. Reagan the night before, he had indicated that a program could be arranged which would include time for meetings between the President and himself, meetings of the working groups, but also one or two days during which the President and Mrs. Reagan could see the country. . . . The President said that perhaps some time before he left office, the General Secretary and Raisa could return, not for a summit but to see the country, and California specifically, since one has not seen America without seeing California.

The old Reagan dream: flying with a Soviet leader over the endless suburbs of Southern California, pointing out that each American family had its own home—and swimming pool! Gorbachev, in fact, was interested. "Yes," he said. "I need deeper knowledge of the United States."

The President opened the doors of the Oval Office at 10:55 that morning, inviting in Vice President Bush, along with Shultz, Carlucci, Powell, and Howard Baker. On the Soviet side, Gorbachev was joined by Shevardnadze and Anatoly Dobrynin, the former ambassador, who had become secretary of the Communist Party. This was the real working session of the summit. Reagan was up and ready this time, better prepared and more focused, working from a written agenda. He began by saying he believed there could be an agreement on long-range strategic missile reduction, with both sides agreeing on reducing their arsenals to fewer than five hundred ballistic missile warheads. There was also hope, he said, of constructive discussion of sea-launched cruise missiles. Finally, Reagan repeated his determination to develop a space-based missile shield.

But SDI was no longer the make-or-break issue it had been at Reykjavik for three reasons: Reagan would be President for only another year, so he would not be making many more final decisions; the new Democratic majority in both houses of Congress had cut research funding by one-third; and, most importantly, Soviet scientists had concluded that no shield system could work. Ironically, the scientist who had the most influence in the Soviet debate was Andrei Sakharov, the man called the father of the Soviet H-bomb, who had become the country's most famous dissident. Sakharov, winner of the Nobel Peace Prize in 1975, had been exiled to the city of Gorky in 1980 for publicly criticizing the Soviet invasion of Afghanistan. Allowed to return to teaching and research in Moscow on Gorbachev's personal orders, he persuaded other scientists and the General Secretary himself that SDI was more dream than threat. It almost certainly would not work, he had told Gorbachev, and if it actually did, it could be easily breached for 10 percent of what it would cost the Americans to develop it, much less deploy it. The key to an effective American space defense, the Soviets concluded, was destroying ballistic missiles soon after they left the ground, before they launched multiple warheads. Thus, an SDI system then could be easily and relatively cheaply defeated by building faster rockets and releasing warheads earlier. "Everything has changed since Reykjavik," the Soviet's deputy foreign minister, Alexander Bessmertnykh, privately told his American counterparts. "All the reports we saw indicated SDI was not realistic from the technical point of view. It looked frightening initially, but it wouldn't work. It could produce some by-products like laser weapons in space, but never a system covering the whole nation. . . . Gorbachev is not nervous about it now."

The key exchange between the leaders, recorded in the official minutes that Wednesday morning, sounded like this:

"*Reagan:* We are going forward with the research and development necessary to see if this is a workable concept. And if it is, we are going to deploy it."

"*Gorbachev:* Mr. President, do what you think you have to do. And if in the end you think you have a system you want to deploy, go ahead and deploy. Who am I to tell you what to do? I think you're

wasting money. I don't think it will work. But if that's what you want
to do, go ahead. We are moving in another direction, and we preserve
our option to do what we think is necessary and in our own national
interest at that time. And we think we can do it less expensively and
with greater effectiveness."

"Now we are entering a new phase," said Gorbachev, "a phase of
reducing strategic offensive arms." In English, the acronym was
START: Strategic Arms Reduction Treaty. The official notes continued: "Gorbachev proposed a straightforward approach: 50 percent
reductions in strategic offensive arms; agreement on a period of non-
withdrawal from the ABM Treaty. . . . But if the President wanted to
link that process to SDI, if it had to involve SDI, there would be no
START treaty, either with the President or his successors."

"It would be better not to link the two concepts," Reagan responded. "One issue [START] should not be made hostage to the
other [ABM]." The talks began to rotate into themselves at that point.
"Secretary Shultz clarified that the President did not mean to suggest
that a START treaty be linked to Soviet acceptance of SDI. In fact, he
had said there should be no linkage to anything. Gorbachev interjected that a START treaty had to be linked to the ABM Treaty. . . .
He asked why the U.S. could not accept the Soviet formula: 50 percent reduction in strategic arms; a ten-year non-withdrawal period."

"Gorbachev said the U.S. side was trying to make things 'foggy.' "

"The President replied with some feeling that it was not he who
was making things foggy. He wanted to make things clear. He did not
want to talk about links to SDI, about 50 percent reductions, about
how the Hell the two sides were to eliminate half their nuclear
weapons. He wanted to talk about how the two leaders could sign an
agreement like the one they had signed the day before—an agreement
that made everyone in the world so damned happy it could be felt in
the room at dinner the night before. 'Let's get started.' . . .

"Gorbachev said he was ready."

Shultz said the ABM details should be set aside. "There is agreement on the concept of a certain period. There is agreement on what
should happen at the end of that period. The two sides were not there
yet on what actions were to be permitted during that period, but that
could be worked out."

"Good," said Gorbachev. "A good conversation."

There was talk about Afghanistan and other regional issues until

Reagan said it was 12:30, and they were supposed to meet their wives, who had been touring the White House. But when they got to the South Portico the women were late. The President set up a joke with Gorbachev, and when their wives arrived a couple of minutes later, both men stood there pointing at their watches.

The Gorbachevs lunched with Shultz at the State Department. The General Secretary offered a toast that impressed the guests greatly: "Urging us on is the will of hundreds of millions of people, who are beginning to understand that as the twentieth century draws to a close, civilization has approached a dividing line, not so much between different systems and ideologies, but between common sense and mankind's feelings of self-preservation on the one hand, and the irresponsibility, national selfishness, prejudice—to put it briefly, old thinking—on the other."

"If a spaceship had landed in the middle of Washington, it could not have caused more commotion," reported Maureen Dowd on the front page of *The New York Times* of December 11. The morning before, Thursday, Gorbachev had breakfasted with Vice President Bush at the Soviet embassy and then rode with him in a motorcade to the White House for the final official meeting with President Reagan. The limousine carrying the two men was driving down busy Connecticut Avenue when Bush remarked: "It's too bad you don't have time to go into one of these stores or greet people."

"Stop the car!" Gorbachev shouted and leaped out of the limousine at L Street, his right hand out. The first hand he reached was attached to a Wang Laboratories account executive named Kimberly Spartin. "I'm still shaking," she told reporters. "It was like the coming of the second Messiah or something." The place went wild with cheering and hands in the air as the crowd surrounded the leader of the Soviet Union. Bush's surprised Secret Service detail plunged into the crowd, frantically shouting: "Keep your hands out of your pockets!" Gorbachev's KGB guards stood frozen for the moment. They were all in front of one of Washington's most popular restaurants, Duke Zeibert's, and the Duke was on a balcony, waving and calling to Gorbachev, inviting him in for borscht.

The President saw it all live on television. "What did you think?" asked a reporter later. "Wait until next summer and he sees what I do with his people," said Reagan, laughing. When Gorbachev finally reached the White House, he and Reagan talked for a few minutes about Afghanistan and Nicaragua—official "regional" problems—in the Oval Office study, then went upstairs to the dining room of the family quarters, sitting down for a working lunch a little after 12:30. The notes of the lunch, written by Mark Parris of the State Department and John Herbst of the NSC, included:

"The President said that perhaps for the joint statement we could note agreement that the Soviet Union would stop supplying arms to Nicaragua. Gorbachev responded that the joint statement could say the two sides accepted and supported the Contadora process and the Guatemala accords."

The General Secretary told Reagan he would announce a one-year withdrawal schedule from Afghanistan, a country where more than twelve thousand Soviet military men had died since the Christmas 1979 invasion, if the United States would stop supplying the mujahideen resisting communist rule. In Nicaragua, too, he said he would stop supplying weapons to the Sandinista government if Reagan would end his support of the contras.

In the end, the "regional" issues were left with the working groups, who were putting together the summit's final statement. Before the lunch ended at 2:10 P.M., the President from Dixon, Illinois, and the General Secretary from Privolnoye, Stavropol, connected on another level. Gorbachev said he loved being inside the crowd of Americans at Connecticut and L. The official notes recorded:

> Gorbachev said he had spent his entire career in the provinces. He had developed this style then. . . . He commented that there was more common sense in the provinces than in a nation's capital. . . .
>
> The President responded that he agreed more completely with this than with anything else the General Secretary had said over the past three days. The President said that he often wondered what would happen if he and the other leaders closed the doors of their offices and quietly slipped away. How long would it be before people missed them?

The final statement, being prepared in the Cabinet Room, was scheduled to be ready for a 2:30 P.M. reading. But it wasn't. Baker left Reagan and Gorbachev alone with their wives and interpreters to see what was taking so long. When he came back, Reagan was telling Gorbachev about something he had read in *People* magazine: "There is this 1,200-pound man who never leaves the bedroom. He went to the bathroom one morning, and he fell in the doorway and got stuck. It frightened him so much he went on a diet."

"Is this a real fact," Gorbachev said to his interpreter.

"Yes," Reagan said. "Since his diet, the man's knee measurements shrank to one and one-third meters around. When the diet is complete, he wants to visit the grave of his mother."

Gorbachev asked how to get to the men's room.

The General Secretary had certainly learned a good deal about Americans in three days, but not that the attention spans of citizens (and reporters) were quite different in democracies than in police states. Before leaving Thursday night, the General Secretary gave a final press conference in the Soviet embassy. It lasted an hour and fifty minutes. His opening statement lasted for an hour and fifteen minutes of that time. Shultz accompanied the Gorbachevs to Andrews Air Force Base that evening—the Secretary of State was flying to Europe to give NATO a summary of the summit—and Shultz told Gorbachev that he had watched the whole thing on television. "What did you think?" asked Gorbachev.

"You went on much too long," said Shultz.

Gorbachev slapped the American on the back and said: "Well, at least there's one guy around here who tells you what he thinks." But Gorbachev could be that kind of guy, too. He had surprised American newspaper editors in a meeting the day before with a burst of candor, comparing the Soviet and American economies and saying: "The Soviet Union is the world's second ranking power."

The summit's joint statement was issued as Gorbachev's jet took off. The grand paragraph included: "The President and the General Secretary . . . continued to be guided by their solemn conviction that a nuclear war cannot be won and must never be fought. They are determined to prevent any war between the United States and the Soviet Union, whether nuclear or conventional. They will not seek to achieve military superiority." On most of the issues that remained between the countries, the language was as general and inoffensive. On "Regional Issues," the conclusion read: "The President and the General Secretary engaged in a wide-ranging, frank and business-like discussion including Afghanistan, the Iran-Iraq War, the Middle East, Cambodia, southern Africa, Central America and other issues." The "Human Rights and Humanitarian Concerns" section was relegated to a single sentence: "The leaders held a thorough and candid discussion of human rights and humanitarian questions and their place in the U.S.-Soviet dialogue."

Diplomatic language aside, no one doubted the three days marked a major event, perhaps a hinge of history. The nation's chief Gorbachev watcher, Ambassador Matlock, said he thought Gorbachev's fear of America and Americans was turned around by his brief encounter with the friendly crowd on Connecticut Avenue. "You know what mattered for Gorbachev?" said Matlock after it was over. "It wasn't seeing our prosperity—he expected that—it was being applauded by Americans. It was not the Manichean world he had grown up studying. He saw that the Americans didn't hate him." The Soviet leader said something like that himself, heresy for a trained Marxist, as he pulled his thoughts together on the flight to Moscow for his first summit report to the Politburo: "In Washington, probably for the first time, we clearly realized how much the human factor means in international politics. . . . These people [the Americans] are guided by the most human motives and feelings."

Reagan, too, was beyond seeing a world of good and evil. The President was euphoric, telling Howard Baker: "See, they underestimated me again. They thought that they could persuade me, they could beat me, and by staying the course, I brought Gorbachev and the Soviets to the table. I got the INF Treaty." He also got a nice bounce in national polls; a *Washington Post*/ABC News poll recorded that his approval rating on foreign policy had jumped to 57 percent, up from 46 percent only ten days before. His overall approval rating in the poll went from 50 percent before the summit to 58 percent in those same ten days.

But the Soviet star got better reviews; "Gorbachev's Tour de Force" was the cover line on *Time* magazine. Inside, among all the color photographs of Reagan and Gorbachev, the report said: "In fact, though the President would wince at the thought, the summit was not so much a triumph of a Reagan revolution in foreign policy as it was a return of the principles of détente: a reduction of tensions between the two superpowers and a recognition that arms control was the fulcrum of relations between the two countries."

The New Republic agreed with that but added some cool cynicism about the President: "At the beginning of his administration, Reagan knew exactly one thing about the Soviet Union: it was the 'evil empire,' the bad guys. And you fight bad guys at every step. What rendered Reagan suddenly conciliatory in mid-administration wasn't any dramatic change in Soviet behavior. . . . What changed Reagan's tune, rather, was the cue he's always responded to: applause. Mikhail Gorbachev had been winning global acclaim by talking peace. Reagan wanted some of the action. It's that simple."

Conservatives were more pointed. William F. Buckley, writing in his *National Review*, said he could not understand how Reagan could put Europe at risk, facing millions of Red Army troops and tanks. Howard Phillips of the Conservative Caucus mocked Reagan as "Nothing more than a useful idiot for Soviet propaganda." The headline over the editorial pages of the *Detroit News* was: "A Day That Will Live in INFamy," then continued: "When the glow of the Washington summit begins to wear off, we are likely to find that we have been sold a bill of goods. The Western position will have been weakened, not strengthened. Few politicians will have the courage to say so. . . . Where is the Winston Churchill of our day?"

In the unkindest cut, the Reagans' friend George Will wrote that the President had accelerated America's "intellectual disarmament," then concluded: "December 8 will be remembered as the day the Cold War was lost."

The glow did fade some as the old year ended with new argument and contradiction, some of it comic, about two old issues, Nicaragua and the federal budget. Even as the General Secretary of the Soviet Union was privately promising the President of the United States that he was willing to end arms shipments to Central America, the Ortega brothers once again found a way to stop Congress from completely cutting off aid to the contras. President Daniel Ortega and Defense Minister Humberto Ortega sounded more like the Marx Brothers than Marxists, as Humberto announced that he intended to increase the size of the Sandinista army to 600,000 men—in a country of only 3.5 million people—and buy a few top-of-the-line Soviet MiG-21s. Trying to calm the predictable uproar in Washington, Daniel said that what Humberto meant was light arms training of reservists. "Like Switzerland," said the brother who was President. But it was too late. Once again, the Congress, in a Senate-House conference, voted for some contra aid, $8.1 million this time, in nonmilitary assistance.

That was seen as a small Reagan victory. But there was bad news for the President, too. As the Reagans were trying to leave town for the holidays, Michael Deaver, who had served them for decades, was convicted of three counts of perjury for lying about illegally using government contacts in his new lobbying business. He was facing up to fifteen years in federal prison. Then, on December 23, a space shuttle scheduled to fly in June, the first flight since the *Challenger* disaster in 1985, failed a series of safety tests as the innards of the steering nozzles cracked under simulated flight pressure. On the same day, in a separate incident, the manufacturer of the nozzle, Morton Thiokol, lost five people when an MX missile exploded as it was being assembled in Utah.

The day before, at 3:30 A.M., the 100th Congress, months behind schedule, with members desperate to get home for the holidays, passed a 1988 federal budget and sent it on to the White House. The big feature of the bill was a $79 billion, two-year deficit-reduction program, including $9 billion in unspecified new taxes. "The flimsy savings from domestic spending programs are more gimmicky and marginal than structural and real," editorialized *The Washington Post,* noting that the 1988 appropriations bill passed the House by a single vote, 209 to 208. "The real problems are going to be shoved off on the next president and the 101st Congress."

On December 27, as the President left town to celebrate the coming of the new year in California, *Time* magazine announced that its man of the old year was . . . Gorbachev. "A ruthless political opportunist and a symbol of hope for a new kind of Soviet Union" was its verdict. But the Fashion Foundation of America named Reagan to its "Best Dressed" list for the fourth straight year, and dropped Gorbachev because he wore a business suit rather than a tuxedo to the formal White House dinner to celebrate the signing of the INF Treaty.

CHAPTER 22

MAY 29, 1988

S ECRETARY OF STATE SHULTZ FLEW TO MOSCOW on February 21, 1988, for a series of meetings to plan for a fourth summit between President Reagan and General Secretary Gorbachev in late May. The original plan had been for ceremonies commemorating the signing and U.S. Senate ratification of the INF Treaty and meetings to advance the negotiation of the more important START Treaty, reducing the number of strategic ballistic missiles in the superpower arsenals. But, in fact, most of the talk was about the remote and poor country time had forgotten more than once: Afghanistan.

Afghanistan had become the Soviets' Vietnam, or worse. On Christmas Day of 1979, the Red Army had invaded the country to preserve a communist government that had taken power in a military coup in April of 1978, bringing their form of Soviet-backed modernism to Kabul—a modernism that included such things as mass education for women. Within less than a year Islamic mujahideen, fighters of holy war, began guerrilla warfare against the outsider occupying their territory and "corrupting" their women.

The invasion and the brutality of the war on both sides had caused President Carter to reevaluate Soviet intentions in the world and led him to begin the military buildup that President Reagan then escalated. The war itself was brutal enough to shock not only Carter, but much of the world. By the end of 1987, more than one million Afghanis had been killed and another three million had fled the country, most to refugee camps in Pakistan, and between twelve thousand and fifteen thousand Soviet soldiers and airmen were dead. With money and arms supplied by the United States and Saudi Arabia, the mujahideen slowly defeated the Red Army, particularly, after Reagan approved a shipment of 75 Stingers, shoulder-fired, heat-seeking aircraft missile systems, to the Afghan resistance in May 1986. On September 25 of that year, mujahideen hiding near a Soviet airbase shot down three HIND assault helicopters. From that day on, Soviet aircraft were forced to fly higher and higher to avoid the Stinger missiles—and without ground support, Red Army soldiers became easy targets for Afghan guerrillas. A video of the first Stinger action was delivered to Reagan in the Oval Office—it was shaky work, but he got the idea.*

On the evening of February 8, the principal Soviet news program *Vremya* had been interrupted as an announcer read a long statement from Gorbachev saying that the 115,000 Soviet troops in Afghanistan would begin leaving on May 15 and the last would be out by March 15, 1989, if . . . The "if" was a settlement in Geneva peace talks with Pakistan and its most important ally, the United States. Gorbachev wanted the friends and patrons of the ferocious mujahideen to end the flow of military supplies to the opposition as the Red Army withdrew. It was the same thing the United States had asked of the Soviet Union as American troops were withdrawn from Vietnam. That had not been a success; Moscow allowed history to take its own course and let the Americans be humiliated.

Though nothing had been made public, Shevardnadze had told Shultz, during early planning for the Washington summit, that the Soviet Union intended to withdraw all its troops from Afghanistan before the end of 1988. Just before he left Washington in December, Gorbachev had repeated that schedule to Reagan, and asked if the United States would end its support of the mujahideen as the Soviets left.

Reagan was surprised and never clearly answered the question. When Soviet intentions became public, many officials in Washington, particularly Senate Republicans led by Jesse Helms of North Carolina, believed Gorbachev's announcement was a trick or a trap of some kind. They were wrong; the Cold War was taking an amazing turn.

When Shultz had gone to Moscow early in the year to plan for Reagan's first visit to the "Evil Empire," the private talks were more

---

* According to studies by the University of Geneva in Switzerland, Afghan war deaths totaled 1,245,000 up to 1988—more than 9 percent of the country's population—and 13,854 Soviet military men were killed. The Stingers, which brought down at least 275 Soviet aircraft, had a kill rate estimated at more than 50 percent.

about Afghanistan than about arms control. The Soviet-American relationship, the Gorbachev-Reagan relationship—or the economic and social problems of the Soviet Union—had reached the point that the Soviets were pulling back and the Americans were in on it.

In terms of Reagan's power and his governance in 1988, the best thing the President had going for him was Gorbachev's determination to get past decades of Soviet mistakes and miscalculations at home. Reagan had reestablished the power and the status of the office during his first term, but by 1987 he had seemed to be running out of both energy and political friends. His 1987 won-loss percentage in Congress was, according to *Congressional Quarterly* tabulations, just 43.5 percent, compared with 82.4 percent in 1981. A striking number of his men—beginning with Deaver, awaiting sentencing, and Meese, still under investigation for helping friends in government dealings—were in legal trouble. Reagan seemed a spent force. One of his old adversaries, California representative Tony Coelho, a Democrat, said the old actor had come to Washington with a six-year script for an eight-year role. Year-end reviews of 1987 and previews of 1988 were mixed at best. The presidential analyst of the Newhouse Newspapers, Miles Benson, put it this way:

> As Ronald Reagan enters the end-game stage of his Presidency, even his buoyant optimism cannot make up for the reality that some goals he set for his Administration seemed to have slipped beyond his grasp. A balanced budget? Forget it. The red ink for the fiscal year will be at least $160 billion. . . . Reagan is almost certain to leave office with the Sandinistas still in control of Nicaragua and the leftist guerrillas waging war in El Salvador and Guatemala. . . . Meanwhile the gyrating stock market, the nation's world trade imbalance, the fast-changing value of the dollar and the rising crescendo of gunfire in the Persian Gulf warn that Reagan's last year in the White House may be a particularly dangerous one.

On the CBS News end-of-the-year roundup program, the network's political analyst, Bruce Morton, had said: "If there is any kind of a crisis . . . you're going to see a President to whom people won't pay much attention to anymore. He won't have a lot of clout with the Congress, he won't have a lot of clout with the voters. They will be looking at the new guys, trying to figure out whom they want to have running the store in 1989." Reacting to that, Senator Alan Simpson, a Wyoming Republican who loved to buck conventional wisdom, said on the eve of Reagan's last State of the Union speech: "He's 76 years old and I've heard the greatest doomsday stuff. . . . Bitburg, that's the end of him. Had his colon taken out, been shot in the chest. . . . Just a string of hideous things that mean the end of Ronald Reagan. And it ain't happened, and it ain't going to happen now."

Perhaps, but Reagan's last State of the Union itself turned out to be the end of even small new ideas from this President. "A Constitutional amendment mandating a balanced budget" . . . "Line-item veto" . . . "Ensure that the Federal government never again legislates against the family and the home" . . . "In a child's education, money can't take the place of basics like discipline, hard work and, yes, homework" . . . "Say no to drugs" . . . "In Nicaragua, the struggle has extra meaning" . . . "So, too, on Afghanistan" . . . "Build a safer peace and reduce the danger of nuclear war." The applause was polite and short.

The Reagan presidency had drifted into ceremony. Democrats were now driving the action in Washington, such as it was, and Gorbachev reigned in the world, or at least in the press of the world, trying to remake the pathetic Soviet economy, withdrawing troops, announcing to Eastern European communist leaders that they were on their own, that the Red Army was never again going to protect them from their own people—because the Red Army and the Soviet Union were admitting that they had worse problems than their satellites did.

President Reagan was playing President now. Sam Donaldson of ABC News got hold of his daily schedule and attendant talking points for February 25. The day started in the usual way: Reagan woke at 7:30 and at breakfast looked at his News Summary and then at the morning newspapers—beginning with the comics in his favorite papers, the conservative *Washington Times* and his home-town *Los Angeles Times*—then went downstairs at exactly 9 A.M. He went first to the Rose Garden, throwing nuts and acorns he had collected at Camp David to waiting White House squirrels. Then he talked about the day's schedule with Howard Baker and sat through the morning national security briefing by his latest National Security Adviser, General Powell. He took some personal time to answer letters from strangers and then picked up his schedule, crossing off each event as it ended:

DROP-BY MEETING WITH CEOS . . . 11:30 A.M. Purpose: To brief CEOS of major corporations on the administration's budget initiatives and ask for their support . . . "I know you've already heard from Colin Powell and from Jim Miller on the budget package. . . . It isn't a perfect agreement but it's a first step. The two-year agreement will reduce the deficit by a total of $76 billion." . . . "I hope you agree on the critical need to fix the budget process and we can count on you." *

PHOTO WITH WAYNE NEWTON Time 1:45 P.M. Purpose: To thank Wayne Newton for his tireless efforts on behalf of America's military men and women. . . . Mr. Newton is the only entertainer to have travelled and performed in Viet Nam, Beirut and now the Persian Gulf.

And so it went: "2:00 P.M. MEETING WITH BIPARTISAN GROUP OF SENATORS" . . . "4:30 PRESENTATION OF EASTER SEALS . . . Talking Points. 'Shawn, congratulations on being selected as the 1988 Easter Seal child' . . . 'Pat Boone, I want to take this opportunity to thank you for all you've done' " . . . "4:45 P.M. RE-CEIVE REPORT OF THE PRESIDENT'S CANCER PANEL . . . 'Thank you, Armand [Hammer] for coming here to present the report.' "

Then the President went back upstairs for dinner, some television, and homework. Office gossip about the President's drifting attention and little naps at big meetings was merging into eyewitness accounts of decline in his mental capacity. One involved a British television crew invited into the Oval Office for a short question-and-answer session on Margaret Thatcher's long service as Prime Minister. The President was already wearing a small microphone on his lapel, and the British technicians heard the conversation between a young press assistant and Reagan. The young man was telling the seventy-seven-year-old President where he was: "You're in the Oval Office, Mr. President. These people are British and they will ask you for a short comment about Prime Minister Thatcher."

On February 25, *The Washington Post* published an interview with Reagan. The paper's senior editors questioned him as if his presidency was already over, and he responded in kind. Asked about the burdens of the doubling of the national debt on his watch, Reagan answered

---

* James Miller III become director of the Office of Management and Budget in 1985.

with a sort of leftist logic: "It's a burden, there's no question about that. . . . One of the major factors about our budget right now is the interest? And you find out that a great many institutions, universities, educational institutions of all kinds that part of their endowment are government bonds. And a lot of that interest is going to them and to individual Americans. So, instead of being something that's just going down a rathole, it's a kind of redistribution of national wealth."

The editors also asked about "the sleaze factor" in his administration. More than one hundred of his appointees, including Meese, Deaver, and Nofziger, had been or were being investigated and, as often as not, convicted for enriching themselves by abusing the power of high office. "I'm saddened of course," he said. "I found those individuals to be the very soul of integrity in the more than 20 years I've known them. I have a feeling that there's a certain amount of politics involved in all this and that I'm really the target."

Nofziger, the former White House communications director who had served Reagan for almost two decades, had been convicted on February 12 of three felony counts of illegal lobbying. Essentially, he had ignored the one-year ban on approaching former government colleagues, going back to the White House seeking favors for three of his public relations clients: the Marine Engineers Union, Fairchild Aircraft, and a company called Wedtech, which was drumming up administration support for a private billion-dollar pipeline from oilfields in Iraq to a port on the Red Sea in Jordan.*

Wedtech was also a part of Meese's legal troubles. The new company was run by his friend and personal attorney, a law school classmate named E. Robert Wallach. A special prosecutor had discovered a 1985 memorandum from Wallach to Meese discussing payoffs to Israeli officials and to Prime Minister Shimon Peres's Labour Party in exchange for not interfering with construction of the proposed pipeline, which would run close to Jordan's border with Israel. In a letter to Peres at the same time, Meese had advised the Prime Minister that Israeli officials should deal only with the National Security Council and avoid discussing the project with the State Department.

On March 28, a month after *Washington Post* editors asked about investigations of Meese, two of the Attorney General's top assistants knocked on the front door of Howard Baker's home at 7 A.M. Deputy

---

* Nofziger's convictions were set aside by a federal appeals court in June of 1989 in a decision that said that the prosecution had offered no evidence that Nofziger knew he was breaking the law.

Attorney General Arnold Burns and Assistant Attorney General William Weld told the White House chief of staff that they and four of their assistants intended to announce that they would be resigning later that day. They told Baker the Justice Department was demoralized and essentially unmanaged, as Meese spent most of his time talking to his private attorneys and making grand jury appearances, fifteen so far. Weld told Baker that if he were still working as a prosecutor back in Massachusetts he would seriously consider indicting Meese for his actions on behalf of Wedtech.*

Calls for Meese's resignation filled newspapers and the nightly news, but the President took little notice. The *Chicago Tribune*, a newspaper normally friendly to the President, called on what they said was a higher power in a lead editorial: "Well, the time has finally come. Nancy Reagan is just going to have to fire Ed Meese. Heaven knows her husband won't do it. . . . Again, she has to save her husband from himself."

On April 22, it was reported that Meese's wife, Ursula, who earned $50,000 a year working for the Multiple Sclerosis Foundation in Washington, was being paid not by the charity but by the Bender Foundation, part of the Bender Partnership, which had recently negotiated $50 million a year in Justice Department office leases, triple the previous rent for the same offices. Three more Meese assistants resigned, and Baker brought Burns and Weld into the White House to meet with the President for forty-five minutes. Weld laid out his hypothetical indictment of his old boss. Reagan listened, told no jokes, and asked no questions. Then the President called in Meese. Reagan said nothing after the meeting as White House aides assured reporters that the Attorney General would not be leaving his job anytime soon.

On May 16, Meese lost another staffer. He fired his press spokesman, Terry Eastland, for not being aggressive enough in his daily defenses of the Attorney General's doings past and present. Meese's chief speechwriter, William Schambra, quit to protest Eastland's dismissal. That was it for Meese's most loyal journalistic defender, the *Washington Times,* which called editorially for his resignation, saying: "Edwin Meese's attempts to vindicate himself have destroyed his department."

The President, who was not seen so much around town anymore, surprised Washington by calling an afternoon press conference the

---

* Weld returned home to Massachusetts and was elected governor of the state in 1990.

next day, May 17. The second question was the first of a half-dozen about the investigations of Meese. Reagan answered: "I have complete confidence in him. . . . I've seen no evidence of any wrongdoing on his part."

The President must have prized that kind of unquestioning loyalty just then because several of the questions he was getting, and dodging as well as he could, came from what was being said and written about him by loyalists who had fallen from his grace. Three of the questions that afternoon were about whether he believed in astrology. His angry former chief of staff Don Regan, in a memoir titled *For the Record,* had gotten even with Nancy Reagan by revealing her interest in astrology, writing: "Virtually every move and decision the Reagans made during my time as White House chief of staff was cleared in advance by a woman in San Francisco who drew up horoscopes to make certain that the planets were in a favorable alignment for the enterprise." He wrote about the multicolored calendar on his desk for bad days and good, judgments made by Joan Quigley, the San Francisco astrologer.

He specifically blamed Reagan's failure to publicly confront the issues raised by the Iran-contra disclosures of early 1987 on the astrologer, who was advising the Reagans that harm might come to the President if he left the White House on certain days—or if he held press conferences. "We were paralyzed by this craziness," said the former Chief of Staff.

Reagan responded to all the questions raised by Regan by going back to the 1981 shooting at the Hilton, saying: "After I'd been shot, which was quite a traumatic experience for my wife," he began, "she was getting a great many calls from friends, and a friend called and said that—or wished that he'd known that what I was going to do that day and so forth because of—he mentioned someone, that all the signs were bad and everything else. And Nancy was—it was a trauma that didn't go away easily. And when suddenly things of the same kind just for a short period there—when I was booked for something of the same kind where the accident occurred, why, she would ask, what does it look like now? And no changes were ever made on the basis of whether I did or did not conduct this. . . . I don't guide my life by it, but I won't answer the question the other way because I don't know enough about it to say is there something to it or not."

He was not making a lot of sense, but he really could not. In fact, the Reagans had fooled around with astrology for thirty years before and after he was in politics—and old acquaintances were suddenly talking. Some talked of the parties he hosted monthly for Carroll Righter, who wrote an astrology column for the *Los Angeles Times* and serviced a list of movie types. Reagan would greet the guests, then call them together to say: "I'd never even think of making an important decision without calling Carroll first." Another West Coast astrologer, Joyce Jillson of Los Angeles, claimed she also worked with the Reagans, saying she was part of the decision to select George Bush as Reagan's running mate in 1980.

For a man as comfortable and charming as he was, Ronald Reagan had few if any deep friendships. He rarely even talked to the men who served him after they left that service. That cool distance, Reagan's penchant for seeing and hearing only what he wanted to see and hear, may have had something to do with the fact that so many of his former aides wrote books or gave interviews praising the great man, but still let show bruised veins of hurt and resentment. David Stockman was cruel and specific in his reminiscences, helping create the image of a befuddled old man who came alive only when the curtain opened and the lights brightened. Former spokesman Larry Speakes wrote *Speaking Out,* which came out at about the same time as Regan's book, revealing that as spokesman he had invented Reagan quotes, speaking his own words rather than whatever his boss might have said or thought. That was hardly news in the White House. Part of the duty of people there is to present a presidency that knows all and comments rather blandly on most of it. But part of that job was to keep quiet about the limitations of the man in the Oval Office. No man can be as big as the presidency; the idea that one human can actually fill the job is an act of faith. Speakes had not kept the faith and he paid a price, losing his job as vice president of public affairs at Merrill Lynch. Regan's old company forced Speakes to quit within a week after his book raised questions about the President.

Speakes had also written that the President did not read newspapers. "Not true," said the President. "I begin with the comics, a lifetime habit, and then my next turn is to the editorial pages." Next up was the administration's first Secretary of Education. Terrell Bell wrote a memoir, *The Thirteenth Man,* talking of the casual racism among midlevel officials in the White House and Office of Management and Budget—men who talked of "Martin Lucifer Coon, Jr." and called Title IX "The Lesbians' Bill of Rights"—as they discussed his department's budget. The astrology revelations—"Yes, I do," Mrs. Reagan answered when Howard Baker asked if she followed the charts—struck dissonant chords few had heard before. Doug Bandow, a former Reagan assistant in the White House who became a senior fellow at the Cato Institute, a libertarian think tank, suggested in his syndicated column that evangelical Christians should rethink their commitment to the President, citing the eighteenth chapter of Deuteronomy, in which God attacks "The abominations . . . of soothsayers and fortune tellers."

As early as the first weeks of 1988, pundits and politicians alike were often treating Reagan as if he were a former President. There were nomination contests in both parties for the men who would be his successor. Vice President Bush and Senator Dole were fighting for the Republican nomination, and a dozen Democrats contending in early primaries topped the front pages and led the nightly news. The incumbent's record and legacy were being chewed up on editorial pages and in campaign books—and they were accentuating the negative. "Legacy? What Legacy?" asked a *New Republic* title.

But at the same time, the President was finally winning some sincere praise on foreign affairs, being lionized a bit for his partnership with Gorbachev. But Gorbachev was coming across as the senior partner in that one. Analyses of domestic achievement were harsher, typified by headlines over economic analyses in *The Washington Post* and the *Financial Times,* both published on February 24. "Requiem for Reaganomics" in the *Post* was by Robert Samuelson, who wrote: "Reagan squandered a chance to recast the economic debate. . . . Reagan might have defined the practical and the possible. Government policies must rest on sound ideas that are widely understood. Mystifying economic theories will not do. . . . He leaves a catchy phrase. In the end, 'Reaganomics' is little more." The *Financial Times* headline was "Final Curtain Falls on Reagan's Fiscal Follies." Those efforts came in a week when a *New York Times*/CBS News poll indicated for the first time in Reagan's tenure that more Americans were expressing pessimism than optimism when asked about the American future.

In a detailed analysis of Reagan's economic governance, Martin Tolchin of *The New York Times* brought David Stockman back to the front page after six quieter years as an investment banker on Wall Street, attacking his President and his own work as budget director:

"In terms of what Ronald Reagan used to flail away at, in terms of an out of control 'welfare' state, the Reagan legacy is not of contraction but consolidation. What Reagan did, essentially, was to pick up the 1981 Democratic budget and complete the job of consolidation, winnowing out minor programs. But the consolidation, combined with deep tax cuts, leaves an untenable and unsustainable fiscal structure and financial burden."

Doing the numbers, Tolchin pointed out that after the shouting died down, only one federal program had been ended during the Reagan years—revenue-sharing with the states. Domestic social programs were cut, eligibility standards had been narrowed, and benefits were cut, but big government lived on. Agricultural subsidies, a Reagan target for decades, almost tripled on his watch, going from $11.3 billion in 1981 to $31 billion in 1988. Civilian government employment went up, too, by 150,000, to 3 million total. What was cut was "discretionary" public spending, mostly redistribution of wealth to the poor and near-poor. That went from 5.7 percent of GNP to 3.7 percent. Education and training funds were cut from $33 billion to $28 billion. Community development funds went from $10.5 billion to $6 billion.

Tolchin concluded that Reagan had succeeded, mostly with words, in lowering expectations of what the federal government could and should do, saying: "His Presidency has made it perilous for any politician to propose new programs without specifying how to pay for them." And he killed or pushed back other men's dreams of such things as mammoth aid to education, national health insurance, and guaranteed incomes. In other words, whatever the thinking behind the massive deficit spending of the Reagan years, the purpose became the slashing of domestic spending.

By the end of May, as if Reagan were already history, the *National Journal* published a full issue on the Reagan presidency, with a final comprehensive article under the title "What Reagan Promised . . . What Reagan Delivered."

Under "Economy," the *Journal* reported that GNP had grown at a mediocre annual rate of 2.6 percent under Reagan—compared with 3.0 percent under Carter—noting that the White House hyped that number by calculating only after the 1981–82 recession; counted that way, growth was a robust 4.2 percent a year. Inflation dropped from 12.5 percent in Carter's last year to an average in the 3 percent range.

"Give him D for deficits," said the report, noting that the deficit had risen to above $200 billion for three of Reagan's eight years and averaged above $150 billion for the other five. Federal taxes accounted for 20 percent of GNP before Reagan's 1981 tax cut and were closer to 19 percent after the big cut and several hidden increases and the loophole closing of the Tax Reform Act of 1986. But, said the *Journal,* "Supply-Side Economics had failed. Reduced taxes did not stimulate additional savings and business investment. Unemployment averaged 7.7 percent under Reagan compared with 6.4 percent under Carter."

On job creation, Reagan had predicted that only 10 million jobs would have been created if Carter were reelected; Reaganomics created fewer than that, 9.2 million. Nominal interest rates were still historically high, but were less than half what they were in 1981. As for federal spending, it consumed more of the GNP under Reagan than under any peacetime President in history, climbing to 24.3 percent in fiscal 1983, then dropping to 22.8 percent in 1987.

On "National Security and Foreign Policy," the *Journal* reported that Reagan's $2 trillion in new Pentagon spending authority had modernized the military, improved morale, and generated reenlistments in the volunteer army. But questions were raised about the emphasis on hardware and the ignoring of runaway costs on one weapons system after another. "Slow, but sure," the writers said in praising Reagan's arms control moves—but added pointed questions about his adherence to SDI and fiddling with the ABM Treaty.

They also mocked his campaign promises "never to pay ransom" for hostages and his inconsistent and erratic use of force against the terrorists plaguing Americans everywhere. On the so-called "Reagan Doctrine" of supporting local wars to check or overthrow communist governments, the *Journal* verdict was "Hit or miss." The writers contrasted effective American action in helping remove President Marcos in the Philippines after a delay, doing the same with Jean-Claude Duvalier in Haiti, possible success in Afghanistan, stalemate in El Salvador and Nicaragua, and failure to remove Panama's military chief, the commander of the Panamanian Defense Forces, Manuel Noriega, after he was indicted by a federal grand jury in Miami in February of 1988 for drug-running.

In "Governing and Regulatory Policy," the *Journal* described Reagan's successes in reducing the number of federal regulations— from 87,000 pages in the *Federal Register* in 1980 to just 47,000 pages in 1986. But they noted, too, that there was still great controversy over the eventual effect of the elimination of hundreds of national environmental standards. In the Reagan administration, the deregulators who did that work were often former industry lobbyists appointed to regulate their old clients. Also, the President failed totally in trying to make good on his pledges to eliminate two Cabinet departments, Education and Energy. As for his promise to "put federal employment on a diet," the report calculated that federal civilian employment *increased* by 4.8 percent on his watch.

On "Social Programs," the *Journal*, like the *Times*, noted that Reagan had some success in eliminating public service jobs programs, but that all of the New Deal and most of the Great Society programs of Franklin Roosevelt and Lyndon Johnson had survived the eight-year conservative purge. They were smaller sometimes, but they were still there. Social Security had survived as well; it just cost taxpayers a lot more. Reagan the candidate had pledged to preserve the program but President Reagan tried and failed to cut back until 1983, when a bipartisan commission he appointed produced a solvency plan to sharply increase payroll taxes (offsetting many income tax cuts) and gradually increasing the age of eligibility from sixty-five to sixty-seven years of age.

Finally, Reagan won a good deal of political admiration in the "Judges and the Courts" section. His Justice Department had lost more often than it won in trying to eliminate affirmative action based on past racial and gender discrimination, but had lost even more times trying to make abortion illegal again, and in trying to weaken civil rights laws. But, the magazine concluded, Reagan, who appointed more than three hundred federal judges, had transformed civil and criminal jurisprudence, concluding: "These appointments could be his most enduring legacy."

Reagan's attitudes toward the courts and toward civil rights were tested one more time that spring. Earlier in the year, Congress had passed the Civil Rights Restoration Act of 1987. The legislation, opposed by the President, was designed to nullify a 1984 Supreme Court decision regarding a Pennsylvania liberal arts school, Grove City College, which had refused to sign compliance orders mandated by Title IX of the Civil Rights Act of 1972, the title that required colleges to offer equal athletic facilities and opportunities for female students. The case turned on the fact that although the Christian-oriented school accepted no federal aid, some of its students did. There was no contention that the school did discriminate against women or anyone else and the court ruled 6 to 3 that it did not have to sign the orders. The new Restoration Act required signing. Reagan vetoed the act on March 16, his sixty-third veto. Six days later, on March 22, both the Senate and House voted to override the veto, only the ninth override of the Reagan years. The vote was 73 to 24 in the Senate, with 21 Republicans ignoring the President and a national campaign by the Moral Majority and other Christian and conservative groups backing the college. The House vote was 292 to 133, with 52 Republicans joining the Democratic majority. "This is just another big government power grab," said Reagan after the vote. "This isn't a civil rights bill. . . . [It is] designed to take control away from states, localities, communities, parents and the private sector and give it to Federal bureaucrats and judges."

The words were vintage Reagan, but they had lost the kind of power they once had. He had connected Americans with a common political language—dumbing down politics in his way—but after six years or so he was repeating himself, as he did in his letters over the years. But if the power was lost, there was still a great deal of love and respect. At Reagan's last Gridiron Dinner, on March 27, the great communicator of the loyal opposition, Governor Mario Cuomo of New York, once again celebrated Reagan from the podium: "As John Kennedy did, Ronald Reagan has striven with considerable success to make Americans feel good about their country. We can all be grateful for that effort. . . . For me, my family, and the whole family of New York, we thank you Mr. President and Mrs. Reagan, for the grand example you have set for us in meeting the small problems of our own lives."

The sentiments were still there, perhaps a form of premature nostalgia. But Reagan's own words were becoming background noise from another time. It looked as if his great dreams would leave Washington with him. Some had left with Weinberger. The President's pledge of a six-hundred-ship Navy was eliminated as the Pentagon began preparing its 1988 budget requests. The new number would be 589. Star Wars budget requests and allocations were also in decline, to the point that the system itself was disappearing.

Five years and more than $12 billion after Reagan's first SDI speech, the Joint Chiefs of Staff were preparing budget proposals based on their own secret studies that the best feasible system, if any system was feasible at all, might have the capacity to block only 30 percent of Soviet warheads in a massive first-strike attack. Their plan was exactly what the President had said it would not be in his 1983 speech, "just another method of protecting missile silos."

There was also only a bit more hope for the Reagan Doctrine and the wars against leftists south of the border in Central America. At the beginning of 1988, his eighth year, the President began pushing again for new contra aid, $270 million this time, to be spent over eighteen months. He argued that the only reason the Sandinista government in Nicaragua was talking peace and democracy with its Central American neighbors—offering to meet the American demand for direct negotiations with the contras—was because of the military pressure of the insurgents and their White House patrons.

The argument was valid enough, but few listened anymore. "There is no question that the contra policy helped turn the Sandinistas around," said one of Reagan's most consistent and articulate critics, William Charles Maynes, the editor of Foreign Policy magazine. "But the most that could ever be done is to soften the Sandinistas, to make them more democratic, rather than democratic. It's hard to see Reagan's contra policy as a success because the contra policy has basically destroyed the Administration."

Soon enough, the $270 million request for contra aid was reduced to $50 million, and then $36 million, over six months. On February 2, the President had made an Oval Office "make or break appeal," his words for the last amount. But all three television networks declined to broadcast it. The request was defeated by a 219 to 211 vote the next day in the House. There was, however, good news for the President that day. The Senate confirmed Anthony Kennedy for the Supreme Court by a 97 to 0 vote.

Events were moving too fast for the President to do much more for his favorite "freedom fighters." On March 16, the federal grand jury empaneled by Lawrence Walsh, the special prosecutor investigating the Iran-contra adventures of early 1987, returned a 101-page, 23-count indictment of Oliver North, John Poindexter, Richard Secord, and Albert Hakim on charges of destroying evidence, conspiracy, fraud, and theft of government property. Sixteen of the counts named North, who, if convicted, might face eighty-five years in prison.

A few days earlier, when McFarlane had pleaded guilty to four lesser charges, including withholding information from Congress, the

President, in a rare show of cynicism, had quipped: "He just pleaded guilty of not telling Congress everything they wanted to know. I've done that myself." This time, he added: "I just have to believe that they are going to be found innocent because I don't think they were guilty of any law-breaking, any crime." At almost the same hour the indictments were announced, large numbers of Sandinista troops, perhaps more than a thousand, crossed the Honduran border in pursuit of contras returning to their camps and supply posts on the Honduran side.

The United States ambassador to Honduras, Everett Briggs, met with the country's president, José Azcona, offering whatever help he needed against the Sandinista units. In Washington, at 9:30 A.M. on March 16, Reagan was briefed on the incursion and Briggs's meetings by his new National Security Adviser, Colin Powell. At 11 A.M. that morning, Powell returned to the Oval Office with Secretary of State Shultz and the Joint Chiefs of Staff for another briefing and with a list of options that included sending in American troops.

That was the option the President chose. He ordered 3,200 American troops, most of them members of the 82nd Airborne Division, onto planes at Fort Bragg, North Carolina, and Fort Ord, California, waiting for a formal request from Azcona. That came at 7:49 P.M.

Powell called the President, then went up to the family quarters. Twelve minutes later, Reagan officially ordered the troops into Honduras. They were to join an "Emergency Deployment Readiness Exercise" at Palmerola Air Force Base near Tegucigalpa, the capital, where three thousand other Americans were already conducting exercises that never actually ended, as American troops were rotated out and in. "This is a signal to the governments and people of Central America," said White House spokesman Marlin Fitzwater at 10 P.M., emphasizing that the Americans at Palmerola were 125 miles from where Honduran troops and planes were exchanging fire with Sandinista regulars returning to Nicaragua.*

---

* I was in Tegucigalpa at the time, working on an article for *The New Yorker* magazine, and the city's hotels were quickly filled with young Americans in civilian clothes, often with Army boots slung over their shoulders. "Why are you here?" I asked one, in an elevator at the Mayan Hotel. He answered: "Vacation. Sir!" Driving out to Palmerola, forty miles southeast of the city, as huge U.S. Air Force cargo planes were landing at the commercial airport, I was stopped at a roadblock. Three planes swept over a low mountain range and the air was suddenly filled with paratroopers floating down near the road. A U.S. Army sergeant, driving a truck loaded with telephone poles, was next to me. "What's this?" I said. "What's what?" he said. "The paratroopers," I said, pointing at them. "What paratroopers?" he said. Then added: "Sir!"

Four days later, voters in El Salvador rejected the Christian Democratic Party of President Duarte, America's man, America's party, giving ARENA, the National Republican Alliance, the party of right-wing death squads, control of the National Assembly and, for the first time in twenty-four years, of the city of San Salvador.

On March 23, General Powell asked for an unusual afternoon appointment with the President. He came to the Oval Office to report that Nicaragua's President Ortega had met with contra leaders in Managua and that both sides had signed a two-month cease-fire and prisoner-release agreement. It came as a complete surprise, said Powell. The NSC analysis speculated that both sides had recognized that they were losing the attention of their Cold War patrons, that American support of the contras might end as Reagan's days ended, and that Gorbachev wanted to focus on his own domestic problems, particularly violence between the peoples of two southern republics, Armenia and Azerbaijan.

The Nicaraguan truce brought together congressional Democrats and Republicans for the first time in more than five years. Leaders of both parties in the House and Senate negotiated a $48 million non-military aid package to cover contra expenses during the cease-fire and the bill passed by overwhelming majorities on March 31.

On April 11, Reagan came into the White House press room to announce that he was sending Secretary of State Shultz to Geneva to sign an agreement with the Soviet Union, the communist government of Afghanistan, and the government of Pakistan, which was representing the mujahideen resistance, for the complete withdrawal of the occupying Red Army from Afghanistan within nine months, after almost nine years of vicious warfare.

In much of the world, the agreement was hailed as an extraordinary victory for American resolve and diplomacy: the end of the Brezhnev Doctrine that the Soviet Union would never cede control over a communist country. But in Washington it was called a "sell-out" by the President's most conservative supporters, led once more by Jesse Helms. It was hardly a definitive peace treaty, simply ignoring the question of whether and how the United States and the Soviet Union would continue to supply arms and other aid as a civil war raged on between the communists in Kabul and the mujahideen in remote valleys and mountains. Everyone involved understood that their signatures would not end the fighting between the Soviet-trained communists in Kabul and the coalitions of warlords, tribal armies, and Islamic militants—armed and trained by the Americans, the Saudis, and the Pakistanis—that had held off Soviet power for almost a decade.

Officially, there was an oral agreement, read in Geneva by Shultz: "It is our hope that the Soviet Union will contribute to this process by ending the flow of arms to its client regime in Kabul. But we have made clear to Soviet leaders that, consistent with our obligations as guarantor, it is our right to provide military aid to the resistance. We are ready to exercise that right, but we are prepared to meet restraint with restraint."

Unofficially, the United States had no intention of ending arms shipments to Pakistan for delivery to Afghanistan—or sales on the black markets of South Asia. The Central Intelligence Agency had already sent more than $2 billion in weaponry, and another $2 billion had come from Saudi Arabia, much of that money supporting "madrassas" (religious schools) training fundamentalist Islamic militants called "taliban" (scholars) in Pakistan's bare deserts and mountains. In fact, most of the insurgents were already denouncing the Geneva accord.

When Shultz and Shevardnadze met a week later in Moscow to plan for the Reagan-Gorbachev summit there at the end of May, the Soviet Foreign Minister said, as recorded in the American minutes: "What worries the Soviets is that the regime in Kabul—whether it ruled well or not was another question—the leaders of that regime signed the Geneva documents. There were also opposition leaders . . . declaring they would fight to the end. They wished to establish a fundamentalist regime. The U.S. should be aware of that, and assess it soberly."

But admitting all that would have been a deal-breaker, and Gorbachev badly wanted a deal. In the end, the details were worked out in a telephone call between Reagan and President Muhammad Zia ul-Haq, the American-backed military ruler of Pakistan. After going over the amount of weaponry, to be paid for by the United States and Saudi Arabia, that would continue to be sent to the mujahideen until they overthrew the Kabul government, Zia said: "Mr. President, we'll just lie about it. That's what we've been doing for eight years. . . . Muslims have the right to lie in a good cause."

Late in May, as the first Soviet units left Afghanistan, Reagan sat for an interview in Washington with Soviet television journalists. He was asked whether he considered Gorbachev a friend. The President circled the question a bit, then said: "Well, I can't help but say 'yes' to that, because the difference that I've found between him and other previous leaders that I have met with is that, yes, we can debate and disagree. . . . But there is never a sense of personal animus." Most of powerful Washington was still talking and thinking Cold War. Richard Perle, commenting after the summit in *U.S. News and World Report,* said: "There is not a shred of evidence that Gorbachev desires respite from the burdens of military spending, a reordering of priorities." The President was beyond that. He believed that Gorbachev was trying, against the odds, to remake communism and the Soviet Union. The Soviet leader had surprised both Reagan and Shultz with an extraordinary ahistorical statement during planning meetings for the summit: "The Soviet Union does not pretend to have the final truth. We do not impose our way of life on other peoples."

For weeks, the Soviets had been remaking Moscow. Crews were painting buildings and paving roads that Reagan might see when he arrived on May 29. A bureaucrat the same size as the six-foot-one Reagan was being driven through the city in a limousine to see what the American would see from the back seat. Lampposts on the road in from the airport were painted to just above the height that Reagan would see from the car.

One of the neighborhoods that was cleaned up and painted over was around the apartment house of a Jewish "refusenik" couple, Tatyana and Yuri Ziman, who had been trying to leave the Soviet Union since 1977 and were on the list of seventeen families Reagan carried with him. As he had in the past, the President intended to give the names to Gorbachev, asking him to consider releasing any of them as a private gesture of goodwill—a human rights gesture the United States would neither announce nor exploit. This time was different, though. Somehow Nancy Reagan had heard about the Zimans and had persuaded her husband that they should stop by the Zimans' apartment as they drove from the airport to the Kremlin.

Hearing that, the Soviet leader dispatched Alexander Bessmertnykh to tell the American ambassador, Jack Matlock, the former NSC Soviet analyst, that Gorbachev would take the apartment visit as a personal insult—and that the Zimans would never get an exit visa if the Reagans went ahead with their little drop-by. While the President rested for three days in Helsinki, Finland, before flying the 560 miles to Moscow, Matlock persuaded Shultz and Howard Baker to cancel the stop.*

There was tension in the American party during the flight to Helsinki and during the three days in the Finnish capital. More and more, Reagan seemed uninterested in much of what was happening around him, more distant, more fumbling than usual. There was more talk than ever among his assistants and the few reporters who occasionally got near him that the President was just another old man who was losing his grip, that he was not ready for another smiling tussle with the younger man from Moscow. But when the President appeared at the door of Air Force One on the afternoon of May 29 at Vnukovo II Airport outside the Soviet capital, he looked as bright and clear as the spring sky above. It was show time.

And the fourth summit was indeed scheduled as a show, a celebration of the new relationship between the superpowers and a welcome break for both leaders from domestic problems and the wars of Afghanistan and Central America. "REAGAN OFF FOR SUMMIT THAT COULD REFURBISH PRESIDENCY" was *The Washington Post*'s headline as Reagan began his mission to Moscow.

At the Kremlin, Reagan and Gorbachev greeted each other as friends, and talked for more than an hour. It was a rambling conversation, mostly about human rights and religion, a Reaganesque hour, heavy on anecdotes and personal reminiscence. Each had an agenda. Gorbachev hoped the President would sign a short joint statement, which he had read in English: "Proceeding from their understanding of the realities that have taken shape in the world today, the two leaders believe that no problem in dispute can be resolved by military means. They regard peaceful coexistence as a universal principle of international relations. Equality of all states, non-interference in internal affairs and freedom of socio-political choices must be recognized as the inalienable and mandatory standards of international relations."

"Sounds okay to me," said Reagan.

Then it was the President's turn. He talked a bit about the names on

---

* Two months after the Moscow summit, the Zimans were given exit visas and moved to Boston.

his list of people, including the Zimans, who wanted to leave the Soviet Union. Then, as recorded in the official notes of the meeting:

> The President continued that he wished to take up another topic that had been a kind of personal dream of his. He had been reluctant to raise it with Gorbachev, but he was going to do it now anyway. . . . If word got out that this was even being discussed, the President would deny he had said anything about it.
>
> Gorbachev could do something of benefit not only to him but to the image of his country worldwide. The Soviet Union had a church—in a recent speech Gorbachev had liberalized some of its rules—the Orthodox Church. The President asked Gorbachev what if he ruled that religious freedom was part of the people's rights, that people of any religion—whether Islam with its mosque, the Jewish faith, Protestants or the Ukrainian church—could go to the church of their choice. . . . If Gorbachev could see his way clear to do what the President had asked, continued the President, he felt very strongly that he would be a hero, and that much of the feeling against his country would disappear like water in hot sun. If there was any one in the room who said he had given such advice, he would say that person was lying, that he had never said it.

Gorbachev said he did not consider religion a big problem. He said there was freedom of religion in the Soviet Union, though he was an atheist himself, and thought atheists were often criticized in the United States.

"My son is an atheist," interrupted Reagan.

That went on for a while and at the end of the session, the President brought it up again, according to the notes: "The President concluded that there was one thing he wished to do for his atheist son. He wanted to serve his son the perfect gourmet dinner, to have him enjoy the meal, and to ask him if he believed there was a cook."

The son, Ronald Reagan Jr., as it happened, had been in Moscow the year before, performing with an American dance troupe, and had told his father about "The Arbat," a reconstructed street newly turned into a pedestrian mall, lined with small shops and cafés, energized by street musicians and artists—a happening place that looked as if it could be in Baltimore or Santa Monica. This would be Reagan's answer to Gorbachev's hand-shaking on Connecticut Avenue.

After the Gorbachev meeting, ignoring Secret Service objections and telling Soviet security services nothing until moments before they arrived, the Reagans suddenly popped out of a car and began walking along the brickway. Astonished Russians, out for a Sunday evening stroll, began to cheer and wave as the Reagans moved along. Then, as the crowds pushed in, the Soviet guards rushed in to form a ring around the President and the other Americans with him—and they were a brutal bunch, punching and kicking anyone who got in their way, including American reporters.

"Leave them alone! These are Americans! These are our press!" shouted Mark Weinberg, a Reagan staffer, calling out again and again. One was swinging at Helen Thomas until the President pulled her in between himself and Nancy. Reagan was stunned, writing in his diary that night: "I've never seen such brutal manhandling as they did on their own people who were in no way getting out of hand. . . . Perestroika or not, some things haven't changed."

"Second day of the Reagan-Gorbachev summit," said CBS News anchor Dan Rather from inside the Kremlin walls. "They are pressing their private agendas. Mr. Reagan is trying to ensure his place in history. General Secretary Gorbachev is trying to ensure he has a future."

The leaders met again in St. Catherine's Hall on the morning of the second day, May 30, but the real grunt work of the summit—continuing negotiations on the substance and details of the proposed START Treaty—was being done in separate meetings by large groups of "experts" in around-the-clock meetings. Reagan was hammering away on human rights issues, particularly freedom of religion, and Gorbachev was trying to change the subject.

That afternoon at Spaso House, the President met with the Zimans and ninety-four other dissidents and Soviet human rights activists for an hour. "I wanted to convey to you that you have the prayers and support of the American people, indeed of people throughout the world," he began. "I've come to Moscow with this human rights agenda because . . . it is our belief that this is a moment of hope. The new Soviet leader appears to grasp the connection between certain freedoms and economic growth. . . . Freedom of religion . . . Freedom of speech . . . Freedom of travel . . . The freedom to keep the fruits of one's labor. . . .

"Here I would like to speak to you not as a head of government but as a man, a fellow human being. I came here hoping to do what I could to give you strength. Yet I already know that it is you who have strengthened me. . . . While we press for human rights through diplomatic channels, you press with your very lives, day in, day out, year after year, risking your jobs, your homes, your all."

Then he told the gourmet dinner and the cook story again. It was a powerful little talk, ending with a quote from Alexander Pushkin, the great poet of pre-Revolution Russia: "It's time my friend, it's time. The heart begs for peace, the days fly past, it's time, my friend, it's time."

His friend, his host, the atheist, was not pleased. At a formal Kremlin dinner that night, the General Secretary in his toast to the President talked of "realism" and socialism: "We see ourselves even more convinced that our Socialist choice was correct, and we cannot conceive of our country developing without socialism—based on any other fundamental values. . . . We want to build contacts among people in all forums. But this should be done without interfering in domestic affairs, without sermonizing or imposing one's views and ways, without turning family or personal problems into a pretext for confrontation between states."

Reagan's head dropped as Gorbachev carried on. He was asleep; Shultz was trying to keep him awake. In his response, the President did sermonize, as he had for a lifetime, speaking of the problems and hopes of the world in personal and family terms. He quoted from folk songs, praising the beauty, the heart, and the courage of Russia and its people, talking of clearing the forests and fighting the Nazis. Then he gave Gorbachev a video recording of the 1956 film *Friendly Persuasion*. He slowly outlined the story of a Quaker family in Indiana dealing with the private and the public terrors of the Civil War.

"I promise not to spoil the outcome for you, but I hope you'll permit me to describe one scene," said the President. "Just as the invading armies come into southern Indiana, one of our states, the Quaker farmer is approached by two of his neighbors. One is also a Quaker who earlier in the story, when times are peaceful, denounces violence and vows never to lift his hand in anger. But now that the enemy has burned his barn, he's on his way to battle and he criticizes his fellow Quaker for not joining him in renouncing his religious beliefs. The other visitor, also on his way to battle, is the intruding but friendly neighbor. Yet it is this neighbor, although a nonbeliever, who says he's proud of the Quaker family's decision not to fight. In the face of the tragedy of war, he's grateful, as he says, that somebody's holding out for a better way of settling things. . . .

"So, Mr. General Secretary, let us also toast the art of friendly persuasion, the hope of peace with freedom, the hope of holding out for a better way of settling things. Thank you, and God Bless You."

CHAPTER 23
JANUARY 11, 1989

G EORGE SHULTZ LOVED SIGHTSEEING. He had been known to disappear in the late hours with his wife, once to see the Taj Mahal in the moonlight after a long day of trying to assess the endless troubles between India and Pakistan. He thought Red Square in Moscow was among the most beautiful places in the world, named long before the communists took over Russia. He liked to tell people "Red" was actually an English translation of a Russian word for beautiful. He wanted Reagan to see it. But political types and image-makers in the White House traveling party thought a photo of the President near Lenin's tomb would hurt him among zealous anti-communists, who were already saying that their old hero was betraying his own ideals by dealing with and going to the "Evil Empire."

So Shultz suggested to Reagan that he tell Gorbachev he wanted to walk around the square. Afraid that Reagan would forget—he was forgetting a lot of things now and television reports talked of his seeming lack of vigor—Shultz personally typed out a card and put it in with the President's talking points: "Mr. General Secretary, I understand that Red Square is quite a sight to see, and sometime during the course of this visit, I'd like to see it."

Gorbachev, of course, said he'd love to take his American friend around the great plaza bordered by castles and old onion-domed churches, places whose architecture, but not their missions, survived revolution. This being the land of Potemkin and his false-fronted villages painted to fool the Czarina as she passed by on her way to the country, the Soviets cleared the streets around the square at the appointed hour. Eight groups of "ordinary Muscovites," twenty-five or so in each group, were then stationed around the square, looking as happy as the pretty children around them. Cameramen and photographers had no trouble catching the General Secretary holding a baby and saying: "Shake hands with Grandfather Reagan."

The twenty-minute walkabout produced a singular moment at the summit. Grandfather Reagan had been ducking "Evil Empire" questions by pretending he could not hear them. But American reporters got to him this time, calling out: "Do you still think you're in an evil empire, Mr. President?"

"No."

"Why not?"

"I was talking about another time in another era."

A few minutes later, obviously tired but relaxed, the President threw an arm around Gorbachev's shoulder as they walked along like a couple of guys coming off the field after the big game. That was just too much for America's anti-communist establishment. The most articulate, William F. Buckley, wrote a commentary he called "So Long, Evil Empire": "We sinners believe, because we were taught to believe and to give internal assent to the mandate, that we must forgive, seventy times seven times. But Mr. Reagan is engaged now not in forgiveness, but in what George Orwell called vaporization. Big Brother decides to change a historical or a present fact, and evidence inconvenient to the new thesis is simply made to—disappear." But, truth be told, that skill, that gift, was at the heart of Reagan's formidable politics. He imagined a past. He imagined a world. And he made people believe in the past he imagined, and a future, too. Friendly persuasion.

Afterward, the President moved on to a lunch hosted by Moscow's literary and cultural elite and then to a monastery and Moscow State University, Gorbachev's alma mater, to speak to two thousand students. Reagan and the round Seal of the President were dwarfed by a giant sculpture of the head of Lenin. His speech to the artists at lunch was short and brilliant. Referencing Russian poets, writers, dancers, and directors, he cast himself as one of them. To make his most revealing point about himself, he quoted the Russian filmmaker Sergei Eisenstein: "The most important thing is to have the vision. The next is to grasp and hold it. You must see and feel what you are thinking. You must see and grasp it. You must hold and fix it in your memory and senses and you must do it at once." Then he said: "That is the very essence of leadership, not only on the movie set where I learned about it, but everywhere."

His speech at the university was another hit. Coming from a visit to the Danilov monastery and a few words with leaders of the state-controlled Russian Orthodox Church, Reagan again talked a good deal about God and religion. But he said more about science and technology and entrepreneurship—a message that confused some Russians, as their nation grew poorer even as it produced some of the greatest mathematicians and theoretical physicists in the world, which was at the core of both Gorbachev's promises and problems. Reagan put it this way: "Like a chrysalis, we're emerging from the Industrial Revolution—an economy confined to and limited by the Earth's resources—into, as one economist titled his book, 'The Economy of the Mind,' in which there are no bounds on human imagination and the freedom to create. . . . Think of that little computer chip. Its value isn't in the sand from which it was made."

The President impressed both students and faculty with standard old stories of America—including a vivid description of the young William Hewlett and David Packard working in that garage near Stanford—parables that had rarely been heard in these parts. He told them: "Democracy is less a system of government than it is a system to keep government limited." . . . "Our Constitution is different and the difference is in three words, 'We, the people.' Our Constitution is a document in which we the people tell the government what its powers are." . . . "It's hard for government planners, no matter how sophisticated, to ever substitute for millions of individuals working day and night to make their dreams come true. . . .

"Your generation is living in one of the most exciting, hopeful times in Soviet history," he told the students. "In this Moscow, this May of 1988, we may be allowed that hope—that freedom, like the fresh green sapling planted over Tolstoy's grave, will blossom forth at last in the rich fertile soil of your people and culture."

There were a couple of unfriendly questions—one about American treatment of Indians—but the President was cheered as if he were at a Republican National Convention. And the old pro left them laughing, saying: "Nobody asked me what it was going to feel like to not be President anymore. I have some understanding, because after I'd been governor for eight years and then stepped down, we'd only been home a few days and someone invited us out to dinner. Nancy and I both went out, got in the back seat of the car, and waited for somebody to get in front and drive us."

In their last session together, on June 2, Gorbachev asked Reagan about the short statement he had agreed to in the first moments of the summit. The President hesitated because his people, led by Shultz, had objected to what they considered the old language of the Cold War and détente, especially the phrase "peaceful coexistence," words that were in the air when the Soviets invaded Afghanistan. "I don't want to do it," Reagan told Gorbachev.

Gorbachev was silent for a moment. Then he stood and smiled. He reached for Reagan's hand and said: "Mr. President, we had a great time." The Russian put his arm around Reagan's shoulder this time and the two of them walked out together.

The President stopped in London on his way back home. He was a tired man. He fell asleep in a meeting with Japanese leaders, and when it was over he shook hands with the interpreter and said, "Well, Mr. Foreign Minister, it sure has been a pleasure." That was Ronald Reagan. So he was, too, when he arrived back in Washington and, in his way, reported on the summit to congressional leaders in the Cabinet Room. Skipping over the issues, great and small, of arms control, regional conflicts, and human rights, he quickly got to the heart of what was happening between himself and Gorbachev, saying:

"We won't be disturbed by the media, so we'll get right to it. . . . The channels of communication I think between our two governments are wide open and I hope we can keep it that way and allow my replacement to build on the achievements so far. I think it's clear that Gorbachev wants to restore the Soviet economy. It's a terrific job and it will take him a long time if he succeeds at all, because he's got opposition there, very obviously so. He also appears to be interested in political reform. . . . In any event, though we've seen progress, yet at the same time we have to consider them an adversary, because of their foreign policy and controlled society at home."

Then he added: "We know the power of the word, and we know the importance of being able to speak directly to the Soviet people without their government in between. I was pleased on my trip to convey the support of the American people directly to the dissidents and refuseniks struggling for their human rights and also to the clergy with regard to freedom of religion."

REAGAN offered his last words to the Republican Party he had remolded and revitalized at the 1988 Republican National Convention in New Orleans on the night of August 15. It was George H. W. Bush's convention this time. After eight years of loyal service, he had rather easily won the party's presidential nomination, defeating Senator Dole in a series of winter and spring primary elections. After Moscow, the selection process in both parties—Massachusetts governor Michael Dukakis had won the Democratic nomination and selected Senator Lloyd Bentsen of Texas as his vice presidential running mate—dominated the news as Reagan kept to a formal schedule that was even lighter than usual.

Only two pieces of business in early July had claimed much of his time: Attorney General Meese, under investigation and pressure for months, finally resigned, saying that he had been "completely vindicated" by a special prosecutor's sealed final report saying he had "probably" broken the law in his personal financial dealings but there would be no prosecution, and, on July 3, a United States warship in the Persian Gulf shot down Iran Air Flight 655, killing 290 passengers and crew. Reagan was at Camp David when the Airbus 300, on a flight to Dubai, was shot out of the air by two missiles. He issued a statement referring reporters to the Department of Defense for details, saying: "I am saddened to report that it appears that in a proper defensive action by the USS *Vincennes* this morning in the Persian Gulf an Iranian airliner was shot down over the Strait of Hormuz. This is a terrible human tragedy. . . . We deeply regret any loss of life. . . . The *Vincennes* followed standing orders and widely publicized procedures, firing to protect itself against possible attack. The only U.S. interest in the Persian Gulf is peace." *

As television news showed the bodies of passengers floating over a wide swath of the Gulf, the President said he had officially apologized to the government of Iran and that the United States would consider paying compensation to the families of the victims, who came from seven countries. Then he added: "This was an understandable accident."

Defense spokesmen in Washington said the *Vincennes*, with the most advanced electronic technology in the world, mistook the airliner for an American-built Iranian F-14, purchased when the Shah was still in power in the 1970s. The chairman of the Joint Chiefs, Admiral William Crowe, rejected comparisons with the Soviet shootdown of Korean Airlines Flight 007 in 1983, saying that the Iranian

---

* Special Prosecutor James McKay reported two weeks later, on July 19, that he did not have enough evidence to ask for an indictment of Meese on his role in the Iraqi pipeline and Wedtech cases, but also concluded that the Attorney General had probably violated the law four times, including the filing of a false income tax return in 1985.

airliner was in a combat zone and was flying low—it had taken off only four minutes before the missiles hit.*

In New Orleans, in the Superdome, the Republicans in the convention cheered and cheered as Reagan cheered them on for the last time:

> God put this land between the two great oceans to be found by special people from every corner of the world who had that extra love for freedom that prompted them to leave their homeland and come to this land to make a brilliant light beam of freedom to the world. It's our gift to have visions, and I want to share that of a young boy who wrote to me shortly after I took office. In his letter he said: "I love America because you can join the Cub Scouts if you want to. You have a right to worship as you please. If you have the ability, you can try to be anything you want to be. And I also like America because we have about 200 flavors of ice cream."

Then he spoke to candidate Bush: "George, just one personal request: Just go out there and win one for the Gipper." And they cheered some more. Well they should have: The old actor up there on the podium had made them the dominant party in the country by turning the political populism of Franklin D. Roosevelt on its ear; the enemy of the working man was no longer big business but big government. The Reagans left for the airport, the Belle Chasse Naval Air Station, to begin the flight to their ranch in the sky. As the President started up the steps, Bush stopped him and whispered the answer to the convention's only question, that his vice presidential nominee would be J. Danforth Quayle, Senator Dan Quayle, a forty-one-year-old senator from Indiana.

The conventional convention wisdom was that that was about the last the party would see of the Gipper. The President had treated the Vice President the way he had treated everyone else, as a hired hand. Reagan and Bush had had lunch most weeks, eating Mexican food, telling dirty jokes, and talking sports most of the time. Reagan liked to make fun of Bush. At one lunch they talked about the country's

---

* At the same time, Vice President Bush was dispatched to the United Nations, saying on August 3 that Iran must bear the principal responsibility for the shootdown because it allowed the airliner to fly in a combat zone. A Navy investigation concluded that the cause of the disaster was human error, that tense crew members misread radio and radar information in the ship's combat command center. No member of the *Vincennes* crew was criticized or disciplined in the Navy's final report.

trade deficit, which, under Reagan's free trade regime, had grown even faster than the budget deficit. Reagan said, "You'll never believe what's one of our most important exports. Condoms."

"I didn't know that," Bush replied.

"Yep, there's a big 'Made in the USA' marked on every one."

"Wow, I didn't know that either."

"Well, you have to unroll them all the way to see it."

Bush and his wife, Barbara, resented the fact that the Reagans had rarely invited them upstairs or to Camp David, and were never big on saying "Thank you" for gifts and services. But the Vice President wanted every word and minute of support and time he could get from the President, whose personal approval ratings had gone from 47 to 57 percent in Gallup polls from January to September as the campaign began with polls showing Bush in a close race with Dukakis.

This Vice President was a close student of Republican politics and well remembered what had happened to Vice President Richard Nixon against John F. Kennedy in 1960 when President Eisenhower's support seemed grudging and uninterested. There was also a bit of tension when the ever-loyal Bush had to distance himself a bit from Reagan to court Republican hard-liners during the primaries, telling reporters that he thought Reagan might be a little too enthusiastic about SDI and about Mikhail Gorbachev, too. "I don't think we know yet what the price tag will be," he said when Gerald Boyd of *The New York Times* asked about SDI in New Orleans. "If you went to a full deployment of a full strategic defense, it would be very expensive."

The conventional wisdom of August was wrong. After the Reagans returned to Washington from California on September 7, he handed out red, white, and blue ties with the legend "Push for Bush" to Cabinet members and told them he expected them to be on the road campaigning for the next two months. Then Reagan headed out, too, campaigning as if he were running himself. And he was, telling a couple of his men that the "Reagan Legacy" would last less than a hundred days if Dukakis took over the White House. He also added a legacy notch on October 13, when he signed the Family Support Act of 1988, the welfare reform bill he had negotiated over two years, turning control of the details over to congressional Democrats, led, ironically, by Senator Bentsen, but meeting his goal of producing the most substantive change in the welfare system in fifty years—the first federally mandated work program for welfare recipients.

The vote on November 8 was not quite the Reagan landslide of four years earlier, but Bush won 54 percent, holding together enough of the Reagan constituency to win 40 states to Dukakis's 10 plus the District of Columbia, giving him an electoral college margin of 426 to 112. The Democrats, however, maintained control of both houses of Congress, gaining 5 seats in the House of Representatives to control it by 262 seats to 173, and gaining 2 Senate seats to control the upper house by 56 to 44. In declaring victory and preparing to take over, the President-elect seemed to vent a bit of hostility to his patron, saying the vote was a victory for "my principles," then pledging "kinder and gentler" government and saying things such as: "I'm going to be a shake-me and wake-me president. I will personally read the Daily Intelligence Briefing every morning." And: "The intelligence community will stay out of the policy business." Within three weeks, on November 25, R. W. Apple Jr. of *The New York Times* was writing on the paper's front page: "Mr. Bush has moved with such dispatch and with such seeming confidence, in fact, that it sometimes seems almost as if he is governing, rather than preparing to govern. . . . It was Mr. Bush and not Mr. Reagan who spoke out last week in an effort to calm the financial markets of the world."

Reagan did seem ready to be seen as "President-emeritus," a phrase used by the *National Journal,* particularly after it became clear that there was no chance that American and Soviet arms control negotiators could come to agreement on a START Treaty before he was to fly west into the sunset come January 21, 1989. Even before the votes were counted on election day, Ken Duberstein, who had replaced Howard Baker as chief of staff in July, briefed reporters on Reagan's plans: "He will very much don the mantle of a professor and an educator and share with the American public, and with his successor, the lessons he has learned over these past eight years."

Six days after the election, "Professor Reagan" gave the first in an announced series of four addresses reflecting on America and his presidency. The class was fifty seventh- and eighth-grade students from Washington-area schools, invited to the East Room for the occasion, and a small national C-SPAN television audience. Reagan gave a short victory speech, saying: "The fact is that an entire planet is watching and following us." Everyone, everywhere, he said, wanted what America had. He began that list with democracy and capitalism and moved easily on to Nobel Prizes, Disneyland, Eddie Murphy, blue jeans, and rock music. Then he asked the students for comments and questions. Reporting in the *National Journal* a week later, Dick Kirschten wrote: "When the kids got the chance to ask questions, Reagan may have been reminded just why it is that it has been almost nine months since he has bothered to hold a formal televised press conference."

A couple of children stood to say they were glad to be part of a country where you can choose what kind of education you want and where the government tried to protect them from dangerous drugs. Then came this question: "I'm Casey Lee, and I'm from St. Stephen's School. And I was wondering what was the most important thing that you wanted to accomplish, but that you weren't able to accomplish as President?"

"I could sum that up very briefly: the Federal deficit," Reagan said. But he was not brief. He blamed the Democrats, then continued with his standard pitches for a constitutional balanced budget amendment and the line-item veto. The students were apparently not satisfied with that. "Hi. My name is Ben Allnutt. I go to Poolesville Junior-Senior High School," said the next one. "I was wondering if the younger generation today is going to have to pay for the world debt in years to come?"

"No," said the President. "I don't believe that it is that big a problem. You mean our Federal deficit? No, I think with this thing we have going along—yes, there will be a time when in the future, when government bonds come due and so forth—whether it be the taxpayers at that time that are paying them off. But if we can get this plan we are working on into effect, that will come along gradually. . . . Truth of the matter is, bad as our Federal debt is, it is much milder than many other countries as a percentage of our gross national product."

"My name is Cameron Fitzhugh, and I'm from St. Agnes School in Alexandria, Virginia. I was wondering if you think that it's possible to decrease the national debt without raising taxes on the public?"

"I do. That's a big argument that's going on in government. . . . I studied economics in college when I was young, and I learned there about a man named ibn-Khaldun, who lived 1,200 years ago in Egypt. He said: 'In the beginning of the empire, the rates were low. The tax rates were low, but the revenue was great. In the end of the empire when the empire was collapsing, the rates were great, and the revenue was low.' So—all right."

The students, twelve- and thirteen-year-olds, kept at the President as he tried to parry questions with convoluted riffs about aid to black colleges and gun control. Finally, Nora Taylor, from St. Agnes, asked when he thought there would be a woman president. He responded that he would be meeting soon with Prime Minister Thatcher. And he would be meeting again with President Gorbachev, who had acquired that new title after aggressively, and controversially, changing both the structure and personnel of the government and the Communist Party of the Soviet Union at a series of party conferences that began after Reagan had left Moscow.

The sweep of Gorbachev-initiated changes could be dramatized by a statistic: The average age of Central Committee members dropped from seventy-one to fifty-eight. The American intelligence community was flooding the White House with contradictory analyses of what was happening in the communist world, but the President saw few of them. He was more confident in his own evaluation of Gorbachev than in papers such as this one, which he did see, from the CIA's Soviet Analysis unit:

> Many Soviets regard Gorbachev's proposal to combine the top state and party jobs as a blatant power grab. . . . Gorbachev has also provided ammunition to opponents eager to portray him as a leader with an inflated ego, excessive personal ambition [imitating] self-promotion techniques of Western politicians . . . some fear his program will erode the old foundations of party rule before solid new foundations are built. He has so far not achieved any significant improvement in the overall economic situation, and there is a widespread perception that living conditions are deteriorating. . . . Yet his radical program is placing such enormous stress on the Soviet system, damaging the vested interests of so many elites, and creating such a high degree of tension in society as a whole that failure to call attention to the potential for leadership conflict to come to a head would reflect a gravely unjustified complacence.

There were also questions about whether the Soviet leader pushing democratic systems on his colleagues and countrymen was more popular in the West than in his own country. He had invited himself to the United States this time, coming to New York on December 6 to address the United Nations. Reagan was delighted; Bush less so. As far as the President-elect was concerned, Gorbachev was Reagan's friend but Bush's adversary, and he was intruding in the midst of a delicate transition. To emphasize that this fifth Reagan-Gorbachev meeting was not a mini-summit, nor even an official event, the Americans arranged a lunch on Governors Island, a Coast Guard station just off the tip of Manhattan. Bush would attend, not as President-elect, but as Vice President.

At the United Nations, the Soviet President talked for forty-five minutes about a new and globalized world. "A new world," he said, "where the use or threat of force no longer can or must be an instrument of foreign policy." He talked of perestroika and made pledges to liberalize immigration laws and human rights practices in his country. Then he said what he had come to say, shocking delegates and officials from around the world:

> Today I can report to you that the Soviet Union has taken a decision to reduce its armed forces. Within the next two years their numerical strength will be reduced by 500,000 men. The number of conventional armaments will also be substantially reduced. This will be done unilaterally. . . . By agreement with our Warsaw Treaty allies, we have decided to withdraw by 1991 six tank divisions from the German Democratic Republic, Czechoslovakia and Hungary, and to disband them. . . . Soviet forces in these countries will be reduced by 50,000 men and their armaments, by 5,000 tanks. . . . At the same time, we shall reduce the numerical strength of the armed forces in this part of our country and in the territories of our European allies will be reduced by 10,000 tanks, 8,500 artillery systems and 800 combat aircraft.

Gorbachev was talking about a 25 percent reduction in the Red Army's forty thousand tanks, which for more than forty years had been the spear point of a potential Soviet invasion of Western Europe. Then he pledged that the Red Army units in Warsaw Pact countries would be reorganized into purely defensive configurations, and that he would begin removing Soviet troops from Asia, beginning in the Mongolian People's Republic.

"A brilliant way to play a losing hand," was *Newsweek*'s take on the speech. That was certainly true, but a *New York Times* editorial put it in a larger context: "Perhaps not since Woodrow Wilson presented his Fourteen Points in 1918 or since Franklin Roosevelt and Winston Churchill promulgated the Atlantic Charter in 1941 has a world figure demonstrated the vision Mikhail Gorbachev displayed at the United Nations." More conservative journals were not impressed.

The *New York Daily News* called Gorbachev the "Soviet Sorcerer" and the *New York Post* editorialized: "The realities of international life require us to deal with Gorbachev. But it is one thing to negotiate with him, another to give him aid and still another to celebrate him. The first proposition is acceptable. The latter two are not."

The speech and its reception were the talk of the town, and of the world. But that was not what Gorbachev talked about during the limousine ride to southern Manhattan and the ferry ride to Governors Island, where the fortieth and forty-first Presidents waited for him. He was being briefed on a tremendous earthquake (6.9 on the Richter Scale) that had hit the Soviet republic of Armenia. Early reports indicated that thousands of people might be dead, and more were trapped under tons of rubble of collapsed buildings, old buildings with none of the steel reinforcing of more modern buildings in the West.

On Governors Island, Reagan, Bush, and Gorbachev and their staffs chatted a bit and then went to lunch at the Coast Guard commandant's house. It was a bit awkward. Reagan wanted to reminisce, Gorbachev wanted to connect with Bush, and Bush did not want to upstage Reagan. Sure enough, Reagan said, "You may have heard this one," remarking that Lyndon Johnson had once said that if he walked across the Potomac River, the press would report, "President can't swim!"

Yes, Gorbachev said with a laugh, Reagan had told him that one before.

Then Reagan gave the Soviet leader a framed photograph of their first meeting in the boathouse in Geneva, with an inscription he had written across the bottom: "We have walked a long way together to clear a path for peace. Geneva—1985. New York—1988."

The Russian asked Reagan what he thought of the U.N. speech. "I heartily approve," Reagan answered.

To Bush, Gorbachev said: "I know what people are telling you now that you've won the election: you've got to go slow, you've got to be careful, you've got to review. That you can't trust us, that we're doing all this for show."

"No serious American believes that," Bush said, with some exaggeration. "No faction, Democratic or Republican, right, left or center believes that."

"Our freedoms allow people to sound off," Reagan interjected. "There is a fringe that still believes Hitler was a nice guy."

Gorbachev took over again: "You'll see soon enough that I'm not doing this for show and I'm not doing this to surprise you or to take advantage of you. I'm playing real politics. I'm doing this because I need to. I'm doing this because there's a revolution taking place in my country. I started it. And they all applauded me when I started in 1986, and now they don't like it so much, but it's going to be a revolution, nonetheless."

As they finished lunch, Reagan raised his wineglass to Gorbachev. "This is my last meeting. I'd like to raise a toast to what we have accomplished and what you and the Vice President will accomplish together after January 20." Bush and Gorbachev raised their glasses, and then the Russian lowered his, looked over the rim to Bush, and said, "This is our first agreement."

The three went outside and posed for photographs with the Statue of Liberty in the background across New York Harbor. Reporters rushed in, shouting questions. Reagan repeated his "hearty approval" line and the next question was: "And, Mr. Vice President, your reaction to the decision?"

"I support what the President says," Bush said and laughed. "Give me a ring on January 21."

"One of the best answers of the year," said Gorbachev, who was laughing, too.

Then Gorbachev was pulled aside and told that the death toll in the Armenia earthquake was being estimated at 50,000, maybe more. Estimates of injuries were as high as 400,000, with rescue workers desperately digging through rubble, trying to reach people calling for help and crying in pain. The Soviet leader had been scheduled to stay in New York for another day and then go on to Cuba for a meeting with Fidel Castro and to London to see Thatcher. Instead, he left Kennedy International Airport the next morning for Moscow and then Armenia. On another part of the airfield, a chartered Boeing 727 was being filled with search-and-rescue machinery and medical supplies to be transported to Armenia, the first American aid the Soviets had accepted since the days just after the end of World War II.

Ronald Reagan, who was long past the days when he wrote most of his own material, told his new chief of staff, Ken Duberstein, to see if he could get Peggy Noonan to work on a Farewell Address. As she went into the Oval Office on December 13, she was not sure the President remembered her. But she was determined to get to know him better than she had when she worked in the White House. They met five times. In one of the Oval Office sessions, Duberstein tried to help her along in prompting Reagan to reflect on the times of his life.*

"Mr. President, I've been wondering what was the most difficult day you ever had in this office?" Duberstein asked.

"Oh well, I don't know, I . . ."

Watching and listening, Noonan thought he had trouble answering because, for him, there were no difficult days.

"I have a feeling," Duberstein tried, "it may have been the day the marines died in the barracks in Lebanon."

"Oh yes."

"And the shuttle explosion," Duberstein said.

"Oh yes."

"And Grenada."

"Yes."

"The marines in Lebanon and the Grenada invasion happened in the same week."

"Oh yes."

Noonan asked: "Didn't you have to call the families of the marines the day they died?"

"I met with so many . . ."

"How does a day like that make you feel? How is that when you're president?"

Reagan hesitated. Then he said: "Well, you feel you are in charge, and they are dead."

Noonan put her thoughts and feelings together in a two-page, single-spaced "Dear Mr. President" note. "These are my thoughts," she said: "We have to remember that this is a tonal speech—a tone poem aimed at subtly reminding the people of what a giant you are, what a phenomenon your career has been, what you have stood for, and how much they will miss you. . . .

"They love you, Mr. President, but you're still a mystery man to them in some respects. We're going to reveal more of you than they've seen in the past, mostly by talking about big things in a personal and anecdotal way. . . . You told me, and you should say in your Farewell Address, that the twin triumphs of your presidency were the economic turnaround the people created, and the fact that America is

---

* Noonan, who was working on President-elect Bush's inaugural address at the same time, worked with Tony Dolan on the Farewell Address from December 13, 1988, to January 16, 1989. She was paid at a day rate of $277 for the Reagan speech, earning $6,479.

once again admired in the world. . . . We should, in this speech, go back to first principles like 'City on a Hill.'

"The speech then: We should open simply, briefly review the past eight years, mention the triumphs and the disappointments, talk about the future regarding the Soviets, talk about how leaving is bittersweet, say that in keeping with the tradition set by Washington and Eisenhower you have a warning to offer, and that it is that our children are not getting the grounding in love of country and understanding of democracy that we did, and how a little more attention to this matter would be in order."

And that was the speech. A little corny, both triumphant and old-fashioned. "We meant to change a nation, and instead, we changed a world," said President Reagan from the Oval Office on January 11, 1989. "Countries across the globe are turning to free markets and free speech."

His "warning" sounded thinner than Washington's fear of foreign entanglements and Eisenhower's wariness about the military-industrial complex, but it was heartfelt: "An informed patriotism is what we want. And are we doing a good enough job teaching our children what America is and what she represents in the long history of the world? . . . Our spirit is back, but . . .

"We've got to do a better job of getting across that America is freedom—freedom of speech, freedom of religion, freedom of enterprise. And children, if your parents haven't been teaching you what it means to be an American, let 'em know and nail 'em on it.

"I've spoken of the shining city all my political life. And how stands the city on this winter night? More prosperous, more secure and happier than it was eight years ago. . . .

"And as I walk off into the city streets, a final word. My friends: We did it. We weren't just marking time. We made a difference. We made the city stronger, we made the city freer, and we left her in good hands.

"All in all, not bad, not bad at all," said Ronald Reagan. "And so, goodbye."

AFTERWORD

I N AUGUST OF 1994, former President Reagan was diagnosed as suffering from Alzheimer's disease, an awful and incurable neurological disorder. His last important public appearance was at the funeral of former President Nixon that April. By the next year he was no longer able to ride. The Reagans sold Rancho del Cielo in August of 1995.

The world was already a different place than it had been when Ronald Reagan left the presidency on January 20, 1989. George H. W. Bush served one term as President. As the national debt continued to increase, he broke a campaign pledge not to raise taxes and was defeated by Governor Bill Clinton, an Arkansas Democrat, in 1992.

Mikhail Gorbachev was elected President of the Soviet Union in April of 1989 in that country's first democratic election, just two months after the withdrawal of the last Red Army troops from Afghanistan. In June 1989, Lech Walesa, the shipyard electrician from Gdansk, was elected President of Poland in a free election. In that same month, elections were announced in four more communist countries: Hungary, Czechoslovakia, Bulgaria, and Romania. On November 9, 1989, the wall that had separated East Berlin from West Berlin since 1961, the wall that Ronald Reagan had demanded Gorbachev tear down, was torn down, beginning the reunification of Germany.

At the beginning of 1990, just after Gorbachev had been awarded the Nobel Peace Prize, the republics that made up the Soviet Union, led by Lithuania and other Baltic states, began to declare independence from Moscow. In June of 1991, Boris Yeltsin, Gorbachev's old friend who had earlier attacked his communist rule, was elected President of the Russian Republic with 57 percent of the vote. On December 15, 1991, President Gorbachev formally dissolved the Soviet Union into its many republics. Ten days later, he resigned as President of the union and ceded the rule he still retained to Yeltsin.

In Central America, President George H. W. Bush continued to advocate humanitarian aid for the contras. But, unlike Reagan, he supported the peace plans initiated by President Oscar Arias of Costa Rica. As part of one of those Arias negotiations, the Sandinista government of Nicaragua, abandoned by Moscow and with inflation of more than 800 percent, called elections in 1990. President Daniel Ortega was defeated by Violeta Chamorro, publisher of *La Prensa,* the candidate of the center-right National Opposition Union. In El Salvador, a United Nations peace and power-sharing treaty was signed in January of 1992 by the right-wing government officials and left-wing insurgents.

The civil war in Lebanon ended in 1990, although Israeli troops remained in the south of the country, and Syrian troops occupied much of the eastern part into the first years of the twenty-first century. The last three American hostages held in Beirut were released in December 1991.

Oliver North was convicted in May of 1989 of three criminal counts: obstruction of Congress, destruction of documents, and accepting illegal gratuities. He was sentenced to two years of probation and fined $150,000. All charges against him were dropped in 1991 when the U.S. Court of Appeals dismissed one count and set aside the others. In a 1991 autobiography, *Under Fire,* North wrote: "Now, five years later, I am even more convinced: *President Reagan knew everything,* about the diversion of monies paid by the Iranian government to the contras." He became the Republican candidate for the United States Senate from Virginia in 1991—Reagan refused to endorse him—losing a close race to the Democratic incumbent, another former Marine officer, Senator Charles Robb. In April of 1994, Admiral John Poindexter was convicted of five criminal charges, including conspiracy, obstruction of Congress, and perjury. He was sentenced to six months in prison. The conviction was overturned on technical grounds by a Federal Appeals Court panel in November of 1991. Robert McFarlane, convicted of four misdemeanors in 1988, was pardoned by the first President Bush. Former Secretary of Defense Caspar Weinberger, who had been indicted on four felony counts of lying to Congress, was also pardoned, in 1992, by President Bush.

Two START treaties were signed by the United States, and by the Soviet Union and its separated republics in 1991 and 1992. If fully implemented—and there were disputes among the former Soviet republics—those treaties would reduce the number of long-range nuclear-tipped missiles by about two-thirds. Funding for the Strategic Defense Initiative decreased each year after President Reagan left office, but like other defense programs it survived. A little money was appropriated for SDI research each year. That legislative device allowed members of Congress to avoid going on record as actually opposing the old Reagan idea.

The Republican Party, which already had a majority in the United States Senate, won a majority of the House of Representatives in the 1994 elections, controlling both houses for the first time since 1955.

By the year 2000, the number of AIDS cases in the United States was approaching one million. One in 250 Americans were infected with HIV (human immunodeficiency virus). Worldwide, more than 40 million people were infected, the greatest number in Africa.

In February of 2000, the Congress voted to rename Washington National Airport. The new name: Ronald Reagan Washington National Airport. The renaming was part of a national conservative campaign by the Ronald Reagan Legacy Project to have one public facility named after the fortieth President in each of the country's 3,067 counties.

More than nine hundred books have been written about Ronald Reagan since he left the White House. Some are picture books, but most are quite serious and tend to enshrine his life and record, with titles such as *Reagan's War: The Epic Story of His Forty-Year Struggle and Final Triumph over Communism* and *Hand of Providence: The Strong and Quiet Faith of Ronald Reagan*. Many are subsidized, principally by the Hoover Institution at Stanford University and the Heritage Foundation in Washington. Both institutions could be described as devoted to promoting the idea of Reagan as one of the great Presidents. There is irony in the persistent conservative glorification of Reagan, because as his Presidency ended they had accused him of adopting liberal-style détente. Many prominent conservatives were in agreement with columnist George Will's assertion, as the Soviet leader left the 1987 Washington summit, that that day would be remembered as the day when the United States "lost" the Cold War.

That same day, December 11, 1987, Howard Phillips, chairman of the Conservative Caucus, wrote on the op-ed page of *The New York*

Times: "President Reagan is little more than the speech-reader-in-chief for the pro-appeasement triumvirate of Howard H. Baker Jr., George P. Shultz, and Frank Carlucci. . . . The summit meeting and the so-called arms control treaties are a cover for the treasonous greed of those who manipulate the Administration. Mr. Reagan is no longer in any way accountable to the millions who recognize that we are in a deadly, strategic end-game with the Soviet Union, militarily the most powerful regime in world history."

On June 5, 2004, President Reagan, whose wife told me he had not opened his eyes in four years, died at his home in Bel Air. His state funeral, planned and managed by Nancy Reagan, moved from Bel Air to the Reagan Presidential Library in Simi Valley, California, to the National Cathedral in Washington, then back to Simi Valley and his final resting place down the hill a bit from the library. The mourning and the services and ceremonies lasted for a week, most of them broadcast day and night on national television. "God, this is impressive," said Steven Weisman, a *New York Times* White House correspondent during the Reagan years. "But the man they're talking about is not the President I covered every day."

NOTES

ABBREVIATIONS:

AAL: Ronald Reagan, *An American Life* (New York: Simon & Schuster, 1990)

AP: Associated Press

Int.:   Interview conducted by author unless otherwise noted

LAT: *Los Angeles Times*

NIE: National Intelligence Estimate

NSA: National Security Archive

NYT: *The New York Times*

PHF: Presidential Handwriting File, Ronald Reagan Presidential Library and Museum (Simi Valley, California)

RRPLM: The Ronald Reagan Presidential Library and Museum (Simi Valley, California)

UPI: United Press International

WHNS: White House News Summary

WHORM: White House Office of Records Management

WHSOF: White House Staff and Office Files

WP: *The Washington Post*

WSJ: *The Wall Street Journal*

WT: *Washington Times*

All references to Ronald Reagan's public speeches, press conferences, or other public appearances, unless otherwise noted, come from *The Public Papers of President Ronald W. Reagan*. These are maintained by the National Archives and Records Administration and compiled for publication by NARA's Federal Register staff, and are available at www.reaganlibrary.com.

All references to the President's activities, unless otherwise noted, are from the Presidential Daily Diary, kept by the Diarist of the United States, and now housed at the Ronald Reagan Presidential Library and Museum. All references to President Reagan's telephone calls, unless otherwise noted, come from the log of Presidential Telephone Calls, in the Presidential Handwriting File, at the Reagan Library. All references to handwriting attributed to President Reagan, unless otherwise noted, can also be located in the Presidential Handwriting File, at the Reagan Library.

The author covered Ronald Reagan on and off over the years, particularly during his presidency and his 1980 and 1984 campaigns. Over those years he interviewed political figures, journalists, and friends of the Reagans, some of them several times. This is a partial list of those interviewed, with interviews done specifically for this book marked with asterisks.

Morton Abramowitz
Representative Les Aspin
Senator Howard Baker
Secretary of State James A. Baker III
James David Barber
William Baroody Jr.
Carl Bernstein *
Representative John Brademas*
Senator Bill Bradley
Governor Edmund "Jerry" Brown
Governor Edmund "Pat" Brown
James McGregor Burns
President George H. W. Bush
Patrick Caddell
Lou Cannon
Governor Hugh Carey
President Jimmy Carter
Senator Clifford Case
Judge William Clark*
President Bill Clinton
Walter Cronkite
Richard Darman*
Michael Deaver*
John "Terry" Dolan
Senator Robert Dole
Sam Donaldson
Amatie Etzioni
President Gerald Ford
Edwin Fuelner Jr.
William A. Galston
Representative Newt Gingrich
Senator Gary Hart
Lee Huebner*
Mark Green*
Tom Griscom
Senator Jacob Javits
Martin Kaplan
Representative Jack Kemp
Senator Edward Kennedy
Senator Robert F. Kennedy
Steve Kroft*
Arthur Laffer

Governor Richard Lamm
Christopher Matthews*
Mayor John V. Lindsay
Senator Charles McC. Mathias
William Maynes
Attorney General Edwin Meese III*
Senator Daniel Patrick Moynihan
John Negroponte*
Richard Neustadt
President Richard Nixon
Lyn Nofziger*
Lord David Owen
Richard Perle
Tully Plesser*
Jerry Rafshoon
Mrs. Nancy Reagan*
Secretary of Labor Robert Reich
James Rentschler*
Alan Riding*
Steven V. Roberts*
Vice President Nelson Rockefeller
Ed Rollins
Hobart Rowen
Secretary of Treasury Robert Rubin*
Alan Ryskind (by Keith Bettinger)*
William Schneider
Robert Shrum
Secretary of State George Shultz*
Walter Slocombe
Stuart Spencer
Robert Squier
Lesley Stahl*
Richard Threlkeld*
Secretary of Defense Caspar
    Weinberger
Steven Weisman*
F. Clifton White
Charles Z. Wick*
Thomas Winter (by Keith Bettinger)*
Christopher Wren*
Mort Zuckerman*

INTRODUCTION

xi I first met: *NYT,* 11/17/67.

xi 1,187 to 1,070: *Ronald Reagan: The Presidential Portfolio* (New York: Public Affairs, 2001), p. 73.

xii magazine story: "Reagan's Campaign Strategy," *New York,* December 15, 1975, p. 39.

xii Pretty soon: The letter is on page 588 of *Reagan: A Life in Letters,* Kiron K. Skinner, Annelise Anderson, and Martin Anderson, eds. (New York: Free Press, 2003).

xii James Lake: *Leadership in the Reagan Presidency,* edited by Kenneth W. Thompson (Lanham, MD: Madison Books, 1992), p. 105.

xiii "First of all": Rollins int.

xiii "In the discharge of the duties": *The Autobiography of Calvin Coolidge* (Plymouth Notch, VT: Calvin Coolidge Memorial Foundation, 1989), p. 196.

xiii Tom Sawyer: *AAL,* p. 29.

xiv "I'm entering the race": Adriana Bosch, *Reagan: An American Story* (New York: TV Books), p. 121

xiv "Reagan's admirers": *Economist,* 6/12/04, p. 19.

xv "I feel very strongly": Deborah Hart Strober and Gerald Strober, *Reagan: The Man and His Presidency* (Boston: Houghton Mifflin, 1998), p. 571.

xv "This is a message": Oval Office videotape made for National Archives, April 1, 1985; William Doyle, *Inside the Oval Office: The White House Tapes from FDR to Clinton* (New York: Kodanasha, 2004).

xv "He treats us all the same": Richard Darman, *Who's in Control: Polar Politics and the Sensible Center* (New York: Simon & Schuster, 1996), p. 59.

xvi "What was the biggest problem": Regan int.

xvi "I want to talk to you": Public Papers of the Presidents, 1979. (Jimmy Carter.)

xvii He had a 63 percent: *National Journal,* 10/23/82, p. 1790.

xvii "Reagan is above the debate": Rubin int.

xvii "We will act": *National Journal,* 4/4/81, p. 562.

CHAPTER 1: JANUARY 20, 1981

1 "We have good news on the hostages": Deaver int.

1 Deaver told President Carter: Deaver int.; Jimmy Carter, *Keeping Faith: Memoirs of a President* (New York: Bantam, 1988), p. 11.

1 "Do I have to?": Deaver int.

2 "It's very close": Deaver int.; Rafshoon int.

2 "Who's Jack Warner?": Rafshoon int.

2 "Not yet": Rafshoon int.; Deaver int.

3 "You've got to get": Rafshoon int.

3 Reagans smiled at them now: Ibid.

3 "We can expect Ronald Reagan": Albert R. Hunt, *The American Election of 1980* (Washington, D.C.: American Enterprise Institute, 1981).

4 "before nine, after five": Daniel Yergin and Joseph Stanislaw, *The Commanding Heights: The Battle for the World Economy* (New York: Simon & Schuster, 1998), p. 329.

4 "The system": RRPLM, Personal Papers of Kenneth Khachigian, Box 1: Inaugural Address, 1/20/81 (4).

4 "It was about Bataan": Ibid., 1/20/81(5).

4 "We have great deeds to do": Ibid.

5 Treptow had kept a diary: Lou Cannon, *President Reagan: The Role of a Lifetime* (New York: Public Affairs, 2000), p. 75.

5 "Put it back in": Khachigian int.

5 "Shitheels!": RRPLM, Personal Papers of Kenneth Khachigian, Box 1: Inaugural Address, 1/20/81 (3); Deaver int.

5 He wrote the final version: The Reagan library has a good copy of Reagan's draft in Personal Papers of Ken Khachigian, Box 1: Inaugural Address 1/20/81 (10).

6 "We win. They lose": Michael Reagan, FrontPageMag.com, 7/5/05.

7 "I find nothing wrong": Cannon, *President Reagan*, p. 746.

8 "I'm sorry, sir": Rafshoon int.

8 "Reagan floated": *WP*, 1/21/81.

8 "An across-the-board rejection": RRPLM, WHNS, 1/21/81.

8 "President Reagan said what needed to be said": Ibid.

8 "What an insult to language and logic!": Ibid.

9 "The deep underlying question": Ibid.

9 "he jumped, clicked his heels": Strober and Strober, *Reagan*, p. 40.

9 "sharp message": Alexander M. Haig Jr., *Caveat: Realism, Reagan, and Foreign Policy* (New York: Scribner, 1984), p. 98.

10 "Poland's Prospects": National Security Archives, NIE 12.6–81.

10 The Soviet limousine was turned away: Cannon, *President Reagan*, p. 256.

10 "I'd kick their balls off": Nofziger int.

11 had paid 91 percent in income tax: Ronald Reagan, *An American Life* (New York: Simon & Schuster, 1990), p. 117.

11 "Voodoo Economics": *WP*, 9/23/80.

11 "Supply Side Economics": *NYT*, 12/17/80.

12 "Surprise swept over the Democrats": *NYT*, 2/20/81.

12 "I just lost that one": David A. Stockman, *The Triumph of Politics: Why the Reagan Revolution Failed* (New York: Harper & Row, 1986), p. 47.

13 "send you to OMB": Ibid., p. 74.

13 "You know, I am Ronald Reagan": Martin Anderson, *Revolution: The Reagan Legacy* (Stanford, CA: Hoover Institution Press, 1990), p. 215.

13 "That's enough, Nancy!": Stuart Spencer int., Strober and Strober, *Reagan*, p. 48.

13 He signed on to "Supply Side": "The Education of David Stockman," *Atlantic Monthly*, December 1981.

13 "I don't feel vulnerable": *NYT*, 3/15/81.

14 "Right, fellas": Stockman, *The Triumph of Politics*, p. 109.

14 "It isn't that he doesn't like people": Strober and Strober, *Reagan*, p. 45.

14 "warmly ruthless man": Anderson, *Revolution*, p. 288; Strober and Strober, *Reagan*, p. 45.

15 "Latin America into a beacon of freedom": Alan Riding int. Riding is former chief Latin American correspondent of the *New York Times*. He was in the room when Reagan appeared.

15 "steps being taken to implement": RRPLM, WHSOF: Executive Secretariat, NSC Country Files, Box 32, Nicaragua, 1/20/81–1/31/82 (3 of 5).

15 "I've just been fired by Haig": Riding int.

16 "Recommended Telephone Call": The Reagan Library, in their Presidential Handwriting File, has a series of boxes called Presidential Telephone Calls 1981–1989. According to the Reagan Library's finding guide, the series consists of memos prepared for the President, which recommended that telephone calls

be made to individuals on a variety of topics. The President would make a note of the result of the telephone conversation on the memos. This series provides insight into the President's efforts to lobby members of Congress to vote for a number of pieces of legislation that were a high priority to the Reagan administration.

16 Darman nodded to the Reagans: Darman int.

16 *Day in the Life of the President:* Transcript, NBC News, 2/10/81.

17 "Here's what the day looks like": Strober and Strober, *Reagan,* p. 96; James Baker int.

17 bare desk: James Baker int.

17 Central Intelligence Agency biography: RRPLM, National Security Briefing, 2/8/81.

18 The agenda in front of him said: RRPLM, Presidential Briefing Papers, 2/10/81.

18 Stockman did know they were wrong: "The Education of David Stockman," *Atlantic Monthly,* December 1981.

20 "If we try for '83": UPI, 2/12/81.

21 "An opening in which": RRPLM, WHSOF: Office of Speechwriting, Drafts, Address to Joint Session/Economy Background.

21 the nineteenth page of his speech draft: RRPLM, WHSOF: Office of Speechwriting, Drafts, 2/18/81.

22 "This was the big night": Reagan diary, 2/18/81.

22 "NOTHING WRONG THAT WE CAN'T FIX": *New Orleans Times-Picayune,* 2/19/81.

22 "REAGAN ROLLS ECONOMIC DICE": *Omaha World Herald,* 2/19/81.

22 "A Bold and Risky Venture": *NYT,* 2/19/81.

22 "figure-studded speech": RRPLM, WHSOF: Office of Speechwriting, Drafts, 2/18/81.

22 "Trying to Repeal Keynes": *NYT,* 2/20/81.

24 "State Department Spreading Marxism in Central America": Albert R. Hunt, "Thunder on the Right: As Ronald Reagan's Star Rises, So Does That of the Conservative Newspaper *Human Events,*" *WSJ,* 7/9/80.

24 "Is Reagan Ignoring Activists?": Rusher, *Human Events,* 2/27/81.

25 "A must-read": Edwin Meese III, *With Reagan* (Washington D.C.: Regnery, 1992), p. 104.

25 more than 2,200 feet above: Darman, *Who's in Control,* p. 67.

25 "or forgetting your lines": On Air Force One pool report.

CHAPTER 2: MARCH 30, 1981

26 "The most trusted man in America": *WP,* 3/7/81.

27 "We all know what the President wants": Meese, *With Reagan,* p. 174.

28 "Now I've done some figuring": Regan int.

28 he concluded there was something wrong with Carter: Deaver int.

28 people began singing "America the Beautiful": *AAL,* p. 253.

28 "Fellas, I promised I wouldn't touch Social Security": March 17 meeting with Republican senators in the Oval Office, Dole int.

28 "Anytime I can get 70 percent": Thompson, *Leadership in the Reagan Presidency,* p. 155.

29 "Mr. President, I hear your theory": Stockman, *The Triumph of Politics,* p. 149; Carey int.

29 Smith reversed OMB's proposal: Stockman, *The Triumph of Politics,* p. 141.

29 "We believe in free trade": Cannon, *President Reagan,* footnote, p. 383.

30 "Second-rate hambones": Ibid., p. 164.

30 "National Security Decision Directive 1": Christopher Simpson, *National Security Directives of the Reagan and Bush Administrations* (Boulder, CO: Westview Press, 1995), pp. 9, 19.

30 Soviet economy: *AAL*, p. 316.

30 "fucking parking lot": Cannon, *President Reagan*, p. 163.

30 "Good God, I can't believe": Ibid.

31 He dictated a resignation letter: *AAL*, p. 61.

32 "Mr. Haig's rush": RRPLM, WHNS, 3/29/81.

32 "The man is dangerous": *Gainesville Sun*, 3/24/81.

32 "So the single voice the Reagan": *NYT*, 3/27/81.

33 "make the news instead of reporting it": *NYT*, 3/26/81.

33 "He will not say what": Lou Cannon, *Reagan* (New York: G.P. Putnam, 1982), p. 384.

34 "What the hell's that?": Herbert L. Abrams int. 7/23/90. Most of the following details of the assassination attempt, the confusion surrounding the crime, and its medical aftermath are taken from Dr. Abrams's 1992 book, *The President Has Been Shot* (New York: W.W. Norton).

35 "I'll walk in": Deaver int.

35 "I don't hear anything": Larry Speakes, *Speaking Out* (New York: Avon, 1989), p. 10; Speakes int.

35 "Oh my God, we've lost him": Abrams, *The President Has Been Shot*, p. 58.

35 "Who's holding my hand?": *AAL*, p. 260; Cannon, *Reagan* (1982), p. 404.

36 the thousand-dollar suit: Speakes, *Speaking Out*, p. 128.

36 "I forgot to duck": *AAL*, p. 260.

36 "The guy's in really bad shape": Ed Rollins, *Bare Knuckles and Back Rooms: My Life in American Politics* (New York: Broadway Books, 1996), p. 92.

36 " 'Think we're going to lose him' ": Speakes, *Speaking Out*, p. 10.

36 "Has the Vice President been called?": Haig, *Caveat*, p. 151.

37 Reagan had not been hit: Nancy Reagan, *My Turn: The Memoirs of Nancy Reagan* (New York: Random House, 1989), p. 3.

37 "George! This is Al Haig": Haig, *Caveat*, p. 152.

37 "Flash. Please deliver": Ibid., p. 155.

37 Haig crossed out: Ibid.

37 "No, of course not": Ibid., p. 157.

37 "This is apt to be a loner": Regan int.

37 "the bullet for evidence": Abrams, *The President Has Been Shot*, p. 63.

37 a hollow .22-caliber slug: Laurence I. Barrett, *Gambling with History* (New York: Doubleday, 1983), p. 111.

37 Aaron inched it out: Abrams, *The President Has Been Shot*, p. 63.

38 The chest cavity was filled with blood: Ibid., p. 130.

38 "The anesthesia affects the mind": Ibid., p. 154.

38 Dr. Aaron decided immediate surgery was necessary: Ibid., p. 62.

38 "I hope you're a Republican": Nancy Reagan, recounting this incident, describes the President as saying, "Please tell me you are all Republicans." Nancy Reagan, *My Turn*, 7.

38 "The football": Speakes int.

38 "the helm is right here": Speakes, *Speaking Out*, p. 3; Speakes int.

39 locking them in his safe: Darman, *Who's in Control*, p. 56.

39 Moynihan of New York: Daniel Patrick Moynihan, *Came the Revolution* (San Diego: Harcourt Brace Jovanovich, 1988), p. 10.

39   "Is the President in surgery": White House press briefing transcript, 3/30/81.

40   "How do you get up to the press room?": Regan int.

40   "They want to know who's running the government": Haig, *Caveat*, p. 159.

40   He thought he might faint: Regan int.

40   "I can't believe this": Donald T. Regan, *For the Record: From Wall Street to Washington* (San Diego: Harcourt Brace Jovanovich, 1988) p. 167.

40   "Is he mad?": Ibid.

41   "Until the Vice President actually arrives here": Speakes int. A March 31 memo to the press office, marked "Background for Larry Speakes," read: "The term 'command authority,' or more properly National Command Authority, refers to the preexisting orders of the Commander-in-chief and the established procedures and chain-of-command to be followed in the event of certain limited military situations. Although these matters are classified, the National Command Authority procedures cover certain delegations from the President to the Vice President and to the Secretary of Defense in the event of specific circumstances. National Command Authority procedures have been adopted by many prior Administrations, as well as by President Reagan when he took office.—Fred Fielding."

41   fished into his pockets: Nofziger int.

41   The surgery was finished: Abrams, *The President Has Been Shot*, p. 64.

41   "We want to make the government": Speakes, *Speaking Out*, p. 15.

42   "What's his beef?": Barrett, *Gambling with History*, p. 123.

42   "Where am I?": Nofziger notes.

CHAPTER 3: APRIL 28, 1981

43   *Washington Post*/ABC News poll: RRPLM, WHNS, 4/1/81.

44   Reagan had dozed: Abrams, *The President Has Been Shot*, p. 66.

44   "What makes you think I'd be happy to hear *that*?": Nofziger int.

44   He received morphine: Abrams, *The President Has Been Shot*, p. 159.

44   "President Reagan's pen": *Los Angeles Herald Examiner*, 4/1/81.

44   "The President's excellent prognosis": *LAT*, 4/1/81.

44   For the rest of the day: Nofziger int.

44   "Oh damn, oh damn": Ibid.

44   still needed oxygen to breathe: Nancy Reagan, *My Turn*, p. 9.

45   "I would abandon": *NYT*, 4/2/81.

45   "A new legend has been born": *WP*, 4/1/81.

46   "During the brief time Monday": *WSJ*, 4/1/81.

46   "We will act as if he were here": *National Journal*, 4/4/81.

46   ending years of suspicion and estrangement: Lesley Stahl, *Reporting Live* (New York: Simon & Schuster, 1999), p. 134.

46   "He's so sick, oh, he may die": Stahl int.

46   fever of almost 103 degrees: Barrett, *Gambling with History*, p. 121; Abrams, *The President Has Been Shot*, p. 67–68.

46   "We've been living in a dream world": Abrams, *The President Has Been Shot*, p. 73.

47   other physicians were more worried: Ibid., p. 74.

47   He slept through most of Saturday and Sunday: Ibid.

47   happily watching television cartoons: Ibid., p. 90.

48   He was shocked: John A. Farrell, *Tip O'Neill and the Democratic Century* (Boston: Little Brown, 2001), p. 553.

48 "Woodrow Wilson": Barrett, *Gambling with History,* p. 123; Darman, *Who's in Control,* p. 61.

48 "Doped up": Farrell, *Tip O'Neill and the Democratic Century,* p. 553.

49 even his wife was having trouble getting him to eat: Nancy Reagan, *My Turn,* p. 14.

49 press pool: Weisman int.

50 "Whatever happens now I owe my life to God": *AAL,* p. 263.

50 how pale and disoriented: Darman, *Who's in Control,* p. 60.

50 "The first full day at home": *AAL,* p. 264.

51 "I've never understood": Darman, *Who's in Control,* p. 60; Darman int.

51 first quarter of 1981 was 6.5 percent: *NYT,* 4/21/81.

51 NBC News/Associated Press survey: RRPLM, WHNS, 4/18/81.

53 His draft: *AAL,* pp. 272–73.

53 "I promised to do it in the campaign, Al": Haig, *Caveat,* p. 111.

54 Haig sent back a State Department rewrite: *AAL,* p. 271.

54 "You know, Mr. President": Deaver, Strober and Strober, *Reagan,* p. 116.

54 "Thank you": Ibid., pp. 115–16.

54 clipped a cover letter in his own hand: *AAL,* pp. 271–73.

55 "We've got some news": Cannon, *President Reagan,* p. 722.

55 "The place went nuts": int. John Chancellor, NBC News.

55n "Blamed the United States": *AAL,* p. 273.

56 "That reception was almost worth getting shot": Ibid., p. 285.

56 Jim Wright of Texas, wrote in his diary: Farrell, *Tip O'Neill and the Democratic Century,* p. 553.

57 "The President has become a hero": Ibid., p. 556.

CHAPTER 4: AUGUST 8, 1981

58 Reagan, wearing a bulletproof vest: He called it "my iron underwear." *AAL,* p. 275.

59 Darman changed the autopenning system: Darman, *Who's in Control,* p. 61.

59 Secret Service was keeping ordinary people: Ibid.; Bosch, *Reagan,* p. 170.

59 weight dropped from 112 pounds to 100: Nancy Reagan, *My Turn,* p. 45.

60 could have prevented the shooting: Ibid., p. 46.

60 "I am so scared": Ibid., p. 46.

60 Then, working through Deaver, Mrs. Reagan: Ibid., pp. 47–48; Deaver int.; Bosch, *Reagan,* p. 169.

60 a happy Nancy meant a happy Ronnie: Nancy Reagan, *My Turn,* pp. 46–47; Deaver int.; Bosch, *Reagan,* p. 169.

60 Ronald Reagan Jr.: Stahl int.

60 "How are you, Mr. Mayor": Stahl, *Reporting Live,* p. 135.

62 hundredth day in office: Cannon, *Reagan* (1982), p. 333.

62 "Let me take this opportunity": RRPLM, 5/18/81.

62 $73,420 a year: *Business Week,* 5/4/81.

62 17,500 men and women: Ibid.

62 forty hours to thirty-two hours: Ibid.

62 October 20, 1980, letter: RRPLM, letter sent to Robert Poli during campaign, later forwarded from Bob Bonitati to Elizabeth Dole on 5/1/81.

63 "This is a letter of understanding": RRPLM, WHSOF: Fuller, Craig: OA 10974, PATCO Strike (1 of 2).

63 "The only illegal strike": *Business Week,* 5/4/81.

64 President's Legislative Strategy Group: Speakes, *Speaking Out,* p. 89.

64 deficit would be $55 billion: RRPLM, WHSOF: Darman, Richard, memo, 5/12/81.

64 "Wide Support in Setting New Course for Nation": *NYT,* 5/1/81.

65 "I have a statement on the Social Security": Farrell, *Tip O'Neill and the Democratic Century,* pp. 571–72.

65 "crazy": Deaver int.

65n advocating privatization options: Ronald Dugger, *On Reagan* (New York: McGraw-Hill, 1983), p. 47.

66 "I don't see any ranch time": Deaver int.

66 The fifteen action items: RRPLM, WHSOF: Cicconi, James W. Series I, Senior Staff Mtgs, May 8, Box 15.

67 "Be dull, Mr. President": Barrett, *Gambling with History,* p. 74.

67 "Mr. President, we know that you are familiar": Thompson, *Leadership in the Reagan Presidency,* p. 174.

67 "Don't worry": Ibid.

68 Gergen: Gergen int.

68 destroyed a nuclear reactor in Iraq: Bernard Gwertzman of the *NYT* reported on June 9, 1981, that "There was some initial uncertainty over what types of American planes were used. Some officials said F-16's, the newest planes in the Israeli Air Force, had done the bombing, but others said later that the raid was carried out by about 15 F-15's and F-4's, with the F-4's, armed with special precision weapons known as 'smart bombs,' doing the actual bombing."

68 "By golly": *Time,* 6/22/81.

69n "That fellow Begin makes it very hard for us to support Israel": Speakes, *Speaking Out,* p. 136.

69n "I can understand his fear": *AAL,* p. 413.

71 "Old Buddy": Farrell, *Tip O'Neill and the Democratic Century,* pp. 574–75.

71 "His philosophical approach": Barrett, *Gambling with History,* p. 15.

71 Reagan had promised to try to find a woman: Cannon, *President Reagan,* p. 722. The candidates listed in May 1981 were: Robert Bork, 54, a professor at Yale Law School and former Solicitor General; Deputy Secretary of State William Clark, 50; Court of Appeals Judge Amalya Kearse, 44; District Court Judge Cornelia Kennedy, 58; California Superior Court Judge Joan Dempsey Klein, 57; University of Chicago Law School Professor Philip Kurland, 59; Nevada Senator Paul Laxalt, 58; Court of Appeals Judge William Mulligan, 63; Brigham Young University President Dallin Harris Oaks, 49; Arizona Appellate Court Judge Sandra Day O'Connor, 51; Duke Law School Professor August Pye, 50; former Attorney General and Secretary of State William Rogers, 68; North Carolina Chief Justice Susie Marshall Sharp, 74; Court of Appeals Judge Joseph Sneed, 61; Circuit Court Judge H. Clifford Wallace, 53; FBI Director William Webster, 57; Court of Appeals Judge Malcolm Wilkey, 63; Yale Law School Professor Ralph Winter, 46. This list of candidates can be found at the RRPLM, in the White House Staff and Office files of Fred Fielding, Supreme Court Nominations 1981 (1), OA 3489.

72 busiest day ever for Reagan: *U.S. News & World Report,* 7/6/81.

72 "Welcome back": Ibid.

72 "Oh, this is the worst!": Ibid.

72 Margaret Heckler: Ibid.

72 four names, all women: Cannon, *Reagan* (1982), p. 314.

73 Richard Darman told him: Darman, *Who's in Charge,* p. 84

73 The President got Breaux's vote: Barrett, *Gambling with History,* pp. 160–61.

73 Century Plaza: Ibid.

74 "Oh, my God": Deaver int.

74 "REAGAN'S AIDES SAY A BALANCED BUDGET IS POSSIBLE BY 1984": *NYT,* 6/28/81.

74 The conversation began with horses: *AAL,* p. 280; Clark int.

74 Reagan liked her immediately: Cannon, *President Reagan,* p. 723.

74 The formal announcement of her nomination: Ibid.

74 quiet flurry of last-minute opposition: Ibid.

74 On July 6, Max Friedersdorf reported: RRPLM, "Congressional Telephone Calls" memo, 7/6/05, Friedersdorf papers.

75 Evans and Novak filed a column: RRPLM, WHSOF: Meese, Edwin III, OA 2408: Appointments—Supreme Court—O'Connor (2).

75 "Kenneth W. Starr": Twenty years later, Starr came to greater public attention as the special prosecutor investigating a series of money and personal charges against President William Clinton.

75 ten to one against O'Connor: *Newsweek,* 7/20/81.

75 "This is the best thing he's done": Ibid.

75 *The Washington Post* editorialized: *WP,* 7/8/81.

75 "Every good Christian": Clark int.

75 "Jerry, I am going to put forth a lady": Strober and Strober, *Reagan,* p. 85.

76 women staffers: Stahl int.

76 Anderson: Anderson, *Revolution,* p. 290.

76 "Maybe we should just brand all the babies": Ibid., pp. 274–77.

77 "I'm not going to get involved in details": *NYT,* 8/7/81.

77 "Political-Economic Turn": *NYT,* 7/30/81.

78 "a riverboat gamble": RRPLM, WHNS, 8/2/81.

78 Item 4 on the senior staff agenda meeting: RRPLM, WHSOF: Cicconi, James W., Series III: Senior Staff Meetings, July 1981 (Action Items) [1 of 2], Box 16.

78 "They cannot": *LAT,* 7/15/81.

79 David Gergen, the communications director: RRPLM, WHSOF: Gergen, David: OA 10520, Air Traffic Controllers.

79 "There is no right to strike against the public safety": *NYT,* 8/9/81.

79 Back inside, Reagan said: Cannon, *President Reagan,* p. 437.

79 more than ten to one: RRPLM, White House telephone log of calls supporting Reagan's stance on PATCO; Deaver int.

79 David Broder, summed it up this way: *WP,* 8/9/81.

79 Tom Fox wrote: RRPLM, WHNS, *Philadelphia Inquirer,* 8/11/81.

80 "While Reagan started out in politics": *WP,* 8/2/81.

80 The Federal Aviation Administration: Federal Register, 11/13/80.

80 Thirteen thousand controllers struck on August 3: Cannon, *President Reagan,* p. 437.

81 "We didn't want to confuse the tax picture": Farrell, *Tip O'Neill and the Democratic Century,* p. 578.

81 "Dave, if what you are saying is true": Ibid.

81 " 'To the rear march!' ": Barrett, *Gambling with History,* p. 171.

82 "Drew, don't worry about me": *Fortune Magazine,* "What Managers Can Learn from Manager Reagan," 9/15/86.

CHAPTER 5: AUGUST 13, 1981

83 "Lassie": Steven Weissman int.
83 "255-4855": Darman, *Who's in Control*, p. 70. Years later Richard Darman wrote: "Looking back now at all the reasons that the imbalanced 1981 program was passed, I am struck the more by how improbable the enactment of the full 1981 tax act really was. Of the ten basic reasons for its enactment, at least six were themselves highly unusual: a dominating anti-government populism; a majority party fear of realignment; Ronald Reagan; an extended honeymoon; David Stockman; and a pragmatist-ideologue alliance. Of these six unusual phenomena, probably a least five were required for enactment. The odds of those five coinciding could reasonably be assessed at something like one in a million."
84 "He won't think about things": Nofziger int., Thompson, *Leadership in the Reagan Presidency*, Vol. 1, p. 82.
84 "A Disengaged Presidency": *Newsweek*, 9/7/81; Stahl, *Reporting Live*, p. 138.
84n 22 to 24 percent range: Darman, *Who's in Control*, p. 78.
84n "record that still stands": Ibid., p. 98.
85 Ronald Hoff: *NYT*, 8/30/81.
85 "Bill Smith is going to be my attorney general": Strober and Strober, *Reagan*, p. 69.
85 "NO TAX INCREASE!": Speakes, *Speaking Out*, p. 137.
86 "I just wanted them to see me standing there": Stahl, *Reporting Live*, p. 194.
86 "Nope": RRPLM, PHF, Series V: WH Mail reports, Box 1, Folder 5.
86 "The Air Strike": *NYT*, 8/14/81, p. 1.
87 "It's a fair warning": *WSJ*, 8/14/81, p. 1.
87 fourteen-page analysis: RRPLM, WHSOF: Meese, Edwin, OA 6518, Wirthlin 1981 (3).
87 CBS was trying to install a telescope: Stahl, *Reporting Live*, p. 138.
87 the president told his wife: Ibid.
87 After fifteen minutes: Christopher Matthews int.
87 "It's like iron": Ibid. This is the same Chris Matthews who turned to television and became the star of NBC News's *Hardball*.
88 "Good work": Meese int.
88 the Navy had raised the question: *AAL*, p. 289.
88 "AIDES LET RON SLEEP ON IT": *New York Daily News*, 8/20/81.
88 "Meese's decision not to notify Reagan": *WP*, 8/20/81.
88 "World War III?": Stahl, *Reporting Live*, p. 138. Humor columnist Art Buch-wald also had his say, writing a mock Reagan diary entry: "We had a lot of fun, I cut brush, cleared out trees, hiked with my best girl, Nancy, and shot down two Libyan planes. I was sleeping when we shot them down, and my best friend, Ed Meese, didn't wake me up at the time. But it was fun hearing about it." (Bosch, *Reagan*, p. 113).
89 "staff members": *Newsweek*, 9/1/81.
89 James Baker took on the task of rebuttal: *Newsweek*, 9/1/81.
89 spent an hour with an old cowboy movie buddy: Press pool report, 9/1/81.
89 Donaldson looked up at the thing and laughed: Donaldson int.
90 $209,508 in new White House china: *NYT*, 10/2/81.
90 "Don't let the President go on vacation next year": *NYT*, 9/7/81.
91 "a nice guy nobody elected and nobody knows": *NYT*, 9/6/81.

91 "wrecking crew": *WP,* 9/4/81.

91 "working as well as it ever has, if not better": Ibid.

91 "We can't hide from reality": *Atlantic Monthly,* December 1981.

92 "If it comes down to": Weinberger int.

92 "What would people think?": Barrett, *Gambling with History,* p. 84.

92 "Left this out": RRPLM, PHF: Presidential speeches, Folder 19, 9/24/81 box.

92 "No easy way to correct with speeches": RRPLM, PHF, 9/22/81.

92n Dick Cheney: Stockman, *The Triumph of Politics,* p. 311.

93 "Tinkering": *NYT,* 9/27/81.

93 "Reagan in Retreat": *Baltimore Sun,* 9/27/81.

93 Reagan endured hours of mock conferences: *WP,* 10/2/81.

93 Speakes placed budget: Ibid.

93 "friendlies": Ibid.

93 "You made me sound like Charlie McCarthy": Speakes, *Speaking Out,* p. 309.

94 "If those Airborne Warning and Control Systems": *NYT,* 4/21/81.

94 "AWACS is dead": RRPLM, WHNS, 10/29/81 (Phil Jones, CBS News).

94 "Ron to Israel": *New York Daily News,* 10/2/81.

94 "I'm going to vote against AWACS, period": *Des Moines Register,* 10/27/81.

94 "We just took Jepsen and beat his brains out": Ibid., 10/29/81.

94 Working on another switcher: Strober and Strober, *Reagan,* p. 31; Falwell int.

95 letter to a friend, George Eccles: RRPLM, WHORM: FG035 (045643).

95 text of letter to Walton: Skinner et al., eds., *Reagan: A Life in Letters,* p. 617.

95 "a slight one": *WP,* 10/22/81.

95 nine million Americans were out of work: *NYT,* 12/25/81.

96 "The Education of David Stockman": *The Atlantic Monthly,* December 1981.

96 "My friend . . . your ass is in a sling": Stockman, *The Triumph of Politics,* p. 4.

96 "Dave, how do you explain this?": Darman, *Who's in Control,* p. 107.

97 Baker and Deaver had a script waiting: Ibid.

97 "David Stockman was not the sinner": *Time,* 12/17/81.

97 "Somewhere along the line": *WP,* 11/18/81.

97 "revenue enhancements": Ibid.

97 Tanks were in the streets: *NYT,* 12/16/81.

97 "We who were going to balance the budget": *AAL,* pp. 312, 314.

98 Israeli Knesset voted 63 to 21: *NYT,* 12/15/81.

98 Haig and Secretary of Defense Weinberger in agreement: *NYT,* 12/16/81.

98 "hard for you to be his friend": Barrett, *Gambling with History,* p. 271.

98 An NBC News "White Paper": 12/27/81.

CHAPTER 6: JUNE 8, 1982

99 "He just doesn't seem to have": *National Journal,* 10/31/81. Dick Cheney would become Secretary of Defense and Vice President of the United States.

99 "What is really back": *WP,* 10/11/82.

99 "explain, dammit!": RRPLM, WHSOF: Executive Secretariat, NSC: Country Files, El Salvador, Vol. II 6/1/81–12/21/81 (3), Box 91363.

99 "I don't honestly know"; *NYT,* 10/21/81.

100 One clarification followed another: *NYT,* 10/22/81.

100 unemployment at 9.5 percent: Gannett News Service, 6/6/82.

100 rejected almost immediately by the Republicans: *WP,* 5/6/82.

100 "EXTREMELY CONFIDENTIAL": RRPLM, WHSOF: Fuller, Craig, Economic/Budget Policy, 3/82, Box 10972 (2 of 2).

100 "The Administration's fiscal program": Ibid.

101   shooting of Israel's ambassador, Shlomo Argov: Shultz, George P., *Turmoil and Triumph* (New York: Scribner, 1993), p. 43.

101   official story that the Israeli Defense Forces: *NYT,* 6/11/82.

102   "Gosh they really are close": *Time,* 10/4/82.

102   Philip Habib: Shultz, *Turmoil and Triumph,* p. 45.

103   "Project High Frontier": *Human Events,* 5/22/82.

104   "bad shape": *AAL,* p. 316.

104   (NSDD 32): May 1982; Simpson, *National Security Directives,* p. 62.

104   The President was determined to go on the offensive in the Cold War: Pipes left the White House to return to Harvard in September 1982. In an exit interview he said: "It was interesting that the way the air controllers' strike was handled impressed the Russians. Seeing a union leader taken away in chains—that surprised them and gave them respect for Reagan. It showed them a man who, when aroused, will go the limit to back up his principles."

105   The backup study: NSSD 1-1982, RRPLM.

105   radio and newspaper commentaries: Kiron K. Skinner, Martin Anderson, and Annelise Anderson, eds., *Reagan's Path to Victory* (New York: Free Press, 2004) p. 243.

106   "His summit partners": *NYT,* 6/7/82.

106   "Yankee Go Home!": RRPLM, WHNS, 6/6/82.

106   "President Reagan is a man of long vision": AP, 6/6/82.

107   Haig, without bothering to wake or tell Reagan: *WP,* 6/6/82.

107   "You don't talk to the company commander": RRPLM, WHNS, 6/6/82.

107   kissed Kirkpatrick: Clark int.

107   "You've caught me a long way from there": RRPLM, WHNS, 6/6/82.

107   "A bunch of amateurs": UPI, 6/8/82.

107   the President and the Pope: Carl Bernstein and Marco Politi, *His Holiness* (New York: Penguin, 1997), p. 355; Bernstein int.

109   "Communism is neither an economic or a political system": May 1975 radio address.

109   "I think there is every indication": June 1980 to editorial writers of the *WP.*

110   "We must keep the heat": Farrell, *Tip O'Neill and the Democratic Century,* p. 607.

110   "The speech was very strong": RRPLM, WHNS, 6/9/82.

110   "Maybe he'll go down": RRPLM, WHNS, 6/6/82.

110   "It was a very hard-hitting speech": RRPLM, WHNS, 6/6/82.

110   hitting harder: The language in the Westminster speech draft reads: "Surely those historians will find in the councils of those who preached the supremacy of the state, who declared its omnipotence over individual man, who predicated its eventual domination of all peoples of the earth, surely historians will see there . . . the focus of evil." RRPLM, WHSOF: Speechwriting, WHO of: Research. OA 13653: Westminster Drafts (6/8/82) (6).

110   *Witness:* Thompson, *Leadership in the Reagan Presidency,* Vol. 1, p. 104.

110   He mixed and matched contact lenses: Ibid.

111   "the nitwit minister": *WP,* 12/14/81; *NYT,* 6/9/82.

111   "Clark is living proof that still waters can run shallow": *NYT,* 10/26/83.

111   "run the building": Clark int.

111   "He doesn't know his ass from third base": Ibid.

111   "That son-of-a-bitch is the worst influence": Ibid.

111   "His staying power is zilch": Ibid.

111   the President's only close friend was his wife: After he left Washington to return

to his California ranch and law practice in Paso Robles, Clark never received another telephone call from the man he served for twenty years. When Reagan's official biographer, Edmund Morris, asked him about that in 1993, Clark began to cry.

111 rapidly losing his hearing: Reagan attributed the beginning of his hearing difficulties to a gun being fired near his head during the filming of a movie.

112 Meese's bulging briefcases: Speakes, *Speaking Out*, p. 86.

112 weekly lunches: RRPLM, WHSOF: Presidential Daily Diary.

112 "No thanks": *WP*, 3/21/82.

112 His next move was to demand: Clark int.; Barrett, *Gambling with History*, p. 234.

112 "FOR THE PRESIDENT": For examples of a Clark memo, see the RRPLM, WHSOF of Clark, William L.

112 The Clark/Reagan style: RRPLM, WHSOF: Executive Secretariat, NSC Country Files, Pakistan: NSC Briefing Book State Visit of President Zia of the Islamic Republic of Pakistan December 6–14, 1982 (2).

113 Deaver had tried to trick: Deaver int.

113 "What am I, a leper?": Deaver int.

113 "This situation with Al is very serious": McFarlane int.; Clark int.; Robert McFarlane with Sofia Smardz, *Special Trust* (New York: Cadell & Davies, 1994), p. 200.

113 700,000 people gathered: *NYT*, 6/13/82.

113 "the noblest concept": *NYT*, 6/18/82.

114 a CIA briefing video that had been prepared for him: Geoffrey Kemp int.: Strober and Strober, *Reagan*, p. 151.

114 Still, Reagan considered Begin a liar: Deaver int.

114 Israeli troops crossed into Lebanon: *NYT*, 6/7/82.

114 the big mistake had been not inviting Begin to the summit: ABC's *This Week with David Brinkley*, 6/6/82; RRPLM, WHNS, 6/7/82.

114 The Israeli takeover of occupied territory in Golan: *NYT*, 12/15/81.

114 The United States had reacted to that takeover: *NYT*, 12/19/81.

114 "What kind of talk is this 'punishing Israel'?": Reuters, 12/21/81; *AAL*, p. 419.

115 In the Oval Office on June 21: *AAL*, p. 424; Clark int.

115 Begin responded with seething passion: Clark int.

115 He decided not to say anything: Ibid.

115 "REAGAN BACKS ISRAEL": *WP*, 6/22/82.

115 "REAGAN AND BEGIN APPEAR IN ACCORD": *NYT*, 6/22/82.

116 "Al, what would you do": Haig, *Caveat*, p. 311.

116 On Wednesday, Clark set up an evening meeting: Clark int.; Deaver int.

116 "Mr. President, I want you to understand": Haig, *Caveat*, p. 311–15.

117 telling Clark and Deaver that he wanted to wait: Deaver int.; Clark int.

117 He handed the Secretary an unsealed envelope: Haig, *Caveat*, p. 314.

118 "Conservatives upset": RRPLM, Darman morning memos, 6/28/82.

118 "Direct RR assurances": Ibid.

118 Nixon, who regularly: Clark int. Clark told me that part of his job was to travel to New Jersey each month to confer with the former President and report back with his advice for Reagan.

118 "It was the toughest going-over": Farrell, *Tip O'Neill and the Democratic Century*, p. 598.

119 distrusted most everything about supply-side theory: Dole int.

119   "South Succotash": *Oklahoma Daily News*, 3/16/82.

119   "Its influence has been reduced": *WP*, 3/21/82.

120   "You know a person told me yesterday": Stahl, *Reporting Live*, p. 146.

120   "anecdotage": *NYT*, 3/8/82.

120   "More disquieting than Reagan's performance": *WP*, 1/21/82.

120   "The President's Mind": *New Republic*, 4/4/82.

120   Baker and Darman were the only Reagan representatives: Barrett, *Gambling with History*, p. 356.

120   "RR needs to seek to meet with O'Neill": RRPLM, WHSOF: Darman, Richard.

120   "Leave the President alone, you fat bastard!": Matthews int.

121   The President opened the meeting with an Irish joke: Farrell, *Tip O'Neill and the Democratic Century*, pp. 587–89.

121   "Mr. President, the nation is in a fiscal mess": *NYT*, 4/29/82.

121   "You can get me to crap a pineapple": Farrell, *Tip O'Neill and the Democratic Century*, p. 588–89.

121   "The President offered a raw deal": *WP*, 4/30/82.

121   "President Reagan attacked his own budget": RRPLM, WHNS, Newhouse Newspapers, 4/30/82.

122   "revenue enhancers": *NYT*, 9/29/82.

122   "The largest revenue-raising bill ever": *NYT*, 8/17/82.

122   "The future of this economy is now": Dole int.

123   To win the votes of three Republican congressmen from Long Island: Rep. Tom Downey, D-NY, int.

123   Americans counted 220 bombing sorties: George P. Shultz, *Turmoil and Triumph*, p. 71.

123   "Watching the Israeli Air Force smashing Beirut": *Newsweek*, 8/18/82.

123   calls from Philip Habib, and from King Fahd: *AAL*, p. 427–28.

123   "I can't be part of this anymore": Deaver int.; Shultz int.

124   "I told Begin it had to stop": *AAL*, p. 428. The President was hardly alone in his concerns about Begin and Sharon as Israel bombarded Beirut that summer. In an August 3 commentary on the *NBC Nightly News*, as Israeli tanks rolled into West Beirut, John Chancellor said: "What's an Israeli army doing here in Beirut? The answer is that we are now dealing with an imperial Israel which is solving its problems in someone else's country—world opinion be damned. . . . The Israel we saw here yesterday is not the Israel we have seen in the past." But public support of Israel as an ally continued to be strong, 73 to 17 percent in a Louis Harris survey conducted between August 5 and August 10.

124   "had that kind of power": Deaver int.

124   The final vote shared front pages: *NYT*, 8/20/82; *WP*, 8/20/82.

124   "Timid Dawn of Peace in Lebanon": *NYT*, 8/20/82.

125   "We have a budget wrapped in deceit": *NYT*, 8/21/82.

125   "The Largest Tax Increase in History": *Human Events*, 7/31/82.

125   coming from loudspeakers: Major Charles Dalgleish, *Recon Marine: An Account of Beirut and Grenada* (Detroit: Harlo Press, 1995), p. 31.

125   "In Strictest Confidence": RRPLM, WHSOF: Meese, Edwin III, OA 9449, Elections 1982 (1 of 2).

126   "The President was ready for this a year ago": Shultz, *Turmoil and Triumph*, p. 90.

126   their families were allowed to stay: Ibid.

127   "Begin must be wondering": RRPLM, WHNS, ABC News, 9/3/82.

127   Alexander Haig, speaking at a dinner: *NYT*, 8/5/82.

128 "We have been betrayed by the Americans": John Boykin, *Cursed Is the Peace-maker* (Belmont, CA: Applegate Press, 2002), p. 169.

128 $250 million in Israeli military aid: *Time,* 9/6/82.

128 Begin had another answer for the Americans: *NYT,* 9/16/82.

128 Gemayel was killed: *WP,* 9/15/82; AP, Reuters, Gannett News Services, 9/15/82.

128 Begin's cabinet: Boykin, *Cursed Is the Peacemaker,* p. 80.

129 In Tel Aviv, 300,000 demonstrators: *NYT,* 9/19/82.

129 "We have a sense that underneath": *NYT,* 9/21/82.

129 "U.S. Marine Landing Force": Dalgleish, *Recon Marine,* p. 50.

129 The rules of engagement: *Report on the DOD Commission on Beirut International Airport Terrorist Act,* October 25, 1983.

130 The desks and buildings: Boykin, *Cursed Is the Peacemaker,* p. 277.

130 unemployment rate had reached 10.1 percent: *Time,* 10/18/82.

130 had dropped to 42 percent by November: Gallup poll, 12/8/82.

130 12 percent: *WP,* 10/14/82.

131 Paul Volcker: RRPLM, WHNS, 10/13/82 (NBC's Mike Jensen).

131 back over 1,000 points in mid-October: *NYT,* 10/12/82.

131 The President watched the election returns: Barrett, *Gambling with History,* p. 5.

131 "Oh dear, I'm sorry": Ibid.

131 "It stands for 'Demagogue' ": Ibid.

132 "Press guidance: The coalition remains intact": RRPLM, WHORM: FG006-01 (108475).

132 "You know we're in a depression now": Darman, *Who's in Control,* p. 113.

132 "Well, the economy is in a hell of a mess": Ibid., p. 114.

132 "What we are witnessing this January": *WP,* 1/12/83.

132 "I'll go out and get shot again": Deaver int.

CHAPTER 7: MARCH 8, 1983

133 "Likely to Start an Unnecessary War": RRPLM, Wirthlin political memos.

133 "Richard Nixon was to China": RRPLM, WHSOF: Meese, Edwin III, OA 9449, Elections 1982 (1 of 2).

134 "We win, they lose": Michael Reagan, *The Bush Doctrine: We Win, They Lose.* FrontPageMagazine.com, 7/5/05.

134 NSDD 75: Simpson, *National Security Directives,* p. 275.

135 The Soviets—whose own cables in that spring of 1982 warned: Matlock int.

136 one hundred MX intercontinental missiles: *NYT,* 11/23/82.

137 It took two days for a *Washington Post* reporter, Michael Getler: *WP,* 11/24/82.

137 "Peacemaker": *NYT,* 11/23/82.

137 House voted 245 to 176 against funding production: *NYT,* 12/8/82.

137 a special commission: *Time,* 1/17/83.

137 the House approved a $2.5 billion appropriation: *NYT,* 12/9/82.

138 So, Nancy Reagan called O'Bie Shultz: Shultz, *Turmoil and Triumph,* p. 164.

138 The President and the ambassador talked for almost two hours: Memorandum of Conversation: President Reagan, Sec. State Shultz, Amb. Dobrynin— 2/15/83—5:10–6:50 pm. The White House; Shultz, *Turmoil and Triumph,* pp. 164–65.

138 "The Pentecostals": *Human Events,* 11/6/82, p. 944.

139 "The Truth and the Strength of America's Deterrent": RRPLM, WHSOF: Clark, William, Box 8: "U.S. Soviet Relations Papers, Working Files: Contains Originals (2).

141 "The Rt. Rev. Ronald Reagan": *Time,* 3/21/83.
141 5-cents-a-gallon national gasoline tax: *NYT,* 11/10/82; 11/24/82; 12/7/82; RRPLM, WHNS, 1/6/83.
141 "a palace coup": *NYT,* 11/24/82.
141 "My dream": Reagan's diary, 2/11/83.
142 "Look, every weapon has resulted in a defense": Cannon, *President Reagan,* p. 285.
142 High Frontier: *Human Events,* 1/29/83.
142 "What if we began to move away from our total reliance": Meeting with Joint Chiefs of Staff, Oval Office, 2/11/83.
142 "Is he serious?": Clark int.
142 McFarlane, had done some research of his own: Cannon, *President Reagan,* p. 281.
143 "What if we were to tell the world": Reagan diary, 2/11/83.
143 "MX plus": Cannon, *President Reagan,* pp. 286–87.
143 "This is lunacy": Ibid., p. 287.
145 948 of the 1,136 callers: RRPLM, WHORM: FG 006-01 (131585).
145 "What this offers is hope": RRPLM, WHNS, 3/25/83.
145 "raise our sights": Ibid.
145 "The President went a little far": Ibid.
145 "Star Wars" . . . "Fantasy Death Ray Gun" . . . "Razzle-Dazzle" . . . "Sophisticated Nonsense": RRPLM, WHNS, 3/25/83, 3/26/83, 3/27/83.
145 "A pipe dream": *NYT,* 3/27/83.
145 "President Reagan used an old debater's trick": *Chicago Tribune,* 3/28/83.
145 "Mr. Reagan's military spending": *Miami Herald,* 3/25/83.
145 "I felt good": Reagan diary, 3/23/83.
146 NSDD 85: "Eliminating the Threat from Ballistic Missiles," signed 3/25/83.
146 "I didn't expect them to cheer": RRPLM, WHNS, 3/25/83 (reported by NBC's Chris Wallace).
146 "Quite irresponsible": Reagan to reporters, 3/30/83.
146 "If this thing works": Deaver int.
147 "Strategic experts within the administration": Leslie H. Gelb, *NYT,* 3/25/83, p. 1.
148 "For obvious reasons": RRPLM, WHORM: WE 007 (11729555).
148 "obtuse Israeli political purposes": *NYT,* 3/18/83.
149 "over my dead body": Eric Hammel, *The Root: The Marines in Beirut* (San Diego: Harcourt Brace Jovanovich, 1985), pp. 63–64.
149 "The evidence is convincing": RRPLM, WHNS, 1/18/83.
149 Sharon resigned on February 11: *NYT,* 2/11/83.
149 "indirect responsibility": *NYT,* 2/9/83.
149 Sharon was back in the cabinet: *NYT,* 11/14/83.
149 the President accepted the resignations: *NYT,* 3/10/83.
150 Watt was announcing: *WP,* 4/6/83.
150 Nancy Reagan loved the Beach Boys: RRPLM, WHNS, 4/8/83 (ABC's Sam Donaldson).
150 "I've had it up to my keister with leaks": Stahl, *Reporting Live,* p. 161.
151 "Assistant to *The New York Times* for Communications": *Newsweek,* 4/4/83.
151 secrecy agreements: *NYT,* 3/12/83.
151 "gag rules": Stahl, *Reporting Live,* p. 161.
151 " 'Ed Nitze' ": Ibid.
151 "If you strap me up": Baker, Strober and Strober, *Reagan,* p. 180.

151 "Mr. President, we have an historic opportunity": Casey to Reagan.

152 "Meeting re: El Salvador": *AAL,* p. 477.

152 at least sixty-nine times since 1850: RRPLM, WHNS, 4/21/83 (Reuters).

152 death squads: One of the more brutal death squad crimes was the killing of four American women, two Maryknoll nuns, an Ursuline nun, and a Catholic humanitarian worker, in December of 1980. The women's bodies were found in a shallow grave near the San Salvador airport. The crime and investigation were closely followed in the United States, particularly by Democrats in the House of Representatives, because a high-ranking Maryknoll sister, Eunice Tolan, was a cousin of Speaker O'Neill.

152 condemn the brutality of government security forces: *Time,* 11/15/82.

152 military rulers of Guatemala: UPI, 12/6/82.

153 "The Reagan administration deplores": *New York Daily News,* editorial, 4/8/83.

153 NSDD 17: RRPLM, WHNS, *NYT,* 4/7/83.

153 John Negroponte, was overseeing the training: *Newsweek,* 11/8/82.

153 "Boland amendments": Ironically, the White House consulted with Boland in the drafting of the first Boland Amendment in December of 1982 to prevent the passage of an even more restrictive amendment sponsored by Representative Tom Harkin, an Iowa Democrat, who proposed barring any and all anti-Sandinista military aid. Like many other members of Congress, Harkin believed "contras" was just a new name for members of Anastasio Somoza Debayle's old Guardia Somoza, the National Guard. Somoza ruled the country for forty-five years before being deposed in 1979 by the leftist guerrillas who called themselves Sandinistas, after Augusto César Sandino, who fought a guerrilla war against American Marines occupying the country in 1927. One of the arguments used by the Reagan administration in maintaining it was not trying to overthrow the government of Nicaragua was that two thousand contras had no realistic chance of overthrowing the 25,000-member Nicaraguan army. Within a few months, however, the CIA informed Congress that the number of contras had reached seven thousand, most of them operating from Honduras and most of them wearing new uniforms and boots and using newer and heavier weaponry than that being used by Sandinista troops. On the question of the Sandinistas' plans, both the President and Secretary of State Shultz repeatedly declared that Sandinista leadership had proclaimed: "Revolution without borders." In fact, to my knowledge, no researcher has been able to show that someone in Nicaragua ever used that phrase. *Time,* 4/18/83.

154 "First we will take Eastern Europe": Reagan often used the quote but researchers inside and outside the White House were unable to confirm that Lenin ever said that.

154 interesting to discover that the Latin countries were different from one another: *WP,* 12/16/82.

154 backup papers of NSDD 17: Simpson, *National Security Directives,* p. 8. Also, RRPLM. The Reagan Library has all the NSDDs, including the NSSDs, in the research room.

155 selling military equipment to Guatemala: *NYT,* 1/8/83.

155 "I have dispatched Ambassador Walters": RRPLM, WHSOF: North, Oliver, Box 62, Guatemala—Oliver L. North, NSC Staff (2 of 3) OLN Middle Upstairs Office Vertical File.

155 An additional note from Clark, read to Ríos Montt: Ibid.

155 "The President [Ríos Montt] launched into": Ibid.

155 More than twenty officials in the White House: *NYT*, 4/22/83.

156 It was never announced: Shultz int., 9/17/02.

156 "Khomeiniville": Dalgleish, *Recon Marine*, p. 290.

156 blue cards with revised rules: Ibid., p. 331.

157 President Truman's address: Public Papers of the President, 1947.

158 Instant analysis: Press commentary from RRPLM, WHNS, 4/28/83, 4/29/83.

159 "I know about the morticians": *NYT*, 4/28/83.

159 "It was suggested that": RRPLM, WHSOF: Cicconi, James W. Series III: Senior staff meetings file, April 1983 (2 of 2) Box 18.

159 "Well, George, in many ways I feel better": *LAT*, 6/7/04.

CHAPTER 8: SEPTEMBER 5, 1983

160 the May 17 Agreement: Dalgleish, *Recon Marine*, p. 196.

161 McFarlane, on a secret three-day trip: Clark int.; McFarlane, *Special Trust*, p. 243.

162 On July 12 . . . "Covert Action Finding on Nicaragua": Roy Gutman, *Banana Diplomacy* (New York: Touchstone, 1989), p. 95.

162 "Top Secret" memo: Memorandum for the Secretary of Defense, from William Howard Taft: "CIA Request for DOD Support of Covert Activities in Nicaragua," 9/2/83.

162 Anticipate a new Presidential Finding: Memorandum for the United States Army Chief of Staff, the United States Navy Chief of Naval Operations, the United States Air Force Chief of Staff, the United States Marine Corps. Commandant, from John W. Vessey, Jr.: "DOD Support for the DCI," 9/6/83.

162 "Provide training support and guidance to Nicaragua resistance forces": Finding 9/19/83, The Iran-Contra Scandal, National Security Archive, 1993.

163 "You can't do this to me": Shultz, *Turmoil and Triumph*, p. 312.

163 He thought Clark was incompetent: Ibid., p. 166; Shultz int.

163 right-wing warmonger: Shultz, *Turmoil and Triumph*, p. 317.

163 "Clark Takes Charge": *Time*, 8/8/83.

164 "Palestinian guerrilla factions": *NYT*, 8/3/83.

164 "enemy forces": *NYT*, 9/4/83.

165 assuring Iraqi leader Saddam Hussein: Theodore Draper, *A Very Thin Line: The Iran Contra Affairs* (New York: Hill and Wang, 1991), p. 554.

166 "Only 25 percent": *NYT*, 7/1/83.

166 $179 billion: *NYT*, 10/27/83.

166 the highest in eighteen months: *WP*, 5/19/83.

167 "frosted": Hammel, *The Root*, p. 135.

167 White House leaked a story: *NYT*, 8/7/83.

167 "That is what they told me to tell you": Shultz, *Turmoil and Triumph*, p. 363.

167 "They have no compunctions": Ibid., p. 364.

168 declaring that the KAL plane was a spy plane: *NYT*, 9/3/83.

168 Standard air maps: *Time*, 9/12/83.

168 French President François Mitterrand: *Liberation*, Paris, 9/6/83.

169 "We didn't elect a dictionary": RRPLM, WHNS, 9/5/83.

169 "airliner out of the skies": RRPLM, WHNS, 9/8/83, *Manchester Union Leader*.

169 "We've got to protect against overreaction": *NYT*, 10/16/83.

169 He crossed out those last ten words: RRPLM, WHSOF: Speech Drafts, Box 106: Address to the Nation (2 of 3) (Elliot), 9/5/83.

170 "I am breaking off attack": RRPLM, WHSOF: Executive Secretariat, NSC:

Records: Subject File, Box 43: Korean Airline Shootdown [8/31/83—Nov. 1983] (8/22).

170 The count of telephone calls: RRPLM, WHSOF: Baker, James, Box 10513 Communications (2 of 4).

170 outweigh negative: Speakes int.

170 "What has been so admirable": *NYT*, 9/7/83.

171 *"Hellcats of the Navy": Time*, 1/10/83. Filmed in 1956, it was the only film in which Reagan and Nancy Davis, the future Mrs. Reagan, worked together.

172 A mortar shell: McFarlane, *Special Trust*, pp. 250–51.

172 an amendment to NSDD 103: Simpson, *National Security Directives*, p. 324.

172 "Our basic strategy": McFarlane, *Special Trust*, p. 251.

173 the frigate *John Rodgers: NYT*, 9/18/83.

173 "There is not a significant danger": Hammel, *The Root*, p. 221.

173 "extremely dangerous signals": *NYT*, 9/17/83.

173 began dropping 338 five-inch rounds: Hammel, *The Root*, p. 222.

173 move the United Nations: *NYT*, 9/20/83.

174 "imminent hostilities": *NYT*, 9/11/83.

174 U.S. ambassador's residence was hit: RRPLM, WHNS, 9/21/83.

174 "It would be unwise": Ibid.

174 "a Jew and a cripple": RRPLM, WHNS, 9/22/83 (CBS's Bruce Morton).

175 martial law in 1972: *Time*, 9/12/83.

175 "We love you": *WP*, Marcos obituary, 9/29/89.

175n Mike Deaver was dispatched to Manila: National Security Archives, Department of State, Telegram: "Assistant to the President Michael Deaver's Call on President Marcos," 10/3/83.

176 "Americans taught us for fifty years": Stanley Karnow, *In Our Own Image* (New York: Ballantine, 1990), p. 401.

176 "the Syrians and the Soviets take over?": *AAL*, p. 462; Shultz int.

176 Soviet military aid to Syria: Ibid.

176 "Khomeiniville": *NYT*, 8/16/83.

176 landing in the American ambassador's compound: McFarlane, *Special Trust*, p. 253.

176 "Jim, I really need your help": Ibid.

176 "Let's go for a swim": Ibid., p. 254.

176 Assad and Gemayel did agree: *NYT*, 9/26/83.

177 French warplanes were attacking: *NYT*, 9/23/83.

177 At a National Security Council meeting: RRPLM, NSC Notes, 10/18/83.

177 He ended that entry: Reagan, *AAL*, p. 446.

177 Bill Clark abruptly resigned: *NYT*, 10/14/83.

178 Clark was replacing Watt: *NYT*, 10/14/83.

178 "The fellas have a real problem with this": Deaver int.

178 "Jim took it well": *AAL*, p. 448.

178 "Memorandum for Administration Spokesman": RRPLM, WHSOF: Duberstein, Ken: Office of Legislative Affairs, OA 8615, Memos to Ken from White House Staff (outside L.A.) (1) Nov. 83–Feb. 82.

178 national holiday in honor of Martin Luther King: *NYT*, 10/20/83.

179 As far back as February: *WP*, 2/27/83 from RRPLM, WHNS, 2/27/83 (reported by NBC).

180 NSDD 105: Simpson, *National Security Directives*, p. 332.

180 "Do it": McFarlane int.

180 drawing up NSDD 110: Simpson, *National Security Directives*, p. 245.

180   "Urgent Fury": Dalgleish, *Recon Marine,* p. 111.

180   was finding maps of the island: Ibid., p. 112.

181   "This is Ronald Reagan": *NYT,* 10/23/83.

181   "Mr. President I have bad news": McFarlane, *Special Trust,* p. 263; McFarlane int.

CHAPTER 9: FEBRUARY 26, 1984

182   More than a million people: *NYT,* 10/23/83.

182   "This is an obvious attempt": McFarlane, *Special Trust,* p. 267.

182   "We will not be intimidated": The final American death toll in the Beirut bombing was 241. The French lost 58 men.

183   detour to Grenada: CBS News, 10/21/83; RRPLM, WHNS, 10/22/83.

183   "Double it": Air Force Chief of Staff Lawrence Welch to friends after meeting.

183   John Poindexter, who lied to him: Speakes int.

184   the 22nd Marine Amphibious Unit: *NYT,* 11/14/83.

184   "You are informing us": Matthews int.

184   a very angry telephone call from Prime Minister Margaret Thatcher: *AAL,* p. 454.

185   "Mr. President, he's not being critical": RRPLM, WHNS, 10/28/83.

185   "patriotism over partisanship": RRPLM, WHSOF: Baroody, Michael, OA 11244, Lebanon/Grenada, Presidential Speeches, 10/27/83 (1 of 5).

185   "Conduct amphibious/helo landing": Dalgleish, *Recon Marine,* pp. 113–14.

186   Then they learned: *NYT,* 11/14/83.

186   thirty hours later: *Time,* 11/21/83.

186   "If I were there, Margaret": RRPLM, WHSOF: Executive Secretariat, NSC Country Files, United Kingdom, Vol. IV, 8/1/82–10/31/83 (4 of 5), Box 91330.

187   "1,900 U.S. TROOPS": *NYT,* 10/26/83.

187   "It appears that Cuban workers": RRPLM, WHSOF: National Security Affairs, Office of the Ass't to the President for: Records: Country File, Grenada Invasion—Oct. 1983 (8), Box 91,365.

187   "One day we've got": RRPLM, WHSOF: Meese, Edwin III, OA 9450, Grenada (1 of 3).

187   "It is no time for the press of America": Ibid.

188   When photographers tried to photograph: *WP,* 10/27/83.

188n   Modica changed his mind: *Newsday,* 10/28/83

189   Their most reliable source was the enemy: Weisman int.

189   "This action raises the suspicion": *LAT,* 10/30/83.

189   "Military-Press Dialogue": RRPLM, WHSOF: Baker, James III: Box 10513, Communications (1 of 4).

189   "Do nothing": Ibid.

189   "This we cannot stand": RRPLM, WHSOF: Executive Secretariat, NSC Country Files, Box 91, 365—Grenada.

189   "Reporters . . . against us": *WP,* 12/12/83.

190   "Uncle Reagan": Dalgleish, *Recon Marines,* p. 138.

190   written by Reagan himself: Speakes int.

191   4,272 were positive: RRPLM, WHSOF: Baroody, Michael, OA 11244 ("Lebanon/Grenada, RR's speech 10/27 [2 of 5]").

191   Congressional reaction was also over the top: Ibid.

191   indicated there was a difference: RRPLM, WHNS, 10/29/83 *(Newsweek, NYT).*

192   mental hospital: *WP,* 11/1/83.

192 "Grenada: What the Captured Documents Prove": RRPLM, WHSOF: National Security Affairs: Office of the Ass't to the President for: Records: Country File, Grenada Invasion—Oct. 1983 (2) Box 91,365; also see *NYT,* 11/5/83.

193 "the troops out of there": RRPLM, WHSOF: Baker, James III, Communications (1 of 4), Box 10513.

193 early November polls: *Time,* 11/21/83.

193 a *USA Today* survey: *USA Today,* 11/1/83.

193 "We can't go with gunboat diplomacy": *NYT,* 10/29/83; *NYT,* 11/9/83.

193 made it personal: Farrell, *Tip O'Neill and the Democratic Century,* p. 618.

194 reelection: Nancy Reagan int.; Clark int.

194 "They hoodwinked me": Farrell, *Tip O'Neill and the Democratic Century,* p. 618.

194 "But he better not try this again": Ibid.

194 Starlifter landed clumsily: *Time,* 11/28/83.

194 "Shame! Shame!": *Time,* 11/28/83.

194 "A lackey of the Americans": *Time,* 11/28/83; RRPLM, WHNS, 11/16/83 (Reuters).

194 first of 572: RRPLM, WHNS, 11/15/83.

195 voted 286 to 226: RRPLM, WHNS, 11/22/83 (CBS's John Blackstone).

195 "They'll be back": RRPLM, WHNS, 11/21/83 (ABC's *This Week with David Brinkley*).

195 Jennings: *ABC World News Tonight,* 12/15/83.

195 In fact, British public opinion: RRPLM, WHNS, 11/15/83 (CBS's Tom Fenton).

196 "To 22nd MAU": Dalgleish, *Recon Marine,* p. 217.

196 determined to get Americans out of Lebanon: McFarlane, *Special Trust,* p. 271.

196 "The President isn't going to understand this, Cap": Ibid.

196 Israeli and French jets bombed: RRPLM, WHNS, 11/18/83 (ABC's Barrie Dunsmore); *NYT,* 11/18/83.

197 two films: Dalgleish, *Recon Marine,* p. 218.

197 "Mole City": Ibid., p. 240.

197 dog tags: Ibid., p. 241.

197 Thanksgiving dinner: RRPLM, WHNS, 11/24/83 (ABC, CBS, NBC).

197 twenty-eight Navy fighter-bombers: RRPLM, WHNS, 12/5/83 (CBS's Bill Lynch). The *NYT* reported on 12/4/83 that "The Pentagon said 24 planes were involved."

197n "The CIA had tracked the source": McFarlane, *Special Trust,* p. 270.

198 But two of the Navy planes were shot down: *NYT,* 12/4/83; *NYT,* 12/5/83.

198 personally authorized the American air strike: McFarlane, *Special Trust,* p. 272.

198 "bleeding to death": RRPLM, WHNS, 12/5/83 (NBC's Tom Brokaw).

198 "We have a trigger-happy President": RRPLM, WHNS, 11/22/83 (*WP*).

198 "we're headed for war": RRPLM, WHNS, 11/20/83 (Reuters).

198 Stansfield Turner, James Schlesinger, and William Colby: *Time,* 1/16/84.

198 Newspaper editorials: RRPLM, WHNS, 12/5/83.

198 "That, in a nutshell": *Baltimore Sun,* 12/6/83.

198 Huge dump trucks and new three-foot-high concrete barriers: *NYT,* 11/29/83.

198n "You don't quarrel with success": *Time,* 1/16/84.

199 NSDDs. Number 111 . . . 115: Simpson, *National Security Directives,* pp. 343, 351.

199 Reagan and Shamir: RRPLM, WHNS, 11/30/83 (CBS's Bill Plante).

199 "The Shadow of Terrorism": *Time,* 12/26/83.

200 "Why do you invade our country": Dalgleish, *Recon Marine,* p. 249.

200 "All Americans must die": Ibid., p. 294.

200 "Suck the big 16-inches": Ibid., p. 310.

201 "deterioration over there": Matthews int.

202 "Retreating tall": *WP,* 11/27/83.

202 Malcolm Kerr, was murdered: *NYT,* 1/19/84.

202 including three congressional leaders: RRPLM, WHSOF: Baker, James III, Box 8, L.A. (7 of 7).

202 Speaker retaliated: *NYT,* 2/4.

203 The last American unit to leave: Dalgleish, *Recon Marine,* p. 328.

203 Dalgleish wondered: Ibid., p. 325.

203n Shultz wrote of the "redeployment": Shultz, *Turmoil and Triumph,* p. 231.

CHAPTER 10: NOVEMBER 6, 1984

204 "Men of the Year": *Time,* 1/2/84.

204 secret United States Information Agency reports: Charles Z. Wick int.

205 longhand: RRPLM, PHF: Speeches, Folder 241, 1/16/84–1/18/84.

205 "Maniacal plans": *Time,* 1/30/84.

205 "I don't want to honor that prick": Jack F. Matlock Jr., *Autopsy on an Empire* (New York: Random House, 1995), p. 87.

207 "Truth is not the same thing": Nofziger int.

207 In a final memo: RRPLM, WHSOF: Baker, James III: Box 10513, Communications (1 of 4).

208 In one of a series of memos: RRPLM, WHSOF: Baker, James III, Political Affairs, 1/84–7/84.

208 "young woman named Peggy Noonan": RRPLM, WHSOF: 2/20/84, Darman, Series 1: Subject file, Speech Writing and Research Office (1 of 5).

208 "OK.RR": Ibid.

209 "Mondale: Going for a Knockout": *Time,* 3/5/84.

211 "The longer the large deficits": RRPLM, WHNS, 12/13/83 (NBC's Mike Jensen).

211 "we can't have the kind": Hobart Rowen int.

211 sat Feldstein down: *Time,* 3/5/84.

212 Koop: Koop int., Strober and Strober, *Reagan,* p. 136.

212 ABC's *Good Morning America.* . . . David Hartman: RRPLM, WHNS, 2/1/84.

213 "Feld-steen" and "Feld-stine": *NYT,* 12/1/83.

214 Hussein said: *NYT,* 3/16/84, p. 1.

214 "Despicable": *Newsweek,* 4/16/84.

214 "To suggest we should not debate policy": *Newsweek,* 4/1/84.

215 the CIA was mining Nicaraguan harbors: *U.S. News & World Report,* 5/13/84.

215 two out of three respondents disapproved: *NYT,* 4/29/84.

216 "I am pissed off": Bob Woodward, *Veil* (New York: Simon & Schuster, 1986), p. 322.

216 Republican David Durenberger: *Time,* 4/23/84.

216 "The mumbling leading the deaf": McFarlane int.

216 "Who's going to interpret": McFarlane, *Special Trust,* p. 283.

216 "God knows what he just approved": Ibid.

217 "Teflon Man": Steven Weisman, *The New York Times Magazine,* 4/29/84.

217 Hugh Sidey of *Time: Time,* 5/10/84.

218 fall asleep during: Christopher Wren int.

219 Kissinger Commission: *Time,* 1/23/84.

219 led with the news from Moscow: RRPLM, WHNS, 5/10/84.

219 By a 212 to 208 vote—56 Democrats sided with the President—the House approved a White House request for $170 million in new military aid for El Salvador: *WP,* 5/1/84.

220 "It is the CIA that won the election: *NYT,* 5/8/84.

220 "did everything but stuff the ballot boxes": *WP,* 5/9/84.

220 "Don't leave me standing alone": *NYT,* 5/23/84.

220 "He's our kind of man": Ibid.

220 "We're not going to send him back empty-handed": Ibid.

220n "The accusation": McFarlane int.

221 "Do everything you can": McFarlane, *Special Trust,* p. 68.

221 McFarlane sat in the living room: Ibid., p. 69.

222 "Mum's the word": Ibid., p. 70.

222 "You don't want to know": Ibid., p. 71.

222 "Reagan's Policies Spell Death For Millions": *NYT,* 6/3/84.

223 "You didn't say that in 1944": Joseph Petro, *Standing Next to History* (New York: St. Martin's, 2005), p. 173.

223 "The purpose of this meeting": McFarlane int.

224 "We need to hold them accountable": Ibid.

225 "Bank Acct #": Oliver North notebook entry, 6/25/84.

225 "You know a while ago": Peggy Noonan, *What I Saw at the Revolution* (New York: Scribner, 1993), p. 67.

226 "This is a down payment": *Christian Science Monitor,* 6/29/84.

226 "The Tax Issue": RRPLM, WHSOF: Baker, James III, Box 8, OA10514, Issues.

227 "Sure, they're unhappy": Int., RTE-Television, Dublin, 5/28/84.

228 "Let's just get together": *NYT,* 6/13/84.

228 "It's been five years": Ibid.

228 "Exit Ronald Reagan": *Time,* 6/25/84.

228 "Behind the Bear's Angry Growl": *Time,* 5/21/84.

228 "The Reagan Administration": Ibid.

228 "My fellow Americans": *NYT,* 8/14/84.

228 "Doing everything": Stahl int.

230 killing two Americans: The Americans were later identified as Dana Parker, a policeman in Huntsville, Alabama, and James Powell III, a flying instructor from Memphis, Tennessee. Both were Vietnam veterans engaged in training contra troops. The CIA later claimed four Cubans were killed in the attack.

230 CIA manual: AP, 10/15/84.

230 "No, no, no, that is not true": *NYT,* 10/17/84.

231 NSDD 138: Simpson, *National Security Directives,* p. 405.

232 "What evidence do we insist upon": Shultz, *Turmoil and Triumph,* p. 646.

232 "It is time to think": Ibid.

232 "We may never have": Ibid., pp. 646–47.

232 "If I'd had as much make-up": *NYT,* 10/29/84.

232 *New York Times*/CBS News poll: *NYT,* 10/18/84, p. 1.

233 The CIA conceded the next day: AP, 10/19/84.

234 "youth and inexperience": *AAL,* p. 329.

CHAPTER 11: MARCH 11, 1985

235 diplomatic relations: RRPLM, WHNS, 11/26/84.

235 CW [Chemical Warfare] production capability: Memo to Shultz 8333438, 11/1/83.

235 Aziz was welcomed: RRPLM, WHNS, 11/26/84.

235 "Analysis of Possible U.S. Shift": Memo to Sulzberger 8330967.

236 called "Bear Spares": Declaration of Howard Teicher in *USA vs. Carlos Cardoen et al*, US District Court, Southern District of Florida, 1/31/95. (Teicher, a former NSC official, accompanied Rumsfeld on Middle East trips and testified under oath in the U.S. prosecution of Cardoen, a Chilean arms dealer.)

236 "Talking Points" stated: Cable AN D830 736-9623 State Department, 12/14/83.

236 returned to Baghdad: Declaration of Howard Teicher.

236 signed NSDD 139: Simpson, *National Security Directives*, p. 366.

236 "A New Approach for the Second Time": RRPLM, WHSOF: Baker, James A. Files, Mis (1 of 4) OA 10514.

238 Shultz was prevailing: Shultz int.

238 "space arms race": *Time*, 1/7/85.

238 "We can do business with him": Ibid.

238 "transfer of the arms race to outer space": Ibid.

238 "SDI is not defensive": Shultz int.

239 Baker and Regan wanted to trade jobs: Regan, *For the Record*, p. 233; Regan int.

239 with his wife: Regan, *For the Record*, p. 229; Nancy Reagan int.

239 "Fuck you and the horse you rode in on": Deaver int.

239 "You're the only friend": Regan, *For the Record*, pp. 218–19.

239 "You know what's wrong with you, Baker?": Ibid., p. 219.

241 "I'm not clear whether the fire is still there": RRPLM, WHNS (Gergen).

241 "Will marble tablets record": *WP*, 1/20/85.

243 "REAGAN BUDGET PURSUES HIS POLITICAL GOALS": *National Journal*, 2/9/85.

244 "I'm not getting anything at all": RRPLM, WHNS, 12/13/84 (CBS evening news).

244 routing mortars: Gutman, *Banana Diplomacy*, p. 309.

244 "highly patriotic" gentlemen: RRPLM, WHORM: CO1114 Nicaragua (309648).

245 "They are our brothers, these freedom fighters": *NYT*, 3/2/85.

245 "I promise": *NYT*, 3/15/85.

245 His blood pressure was recorded as 130 over 74: *U.S. News & World Report*, 3/25/85.

246 "We used to be told the MX was needed": RRPLM, WHNS, 3/25/1985.

246 "I would like you to visit me in Washington": *AAL*, p. 612.

246 Gorbachev responded within two weeks: RRPLM, Executive Secretariat, NSC: Head of State File, Box 39, U.S.S.R.: General Secretary Gorbachev 8590475-8590495.

246 "I look forward to meeting you personally": *AAL*, p. 616; Jack F. Matlock, *Reagan and Gorbachev: How the Cold War Ended* (New York: Random House, 2004), p. 122.

247 "A vote against this proposal": RRPLM, WHNS, 4/16/85.

247 *"Viva Nicaragua Libre!"*: Later audits of the Nicaragua Refugee Fund and the dinner, both part of a $750,000 public relations plan coordinated by the White House, as reported by the *Los Angeles Times* on December 16, 1986, showed that only $1,000 of the $219,525 reached the contras. The audit showed costs totaling $218,376, including $116,938 in consulting fees and $71,163 to feed the nearly seven hundred people at the dinner. According to the audit, $50,000 went to public relations firm Miner & Fraser, and another $10,000 went to

Daniel Conrad, a fund-raiser for the National Endowment for the Preservation of Liberty, a conservative group that North reportedly assisted in preparing pro-contra television commercials.

247 $7,000 a month by the CIA: Report of the Congressional Committees Investigating The Iran Contra Affair, 11/13/89.

247 account funded by Saudi Arabia: Ibid.

247 $50,000 to a retired British officer: Ibid.

247 And North was urging McFarlane: Ibid.

248 "Fallback Plan for the Nicaraguan Resistance": Ibid.

248n In 1974, when North: Constantine C. Menges, *Inside the National Security Council* (New York: Simon & Schuster, 1988), p. 357.

249 "Succumbing to the pressure of the Jews": Cannon, *President Reagan,* pp. 510–12.

249 "DON'T COMMEMORATE BUTCHERS": *Denver Post,* 4/19/85.

250 "The press has the bit": *AAL,* p. 378.

250 The President was sitting five feet from Wiesel: Public Papers of the President, 1985, pp. 459–62.

251 "My Dreyfus case": *AAL,* p. 378.

251 "The press is still chewing on the Bitburg business": Ibid., p. 379. Reagan received daily packets of mail about the visit. One from a five-year-old read: "Dear Mr. President: I have seen *The Sound of Music.* The Nazis don't look like nice people. Please don't go to their cemetery." It was signed: "Chelsea Clinton, Little Rock, Ark." (*St. Louis Post-Dispatch,* 6/6/2004.)

251 "I'm worried about Nancy": *AAL,* p. 379.

251 "We are going to Bitburg, period": RRPLM, WHNS, 4/25/85.

251 She had Deaver call her astrologer: Deaver int.

251 "We're talking about my husband's life": Ibid.

251 "the chairman of the board": Regan int.

252 "the mice": Noonan, *What I Saw at the Revolution,* p. 229.

252 "I have become distressed": RRPLM, WHORM: PR00701 (292198).

252 International Business Communications: Draper, *A Very Thin Line,* p. 52.

252 As hundreds of anti-contra demonstrators: RRPLM, WHNS, 4/23/85 (NBC's Chris Wallace).

253 "The real issue here": RRPLM, WHNS, 4/22/85.

253 "For the life of me": RRPLM, WHNS, 4/23/85 (ABC's Sam Donaldson).

253 "The President of the United States": RRPLM, WHNS, 4/23/85 (ABC's Sam Donaldson).

253 "It isn't a question of $14 million": Ibid. (CBS's Phil Jones).

253 "We are being asked": RRPLM, WHNS, 4/24/85 (ABC's Brit Hume).

253 "So they'll die": Ibid. (ABC's Brit Hume and NBC's John Dancy).

254 "Got a problem": RRPLM. WHNS, 4/24/83 (CBS, Morton Dean).

254 "The President's address followed": WP, 4/24/83.

254 "Can he win this time?": RRPLM, WHNS, 4/25/85 (CBS's Lesley Stahl).

254 "It is imperative that you make clear": Draper, *A Very Thin Line,* p. 108.

254 "Expressed his support": RRPLM, PHF.

255 Reagan did sign off on $4.5 million: Draper, *A Very Thin Line,* p. 109.

255 Reagan was greeted by huge: *AAL,* p. 383.

256 "Mission Accomplished": Deaver int.

256 "Israeli leaders across the political spectrum": *NYT,* 5/7/85.

256 "We see similar Soviet": RRPLM, WHNS, 5/9/85.

256 "Gorbachev used some of the harshest": Ibid.

258 "Trying to tax people": Rostenkowski news conference, 5/29/85.

258 "Jesus": Regan int.

258 At 8 A.M. the next morning: Dan Rather of CBS reported on May 29 that "It took a 461-page, $18 book to explain fully and officially for the first time exactly how President Reagan says he would make the federal tax system more simple and more fair. All that fine print failed to satisfy various voices of opposion who say it still gives some of the biggest tax breaks to some of the richest Americans while imposing taxes for the first time ever on the unemployment checks of all Americans."

258 "They also don't pay as much": RRPLM, WHNS, 5/29/85.

258 "I know this is a conservative era": Ibid.

259 "The first year of a first term of a new president:" Ibid. (ABC's Peter Jennings int. with George Will).

259 $27 million in humanitarian aid: NYT, 6/13/85.

260 Reagan was wakened before 7 A.M.: AAL, p. 493.

260 "You have not permission": NYT, 6/15/85.

260 "He just killed a passenger!": Ibid.

260 "Status Report on the TWA Hijacking": RRPLM, WHSOF: Executive Secretariat, NSC: Records System File (8590671).

260 "For their own safety": NYT, 6/16/85.

260 "We do not make concessions": NYT, 6/18/85.

261 "New Jersey!": Cannon, President Reagan, p. 536.

261 "Captain": RRPLM, WHNS, 6/20/85.

261 "That captain": AAL, p. 495.

262 anchormen intoned: ABC's Barry Serafin reported on June 19 that "Ronald Reagan came into office talking tough about terrorism as he welcomed home the hostages from Iran. . . . But there was no retribution—then nor nearly a year later when the U.S. Embassy was bombed again. There were, said the President, difficult considerations."

262 "long on talk and short on action": RRPLM, WHNS, 7/12/85.

262 canceling his vacation: NYT, 6/25/85.

262 "The demand is still": AAL, p. 494.

263 Awoke with the knowledge: Ibid., p. 497.

263 improved relations with the Iranian government: McFarlane, Special Trust, p. 17.

263 four U.S. Marines and two American businessmen: NYT, 6/23/85.

264 "By establishing as his 'primary goal' ": NYT, 7/20/85.

264 near-record 67 percent: RRPLM, WHNS, 6/25/85 (ABC News/WP Poll).

264 "Our expectations are not great at all": NYT, 7/3/85.

CHAPTER 12: NOVEMBER 16, 1985

265 "The new international version of Murder, Incorporated": NYT, 7/9/85.

265 Syria was dropped: Ibid.

266 "We are violating badly": National Journal, 7/13/85; NYT, 6/30/85.

266 "Let me be": Colonel John Hulton int., Strober and Strober, Reagan, p. 45.

266 "Acting President": NYT, 7/14/85.

266 "I feel fit as a fiddle": Ibid.

266 "The President has cancer": WP, 7/16/85.

267 Bill Garner: RRPLM, WHNS, 7/17/85.

267 visibly annoyed by the chief of staff's performance: Regan int.

267 Christa McAuliffe: NYT, 7/20/85.

267   NASA officials quickly dismissed: *NYT*, 7/31/85.

267   "Miracle of miracles": *AAL*, p. 501.

268   "What do you think?": McFarlane, *Special Trust*, p. 26.

269   "Get the guys together": Ibid., p. 28.

269   "I think this is a very bad idea": Shultz int.

269   "fabricator notice": Draper, *A Very Thin Line*, p. 127.

269   "Bud, I've been thinking": McFarlane, *Special Trust*, p. 26.

269n six-page memo: Shultz, *Turmoil and Triumph*, pp. 794–95.

270   "First I had to give up popcorn": *AAL*, p. 502.

270   turned on CBS News: Lesley Stahl int.

270   unloaded at Mehrabad International Airport: Draper, *A Very Thin Line*, p. 170.

270   William P. Goode: Oliver L. North with William Novak, *Under Fire: An American Story* (New York: Harper Collins, 1991) p. 293.

270   "The situation today": *Time*, 9/9/85; *NYT*, 9/2/85.

271   Then on September 10: *NYT*, 9/11/85.

272   "In so doing": *WP*, 9/10/85.

273   Rock Hudson: *WP*, 10/3/1985. The President's statement read: "Nancy and I are saddened by the news of Rock Hudson's death. He will always be remembered for his dynamic impact on the film industry and fans all over the world will certainly mourn his loss. He will be remembered for his humanity, his sympathetic spirit, and well-deserved reputation for kindliness. May God rest his soul."

273   this one delivering 408 TOW missiles: Iran-Contra Scandal, National Security Archive, p. 393.

273   Kimche, called McFarlane: McFarlane, *Special Trust*, p. 37.

274   "They have one demand": Ibid., p. 39.

274   a meeting in a Chicago high school: *AAL*, p. 496.

274   "Why won't you at least try to negotiate?": Jane Mayer and Doyle McManus, *Landslide: The Unmaking of the President* (Boston: Houghton Mifflin, 1988), p. 101.

274   "Stop those motherfuckers!": Mayer and McManus int.

274   a two-sentence "FLASH" message: RRPLM, WHNS, 10/8/84.

275   "The ship . . . has broken radio contact": RRPLM, Crisis Management Center, NSC: Records, Achille Lauro (1 of 23) Box 91131.

275   "commander": *Time*, 10/21/85.

276   "Fish or Cut Bait, Mr. President!": *WT*, 10/10/85.

276   "Go ahead!": *Time*, 10/21/85.

276   a ham radio operator: *NYT*, 10/15/85.

276   "I don't care what it takes": *Time*, 10/21/85.

277   "at Sigonella": Ibid.

277   "Admiral, I salute the Navy!": *Time*, 10/21/85.

277   "WE GOT 'EM": *Time*, 10/21/85.

277   "Thank God we finally won one": *Time*, 10/21/85.

277   "You have my gratitude": McFarlane int.

277   The American cheers did not travel well: RRPLM, Crisis Management Center, NSC: Records. *Achille Lauro* (23 of 23), box 91131. The reactions from foreign newspapers were summarized in a special report from the United States Information Agency. The report begins: "World media divided sharply on the U.S. interception of the Palestinian hijackers of the Italian Cruise ship *Achille Lauro*

with applause tempered by fears and reservations of the United States and Israel in the Middle East and South Asia."

278   But many other governments: RRPLM, WHNS, 10/22/85–10/25/85.

278   "I am deeply wounded": *Time,* 10/28/85.

CHAPTER 13: NOVEMBER 19, 1985

Geneva Summit: All official records from the Geneva summit come from the RRPLM. They are found in the Executive Secretariat System files or in the White House Staff and Office Files of Jack Matlock, Series II: US-USSR Summits. Unfortunately, at this time the Reagan Library has not made available for research purposes a finding guide for Jack Matlock.

280   "The Super-Summit": UPI, 10/7/85.

280   more than three thousand reporters: Speakes int.

280   Inside that mansion: Cannon, *Ronald Reagan,* p. 674.

280   Matlock played Gorbachev: Matlock int.; Abramowitz int.

281   "That's fine": Matlock int.

281   "Soviet Union 101": Jack Matlock int.; Matlock, *Reagan and Gorbachev,* pp. 133–34.

281   *svoboda: Time,* 11/18/85.

281   The President also talked for hours with Suzanne Massie: Matlock, *Reagan and Gorbachev,* pp. 92–93.

281   personal guidance from former President Nixon: Matlock int.

281   the soviets had been leaking stories that Gorbachev: McFarlane int.

281   "secret" letter to Reagan: *NYT,* 11/16/85.

282   McFarlane, off the record: McFarlane int.

282   "You ask": *NYT,* 11/19/85.

282   American commentator: Richard Reeves, 9/25/85. The words were my own. Searching through Reagan's presidential papers, I came across a presidential briefing package which included my own syndicated column, published on September 25, 1985, written after covering a Gorbachev trip to Paris. "Americans, from President Reagan on down, have become so hung up on the image of Soviet leader Mikhail Gorbachev that we are in danger of forgetting that substantively it is the Soviet Union, not the United States, that is on the defensive on the dominant issue of our times, arms control. . . . It is Gorbachev who is having a fine time these days waving to the crowds from the back, but it is Reagan who is in the driver's seat as both men start down the road to Geneva. Reagan has what former President Nixon has called 'the ultimate bargaining chip' in the Strategic Defense Initiative because whether the system works or not, developing it would break the Soviet economy long before it would break the American one."

282   "the ultimate bargaining chip": Nixon int.

282   "USSR: A Society in Trouble": Dept. of State, Intelligence and Research Office.

284   "I've had made a special model": *WP,* 11/22/85.

284   "irresistible force meeting an immovable object": *AAL,* p. 631.

284   "Lord, I hope I'm ready": Ibid., p. 11.

284   "Oh, Lordy": Ibid., p. 640.

284   Round one to the American: Ibid., p. 635.

285   "You're right. I did like him": Matlock int.

285   as he spoke of trade: Matlock, *Reagan and Gorbachev,* p. 156.

285   "will all come to nothing": Gorbachev specifically mentioned the Heritage

Foundation, a think tank whose staff included many conservative scholars and advocates who did believe the Soviets could be spent into oblivion.

286 Matlock's notes described: RRPLM, WHSOF: Matlock, Jack, Series II: US-USSR Summits.

287 "He was another guy immediately": Bosch, *Reagan*, p. 264.

287n Kornienko, immediately told Shultz: Shultz, *Turmoil and Triumph*, p. 600.

288 "Hymietown": *WP*, 2/13/85. Campaigning for the Democratic presidential nomination in 1984, Jackson called New York City "Hymietown" because of its large Jewish population, in private conversation with reporters.

288 "Those who talk": Speakes int.

288 " 'There is much that divides us' ": Speakes, *Speaking Out*, p. 170; RRPLM, WHNS, 11/21/85.

289 "who can bring peace to the world": Bosch, *Reagan*, p. 263.

289 Memorandum of Conversation: RRPLM, WHSOF: Executive Secretariat, NSC System Files, 85104 (1).

291 "Dr.": Nancy Reagan int.

291 16th Book of Acts: He meant Acts 17:26, which says in the King James Version: "And hath made of one blood all nations of men for to dwell on all the face of the earth, and hath determined the times before appointed, and the bounds of their habitation."

292 Dimitry Zarechnak was shocked: Matlock int.

293 until past 4:30 A.M.: Cannon, *President Reagan*, p. 677.

293 "Pat, this has been a good meeting": Buchanan int.

293 "Dear Friends": Reagan to Hussain Aga Khan, 11/21/85, provided to Edmund Morris by Nancy Reagan. Morris, *Dutch: A Memoir of Ronald Reagan* (New York: Random House, 1999), p. 575.

293 "few concrete results": RRPLM, WHNS, 11/22/85.

294 "appropriately applied": Cannon, *President Reagan*, p. 677.

294 I bet the hard-liners": Ibid.

294 83 percent of respondents approved: RRPLM, WHNS, 11/22/85.

294 I haven't gotten such": *AAL*, p. 641.

CHAPTER 14: JANUARY 28, 1986

295 "He changes them like he changes his underwear": Speakes int.

295 "bone-tired" he said: McFarlane int.

295 "You know it's pointless": McFarlane int.; McFarlane, *Special Trust*, p. 324.

295 nervous breakdown: Ledeen int., Strober and Strober, *Reagan*, p. 309. In the summer and fall of 1985, McFarlane had a nervous breakdown—or what in the old days you would have called a nervous breakdown. He just collapsed, in part because of frustration. He felt he wasn't getting through to Reagan; he felt that he, personally, was the wrong sort of person to deal with Reagan. "All the other people there had a great rapport with Reagan. They went back a long way with him; they were all self-made men—wealthy people, business people, people of the world. McFarlane was a military guy—a marine colonel."

297 "This is outrageous": McFarlane, *Special Trust*, p. 327.

297 "You should know": Ibid., p. 46.

297 "NSC briefing": *AAL*, p. 509.

298 Poindexter . . . briefing: Joint Hearing, Select Committee, Series 100, Vol. 8, pp. 124, 164.

298 "We're not dealing with terrorists": McFarlane, *Special Trust*, p. 46.

298   "Go ahead": Ibid., p. 47.

298   "That's not paying ransom to kidnappers": *AAL*, p. 512.

298   "[A] complex plan": Ibid.

298   Three Israelis: McFarlane, *Special Trust*, p. 47.

299   "I don't believe": Ibid., pp. 48–49.

299   He thought North may have briefed Ghorbanifar: Ibid., p. 49.

299   "Bud's right, Mr. President": Ibid., p. 50.

299   "I'm sorry to hear this": Ibid., p. 51.

299   "It's risky": Ibid.

299   "Bud is back": *AAL*, p. 510.

299   "Go between": Ibid.

299   McFarlane came away: McFarlane int.

299   "Gramm Rudman Hollings": *AAL*, p. 510.

301   Kemp said: *NYT*, 12/12/85.

301   "Reagan Being Viewed as Irrelevant": *National Journal*, 12/21/85.

301   "All of us": Ibid.

301   248 young men: *NYT*, 12/17/85.

302   "The worst I have seen": *NYT*, 12/22/85.

303   "According to Democrats": *Baltimore Sun*, 12/10/85.

303   "This bill is designed": *Philadelphia Inquirer*, 12/11/85.

303   November 1 . . . lie detector tests: Shultz, *Turmoil and Triumph*, p. 801.

303   March of 1982: Cannon, *President Reagan*, p. 371.

303   "The minute in this government": *NYT*, 12/20/85.

304   "In World War II": Stanley Karnow, *In Our Image*, p. 407.

304   "fraudulent and absurd": *NYT*, 11/23/86.

304   "The old man is confusing Marcos": Speakes int.

304   "Mrs. Aquino is an empty-headed housewife": Shultz, *Turmoil and Triumph*, p. 616.

305   terrorist attacks inside the Rome and Vienna international airports: *NYT*, 12/28/85.

305   Don Regan and his men: Noonan, *What I Saw at the Revolution*, p. 214.

305   "This speech doesn't read like a Ronald Reagan speech": RRPLM, WHORM: SP230-86 (379864).

305   "in crayon": Noonan exit int.

306   "great disservice to the President": Ben Elliot memo re the "Regan comments" on 1986 State of the Union drafts.

306   Public Health: *WP*, 3/19/86.

306   The President wanted: Minutes, Domestic Policy Council, 12/17/85.

306   "Sir, the *Challenger* just blew up!": Speakes, *Speaking Out*, p. 117.

307   "They're all citizens": Karna Small writing this after *Challenger* destruction; Noonan, *What I Saw at the Revolution*, p. 25.

308   He was afraid: Post-*Challenger* address on national television; Noonan int.

308   "As the old dictator": *NYT*, 2/6/86.

308   fly him and his family to exile in France: *NYT*, 2/8/86.

309   both President Marcos and Cory Aquino claiming victory: *NYT*, 2/16/86.

309   widespread fraud and violence: *NYT*, 2/10/86.

309   Lugar estimated that Aquino had actually won: *NYT*, 2/13/86.

309   "sons of bitches": Speakes int. Reagan did not dislike the press and he only knew the names of a few reporters beginning with Lou Cannon and Sam Donaldson. Nancy Reagan was different. Richard Threlkeld, then of CBS, remembers vividly a night in Sacramento when reporters gathered outside her home for one reason or another. When Reagan arrived he stepped from his car and

began answering questions. His wife appeared at the door and said: "Ronnie, don't you dare talk to those cocksuckers."

309   "The bottom line is inescapable": Bosworth cable to State.
309   Habib out of retirement: *NYT,* 2/12/86.
309   Shultz called Reagan: Shultz, *Turmoil and Triumph,* p. 629.
310   "The President is the President": Ibid.
310   "The Marcos era has ended": Ibid., p. 635.
310   "All we can do is send the message": *AAL,* p. 365.
310   "The situation in the Philippines": Ibid.
311   "We are ordering our ambassador": Ibid.
311   the President throwing snowballs: Shultz, *Turmoil and Triumph,* p. 638.
311   "Wait a minute!": Ibid.
311n Mrs. Reagan told Mrs. Marcos: *AAL,* p. 365.
312   "Try not to forget": *Time,* 3/10/86.
312   "The President's earlier equivocations": *Baltimore Sun,* 2/25/86.
312   "The Reagan administration appears": *Detroit News,* 2/25/86.
312   "It has been a good month": *Newsday,* 2/26/86.
312   "Reagan acted intelligently": *Quotidien,* 2/25/86.
312   "It seems incredible": *La Stampa,* 2/25/86.
312   *Volksblatt* speculated: RRPLM, WHNS, 2/26/86.
313   $70 million of that earmarked: *NYT,* 8/11/84.
313   "With the vote on contra aid": *WP,* 3/12/86.
314   "Because of the extreme sensitivity": Iran-Contra Affair, p. 208, Doc. 64: Finding regarding Iran.
314   At the bottom: Menges, *Inside the National Security Council,* p. 347.
315   "irrefutable evidence": *NYT,* 1/8/86.
315   The President ordered the Sixth Fleet: *NYT,* 1/25/86.
315   "Could this lead us into trouble?": *Time,* 4/7/86.
315   As he had: John Whitehead int., Strober and Strober, *Reagan,* pp. 381–82.
316   "I would like to ask": RRPLM, Minutes, Domestic Policy Council, 12/19/85, p. 3, Whitehead papers, Box 17.
316   the Navy wanted to wait: Shultz, *Turmoil and Triumph,* p. 476.
316   Even Margaret Thatcher urged: *NYT,* 1/11/86.
316   the United States embassy in Moscow: Matlock int.
316   A Soviet communications ship: *Time,* 4/22/86.
317   "Within 48 hours of the House rejection": RRPLM, WHNS, 3/25/86.
317   62 to 28 percent: RRPLM, WHNS, 4/15/86.
318   Ferch, sick with the flu: Gutman, *Banana Diplomacy,* p. 324.
318   Senate voted 53 to 47: *NYT,* 3/28/86.
318   La Belle Club: *NYT,* 4/6/86.
318   "Tripoli will be happy": Shultz, *Turmoil and Triumph,* p. 683.
319   "Maybe we could stop the terror": Speakes int.
320   The Tripoli-area targets: *Economist,* 4/19/86.
320   "For Europe, Qaddafi": RRPLM, WHNS, 4/15/86.
320   "He asked for it": *Dallas Morning News,* 4/15/86.
320   "Even the most scrupulous": *NYT,* 4/15/86.
320   "The U.S. cannot fight a world war against terrorism by itself": *Milwaukee Sentinel,* 4/9/86.
320   "You ask yourself": *NYT,* 4/20/86.

CHAPTER 15: JUNE 17, 1986

322 "The President knows how to steal a headline": *NYT,* 5/9/86.

323 The committee vote: RRPLM, WHNS, 5/9/86.

324 "Either we get funding": RRPLM, Casey memo on April 23.

324 "Look, I don't want to pull": Ibid.

324 Reagan publicly requested: *NYT,* 5/11/86.

324 221 ayes and 209 nays: *NYT,* 6/26/86.

325 "The economic, as opposed to the social face": "The Public Philosophy of Ronald Reagan," presented March 28, 2002, Conference on the Reagan Presidency at UC Santa Barbara.

325 "the bookend presidents": Ibid.

326 "More Vigor for the Right": *NYT,* 6/18/86.

326 "Both men have": *WP,* 6/18/86.

327 "If this means the Supreme Court": *Dallas Morning News,* 6/18/86.

327 "To many people": *Dallas Times Herald,* 6/18/86.

327 exit interview: The RRPLM has an entire collection of exit interviews, including Peggy Noonan's.

328 looked shriveled to her: Stahl, *Reporting Live,* p. 257.

329 reopening of the Statue of Liberty: *NYT,* 7/5/86.

329 "persistent or egregious discrimination": The two cases are *Local Number 93, International Asso. of Firefighters, etc. v. Cleveland,* No. 84-1999, SUPREME COURT OF THE UNITED STATES, 478 U.S. 501, and *Local 28 of Sheet Metal Workers' Int'l Ass'n v. EEOC,* No. 84-1656, SUPREME COURT OF THE UNITED STATES, 478 U.S. 421.

329 "There is no individual in this country": Meese int.

330 unmarked white Boeing 707: McFarlane, *Special Trust,* p. 56.

330 carried a pallet of HAWK missile parts: Ibid., p. 55.

330 four remaining American hostages: One of the original seven American hostages in Beirut, Peter Kilburn, the librarian of the American University, was found shot to death three days after the United States bombing raid on Libya. Intelligence agencies later concluded that Libyans had paid a ransom to the kidnappers to kill Kilburn in retaliation for the April 14, 1986 raid. *AAL,* p. 520, and McFarlane, *Special Trust,* p. 57.

330 They sat in the terminal for two hours: McFarlane, *Special Trust,* p. 57.

330 "We are emissaries": *Time,* 12/8/86.

330 No one but bureaucrats: Ibid., p. 58.

330 taken the HAWK parts: Ibid.

331 Reagan himself had come: *AAL,* p. 520.

331 "Bud's the man on the scene": McFarlane, *Special Trust,* p. 63.

331 was now being used in Central America: Ibid., p. 56.

331 "It was a heart breaking disappointment": *AAL,* p. 521.

331 "This release of Jenco": Ibid., p. 522.

331 "Father Jenco's release": *Newark Star-Ledger,* 7/30/86.

331n "We were *not* trading arms for hostages": Ibid., p. 523.

332 "any member of the Hebrew race": *NYT,* 8/8/86.

332 "He is too extreme on race": RRPLM, WHNS, 7/30/86.

332 Bill Moyers: RRPLM, WHNS, 8/6/86.

332 whether there was going to be a 1986 summit: RRPLM, WHSOF: Ross, Dennis, Box 6: Chron File September 1986 (1).

334 "Our hearts go out": RRPLM, WHSOF: Executive Secretariat, NSC: Head of State File, Box 40, U.S.S.R.: General Secretary Gorbachev (8690389-8690433).

334 Gennady Zakharov: *NYT*, 9/10/86; Matlock, *Reagan and Gorbachev*, pp. 197–202.

334 "I can give you my personal assurance": RRPLM, WHSOF: Executive Secretariat, NSC: Head of State File, Box 40, U.S.S.R.: General Secretary Gorbachev (8690616-8690659).

334 "Regarding the question you raised": Ibid.

335 "I'm mad as hell": *AAL,* p. 667.

335 "Sept. 9": Ibid.

335 "We don't allow KGB": Ibid. p. 668.

335 "The U.S. side has unduly dramatized": RRPLM, WHSOF: Executive Secretariat, NSC: Head of State File. Box 40, U.S.S.R.: General Secretary Gorbachev (8690616-8690659).

336 "I opted for Iceland": *AAL,* p. 669.

336 walked in behind him and said: *WP,* 10/1/86.

336 "A Humiliation for the President": *San Diego Union,* 9/30/86.

336 "Justice is not served": *WT,* 9/30/86.

336 "George Shultz is a complete sellout": RRPLM, WHNS, 10/1/86.

336 "What we seem to have tonight": Ibid.

337 to override Reagan's veto of sanctions: *NYT,* 10/3/86.

337 an unmarked cargo plane was reported missing: President's Intelligence Briefing, 10/5/86.

338 paying $3,000 a month: RRPLM, WHNS, 10/10/86.

338 "Situation requires that we do necessary damage control": Cable from Fernandez to Washington.

338 North . . . lying: Speakes, *Speaking Out,* p. 347.

338 North at Camp David: Draper, *A Very Thin Line,* p. 422.

339 "Two Cuban naturalized Americans": *NYT,* 10/10/86.

CHAPTER 16: OCTOBER 12, 1986

Reykjavik: All official notes and memorandums of conversation can be accessed at the RRPLM, in the Executive Secretariat, System Files, 8690725 (1).

340 "When you stop trying": Speakes int.

340 "If we are still trying": Anatoly Chernyaev, *My Six Years with Gorbachev* (College Station, PA: Pennsylvania State University Press, 2000), p. 83.

340 "You have reserved": Matlock, *Reagan and Gorbachev,* p. 214.

341 "Concept Paper": Dan Oberdorfer, *The Turn: From the Cold War to a New Era* (New York: Touchstone, 1992) p. 188.

341 Gorbachev had also been asking questions: Matlock, *Reagan and Gorbachev,* p. 192; Matlock int.

341 he was the one making the decisions: Ibid.

341 "Not withstanding his political past": Jacques Attali, *Verbatim,* Vol. 2, 1986–88 (Paris: Fayard, 1995), p. 112.

342n In a 1985 interview with Marguerite Duras: Transcript from James Rentschler, 11/30/2002.

343 "Gorbachev indicated that": RRPLM, WHNS (Matlock notes), 10/11/86.

343 "They're coming our way": Oberdorfer, *The Turn,* p. 191.

343n "Don't be ridiculous": Matlock int.

344 "I'm afraid he's going after SDI": Ibid.

345 Not as much: Kampelman int., Strober and Strober, *Reagan*, p. 238.

346 "Literally a miracle": Oberdorfer int. with Reagan, 3/27/90.

348 "a creative person": Oberdorfer, *The Turn*, p. 197.

349 "He gets his precious ABM Treaty": Ibid., p. 199.

349 "If we agree to the Gorbachev limitations": Richard Perle int. with Austin Hoyt.

351 "Everything could be decided right now": Oberdorfer, *The Turn*, p. 201.

351 "Oh, shit!": Matlock, *Reagan and Gorbachev*, p. 232.

351 told his wife: Nancy Reagan int.

351 "Let's do it!": Matlock int.

352 "No statement": Speakes, *Speaking Out*, p. 178.

352 "Goddamnit!": Shultz int.

353 "Mr. President": Oberdorfer, *The Turn*, p. 207.

353 "No one who attended the summit": *WP*, 10/17/86.

353 "Shultz looks like his dog": Sam Donaldson int.

353 "FAILURE!": Matlock, *Reagan and Gorbachev*, p. 238

353 "I hope you're right": Charles Wick int.; Regan int.

353 the President was failing mentally: Regan int.

353 "World Series": Wick int.

354 "Somber, weary but eager to explain": RRPLM, WHSOF: Regan, Donald T.: Files (Reading file for Regan/Iceland Summit) (4 of 5) OA 14013.

355 "A turn in world history failed": *NYT*, 10/15/86.

355 secret Kremlin meeting: *National Security Archive*, "A Meeting of the Politburo of the CC CPSU," 10/14/85.

357 "When one side suddenly": RRPLM, WHNS, 10/15/86.

357 Schlesinger, spoke for: *NYT*, 10/16/86.

357 Prime Minister Thatcher: Charles Powell int.

358 "Mr. President, we have concluded": Oberdorfer, *The Turn*, p. 207.

358 71 percent favorable: RRPLM, WHNS, 10/16/86.

358 "I saw his human hesitation": Matlock int.

358 "I am an eyewitness": Ibid.

359 "We saw their bottom line": Ibid.

359 deficit was $220.7 billion: RRPLM, WHNS, 10/24/86.

359 "Beirut publication": *NYT*, 11/3/86.

359n "I said to him": George Shultz int. with Austin Hoyt.

360 "Fanciful stuff": *NYT*, 11/5/86.

361 "I'm not going into all that": RRPLM, WHNS, 11/5/86.

361 "bilge": *AAL*, p. 528.

CHAPTER 17: NOVEMBER 25, 1986

362 an Oval Office meeting: RRPLM, Keel notes, Vol. 14, Appendix B 974 1023; Testimony, Select Committee, 1987; Regan notes, Vol. 10, 100 Series.

362 January 17, 1986: The "Finding" was written by North and Poindexter after three Israeli shipments of arms to Iran, and designed to show the deals were not arms for hostages exchanges. The reasons listed in the "Finding" were: (1) establishing a more moderate government in Iran; (2) obtaining from them significant intelligence not otherwise obtainable. . . . ; (3) furthering the release of the American hostages in Beirut. . . ." Released 1/9/87, published in the *NYT*, 1/10/87, p. 5.

363 Actually Iran: Cable from the AmEmb Tel Aviv to Sec State WashDC: AM: 0820270-0562; *NYT*, 5/26/82.

363   "Our policy": *NYT,* 11/11/86.

364   only 22 percent of respondents approved: RRPLM, WHNS, 11/13/86.

365   Americans believed the President was lying: *LAT,* 11/16/86, p. 1.

365   14 percent of respondents believed: *LAT,* 11/18/86.

365   "shovel brigade": *NYT,* 11/16/86.

365   "authority to speak": Stahl, *Reporting Live,* p. 268.

365   "I never should": Shultz, *Turmoil and Triumph,* p. 823.

365   "I'm not firing anybody": *NYT,* 11/25/86.

366   "We have been deceived": Shultz, *Turmoil and Triumph,* p. 828.

366   Regan had at least twice hung up on her: Regan int.

367   "A shredding party": Mayer and McManus, *Landslide,* p. 327; Report of Select Committee, pp. 301–307.

367   Hasenfus: *NYT,* 12/18/86.

368   Poindexter opened the safe: Testimony of Adm. Poindexter Before the Joint Committee Investigating the Iran-Contra Affair.

368   the resigning began: *NYT,* 11/26/86.

369   "Mr. President, I assume": Report of the Select Committees Investigating Iran-contra, Vol. 8, Series 100, p. 1235.

369   The three top leaders: *NYT,* 12/1/86.

369n   "Meese . . . investigation": Walsh, final report, Vol. I, p. xvii.

370   "You're an American hero": McFarlane int.

370   "Not funny": Speakes, *Speaking Out,* p. 351.

370   "Is it conceivable?": RRPLM, WHNS, 11/26/86.

370   "that I wasn't told everything": *Time,* 12/8/86.

371   "second-rate minds": *Philadelphia Daily News,* 11/25/86.

371   only 28 percent of respondents: RRPLM, WHNS, 12/5/86.

371   Ross Perot: *WP,* 12/2/86. Bob Woodward also reported this on Perot, who was a member of President Reagan's Foreign Intelligence Advisory Board until June 1985: "Perot's efforts to help the Reagan administration free Americans held abroad predates the string of Beirut kidnappings. Early in 1982—again at North's request—the Texas billionaire wired $500,000 to an Italian bank to pay for the release of Brig. Gen. James L. Dozier, a ransom attempt that also failed. . . . Perot's secret activities on behalf of the U.S. government date at least to 1969, when he agreed to work behind the scenes for the Nixon administration in an effort to improve treatment of American prisoners of war in Vietnam." That was in addition to the $200,000 he contributed in April 1985, to be used as ransom money in Beirut.

371   EX-AIDE TO REAGAN: *NYT,* 12/5/86.

371   broken into the office of Robert White: RRPLM, WHNS, 12/2/86.

372   Both North and Poindexter: Ibid., 12/4/86.

372   The Israeli government confirmed: *WP,* 12/4/86.

372   "duped by arms dealers": RRPLM, WHNS, 12/8/86; *WT,* 12/8/86.

372   "That's slammer time": *WP,* 6/14/87. As recorded in the *Post:*

> Senator Eagleton: Were you in the fund-raising business?
>
> Mr. Abrams: I would say we were in the fund-raising business. I take your point.
>
> Senator Eagleton: Take my point? Under oath, my friend, that's perjury. Had you been under oath, that's perjury.
>
> Mr. Abrams: Well, I don't agree with that.
>
> Senator Eagleton: That's slammer time.
>
> Mr. Abrams: I don't agree with that, Senator.

Senator Eagleton: Oh, Elliott, you're too damn smart not to know—

Mr. Abrams: I think that the—

Senator Eagleton: . . . You were in the fund-raising business, you and Ollie. You were opening accounts, you had account cards, you had two accounts and didn't know which account they were going to put it into.

Mr. Abrams: You've heard my testimony.

Senator Eagleton: I've heard it, and I want to puke.

372   "Savvy and well-schooled": *WP*, 12/3/86.

372   "This signals the end of": *WT*, 12/3/86.

372   "the most fun we've had since Watergate": *WP*, 12/8/86.

373   "brought us back from Watergate?": *WP*, 12/8/86.

373   "Remarks for Administration Surrogates": RRPLM, WHSOF: Ball, William, Iran Contra Staffing Memos (2 of 2) OA 15,333.

373   "Question 9": RRPLM, WHORM, C0071 Iran 1 of 2.

373   "Question 3": Ibid.

373   "Who is picking this fight?": Ibid.

374   The press was alive: Oliver North and his schemes were largely ignored in the press, partly because suspicious reporters (including me) were told by Speakes that if North's name appeared, his life might be endangered.

374   Adnan Khashoggi: *NYT*, 12/15/86.

374   "use immunity": *NYT*, 12/17/86.

374   Casey collapsed in his office: *NYT*, 12/16/86.

374   a direct contradiction: *NYT*, 12/19/86.

374   "Independent Counsel": *NYT*, 12/20/86.

375   he had a secret reservation: Lawrence E. Walsh, *Firewall: The Iran-Contra Conspiracy and Cover-up* (New York: W.W. Norton, 1997), p. 25.

375   "Virtual seclusion": *WSJ*, 1/27/87.

375   arms-for-hostage deal: RRPLM, WHNS, 1/30/87.

375   approved every significant move: RRPLM, WHNS, 1/29/87.

376   The document listed dozens of lies: *NYT*, 1/29/87; *WP*, 2/8/87.

376   Poindexter lied to Charles Price: *WP*, 2/8/87.

376   resigned as CIA director: *NYT*, 2/3/87.

376   McFarlane attempted suicide: McFarlane, *Special Trust*, pp. 14–16, 337.

CHAPTER 18: JUNE 12, 1987

378   Reagan wanted to change his story: Cannon, *President Reagan*, p. 631.

379   Peter Wallison had written another reminder: Cannon, *President Reagan*, p. 631.

379   "God, it was just terrible": Ibid., p. 632.

379   "Any whispers by people": RRPLM, WHNS, 2/2/87.

379   "Nancy Reagan's campaign": *WP*, 2/27/87.

380   "Get off my goddamn back": Strober and Strober, *Reagan*, p. 48.

380   "I think I'm aware of people": RRPLM, WHNS, 6/25/85.

380   "The First Lady is no longer speaking to Regan": *WP*, 2/18/87.

380   "President Reagan is being weakened": *NYT*, 3/2/87.

380   "The Myth of the Decisive President": *WP*, 2/23/87.

381   " 'I will be glad to take the heat for that' ": *Newsweek*, 3/9/87.

381   "I'm afraid that": Ibid.

382   "INQUIRY FINDS": *NYT*, 2/27/87.

382   "The President clearly did not": *NYT*, 2/27/87.

382   "The problem": Ibid.

383   PROFS e-mail: *Newsweek*, 3/9/87; *National Journal*, 3/7/87.

383   Naval Academy graduates: Poindexter, class of 1958; McFarlane 1959; North, 1968.

383   "well beyond my charter": *National Journal*, 3/7/87.

384   "North secretly ran": RRPLM, WHNS, 2/27/87.

384   more than $33 million was missing: *WT*, 3/2/87.

384   dropping ten points to 42 percent: (NYT/CBS Poll).

384   "I've just had lunch with the President": Regan, *For the Record*, p. 369.

385   "My prayers": *AAL*, p. 538.

385   Howard Baker: Baker int.

385   considering a run: *NYT*, 2/28/87.

386   "I hearby resign": Regan int.

386   Meese called: Meese int.

386   "There's no one in charge": Meese int.

386   "inattentive": Mayer and McManus, *Landslide*, p. ix.

386   "dragon lady": *NYT*, 3/5/87.

386   written by Landon Parvin: *WP*, 5/31/87.

387   "As televised congressional hearings": *Time*, 3/16/87.

387   "I've lost my voice": RRPLM, WHNS, 3/12/87.

387   "A despondent and demoralized man": *NYT*, 3/15/87.

388   Mike Deaver was indicted: *NYT*, 3/19/87.

389   "The Federal role": *WP*, 4/2/87.

389   Avoiding the words "sex" and "condoms": *USA Today*, 4/12/87.

389   " 'value neutral' ": Ibid.

389   "We can no longer": *NYT*, 4/7/87.

389   "Until the Reagan Administration": RRPLM, WHNS, 4/1/87.

389   "Ronald Reagan finally uttered": *Philadelphia Daily News*, 4/6/87.

390   "I beg you to vote with me": RRPLM, WHNS, 4/3/87.

390   bought the Reagans a $2.5 million Bel Air house: *WP*, 4/15/87.

390   "The President walks": *WP*, 4/13/87.

390   friendly letter to Gorbachev: RRPLM, WHSOF: Executive Secretariat, NSC Head of State File, U.S.S.R.: General Secretary Gorbachev, 8790364, Box 41.

391   "Gorbachev more clearly": National Security Archives, State Intelligence Research Report, 4/7/87.

391   frightened European leaders: *Time*, 5/11/87.

391   "I often fantasize": Barrett, *Gambling with History*, p. 30.

392   Staffers of the joint committee: *Time*, 5/11/87.

392   Carl "Spitz" Channell pleaded guilty: *NYT*, 4/30/87.

392   Inouye, said on Sunday television: RRPLM, WHNS, 5/4/87.

393   "Secord Stated that the administration": RRPLM, WHSOF: Duberstein, Kenneth, Office of the Chief of Staff, Box 2: Iran/Contra Issues # 2 of 2 (2).

393   summer of 1984: Ibid.

393   Fitzwater's first press memo: RRPLM, WHORM: FG 037 (500879).

394   "Casey asked me": RRPLM, WHNS, 5/6/87.

394   "Did Ollie North tell": RRPLM, WHSOF: Duberstein, Kenneth, Office of the Chief of Staff, Box 2: Iran/Contra Issues # 1 of 2 (1).

394   The Culvahouse memo to the President: Ibid.

394   "Our response is": Ibid.

394   "Secord stated that": RRPLM, WHSOF: Duberstein, Kenneth, Office of the Chief of Staff, Box 2: Iran/Contra Issues # 2 of 2 (2).

394   "McFarlane learned of the diversion": RRPLM, WHSOF: Ball, William L. III, OA 15331: "Iran/Contra Staffing Memos" (2 of 3).

395 Sultan of Brunei: *NYT,* 5/13/87.
396 "From now on": RRPLM, WHNS, 5/20/87.
396 "the villain in this piece": *WP,* 5/20/87.
396 *Lady Ellen:* RRPLM, WHSOF: Duberstein, Kenneth, Office of the Chief of Staff, Box 2: Iran/Contra Issues # 2 of 2 (2).
396 Joseph Coors: Ibid.
396 William O'Boyle: Ibid.
396 Adolfo Calero: *WSJ,* 5/21/87; *Christian Science Monitor,* 5/21/87; RRPLM, WHNS, 5/21/87.
396 "Chairman Inouye was upset": RRPLM, WHSOF: Ball, William L. III, OA 15331: "Iran/Contra Staffing Memos" [2 of 3].
397 Abrams was the next witness: RRPLM, WHNS, 6/3/87.
397 demanding that Abrams be fired: RRPLM, WHNS, 6/4/87.
398 "Elliott Abrams has": RRPLM, WHNS, 6/4/87.
398 69 percent thought Reagan was lying: RRPLM, WHNS, 6/3/87.
398 "MARKETS SURPRISED": *NYT,* 6/3/87.
398 "Anti-Inflation Legacy": Ibid.
398 "Greenspan faces a daunting challenge": *WSJ,* 6/3/87.
398n Alan Fiers testified: RRPLM, WHNS, 8/26/87.
399n The 1981 income tax cut: Office of Tax Analysis Working Paper 81, "Revenue Effects on Major Tax Bills," Jerry Tempalski, Dept. of Treas.
400 Census Bureau: Mark Hertsgaard, *On Bended Knee* (New York: Schocken Books, 1989), p. 135.
400 Poindexter and North would be summoned: *WP,* 6/11/87.
400 Secord had used $200,000: *WP,* 6/11/87.
400 "There are times": *WP,* 6/10/87.
401 "Now, I'm the President, aren't I?": *On the Record with Greta Van Susteren,* 6/6/02.
401 Brandenburg Gate: *WP,* 6/11/87.
401 "We hear much from Moscow": *WT,* 6/12/87.
401 "General Secretary Gorbachev": AP, 6/12/87.

CHAPTER 19: JULY 7, 1987

402 Charles J. Cooper: *NYT,* 6/26/87.
402 "Would you believe": RRPLM, WHNS, 6/26/87.
403 "Reagan's Ability to Lead Nation": *NYT,* 6/28/87.
403 memory: Dr. Lawrence Altman, *NYT,* 10/5/94.
404 "He is widely regarded": *WP,* 7/1/87.
404 "Bork's America": RRPLM, WHNS, 7/2/87.
404 "Reagan could search": *Baltimore Evening Sun,* 6/29/87.
404 "LtCol North repeatedly": RRPLM, WHSOF: Duberstein, Kenneth. Office of the Chief of Staff. Series I. Subject File. Box 2: Iran/Contra Issues # 2 of 2 (1).
404 "diversion": RRPLM, WHSOF: Ball, William, Iran-Contra Staffing Memos (1 of 2) OA 15,331.
405 Attorney General Meese was in the room: RRPLM, WHNS, 6/8/87.
405 signed presidential finding: RRPLM, WHNS, 7/8/87.
405 "First of all": Ibid.
405 "political theater": Ibid.
406 "There is great deception": Ibid.
406 "Perhaps the most noteworthy": RRPLM, WHSOF: Duberstein, Kenneth, Of-

fice of the Chief of Staff, Series I, Subject File, Box 2: Iran/Contra Issues # 2 of 2 (1).

406 "North admitted": RRPLM, WHSOF: Ibid.

406 "elected representatives": RRPLM, WHSOF: Ball, William, Iran Contra Staffing Memos (1 of 2) OA 15,333.

406 "lies and lives": RRPLM, WHNS, 7/9/87.

406 "Testimony about North's Alleged Misuse of Funds": RRPLM, WHSOF: Duberstein, Kenneth, Office of the Chief of Staff, Series I, Subject File, Box 2: Iran/Contra Issues # 2 of 2 (1).

407 "I often used my own paycheck": RRPLM, WHNS, 7/9/87.

407 "get rid of things": RRPLM, WHNS, 7/9/87.

407 "I'll be glad to meet Abu Nidal": RRPLM, WHNS, 7/8/87.

407 "The most popular soap opera": RRPLM, WHNS, 7/9/87.

407 "Ollie North craze": RRPLM, WHNS, 7/9/87.

407 on their covers: *Time* 7/27/87; *Newsweek,* 7/27/87.

407 personal checks: *WP,* 7/10/87.

407 " 'Olliemania' Sweeps USA": *USA Today,* 7/9/87, p. 1.

407 "North's Brazen Lies": *New York Daily News,* 7/8/87.

408 "Lt. Col. North read an opening statement": RRPLM, WHSOF: Ball, William, Iran Contra Staffing Memos (1 of 2) OA 15,333.

408 "They were working": RRPLM: WHNS, 7/10/87.

408n the Justice Department denied: Ibid.

409 "North is obviously": RRPLM, WHNS, 7/13/87.

409 "I think what you have": Ibid.

409 "He's Rocky": Ibid.

409 he had rejected the money: RRPLM, WHSOF: Duberstein, Kenneth, Office of the Chief of Staff, Series I, Subject File, Box 2: Iran/Contra Issues # 2 of 2 (1).

409 "The Congressional committee investigating": *NYT,* 7/14/87.

409 "I don't want you prosecuted": RRPLM, WHNS, 7/14/87.

409 "a series of lies": Ibid.

410 "The principle was so important": *WT,* 7/15/87.

410 "Ethnic slurs have no place in America": RRPLM, WHNS, 7/14/87.

410 "His testimony that": *NYT,* 7/14/87.

410 "I was convinced": RRPLM, WHNS, 7/15/87.

411 "Poindexter found the concept": RRPLM, WHSOF: Ball, William, Iran Contra Staffing Memos (1 of 2) OA 15,333.

411 "I wanted to protect him": AP, 7/16/87.

411 placing himself between President Reagan and the American people: RRPLM, WHNS, 7/22/87.

411 secrecy was necessary: Ibid.

411 "If the President": *WP,* 7/22/87.

411 "head held high": RRPLM, WHNS, 7/22/87.

412 "The admiral fell": *USA Today,* 7/16/87.

412 Its anonymous source: *WP,* 7/20/87.

412 threatened to quit three times: *WP,* 7/24/87.

412 "SHULTZ ANGRILY TELLS INQUIRY": *NYT,* 7/24/87.

413 "MEESE SAYS NORTH": *NYT,* 7/30/87.

413 "REGAN TESTIFIES": *NYT,* 7/31/87.

413 "WEINBERGER SAYS": *NYT,* 8/1/87.

413 "The story has now been told": RRPLM, WHNS, 8/4/87.

413 "I'm not going to comment": RRPLM, WHNS, 8/12/87.

413 "These past nine months": RRPLM, WHSOF: Powell, Colin L., Box 92476: CHRON—Official 1987(10).

414 "clean out this desk": *USA Today,* 8/13/87.

414 has aged visibly: *WSJ,* 8/12/87.

414 twenty-five-day vacation: RRPLM, WHNS, 8/21/87.

414n 46 percent of respondents: RRPLM, WHNS, 8/14/87 (ABC News, Ted Koppell, 8/13/87).

415 "Bork's only a little better than 50-50": Dole int.

415 summit meeting between Reagan and Gorbachev: *NYT,* 9/19/87.

415 "Gorbachev: Steering the USSR": National Security Archives, July 1987.

416 Gorbachev needed his *peredyshka:* Strobe Talbot, *Foreign Affairs* (Fall 1988), p. 49.

416 "Regarding the INF agreement": RRPLM, WHSOF: Duberstein, Kenneth, Office of the Chief of Staff, Box 1: Aid to the Contras.

416 dropping his Reykjavik demand: *WP,* 8/31/87.

416 thirteen minutes after launch: RRPLM, WHNS, 8/31/87.

416 "What I want": *NYT,* 8/27/87.

417 "The situation has obviously changed": *NYT,* 8/28/87.

417 to scrap 1,015 missiles: *Toronto Star,* 9/18/87.

417 "Something's happened": Shultz, *Turmoil and Triumph,* p. 1001.

418 "One of my most characteristic": *Time,* 11/23/87.

CHAPTER 20: OCTOBER 19, 1987

419 "This is the main event": *U.S. News & World Report,* 9/14/87.

419 "the judge's goal": Ibid.

419 "He defended poll taxes": *LAT,* 10/15/87.

419 "He is probably the greatest": RRPLM, WHNS, 9/15/87.

420 "the freedom of the individual": *U.S. News & World Report,* 9/14/87.

420 "I was in my libertarian phase": Ibid.

420 opposing "one man, one vote": Ibid.

420 "freedom of speech": Ibid.

420 "wrongly decided": Ibid.

420 "I don't think abortion": Ibid.

420 "intellectual errors": *LAT,* 8/26/87.

420 "absurd" and "unprincipled": *U.S. News & World Report,* 9/14/87.

420 "He believes": *WP,* 9/1/87.

420 "Well Qualified": *WP,* 9/10/87.

420 "Not Qualified": RRPLM, WHNS, 9/15/87. The White House News Summary of September 14, 1987, took note of my syndicated column on the Bork nomination: "I am against Judge Robert Bork's nomination for the Supreme Court because he is against something I hold dear: the right to a day in court. The last resort for Americans has always been to sue the so-and-sos. You might win. You might lose. But you got your chance. . . . My objection to Judge Bork is that he has, whenever he could, denied access to the courts to any individuals or groups challenging established government authority. There have been 16 split-decisions involving access—the right to bring suit—during Judge Bork's tenure on the U.S. Court of Appeals, and 16 times he voted against the plaintiffs."

420 "soul of the U.S. Supreme Court": RRPLM, WHNS, 9/15/87.

420 "Talk about your pillow fights": *WP,* 9/16/87.

421 The nominee began: RRPLM, WHNS, *ABC World News Tonight,* 9/16/87.

421   "My philosophy": *NYT,* 9/16/87.

421   Arlen Specter: *NYT,* 9/18/87.

421   "I've been getting criticism": *WP,* 9/18/87.

422   "Over my dead body": *WP,* 10/6/87.

422   "The process of appointing": RRPLM, WHNS, 10/14/87.

422   "And on Capitol Hill, too": *WT,* 10/6/87.

422   Judiciary Committee voted 9 to 5: *NYT,* 10/7/87.

422   "His opponents": RRPLM, WHNS, 10/7/87.

423   new top-of-the-page news: *NYT,* 10/10/87.

423   The hopes of peace: *Time,* 10/5/87.

423   Arias was awarded the Nobel Peace Prize: *NYT,* 10/14/87.

423   *Sea Isle City: NYT,* 10/17/87.

423   Dow Jones index dropped 108 points: Ibid.

423   The theories of the day: *Time,* 10/5/87.

423   a matter of emotion: Ibid.

424   On Monday, October 19: *WP,* 10/20/87.

424   Iranian oil platforms: Ibid.

424   "Stated Reasons for Stock Market Decline": RRPLM, WHSOF: Duberstein, Kenneth, Office of the Chief of Staff, Box 3: Stock Market Issues/National Economic Commission.

424   "For months": *WP,* 10/20/87.

425   He answered four questions: *NYT,* 10/22/87.

427   "In a bid to calm": *NYT,* 10/23/87.

427   "Like many Americans": RRPLM, WHNS, 10/24/87.

427   rejected by the Senate, 58 to 42: *NYT,* 10/24/87.

427   Dow Jones dropped 157 points: *NYT,* 10/27/87.

427   "Eager not to disappoint": *NYT,* 10/28/87.

428   marijuana occasionally in the 1960s and 1970s: *WP,* 11/6/87.

428   "It's about time": *WT,* 11/5/87.

428   Meese . . . Deaver . . . North: *USA Today,* 11/5/87.

428   North was taking the Fifth Amendment: AP, 11/5/87.

428   "He stopped going for the home run": *Time,* 11/23/87.

428   Weinberger had told Reagan: *NYT,* 11/3/87.

428   Colin Powell: *WP,* 11/5/87.

429   "The Reagan Revolution": RRPLM, WHNS, 11/16/87.

429   "The majority report": RRPLM, WHSOF: Duberstein, Kenneth: Office of the Chief of Staff, Series I, Subject File, Box 2: Iran/Contra Issues # 1 of 2 (1).

429   which the President did not read: RRPLM, WHNS, 11/19/87.

429n Eighteen members: *Time,* 11/23/87.

430   "The report today is an aftershock": Ibid.

430   "They ran a government": RRPLM, WHNS, 11/18/87.

430   the Dow Jones had lost 44 points: Reuters, 11/20/87.

431   a plan to reduce the deficit by $30 billion: *NYT,* 11/21/87.

431   "Make cuts": *WP,* 11/17/87.

431   "What's wrong": *WP,* 12/4/87.

431   "Reagan Now Viewed": *National Journal,* 11/28/87.

432   "Gorbachev's a Hit with the American Public": *NYT,* 12/4/87.

432   "Summits are moments of high expectations": RRPLM, WHSOF: Powell, Colin.L. Box 92476L CHRON—Official 1987(13).

432   "Gorbachev's Gameplan": According to the memorandum, William Webster sent Gates's intelligence report to the President, the Vice President, the Secre-

taries of State and Defense, the assistant to the President for National Security Affairs, and the chairman of the Joint Chiefs of Staff on 11/24/87, National Security Archives.

433   a one-hour interview with Tom Brokaw: RRPLM, WHNS, 12/3/87.

433   "While talking friendship": Ibid.

CHAPTER 21: DECEMBER 8, 1987

435   "Knock 'em dead": *Newsweek*, 12/21/87, p. 19.

435   The time was chosen by Joan Quigley: Selwa Roosevelt, *Keeper of the Gate* (New York: Simon & Schuster, 1990), p. 245; Oberdorfer, *The Turn*, p. 259.

435   "I'm not on trial here": *Time*, 12/21/87.

435   "There's a big difference": *Newsweek*, 12/21/87.

436   With 250 invited guests: *Time*, 12/21/87.

436   1,752 Soviet missiles and 859 American weapons: *Newsweek*, 12/21/87.

436   "You say that every time": *Time*, 12/21/87.

436   escalation of military tensions: RRPLM, WHSOF: Executive Secretariat, NSC System files: 8791377.

436   "The United States was still proposing": Ibid.

437   any country with a fertilizer plant: Ibid.

437   "Compared to American expansionism": Ibid.

437   Reagan told a long joke: Ibid.

437   the Soviet embassy for tea: *WT*, 12/9/87.

437   "That was terrible": Oberdorfer, *The Turn*, p. 263.

438   "I better go home": Frances FitzGerald, *Way Out There in the Blue: Reagan, Star Wars and the End of the Cold War* (New York: Simon & Schuster, 2000), p. 431; Shultz, *Turmoil and Triumph*, p. 1011.

438   "We missed you": Nancy Reagan int.

438   Perle, in private business now . . . asking: *Newsweek*, 12/28/87.

438   "I know": *Newsweek*, 12/21/87.

438   "My country is in trouble": Shultz, *Turmoil and Triumph*, p. 1011.

438   "Moscow Nights": *Time*, 12/21/87.

439   "That song just cost you 200 ships": Ibid.

439   Joe DiMaggio: *Newsweek*, 12/21/87.

439   "Gorbachev said that in his conversation": RRPLM, WHSOF: Executive Secretariat, NSC System files: 8791384.

440   "Everything has changed": Shultz int.

440   "We are going forward": *Time*, 12/21/87.

441   "Now we are entering a new phase": RRPLM, WHSOF: Executive Secretariat, NSC System files: 8791377.

442   "It's too bad": Bush breakfast with reporters, 12/11/87, as reported by Oberdorfer, *The Turn*, p. 468.

442   "Keep your hands out of your pockets!": *WP*, 12/11/87.

442   "Wait until next summer": *WP*, 12/13/87; *AAL*, p. 701.

443   Stop supplying the mujahideen: Morton Abramowitz int.

443   "There is this 1,200-pound man": FitzGerald, *Way Out There in the Blue*, p. 432.

444   "What did you think": Shultz, *Turmoil and Triumph*, p. 1015.

445   "You know what mattered for Gorbachev?": Matlock int.

445   "human motives and feelings": Anatoly Chernyaev, *My Six Years with Gorbachev*, p. 142.

445   "See, they underestimated me again": Bosch, *Reagan*, p. 320.

445 had jumped to 57 percent: RRPLM, WHNS, 12/15/87.

445 "Gorbachev's Tour de Force": *Time,* 12/21/87.

445 "At the beginning": *New Republic,* 12/21/87.

446 Buckley: *National Review,* 12/21/87.

446 Phillips: *NYT,* 12/11/87.

446 "A Day That Will Live in INFamy": *Detroit News,* 12/10/87.

446 Will: *WP,* 12/11/87.

446 Humberto announced: RRPLM, WHNS, 12/14/87.

447 convicted of three counts of perjury: *NYT,* 12/17/87.

447 failed a series of safety tests: RRPLM, WHNS, 12/23/87.

447 an MX missile exploded: AP, 12/23/87.

447 The day before, at 3:30 A.M.: *NYT,* 12/23/87.

447 "The flimsy savings": *WP,* 12/24/87.

447 man of the old year: *Time,* 1/4/88.

447 "Best Dressed": UPI, 12/28/87.

CHAPTER 22: MAY 29, 1988

449 Stingers: Christopher Andrew, *For the President's Eyes Only: Secret Intelligence and the American Presidency* (New York: HarperCollins, 1995).

449 On the evening: Oberdorfer, *The Turn,* p. 275.

449 Though nothing had been made public: Shultz, *Turmoil and Triumph,* p. 1087.

449n According to studies: Alexander Alexieu, "The United States and The War in Afghanistan," RAND Institute, January 1988.

450 a six-year script: Coehlo int.

450 "As Ronald Reagan enters": *Kansas City Times,* 1/2/88.

450 "If there is any": RRPLM, WHNS, 1/4/88.

451 Sam Donaldson of ABC News: The President's Daily Schedule, 2/25/88.

452 "You're in the Oval Office": Confidential source/television crew.

453 More than one hundred: RRPLM, WHNS, 2/12/88.

453 convicted on February 12 of three felony counts: RRPLM, WHNS, 2/12/88.

454 consider indicting Meese: *NYT,* 3/31/88.

454 "save her husband from himself": *Chicago Tribune,* 3/31/88.

454 He fired his press spokesman: *NYT,* 5/17/88.

454 "destroyed his department": RRPLM, WHNS, 5/17/88.

455 "I have complete confidence": *NYT,* 5/18/88.

456 Carroll Righter: Ira Reiner, former District Attorney of Los Angeles County, described the parties in an interview with the author.

456 "Not true": RRPLM, WHNS, 4/14/88.

456 "Martin Lucifer Coon, Jr.": Terrel H. Bell, *Thirteenth Man: A Reagan Cabinet Memoir* (New York: Free Press, 1988), p. 104.

457 "The abominations": RRPLM, WHNS, 5/29/88.

457 pessimism than optimism: *NYT,* 2/21/88.

458 "In terms of what Ronald Reagan": *NYT,* 2/16/88.

458 "What Reagan Promised": *National Journal,* 5/14/88.

461 ninth override of the Reagan years: *NYT,* 3/23/88.

461 The vote was 73 to 84: *LAT,* 3/23/88.

461 "This is just another": RRPLM, WHNS, 3/23/88 (ABC News transcript).

461 "As John Kennedy did": *WP,* 3/28/88.

461 six-hundred-ship Navy: *WP,* 2/8/88.

462 only 30 percent of Soviet warheads: *WP,* 3/27/88.

462 William Charles Maynes: *National Journal,* 1/12/88.

463 "He just pleaded guilty": *WP,* 3/17/88.

463 "This is a signal": Fitzwater statement, 3/16/88.

465 "restraint with restraint": Shultz, *Turmoil and Triumph,* p. 1093.

465 "Mr. President, we'll just lie about it": Oberdorfer, *The Turn,* p. 280.

466 Perle: *U.S. News & World Report,* 12/11/87.

466 "We do not impose": Oberdorfer, *The Turn,* p. 287.

466 For weeks, the Soviets: Author's reporting from Moscow, 5/88.

466 persuaded her husband: Nancy Reagan, *My Turn,* p. 353.

467 more distant, more fumbling than usual: Stahl, *Reporting Live,* p. 137.

467 It was show time: Ibid., p. 279.

467 "REAGAN OFF FOR SUMMIT": *WP,* 5/25/88.

467 "Proceeding from their understanding": RRPLM, WHSOF, Executive Secretariat, NSC System files: 8890511.

468 "The President concluded": Memocon 8890497 Executive Secretariat, NSC, 5/29/88, p. 3.

468 "The Arbat": *AAL,* p. 709; Matlock int.

469 "Leave them alone": Oberdorfer, *The Turn,* p. 296.

469 "Second day": RRPLM, WHNS, 5/30/88 (Moscow).

CHAPTER 23: JANUARY 11, 1989

472 Taj Mahal: Author reporting from Peshwar, Pakistan.

472 "Red": Shultz, *Turmoil and Triumph,* p. 1103.

473 "Shake hands": RRPLM, WHNS, 6/1/88.

473 "Do you still think": RRPLM, WHNS, 5/31/88, 6/1/88.

473 "So Long, Evil Empire": *National Review,* 7/8/88.

473 two thousand students: AP, 6/1/88.

475 "I don't want to do it": Memorandum of Conversation 90511, Second Plenary Meeting, Moscow 6/1/88, p. 17.

475 He fell asleep: Shultz int.

475 "We won't be disturbed": RRPLM, 6/14/88 (9:30 A.M., Cabinet Room).

476 "completely vindicated": *WP,* 7/6/88.

476n Special Prosecutor James McKay: *WP,* 7/17/88.

478 "You'll never believe": Edmund Morris int.

478 from 47 to 57 percent: *National Journal,* 10/8/88.

478 "I don't think we know yet": *NYT,* 8/17/88.

479 "my principles": *NYT,* 11/16/88.

480 "When the kids" *National Journal,* 11/21/88.

481 "Many Soviets regard": CIA Memo, Leadership Situation in the USSR, 9/27/1988.

482 "A new world": *NYT,* 12/7/88.

482 "A brilliant way to play": *Newsweek,* 12/19/88.

482 "Perhaps not since": *NYT,* 12/18/88.

483 "Soviet Sorcerer": *New York Daily News* 12/8/88.

483 "The realities": *New York Post,* 12/8/88.

483 "We have walked": AAL, p. 720.

484 They met five times . . . : Noonan, *What I Saw at the Revolution,* pp. 326–28.

485 "Dear Mr. President": RRPLM, WHORM: SP1314: 589277 (8/8). Additionally, Tony Dolan's speech drafts are available at the Reagan Library in Box 69 of Dolan's White House Staff and Office files.

AFTERWORD

489   By the year 2000: *Newsday,* 6/9/04.
489   More than nine hundred books: Amazon.com listings for Ronald Reagan.
489   "lost" the Cold War: *WP,* 12/11/87.
490   "God, this is impressive": Weisman int.

BIBLIOGRAPHIC ESSAY

According to Amazon.com more than nine hundred books have been written about Ronald Reagan. Of these, there are three books that are especially important for understanding Reagan. The first, Ronald Reagan's own, *An American Life* (New York: Simon & Schuster, 1990), is Reagan's own version of his life and times, and is as interesting for what is left out as for what is included. The book's strength is also its flaw, for research purposes: His diary entries are part of Reagan's selective version of events and experiences. While his recollections are self-selected, however, they do provide considerable information on what the President knew and when he knew it. In the second work, Lou Cannon's *President Reagan: The Role of a Lifetime* (New York: Public Affairs, 2000), the author who covered Reagan throughout his political career, beginning in 1966, produces a detailed account of Reagan and the people in his orbit. For other writers, Cannon is more than a journalist. He is a character in this history, a trusted eyewitness. The third book, Edmund Morris's *Dutch: A Memoir of Ronald Reagan* (New York: Random House, 2000), is the first authorized biography of a sitting President. A fascinating book by a brilliant writer, it was unnecessarily flawed by a Reaganesque mixing of nonfiction and fiction.

Several other significant books view Reagan from different perspectives. Adriana Bosch's *Reagan: An American Story* (New York: TV Books, 2000) is an excellent, concise biography, the product of interviews with many and varied sources; Lou Cannon's *Reagan* (New York: Putnam, 1982) is an earlier work of the journalist; and Garry Wills's *Reagan's America* (New York: Penguin, 2000) examines the forces and institutions that shaped Reagan and all the rest of us.

Early analyses of the Reagan administration by journalists were usually critical, even dismissive. Those works include Laurence Barrett's very professional overview of the Reagan administration's first year, *Gambling with History: Reagan in the White House* (New York: Doubleday, 1983); Sidney Blumenthal's *The Rise of the Counter-Establishment: From Conservative Ideology to Political Power* (New York: Times Books, 1986) and Lesley Stahl's *Reporting Live* (New York: Simon & Schuster, 1999), a delightful and incisive journalist's memoir.

Additional contemporary views of Reagan from the press include Rowland Evans and Robert Novak, *Reagan Revolution* (New York: Dutton, 1981); Jane Mayer and Doyle McManus, *Landslide: The Unmaking of the President* (Boston: Houghton Mifflin, 1988); Mark Hertsgaard, *On Bended Knee* (New York: Schocken, 1989); Haynes Johnson, *Sleepwalking Through History* (New York: Anchor, 1992);

Richard Reeves, *The Reagan Detour* (New York: Simon & Schuster, 1985); and Bob Schieffer and Gary Paul Gates, *The Acting President* (New York: Dutton, 1989).

While academic criticism of Reagan tended to be published after the presidency (Walter Williams, *Reaganism and the Death of Representative Democracy* [Washington, D.C.: Georgetown University Press, 2003], is an example), relatively neutral works have been produced as well, including Larry Berman, ed., *Looking Back on the Reagan Presidency* (Baltimore: Johns Hopkins University Press, 1990); Paul Boyer, ed., *Reagan As President* (Chicago: Ivan R. Dee, 1990); W. Elliot Brownlee and Hugh Davis Graham, eds., *The Reagan Presidency* (Lawrence: University Press of Kansas, 2003); and Eric J. Schmertz, Natalie Datlof, and Alexej Ugrinsky, eds., *Ronald Reagan's America* (Westport, CT: Greenwood Press, 1997).

There is a full and growing Reagan literature, most of it celebratory, by men and women who served or admired him. Many are obvious attempts to build a case for his historical greatness, though some have touches of vengeance in them: Martin Anderson, *Revolution: The Reagan Legacy* (Stanford, CA: Hoover Institution Press, 1990); Terrell H. Bell, *The Thirteenth Man: A Reagan Cabinet Memoir* (New York: Free Press, 1988); Richard Darman, *Who's in Control: Polar Politics and the Sensible Center* (New York: Simon & Schuster, 1996); Michael K. Deaver, *Behind the Scenes* (New York: William Morrow, 1988); Michael K. Deaver, *A Different Drummer: My Thirty Years with Ronald Reagan* (New York: HarperCollins, 2001); Donald J. Devine, *Reagan's Terrible Swift Sword: Reforming and Controlling the Federal Bureaucracy* (Ottawa, IL: Jameson Books, 1991); Dinesh D'Souza, *Ronald Reagan: How an Ordinary Man Became an Extraordinary Leader* (New York: Free Press, 1999); David Gergen, *Eyewitness to Power* (New York: Simon & Schuster, 2000); Steven Greffenius, *The Last Jeffersonian* (New York: American Book Publishing, 2001); Alexander Haig, *Caveat: Realism, Reagan and Foreign Policy* (New York: Scribner, 1984); C. Everett Koop, *Koop* (New York: Random House, 1991); Jim Kuhn, *Ronald Reagan in Private* (New York: Sentinel, 2004); Robert C. McFarlane with Sofia Smardz, *Special Trust* (New York: Cadell & Davies, 1994); Edwin Meese III, *With Reagan* (Washington, D.C.: Regnery, 1992); Lyn Nofziger, *Nofziger* (Washington, D.C.: Regnery, 1992); Peggy Noonan's captivating *What I Saw at the Revolution* (New York: Scribner, 1993); Peggy Noonan, *When Character Was King* (New York: Penguin, 2002); Oliver L. North with William Novak, *Under Fire: An American Story* (New York: HarperCollins, 1991); Donald T. Regan, *For the Record: From Wall Street to Washington* (San Diego: Harcourt Brace Jovanovich, 1988); Peter Robinson, *How Ronald Reagan Changed My Life* (New York: Regan Books, 2003); Ed Rollins, *Bare Knuckles and Back Rooms: My Life in American Politics* (New York: Broadway Books, 1996); Selwa Roosevelt, *Keeper of the Gate* (New York: Simon & Schuster, 1990); William French Smith, *Law and Justice in the Reagan Administration* (Stanford, CA: Hoover Institution Press, 1991); Larry Speakes, *Speaking Out* (New York: Avon, 1989), a candid assessment of staffers and cabinet members; David A. Stockman, *The Triumph of Politics: Why the Reagan Revolution Failed* (New York: Harper & Row, 1986), a sensation in its time; Peter J. Wallison, *Ronald Reagan: The Power of Conviction and the Success of His Presidency* (New York: Perseus, 2002); and Caspar Weinberger, *Fighting for Peace: Seven Critical Years in the Pentagon* (New York: Warner Books, 1990).

Books on Nancy Reagan, or primarily concerned with the First Lady, include Nancy Reagan, *My Turn: The Memoirs of Nancy Reagan* (New York: Random House, 1989); Kitty Kelley, *Nancy Reagan* (New York: Pocket Books, 1992), a detailed book attacked for inaccuracies; and Joan Quigley, *What Does Joan Say?* (New York: Pinnacle, 1991), a slight book by the First Lady's favorite astrologer.

An eyewitness account of John Hinckley Jr.'s assassination attempt on the President is presented by Joseph Petro with Jeffrey Robinson in *Standing Next to History* (New York: Thomas Dunne Books, 2005). The seriousness of the President's condition and behind-the-scenes confusion in the aftermath of the shooting is documented in Herbert Abrams, *The President Has Been Shot* (New York: W. W. Norton, 1992).

Related memoirs and biographies of congressmen include John M. Barry, *The Ambition and the Power* (New York: Viking, 1989), a biography of Jim Wright; John A. Farrell, *Tip O'Neill and the Democratic Century* (Boston: Little, Brown, 2001); and Thomas P. "Tip" O'Neill with William Novak, *Man of the House: The Life and Memoirs of Speaker Tip O'Neill* (New York: Random House, 1987).

Other sources providing insight from within or near the administration include Deborah Hart Strober and Gerald S. Strober, *Reagan: The Man and His Presidency* (Boston: Houghton Mifflin, 1998), a sympathetic and very valuable oral history; and Kenneth W. Thompson, ed., *Leadership in the Reagan Presidency: Seven Intimate Perspectives* (Lanham, MD: Madison Books, 2000), which was more balanced.

Ronald Reagan's high regard for words and ideas are reflected in volumes on his letters and speeches. The collections of letters are his correspondence with the nation: Kiron K. Skinner, Annelise Anderson, and Martin Anderson, eds., *Reagan in His Own Hand* (New York: Free Press, 2001); Kiron K. Skinner, Annelise Anderson, and Martin Anderson, eds., *Reagan: A Life in Letters* (New York: Free Press, 2003); Ralph E. Weber and Ralph A. Weber, eds., *Dear Americans: Letters from the Desk of Ronald Reagan* (New York: Doubleday, 2003).

Collections and studies of his speeches and rhetoric can be found in Ronald Reagan and D. Erik Felten, *A Shining City* (New York: Simon & Schuster, 1998), a collection of speeches and tributes; Carol Gelderman, *All the Presidents' Words: The Bully Pulpit and the Creation of the Virtual Presidency* (New York: Walker, 1997); William Ker Muir, *The Bully Pulpit: The Presidential Leadership of Ronald Reagan* (San Francisco: ICS Press, 1992); and Mary E. Stuckey, *Playing the Game: The Presidential Rhetoric of Ronald Reagan* (New York: Praeger, 1990).

Works by and about previous Presidents help put Reagan's presidency into context. Those works begin with the President's own favorites, Calvin Coolidge, *The Autobiography of Calvin Coolidge* (Plymouth Notch, VT: Calvin Coolidge Memorial Foundation, 1989); and Jane Curtis and Will Curtis with Frank Lieberman, *Return to These Hills: The Vermont Years of Calvin* Coolidge (Woodstock, VT: Curtis Lieberman Books, 1985), which Reagan was reading in 1985 when doctors came into his hospital room to tell him his colon cancer operation was a success. Other relevant works include Fred I. Greenstein, *The Hidden-Hand Presidency: Eisenhower as a Leader* (New York: Basic Books, 1982); and Jimmy Carter, *Keeping Faith: Memoirs of a President* (New York: Bantam, 1982).

More general studies of the presidency include James David Barber, *Presidential Character: Predicting Performance in the White House* (Englewood Cliffs, NJ: Prentice Hall, 1992); Richard G. Hutcheson *God in the White House: How Religion Has Changed the Modern Presidency* (New York: Macmillan, 1989); William W. Lammers and Michael A. Genovese, *The Presidency and Domestic Policy* (Washington, D.C.: Congressional Quarterly Books, 2000); Marc Landy and Sidney M. Milkis, *Presidential Greatness* (Lawrence: University Press of Kansas, 2001); and William E. Leuchtenberg, *In the Shadow of FDR: From Harry Truman to Ronald Reagan* (Ithaca: Cornell University Press, 1989).

For first-person accounts of the Cold War from the United States's perspective, see George P. Shultz, *Turmoil and Triumph* (New York: Scribner, 1993); Paul H. Nitze, Steven L. Rearden, and Ann M. Smith, *From Hiroshima to Glasnost: At the Center of*

Decision (New York: Grove Press, 1989); Jack F. Matlock Jr., *Autopsy on an Empire* (New York: Random House, 1995); and Jack F. Matlock Jr., *Reagan and Gorbachev: How the Cold War Ended* (New York: Random House, 2004).

For a first-person view from the Soviet side, see Anatoly Dobrynin, *In Confidence: Moscow's Ambassador to Six Cold War Presidents* (New York: Times Books, 1995); Andrei Gromyko, *Memoirs* (New York: Doubleday, 1990); and Eduard Shevard- nadze and Catherine A. Fitzpatrick (translator), *The Future Belongs to Freedom* (New York: Free Press, 1991).

Eyewitness perspectives on Mikhail Gorbachev are also available: Anatoly Che- myaev, *My Six Years with Gorbachev* (University Park: Pennsylvania State University Press, 2000); and Valery Boldin and Eveylin Rossiter (translator), *Ten Years That Shook the World: The Gorbachev Era as Witnessed by His Chief of Staff* (New York: Basic Books, 1994).

Works analyzing the Cold War include, most valuably, Don Oberdorfer, *The Turn: From the Cold War to a New Era* (New York: Touchstone, 1992); Carl Bernstein and Marco Politi, *His Holiness* (New York: Penguin, 1997); Michael R. Beschloss and Strobe Talbott, *At the Highest Levels: The Inside Story of the End of the Cold War* (Boston: Back Bay Books, 1994); Sidney Blumenthal, *Pledging Allegiance: The Last Campaign of the Cold War* (New York: HarperCollins, 1992); Stephen F. Cohen, *So- vieticus* (New York: W. W. Norton, 1986); Steven Kotkin, *Armageddon Averted: The Soviet Collapse, 1970–2000* (Oxford: Oxford University Press, 2001); Derek Lee- baert, *The Fifty-Year Wound: How America's Cold War Victory Has Shaped Our World* (Boston: Little, Brown, 2002); Michael Mandelbaum, *The Dawn of Peace in Europe* (New York: Twentieth Century Foundation, 1996); Michael Mandelbaum, *Ideas That Conquered the World: Peace, Democracy, and Free Markets in the Twenty-First Century* (New York: Public Affairs, 2002); David Pryce-Jones, *The Strange Death of the Soviet Empire* (New York: Metropolitan Books, Henry Holt, 1995); Strobe Talbott, *The Russians and Reagan* (New York: Vintage, 1984); and Jay Winik, *On the Brink: The Dramatic Behind the Scenes Saga of the Reagan Era and the Men and Women Who Won the Cold War* (New York: Simon & Schuster, 1996).

On arms control, see Kenneth L. Adelman, *The Great Universal Embrace* (New York: Simon & Schuster, 1989); Robert Scheer, *With Enough Shovels* (New York: Vintage, 1983); and Strobe Talbott, *The Master of the Game* (New York: Alfred A. Knopf, 1988).

For the Strategic Defense Initiative, see Scott Armstrong and Peter Grier, *Strategic Defense Initiative: Splendid Defense or Pipe Dream* (New York: Foreign Policy Asso- ciation, 1986); Rebecca S. Bjork, *The Strategic Defense Initiative* (New York: State University of New York Press, 1992); and Frances FitzGerald, *Way Out There in the Blue* (New York: Simon & Schuster, 2001), which uses the idea as a wedge for deep exploration of Reagan as a public figure.

A reconstruction of the events surrounding the Soviet destruction of Korean Air- lines Flight 007 is presented in Seymour Hersh, *The Target Is Destroyed* (New York: Random House, 1986). Other works regarding KAL 007 include Michael Brun, *Inci- dent at Sakhalin* (New York: Four Walls Eight Windows, 1996); Oliver Clubb, *KAL Flight 007: The Hidden Story* (New York: Permanent Press, 1985); Alexander Dallin, *Black Box: KAL and the Superpowers* (Berkeley: University of California Press, 1985); David E. Pearson, *KAL 007—The Cover-Up* (New York, Simon & Schuster, 1987); and Jeffrey St. John, *Day of the Cobra* (Nashville: Thomas Nelson, 1984).

Key sources on American intelligence include Robert M. Gates, *From the Shad- ows: The Ultimate Insider's Story of Five Presidents and How They Won the Cold War* (New York: Simon & Schuster, 1996); John Ranelagh, *The Agency: The Rise and Decline of the CIA from Wild Bill Donovan to William Casey* (New York: Simon & Schuster, 1986); and Bob Woodward, *Veil: The Secret Wars of the CIA, 1981–1987* (New York: Simon & Schuster, 1987).

Reagan's interactions with the world community are presented in Eric J. Schmertz, Natalie Datlof, and Alexej Ugrinsky, eds., *President Reagan and the World* (Westport, CT: Greenwood Press, 1997). Other works regarding diplomacy and foreign policy include Coral Bell, *The Reagan Paradox* (New Brunswick: Rutgers University Press, 1989); George Crile, *Charlie Wilson's War* (New York: Atlantic Monthly Press, 2003); Sterling Kernek, Caspar Weinberger, and Max M. Kampelman, *Foreign Policy in the Reagan Presidency* (Lanham, MD: University Press of America, 1993); Jeane J. Kirkpatrick, *The Reagan Phenomenon and Other Speeches on Foreign Policy* (Washington, D.C.: AEI Press, 1983); James M. Scott, *Deciding to Intervene: The Reagan Doctrine and Foreign Policy* (Durham: Duke University Press, 1996); and Christopher Simpson, *National Security Directives of the Reagan and Bush Administrations* (Boulder, CO: Westview Press, 1995).

For the Middle East, see Daniel Yergin, *The Prize* (New York: Free Press, 1993); Thomas L. Friedman, *From Beirut to Jerusalem* (New York: Anchor, 1990); Anita Miller, Jordan Miller, and Sigalit Zetouni, *Sharon: Israel's Warrior-Politician* (Chicago: Academy Chicago Publishers, 2002); and Ariel Sharon and David Chanoff, *Warrior: An Autobiography* (New York: Simon & Schuster, 2001). Works primarily concerning the American presence in Lebanon include John Boykin, *Cursed Is the Peacemaker* (Belmont, CA: Applegate Press, 2002); and Eric Hammel, *The Root: The Marines in Beirut, August 1982–February 1984* (San Diego: Harcourt Brace Jovanovich, 1985). On Grenada, see Gregory Sanford and Richard Vigilante, *Grenada: The Untold Story* (Lanham, MD: Madison Books, 1984); and for an eyewitness account of both Beirut and Grenada, see Major Charles Dalgleish, *Recon Marine: An Account of Beirut and Grenada* (Detroit: Harlo Press, 1995).

Works concerning the United States and Central America include Raymond Bonner, *Weakness and Deceit* (New York: Times Books, 1984); Kevin Buckley, *Panama* (New York: Simon & Schuster, 1991); Christopher Dickey, *With the Contras* (New York: Simon & Schuster, 1986); Roy Gutman, *Banana Diplomacy* (New York: Touchstone, 1989); and Walter La Feber's estimable *Inevitable Revolutions* (New York: W. W. Norton, 1993).

The most valuable sources concerning the Iran-contra scandal are Theodore Draper, *A Very Thin Line: The Iran-Contra Affairs* (New York: Hill and Wang, 1991); and Peter Kornbluh and Malcolm Byrne, eds., *The Iran-Contra Scandal: The Declassified History* (New York: New Press, 1993), an essential collection of significant documents.

Accounts and memoirs from Iran-contra participants not previously mentioned include Elliott Abrams, *Undue Process* (New York: Free Press, 1992); and Robert Timberg, *The Nightingale's Song* (New York: Simon & Schuster, 1995), in which the author, a veteran of the Vietnam War, investigates the connection between Iran-contra and Vietnam through the stories of five Annapolis graduates, McFarlane, Poindexter, North, Senator John McCain, and Secretary of the Navy James Webb.

For official reports on Iran-contra, see Daniel K. Inouye and Lee H. Hamilton, *Iran-Contra Affair: Report of the Congressional Committees* (New York: Three Rivers Press, 1988); and John Tower, Edmund Muskie, and Brent Scowcroft, *The Tower Commission Report* (New York: Random House, 1987).

Additional analysis of Reagan's foreign policy and the Iran-contra affair is available in Constantine C. Menges's interesting volume *Inside the National Security Council: The True Story of the Making and Unmaking of Reagan's Foreign Policy*

(New York: Touchstone, 1989); and Lawrence E. Walsh, *Firewall: The Iran-Contra Conspiracy and Cover-up* (New York: W. W. Norton, 1997).

For background on the economy in the Reagan years see Paul Craig Roberts, *Supply-Side Revolution: An Insider's Account of Policymaking in Washington* (Cambridge: Harvard University Press, 1984); Herbert Stein, *Presidential Economics* (New York: Simon & Schuster, 1984); Paul A. Volcker and Toyoo Gyohten, *Changing Fortunes* (New York: Times Books, 1992); and Jude Wanniski, *The Way the World Works* (New York: Basic Books, 1978).

Favorable analyses of Reagan's economic policies include Jeffrey H. Birnbaum and Alan S. Murray, *Showdown at Gucci Gulch: Lawmakers, Lobbyists, and the Unlikely Triumph of Tax Reform* (New York: Random House, 1987); Michael J. Boskin, *Reagan and the Economy: The Successes, Failures and Unfinished Agenda* (San Francisco: Institute for Contemporary Studies, 1988); and Bruce R. Bartlett, *Reaganomics: Supply-Side Economics in Action* (New York: Quill, 1982).

Critical views of Reagan's economic policies include Frank Ackerman, *Reaganomics: Rhetoric vs. Reality* (Boston: South End Press, 1982); Frank Ackerman, *Hazardous to Our Wealth: Economic Policy in the 1980s* (Boston: South End Press, 1984); Daniel Patrick Moynihan, *Came the Revolution* (San Diego: Harcourt Brace Jovanovich, 1988), on the welfare system; Peter G. Peterson and Neil Howe, *On Borrowed Time: How Growth in Entitlement Spending Threatens America's Future* (San Francisco: ICS Press, 1988); Elton Rayack, *Not So Free to Choose: The Political Economy of Milton Friedman and Ronald Reagan* (New York: Praeger, 1986); Hobart Rowen, *Self-Inflicted Wounds* (New York: Times Books, 1994); and Daniel Yergin and Joseph Stanislaw, *The Commanding Heights: The Battle for the World Economy* (New York: Simon & Schuster, 1998).

On conservatives and conservatism the most important and interesting books are George H. Nash, *The Conservative Intellectual Movement in America Since 1945* (Wilmington: Intercollegiate Studies Institute, 1998); and Whittaker Chambers, *Witness* (Washington, D.C.: Regnery, 1980). Other relevant works include Matthew Dallek, *The Right Moment: Ronald Reagan's First Victory and the Decisive Turning Point in American Politics* (New York: Free Press, 2000); Lee Edwards, *The Conservative Revolution* (New York: Free Press, 1999); John Micklethwait and Adrian Wooldridge, *The Right Nation: Conservative Power in America* (New York: Penguin, 2004); and David G. Savage, *Turning Right: The Making of the Rehnquist Supreme Court* (New York: John Wiley & Sons, 1992).

Highly recommended books that do not fall into the above categories include Jacques Attali, *Verbatim, Vol. 2: 1986–1988* (Paris: Fayard, 1995); Fred Barnes, *A Cartoon History of the Reagan Years* (Washington, D.C.: Regnery, 1988); Robert H. Bork, *The Tempting of America* (New York: Free Press, 1997); John E. Chubb and Paul E. Peterson, eds., *The New Direction in American Politics* (Washington, D.C.: Brookings Institution Press, 1985); Jonathan Lash, *A Season of Spoils: Ronald Reagan's Attack on the Environment* (New York: Pantheon, 1984); Peter B. Levy, *Encyclopedia of the Reagan-Bush Years* (Westport, CT: Greenwood Press, 1996); and David C. Martin and John Walcott, *Best Laid Plans: The Inside Story of America's War Against Terrorism* (New York: Touchstone, 1989).

Chas Budnick
Washington, D.C.
August 2005

ARCHIVES ESSAY

The Ronald Reagan Presidential Library and Museum is the first presidential library to fall under the 1978 Presidential Records Act (PRA), which states that "The United States shall reserve and retain complete ownership, possession, and control of Presidential records." Those records were further defined as "documentary materials, or any reasonably segregable portion thereof, created or received by the President, his immediate staff, or a unit or individual of the Executive Office of the President whose function is to advise and assist the President, in the course of conducting activities which relate to or have an effect upon the carrying out of the constitutional, statutory, or other official or ceremonial duties of the President." (44 U.S.C. Chapter 22.)

On November 1, 2001, after long delays in the mandatory release of about 68,000 pages of President Reagan's presidential papers (see *A.H.A. v. NARA,* 310 F. Supp. 2d 216), President George W. Bush signed Executive Order 13,233, *Further Implementation of the Presidential Records Act.* When enacted, E.O. 13,233 eliminated the provision of the PRA which provided that upon a petition for a presidential record, the Archivist of the United States would determine that a presidential record should be declassified, and following a thirty-day notification period during which an incumbent President and the former President (or designee) are given a chance to claim executive privilege over the records; without a claim of executive privilege the records would be released. If executive privilege were claimed, and the Archivist still deemed that the records were exempt from executive privilege, it would be up to the incumbent President or former President (or designee) to challenge the decision of the Archivist.

Now, under E.O. 13,233, when a claim of executive privilege is made, it is not subject to review by the Archivist of the United States, and instead is left up to the original petitioner to challenge the claim of executive privilege in court. Additionally, to successfully challenge a claim of executive privilege, the petitioner must show "a demonstrated, specific need" for the records sought. Last, E.O. 13,233 extended the notification period from thirty days to "for no longer than 90 days for requests that are not unduly burdensome."

GENERALLY, in order to petition the government for the release of presidential records, a researcher fills out a Freedom of Information Act (FOIA) request specifying the particular records they seek to be declassified. Next, the archivist determines if they have classified or unprocessed records relating to the FOIA request. If so, the archivist informs the researcher that they have identified records relating to the FOIA request, and gives an estimate of time required to process the records. That processing works two ways: 1) For records identified as unprocessed, archivists must go through every document to see if there are any FOIA restrictions that apply and prevent the library from releasing the records. Next, records are organized into boxes and then folders within each box. 2) For records that have been processed but are for some reason still classified, the archivist must determine whether the records still merit classification, or depending on the classification, refer the question to the agency that originally classified the material.

In both cases, the next step is called notification. Notification involves informing both the former President or his designee and the incumbent President that a petition has been filed for the release of those specific records. During the notification period, the incumbent President and the former President, or designee, may claim executive privilege, thereby denying the petitioner their FOIA request. The notification period is supposed to last for no longer than ninety days, but this period can be delayed indefinitely if the Presidents or their designees declare that the deadline is "unduly burdensome." If executive privilege is claimed, the petitioner may challenge the claim in court.

Additionally, for records that are classified for national security reasons, there is a mandatory review (MR) request that is available to researchers. An MR request is different in that the document requested has already been identified by the library but kept out of the file. In its place, the archivists put a "withdrawal slip" identifying the document and stating that it is being withheld for national security reasons. After filling out an MR request the document is then sent back to the agency that first classified the document.

WE BEGAN research at the Reagan Library for *President Reagan: The Triumph of Imagination,* in December 2001, just one month after E.O. 13,233 was signed into law. At that time, the Reagan Library estimated that five million of their 50 million pages of presidential records were available for research. The library still estimates that they have processed only 10 percent of their collection.

We started our research by familiarizing ourselves with the hundreds of collections of files that the library had already categorized. Then we focused on specific topics and collections that we identified as being of particular interest to our research.

An example of a topic of particular interest would be exploring our hypothesis that the key to President Reagan's leadership was in his speeches. We studied drafts of all major speeches. Those speech files, in total 652 feet of paper, were found in three places: 1) White House Office of Speech Drafts, 2) White House Office of Speech Research, and 3) White House Office of Records Management. Together, these three series of collections total more than one million pages of presidential records.

We also searched for topics we considered to be of general interest, such as meetings between President Reagan and foreign leaders. Other topics of interest would be the Strategic Defense Initiative, the downing of Korean Airlines Flight 007, the United States invasion of Grenada, the sending of the United States Marines into Beirut, and so forth.

After identifying topics as either of particular interest or general interest, we realized that many topics of general interest had already been researched at the library, which meant that either someone else had filed a FOIA request on that topic, or the library had initiated the release of documents relating to a particular topic.

We quickly learned that topics of specific interest were generally unavailable for research, and to gain access to these records, we would have to file a FOIA request to petition for the release of these records. As mentioned the filing of a FOIA request is a cumbersome process that cannot be relied upon for timely research. Nevertheless, we filed nearly fifty FOIA requests and hundreds of mandatory review requests. Our FOIA requests date back to December 2001 or early 2002 and our MR requests to the middle of 2002. In most cases, we never heard back on those requests.

AFTER almost four years of research, it seems apparent that the FOIA and MR request systems are of little value to most researchers. At the Reagan Library, the queue is currently sixty months before the archivists begin processing a FOIA request for classified material, and forty-two months for nonclassified material.

The five-year wait can defeat many researchers. In our case, we might have been able to work effectively within this time frame. After all, *President Kennedy* took eight years to complete, while *President Nixon* took seven years.

There are, however, exceptions. President Reagan's official biographer, Edmund Morris, was given more access to the President's personal papers. Other writers, including Martin Anderson, Annelise Anderson, and Kiron Skinner, who have recently published books on Reagan's letters and radio addresses, have also been given greater access to President Reagan's personal papers.

Jason Ebin
Simi Valley, California
August 2005

ACKNOWLEDGMENTS

This book would not have been possible without the contributions of three talented young men who worked with me over the past five years. Keith Bettinger, now living and working in Malaysia with his new wife and daughter, organized research material (and me) for almost three years. He was replaced by Chas Budnick, now headed for New York University School of Law, who held the work together and then some as I wrote in cities around the world. Jason Ebin, now at the University of Wisconsin School of Law, practically lived at the Ronald Reagan Presidential Library in Simi Valley, California. Without them, I would be working now on about Chapter 3.

This is the sixth book I have done with (or for) Alice Mayhew, at Simon & Schuster. I am grateful to her one more time for knowing the right questions and almost all the answers as well. My agent and friend, Amanda Urban of International Creative Management, was more than creative in keeping the Reeves family eating all these years. And Mayhew's deputy, Roger Labrie, practically became a member of that family. My friends Richard Ashthalter and John Phillips made it possible for me to write parts of the book in Paris and Italy.

Not for the first time, I am greatly indebted to archivists, particularly to Greg Cummings and Shelly Jacobs at the Reagan Presidential Library in Simi Valley, California (Cummings has moved to the Nixon Library, as it finally becomes part of the National Archives). Mike Duggan, Ben Pezzillo, and Meghan Lee (who has also moved to the Nixon Library) also deserve substantial credit for this book. Others at the library who contributed to this work include: Diane Barry, Kelly Barton, Steve Branch, David Bridge, Sherrie Fletcher, Lisa Jones, Ira Pemstein, Bruce Scott, Cate Sewell, Jenny Sternaman, Josh Tenenbaum, and Raymond Wilson.

Having said that, I would like to note that archival research on this book was much more difficult than on either *President Kennedy: Profile of Power* or *President Nixon: Alone in the White House,* a subject discussed in the separate "Archives Essay" in this volume. The Reagan Library is in many ways user-friendly, but it is hard to escape the conclusion that some users are more equal than others. I probably did not help matters by becoming part of a group of historians and scholars who, in April of 2002, testified critically before the Committee on Government Reform of the House of Representatives about restrictions imposed by the administration of President George W. Bush on access to the records of President Reagan and President George H. W. Bush, who also served as Reagan's Vice President. One example was the refusal to open "Press Pool" reports to researchers, even enough those reports, written for the larger press corps by a half-dozen or so pool reporters allowed more access to the President, were never actually government records.

Because of all that, I am extremely grateful to the number of Reagan people who took the time to talk with me over these years, beginning with Nancy Reagan. As mentioned in the Introduction to this book, my personal politics were quite different from those of the President I was studying. When my first pages arrived at Simon & Schuster, one of the bosses there (not Alice Mayhew) said, "My God, Reeves sounds sympathetic to Reagan." I took that as a compliment, although I thought that I was sympathetic not to a man but to a President. For me, this book was the end of a trilogy on three very different men, Kennedy, Nixon, and Reagan, and I have come to respect greatly the presidency itself.

I am grateful, too, for the help of Alexandra Truitt, who did the photo research for this book and to Bette Butler and Steven Missildine, who helped copy documents for me at the Reagan Library.

Finally, I could not have done this book without the extraordinary understanding and unselfishness of my wife, Catherine O'Neill. But then I'm not sure I could do much of anything without her. There may be things I did not understand about President Reagan, but it was never hard for me to understand the love shared by Ronald and Nancy Reagan.

Richard Reeves
Sag Harbor, New York
August 2005

INDEX

ABOUT THE AUTHOR

RICHARD REEVES is the author of *President Kennedy: Profile of Power* and *President Nixon: Alone in the White House.* This is his eleventh book. He is a syndicated columnist and a professor at the Annenberg School for Communication at the University of Southern California. His television films have won Emmy, duPont-Columbia, and Peabody awards.